Education at a Glance 2007

OECD INDICATORS

OECD

ORGANISATION FOR ECONOMIC CO-OPERATION AND DEVELOPMENT

ORGANISATION FOR ECONOMIC CO-OPERATION AND DEVELOPMENT

The OECD is a unique forum where the governments of 30 democracies work together to address the economic, social and environmental challenges of globalisation. The OECD is also at the forefront of efforts to understand and to help governments respond to new developments and concerns, such as corporate governance, the information economy and the challenges of an ageing population. The Organisation provides a setting where governments can compare policy experiences, seek answers to common problems, identify good practice and work to co-ordinate domestic and international policies.

The OECD member countries are: Australia, Austria, Belgium, Canada, the Czech Republic, Denmark, Finland, France, Germany, Greece, Hungary, Iceland, Ireland, Italy, Japan, Korea, Luxembourg, Mexico, the Netherlands, New Zealand, Norway, Poland, Portugal, the Slovak Republic, Spain, Sweden, Switzerland, Turkey, the United Kingdom and the United States. The Commission of the European Communities takes part in the work of the OECD.

OECD Publishing disseminates widely the results of the Organisation's statistics gathering and research on economic, social and environmental issues, as well as the conventions, guidelines and standards agreed by its members.

This work is published on the responsibility of the Secretary-General of the OECD. The opinions expressed and arguments employed herein do not necessarily reflect the official views of the Organisation or of the governments of its member countries.

Also available in french under the title:
Regards sur l'éducation 2007
LES INDICATEURS DE L'OCDE

FOREWORD

Governments are paying increasing attention to international comparisons as they search for effective policies that enhance individuals' social and economic prospects, provide incentives for greater efficiency in schooling, and help to mobilise resources to meet rising demands. As part of its response, the OECD Directorate for Education devotes a major effort to the development and analysis of the quantitative, internationally comparable indicators that it publishes annually in *Education at a Glance*. These indicators enable educational policy makers and practitioners alike to see their education systems in the light of other countries' performances and, together with OECD's country policy reviews, are designed to support and review the efforts that governments are making towards policy reform.

Education at a Glance addresses the needs of a range of users, from governments seeking to learn policy lessons to academics requiring data for further analysis to the general public wanting to monitor how its nation's schools are progressing in producing world-class students. The publication examines the quality of learning outcomes, the policy levers and contextual factors that shape these outcomes, and the broader private and social returns that accrue to investments in education.

Education at a Glance is the product of a long-standing, collaborative effort between OECD governments, the experts and institutions working within the framework of the OECD's indicators of education systems (INES) programme and the OECD Secretariat. The publication was drafted by the Indicators and Analysis Division of the OECD Directorate for Education, under the responsibility of Andreas Schleicher, in co-operation with Etienne Albiser, Eric Charbonnier, Michael Davidson, Bo Hansson, Corinne Heckmann, Ben Jensen, Karinne Logez, Sophie Vayssettes and Jean Yip. Administrative support was provided by Cécile Bily and editorial support was provided by Kate Lancaster. The development of the publication was steered by INES National Co-ordinators in member countries and facilitated by the financial and material support of the three countries responsible for co-ordinating the INES Networks – the Netherlands, Sweden and the United States. The members of the various bodies as well as the individual experts who have contributed to this publication and to OECD INES more generally are listed at the end of the book.

While much progress has been accomplished in recent years, member countries and the OECD continue to strengthen the link between policy needs and the best available internationally comparable data. In doing so, various challenges and trade-offs must be faced. First, the indicators need to respond to educational issues that are high on national policy agendas, and where the international comparative perspective can offer important added value to what can be accomplished through national analysis and evaluation. Second, while the indicators need to be as comparable as possible, they also need to be as country-specific as is necessary to allow for historical, systemic and cultural differences between countries. Third, the indicators need to be presented in as straightforward a manner as possible, while remaining sufficiently complex to reflect multi-faceted educational realities. Fourth, there is a general desire to keep the indicator set as small as possible, but it needs to be large enough to be useful to policy makers across countries that face different educational challenges.

The OECD will continue to address these challenges vigorously and to pursue not just the development of indicators in areas where it is feasible and promising to develop data, but also to advance in areas where a considerable investment still needs to be made in conceptual work. The further development of the OECD Programme for International Student Assessment (PISA) and its extension through the OECD Programme for the International Assessment of Adult Competencies (PIAAC), as well as the launch of the OECD Teaching and Learning International Survey (TALIS) will be major efforts to this end.

The report is published on the responsibility of the Secretary-General of the OECD.

TABLE OF CONTENTS

Name of
the indicator
in the
2006 edition

EDITORIAL

By Barbara Ischinger, Director for Education

The effects of tertiary education expansion: a high-calibre workforce or the overqualified crowding out the lesser qualified?

Higher education graduation rates have grown massively in OECD countries in recent decades. But what is the impact of this on labour markets? Has the increasing supply of well-educated labour been matched by the creation of an equivalent number of high-paying jobs? Or one day will everyone have a university degree and work for the minimum wage? The analysis below of this year's edition of *Education at a Glance* suggests that the expansion has had a positive impact for individuals and economies and that there are, as yet, no signs of an "inflation" of the value of qualifications. The sustainability of the continued expansion will, however, depend on re-thinking how it is financed and how to ensure that it is more efficient.

In most OECD countries, among adults aged 55 to 64 (who entered the workforce in the 1960s and early 1970s) between 7 and 27% have completed higher education (have tertiary qualifications), except in Canada and the United States where more than 30% have done so. Among younger adults aged 25 to 34, at least 30% have obtained tertiary qualifications in 19 countries and over 40% have in 6 countries (Indicator A1). The proportion of the population with tertiary qualifications has risen from 19 to 32% of the population between these two groups.

Although most countries have seen at least some growth in tertiary enrolments (Indicator C2) and in tertiary attainment, the rate of expansion has varied widely from one country to another and from one time period to another. Much of the growth has come from periods of rapid, policy-driven expansion in certain countries. Korea, Ireland and Spain, for example, more than doubled the proportion of tertiary graduates entering the workforce between the late 1970s and the late 1990s from initially low levels, whereas in the United States and Germany the proportion remained largely unchanged, with relatively high levels in the United States and comparatively low levels in Germany (Indicator A1).

Governments pursuing an expansion of tertiary education have often acknowledged doing this in the understanding that more high-level skills are needed in an advanced knowledge economy, requiring a much greater proportion of the workforce than previously to be educated beyond the secondary school level. And indeed, in many countries there has been significant growth of jobs and industries in sectors dependent on a more skilled workforce. However, the question remains – what will be the effect increasing the supply of the well-educated on the labour market? It is certainly conceivable that at least some of the new graduates end up doing jobs that do not require graduate skills and that they obtain these jobs at the expense of less highly qualified workers. Such a crowding out effect may be associated with a relative rise in unemployment among people with low qualifications (as higher-qualified workers take their jobs), but also potentially with a reduction in the pay premium associated with tertiary qualifications (as a rise in graduate supply outstrips any rise in demand for graduate skills).

Improved coverage of international trend data linking educational qualifications and labour market outcomes makes it possible to investigate this issue in *Education at a Glance 2007* in a way that was not possible in the past. The analysis below draws on Indicator A1, which shows that there are substantial rewards associated with attaining tertiary education and substantial penalties associated with failing to reach at least the upper secondary standard.

In all OECD countries, the average earnings premium associated with tertiary compared to upper secondary education is more than 25% and in some is more than 100% (Indicator A9). In addition, the average unemployment rate among those only with lower secondary education is 5 percentage points higher than those whose highest level is upper secondary, and 7 points higher than those with tertiary education (Indicator A8). Analysis also shows that while unemployment is substantially higher than the average among those with low qualifications, this penalty has not deteriorated in those countries that have expanded tertiary education, as the crowding-out hypothesis would have suggested. On the contrary, in the countries expanding most rapidly, a small rise in the relative risk in the late 1990s was followed by a fall in the early 2000s. However, in those countries that did not expand tertiary education, there has been a rise in the relative risk of unemployment. Indeed, in these countries a failure to complete upper secondary education is now associated with an 80% greater probability of being unemployed, compared to less than 50% in those countries that have increased tertiary education the most.

Equally important, countries expanding tertiary education attainment more in the late 1990s tended to have a greater fall (or smaller rise) in unemployment between 1995 and 2004 than countries with less tertiary expansion. For example, France, Ireland and Korea had the fastest growth in tertiary attainment and close to zero or negative growth in unemployment, whereas Germany, the Czech Republic and the Slovak Republic had low or no growth in tertiary attainment but substantial growth in unemployment among the unqualified. While there is not a perfect match – Finland had no tertiary expansion but a fall in unemployment, Poland expanded tertiary education but unemployment rose too – the general trend is again the opposite of what one would expect according to the crowding-out hypothesis (Indicator A1).

The data provide thus no evidence that the lesser qualified are crowded out from the labour market and there is much to point to the opposite: that the least educated individuals benefit in terms of better employment opportunities when more people enter higher education. It may be that the expansion of the high end of the educational ladder is, apart from generating growth, also providing more equitable employment opportunities. In addition, an analysis of trends in the absolute level of unemployment for upper-secondary educated adults suggests that changes in the level of unemployment during the period 1995 to 2004 are unrelated to changes in tertiary attainment levels. In fact, for both upper and lower secondary unemployment, there is no statistically significant correlation between an expansion in tertiary attainment and movement in unemployment rates after controlling for growth in GDP.

Indeed, GDP and productivity seem to drive unemployment prospects regardless of changes in tertiary attainment. There is, however, a significant correlation between increases in tertiary and upper secondary attainments and the fall in relative unemployment for lower-secondary educated adults. All this suggests that employment prospects among the least well-educated are principally tied to growth in the economy and in general to productivity, to which an adequate supply of high-skilled labour can potentially contribute. Strong overall economic health would appear to more than compensate for any crowding out effects, with the net outcomes for relatively less-educated groups being positive. The positive employment impact of economic growth is greater for those without tertiary qualifications than for graduates, perhaps because employers are more willing to meet the cost of retaining those with higher qualifications during difficult economic times.

Furthermore, analysis also suggests that oversupply of skills does not create unemployment among those with tertiary qualifications or a slump in their pay. Although this does not imply that tertiary graduates enter jobs in line with their qualifications, it still indicates that the benefits of higher education have not deteriorated as higher education has expanded. And while there have been some small rises in the relative risk of unemployment for graduates, this has been no worse where tertiary attainment has expanded fastest. Indeed, in all OECD countries graduates face much lower levels of unemployment than do other groups. In terms of pay, the data suggest some curbing of an increasing advantage for tertiary graduates where their supply has risen fastest, but not a general fall. This evidence corroborates similar results from cross-sectional studies, suggesting that lower-educated groups share in the benefit of more tertiary education and that the extra skills produced have largely been absorbed by the labour market. In tracking these phenomena over time, it is interesting to note that positive effects seem to be more pronounced in recent years, contradicting the notion that tertiary education, so far, is expanding too rapidly.

It is hard to predict the future from these past trends. Will the expansion of higher education continue at this rapid pace, driven by an ever-rising demand for the highly skilled? Or will it level off and will relative earnings decline? At the beginning of the 20th century, few would have predicted that, among OECD countries, upper secondary education would be largely universal by the end of the century. So it is equally difficult to predict how tertiary qualifications will have evolved by the end of the 21st century.

What is clear is that, for now at least, the demand for more and better education continues to rise, with still substantial payoffs in terms of earnings and productivity gains. And enrolments continue to grow in OECD countries, with more than 50% – in some countries more than 75% – of high school graduates now entering university-level education (Indicator C2).

How will countries pay for this expansion, given that spending per student has already begun to decline in some countries, as enrolments rose faster than spending on tertiary education (Indicator B1)? Establishing innovative financing and student support policies that mobilise additional public and private funding in ways that better reflect the social and private benefits of tertiary education will certainly be part of the answer. And many countries are moving successfully in this direction, some without creating barriers for student participation (Indicator B5).

So far, the Nordic countries have achieved expansion by viewing massive public spending on higher education, including both support of institutions and support of students and households, as an investment that pays high dividends to individuals and society. Australia, Japan, Korea, New Zealand, and the United Kingdom have expanded participation in tertiary education by shifting some of the burden of financial provision to students. In Australia, for example, a risk-free loan programme that suppressed liquidity constraints for poorer students was introduced; this has not, however, had a negative effect on the equity of access for students from low socio-economic backgrounds. In contrast, many European countries are not increasing public investments in their universities nor are universities allowed to charge tuition fees, with the result that the European average for spending per tertiary student is now well below half the level of spending in the United States (Indicator B1).

But it is equally clear that more money alone will not be enough. Investments in education will need to become much more efficient too. For the first time, *Education at a Glance* examines this question and estimates that, on average across OECD countries, taxpayers could expect 22% more output for current inputs (Indicator B7). This efficiency indicator is exploratory at this stage; it covers only elementary and secondary schooling and it will require substantial further development over the years to come, not least to capture a wider range of educational outcomes. However, it indicates the scale of effort that is needed for education to re-invent itself in ways that other professions have already done and to provide better value for money.

For tertiary education, this means creating and maintaining a system of diverse, sustainable and high-quality institutions with the freedom to respond to demand and accountability for outcomes they produce. It means ensuring that the growth and development of tertiary educational systems are managed in ways that improve access and enhance quality. And it means that universities will have to evolve so that their leadership and management capacity matches that of modern enterprises. Much greater use needs to be made of appropriate strategic financial and human-resource management techniques in order to ensure long-term financial sustainability and meet accountability requirements. Institutions must be governed by bodies that have the ability to think strategically and reflect a much wider range of stakeholder interests than only the academic community. Such change may not come easily, but the need for it cannot be ignored nor the risk of complacency denied. The OECD will continue to monitor progress in this area with the aim of helping countries rise to the challenges.

Barbara Ischinger

INTRODUCTION: THE INDICATORS AND THEIR FRAMEWORK

■ The organising framework

Education at a Glance – OECD Indicators 2007 provides a rich, comparable and up-to-date array of indicators that reflect a consensus among professionals on how to measure the current state of education internationally. The indicators provide information on the human and financial resources invested in education, on how education and learning systems operate and evolve, and on the returns to educational investments. The indicators are organised thematically, and each is accompanied by information on the policy context and the interpretation of the data. The education indicators are presented within an organising framework that:

■ Distinguishes between the actors in education systems: individual learners, instructional settings and learning environments, educational service providers, and the education system as a whole;

■ Groups the indicators according to whether they speak to learning outcomes for individuals or countries, policy levers or circumstances that shape these outcomes, or to antecedents or constraints that set policy choices into context; and

■ Identifies the policy issues to which the indicators relate, with three major categories distinguishing between the quality of educational outcomes and educational provision, issues of equity in educational outcomes and educational opportunities, and the adequacy and effectiveness of resource management.

The following matrix describes the first two dimensions:

	1. Education and learning outputs and outcomes	2. Policy levers and contexts shaping educational outcomes	3. Antecedents or constraints that contextualise policy
I. Individual participants in education and learning	1.I The quality and distribution of individual educational outcomes	2.I Individual attitudes, engagement and behaviour	3.I Background characteristics of the individual learners
II. Instructional settings	1.II The quality of instructional delivery	2.II Pedagogy and learning practices and classroom climate	3.II Student learning conditions and teacher working conditions
III. Providers of educational services	1.III The output of educational institutions and institutional performance	2.III School environment and organisation	3.III Characteristics of the service providers and their communities
IV. The education system as a whole	1.IV The overall performance of the education system	2.IV System-wide institutional settings, resource allocations and policies	3.IV The national educational, social, economic and demographic contexts

The following sections discuss the matrix dimensions in more detail:

■ *Actors in education systems*

The OECD indicators of education systems programme (INES) seeks to gauge the performance of national education systems as a whole, rather than to compare individual institutional or other sub-national entities. However, there is increasing recognition that many important features of the development, functioning and impact of education systems can only be assessed through an understanding of learning outcomes and their relationships to inputs and processes at the level of individuals and institutions. To account for this, the indicator framework distinguishes between a macro level, two meso-levels and a micro-level of education systems. These relate to:

- The education system as a whole;
- The educational institutions and providers of educational services;
- The instructional setting and the learning environment within the institutions; and
- The individual participants in education and learning.

To some extent, these levels correspond to the entities from which data are being collected but their importance mainly centres on the fact that many features of the education system play out quite differently at different levels of the system, which needs to be taken into account when interpreting the indicators. For example, at the level of students within a classroom, the relationship between student achievement and class size may be negative, if students in small classes benefit from improved contact with teachers. At the class or school level, however, students are often intentionally grouped such that weaker or disadvantaged students are placed in smaller classes so that they receive more individual attention. At the school level, therefore, the observed relationship between class size and student achievement is often positive (suggesting that students in larger classes perform better than students in smaller classes). At higher aggregated levels of education systems, the relationship between student achievement and class size is further confounded, *e.g.* by the socio-economic intake of schools or by factors relating to the learning culture in different countries. Past analyses which have relied on macro-level data alone have therefore sometimes led to misleading conclusions.

■ *Outcomes, policy levers and antecedents*

The second dimension in the organising framework further groups the indicators at each of the above levels:

- Indicators on observed outputs of education systems, as well as indicators related to the impact of knowledge and skills for individuals, societies and economies, are grouped under the sub-heading *output and outcomes of education and learning;*
- The sub-heading *policy levers and contexts* groups activities seeking information on the policy levers or circumstances which shape the outputs and outcomes at each level; and
- These policy levers and contexts typically have *antecedents* – factors that define or constrain policy. These are represented by the sub-heading *antecedents and constraints*. It should be noted that the antecedents or constraints are usually specific for a given level of the education system and that antecedents at a lower level of the system may well be policy levers at a higher level. For teachers and students in a school, for example, teacher qualifications are a given constraint while, at the level of the education system, professional development of teachers is a key policy lever.

■ Policy issues

Each of the resulting cells in the framework can then be used to address a variety of issues from different policy perspectives. For the purpose of this framework, policy perspectives are grouped into three classes which constitute the third dimension in the organising framework for INES:

- Quality of educational outcomes and educational provision;

- Equality of educational outcomes and equity in educational opportunities; and

- Adequacy, effectiveness and efficiency of resource management.

In addition to the dimensions mentioned above, the time perspective as an additional dimension in the framework, allows dynamic aspects in the development of education systems to be modelled also.

The indicators that are published in *Education at a Glance 2007* fit within this framework, though often they speak to more than one cell.

Most of the indicators in **Chapter A** *The output of educational institutions and impact of learning* relate to the first column of the matrix describing outputs and outcomes of education. Even so, indicators in **Chapter A** measuring educational attainment for different generations, for instance, not only provide a measure of the output of the educational system, but also provide context for current educational policies, helping to shape polices on, for example, lifelong learning.

Chapter B *Financial and human resources invested in education* provides indicators that are either policy levers or antecedents to policy, or sometimes both. For example, expenditure per student is a key policy measure which most directly impacts on the individual learner as it acts as a constraint on the learning environment in schools and student learning conditions in the classroom.

Chapter C *Access to education, participation and progression* provides indicators that are a mixture of outcome indicators, policy levers and context indicators. Entry rates and progression rates are, for instance, outcomes measures to the extent that they indicate the results of policies and practices in the classroom, school and system levels. But they can also provide contexts for establishing policy by identifying areas where policy intervention is necessary to, for instance, address issues of inequity.

Chapter D *Learning environment and organisation of schools* provides indicators on instruction time, teachers working time and teachers' salaries not only represent policy levers which can be manipulated but also provide contexts for the quality of instruction in instructional settings and for the outcomes of learners at the individual level.

READER'S GUIDE

Coverage of the statistics

Although a lack of data still limits the scope of the indicators in many countries, the coverage extends, in principle, to the entire national education system (within the national territory) regardless of the ownership or sponsorship of the institutions concerned and regardless of education delivery mechanisms. With one exception described below, all types of students and all age groups are meant to be included: children (including students with special needs), adults, nationals, foreigners, as well as students in open distance learning, in special education programmes or in educational programmes organised by ministries other than the Ministry of Education, provided the main aim of the programme is the educational development of the individual. However, vocational and technical training in the workplace, with the exception of combined school and work-based programmes that are explicitly deemed to be parts of the education system, is not included in the basic education expenditure and enrolment data.

Educational activities classified as "adult" or "non-regular" are covered, provided that the activities involve studies or have a subject matter content similar to "regular" education studies or that the underlying programmes lead to potential qualifications similar to corresponding regular educational programmes. Courses for adults that are primarily for general interest, personal enrichment, leisure or recreation are excluded.

Calculation of international means

For many indicators an OECD average is presented and for some an OECD total.

The OECD average is calculated as the unweighted mean of the data values of all OECD countries for which data are available or can be estimated. The OECD average therefore refers to an average of data values at the level of the national systems and can be used to answer the question of how an indicator value for a given country compares with the value for a typical or average country. It does not take into account the absolute size of the education system in each country.

The OECD total is calculated as a weighted mean of the data values of all OECD countries for which data are available or can be estimated. It reflects the value for a given indicator when the OECD area is considered as a whole. This approach is taken for the purpose of comparing, for example, expenditure charts for individual countries with those of the entire OECD area for which valid data are available, with this area considered as a single entity.

Note that both the OECD average and the OECD total can be significantly affected by missing data. Given the relatively small number of countries, no statistical methods are used to compensate for this. In cases where a category is not applicable (code "a") in a country or where the data value is negligible (code "n") for the corresponding calculation, the value zero is imputed for the purpose of calculating OECD averages. In cases where both the numerator and the denominator of a ratio are not applicable (code "a") for a certain country, this country is not included in the OECD average.

For financial tables using 1995 data, both the OECD average and OECD total are calculated for countries providing both 1995 and 2004 data. This allows comparison of the OECD average and OECD total over time with no distortion due to the exclusion of certain countries in the different years.

For many indicators an EU19 average is also presented. It is calculated as the unweighted mean of the data values of the 19 OECD countries that are members of the European Union for which data are available or can be estimated. These 19 countries are Austria, Belgium, the Czech Republic, Denmark, Finland, France, Germany, Greece, Hungary, Italy, Ireland, Luxembourg, the Netherlands, Poland, Portugal, the Slovak Republic, Spain, Sweden and the United Kingdom.

Classification of levels of education

The classification of the levels of education is based on the revised International Standard Classification of Education (ISCED-97). The biggest change between the revised ISCED and the former ISCED (ISCED-76) is the introduction of a multi-dimensional classification framework, allowing for the alignment of the educational content of programmes using multiple classification criteria. ISCED is an instrument for compiling statistics on education internationally and distinguishes among six levels of education. The glossary available at *www.oecd.org/edu/eag2007* describes in detail the ISCED levels of education, and Annex 1 shows corresponding typical graduation ages of the main educational programmes by ISCED level.

Symbols for missing data

Six symbols are employed in the tables and charts to denote missing data:

a Data is not applicable because the category does not apply.

c There are too few observations to provide reliable estimates (*i.e.* there are fewer than 3% of students for this cell or too few schools for valid inferences). However, these statistics were included in the calculation of cross-country averages.

m Data is not available.

n Magnitude is either negligible or zero.

w Data has been withdrawn at the request of the country concerned.

x Data included in another category or column of the table (*e.g. x(2)* means that data are included in column 2 of the table).

~ Average is not comparable with other levels of education.

Further resources

The website *www.oecd.org/edu/eag2007* provides a rich source of information on the methods employed for the calculation of the indicators, the interpretation of the indicators in the respective national contexts and the data sources involved. The website also provides access to the data underlying the indicators as well as to a comprehensive glossary for technical terms used in this publication.

Any post-production changes to this publication are listed at *www.oecd.org/edu/eag2007*.

The website *www.pisa.oecd.org* provides information on the OECD Programme for International Student Assessment (PISA), on which many of the indicators in this publication draw.

Education at a Glance uses the OECD's StatLinks service. Below each table and chart in *Education at a Glance 2007* is a url which leads to a corresponding Excel workbook containing the underlying data for the indicator. These urls are stable and will remain unchanged over time. In addition, readers of the *Education at a Glance* e-book will be able to click directly on these links and the workbook will open in a separate window.

Codes used for territorial entities

These codes are used in certain charts. Country or territorial entity names are used in the text. Note that in the text the Flemish Community of Belgium is referred to as "Belgium (Fl.)" and the French Community of Belgium as "Belgium (Fr.)".

AUS	Australia	ITA	Italy
AUT	Austria	JPN	Japan
BEL	Belgium	KOR	Korea
BFL	Belgium (Flemish Community)	LUX	Luxembourg
BFR	Belgium (French Community)	MEX	Mexico
BRA	Brazil	NLD	Netherlands
CAN	Canada	NZL	New Zealand
CHL	Chile	NOR	Norway
CZE	Czech Republic	POL	Poland
DNK	Denmark	PRT	Portugal
ENG	England	RUS	Russian Federation
EST	Estonia	SCO	Scotland
FIN	Finland	SVK	Slovak Republic
FRA	France	SVN	Slovenia
DEU	Germany	ESP	Spain
GRC	Greece	SWE	Sweden
HUN	Hungary	CHE	Switzerland
ISL	Iceland	TUR	Turkey
IRL	Ireland	UKM	United Kingdom
ISR	Israel	USA	United States

Chapter

THE OUTPUT OF EDUCATIONAL INSTITUTIONS AND THE IMPACT OF LEARNING

TO WHAT LEVEL HAVE ADULTS STUDIED?

This indicator profiles the educational attainment of the adult population, as captured through formal educational qualifications. As such it provides a proxy for the knowledge and skills available to national economies and societies. Data on attainment by fields of education and by age groups are also used in this indicator both to examine the distribution of skills in the population and to have a rough measure of what skills have recently entered the labour market and of what skills will be leaving the labour market in the coming years. It also looks at the effects of tertiary education expansion and asks whether this leads to the overqualified crowding out the lesser qualified.

Key results

Chart A1.1. **Picture of generational difference in science and in engineering (2004)**

This chart depicts the ratio of 25-to-34-year-olds with an ISCED 5A level of education and 30-to-39-year-olds with an ISCED 6 level of education to 55-to-64-year-olds with ISCED 5A and 6 levels of education in science and engineering (2004).

■ Science   ▨ Engineering

In all OECD countries the number of individuals holding a science degree in the younger age group outnumbers those who are leaving the labour market in the coming years, on average by three to one. This ratio falls to below two (1.9) for engineering. For four countries – Denmark, Germany, Hungary and Norway – this ratio is below one, indicating that more people with engineering degrees are likely to leave the labour market than the number of those recently entering the labour market with these degrees.

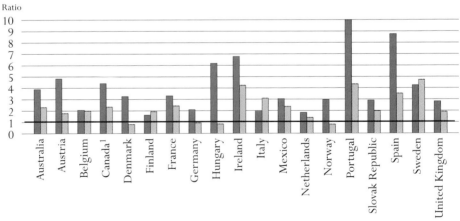

1. Year of reference 2001.
Note: The numerator includes population aged 25 to 34 with an ISCED 5A level of education and aged 30 to 39 with an ISCED 6 level of education. The denominator includes population aged 55 to 64 with ISCED 5A and 6 levels of education.
Source: OECD. Table A1.5. See Annex 3 for notes (*www.oecd.org/edu/eag2007*).
StatLink ⫲⫲ http://dx.doi.org/10.1787/068015451617

Other highlights of this indicator

- The proportion of individuals who have completed upper secondary education has been growing in almost all OECD countries, becoming the norm of youth cohorts. As of 2005, in 22 OECD countries, the proportion of 25-to-34-year-olds who have completed upper secondary education ranges from 73 to 97%. This increase has been particularly rapid in countries such as Korea and Ireland, and so countries with traditionally low levels of education are catching up to countries that have traditionally had higher levels of education.

- Social sciences, business and law are the major educational fields in most countries. They constitute 29% of the overall ISCED 5A and 6 levels of educational attainment in the population among the OECD countries. This may be due to these subjects' popularity among younger individuals. On average, there are three and one-half times as many individuals with degrees in these subjects among 25-to-34-year-olds with an ISCED 5A level of education and 30-to-39-year-olds with an ISCED 6 level of education than there are 55-to-64-year-olds with ISCED 5A and 6 levels of education in these subjects.

- The ratio of younger to older age groups with education as a field of study (ISCED 5A and 6 levels of education) is close to 1 among the OECD countries. For Denmark, Germany, Netherlands, Sweden and United Kingdom, this ratio is below 1, which might signal a potential problem of finding replacements as the older generation retires in the coming years.

- Data shows that increasing levels of tertiary education have not had a negative effect on employment. On the contrary, in the countries where tertiary education expanded most rapidly, a small rise in the relative risk of unemployment in the late 1990s was followed by a fall in the early 2000s. Nor has growth in tertiary attainment generally caused a slump in graduate pay, although on average it has not risen faster than pay generally.

A1

Policy context

A well-educated and well-trained population is essential for the social and economic well-being of countries and individuals. Education plays a key role in providing individuals with the knowledge, skills and competencies needed to participate effectively in society and in the economy. Education also contributes to an expansion of scientific and cultural knowledge. The level of educational attainment of the population is a commonly used proxy for the stock of "human capital", that is, the skills available in the population and labour force. It must be noted, however, that comparing different countries' educational attainment levels presupposes that the amount of skills and knowledge imparted at each level of education are similar in each country.

The skill composition of the human capital stock varies substantially between different countries depending on industry structure and the general level of economic development. The mix of skills as well as changes in this skill structure between different age groups is important to understand to have an idea of the current and future supply of skills in the labour market. One way to track the supply of skills in different subject areas is to examine replacement ratios in different educational fields of those who recently entered the labour market with those leaving the labour market in the coming years. In gauging potential effects of these changes in the composition of skills in the labour market, the overall volume of individuals within a certain field, the current and future industry composition, and to what extent lifelong learning provides an alternative to accumulate specific skills must all be considered.

In addition, it is also important to examine the effects of tertiary education expansion. In many OECD countries, tertiary attainment grew massively between the late 1970s and the late 1990s, although the increase was smaller between the early and the late 1990s. But does the effect of increasing the supply of well-educated labour match the creation of an equivalent number of highly skilled jobs or do some of the extra graduates end up doing jobs that do not require graduate skills, thus crowding out less highly qualified workers from the labour market? And do rising tertiary education levels among citizens reduce the earnings of those with tertiary education?

Evidence and explanations

Attainment levels in OECD countries

On average, across OECD countries, less than one-third of adults (29%) have obtained only primary or lower secondary levels of education, 41% of the adult population has completed an upper secondary education and one-quarter (26%) have achieved a tertiary level of education (Table A1.1a). However, countries differ widely in the distribution of educational attainment across their populations.

In 22 out of the 29 OECD countries – as well as in the partner economies Estonia, Israel, the Russian Federation and Slovenia – 60% or more of the population aged 25 to 64 years has completed at least upper secondary education (Table A1.2a). Some countries show a different profile, however. For instance, in Mexico, Portugal, Spain and Turkey, more than 50% of the population aged 25 to 64 years has not completed upper secondary education. Overall, a comparison of the levels of educational attainment in younger and older age groups indicates marked progress with regard to the achievement of upper secondary education (Chart A1.2). On average across OECD member countries, the proportion of 25-to-34-year-olds having attained

A1

Chart A1.2. Population that has attained at least upper secondary education¹ (2005)
Percentage, by age group

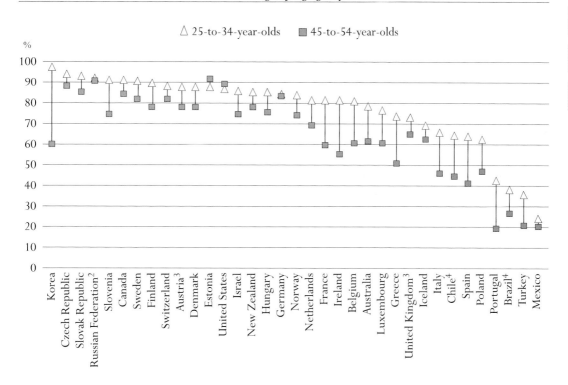

△ 25-to-34-year-olds   ■ 45-to-54-year-olds

1. Excluding ISCED 3C short programmes.
2. Year of reference 2003.
3. Including some ISCED 3C short programmes.
4. Year of reference 2004.
Countries are ranked in descending order of the percentage of 25-to-34-year-olds who have attained at least upper secondary education.
Source: OECD. Table A1.2a. See Annex 3 for notes (*www.oecd.org/edu/eag2007*).
StatLink http://dx.doi.org/10.1787/068015451617

upper secondary education is 13 percentage points higher than that of the 45-to-54-year-old age group. This increase has been particularly dramatic in Belgium, France, Greece, Ireland, Italy, Korea, Portugal and Spain, as well as the partner economy Chile, which have all seen growth of 20 or more percentage points across these age groups.

In countries whose adult population generally has a high attainment level, differences among age groups in the level of educational attainment are less pronounced (Table A1.2a). In countries where more than 80% of 25-to-64-year-olds achieve at least upper secondary attainment, the difference in the share of 25-to-34-year-olds who have attained the upper secondary level and the share of 45-to-54-year-olds who have attained this level is, on average, only 6 percentage points. In Germany and in the United States, the proportion of upper secondary attainment is almost the same for the three youngest age groups. For other countries, where there is more room for increase, the average gain in attainment between these age groups is 16 percentage points, including some very different situations: on the one hand, in Mexico the difference in upper secondary attainment between those aged 25 to 34 years and those aged 45 to 54 years is below 4 percentage points, but on the other hand, the difference reaches 37 percentage points in Korea.

A1

Box A1.1. European Human Capital Index

The link between investment in people and economic performance seems intuitive but is difficult to prove empirically and consistently. Measuring human capital comprehensively requires consideration of people's generic and specific skills, formal educational attainment, adult learning and work practices. Quantifiable translations are also difficult: how much learning on the job is needed to substitute for a month of formal adult education? What is more effective in generating human capital: spending to reduce the student-to-teacher ratio for immigrant children or to retrain the unemployed? Measurement is also complicated by the fact that different sorts of human capital investments have various rates of return for stakeholders and widely divergent pay-back periods. If human capital and its impact were more readily quantified, human capital investment might play a larger role in economic decision making. The Lisbon Council, a Brussels-based independent think tank, recently issued a human capital accounting model using time-based measurements to quantify economically relevant human capital. The methodology captures five different types of learning with economic value: learning from parents; compulsory education; tertiary education received; adult informal and non-formal learning; and learning by doing on the job. Further characteristics of the methodology are:

Consistency across type, time and country: The investment in each type of learning is expressed in the same unit, inflation-adjusted purchasing power parity US dollars, so that the economic value of all learning is comparable across time and place.

Allowance for depreciation: Based on empirical evidence of forgetting rates and knowledge obsolescence rates, the model depreciates different human capital investments over different periods of time and at different rates.

Accounting for input costs: The value of the investment in learning is primarily measured by the effective time spent on learning. This investment of time is given a monetary value. For learning from parents, this is the earned income that parents forego when educating their children. For compulsory education, it is the gross cost of teaching. For tertiary education, it is teachers' gross cost plus the earned income that students forego when studying. For adult non- and informal learning it is the learner's opportunity cost of time. The cost of time spent learning by doing is calculated using the gross salary of the employee. This approach draws on the insight that, under certain conditions, the individual's cost of time for human capital creation is equivalent to the individual's income from existing human capital. For example, an adult will only invest time in non-formal education to the extent that this yields a suitable return – a higher salary. If not, the adult would prefer to spend time generating returns from existing human and financial capital.

A first application of the model has resulted in a European Human Capital Index measuring human capital stock, deployment, utilization and evolution in 13 EU countries. However, significant methodological challenges still exist in applying such a model. The OECD is currently initiating discussion with member countries on both methodology and data availability, with a view to possibly replicating such an index across OECD countries.

For more information, see *www.lisboncouncil.net.*

A1

Expansion of tertiary education

Governments pursuing an expansion of tertiary education have often been driven by the belief that an advanced knowledge economy needs more high-level skills and thus requires a much greater proportion of the workforce than previously to be educated beyond the secondary-school level. However, the question remains whether an increasingly well-educated labour supply is being matched by the creation of an equivalent number of highly skilled jobs or whether at least some of the extra graduates end up in jobs that do not require graduate skills, at the expense of less highly qualified workers. Such a crowding out effect may be associated with a relative rise in unemployment among people with low qualifications (as higher-qualified workers take their jobs), but also potentially with a reduction in the pay premium associated with tertiary qualifications (as a rise in graduate supply outstrips any rise in demand for graduate skills).

An estimate of the expanding rate at which successive cohorts entering the labour market have attained tertiary education can be obtained by looking at the highest qualification held by adults of various ages today. Table A1.3 and Chart A1.3 shows the percentage of the population in OECD countries that has attained tertiary education, by ten-year age ranges.

Chart A1.3. Population that has attained at least tertiary education (2005)
Percentage, by age group

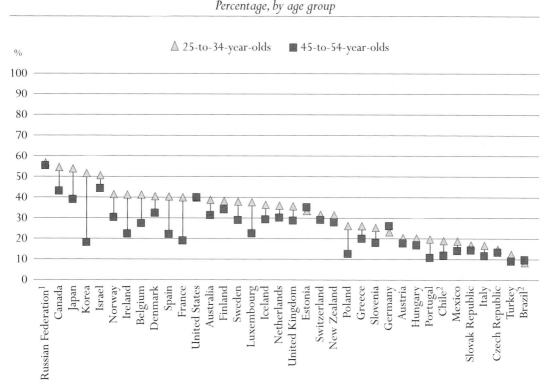

1. Year of reference 2003.
2. Year of reference 2004.
Countries are ranked in descending order of the percentage of 25-to-34-year-olds who have attained tertiary education.
Source: OECD. Table A1.3a. See Annex 3 for notes (*www.oecd.org/edu/eag2007*).
StatLink ⌗⌐ http://dx.doi.org/10.1787/068015451617

A1

When looking at tertiary attainment by five-year age ranges, it becomes clear that there have been large increases in many countries between attainment among cohorts entering the labour market in the late 1970s and the late 1990s. Table A1.6 shows continuing, but overall much smaller, increases between the early and the late 1990s, and divides countries into three groups according to this latter increase.

In general, countries in the first group have seen attainment rise more than other countries during the late 1970s and the late 1990s as a whole, as well as during the later part of this period: on average in these countries, attainment of tertiary qualifications has risen from 23 to 39% over 20 years. An exception is Australia, for which most of the 20-year increase occurred in the 1990s. In Norway and Finland, however, large rises occurred over the period as a whole, but principally between the late 1980s and early 1990s.

A striking observation from Table A1.6 is that the average tertiary attainment rates for the oldest cohort shown, those entering the labour market in the late1960s, is almost identical for the three groups of countries, at 16% to 17%. Yet in the youngest cohort shown, the average attainment in the top group of countries was 39% and in the lowest only 25%. Thus, the countries that during the 1990s were most vigorously expanding tertiary education had opened up a wide gap in attainment compared with the group with no significant expansion in the 1990s.

Data show clearly that there are substantial rewards associated with attaining tertiary education, and substantial penalties associated with failing to reach at least upper secondary education. The average earnings premium associated with tertiary compared to upper secondary education is everywhere more than 25% and in some countries more than 100% (Indicator A9). Across OECD countries, the average unemployment rate among those only with lower secondary education is 5 percentage points higher than those whose highest level is upper secondary, and seven points higher than those with tertiary education (Indicator A8).

Another way to look at trends over time is to consider countries not individually but as groups classified according to how quickly tertiary education has been expanding. The following analysis uses averages for the three groups of countries shown in Table A1.6 above. These three groups represent, respectively, countries for which tertiary attainment among people entering the labour market in the 1990s grew quickly, grew slowly and did not grow to any significant extent.

To consider the crowding-out hypothesis, Chart A1.4 looks at trends in relative unemployment rates by educational qualification among countries with fast, slow and negligible rates of tertiary attainment growth in the 1990s.

Chart A1.4 shows that, while unemployment is substantially higher than the average among those with low qualifications, this penalty has not increased in those countries that have expanded tertiary education, as the crowding-out hypothesis would have suggested. On the contrary, in the countries expanding most rapidly, a small rise in the relative risk in the late 1990s was followed by a fall in the early 2000s. However, in those countries that did not expand tertiary education (the bottom group), there has been a rise in the relative risk and failure to complete upper secondary education is in these countries now associated with an 80% greater probability of being unemployed, compared to less than 50% in the top group.

Chart A1.4. **Relative unemployment rate of adults with lower secondary attainment between 1995 and 2004**

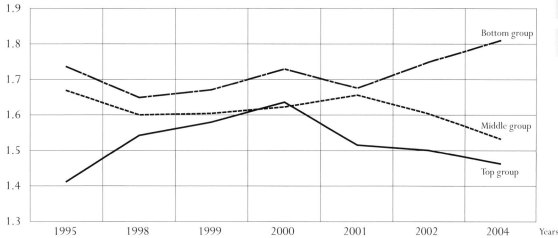

Lower secondary unemployment rate
as a ratio of upper secondary unemployment rate

Note: "Top group" refers to the nine countries that increased tertiary education most in the 1990s (on average 5.9%); "Middle group" refers to the eight countries that experienced modest increases in tertiary education in the 1990s (on average 2.4%); "Bottom group" refers to the nine countries that increased their tertiary education least over the 1990s (on average 0.1%).

Source: OECD. *Education at a Glance 2006*, Indicators A1 and A8.

 StatLink http://dx.doi.org/10.1787/068015451617

This finding is reinforced by Chart A1.5, showing that countries expanding higher education attainment more in the late 1990s tended to have a greater decline (or smaller increase) in unemployment among the lower educated between 1995 and 2004 than countries with less tertiary expansion. For example, Ireland, France and Korea had the fastest growth in tertiary attainment and close to zero or negative growth in unemployment, whereas Germany, the Czech Republic and the Slovak Republic had low or no growth in tertiary attainment but substantial growth in unemployment among the lower educated. While there is not a perfect match – Finland had no tertiary expansion but a fall in unemployment, Poland expanded tertiary education but unemployment rose too – the general trend is again the opposite of what one would expect according to the crowding-out hypothesis. Note also that the relationship is stronger when outliers are removed from the figure.

The data provide thus no evidence that the lesser qualified are crowded out from the labour market and much to point to the opposite: that the least educated individuals benefits in terms of better employment opportunities when more people go into higher education. It may be that the expansion of the high end of educational ladder is, apart from generating growth, also providing more equitable employment opportunities. Last but not least, an analysis of trends in the absolute level of unemployment for upper-secondary educated adults suggests that changes in the level of unemployment during the period 1995 to 2004 are unrelated to changes in tertiary attainment levels.

A1

Chart A1.5. Changes in tertiary education and changes in unemployment for lower secondary educated adults: late 1990s and early 2000s

Percentage point change within the periods

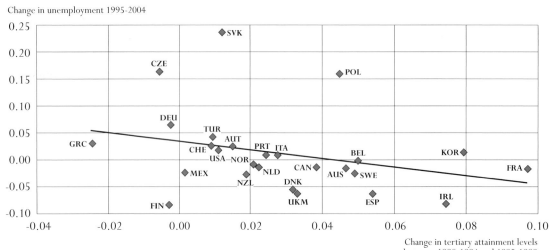

Change in unemployment 1995-2004

Change in tertiary attainment levels
between 1990-1994 and 1995-1999

Source: OECD. *Education at a Glance 2006*, Indicators A1 and A8.
StatLink http://dx.doi.org/10.1787/068015451617

In the case of unemployment and tertiary education, the picture is less clear-cut. Chart A1.6 shows that the extent to which a tertiary degree protects against unemployment risk has deteriorated slightly in the countries with the fastest rates of tertiary expansion, from 37% to 31% less than the risk among those with only upper secondary education. However, the same rate of deterioration has also occurred among countries with the lowest expansion rates, and a faster deterioration occurred among the countries that expanded slowly in the 1990s.

Chart A1.6. Relative unemployment rate of adults with tertiary level attainment between 1995 and 2004

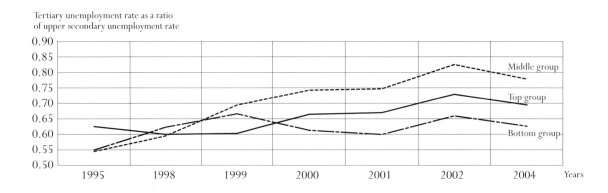

Tertiary unemployment rate as a ratio
of upper secondary unemployment rate

Note: "Top group" refers to the nine countries that increased tertiary education most in the 1990s (on average 5.9%); "Middle group" refers to the eight countries that experienced modest increases in tertiary education in the 1990s (on average 2.4%); "Bottom group" refers to the nine countries that increased their tertiary education least over the 1990s (on average 0.1%).
Source: OECD. *Education at a Glance 2006*, Indicators A1 and A8.
StatLink http://dx.doi.org/10.1787/068015451617

Graduates in the first group of countries, where on average 38% of adults in their late 20s and early 30s have tertiary education, face relative unemployment rates only slightly less favourable than the lower group where 25% are graduates, and more favourable than the middle group where 28% are graduates. There is thus no obvious link between a rising or a high number of graduates and relatively poor or deteriorating unemployment risks for those holding degrees. Overall Chart A1.6 also indicates that upper secondary educated individuals have strengthen their labour market position relative to tertiary educated individuals as their unemployment rates relatively speaking have moved in a positive directions over the period, suggesting once more that higher educated on the whole have not displaced lower educated from the labour market.

An important question is whether rising tertiary education levels among citizens lead to an inflation of the labour-market value of qualifications. Indicator A9 shows that this hypothesis is improbable. Among the countries in which the tertiary attainment grew by 5 percentage points or more between 35-to-44-year-olds and 25-to-34-year-olds, Spain is the only country in which the rapid expansion in tertiary attainment was associated with a significant decline in the wage premium that tertiary attainment attracts, during the period 1997 to 2004. In contrast, countries with fast growing relative earnings returns to tertiary qualifications have been Germany (20 percentage points), Hungary (38 percentage points), Ireland (17 percentage points) and Switzerland (12 percentage points). While improvements in supply have not generally caused a slump in graduate pay, the data show that on average it does not rise faster than pay generally.

When more individuals enter higher education it is obvious to ask whether this will affect the earnings of both those with upper secondary education and tertiary education. In particular, will the intake of more students with lower school performance likely influence the earnings received by those with tertiary education if the higher educational system is not able provide enough support for those with poorer school backgrounds? This question would require an analysis of earnings distributions within each educational group but as such this potential estimation problem will be balanced out in relative earnings as the skills (school performance) in all likelihood declines consistently among those with upper secondary education leaving the impact on relative earnings fairly constant stable when moving more people into higher education.

Variation in attainment levels by fields of study

As shown above, tertiary attainment levels have risen among younger age groups and sharply so in many countries. However, this increase in tertiary attainment is not evenly spread among different fields of education. As depicted in Chart A1.1 there is large variation between countries in the extent to which younger individuals have chosen science or engineering fields in comparison to the older age group. In these key educational fields, there is also substantial variation within countries where supply levels within science have risen more relative to engineering in all OECD countries except in Finland, Italy, and Sweden.

In the case of Denmark, Hungary, and Norway, some of the increases in supply levels in science relative to engineering can be explained by the fact that science is a relative small educational field with few individuals holding a degree from this course of study in the working age population. Table A1.4 shows the distribution of adults at ISCED 5A and 6 levels by fields of education. Social

A1

sciences, business, and law form the main educational field in most countries, with the exception of Ireland where science is the main field and Hungary as well as Norway, where education is the main field, Finland, and the Slovak Republic where engineering make up the main field, and Denmark where health and welfare has been the main course of study for adults.

Among the countries in Table A1.4, social sciences, business, and law make up 29% of the population with ISCED 5A and 6 levels of education. For education this figure is 15%, engineering 14%, art and humanities 13%, and science as a field constitutes 11% of those with ISCED 5A and 6 levels of education. The predominance of social sciences, business, and law is largely driven by increases in these fields of education in recent years. The ratios in Table A1.5 provide an indication of these shifts by comparing the number of 25-to-34-year-olds with an ISCED 5A level of education and 30-to-39-year-olds with an ISCED 6 level of education to the number of 55-to-64-year-olds with ISCED 5A and 6 levels of education, for each field of education. Social sciences, business and law has attracted a substantial amount of young individuals with three and half times as many young adults with degrees in this field as in the older age group. This change reflects increases in attainment levels in general, but it is also a reflection of the fact that many younger individuals have been attracted to this field of study. More than four times as many young individuals have attained a degree in social sciences, business and law compared with the older age group in France, Ireland, Italy, Portugal and Spain.

Education is the field of study where supply has, on average, not increased when comparing younger and older age groups. This largely reflects the relatively stable conditions in which most countries' education systems find themselves. However, for Denmark, Germany, Netherlands, Sweden and United Kingdom the replacement ratio is below 1, which could signal a potential problem for these countries when the older generation retires in coming years. In France, the low level of this ratio reflects changes within the professional training of teachers at the primary level.

Definitions and methodologies

Data on population and educational attainment are taken from OECD and EUROSTAT databases, which are compiled from National Labour Force Surveys. See Annex 3 (*www.oecd.org/edu/ eag2007*) for national sources.

Attainment profiles are based on the percentage of the population aged 25 to 64 years that has completed a specified level of education. The International Standard Classification of Education (ISCED-97) is used to define the levels of education. See Annex 3 (*www.oecd.org/edu/eag2007*) for a description of ISCED-97 education programmes and attainment levels and their mappings for each country.

Successful completion of upper secondary education means the achievement of upper secondary programmes type A, B or C of a similar length; completion of type C programmes (labour market destination) of significantly shorter duration is not classified as upper secondary attainment.

The data for Tables A1.4 and A1.5 originate from a special data collection by the Supply of Skills working group of INES Network B. Data on the distribution by fields of education among the population with tertiary-type 5A/6 levels of education was collected in most cases from Eurostat labour force survey or national labour force surveys.

A1

Further references

For further information on tertiary expansion, see the OECD Education Working Paper "Effects of Tertiary Expansion: Crowding-out effects and labour market matches for the higher educated" (forthcoming on line at *www.oecd.org/edu/workingpapers*).

The following additional material relevant to this indicator is available on line at:

StatLink http://dx.doi.org/10.1787/068015451617

- *Educational attainment: adult population, by gender (2005)*
  Table A1.1b: Males
  Table A1.1c: Females

- *Population that has attained at least upper secondary education, by gender (2005)*
  Table A1.2b: Males
  Table A1.2c: Females

- *Population that has attained tertiary education, by gender (2005)*
  Table A1.3b: Males
  Table A1.3c: Females

- *Attainment of tertiary education, by age (2004)*
  Table A1.6

A1

Table A1.1a.
Educational attainment: adult population (2005)
Distribution of the 25-to-64-year-old population, by highest level of education attained

| | Pre-primary and primary education | Lower secondary education | Upper secondary education | | | Post-secondary non-tertiary education | Tertiary education | | | All levels of education |
			ISCED 3C Short	ISCED 3C Long/3B	ISCED 3A		Type B	Type A	Advanced research programmes	
	(1)	(2)	(3)	(4)	(5)	(6)	(7)	(8)	(9)	(10)
OECD countries										
Australia	9	26	a	a	31	3	9	23	x(8)	100
Austria	x(2)	19	a	48	6	9	9	9	x(8)	100
Belgium	15	18	a	9	24	2	17	13	n	100
Canada	5	10	a	x(5)	27	12	23	23	x(8)	100
Czech Republic	n	10	a	43	34	a	x(8)	13	x(8)	100
Denmark	1	16	2	44	4	n	8	26	n	100
Finland	11	10	a	a	44	n	17	17	1	100
France	14	19	a	31	11	n	10	14	1	100
Germany	3	14	a	49	3	6	10	14	1	100
Greece	29	11	3	3	26	7	7	14	n	100
Hungary	2	22	a	30	28	2	n	17	n	99
Iceland	3	28	7	21	9	3	5	26	x(8)	100
Ireland	17	18	n	a	25	11	11	18	n	99
Italy	17	32	1	7	29	1	1	12	n	100
Japan	x(5)	x(5)	x(5)	x(5)	60	a	18	22	x(8)	100
Korea	12	13	a	x(5)	44	a	9	23	x(8)	100
Luxembourg	19	9	6	18	18	4	10	16	1	100
Mexico	50	29	a	6	x(2)	a	1	14	x(8)	100
Netherlands	8	21	x(4)	15	23	3	2	28	1	100
New Zealand	x(2)	21	a	22	19	11	7	20	x(8)	100
Norway	n	22	a	30	11	4	2	30	1	100
Poland	x(2)	15	34	a	31	4	x(8)	17	x(8)	100
Portugal	59	15	x(5)	x(5)	13	1	x(8)	12	1	100
Slovak Republic	1	14	x(4)	35	37	x(5)	1	13	n	100
Spain	24	27	a	7	13	n	8	19	1	100
Sweden	7	10	a	x(5)	48	6	9	21	x(8)	100
Switzerland	3	10	4	45	6	3	10	17	2	100
Turkey	63	10	a	7	10	a	x(8)	10	x(8)	100
United Kingdom	n	14	19	21	16	a	9	15	6	100
United States	5	8	x(5)	x(5)	49	x(5)	9	28	1	100

	Attained lower secondary level of education or below	Attained upper secondary level of education		Attained tertiary level of education	
OECD average	29	41		26	
EU19 average	29	44		24	

Partner economies										
Brazil[1]	57	14	x(5)	x(5)	22	a	x(8)	8	x(8)	100
Chile[1]	24	26	x(5)	x(5)	37	a	3	10	x(8)	100
Estonia	1	10	a	7	42	7	11	22	1	100
Israel	x(2)	21	a	x(5)	33	a	16	29	1	100
Russian Federation[2]	3	8	x(5)	x(5)	34	x(5)	34	21	x(8)	100
Slovenia	2	17	a	28	32	a	10	9	1	100

1. Year of reference 2004.
2. Year of reference 2003.
Source: OECD. See Annex 3 for notes *(www.oecd.org/edu/eag2007).*
Please refer to the Reader's Guide for information concerning the symbols replacing missing data.
StatLink ⌦ http://dx.doi.org/10.1787/068015451617

A1

Table A1.2a.
Population that has attained at least upper secondary education[1] (2005)
Percentage, by age group

		Age group				
		25-64	25-34	35-44	45-54	55-64
OECD countries	Australia	65	79	66	61	50
	Austria[2]	81	87	84	78	70
	Belgium	66	81	72	60	48
	Canada	85	91	88	84	75
	Czech Republic	90	94	93	88	83
	Denmark	81	87	83	78	75
	Finland	79	89	87	78	61
	France	66	81	71	60	51
	Germany	83	84	85	84	79
	Greece	57	74	65	51	32
	Hungary	76	85	81	76	61
	Iceland	63	69	67	63	49
	Ireland	65	81	70	55	40
	Italy	50	66	54	46	30
	Korea	76	97	88	60	35
	Luxembourg	66	77	68	60	55
	Mexico	21	24	23	20	12
	Netherlands	72	81	76	69	59
	New Zealand	79	85	82	78	66
	Norway	77	83	78	74	73
	Poland	51	62	50	47	43
	Portugal	26	43	26	19	13
	Slovak Republic	86	93	92	85	68
	Spain	49	64	54	41	26
	Sweden	84	91	90	82	72
	Switzerland	83	88	85	82	77
	Turkey	27	36	25	21	15
	United Kingdom[2]	67	73	67	65	60
	United States	88	87	88	89	86
	OECD average	*68*	*77*	*71*	*64*	*54*
	EU19 average	*68*	*79*	*72*	*64*	*54*
Partner economies	Brazil[3]	30	38	32	27	11
	Chile[3]	50	64	52	44	32
	Estonia	89	87	95	92	80
	Israel	79	86	82	75	69
	Russian Federation[4]	89	92	95	90	72
	Slovenia	80	91	84	75	69

1. Excluding ISCED 3C short programmes.
2. Including some ISCED 3C short programmes.
3. Year of reference 2004.
4. Year of reference 2003.
Source: OECD. See Annex 3 for notes *(www.oecd.org/edu/eag2007).*
StatLink 🔗 http://dx.doi.org/10.1787/068015451617

A1

Table A1.3a.
Population that has attained tertiary education (2005)
Percentage of the population that has attained tertiary-type B education or tertiary-type A and advanced research programmes, by age group

	Tertiary-type B education					Tertiary-type A and Advanced research programmes					Total Tertiary				
	25-64	25-34	35-44	45-54	55-64	25-64	25-34	35-44	45-54	55-64	25-64	25-34	35-44	45-54	55-64
	(1)	(2)	(3)	(4)	(5)	(6)	(7)	(8)	(9)	(10)	(11)	(12)	(13)	(14)	(15)
Australia	9	9	9	9	8	23	29	23	21	16	32	38	32	31	24
Austria	9	8	9	10	8	9	12	10	8	6	18	20	19	17	14
Belgium	17	21	19	15	13	14	19	14	12	9	31	41	33	27	22
Canada	23	26	25	22	18	23	28	25	21	19	46	54	50	43	36
Czech Republic	x(11)	x(12)	x(13)	x(14)	x(15)	13	14	14	13	11	13	14	14	13	11
Denmark	8	9	8	6	7	26	31	27	26	21	34	40	35	32	27
Finland	17	11	22	19	14	18	27	19	15	13	35	38	41	34	27
France	10	17	10	7	5	15	22	14	11	11	25	39	25	18	16
Germany	10	7	11	10	10	15	15	16	15	13	25	22	26	26	23
Greece	7	8	8	6	3	15	17	17	14	8	21	25	26	19	12
Hungary	0	1	0	0	0	17	19	17	16	15	17	20	17	16	15
Iceland	5	3	5	6	3	26	33	29	22	17	31	36	34	29	21
Ireland	11	14	11	8	6	18	26	19	14	11	29	41	30	22	17
Italy	1	1	1	0	0	12	15	12	11	8	12	16	13	11	8
Japan	18	25	21	15	8	22	28	25	23	13	40	53	47	38	22
Korea	9	19	8	3	1	23	32	27	15	9	32	51	36	18	10
Luxembourg	10	13	10	7	8	17	24	17	15	11	27	37	27	22	19
Mexico	1	1	1	1	1	14	17	14	13	7	15	18	16	14	8
Netherlands	2	2	2	2	2	28	34	28	28	23	30	35	30	30	24
New Zealand	7	5	6	10	10	20	26	22	17	11	27	31	28	27	21
Norway	2	2	2	3	2	30	39	33	26	22	33	41	35	30	24
Poland	x(11)	x(12)	x(13)	x(14)	x(15)	17	26	16	12	13	17	26	16	12	13
Portugal	x(11)	x(12)	x(13)	x(14)	x(15)	13	19	13	10	7	13	19	13	10	7
Slovak Republic	1	1	1	1	1	13	15	12	13	10	14	16	13	14	11
Spain	8	13	10	5	3	20	27	20	17	11	28	40	30	22	14
Sweden	9	9	8	11	8	21	28	20	18	17	30	37	28	28	25
Switzerland	10	9	12	10	8	19	22	20	19	14	29	31	32	29	22
Turkey	x(11)	x(12)	x(13)	x(14)	x(15)	10	12	8	9	7	10	12	8	9	7
United Kingdom	9	8	10	9	7	21	27	20	19	16	30	35	30	28	24
United States	9	9	10	10	8	30	30	30	30	28	39	39	40	39	37
OECD average	*8*	*10*	*9*	*8*	*6*	*19*	*24*	*19*	*17*	*13*	*26*	*32*	*27*	*24*	*19*
EU19 average	*8*	*9*	*9*	*7*	*6*	*17*	*22*	*17*	*15*	*12*	*24*	*30*	*25*	*21*	*17*
Brazil[1]	x(11)	x(12)	x(13)	x(14)	x(15)	x(11)	x(12)	x(13)	x(14)	x(15)	8	8	9	9	4
Chile[1]	3	4	3	2	1	10	14	9	9	8	13	18	13	11	9
Estonia	11	9	12	13	10	22	24	23	22	19	33	33	36	35	29
Israel	16	15	16	17	16	30	35	28	27	26	46	50	44	44	43
Russian Federation[2]	34	35	37	34	26	21	22	22	20	19	55	56	59	55	45
Slovenia	10	9	10	9	10	11	15	11	8	7	20	25	21	17	16

1. Year of reference 2004.
2. Year of reference 2003.
Source: OECD. See Annex 3 for notes *(www.oecd.org/edu/eag2007)*.
Please refer to the Reader's Guide for information concerning the symbols replacing missing data.
StatLink ⟨≡⟩ http://dx.doi.org/10.1787/068015451617

A1

Table A1.4.
Fields of education (2004)
Distribution by fields of education for the 20-to-64-year-old population with ISCED 5A and 6 levels of educational attainment (percentage)

<table>
<tr><th></th><th></th><th>Education</th><th>Arts and Humanities</th><th>Social sciences, business and law</th><th>Science</th><th>Engineering</th><th>Agriculture</th><th>Health and welfare</th><th>Services</th><th>Other fields</th><th>Total</th></tr>
<tr><th></th><th></th><th>(1)</th><th>(2)</th><th>(3)</th><th>(4)</th><th>(5)</th><th>(6)</th><th>(7)</th><th>(8)</th><th>(9)</th><th>(10)</th></tr>
<tr><td rowspan="30">OECD countries</td><td>Australia</td><td>15</td><td>11</td><td>32</td><td>11</td><td>10</td><td>1</td><td>17</td><td>2</td><td>1</td><td>100</td></tr>
<tr><td>Austria</td><td>10</td><td>15</td><td>34</td><td>9</td><td>15</td><td>2</td><td>13</td><td>2</td><td>0</td><td>100</td></tr>
<tr><td>Belgium</td><td>4</td><td>15</td><td>30</td><td>13</td><td>19</td><td>2</td><td>12</td><td>2</td><td>3</td><td>100</td></tr>
<tr><td>Canada[1]</td><td>16</td><td>12</td><td>34</td><td>12</td><td>11</td><td>2</td><td>12</td><td>2</td><td>0</td><td>100</td></tr>
<tr><td>Czech Republic</td><td>m</td><td>m</td><td>m</td><td>m</td><td>m</td><td>m</td><td>m</td><td>m</td><td>m</td><td>m</td></tr>
<tr><td>Denmark</td><td>16</td><td>11</td><td>19</td><td>4</td><td>13</td><td>1</td><td>34</td><td>1</td><td>0</td><td>100</td></tr>
<tr><td>Finland</td><td>12</td><td>12</td><td>22</td><td>7</td><td>27</td><td>4</td><td>12</td><td>4</td><td>0</td><td>100</td></tr>
<tr><td>France</td><td>9</td><td>19</td><td>35</td><td>15</td><td>10</td><td>1</td><td>7</td><td>3</td><td>1</td><td>100</td></tr>
<tr><td>Germany</td><td>22</td><td>9</td><td>22</td><td>8</td><td>22</td><td>2</td><td>12</td><td>2</td><td>0</td><td>100</td></tr>
<tr><td>Greece</td><td>m</td><td>m</td><td>m</td><td>m</td><td>m</td><td>m</td><td>m</td><td>m</td><td>m</td><td>m</td></tr>
<tr><td>Hungary</td><td>27</td><td>5</td><td>23</td><td>4</td><td>21</td><td>6</td><td>9</td><td>5</td><td>0</td><td>100</td></tr>
<tr><td>Iceland</td><td>13</td><td>13</td><td>32</td><td>8</td><td>13</td><td>c</td><td>16</td><td>5</td><td>0</td><td>100</td></tr>
<tr><td>Ireland</td><td>12</td><td>13</td><td>22</td><td>23</td><td>11</td><td>2</td><td>10</td><td>3</td><td>5</td><td>100</td></tr>
<tr><td>Italy</td><td>4</td><td>19</td><td>33</td><td>12</td><td>14</td><td>2</td><td>15</td><td>1</td><td>0</td><td>100</td></tr>
<tr><td>Japan</td><td>m</td><td>m</td><td>m</td><td>m</td><td>m</td><td>m</td><td>m</td><td>m</td><td>m</td><td>m</td></tr>
<tr><td>Korea</td><td>m</td><td>m</td><td>m</td><td>m</td><td>m</td><td>m</td><td>m</td><td>m</td><td>m</td><td>m</td></tr>
<tr><td>Luxembourg</td><td>2</td><td>17</td><td>36</td><td>12</td><td>19</td><td>c</td><td>10</td><td>c</td><td>3</td><td>100</td></tr>
<tr><td>Mexico</td><td>5</td><td>17</td><td>31</td><td>11</td><td>13</td><td>3</td><td>11</td><td>7</td><td>1</td><td>100</td></tr>
<tr><td>Netherlands</td><td>20</td><td>8</td><td>30</td><td>6</td><td>12</td><td>2</td><td>17</td><td>3</td><td>2</td><td>100</td></tr>
<tr><td>New Zealand</td><td>m</td><td>m</td><td>m</td><td>m</td><td>m</td><td>m</td><td>m</td><td>m</td><td>m</td><td>m</td></tr>
<tr><td>Norway</td><td>20</td><td>7</td><td>18</td><td>4</td><td>6</td><td>1</td><td>12</td><td>3</td><td>29</td><td>100</td></tr>
<tr><td>Poland</td><td>m</td><td>m</td><td>m</td><td>m</td><td>m</td><td>m</td><td>m</td><td>m</td><td>m</td><td>m</td></tr>
<tr><td>Portugal</td><td>16</td><td>12</td><td>27</td><td>13</td><td>14</td><td>2</td><td>12</td><td>3</td><td>1</td><td>100</td></tr>
<tr><td>Slovak Republic</td><td>20</td><td>6</td><td>22</td><td>8</td><td>26</td><td>6</td><td>7</td><td>4</td><td>0</td><td>100</td></tr>
<tr><td>Spain</td><td>15</td><td>11</td><td>32</td><td>10</td><td>12</td><td>2</td><td>12</td><td>4</td><td>0</td><td>100</td></tr>
<tr><td>Sweden</td><td>22</td><td>7</td><td>24</td><td>7</td><td>15</td><td>1</td><td>19</td><td>3</td><td>1</td><td>100</td></tr>
<tr><td>Switzerland</td><td>m</td><td>m</td><td>m</td><td>m</td><td>m</td><td>m</td><td>m</td><td>m</td><td>m</td><td>m</td></tr>
<tr><td>Turkey</td><td>m</td><td>m</td><td>m</td><td>m</td><td>m</td><td>m</td><td>m</td><td>m</td><td>m</td><td>m</td></tr>
<tr><td>United Kingdom</td><td>14</td><td>18</td><td>28</td><td>18</td><td>11</td><td>1</td><td>8</td><td>1</td><td>0</td><td>100</td></tr>
<tr><td>United States</td><td>m</td><td>m</td><td>m</td><td>m</td><td>m</td><td>m</td><td>m</td><td>m</td><td>m</td><td>m</td></tr>
<tr><td colspan="2">OECD average</td><td>15</td><td>13</td><td>29</td><td>11</td><td>14</td><td>2</td><td>12</td><td>2</td><td>1</td><td>100</td></tr>
</table>

Note: Science includes life sciences, mathematics and statistics, computer science and use.
1. Year of reference 2001. Only ISCED 5A of educational attainment.
Source: OECD, Network B special data collection, Supply of Skills working group.
Please refer to the Reader's Guide for information concerning the symbols replacing missing data.
StatLink ⧉ http://dx.doi.org/10.1787/068015451617

A1

Table A1.5.
Ratio of 25-to-34-year-olds with ISCED 5A and 30-to-39-year-olds with ISCED 6 levels of education
to 55-to-64-year-olds with ISCED 5A and 6 levels of education, by fields of education (2004)

	Education	Arts and Humanities	Social sciences, business and law	Science	Engineering	Agriculture	Health and welfare	Services	Other fields	Total
	(1)	(2)	(3)	(4)	(5)	(6)	(7)	(8)	(9)	(10)
Australia	1.9	2.2	3.4	3.9	2.3	2.7	1.9	x(10)	2.9	2.6
Austria	1.0	1.8	2.0	4.8	1.8	1.6	1.4	x(10)	0.5	1.9
Belgium	x(10)	3.4	3.9	2.1	2.0	x(10)	2.4	x(10)	2.7	2.6
Canada [1]	1.1	2.1	3.2	4.4	2.3	2.1	1.9	5.3	0.0	2.3
Czech Republic	m	m	m	m	m	m	m	m	m	m
Denmark	0.8	2.3	2.5	3.3	0.8	0.6	1.2	x(10)	0.0	1.4
Finland	1.3	1.3	1.6	1.6	1.9	1.4	3.9	2.0	0.0	1.8
France	0.6	3.0	4.7	3.3	2.4	2.0	1.1	4.9	2.8	2.8
Germany	0.6	1.4	1.8	2.1	0.9	1.0	1.3	1.6	1.1	1.2
Greece	m	m	m	m	m	m	m	m	m	m
Hungary	1.9	2.7	2.4	6.2	0.8	0.9	1.4	1.3	0.0	1.7
Iceland	x(10)	x(10)	x(10)	x(10)	x(10)	x(10)	x(10)	x(10)	x(10)	2.7
Ireland	1.5	3.4	7.3	6.8	4.2	1.6	3.9	11.5	3.0	4.3
Italy	2.1	1.4	4.0	2.0	3.1	4.4	2.1	3.7	0.0	2.5
Japan	m	m	m	m	m	m	m	m	m	m
Korea	m	m	m	m	m	m	m	m	m	m
Luxembourg	x(10)	x(10)	x(10)	x(10)	x(10)	x(10)	x(10)	x(10)	x(10)	2.4
Mexico	x(10)	3.9	2.2	3.0	2.4	2.8	1.4	2.9	6.5	2.7
Netherlands	0.7	1.7	3.2	1.8	1.4	1.9	1.7	1.6	5.7	1.7
New Zealand	m	m	m	m	m	m	m	m	m	m
Norway	1.0	0.9	2.4	3.0	0.8	0.7	1.2	x(10)	9.0	2.2
Poland	m	m	m	m	m	m	m	m	m	m
Portugal	3.9	2.7	7.3	10.0	4.3	10.3	4.9	8.5	0.6	5.3
Slovak Republic	1.5	2.8	3.9	2.9	2.0	1.5	2.4	3.5	0.0	2.3
Spain	2.0	4.0	7.8	8.8	3.5	6.0	3.8	5.2	3.5	4.7
Sweden	0.9	1.9	1.7	4.3	4.7	2.5	1.3	x(10)	1.2	1.7
Switzerland	m	m	m	m	m	m	m	m	m	m
Turkey	m	m	m	m	m	m	m	m	m	m
United Kingdom	0.8	2.5	3.0	2.8	1.9	x(10)	2.8	x(10)	1.6	2.2
United States	m	m	m	m	m	m	m	m	m	m
OECD average	1.0	2.2	3.5	3.0	1.9	2.2	1.9	3.1	4.5	2.3

Note: Science includes life sciences, mathematics and statistics, computer science and use.
1. Year of reference 2001. Only ISCED 5A of educational attainment.
Source: OECD, Network B special data collection, Supply of Skills working group.
Please refer to the Reader's Guide for information concerning the symbols replacing missing data.
StatLink 〠🔢 http://dx.doi.org/10.1787/068015451617

HOW MANY STUDENTS FINISH SECONDARY EDUCATION?

This indicator shows the current upper secondary graduate output of education systems, *i.e.* the percentage of the typical population of upper secondary school age that follows and successfully completes upper secondary programmes.

Key results

Chart A2.1. **Upper secondary graduation rates (1995, 2005)**

The chart shows the number of students completing upper secondary education programmes for the first time in 1995 and 2005, as a percentage of the age group normally completing this level; it gives an indication of how many young people complete upper secondary education compared to ten years before.

■ 2005   ▲ 1995

In the last ten years, the proportion of students who graduate from upper secondary programmes has progressed by 7 percentage points on average in OECD countries with comparable data. In 21 of 24 OECD countries and the three partner economies for which comparable data are available, the ratio of upper secondary graduates to the population at the typical age of graduation exceeds 70%. In Finland, Germany, Greece, Ireland, Japan, Korea and Norway, graduation rates equal or exceed 90%.

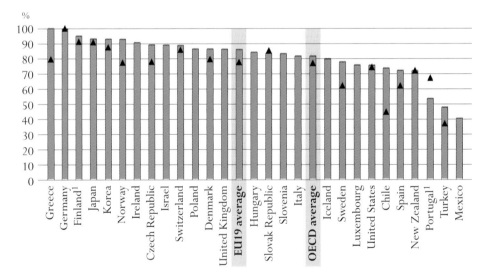

1. Year of reference 2004.
Countries are ranked in descending order of upper secondary graduation rates in 2005.
Source: OECD. Table A2.1. See Annex 3 for notes (*www.oecd.org/edu/eag2007*).
StatLink ᗄᒲᔕᑊ http://dx.doi.org/10.1787/068023602135

Other highlights of this indicator

▪ Females are now more likely to complete upper secondary education than males in almost all OECD countries and partner economies, a reversal of the historical pattern. Today, graduation rates for females are below those for males only in Korea, Switzerland and Turkey and are equal only in the partner economy Slovenia.

▪ In many countries, males are more likely to be on vocational courses. Still, in nearly one-half of the countries represented there is either no gender difference or a higher proportion of females on such courses.

▪ The vast majority of students who graduate from upper secondary programmes graduate from programmes that are designed to provide access to further tertiary education.

▪ Most students obtain upper secondary qualifications giving them access to university-level study (ISCED 5A), although the extent to which students go on to take up such study varies significantly between countries.

▪ In some countries, a significant proportion of students broaden their knowledge at the post-secondary non-tertiary level after completing a first upper secondary programme. In the Czech Republic and Hungary, 20% or more of a typical age cohort complete a post-secondary non-tertiary programme.

Policy context

Rising skill demands in OECD countries have made qualifications at the upper secondary level the minimum credential for successful labour market entry. Upper secondary education serves as the foundation for advanced learning and training opportunities, as well as preparation for direct entry into the labour market. Although many countries do allow students to leave the education system at the end of the lower secondary level, young people in OECD countries who leave without an upper secondary qualification tend to face severe difficulties in entering the labour market (see Indicators A8 and A9).

High upper secondary graduation rates do not guarantee that an education system has adequately equipped its graduates with the basic skills and knowledge necessary to enter the labour market because this indicator does not capture the quality of educational outcomes. But these graduation rates do give an indication of the extent to which educational systems succeed in preparing students to meet the minimum requirements of the labour market.

Evidence and explanations

Graduation from upper secondary education is becoming the norm in most OECD countries. Since 1995, the upper secondary graduation rate has increased by 7 percentage points on average across the OECD countries with comparable data. The highest growth occurred in Greece, Norway and Sweden and in the partner economy Chile, whereas the level of Germany, Japan, New Zealand, the Slovak Republic, Switzerland and the United States has been stable over the last ten years. In Mexico and Turkey, the proportion of students graduating at upper secondary level has strongly progressed since 2000 and thus has reduced the gap between these and other OECD countries.

In 21 of 24 OECD countries and the three partner economies for which comparable data are available, upper secondary graduation rates exceed 70% (Chart A2.1). In Finland, Germany, Greece, Ireland, Japan, Korea and Norway graduation rates equal or exceed 90%.

Gender differences

The balance of educational attainment between males and females in the adult population is unequal in most countries. In the past, females did not have sufficient opportunities and/ or incentives to reach the same level of education as males. Females have generally been overrepresented among those who did not proceed to upper secondary education and underrepresented at the higher levels of education. However, these gender differences are most evident in older age groups and have been significantly reduced or reversed among younger age groups (see Indicator A1).

Today, it is males who trail behind females in upper secondary graduation in almost every OECD country (Table A2.1). Graduation rates for females exceed those for males in 20 of 23 OECD countries and in 2 of the 3 partner economies for which total upper secondary graduation rates can be compared between the genders. The exceptions are Korea, Switzerland and Turkey, where graduation rates are higher for males. In the partner economy Slovenia, graduation rates are similar for both genders. The gender gap is greatest in Denmark, Finland, Iceland, Ireland, Luxembourg, New Zealand, Norway, Poland, Spain and the United States, where female graduation rates exceed those of males by more than 10 percentage points.

A2

Transitions following upper secondary educational programmes

Graduation from upper secondary education is becoming the norm in most OECD and partner economies, but curriculum content in upper secondary programmes can vary depending on the type of education or occupation for which the programmes are designed. Most upper secondary programmes in OECD countries and partner economies are designed primarily to prepare students for tertiary studies, and their orientation can be general, pre-vocational or vocational.

The vast majority of students who graduate from upper secondary programmes graduate from programmes that are designed to provide access to further tertiary education (ISCED 3A and 3B). Programmes to facilitate direct entry into tertiary-type A education are preferred by students in all countries, except in Austria, Germany and Switzerland and the partner economy Slovenia where both female and male students are more likely to graduate from upper secondary programmes leading to tertiary-type B programmes (Table A2.1).

The graduation rate for ISCED 3C (long) programmes is less than 20% on average in the OECD countries.

Chart A2.2. **Access to tertiary-type A education for upper secondary graduates (2005)**

Comparison of graduation rates from upper secondary programmes designed for tertiary-type A entry with actual entry rates to tertiary-type A education

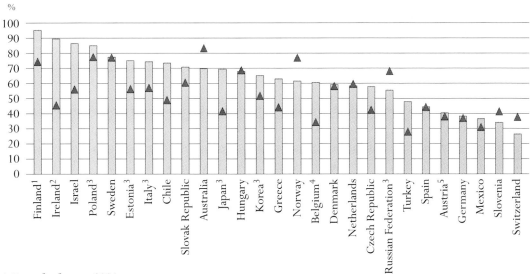

1. Year of reference 2004.
2. Full-time entrants only.
3. Entry rate for tertiary-type A programmes calculated as gross entry rate.
4. Excludes the German-speaking Community of Belgium.
5. Includes ISCED 4A programmes ("Berufsbildende Höhere Schulen").
Countries are ranked in descending order of graduation rates from upper secondary programmes designed to prepare students for tertiary-type A education in 2005.
Source: OECD. Tables A2.1. and C2.1. See Annex 3 for notes (*www.oecd.org/edu/eag2007*).
StatLink ᐽᔍᓯᔍ http://dx.doi.org/10.1787/068023602135

It is interesting, however, to contrast the proportion of students who graduate from programmes designed for entry into tertiary-type A programmes with the proportion who actually do enter these programmes. Chart A2.2 shows this comparison and demonstrates significant variation among countries. For instance, in the OECD countries Belgium, Finland, Ireland, Japan and Turkey, and the partner economies Chile and Israel, the difference between graduation rates from upper secondary programmes designed for tertiary-type A programmes and the eventual entry rate to these tertiary-type A programmes is relatively large (more than 20 percentage points). This suggests that many students who achieve qualifications designed for university level entrance do not in fact go on to take up university studies, although at least in Belgium and Israel such upper secondary programmes also give access to tertiary-type B programmes. In the case of Israel, the difference may be explained by the very varied ages of entry to university, which is partially due to the two to three years of military service students undertake before entering higher education.

In contrast, in countries such as Australia, Norway and Switzerland and in the partner economies the Russian Federation and Slovenia, the upper secondary graduation rate is lower than entry rates. For some countries such as Australia or Norway, this could be explained by a high proportion of international/foreign students (see Indicator C3).

Gender differences by type of programmes

In most OECD countries and partner economies, students do not follow a uniform curriculum at the upper secondary level. Programmes at the upper secondary level can be subdivided into general, pre-vocational and vocational programmes (see Indicator C1).

Chart A2.3. Upper secondary graduation rates for general programmes, by gender (2005)

Percentage of graduates to the population at the typical age of graduation

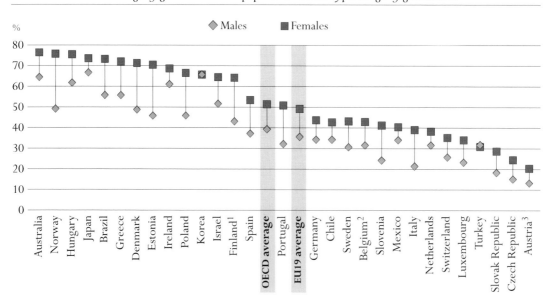

1. Year of reference 2004.
2. Excludes the German-speaking Community of Belgium.
3. Excludes ISCED 4A programmes ("Berufsbildende Höhere Schulen").
Countries are ranked in descending order of upper secondary graduation rates for general programmes for females.
Source: OECD. Table A2.1. See Annex 3 for notes (*www.oecd.org/edu/eag2007*).
StatLink ᗑᔕ http://dx.doi.org/10.1787/068023602135

For all OECD countries and partner economies for which comparable data are available, graduation rates in general programmes for females exceed those for males, with the exception of Korea and Turkey. The OECD average graduation rate from general programmes is 51% for women and 39% for men. The difference is 25 percentage points higher in Norway and in the partner economy Estonia.

There is no clear gender trend for pre-vocational and vocational upper secondary graduation rates. Although vocational programmes are most common for males – 50% of males in OECD countries graduate compared to 47% for females – females students in such programmes outnumber males in Australia, Belgium, Denmark, Finland, Luxembourg, the Netherlands and Spain and the partner economy Brazil (Chart A2.4).

Graduation from post-secondary non-tertiary programmes

Post-secondary non-tertiary programmes of various kinds are offered in 26 OECD countries and 4 partner economies. From an international comparative point of view such programmes straddle the boundary between upper secondary and post-secondary education, even though they might clearly be considered either upper secondary or post-secondary programmes in a national context. Although the content of these programmes may not be significantly more advanced

Chart A2.4. Upper secondary graduation rates for pre-vocational/vocational programmes, by gender (2005)

Percentage of graduates to the population at the typical age of graduation

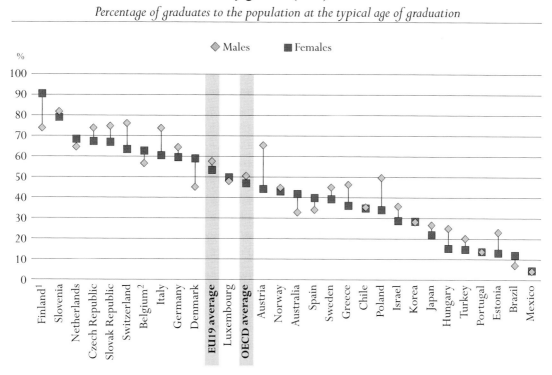

1. Year of reference 2004.
2. Excludes the German-speaking Community of Belgium.
Countries are ranked in descending order of upper secondary graduation rates for pre-vocational/vocational programmes for females.
Source: OECD. Table A2.1. See Annex 3 for notes (*www.oecd.org/edu/eag2007*).
StatLink ꞏꞏꞏ http://dx.doi.org/10.1787/068023602135

than upper secondary programmes, post-secondary non-tertiary programmes serve to broaden the knowledge of participants who have already gained an upper secondary qualification. The students tend to be older than those enrolled at the upper secondary level.

Typical examples of such programmes are trade and vocational certificates, nursery teacher training in Austria and Switzerland, or vocational training in the dual system for holders of general upper secondary qualifications in Germany. In most countries, post-secondary non-tertiary programmes are vocationally oriented.

In the Czech Republic and Hungary, 20% or more of a typical age cohort complete a post-secondary non-tertiary programme.

In 13 of the 24 OECD countries with available data and two partner economies, the majority of, if not all, post-secondary non-tertiary students graduate from ISCED 4C programmes, which are designed primarily to prepare graduates for direct entry into the labour market. Although the gender difference is not apparent at the level of the OECD average, the proportion of males and females participating in such programmes in each country is very different. Poland and the partner economy Estonia count 50% more females who have completed an ISCED 4C programme than males, while the opposite trend exists in Ireland, where women represent four times less graduates than men (Table A2.3).

Apprenticeships that are designed for students who have already graduated from an upper secondary programme are also included in the post-secondary non-tertiary programmes. However, in 7 out of 24 OECD countries and one partner economy, 50% or more of post-secondary non-tertiary graduates have completed programmes designed to provide direct access to either tertiary-type A or B education. In Switzerland, 72% of graduates complete ISCED 4B programmes (Table A2.3).

Definitions and methodologies

The data for the school year 2004-2005 are based on the UOE data collection on education statistics administered annually by the OECD.

In Table A2.1, upper secondary graduates are those who successfully complete the final year of upper secondary education, regardless of age. In some countries, successful completion requires a final examination, and in others it does not (see Annex 1).

Upper secondary graduation rates are estimated as the number of students, regardless of age, who graduate for the first time from upper secondary programmes, divided by the population at the age at which students typically graduate from upper secondary education (see Annex 1). The graduation rates take into account students graduating from upper secondary education at the typical (modal) graduation ages, as well as older students (*e.g.* those in "second chance" programmes) or younger students. The unduplicated total count of graduates is calculated by netting out those students who have graduated from another upper secondary programme in a previous year.

Counts of graduates for ISCED 3A, 3B and 3C programmes are not unduplicated. Therefore, gross graduation rates cannot be added, as some individuals graduate from more than one upper secondary programme and would thus be counted twice. The same applies for graduation rates by programme orientation, *i.e.* general or vocational. Moreover, the typical graduation ages are not necessarily the same for the different programme types.

A2

Pre-vocational and vocational programmes include both school-based programmes and combined school- and work-based programmes that are recognised as part of the education system. Entirely work-based education and training that is not overseen by a formal education authority is not taken into account.

In Table A2.2, data on trends in graduation rates at upper secondary level for the years 1995, 2000, 2001, 2002, 2003 and 2004 are based on a special survey carried out in the OECD countries and four of the six partner economies in January 2007.

In Table A2.3, post-secondary non-tertiary graduates are those who successfully complete the final year of post-secondary non-tertiary education, regardless of age. In some countries, successful completion requires a final examination, and in others it does not.

Post-secondary non-tertiary graduation rates are estimated as the number of students, regardless of age, who graduate for the first time from post-secondary non-tertiary programmes, divided by the population at the age at which students typically graduate from these programmes (see Annex 1). The graduation rates take into account students graduating at the typical (modal) graduation ages, as well as older or younger students. The unduplicated total count of graduates is calculated by netting out those students who have graduated from another post-secondary non-tertiary programme in a previous year.

For some countries, an unduplicated count of post-secondary non-tertiary graduates is unavailable and graduation rates may be overestimated because of graduates who have completed multiple programmes at the same level. Counts of graduates for ISCED 4A, 4B and 4C programmes are not unduplicated. Gross graduation rates cannot be added, as some individuals graduate from more than one post-secondary non-tertiary programme and would thus be counted twice. Moreover, the typical graduation ages are not necessarily the same for the different programme types.

A2

Table A2.1.
Upper secondary graduation rates (2005)
Percentage of upper secondary graduates to the population at the typical age of graduation, by programme destination, programme orientation and gender

	Total (unduplicated)			ISCED 3A (designed to prepare for direct entry to tertiary-type A education)		ISCED 3B (designed to prepare for direct entry to tertiary-type B education)		ISCED 3C (long) similar to duration of typical 3A or 3B programmes		ISCED 3C (short) shorter than duration of typical 3A or 3B programmes		General programmes		Pre-vocational/ vocational programmes	
	M + F	Males	Females	M + F	Females	M + F	Females	M + F	Females	M + F	Females	M + F	Females	M + F	Females
	(1)	(2)	(3)	(4)	(5)	(6)	(7)	(8)	(9)	(10)	(11)	(12)	(13)	(14)	(15)
Australia	m	m	m	70	76	x(8)	x(9)	37	41	x(8)	x(9)	70	76	37	41
Austria	m	m	m	16	20	52	40	n	n	2	4	16	20	55	44
Belgium[1]	m	m	m	60	66	a	a	19	18	16	20	36	42	59	62
Canada	m	m	m	m	m	m	m	m	m	m	m	m	m	m	m
Czech Republic	89	88	91	58	68	n	1	31	22	a	a	19	24	70	67
Denmark	86	77	96	59	70	a	a	51	58	n	n	59	70	51	58
Finland[2]	95	89	101	95	101	a	a	a	a	a	a	53	63	81	90
France	m	m	m	m	m	m	m	m	m	m	m	m	m	m	m
Germany	100	98	102	38	43	61	58	a	a	1	1	38	43	62	59
Greece	102	99	106	63	71	a	a	40	35	x(8)	x(9)	63	71	41	36
Hungary	84	81	87	68	75	a	a	19	14	x(8)	x(9)	68	75	20	15
Iceland	80	68	92	55	68	1	2	37	29	17	21	56	68	54	50
Ireland	91	84	98	89	97	a	a	5	6	81	65	64	68	100	100
Italy	82	80	83	74	77	2	3	a	a	21	19	29	38	67	60
Japan	93	92	94	69	73	1	n	23	21	x(8)	x(9)	69	73	24	21
Korea	93	94	92	65	65	a	a	28	28	a	a	65	65	28	28
Luxembourg	76	70	82	43	52	9	8	21	20	3	2	28	33	48	49
Mexico	40	37	44	36	40	a	a	4	4	a	a	36	40	4	4
Netherlands	m	m	m	58	65	a	a	20	22	22	18	34	37	66	68
New Zealand	72	61	83	x(1)	x(3)	x(1)	x(3)	x(1)	x(3)	x(1)	x(3)	x(1)	x(3)	x(1)	x(3)
Norway	93	82	104	61	75	a	a	43	42	m	m	61	75	43	42
Poland	86	81	92	85	91	a	a	13	9	a	a	55	66	41	33
Portugal	m	m	m	54	63	x(4)	x(5)	x(4)	x(5)	x(4)	x(5)	41	50	13	13
Slovak Republic	84	81	86	71	77	a	a	21	15	1	1	23	28	70	66
Spain	72	65	80	44	53	a	a	18	19	19	20	44	53	36	39
Sweden	78	74	81	77	81	a	a	1	n.	n	n	36	42	42	39
Switzerland	89	90	88	26	29	62	55	10	14	m	m	30	34	69	63
Turkey	48	51	44	48	44	a	a	a	a	m	m	31	30	17	14
United Kingdom	86	83	90	m	m	m	m	m	m	m	m	m	m	m	m
United States	76	70	82	m	m	m	m	m	m	m	m	m	m	m	m
OECD average	*82*	*78*	*87*	*59*	*66*	*8*	*7*	*18*	*17*	*11*	*10*	*45*	*51*	*48*	*47*
EU19 average	*87*	*82*	*91*	*62*	*69*	*8*	*7*	*16*	*15*	*12*	*11*	*42*	*48*	*54*	*53*
Brazil	m	m	m	64	72	9	11	a	a	a	a	64	72	9	11
Chile	73	69	77	73	77	a	a	a	a	a	a	38	43	35	34
Estonia	m	m	m	75	82	a	a	a	a	a	a	57	70	18	13
Israel	89	86	92	86	91	a	a	3	1	a	a	57	64	32	28
Russian Federation	m	m	m	55	x(4)	12	x(6)	18	10	3	2	55	x(12)	33	x(14)
Slovenia	83	83	83	34	42	46	50	n	n	32	28	32	40	80	78

Note: Mismatches between the coverage of the population data and the student/graduate data mean that the participation/graduation rates for those countries that are net exporters of students may be underestimated (for instance, Luxembourg) and those that are net importers may be overestimated.
1. Excludes the German-speaking Community of Belgium.
2. Year of reference 2004.
Source: OECD. See Annex 3 for notes (*www.oecd.org/edu/eag2007*).
Please refer to the Reader's Guide for information concerning the symbols replacing missing data.
StatLink ⎯⎯ http://dx.doi.org/10.1787/068023602135

Table A2.2.
Trends in graduation rates at upper secondary level (1995-2005)
Percentage of upper secondary graduates to the population at the typical age of graduation (1995, 2000, 2001, 2002, 2003, 2004, 2005)

	Typical Age	1995	2000	2001	2002	2003	2004	2005
	(1)	(2)	(3)	(4)	(5)	(6)	(7)	(8)
Australia	18-20	m	m	m	m	m	m	m
Austria	18	m	m	m	m	m	m	m
Belgium	18	m	m	m	m	m	m	m
Canada	m	m	m	m	m	m	m	m
Czech Republic	18-19	78	m	84	83	88	87	89
Denmark	19-20	80	90	91	93	87	90	86
Finland	19	91	91	85	84	90	95	m
France	17-20	m	m	m	m	m	m	m
Germany	19	101	92	92	94	97	99	100
Greece	17-18	80	54	76	85	96	93	102
Hungary	18	m	m	m	m	m	m	84
Iceland	20	m	67	67	79	79	84	80
Ireland	17-18	m	74	77	78	91	92	91
Italy	19	m	78	81	78	m	82	82
Japan	18	91	94	93	92	91	91	93
Korea	17-18	88	96	100	99	92	94	93
Luxembourg	17-19	m	m	m	69	71	69	76
Mexico	18	m	33	34	35	37	39	40
Netherlands	18-20	m	m	m	m	m	m	m
New Zealand	17-18	72	80	79	77	78	75	72
Norway	18-19	77	99	105	97	92	100	93
Poland	18-20	m	90	93	91	86	79	86
Portugal	17	67	52	48	50	59	53	m
Slovak Republic	18-20	85	87	72	60	56	83	84
Spain	17	62	60	66	66	67	66	72
Sweden	19	62	75	71	72	76	78	78
Switzerland	18-20	86	88	91	92	89	87	89
Turkey	16-17	37	37	37	37	41	55	48
United Kingdom	18	m	m	m	m	m	m	86
United States	18	74	74	70	72	75	74	76
OECD average		77	76	77	77	78	80	82
OECD average for countries with 1995 and 2005 data		77						84
EU19 average		78	76	79	79	82	82	86
Brazil	17-18	m	m	m	m	m	m	m
Chile	18	46	63	m	61	64	66	73
Estonia	m	m	m	m	m	m	m	m
Israel	18	m	m	m	90	89	93	89
Russian Federation	17	m	m	m	m	m	m	m
Slovenia	m	m	m	m	m	m	m	83

Source: OECD. See Annex 3 for notes (*www.oecd.org/edu/eag2007*).
Please refer to the Reader's Guide for information concerning the symbols replacing missing data.
StatLink ᐧᐧᑌᔑᐧ http://dx.doi.org/10.1787/068023602135

Table A2.3.

Post-secondary non-tertiary graduation rates (2005)

Percentage of post-secondary non-tertiary graduates to the population at the typical age of graduation, by programme destination and gender

		Total (unduplicated)			ISCED 4A (designed to prepare for direct entry to tertiary-type A education)		ISCED 4B (designed to prepare for direct entry to tertiary-type B education)		ISCED 4C	
		M + F	Males	Females	M + F	Females	M + F	Females	M + F	Females
		(1)	(2)	(3)	(4)	(5)	(6)	(7)	(8)	(9)
OECD countries	**Australia**	m	m	m	a	a	a	a	19.0	22.6
	Austria	m	m	m	24.3	28.5	3.2	5.5	1.7	2.9
	Belgium[1]	m	m	m	7.7	7.5	3.1	3.3	9.1	10.7
	Canada	m	m	m	m	m	m	m	m	m
	Czech Republic	26.2	24.2	28.4	23.3	25.9	a	a	2.9	2.5
	Denmark	1.2	1.6	0.8	1.2	0.8	a	a	a	a
	Finland[2]	2.6	2.5	2.8	a	a	a	a	5.4	5.9
	France	m	m	m	m	m	m	m	m	m
	Germany	16.4	17.7	15.1	11.2	10.6	5.2	4.6	a	a
	Greece	10.7	10.0	11.4	a	a	a	a	10.8	11.6
	Hungary	20.4	19.2	21.6	a	a	a	a	26.3	28.2
	Iceland	7.4	7.5	7.3	n	n	n	n	7.7	7.4
	Ireland	14.3	23.0	5.2	a	a	a	a	14.3	5.2
	Italy	6.9	5.2	8.6	a	a	a	a	6.9	8.6
	Japan	m	m	m	m	m	m	m	m	m
	Korea	a	a	a	a	a	a	a	a	a
	Luxembourg	2.6	4.2	0.9	a	a	a	a	2.6	0.9
	Mexico	a	a	a	a	a	a	a	a	a
	Netherlands	m	m	m	a	a	a	a	1.3	0.7
	New Zealand	18.2	11.5	25.3	x(1)	x(3)	x(1)	x(3)	x(1)	x(3)
	Norway	5.1	7.1	3.0	1.0	0.3	a	a	4.6	2.9
	Poland	13.3	10.2	16.6	a	a	a	a	13.3	16.6
	Portugal	m	m	m	m	m	m	m	m	m
	Slovak Republic	2.8	3.1	2.5	2.8	2.5	a	a	a	a
	Spain	a	a	a	a	a	a	a	a	a
	Sweden	0.8	0.7	0.9	a	a	a	a	0.8	0.9
	Switzerland	15.3	11.5	19.0	5.3	4.7	11.0	15.7	a	a
	Turkey	a	a	a	a	a	a	a	a	a
	United Kingdom	m	m	m	m	m	m	m	m	m
	United States	m	m	m	m	m	m	m	m	m
	OECD average	*8.2*	*8.0*	*8.5*	*3.3*	*3.5*	*1.0*	*1.3*	*5.5*	*5.5*
	EU19 average	*9.1*	*9.4*	*8.8*	*4.4*	*4.7*	*0.7*	*0.8*	*6.0*	*5.9*
Partner economies	**Brazil**	a	a	a	a	a	a	a	a	a
	Chile	a	a	a	a	a	a	a	a	a
	Estonia	m	m	m	a	a	a	a	18.0	22.3
	Israel	m	m	m	m	m	m	m	a	a
	Russian Federation	m	m	m	a	a	a	a	6.2	6.3
	Slovenia	2.6	1.4	3.9	2.0	2.8	0.7	1.1	n	n

Note: Mismatches between the coverage of the population data and the student/graduate data mean that the participation/graduation rates for those countries that are net exporters of students may be underestimated (for instance, Luxembourg) and those that are net importers may be overestimated.

1. Excludes the German-speaking Community of Belgium.

2. Year of reference 2004.

Source: OECD. See Annex 3 for notes (*www.oecd.org/edu/eag2007*).

StatLink http://dx.doi.org/10.1787/068023602135

HOW MANY STUDENTS FINISH TERTIARY EDUCATION?

This indicator first shows the current tertiary graduate output of educational systems, *i.e.* the percentage of the population in the typical age cohort for tertiary education that follows and successfully completes tertiary programmes, as well as the distribution of tertiary graduates across fields of education. The indicator then examines the number of science graduates in relation to employed persons. It also considers whether gender differences concerning motivation in mathematics at the age of 15 may affect tertiary graduation rates. Finally, the indicator shows survival rates at the tertiary level, *i.e.* the proportion of new entrants into the specified level of education who successfully complete a first qualification.

Tertiary education covers a wide range of programmes, but overall serves as an indicator of the rate at which countries produce advanced knowledge. A traditional university degree is associated with completion of "type A" tertiary courses; "type B" generally refers to shorter and often vocationally oriented courses. The indicator also sheds light on the internal efficiency of tertiary educational systems.

Key results

Chart A3.1. **Tertiary-type A graduation rates (1995, 2000, 2005)**

The chart shows the number of students completing tertiary-type A programmes for the first time, in 1995, 2000 and 2005, as a percentage of the relevant group.

▨ 2005　　● 2000　　△ 1995

On average across the 24 OECD countries with comparable data, 36% of students have completed tertiary-type A level education. The proportion of the population cohort completing their tertiary-type A qualifications has increased by 12 percentage points over the past decade. Graduation rates have doubled or more during the past ten years in Austria, Finland, Portugal, the Slovak Republic and Switzerland, but have been stable in the United States, which – along with New Zealand – had the highest rate in 1995.

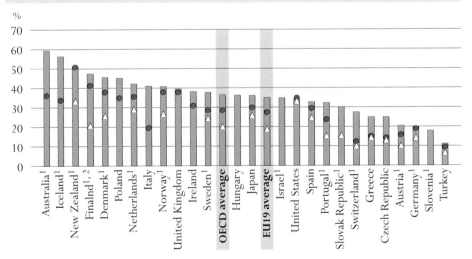

1. Net graduation rate is calculated by summing the graduation rates by single year of age in 2005.
2. Year of reference 2004.
Countries are ranked in descending order of the graduation rates for tertiary-type A education in 2005.
Source: OECD. Table A3.2. See Annex 3 for notes (*www.oecd.org/edu/eag2007*).
StatLink ᵐˢ᷈᷈ http://dx.doi.org/10.1787/068037263103

Other highlights of this indicator

▪ Tertiary-type A graduation rates figures range from around 20% or less in Austria, Germany and Turkey and the partner economy Slovenia, to more than 40% in Australia, Denmark, Finland, Iceland, Italy, the Netherlands, New Zealand, Norway and Poland.

▪ Tertiary-type A graduation rates tend to be higher in countries where the programmes provided are mainly of shorter duration.

▪ The graduation rate is 9% at the tertiary-type B level and 1.3% for programmes leading to advanced research qualifications.

▪ The survival rates in tertiary education represent the proportion of those who enter a tertiary-type A or a tertiary-type B programme, who go on to graduate from either a tertiary-type A or a tertiary-type B programme. On average across 19 OECD countries for which data are available, some 30% of tertiary students fail to successfully complete a programme equivalent to this level of education. Survival rates differ widely among OECD countries. In Greece and New Zealand, less than 60% of those who have entered tertiary programmes will graduate from either a tertiary-type A or a tertiary-type B programme in contrast to their counterparts in Flemish community of Belgium, France, Ireland and Japan where the survival rates is at or above 76%.

A3

Policy context

Upper secondary graduation is becoming the norm in most countries today and in addition the majority of students are graduating from upper secondary programmes designed to provide access to tertiary education, which is leading to increased enrolment in tertiary programmes (see Indicators A2 and C2). Countries with high graduation rates at the tertiary level are also the ones most likely to be developing or maintaining a highly skilled labour force.

Moreover, specific skills and knowledge in science are of particular interest as they increasingly represent a principal source of innovation and growth in knowledge-based economies. Differences among countries in the output of tertiary graduates by field of education are likely to be influenced by the relative rewards in the labour market for different fields, as well as the degree to which the market drives field selection in a particular country.

Tertiary level drop out and survival rates can be useful indicators of the internal efficiency of tertiary education systems. However, students' specific reasons for leaving a tertiary programme are varied: students may realise that they have chosen the wrong subject or educational programme; they may fail to meet the standards set by their educational institution, particularly in tertiary systems that provide relatively broad access; or they may find attractive employment before completing their programme. Dropping out is not necessarily an indication of failure by individual students, but high dropout rates may well indicate that the education system is not meeting the needs of its clients. Students may not find that the educational programmes offered meet their expectations or their labour market needs. It may also be that programmes take longer than the number of years for which students can justify being outside the labour market.

Evidence and explanations

Tertiary graduation rates show the rate at which each country's education system produces advanced knowledge. But tertiary programmes vary widely in structure and scope among countries. Tertiary graduation rates are influenced both by the degree of access to tertiary programmes and by the demand for higher skills in the labour market. They are also affected by the way in which the degree and qualification structures are organised within countries.

Graduation rates at the tertiary level

This indicator distinguishes among three different categories of tertiary qualifications: degrees at the tertiary-type B level (ISCED 5B); degrees at the tertiary-type A level (ISCED 5A); and advanced research qualifications at the doctorate level (ISCED 6).

Tertiary-type A programmes are largely theoretically based and are designed to provide qualifications for entry into advanced research programmes and professions with high skill requirements. Countries differ in the way in which tertiary-type A programmes are organised. The institutional framework may be universities or other institutions. The duration of programmes leading to a first tertiary-type A qualification ranges from three years (*e.g.* the Bachelor's degree in many colleges in Ireland and the United Kingdom in most fields of education, and the *Licence* in France) to five years or more (*e.g.* the *Diplom* in Germany).

Whereas in many countries there is a clear distinction between first and second university degrees, (*i.e.* undergraduate and graduate programmes), this distinction does not exist everywhere.

A3

In some systems, degrees that are comparable internationally to a Master's degree level are obtained through a single programme of long duration. To ensure international comparability, it is therefore necessary to compare degree programmes of similar cumulative duration, as well as completion rates for first-degree programmes.

To allow for comparisons that are independent of differences in national degree structures, tertiary-type A degrees are subdivided in accordance with their total theoretical durations of studies. Specifically, the OECD classification divides degrees into those of medium (three to less than five years), long (five to six years) and very long (more than six years) duration. Degrees obtained from short programmes of less than three years' duration are not considered equivalent to the completion of the tertiary-type A level of education and are therefore not included in this indicator. Second-degree programmes are classified according to the cumulative duration of the first- and second-degree programmes. Those individuals who already hold a first degree are netted out.

Tertiary-type A graduation rates

On average across the 24 OECD countries with comparable data, 36% of persons at the typical age of graduation completed tertiary-type A education in 2005. This figure ranged from around 20% or less in Austria, Germany, Turkey and in the partner economy Slovenia to more than 40% in Australia, Denmark, Finland, Iceland, Italy, the Netherlands, New Zealand, Norway and Poland (Table A3.1).

On average in OECD countries, the tertiary-type A graduation rate has known a significant increase of 12 percentage points over the ten last year. In virtually every country for which comparable data are available, tertiary-type A graduation rates increased between 1995 and 2005, often quite substantially. One of the most significant increase in type A graduation rates was reported in Italy where the rate doubled to 41% between 2000 and 2005, though this was largely a result of structural change. Reform in the Italian tertiary system in 2002 allowed university students who had originally enrolled on programmes with a long duration to attain a degree after three years of study (Chart A3.1 and Table A3.2).

Similarly, in Switzerland, the increase in tertiary-type A graduation rates is largely due to reforms in the system which not only shortened the duration of the first degree but also created new universities focusing on applied sciences.

Over the period 1995 to 2005, tertiary graduation rates evolved quite differently in OECD countries and partner economies. Increase was more marked between 1995 and 2000 than from 2000 to 2005, for some countries (such as New Zealand and Norway). The reverse was observed in the Czech Republic, Greece, Japan and Switzerland, where the increase in graduation rate has occurred mainly in the last five years (Table A3.2).

Tertiary-type A: the shorter the programme, the higher the participation and graduation rates

The duration of tertiary studies tends to be longer in EU countries than in other OECD countries. More than two thirds of all OECD students graduate from programmes with a duration of three to less than five years, whereas the proportion is less than 60% in EU countries (Table A3.1).

A3

It is evident that, overall, tertiary-type A graduation rates tend to be higher in countries where the programmes provided are mainly of a shorter duration. For example, in Austria, the Czech Republic, Germany and the Slovak Republic, the majority of students complete programmes of at least five years' duration and the tertiary-type A graduation rates are at or below 30%. In contrast, tertiary-type A graduation rates are around 40% or more in Australia, New Zealand and the United Kingdom, where programmes of three to less than five years are the norm (more than 90% of graduates following programmes with durations of three to less than five years). Poland provides a notable exception to this trend: despite typically providing long tertiary-type A programmes, its tertiary-type A graduation rate is over 40%.

Chart A3.2. Tertiary-type A graduation rates, by duration of programme (2005)

Percentage of tertiary-type A graduates to the population at the typical age of graduation

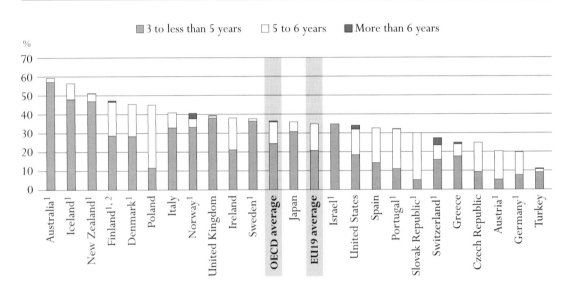

1. Net graduation rate is calculated by summing the graduation rates by single year of age in 2005.
2. Year of reference 2004.
Countries are ranked in descending order of tertiary-type A graduation rates.
Source: OECD. Table A3.1. See Annex 3 for notes (*www.oecd.org/edu/eag2007*).
StatLink ᴍ🖼🐒 http://dx.doi.org/10.1787/068037263103

Tertiary-type B graduation rates

Tertiary-type B programmes are classified at the same level of competencies as tertiary-type A programmes, but are more occupationally oriented and usually lead to direct labour market access. The programmes are typically of shorter duration than type A programmes – usually two to three years – and generally are not intended to lead to university-level degrees. Graduation rates for tertiary-type B programmes averaged some 9% of an age cohort amongst the 22 OECD countries with comparable data (Table A3.1). In fact, graduation from tertiary-type B programmes is a sizeable feature of the tertiary system in only a few OECD countries, most notably in Ireland, Japan and New Zealand and in the partner economy Slovenia, where over 20% of the age cohort obtained tertiary-type B qualifications in 2005.

Chart A3.3. **Tertiary-type B graduation rates (1995, 2000, 2005)**

Percentage of tertiary-type B graduates to the population at the typical age of graduation

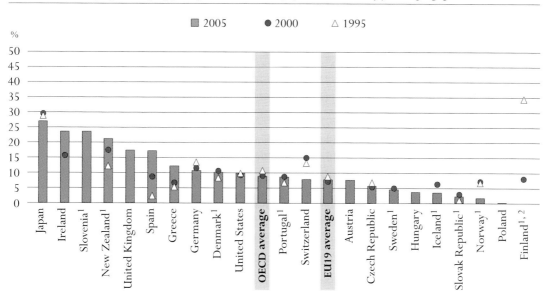

1. Net graduation rate is calculated by summing the graduation rates by single year of age in 2005.
2. Year of reference 2004.
Countries are ranked in descending order of the graduation rates for tertiary-type B education in 2005.
Source: OECD. Table A3.2. See Annex 3 for notes (*www.oecd.org/edu/eag2007*).
StatLink http://dx.doi.org/10.1787/068037263103

Trends in the provision of and graduation from tertiary-type B programmes are variable among countries even though the OECD average has been stable during the past ten years (Chart A3.3). For instance, in Spain, a sharp rise in type B graduation rates between 1995 and 2005 is attributable to the development of new advanced level, specific vocational training programmes. In contrast, type B programmes in Finland are being phased out and the proportion of the age cohort graduating from these programmes has consequently fallen rapidly over the same period.

Advanced research qualification rates

Across the 27 OECD countries with comparable data, an average of 1.3% of the population obtained an advanced research qualification (such as a Ph.D.) in 2005. The percentages range from 0.1% in Mexico and in the partner economy Chile to more than 2% in Germany, Portugal, Sweden and Switzerland (Table A3.1).

Graduations by field of education

Changing opportunities in the job market, differences in earnings among occupations and sectors, and the admission policies and practices of tertiary education institutions may all affect in which field students choose to study. In turn, the relative popularity of the various fields of education affects the demand for courses and teaching staff, as well as the supply of new graduates. The distribution of tertiary graduates across fields sheds light on the relative importance of the different fields from country to country, as well as on the relative proportion of female graduates in those fields.

In 23 of the 29 countries providing data, the largest concentration of tertiary-type A and advanced research qualifications awarded is in the combined fields of social sciences, business, law and services (Table A3.3). On average in OECD countries, more than one-third of tertiary-type A graduations is a degree in social sciences, business, law or services. The percentage of tertiary-type A qualifications awarded in social sciences, business, law and services ranges from less than 30% in Denmark, Finland, Korea, Norway, Sweden and Turkey, to more than 50% in Hungary and Poland and in the partner economy the Russian Federation. The largest concentration of tertiary-type A and advanced research qualifications awarded is in the field of humanities, art and education in Ireland and Turkey; in the fields of engineering, manufacturing and construction in Korea; and in the fields of health and welfare in Denmark, Norway and Sweden.

An average of 25% of tertiary-type A and advanced research students receive qualifications in science-related fields (engineering, manufacturing and construction, life sciences, physical sciences and agriculture, mathematics and computing, but not including health and welfare) in OECD countries. This includes percentages of less than 16% in Hungary, Poland and in the partner economy Brazil, to more than 30% in Finland, Germany, Greece and the Slovak Republic, and nearly 40% in Korea. Similarly popular on average in OECD countries are the fields of humanities, arts and education, from which 25% of tertiary-type A and advanced research students graduate.

The distribution of qualifications awarded by field of study is driven by the relative popularity of these fields among students, the relative number of students admitted to these fields in universities and equivalent institutions, and the degree structure of the various disciplines in a particular country.

Part of the variation in graduation rates among countries (Table A3.1) can also be accounted for by differences in the number of tertiary-type A degrees earned in the fields of humanities, arts and education. Countries with high graduation rates, on average, have a higher proportion of graduates in education and humanities and a lower proportion of graduates in science-related fields. In other words, there is less variation in graduation rates in science-related fields among countries than in overall graduation rates.

The picture is similar for tertiary-type B education, where programmes are more occupationally oriented: the fields of social sciences, business, law and services have the largest concentration of graduates (38%), followed by science-related fields (23%), and the fields of humanities, arts and education (23%) (Table A3.3).

The selection of a field of study at this level is heavily dependent on opportunities to study similar subject matters, or to prepare for similar occupations at the post-secondary non-tertiary or tertiary-type A level. For example, if nurses in a particular country were trained primarily in tertiary-type B programmes, the proportion of students graduating with qualifications in medical sciences from that level would be higher than if nurses were primarily trained in upper secondary or tertiary-type A programmes.

Science graduates among those in employment

Examining the number of science graduates per 100 000 25-to-34-year-olds in employment provides another way of gauging the recent output of high-level skills from different education systems. The number of science graduates (all tertiary levels) per 100 000 employed persons ranges from below 700 in Hungary to above 2 200 in Australia, Finland, France, Ireland, Korea, New Zealand and the United Kingdom (Table A3.4).

The variation of the number of females science graduates for tertiary-type A education and advanced research programmes per 100 000 25-to-34-year-olds in employment is largely lower than that of males. The number ranges from below 500 in Austria, Hungary, Japan, the Netherlands and Switzerland to above 1 500 in Australia, Finland, France, Korea and New Zealand. The OECD average is 970 female science graduates per 100 000 25-to-34-year-olds in employment compared to approximately 1 560 for males (Table A3.4).

This indicator does not, however, provide information on the number of graduates actually employed in scientific fields or, more generally, the number of those using their degree-related skills and knowledge at work.

Chart A3.4. **Number of tertiary science graduates
per 100 000 employed 25-to-34-year-olds (2005)**

Tertiary-type A, tertiary-type B and advanced research programmes, by gender

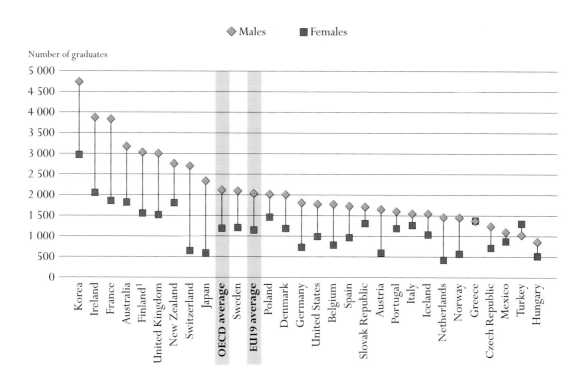

1. Year of reference 2004.
Note: Science fields include life sciences; physical sciences; mathematics and statistics; computing; engineering and engineering trades; manufacturing and processing; architecture and building.
Countries are ranked in descending order of the share of the number of male science graduates in the total number of male and female science graduates in tertiary programmes.
Source: OECD. Table A3.4. See Annex 3 for notes (*www.oecd.org/edu/eag2007*).
StatLink ⫶ http://dx.doi.org/10.1787/068037263103

A3

Impact of gender differences in motivation in mathematics on graduation rates

Beyond a general interest in mathematics, how do 15-year-olds assess the relevance of mathematics to their own lives and what role does such external motivation play with regard to their mathematics performance? The OECD's Programme for International Student Assessment (PISA) provides an index of the instrumental motivation of 15-year-olds that is based on students' responses to questions describing to what extent they were encouraged to learn by external rewards such as good job prospects. Specifically, students were asked to what extent they agreed with the following statements: "Making an effort in mathematics is worth it because it will help me in the work that I want to do later", "Learning mathematics is worthwhile for me because it will improve my career prospects", "Mathematics is an important subject for me because I need it for what I want to study later on", and "I will learn many things in mathematics that will help me get a job". The lower the index is, the lower the instrumental motivation of students can be considered to be. The index varies greatly among OECD countries and ranges from less than minus 0.25 in Austria, Belgium, Japan, Korea, Luxembourg and the Netherlands to more than 0.30 in Denmark, Iceland and Mexico and in the partner economy Brazil (Table A3.5). Although the results of PISA 2003 show that the relationship between performance and instrumental motivation is much weaker than with intrinsic motivation (*i.e.* interest in and enjoyment of mathematics), instrumental or extrinsic motivation has been found to be an important predictor for course selection, career choice and performance (Eccles, 1994).

Chart A3.5. Gender difference in instrumental motivation and tertiary-type graduates in mathematics

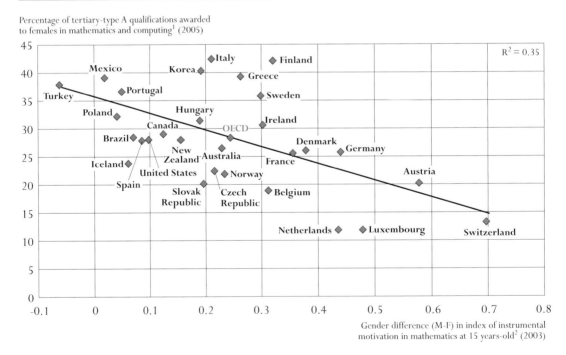

Percentage of tertiary-type A qualifications awarded to females in mathematics and computing[1] (2005)

Gender difference (M-F) in index of instrumental motivation in mathematics at 15 years-old[2] (2003)

1. Percentage of females graduated in mathematics and computing for tertiary-type A and advance research programmes.
2. The greater the gender difference, the less females are motivated compared to males.
Source: PISA database 2003 and OECD. Table A3.5. See Annex 3 for notes (*www.oecd.org/edu/eag2007*).
StatLink ᐧᐧᐧᔿ http://dx.doi.org/10.1787/068037263103

Difference by gender in terms of instrumental motivation can have an influence on the choice to pursue study in the fields of mathematics and computing. Table A3.5 shows that in all the 28 OECD countries for which data are available, the proportion of females graduating from tertiary-type A programmes in mathematics and computing is lower than for all the fields of education. In Belgium, Denmark, Iceland, the Netherlands, Norway and the Slovak Republic, and in the partner economies Brazil and Slovenia, the difference between the proportion of females graduating in mathematics and computing and the proportion of females graduating in all fields is of 35 percentage points or more.

Chart A3.5 shows that in the OECD countries where the difference in instrumental motivation between males and females is largest – namely Austria, Germany, Luxembourg, the Netherlands and Switzerland – the share of women graduating from tertiary-type A programmes in mathematics or computing is also below the OECD average and in some of these countries it is significantly below this benchmark. The gender difference in instrumental motivation in mathematics accounts for 35% of the cross-country variation in the percentage of tertiary mathematics and computing qualifications awarded to women. There is no direct connection between the 15-year-olds assessed by PISA and the older age cohorts leaving university studies. Nevertheless, to the extent that the motivational patterns revealed by PISA were similar also in the past, this suggests that gender differences in instrumental motivation among students in school may, combined with other influences, be predictive of the future study and career choice of males and females.

Survival rates at the tertiary level

The overall tertiary survival rates count as "survival" students those who enter a tertiary-type A programme and who graduate with either a tertiary-type A or a type B qualification or those who enter a tertiary-type B programme and who graduate with either a tertiary-type A or a type B qualification. On average across 19 OECD countries for which data are available, some 30% of tertiary students fail to successfully complete a programme equivalent to this level of education. Survival rates differ widely among OECD countries. In Greece and New Zealand, less than 60% of those who enter tertiary programme are graduated from either a tertiary-type A or a tertiary-type B programme in contrast to their counterparts in Flemish community of Belgium, France, Ireland and Japan where the survival rates is above 76 % (Chart A3.6).

On average across 23 OECD countries for which data are available, some 29% of tertiary-type A students fail to successfully complete the programmes they undertake. Survival rates differ widely among OECD countries. In New Zealand and the United States only just over 50% of those who enter tertiary-type A programme go on to successfully complete their programmes in contrast to their counterparts in Ireland and Korea where the survival rates are 83% and in Japan where the rate is 91% (Table A3.6).

Interestingly, entry rates to tertiary-type A programmes for these countries are below the OECD average, whereas in New Zealand, Sweden and the United States – where survival rates are among the lowest in comparison – entry rates are relatively high. Mexico, on the other hand, has one of the lowest entry rates to type-A programmes among OECD countries and a failure rate at the level of the OECD average for these programmes (Tables A3.6 and C2.4).

A3

Chart A3.6. Survival rates in tertiary education[1] (2004)

*Number of graduates divided by the number of new entrants in the typical year of entrance
to the specified programme*

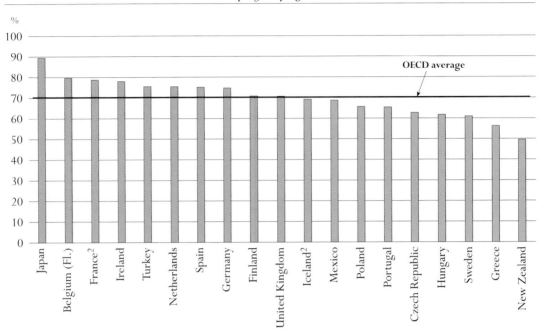

1. The survival rates in tertiary education represent the proportion of those who enter a tertiary-type A or a tertiary-type B programme, who go on to graduate from either a tertiary-type A or a tertiary-type B programme.
2. Survival rates based on panel data.
Countries are ranked in descending order of tertiary-survival rates.
Source: OECD. Table A3.6. See Annex 3 for notes (*www.oecd.org/edu/eag2007*).
StatLink ᗧᔜ http://dx.doi.org/10.1787/068037263103

Tertiary-type B survival rates are, at 67%, somewhat lower than those for tertiary-type A programmes, and again there is wide country variation. Type B survival rates range from above 80% in the Flemish Community of Belgium and Japan to below 40% in Greece. In general, tertiary-type B programmes are of a shorter duration than tertiary-type A programmes. However, interestingly, in the Flemish Community of Belgium, the majority of students graduate from medium length type B programmes (the only tertiary-type B programme option) and the country has the second highest survival rates at the tertiary-type B level, just after Japan, for which the breakdown by the duration of studies is not available (Table A3.6).

Among the 12 OECD countries with comparable data, survival rates from advanced research programmes range from 34% in Greece to around 90% in Italy, Japan and Mexico.

Definitions and methodologies

The data for the academic year 2004-2005 are based on the UOE data collection on education statistics that is administered annually by the OECD.

Tertiary graduates are those who obtain a tertiary qualification in the specified reference year. This indicator distinguishes among different categories of tertiary qualifications: *i)* tertiary-type B qualifications (ISCED 5B); *ii)* tertiary-type A qualifications (ISCED 5A); and *iii)* advanced research degrees of doctorate standard (ISCED 6). For some countries, data are not available for the categories requested. In such cases, the OECD has assigned graduates to the most appropriate category (see Annex 3 at *www.oecd.org/edu/eag2007* for a list of programmes included for each country at the tertiary-type A and tertiary-type B levels). Tertiary-type A degrees are also subdivided by their corresponding total theoretical duration of studies, to allow for comparisons that are independent of differences in national degree structures.

In Table A3.1, graduation rates for first tertiary programmes (tertiary-type A, tertiary-type B and advanced research programmes) are calculated as net graduation rates as the sum of age-specific graduation rates. Gross graduation rates are presented for those countries that cannot provide such detailed data. In order to calculate gross graduation rates, countries identify the age at which graduation typically occurs (see Annex 1). The number of graduates, regardless of their age, is divided by the population at the typical graduation age. In many countries, defining a typical age of graduation is difficult, however, because graduates are dispersed over a wide range of ages.

In Table A3.2, data on trends in graduation rate at tertiary level for the years 1995, 2000, 2001, 2002, 2003 and 2004 are based on a special survey carried out in the OECD countries and four of the six partner economies in January 2007.

In Table A3.3, tertiary graduates who receive their qualification in the reference year are classified by fields of education based on their subject of specialisation. These figures cover graduates from all tertiary degrees reported in Table A3.1. The 25 fields of education used in the UOE data collection instruments follow the revised ISCED classification by field of education. The same classification by field of education is used for all levels of education.

The labour force data used in Table A3.4 are taken from the OECD Labour Force database, compiled from National Labour Force Surveys and the European Labour Force Survey.

The OECD Programme for International Student Assessment (PISA) index of instrumental motivation in mathematics used in the Table A3.5 was derived from 15 year-old students' responses to a series of related questions and has been undertaken by the OECD. The most recent available results come from PISA 2003. A four-point scale with the response categories "strongly agree", "agree", "disagree" and "strongly disagree" was used. All items were inverted for scaling and positive values on this index indicate higher levels of instrumental motivation to learn mathematics. This index was constructed using an item response model (OECD, 2004a).

The survival rate in Table A3.6 is calculated as the ratio of the number of students who graduated from an initial degree during the reference year to the number of new entrants into this degree *n* years before, with *n* being the number of years of full-time study required to complete the degree. The calculation of the survival rate is not defined from a cohort analysis except in France, Iceland and Switzerland that provided data based on a cohort survey (see Annex 3 at *www.oecd.org/edu/eag2007*). This estimation for the other countries assumes constant student flows at the tertiary level, implied by the need for consistency between the graduate cohort in the reference year with the entrant cohort *n* years before. This assumption may be an oversimplification of the reality in countries (see Annex 3 at *www.oecd.org/edu/eag2007*).

A3

Dropouts are defined as those students who leave the specified level without graduating from a first qualification at that level. The first qualification refers to any degree, regardless of the duration of study, obtained at the end of a programme which does not have a previous degree at the same level as a pre-requisite.

Further references

The following additional material relevant to this indicator is available on line at:

StatLink 🔗 http://dx.doi.org/10.1787/068037263103

- *Table A3.7. Trends in net graduation rates at advanced research qualification rates (1995-2005)*
- *Table A3.8. Percentage of tertiary qualifications awarded to females, by type of tertiary education and field of education (2005)*

Table A3.1.
Graduation rates in tertiary education (2005)
Sum of graduation rates for single year of age by programme destination and duration.

A3

	Tertiary-type B programmes (first-time graduation)	Tertiary-type A programmes (first-time graduation)				Advanced research programmes[2]
		All programmes	Proportion of graduates by duration of programmes (in %)			Ph.D. or equivalent
			3 to less than 5 years	5 to 6 years[1]	More than 6 years	
	(1)	(2)	(3)	(4)	(5)	(6)
OECD countries						
Australia	m	59.4	96	4	n	1.7
Austria[3]	7.6	20.4	26	74	n	2.0
Belgium	m	m	m	m	m	1.2
Canada	m	m	m	m	m	m
Czech Republic[4]	5.7	24.9	38	62	n	1.2
Denmark	10.1	45.5	63	37	n	1.2
Finland[5]	0.2	47.3	61	38	1	2.0
France[4]	m	m	m	m	m	m
Germany[3]	10.7	19.9	39	61	n	2.4
Greece[4]	12.2	24.9	71	26	3	0.7
Hungary[4]	3.7	36.2	m	m	m	0.7
Iceland	3.5	56.3	85	15	n	0.3
Ireland[4]	23.6	38.2	56	44	n	1.2
Italy[4]	n	41.0	81	19	n	1.0
Japan[4]	27.0	36.1	86	14	a	0.9
Korea	m	m	m	m	m	1.1
Luxembourg	m	m	m	m	m	m
Mexico	m	m	m	m	m	0.1
Netherlands	n	42.1	m	m	m	1.5
New Zealand	21.2	51.3	92	8	n	1.1
Norway	1.7	40.7	82	11	7	1.2
Poland[4]	0.1	45.1	26	74	n	0.9
Portugal	8.6	32.3	34	65	n	2.6
Slovak Republic	2.3	30.1	17	83	n	1.3
Spain[4]	17.2	32.7	44	56	n	1.0
Sweden	4.5	37.7	97	3	n	2.2
Switzerland[3]	7.8	27.4	58	28	14	3.1
Turkey[4]	m	11.2	82	16	3	0.2
United Kingdom[4,6]	17.4	39.4	97	3	n	2.0
United States[4]	9.9	34.2	54	40	6	1.3
OECD average	*8.9*	*36.4*	*67*	*32*	*1*	*1.3*
EU19 average	*7.7*	*34.9*	*59*	*41*	*n*	*1.5*
Partner economies						
Brazil	m	m	m	m	m	1.3
Chile	m	m	m	m	m	0.1
Estonia	m	m	m	m	m	0.7
Israel	m	34.8	100	n	n	1.3
Russian Federation	m	m	m	m	m	1.9
Slovenia	23.6	17.8	m	m	m	1.2

Notes: Mismatches between the coverage of the population data and the student/graduate data mean that the participation/graduation rates for those countries that are net exporters of students may be underestimated (for instance, Luxembourg) and those that are net importers may be overestimated.
1. Excluding students who subsequently completed a longer programme.
2. Gross calculation rate is calculated for Chile, Estonia, Ireland, Italy, Japan, Korea, Mexico, the Netherlands, Poland, the Russian Federation, the United Kingdom and the United States.
3. Gross graduation rate is calculated for tertiary-type 5B.
4. Gross graduation rate is calculated for tertiary-type 5A and 5B.
5. Year of reference 2004.
6. The graduation rate for tertiary-type B programmes includes some graduates who have previously graduated at this level and it therefore represents an over-estimate of first-time graduation.
Source: OECD. See Annex 3 for notes (*www.oecd.org/edu/eag2007*).
Please refer to the Reader's Guide for information concerning the symbols replacing missing data.
StatLink ⟨⟨⟨⟨ http://dx.doi.org/10.1787/068037263103

A3

Table A3.2.
Trends in tertiary graduation rates (1995-2005)
Percentage of tertiary graduates (first-time graduation, tertiary-type 5A and 5B) to the population at the typical age of graduation
(1995, 2000, 2001, 2002, 2003, 2004, 2005)

		Tertiary 5A							Tertiary 5B							
	Typical age of graduation	1995	2000	2001	2002	2003	2004	2005[1]	Typical age of graduation	1995	2000	2001	2002	2003	2004	2005[2]
	(1)	(2)	(3)	(4)	(5)	(6)	(7)	(8)	(9)	(10)	(11)	(12)	(13)	(14)	(15)	(16)
OECD countries																
Australia	20-25	m	36	42	46	50	47	59	23-29	m	1	1	m	m	m	m
Austria	23-25	10	15	17	18	19	20	20	20-22	m	m	m	m	m	7	8
Belgium	m	m	m	m	m	m	m	m	m	m	m	m	m	m	m	m
Canada	22-25	m	28	m	m	m	m	m	m	m	m	m	m	m	m	m
Czech Republic	23-24	13	14	14	15	17	20	25	23-24	6	5	5	4	4	5	6
Denmark	22-27	25	37	39	41	43	44	46	21-25	8	10	12	13	14	11	10
Finland	25-29	20	41	45	49	48	47	m	21-22	34	7	4	2	1	a	a
France	m	m	m	m	m	m	m	m	m	m	m	m	m	m	m	m
Germany	25-26	14	18	18	18	18	19	20	21-22	13	11	11	10	10	10	11
Greece	25	14	15	16	18	20	24	25	24	5	6	6	7	9	11	12
Hungary	21-25	m	m	m	m	m	29	36	21	m	m	m	m	m	3	4
Iceland	23-25	m	33	38	41	45	51	56	22-24	m	6	8	6	7	5	4
Ireland	21	m	30	29	32	37	39	38	20	m	15	20	13	19	20	24
Italy	23-25	m	19	21	25	m	36	41	22-23	m	n	1	1	m	n	n
Japan	22-24	25	29	32	33	34	35	36	20	28	29	27	27	26	26	27
Korea	m	m	m	m	m	m	m	m	m	m	m	m	m	m	m	m
Luxembourg	m	m	m	m	m	m	m	m	m	m	m	m	m	m	m	m
Mexico	m	m	m	m	m	m	m	m	m	m	m	m	m	m	m	m
Netherlands	22-23	29	35	35	37	38	40	42	19-20	n	n	n	n	n	n	n
New Zealand	21-24	33	50	51	46	49	50	51	20	12	17	17	18	20	21	21
Norway	22-25	26	37	40	38	39	45	41	20	6	6	6	5	5	3	2
Poland	24-25	m	34	40	43	44	45	45	24-25	m	m	m	n	n	n	n
Portugal	22-26	15	23	28	30	33	32	32	21	6	8	8	7	7	8	9
Slovak Republic	22-25	15	m	m	23	25	28	30	21-22	1	2	2	3	2	3	2
Spain	20-22	24	30	31	32	32	33	33	19	2	8	11	13	16	17	17
Sweden	23-26	24	28	29	32	35	37	38	22-23	m	4	4	4	4	4	5
Switzerland	23-26	9	12	19	21	22	26	27	23-29	13	14	11	11	12	12	8
Turkey	22-24	6	9	9	10	11	11	11	m	m	m	m	m	m	m	m
United Kingdom[3]	20-21	m	37	37	37	38	39	39	20-21	m	m	12	12	14	16	17
United States	22	33	34	33	32	32	33	34	20	9	8	8	8	9	9	10
OECD average		*20*	*28*	*30*	*31*	*33*	*35*	*36*		*10*	*8*	*9*	*8*	*9*	*9*	*9*
OECD average for countries with 1995 and 2005 data		*20*						*32*		*10*						*10*
EU19 average		*18*	*27*	*29*	*30*	*32*	*33*	*35*		*8*	*6*	*7*	*6*	*8*	*7*	*8*
Partner economies																
Brazil	23	m	10	10	13	15	m	m	m	m	m	m	m	m	m	m
Chile	m	m	m	m	m	m	m	m	m	m	m	m	m	m	m	m
Estonia	m	m	m	m	m	m	m	m	m	m	m	m	m	m	m	m
Israel	22-26	m	m	m	29	31	32	35	m	m	m	m	m	m	m	m
Russian Federation	m	m	m	m	m	m	m	m	m	m	m	m	m	m	m	m
Slovenia	24-26	m	m	m	m	m	m	18	21-23	m	m	m	m	m	m	24

1. Net graduation rates is calculated in 2005 for Australia, Austria, Denmark, Finland, Germany, Iceland, the Netherlands, New Zealand, Norway, Portugal, the Slovak Republic, Sweden, Switzerland, Israel and Slovenia.
2. Net graduation rates is calculated in 2005 for Denmark, Finland, Iceland, New Zealand, Norway, Portugal, the Slovak Republic, Sweden and Slovenia.
3. The graduation rate for tertiary-type B programmes includes some graduates who have previously graduated at this level and it therefore represents an overestimate of first-time graduation.
Source: OECD. See Annex 3 for notes (*www.oecd.org/edu/eag2007*).
Please refer to the Reader's Guide for information concerning the symbols replacing missing data.
StatLink ⏱ http://dx.doi.org/10.1787/068037263103

Table A3.3.
Percentage of tertiary graduates, by field of education (2005)

		Health and welfare	Life sciences, physical sciences & agriculture	Mathematics and computer science	Humanities, arts and education	Social sciences, business, law and services	Engineering, manufacturing and construction	Unknown or unspecified
		(1)	(2)	(3)	(4)	(5)	(6)	(7)	(8)
		(2)	(3)	(4)	(5)	(6)	(7)	(8)
Australia	A	13.2	6.1	8.3	22.0	43.0	7.2	n
	B	14.6	4.1	9.0	10.9	49.4	11.7	0.3
Austria	A	8.7	8.3	7.1	19.8	41.6	14.5	0.1
	B	14.5	n	n	32.7	10.2	38.1	n
Belgium[1]	A	13.2	10.4	4.5	24.4	36.5	10.9	0.2
	B	21.8	1.4	4.1	31.3	25.2	8.2	8.1
Canada[2]	A	10.5	7.1	5.4	28.2	40.1	8.6	n
	B	m	m	m	m	m	m	m
Czech Republic	A	6.7	7.9	3.7	28.3	34.5	16.3	2.5
	B	32.3	4.8	4.8	7.7	34.4	5.8	10.2
Denmark	A	28.2	4.8	4.7	25.5	27.1	9.8	n
	B	2.4	6.3	8.3	4.7	63.6	14.7	n
Finland[2]	A	19.0	5.6	5.5	19.9	28.8	21.3	n
	B	0.7	n	n	13.9	82.1	3.3	n
France	A	8.1	9.8	6.1	18.9	45.1	11.9	n
	B	21.4	0.6	5.5	3.8	47.9	20.8	n
Germany	A	13.1	9.8	7.6	22.3	31.3	15.9	n
	B	49.5	2.9	0.5	7.8	20.7	17.2	1.3
Greece	A	4.8	13.1	7.9	31.7	32.3	10.2	n
	B	21.3	6.1	6.7	2.4	46.2	17.3	n
Hungary	A	7.9	4.0	2.2	27.1	52.2	6.6	n
	B	4.0	0.5	4.1	0.8	78.5	12.2	n
Iceland	A	11.8	6.2	3.5	37.0	35.4	6.1	n
	B	n	n	8.9	82.9	8.2	n	n
Ireland	A	14.1	4.8	5.5	35.4	30.8	9.4	n
	B	6.9	1.3	0.5	24.9	45.0	21.5	n
Italy	A	14.3	6.4	2.5	23.0	38.0	15.1	0.7
	B	a	a	a	a	a	a	a
Japan	A	6.5	7.9	x(3)	23.5	38.0	20.1	4.0
	B	22.0	0.6	x(3)	20.7	33.5	15.8	7.4
Korea	A	8.4	7.6	5.0	25.9	26.1	27.1	n
	B	12.4	1.1	3.7	26.4	24.6	31.9	n
Luxembourg	A	m	m	m	m	m	m	m
	B	m	m	m	m	m	m	m
Mexico	A	8.4	4.8	8.5	16.1	46.8	14.3	1.0
	B	5.7	1.2	19.1	2.3	36.6	34.7	0.4
Netherlands	A	17.0	4.9	4.3	24.9	40.5	8.4	n
	B	n	n	n	n	n	n	n
New Zealand	A	14.2	7.7	6.8	25.8	39.4	5.2	0.9
	B	10.1	2.9	8.5	31.7	39.4	5.7	1.6
Norway	A	26.5	3.3	6.0	26.6	28.9	7.8	0.7
	B	1.8	0.3	8.4	6.5	80.4	2.7	n
Poland	A	7.2	3.6	4.7	24.4	52.7	7.4	n
	B	a	a	a	100.0	a	a	n
Portugal	A	17.7	7.5	5.7	27.4	30.5	11.3	n
	B	18.2	2.7	6.4	13.0	39.1	20.6	n
Slovak Republic	A	10.8	8.9	4.3	21.5	36.8	17.6	n
	B	70.3	1.0	0.8	14.5	12.8	0.6	n
Spain	A	14.6	7.6	5.1	22.9	35.4	14.3	0.1
	B	12.9	0.6	11.8	14.0	39.0	21.7	n
Sweden	A	25.7	4.7	3.8	23.5	24.4	17.9	n
	B	11.5	4.4	9.2	15.3	42.1	17.4	n
Switzerland	A	8.2	9.8	4.3	20.8	42.6	14.0	0.3
	B	11.3	4.9	6.1	10.0	54.5	13.2	n
Turkey	A	9.5	9.7	4.0	40.0	25.0	11.9	n
	B	6.3	5.6	6.8	1.7	47.0	32.6	n
United Kingdom	A	12.0	8.7	7.3	27.3	34.7	8.7	1.3
	B	39.3	8.9	6.7	20.3	18.4	5.2	1.2
United States	A	9.3	6.1	4.3	28.6	45.3	6.3	n
	B	31.3	2.2	9.0	3.4	40.8	13.2	n
OECD average	*A*	*12.7*	*7.4*	*5.4*	*25.3*	*36.6*	*12.2*	*0.4*
	B	*15.1*	*2.3*	*5.9*	*22.7*	*38.2*	*14.7*	*1.1*
Brazil	A	12.1	4.6	3.3	31.7	38.1	4.5	5.7
	B	1.8	26.3	23.2	3.6	32.5	12.7	n
Chile	A	9.1	8.7	2.5	29.3	34.9	15.6	n
	B	13.1	3.6	9.5	11.0	38.6	24.2	n
Estonia	A	5.1	10.8	5.9	26.0	41.4	10.8	n
	B	20.8	0.9	5.6	14.6	50.6	7.6	n
Israel	A	8.2	6.9	6.3	27.9	38.9	11.8	n
	B	m	m	m	m	m	m	m
Russian Federation	A	3.6	7.6	x(3)	17.9	53.7	17.2	n
	B	9.8	7.9	x(3)	11.6	43.0	25.0	2.7
Slovenia	A	10.7	6.9	2.4	27.3	40.6	12.0	n
	B	11.1	2.5	1.4	5.1	63.5	16.4	n

Note: Column 1 specifies the level of education, where A equals tertiary-type A and advanced research programmes, and B equals tertiary-type B programmes.
1. Excludes the German-speaking Community of Belgium.
2. Year of reference 2004.
Source: OECD. See Annex 3 for notes (*www.oecd.org/edu/eag2007*).
Please refer to the Reader's Guide for information concerning the symbols replacing missing data.
StatLink ᴴᵐˢᴸ http://dx.doi.org/10.1787/068037263103

A3

Table A3.4.
Science graduates, by gender (2005)
Per 100 000 employed 25-to-34-year-olds

	Tertiary-type B			Tertiary-type A and advanced research programmes			All tertiary education		
	M + F	Males	Females	M + F	Males	Females	M + F	Males	Females
	(1)	(2)	(3)	(4)	(5)	(6)	(7)	(8)	(9)
Australia	408	562	214	2 141	2 580	1 589	2 549	3 142	1 803
Austria	350	565	98	788	1 051	479	1 139	1 617	577
Belgium[1]	479	732	179	816	1 006	591	1 295	1 738	772
Canada[2]	m	m	m	1 163	1 406	888	m	m	m
Czech Republic	77	95	50	928	1 111	647	1 005	1 206	697
Denmark	295	337	246	1 307	1 634	928	1 602	1 970	1 174
Finland[2]	n	n	n	2 290	2 936	1 506	2 340	2 997	1 540
France	874	1 334	313	2 043	2 465	1 527	2 917	3 799	1 840
Germany	257	432	38	1 045	1 341	676	1 302	1 773	713
Greece	355	381	318	991	952	1 047	1 346	1 333	1 365
Hungary	75	94	48	620	734	456	695	828	505
Iceland	42	67	13	1 240	1 442	1 009	1 282	1 509	1 022
Ireland	1 233	1 758	596	1 789	2 078	1 440	3 022	3 836	2 036
Italy	n	n	n	1 401	1 509	1 249	1 401	1 509	1 249
Japan	453	640	183	1 143	1 662	390	1 596	2 302	573
Korea	1 942	2 317	1 365	2 072	2 384	1 592	4 014	4 701	2 957
Luxembourg	m	m	m	m	m	m	m	m	m
Mexico	116	134	85	868	927	774	984	1 061	859
Netherlands	n	n	n	948	1 424	410	948	1 424	410
New Zealand	521	717	287	1 777	2 005	1 504	2 298	2 722	1 791
Norway	24	36	10	985	1 380	546	1 009	1 416	556
Poland	a	a	a	1 746	1 981	1 445	1 746	1 981	1 445
Portugal	301	404	184	996	1 080	901	1 381	1 568	1 171
Slovak Republic	4	7	n	1 515	1 670	1 297	1 520	1 677	1 297
Spain	501	712	220	874	982	730	1 375	1 694	950
Sweden	161	237	76	1 495	1 824	1 120	1 656	2 061	1 195
Switzerland	736	1242	143	994	1 426	488	1 730	2 668	631
Turkey	506	508	501	556	484	790	1 062	992	1 291
United Kingdom	348	474	205	1 935	2 493	1 298	2 283	2 967	1 503
United States	301	437	132	1 100	1 306	844	1 401	1 742	976
OECD average	*384*	*527*	*204*	*1 295*	*1 561*	*971*	*1 675*	*2 080*	*1 175*
EU19 average	*295*	*420*	*143*	*1 307*	*1 571*	*986*	*1 610*	*1 999*	*1 136*
Brazil	m	m	m	m	m	m	m	m	m
Chile	m	m	m	m	m	m	m	m	m
Estonia	m	m	m	m	m	m	m	m	m
Israel	m	m	m	m	m	m	m	m	m
Russian Federation	m	m	m	m	m	m	m	m	m
Slovenia	m	m	m	m	m	m	m	m	m

Note: Science fields include life sciences; physical sciences, mathematics and statistics; computing; engineering and engineering trades, manufacturing and processing, architecture and building.
1. Excludes the German-speaking Community of Belgium.
2. Year of reference 2004.
Source: OECD. See Annex 3 for notes (*www.oecd.org/edu/eag2007*).
Please refer to the Reader's Guide for information concerning the symbols replacing missing data.
StatLink ⫘ http://dx.doi.org/10.1787/068037263103

Table A3.5.
Relationship between motivation in mathematics at 15 years old (PISA 2003) and tertiary-type A graduation rates, by gender
Results based on students' self-reports

		Index of instrumental motivation in mathematics at 15 years old (2003)			Percentage of tertiary-type 5A/6 qualifications awarded to females in mathematics and computing	Percentage of tertiary-type 5A/6 qualifications awarded to females in sciences[3]	Percentage of tertiary-type 5A/6 qualifications awarded to females in all fields of education
		All students	Males	Females	Gender difference (M - F)			
		(1)	(2)	(3)	(4)	(5)	(6)	(7)
OECD Countries	Australia	0.23	0.34	0.11	0.23	26	34	56
	Austria	-0.49	-0.20	-0.78	0.58	20	30	52
	Belgium[1]	-0.32	-0.17	-0.49	0.32	19	35	54
	Canada	0.23	0.30	0.17	0.13	29	37	59
	Czech Republic	0.01	0.12	-0.10	0.22	22	31	54
	Denmark	0.37	0.57	0.19	0.38	26	34	61
	Finland[2]	0.06	0.22	-0.10	0.32	42	31	62
	France	-0.08	0.11	-0.25	0.36	26	34	55
	Germany	-0.04	0.18	-0.26	0.44	26	30	49
	Greece	-0.05	0.09	-0.18	0.27	39	43	62
	Hungary	-0.11	-0.02	-0.22	0.19	31	35	64
	Iceland	0.31	0.34	0.28	0.06	24	38	68
	Ireland	0.10	0.25	-0.06	0.31	31	37	59
	Italy	-0.15	-0.04	-0.26	0.21	42	38	59
	Japan	-0.66	-0.49	-0.81	0.32	x(6)	17	41
	Korea	-0.44	-0.36	-0.55	0.20	40	31	48
	Luxembourg	-0.41	-0.16	-0.64	0.48	12	m	m
	Mexico	0.58	0.59	0.57	0.02	39	34	55
	Netherlands	-0.26	-0.04	-0.48	0.44	12	24	56
	New Zealand	0.29	0.37	0.21	0.16	28	39	61
	Norway	0.15	0.27	0.03	0.24	22	28	62
	Poland	0.04	0.06	0.02	0.04	32	39	66
	Portugal	0.27	0.30	0.25	0.05	37	44	67
	Slovak Republic	-0.05	0.05	-0.15	0.20	20	36	56
	Spain	-0.05	0.00	-0.09	0.09	28	37	60
	Sweden	0.02	0.17	-0.13	0.30	36	36	64
	Switzerland	-0.04	0.30	-0.40	0.70	13	24	43
	Turkey	0.23	0.20	0.26	-0.06	38	34	46
	United Kingdom	m	m	m	m	26	32	56
	United States	0.17	0.22	0.12	0.10	28	35	57
	OECD average	**0.00**	**0.12**	**-0.12**	**0.25**	**28.0**	**33.7**	**57.0**
Partner economies	Brazil	0.48	0.52	0.44	0.07	28	39	63
	Chile	m	m	m	m	26	36	56
	Estonia	m	m	m	m	36	48	68
	Israel	m	m	m	m	32	36	60
	Russian Federation	-0.01	0.04	-0.05	0.08	m	m	m
	Slovenia	m	m	m	m	23	37	63

1. Excludes the German-speaking Community of Belgium for columns (5), (6) and (7).
2. Year of reference 2004.
3. Sciences include life sciences, physical sciences, mathematics, statistics, computing, engineering, manufacturing, construction and agriculture.
Source: PISA database 2003 and OECD. See Annex 3 for notes (*www.oecd.org/edu/eag2007*).
Please refer to the Reader's Guide for information concerning the symbols replacing missing data.
StatLink ᵐˢᵖ http://dx.doi.org/10.1787/068037263103

Table A3.6.

Survival rates in tertiary education (2004)

Calculated separately for tertiary-type A and tertiary-type B programmes: Number of graduates from these programmes divided by the number of new entrants to these programmes in the typical year of entrance, by programme destination and duration of programme

	Survival rates in tertiary education[1]	Survival rates in tertiary-type A education[2]				Survival rates in tertiary-type B education[3]				Advanced research programmes
			Duration of programmes				Duration of programmes			
		All programmes	3 to less than 5 years	5 to 6 years	More than 6 years	All programmes	2 to less than 3 years	3 to less than 5 years	5 years or more	
	(1)	(2)	(3)	(4)	(5)	(6)	(7)	(8)	(9)	(10)
OECD countries										
Australia	m	67	x(2)	x(2)	x(2)	m	m	m	m	67
Austria	m	65	x(2)	x(2)	a	m	m	m	a	m
Belgium (Fl.)	80	74	75	71	82	85	a	85	a	m
Canada	m	m	m	m	m	m	m	m	m	m
Czech Republic	63	65	74	60	a	61	66	60	a	44
Denmark	m	m	m	m	m	m	m	m	m	m
Finland	71	71	x(2)	x(2)	x(2)	n	n	a	a	m
France[4]	79	m	m	m	m	m	m	m	a	m
Germany	75	73	92	65	a	79	87	72	a	m
Greece	56	79	78	83	a	35	a	35	a	34
Hungary	62	64	64	x(3)	x(3)	48	48	m	a	37
Iceland[4]	69	67	m	m	m	76	m	m	m	m
Ireland	78	83	x(2)	x(2)	x(2)	69	x(6)	x(6)	x(6)	m
Italy	m	m	m	m	m	m	m	m	m	88
Japan	90	91	91	90	a	87	87	x(7)	a	89
Korea	m	83	83	100	a	m	m	m	a	76
Luxembourg	m	m	m	m	m	m	m	m	m	m
Mexico	69	69	69	x(3)	x(3)	63	63	a	a	90
Netherlands	76	76	76	x(3)	a	a	a	a	a	m
New Zealand	50	54	55	m	m	42	42	x(7)	x(7)	66
Norway	m	m	m	m	m	m	m	m	m	m
Poland	66	66	65	66	a	74	a	74	a	m
Portugal	66	68	62	72	a	58	a	58	a	65
Slovak Republic	m	m	m	m	a	77	80	69	a	m
Spain	75	74	71	76	a	79	79	a	a	m
Sweden	61	60	x(2)	x(2)	a	68	x(6)	a	a	m
Switzerland[4]	m	69	72	68	m	m	m	m	m	m
Turkey	76	74	74	x(3)	a	79	79	a	a	75
United Kingdom	71	78	78	84	53	53	x(6)	x(6)	x(6)	70
United States	m	54	x(2)	m	a	m	m	m	m	m
OECD average	***70***	***71***	~	~	~	***67***	~	~	~	***67***
EU19 average	***69***	***71***	~	~	~	***68***	~	~	~	***64***

1. The survival rates in tertiary education represent the proportion of those who enter a tertiary-type A or a tertiary-type B programme, who go on to graduate from either a tertiary-type A or a tertiary-type B programme.
2. Survival rates in tertiary-type A education represent the proportion of those who enter a tertiary-type A programme, who go on to graduate from a tertiary-type A programme.
3. Survival rates in tertiary-type B education represent the proportion of those who enter a tertiary-type B programme, who go on to graduate from a tertiary-type B programme.
4. Survival rates based on panel data.

Source: OECD. See Annex 3 for notes (*www.oecd.org/edu/eag2007*).

Please refer to the Reader's Guide for information concerning the symbols replacing missing data.

StatLink http://dx.doi.org/10.1787/068037263103

WHAT ARE STUDENTS' EXPECTATIONS FOR EDUCATION?

Drawing on data from the Programme for International Student Assessment (PISA) 2003 survey, this indicator presents the highest level of education that 15-year-old students report they expect to complete. The indicator first provides an overall picture of students' academic expectations in OECD countries and then examines relationships between expectations for tertiary education (ISCED 5 or 6) and variables such as individual performance levels, gender, socio-economic status and immigrant status, in order to shed light on equity issues.

Key results

- At the country level, there is wide variation in students' educational expectations, likely the result of the complex interaction of social, economic, and educational factors in each national context. Fifteen-year-old students' expectations for completing at least a tertiary level education (ISCED 5B, 5A or 6) vary from 21 to 95%, and these expectations are not necessarily related to countries' overall performance or attainment levels.

- PISA 2003 data shows that 15-year-old students' expectations for completing a university-level programme (ISCED 5A or 6) are closely associated with their performance in mathematics and reading. Within every OECD country, students' expectations for their educational attainment rise with their performance level in mathematics and reading. In a number of countries, there are particularly large percentage point differences between the expectation rates for those students at the highest levels of mathematics and reading proficiency and those at the lowest levels.

- In over two-thirds of OECD countries, 15-year-old female students are more likely than males to expect to complete ISCED 5A or 6.

- 15-year-old students from lower socio-economic backgrounds are less likely to expect to complete ISCED 5A or 6 than students from higher socio-economic backgrounds. Even after controlling for mathematics performance, *i.e.* comparing students of similar ability, students with lower socio-economic backgrounds remain less likely to expect to complete these levels of education.

- In most countries, 15-year-old students from an immigrant background have high expectations regarding their education and are more likely to expect to complete ISCED 5A or 6 than their native counterparts. In addition, the relative expectations of these students are even higher when controlling for mathematics performance and socio-economic status.

Policy context

Throughout OECD countries, university-level qualifications are associated with a high premium in the labour market (see Indicators A8 and A9). With skill requirements of OECD labour markets continuing to rise, the capacity and motivation of young people to pursue a university-level qualification remains an important goal for education systems. Indicator A1 examined current levels of educational attainment in the adult population and Indicator A3 compared rates of graduation from tertiary institutions as proxies of countries' production rates of advanced knowledge and skills. This indicator examines what students nearing the end of their compulsory education expect their own educational attainment to be. While the indicator first provides an overview of the percentages of 15-year-old students aspiring to various levels and types of education, the bulk of the indicator focuses more specifically on those 15-year-old students who expect to complete ISCED 5A or 6, *i.e.* those students who expect to obtain a theoretically oriented university-level degree or post-graduate education.

Evidence and explanations

The indicator reports the responses of 15-year-old students (referred to as students below) to a question in the PISA 2003 student background questionnaire: "What is the highest level of education you expect to complete?" For the purposes of comparisons across countries, education levels were classified according to ISCED levels. This indicator groups students by the percentages who expect to complete, as their highest level of education:

• ISCED 2: lower secondary education

• ISCED 3B or 3C: vocational or prevocational upper secondary education

• ISCED 3A or 4: upper secondary or non-tertiary post-secondary education

• ISCED 5B: shorter practically, technically or occupationally oriented tertiary education for direct entry into the labour market

• ISCED 5A or 6: theoretically oriented tertiary education and advanced research programmes

The indicator draws on self-reported data and the possible inaccuracies typically associated with this type of data should be kept in mind. Additionally, there may be cross-national and cross-cultural differences in how students perceived the question and what they may have considered to be a socially desirable response.

Students' expectations for education – comparing countries

Chart A4.1 shows the percentage of students in each OECD country who aspire to complete a tertiary qualification (ISCED 5A, 5B or 6), with countries sorted in descending order of the percentage of students who aspire to complete these levels. Table A4.1a provides the corresponding data for the chart, as well as data on the percentages of students aspiring to other ISCED levels.

Across OECD countries, over one-half (57%) of students on average expect to complete an ISCED 5 or 6 (tertiary) level of education. As the chart shows, this rate varies widely across countries, from a high of 95% of students expecting to complete tertiary education in Korea to a low of 21% expecting to complete at least this level in Germany.

Looking more specifically at the subcategories in the chart, an average of 45% of students across OECD countries expect to complete a university-level tertiary education (ISCED 5A) or

Chart A4.1. Percentage of students expecting to complete different levels of education (2003)

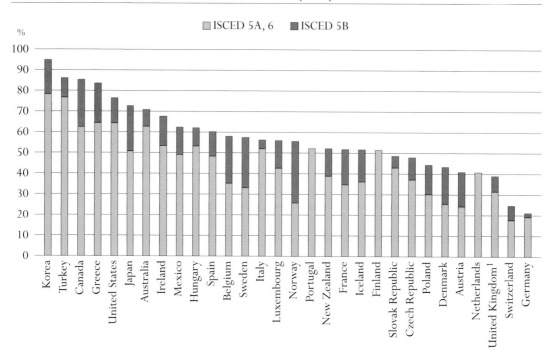

1. Response rate too low to ensure comparability.
Countries are presented in descending order of the percentages of their students who expect to complete tertiary education.
Source: OECD PISA 2003. Table A4.1a.
StatLink 🏅🖬🗐 http://dx.doi.org/10.1787/068053630540

possibly advanced research programmes (ISCED 6). Students' expectations of completing these levels of education again range widely, from approximately 18% in Switzerland to 78% in Korea. Students aspiring to complete a more occupationally oriented education, ISCED 5B, represent on average 13% in OECD countries. And while there also is variation in the expectations rates for ISCED 5B, it is significantly less than for ISCED 5A and 6, ranging from a low of 2% of students in Germany to a high of 30% of students in Norway (for the 27 countries in which this type of education is part of the national system). The countries for which tertiary-type B education makes up a relatively greater percentage of the overall students aiming for tertiary education are Austria, Belgium, Denmark, France, Iceland, Norway, Poland and Sweden.

Students who expect to complete vocational or technical upper secondary (ISCED 3B or 3C) or general upper secondary or non-tertiary post-secondary education (ISCED 3A or 4) as their highest level of education represent nearly 37% of students in OECD countries. Across OECD countries, looking cumulatively across the ISCED levels, this is the level at which the vast majority (frequently well over 90%) of students aspire to complete as a minimum level of education (except Germany with 57%, Mexico with 88%, the Netherlands with 70% and Portugal with 88%).

While this wide variation in students' expectations for completing ISCED 5A or 6 may at first be surprising, it should be noted that students' expectations are formed, in large part, by the social and economic context in which education and learning take place. These economic and social forces include the differential availability of well-paying jobs for individuals with varying levels of education, cost-benefit ratios for students in different countries to pursue higher education, availability of public and private funding, and the nature and structure of the education systems (*e.g.* all students can attend any school of their choosing, students have some choice regarding the school they attend or students are tracked and placed in certain schools). Moreover, the differing relevance of the question for students at the age of 15 – or, in other words, the proximity of that age to an actual decision point about higher education in different countries – may also play a role in the results displayed. Finally, the differences may reflect differing structures in the supply of educational opportunities. For example, in countries where a large proportion of school-leavers traditionally enter vocational programmes, student aspirations for academic programmes may be lower.

One obvious question, when looking at the variation in expectations across countries, relates to how students' expectations relate to their performance on the PISA mathematics assessment.

Chart A4.2 displays the relationship between countries' average mathematics scores and the percentage of students expecting to complete ISCED 5A or 6, and shows that students' expectations are not necessarily congruent with countries' overall performance.

For example, Austria, Denmark, Germany, Norway and Switzerland have average or above-average mathematics performance and, at the same time, well below-average percentages of students who expect to complete ISCED 5A or 6. Of the countries on this list, the three

Chart A4.2. **Relationship between students' expectations for education and countries' mathematics performance (2003)**

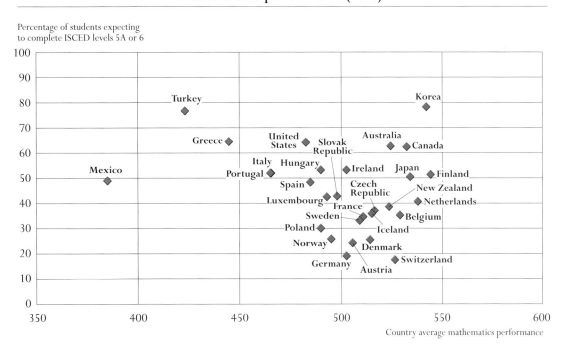

Source: OECD PISA 2003. Table A4.2a.
StatLink ᵐˢ🔗 http://dx.doi.org/10.1787/068053630540

A4

German-speaking countries have highly structured education systems in which students are tracked into different educational pathways (*e.g.* academic, vocational) relatively earlier in their careers, which may influence the expectations of students. There are other countries with similar performance levels whose students have above-average expectation rates (*e.g.* Australia, Hungary) and also those with below-average performance but yet high expectation rates among students (*e.g.* Turkey, Mexico).

It also is interesting to examine how student expectations compare with actual records of educational attainment at the country level. Table A4.1b examines the percentage of students who expect to complete ISCED 5A or 6 with the actual proportion of graduates in the country's adult population from these levels (as reported in Indicator A1). More specifically, the table calculates the difference in the percentage of students expecting to complete ISCED 5A or 6 with the percentage of adults aged 25 to 34 who have completed at least ISCED 5A. This is the segment of the population that is closest in age to the PISA students and with perhaps the most similar historical conditions affecting their educational choices.

The table shows that the actual completion rates among 25-to-34-year-olds in OECD countries vary much less widely across countries than do expectation rates, from 12 to 39%, with most countries having completion rates between one-fifth and one-third of individuals in that age bracket.

The table also shows that there can be large differences between the percentage of students expecting to complete ISCED 5A or 6 and an individual country's actual proportion of graduates for these levels. These differences tend to be the largest for those countries with the highest expectation rates in the first place. In these countries (*e.g.* Australia, Canada, Greece, Korea, and the United States), many students may expect to complete a certain level of education, but a relatively larger percentage of those who expect to may not ultimately do so. Conversely, the differences tend to be the smallest in those countries with relatively lower expectation rates at the start. In these countries (*e.g.* Denmark, Germany, Switzerland), students may be projecting a realistic vision of their chances for this type of education and perhaps are adjusting their expectations according to their national realities or their current place within a tracked education system (such as in Switzerland). Alternatively, the relatively lower rates of graduation from that level may be influenced by the overall low rates of aspiration to that level.

Student characteristics associated with expectations for education

This section first examines the relationship between 15-year-old students' expectations for an ISCED 5A or 6 level of education and their mathematics and reading performance at the student level. Afterwards, it compares the expectations of different subgroups of students, including males and females, students of differing socio-economic status, and native students and those with an immigrant background.

Students' expectations and their performance in mathematics and reading

Table A4.2a examines the relationship between students' expectations and their academic performance at the individual level and shows, for each country, the percentage of students at different levels of mathematics performance who expect to complete ISCED 5A or 6. The data show a strong relationship between mathematics performance and student expectations:

A4

within every OECD country students' expectations for their educational attainment rise with their performance level in mathematics.

The column at the far right of the table reports the difference between the minimum expectation rate for ISCED 5A or 6 (which in all countries is found among students performing at or below Level 1 on the mathematics proficiency scale) and the maximum expectation rate for ISCED 5A or 6 (which in all countries is found among students performing at Level 5 or 6). This is another way to examine the role of mathematics achievement in students' expectations.

These differences in expectations regarding completion of ISCED 5A or 6 among students of different performance levels are especially large in Hungary, Portugal, the Slovak Republic, and Spain. In each of these countries, there is at least a 70-percentage point difference between the expectation rate for those students at the highest levels of mathematics proficiency and those at the lowest levels. In these countries, the vast majority of high-performing students expect to complete ISCED 5A or 6 whereas roughly one-quarter or less of the lowest-performing students shares that expectation. By contrast, the difference between the expectation rate for this level of education between the highest and lowest mathematics performers in Finland, Norway, Sweden, Switzerland and Turkey is less than 40 percentage points.

Some of the variation in the relationship between achievement and expectation at the student level may reflect the degree to which ISCED 5A is a predominant part of the degree and qualification system in a country, as well as the degree to which such an education is perceived as open to everyone. In some countries there are a large number of ISCED 5A institutions catering to students with a wide range of competency levels. In other countries, institutions providing ISCED 5A qualifications are academically highly selective or a university-level education is only one of several common pathways to develop advanced knowledge and skills for the labor market.

Table A4.2b shows a similarly strong relationship between reading performance and expectations as there is between mathematics and expectations. Within every OECD country, for each successively higher reading performance level, a greater percentage of students report they expect to complete ISCED 5A or 6. In addition, differences in expectations to complete ISCED 5A or 6 among students of different reading performance levels are the highest in the same countries where the differences in expectations to complete ISCED 5A or 6 among students of different mathematics levels are the highest (*e.g.* Hungary, Portugal, the Slovak Republic, and Spain). For both reading and mathematics, Finland, Norway, Sweden, and Switzerland have the smallest differences among expectation rates for this level of education between the highest and lowest performing students.

Students' expectations by gender

Table A4.3a compares the percentages of females and males who expect to complete ISCED 5A or 6. In 21 of the OECD countries, there are statistically significant differences in the percentages of females versus males expecting to complete ISCED 5A or 6, with expectations for completing this level more prevalent among females in all but one of those countries (Japan). On average, across OECD countries, 48% of females expect they will complete ISCED 5A or 6 compared with 41% of males who expect to do so. The differences in expectations rates between females and males are over 16 percentage points in Hungary, Ireland, Italy and Portugal.

For Japan – which was the one exception above – the greater expectation for this level of education among males may be related to historical trends in graduation rates. As shown in Indicator A1.3, in Japan the proportion of the 25-to-34-year-old and 35-to-44-year-old males attaining ISCED 5A or 6 exceeds that of females in the same age ranges by the largest amount of any OECD country. This is in contrast to other countries, where the generally higher expectations of females tend to mirror the similar or overall higher proportion of graduates among females, particularly in the lowest age bracket.

Table A4.3b provides another view on students' expectations, showing that in 18 OECD countries females also have higher expectations in terms of the job market (*e.g.* to obtain a white-collar high-skilled job by the age of 30) than do males. This is an interesting complementary statistic because it shows that, in addition to females and males envisioning different educational pathways (to some extent), they also envision different career pathways. However, this may also reflect the extent to which males have greater access than females to lower skilled but relatively high paying jobs.

Overall, these results mirror other attainment-related statistics. Females today are far more likely to have completed tertiary education than females 30 years ago with more than twice as many females aged 25 to 34 having completed tertiary education than females aged 55 to 64. University-level graduation rates for females also now equal or exceed those for males in 21 of the 27 OECD countries for which data are comparable.

These factors most likely play a role in fostering the high expectations females have in terms of education and a future career, reported in this indicator. It appears that public policies over the past twenty years that have tried to foster gender equality have made an impression on young females. However, while females are generally doing better academically and generally have higher expectations, there are equity issues with regard to gender that remain with us: males continue to perform better in mathematics in most OECD countries while females outperform males in reading.

Considering the impact students' beliefs have been shown to have on their self-concepts, motivation to achieve, course taking behaviors, and ultimately on academic success, it is important to remember that more females than males indicate that they believe they are not good at mathematics and that females have shown a significantly lower self-concept in mathematics, as well as significantly higher levels of mathematics anxiety. These factors likely play a role in females' behaviors and choices in terms of field of study, resulting in the fact that on average among OECD countries females make up only 30% of university graduates in mathematics and computer science (Table A3.8, available on line at: *http://dx.doi.org/10.1787/068053630540*).

The role of gender in educational expectations and attainment is complex. However, as the data show, gender differences are not inevitable and policies can have an impact on expectations as well as on the achievement outcomes of males and females.

Students' expectations and their socio-economic status

Table A4.4 examines the relationship between students' backgrounds – using PISA's index of economic, social, and cultural status (ESCS) – and their expectations for achieving higher levels of education. Odds ratios are used to examine the probability that students expect to complete ISCED 5A or 6. Box A4.1 gives an explanation of odds ratios.

> ## Box A4.1. **Explanation and interpretation of odds ratios**
>
> An odds ratio compares the probability (expressed as odds) of an event occurring for two different groups. The odds ratio takes values between zero (0) and infinity. One (1) is the neutral value and means that there is no difference between the groups compared; close to zero or infinity means a large difference. An odds ratio larger than one means that group one has larger odds than group two (*i.e.* the event is more likely to occur for group one than for group two) - if the opposite is true the odds ratio will be smaller than one.

In Table A4.4, an odds ratio of 1 indicates that students of both high and low socio-economic status are equally likely to expect to complete a university-level programme (ISCED 5A or 6). An odds ratio greater than 1 means that students with high socio-economic status are more likely to expect to complete ISCED 5A or 6 than students with low socio-economic status. Conversely, an odds ratio of less than 1 means that students with low socio-economic status are more likely to expect to complete ISCED 5A or 6 than students with high socio-economic status. Therefore, odds ratios that differ from one indicate that socio-economic status plays an influential role in students' aspirations and points to potential inequities in the educational system.

The first column in the table describes the relationship (using the odds ratio) between socio-economic status on students' expectations to complete ISCED 5A or 6. The second column describes the relationship between socio-economic status and students' expectations to complete ISCED 5A or 6, after controlling for their mathematics performance.

The first column shows that students with a relatively higher socio-economic status were at least twice as likely, compared to those with a relatively lower socio-economic status, to expect to complete ISCED 5A or 6 in all but one country. In six countries, this figure was as high as 3 times as likely, and in Hungary, it was 4 times as likely.

The second column shows that in all countries after controlling for mathematics scores the likelihood of students with a relatively higher socioeconomic status to expect to complete ISCED 5A or 6 remains at least 1.5 times greater compared to those with a relatively lower socioeconomic status. Therefore, among students with similar performance levels those from higher socio-economic backgrounds are more likely to have high educational expectations.

This is an important finding and is consistent with much previous research, including analyses of PISA data, which shows that students' home backgrounds are strongly related to their academic beliefs and outcomes. The fact that even when students have the same ability level, students from lower socio-economic backgrounds are still less likely to expect to complete a high level of education than are students from more advantaged backgrounds may reflect the fact that students with lower socio-economic status have made choices in terms of educational programmes or institutions that constrain their educational potential.

Students' expectations and their immigrant status

Table A4.5 shows the odds ratios that first- and second-generation students expect to complete ISCED 5A or 6 compared to native-born students both before controlling for mathematics performance and socio-economic status and after.

Box A4.2. Terminology used for describing students' immigrant background

Native students: Students with at least one parent born in the country of assessment. Students born in the country who have one foreign-born parent (children of "combined" families) are included in the native category, as previous research indicates that these students perform similarly to native students.

First-generation students: Students born outside of the country of assessment whose parents are also foreign-born.

Second-generation students: Students born in the country of assessment with foreign-born parents.

The first and third columns in the table show that in at least half of the 14 OECD countries with sizeable population with an immigrant background among 15-year-olds, both first- and second-generation students are more likely to expect to complete ISCED 5A or 6 than are their native-born counterparts. The odds that first- and second-generation students will have higher expectations relative to native-born students are especially high in Australia and Canada – where these students are at least two times more likely to have such educational expectations.

The second and fourth columns show that the relationship between immigrant status and expectation for ISCED 5A or 6 education is stronger (and statistically significant in all of the OECD countries for which there are data) after controlling for performance and socio-economic status. In other words, among students of similar achievement levels and socio-economic means, immigrant students are much more likely to expect to complete a theoretically oriented tertiary education. In some countries, this expectation is more prevalent among first-generation students and in other countries, among second-generation students, for reasons that may be related to differing patterns of immigration in the countries.

These findings are consistent with other research and analyses that show immigrant students are motivated and have positive attitudes toward school (OECD, 2006b). Enhancing and nurturing these positive attitudes and expectations may be one avenue for educators and policy makers in working to overcome some of the performance differences (influenced partly but not entirely by differing socio-economic status and native language familiarity or ability) between immigrant students and their native counterparts.

Definitions and methodologies

PISA was most recently administered in 2006; however, since those data are not yet available, this indicator is based on data from the PISA 2003 survey.

The target population for this indicator was all 15-year-old students (in participating countries) enrolled in educational institutions at the secondary-school level regardless of grade level, type of institution, and part- or full-time enrolment status. Fifteen-year-olds were defined as students who were between 15 years and 3 months to 16 years and 2 months at the beginning of the PISA testing period. The term "student" is frequently used to denote this target population.

The tables in this indicator provide an OECD average and an OECD total, per the standard PISA reporting conventions. The OECD average takes the OECD countries as a single entity, to which each country contributes with equal weight. For statistics such as percentages or mean scores, the OECD average corresponds to the arithmetic mean of the respective country statistics. In contrast, for statistics relating to variation, the OECD average may differ from the arithmetic mean of the country statistics because it not only reflects variation within countries, but also variation that lies between countries. The OECD total, rather, takes OECD countries as a single entity, to which each country contributes in proportion to the number of 15-year-olds enrolled in its schools. It illustrates how a country compares with the OECD as a whole and may be used to refer to the stock of human capital in the OECD region. As in the indicator, the average is used when the focus is on comparing performance or other attributes across countries. All averages include data for the United Kingdom, even when the data are not shown in the tables.

The United Kingdom did not reach PISA's unit response rate standard, which precludes its comparison with the other countries on whole population analyses. Estimates for the United Kingdom are still reported in charts and tables dealing with subsets of the population for the purposes of comparison within the country. When estimates for the United Kingdom are reported, they are reported at the end of charts and tables separate from the estimates of other countries as a cautionary reminder that the estimate may not be as reliable as the estimates of countries that met PISA's unit response rate standard.

Further references

The following additional material relevant to this indicator is available on line at:

StatLink 🛢️ http://dx.doi.org/10.1787/068053630540

- *Table A4.1b. Comparing students' expectation rates and population attainment for ISCED levels 5A or 6*

- *Table A4.2b. Percentage of students who expect to complete ISCED levels 5A or 6, by reading performance level*

- *Table A4.3b. Percentage of students expecting a white-collar high-skilled occupation at age 30, by gender*

For further information about PISA 2003, see *Learning for Tomorrow's World — First Results from PISA 2003* (OECD, 2004a) and the *PISA 2003 Technical Report* (OECD, 2005b). For further information about the expectations and attitudes of students from an immigrant background, see *Where Immigrants Succeed: A Comparative Review of Performance and Engagement in PISA 2003* (OECD, 2006b). PISA data are also available on the PISA website: *www.pisa.oecd.org.*

A4

Table A4.1a.
Percentage of students expecting to complete different levels of education (2003)

	Highest level students expect to complete									
	ISCED 2		ISCED 3B, 3C		ISCED 3A, 4		ISCED 5B		ISCED 5A, 6	
	%	S.E.	%	S.E.	%	S.E.	%	S.E.	%	S.E.
Australia	2.7	0.2	3.7	0.2	22.8	0.6	8.0	0.3	62.8	0.8
Austria	3.6	0.3	27.5	1.4	28.1	1.0	16.6	0.8	24.3	1.3
Belgium	6.7	0.4	7.5	0.4	27.8	0.9	22.7	0.7	35.3	1.0
Canada	0.7	0.1	6.5	0.3	7.5	0.3	22.7	0.6	62.5	0.8
Czech Republic	0.8	0.1	11.6	0.7	39.7	1.1	10.7	0.6	37.2	1.1
Denmark	9.6	0.5	12.3	0.6	34.8	0.7	17.8	0.7	25.5	0.9
Finland	2.8	0.3	a	a	45.7	0.9	a	a	51.5	0.9
France	1.7	0.2	24.4	1.0	22.2	0.9	17.1	0.8	34.7	0.9
Germany	43.4	1.6	3.4	0.3	32.2	1.0	1.9	0.2	19.1	0.9
Greece	0.8	0.1	8.1	0.7	7.6	0.7	19.0	1.5	64.5	1.9
Hungary	0.3	0.1	9.5	0.8	28.2	1.1	8.8	0.5	53.2	1.4
Iceland	1.6	0.2	8.2	0.5	38.6	0.8	15.6	0.6	36.1	0.8
Ireland	3.6	0.4	7.5	0.5	21.3	0.8	14.1	0.6	53.5	1.1
Italy	2.4	0.4	5.6	0.6	35.8	0.9	4.2	0.4	52.1	1.2
Japan	a	a	13.1	1.1	14.3	0.8	21.9	1.1	50.7	1.3
Korea	0.1	0.0	4.0	0.4	1.0	0.2	16.6	0.8	78.3	1.0
Luxembourg	5.7	0.4	19.4	0.6	18.9	0.6	13.4	0.5	42.6	0.6
Mexico	11.7	1.3	6.7	0.6	19.3	0.8	13.2	0.5	49.1	1.5
Netherlands	30.3	1.6	a	a	28.9	1.2	a	a	40.8	1.5
New Zealand	1.7	0.2	12.1	0.6	34.2	0.7	13.3	0.5	38.8	0.9
Norway	1.0	0.2	25.2	0.8	18.2	0.7	29.8	0.7	25.8	0.9
Poland	6.7	0.5	23.1	0.9	25.9	0.9	14.2	0.6	30.1	1.0
Portugal	12.0	0.9	10.4	0.7	25.4	0.7	a	a	52.2	1.4
Slovak Republic	3.8	0.5	8.5	0.9	39.1	1.2	5.6	0.4	43.0	1.3
Spain	13.8	0.9	11.8	0.6	14.2	0.5	11.9	0.4	48.4	1.2
Sweden	4.2	0.3	23.0	0.7	15.3	0.7	24.3	0.7	33.2	1.1
Switzerland	8.7	0.6	48.7	1.7	17.9	0.7	7.0	0.5	17.6	1.4
Turkey	1.9	0.7	0.9	0.2	11.1	1.0	9.4	0.9	76.7	1.8
United States	0.8	0.1	a	a	22.8	0.7	12.0	0.5	64.4	0.9
OECD total	*6.4*	*0.2*	*8.7*	*0.2*	*21.7*	*0.3*	*12.5*	*0.2*	*50.7*	*0.3*
OECD average	*6.2*	*0.1*	*12.1*	*0.2*	*24.5*	*0.2*	*12.6*	*0.1*	*44.5*	*0.2*
United Kingdom[1]	3.1	0.3	29.4	0.8	28.6	0.7	7.4	0.5	31.5	1.2

1. Response rate too low to ensure comparability.
Source: OECD PISA 2003.
Please refer to the Reader's Guide for information concerning the symbols replacing missing data.
StatLink http://dx.doi.org/10.1787/068053630540

Table A4.2a.
Percentage of students expecting to complete ISCED levels 5A or 6, by mathematics performance level (2003)

A4

	PISA mathematics performance levels												Difference between maximum and minimum expectation rates	Mathematics scores	
	All levels		Level 1 and below		Level 2		Level 3		Level 4		Levels 5 and 6			Mean score	
	%	S.E.	%	S.E.	%	S.E.	%	S.E.	%	S.E.	%	S.E.			S.E.
Australia	62.8	(0.8)	33.0	(1.8)	46.0	(1.6)	60.8	(1.3)	74.2	(1.4)	88.4	(1.0)	55.5	524	(2.1)
Austria	24.3	(1.3)	5.4	(1.1)	8.6	(1.2)	19.6	(1.6)	38.7	(2.4)	58.4	(2.5)	53.0	506	(3.3)
Belgium	35.3	(1.0)	7.7	(1.2)	12.5	(1.3)	24.8	(1.6)	41.3	(1.7)	65.2	(1.3)	57.4	529	(2.3)
Canada	62.5	(0.8)	35.2	(1.6)	44.9	(1.5)	58.2	(1.7)	71.4	(1.3)	83.2	(1.1)	48.0	532	(1.8)
Czech Republic	37.2	(1.1)	6.5	(1.2)	15.1	(1.8)	30.6	(2.3)	50.2	(2.0)	75.7	(1.7)	69.2	516	(3.5)
Denmark	25.5	(0.9)	8.0	(1.4)	14.5	(1.6)	22.5	(1.8)	33.7	(2.0)	49.9	(2.5)	41.9	514	(2.7)
Finland	51.5	(0.9)	35.7	(2.7)	36.8	(2.3)	44.9	(1.8)	53.9	(1.6)	71.1	(1.7)	35.4	544	(1.9)
France	34.7	(0.9)	6.5	(1.1)	17.7	(1.9)	32.2	(2.2)	49.0	(2.5)	68.8	(1.9)	62.3	511	(2.5)
Germany	19.1	(0.9)	3.0	(0.8)	6.2	(1.1)	13.4	(1.3)	27.3	(1.8)	48.3	(1.9)	45.3	503	(3.3)
Greece	64.5	(1.9)	38.4	(1.9)	69.8	(2.5)	85.4	(1.6)	93.6	(1.5)	98.5	(1.1)	60.1	445	(3.9)
Hungary	53.2	(1.4)	15.7	(1.6)	41.1	(2.1)	62.6	(2.3)	80.1	(1.7)	93.1	(1.2)	77.4	490	(2.8)
Iceland	36.1	(0.8)	13.7	(1.9)	21.4	(1.9)	33.0	(1.9)	48.6	(2.2)	63.4	(2.6)	49.7	515	(1.4)
Ireland	53.5	(1.1)	24.8	(2.0)	41.2	(2.3)	58.2	(2.5)	69.9	(2.0)	79.7	(2.3)	54.9	503	(2.4)
Italy	52.1	(1.2)	34.5	(2.6)	50.5	(1.9)	60.4	(1.8)	68.2	(1.9)	78.3	(2.3)	43.8	466	(3.1)
Japan	50.7	(1.3)	14.7	(1.9)	26.5	(2.0)	43.4	(2.4)	60.4	(2.1)	82.6	(1.9)	67.9	534	(4.0)
Korea	78.3	(1.0)	39.7	(3.2)	61.1	(2.1)	76.3	(1.8)	88.6	(1.4)	96.3	(0.8)	56.6	542	(3.2)
Luxembourg	42.6	(0.6)	11.9	(1.4)	28.2	(1.7)	47.7	(1.7)	62.8	(2.2)	80.7	(2.5)	68.8	493	(1.0)
Mexico	49.1	(1.5)	38.6	(1.3)	64.4	(1.8)	74.7	(2.1)	82.0	(4.2)	92.7	(4.3)	54.0	385	(3.6)
Netherlands	40.8	(1.5)	9.3	(2.0)	14.0	(2.3)	22.2	(2.2)	49.7	(2.3)	78.0	(1.6)	68.7	538	(3.1)
New Zealand	38.8	(0.9)	18.9	(1.9)	23.1	(1.9)	33.1	(1.8)	45.4	(2.0)	66.3	(1.8)	47.4	523	(2.3)
Norway	25.8	(0.9)	11.2	(1.2)	16.2	(1.7)	26.2	(2.0)	38.0	(2.1)	50.5	(2.7)	39.3	495	(2.4)
Poland	30.1	(1.0)	7.7	(1.2)	18.8	(1.3)	33.3	(1.7)	49.6	(1.9)	64.8	(3.2)	57.0	490	(2.5)
Portugal	52.2	(1.4)	22.4	(1.5)	47.7	(2.1)	66.3	(1.8)	82.4	(2.1)	92.5	(2.4)	70.2	466	(3.4)
Slovak Republic	43.0	(1.3)	8.7	(1.3)	24.8	(1.7)	45.8	(2.2)	68.3	(2.1)	85.1	(2.1)	76.4	498	(3.3)
Spain	48.4	(1.2)	15.6	(1.8)	37.2	(2.0)	56.3	(1.8)	75.6	(2.0)	88.2	(2.3)	72.7	485	(2.4)
Sweden	33.2	(1.1)	19.1	(1.6)	21.9	(1.9)	30.9	(1.7)	42.4	(2.2)	55.2	(2.2)	36.1	509	(2.6)
Switzerland	17.6	(1.4)	3.8	(0.8)	5.0	(1.1)	10.5	(1.4)	19.9	(1.8)	42.9	(2.9)	39.1	527	(3.4)
Turkey	76.7	(1.8)	63.5	(2.4)	84.8	(1.8)	94.4	(1.5)	97.1	(1.7)	99.3	(0.4)	35.8	423	(6.7)
United States	64.4	(0.9)	43.9	(1.6)	59.6	(1.7)	70.7	(1.7)	79.5	(1.5)	86.7	(2.3)	42.8	483	(2.9)
OECD total	*50.7*	*(0.3)*	*32.9*	*(0.6)*	*42.9*	*(0.7)*	*52.1*	*(0.7)*	*63.0*	*(0.6)*	*77.7*	*(0.7)*	*44.9*	*489*	*(1.1)*
OECD average	*44.5*	*(0.2)*	*24.8*	*(0.4)*	*33.4*	*(0.4)*	*44.0*	*(0.4)*	*56.6*	*(0.4)*	*72.5*	*(0.4)*	*47.7*	*500*	*(0.6)*
United Kingdom[1]	31.5	(1.2)	8.2	(1.4)	15.6	(1.7)	28.8	(1.7)	44.0	(2.1)	68.7	(2.2)	60.5	m	m

1. Response rate too low to ensure comparability.
Source: OECD PISA 2003.
Please refer to the Reader's Guide for information concerning the symbols replacing missing data.
StatLink ⬛🇸🇱 http://dx.doi.org/10.1787/068053630540

A4

Table A4.3a.
Percentage of students expecting to complete ISCED levels 5A or 6, by gender (2003)

	All students		Boys		Girls		Statistically significant difference
	%	S.E.	%	S.E.	%	S.E.	
Australia	62.8	(0.8)	56.6	(1.3)	69.1	(0.9)	G>B
Austria	24.3	(1.3)	22.8	(1.4)	25.7	(2.0)	
Belgium	35.3	(1.0)	32.4	(1.4)	38.5	(1.4)	G>B
Canada	62.5	(0.8)	56.1	(1.0)	68.7	(0.9)	G>B
Czech Republic	37.2	(1.1)	32.0	(1.4)	42.6	(1.7)	G>B
Denmark	25.5	(0.9)	24.6	(1.2)	26.4	(1.0)	
Finland	51.5	(0.9)	49.6	(1.2)	53.5	(1.1)	G>B
France	34.7	(0.9)	29.2	(1.4)	39.7	(1.2)	G>B
Germany	19.1	(0.9)	17.7	(1.3)	20.5	(1.0)	
Greece	64.5	(1.9)	58.5	(2.5)	70.1	(1.8)	G>B
Hungary	53.2	(1.4)	45.5	(1.8)	61.8	(1.8)	G>B
Iceland	36.1	(0.8)	30.7	(1.1)	41.8	(1.3)	G>B
Ireland	53.5	(1.1)	45.3	(1.6)	61.8	(1.4)	G>B
Italy	52.1	(1.2)	43.0	(1.7)	60.4	(1.6)	G>B
Japan	50.7	(1.3)	54.1	(2.1)	47.6	(2.2)	B>G
Korea	78.3	(1.0)	78.9	(2.0)	77.5	(2.0)	
Luxembourg	42.6	(0.6)	41.3	(1.0)	43.9	(1.1)	
Mexico	49.1	(1.5)	41.8	(1.7)	55.8	(1.6)	G>B
Netherlands	40.8	(1.5)	38.7	(2.0)	42.9	(1.6)	
New Zealand	38.8	(0.9)	38.2	(1.3)	39.5	(1.4)	
Norway	25.8	(0.9)	22.4	(1.0)	29.3	(1.2)	G>B
Poland	30.1	(1.0)	23.4	(1.1)	36.8	(1.2)	G>B
Portugal	52.2	(1.4)	43.7	(1.5)	59.9	(1.5)	G>B
Slovak Republic	43.0	(1.3)	37.9	(1.7)	48.3	(1.8)	G>B
Spain	48.4	(1.2)	40.7	(1.7)	55.7	(1.3)	G>B
Sweden	33.2	(1.1)	28.8	(1.2)	37.5	(1.4)	G>B
Switzerland	17.6	(1.4)	16.7	(1.6)	18.6	(1.4)	
Turkey	76.7	(1.8)	72.3	(2.4)	82.1	(1.9)	G>B
United States	64.4	(0.9)	61.2	(1.1)	67.6	(1.2)	G>B
OECD total	*50.7*	*(0.3)*	*47.6*	*(0.5)*	*53.8*	*(0.5)*	*G>B*
OECD average	*44.5*	*(0.2)*	*40.7*	*(0.3)*	*48.4*	*(0.3)*	*G>B*
United Kingdom[1]	31.5	(1.2)	27.0	(1.4)	35.4	(1.7)	G>B

1. Response rate too low to ensure comparability.
Source: OECD PISA 2003.
Please refer to the Reader's Guide for information concerning the symbols replacing missing data.
StatLink ᐊᎶᏏᏞ http://dx.doi.org/10.1787/068053630540

A4

Table A4.4.
Odds ratios that students expect to complete ISCED levels 5A or 6 by socio-economic status (2003)

	(A) Odds before taking into account the mathematics score	S.E.	(B) Odds after taking into account the mathematics score	S.E.	Difference (A)-(B)/(A)
Australia	2.2	(0.10)	1.8	(0.08)	0.186
Austria	3.0	(0.17)	2.4	(0.13)	0.211
Belgium	3.0	(0.13)	2.2	(0.09)	0.274
Canada	2.2	(0.06)	1.9	(0.06)	0.129
Czech Reublic	2.9	(0.11)	2.2	(0.09)	0.247
Denmark	2.2	(0.13)	1.8	(0.11)	0.192
Finland	1.8	(0.06)	1.7	(0.06)	0.104
France	2.3	(0.15)	1.7	(0.12)	0.264
Germany	3.2	(0.21)	2.3	(0.16)	0.280
Greece	3.0	(0.17)	2.3	(0.13)	0.206
Hungary	4.0	(0.22)	2.7	(0.15)	0.313
Iceland	2.1	(0.09)	1.8	(0.09)	0.111
Ireland	2.2	(0.11)	1.8	(0.10)	0.183
Italy	2.5	(0.11)	2.2	(0.10)	0.119
Japan	2.5	(0.15)	2.1	(0.12)	0.168
Korea	2.5	(0.11)	2.0	(0.08)	0.211
Luxembourg	2.5	(0.11)	1.8	(0.09)	0.250
Mexico	2.2	(0.10)	1.8	(0.07)	0.174
Netherlands	2.2	(0.12)	1.5	(0.10)	0.309
New Zealand	2.0	(0.10)	1.6	(0.08)	0.197
Norway	2.4	(0.12)	2.0	(0.11)	0.146
Poland	2.8	(0.11)	2.2	(0.09)	0.202
Portugal	2.3	(0.09)	1.8	(0.07)	0.233
Slovak Republic	3.1	(0.14)	2.3	(0.10)	0.279
Spain	2.5	(0.11)	2.0	(0.09)	0.197
Sweden	2.1	(0.10)	1.8	(0.08)	0.129
Switzerland	3.1	(0.24)	2.5	(0.21)	0.213
Turkey	2.2	(0.17)	1.6	(0.12)	0.241
United States	2.2	(0.08)	1.9	(0.08)	0.167
United Kingdom[1]	2.4	(0.10)	1.8	(0.07)	0.265

OECD countries (side label)

Notes: Bold indicates odds ratio is statistically significantly different than 1. The calculations in this table compare the odds ratio for students whose scores on the ESCS index are within one standard deviation of the mean value for the country and those that are not. This was to make the analysis more comparable with that for immigration status.
1. Response rate too low to ensure comparability.
Source: OECD PISA 2003.
Please refer to the Reader's Guide for information concerning the symbols replacing missing data.
StatLink ꙮ http://dx.doi.org/10.1787/068053630540

A4

Table A4.5.
Odds ratios that students expect to complete ISCED levels 5A or 6, by immigrant status (2003)

	First generation		Second generation	
	Odds ratio before taking into account mathematics performance and ESCS index	Odds ratio after taking into account mathematics performance and ESCS index	Odds ratio before taking into account mathematics performance and ESCS index	Odds ratio after taking into account mathematics performance and ESCS index
Australia	2.39	3.16	2.03	2.92
Austria	0.70	2.39	1.04	3.49
Belgium	0.70	2.56	0.60	2.41
Canada	3.22	3.90	2.29	2.77
Denmark	2.23	6.96	1.77	6.23
France	0.85	2.64	1.19	3.63
Germany	0.70	3.03	0.58	3.16
Luxembourg	1.01	3.35	1.02	2.34
Netherlands	0.97	5.21	1.16	5.47
New Zealand	2.36	2.77	1.75	3.19
Norway	1.13	2.44	1.95	3.86
Sweden	1.93	5.70	1.70	3.29
Switzerland	0.90	3.67	0.87	2.66
United States	0.76	1.43	1.15	2.05

OECD countries (vertical label at left)

Note: Bold indicates odds ratio is statistically significantly different from 1. ESCS = the PISA index of economic, social and cultural status.
Source: OECD PISA 2003.
Please refer to the Reader's Guide for information concerning the symbols replacing missing data.
StatLink ⌐⌐⌐ http://dx.doi.org/10.1787/068053630540

WHAT ARE STUDENTS' ATTITUDES TOWARDS MATHEMATICS?

This indicator examines how 15-year-old students' attitudes toward and approaches to learning and school vary across countries and across groups of countries, as well as the relationship between these characteristics and students' performance in mathematics. The indicator draws on data from the OECD Programme for International Student Assessment's (PISA) 2003 survey.

Key results

- Students from countries that are in close geographical or cultural proximity to one another tend to share similar attitudes toward learning and similar school contexts, though the attitudes and characteristics bringing them together differ across subgroups of countries. The strength of the relationship between students' attitudes toward mathematics, approaches to learning and school contexts and their mathematics performance vary in similar ways across groups of countries.

- In Denmark, Finland and Sweden, students' attitudes toward mathematics have a strong relationship with students' achievement in mathematics. In these countries above-average positive relationship between interest, instrumental motivation, and self-concept with performance and an above-average negative relationship between anxiety and mathematics performance can be observed.

- Japan and Korea, as well as the Nordic countries, show above-average positive associations between at least two of the PISA 2003 indices of students' approaches to learning and their mathematics performance, indicating the importance of strategic learning techniques for students in these countries.

- Of the school-related indices, disciplinary climate consistently has the largest positive effect on mathematics performance across countries. Among the other school-related indices, the largest positive associations are between students' attitudes toward school and teacher support in the countries in the two subgroups that represent most of the Anglophone and Nordic countries in the sample.

A5

Policy context

PISA measures several facets of students' attitudes and approaches to learning and the contexts in which they learn. PISA's conceptual framework is founded on a general model of student learning in which students are active participants in the learning process, with learning involving the strategic engagement of one's cognitive, affective and behavioural processes within their particular cultural, social, and school contexts. In PISA, 15-year-olds' attitudes and approaches to learning are treated as important outcomes in their own right, as well as factors that account for variation in cognitive performance.

There is considerable empirical support for the influence of students' learning attitudes and approaches on academic performance, and vice versa. At the same time, however, it is important to note that the extent and nature of such relationships may differ across countries and cultures. Students' attitudes toward learning and their perceptions of their abilities to regulate their own learning and select appropriate strategies for achieving their goals are shaped in part by their outside environment – the society and culture in which they live and the schools they attend. Education systems differ in the extent to which they value particular learning attitudes or courses of action. For example, in countries that may place a high premium on academic performance, particularly in mathematics, students may display considerably higher levels of anxiety about their performance in mathematics than in countries that do not share this goal.

This indicator examines how 15-year-old students' attitudes toward and approaches toward learning and the school contexts of learning vary across countries and across groups of countries, and also the relationship between these characteristics and students' performance in mathematics.

Evidence and explanations

The indicator is based on the PISA 2003 survey and draws on eight composite scales describing students' attitudes towards mathematics and their approaches to learning, as well as four school-related scales describing the social contexts and climates in which learning occurs. Each of the 12 scales is based on a number of survey items that provide ordinal values, which are summarised into composite scales, with varying but reasonable levels of scale reliabilities. (See *Learning for Tomorrow's World: First Results from PISA 2003* [OECD 2004a] for additional information on the construction of these scales.)

Students' attitudes include their interest in and enjoyment of mathematics, instrumental motivation, self-concept in mathematics, self-efficacy in mathematics, and anxiety in mathematics. Learning approaches include students' reported use of control strategies, memorisation strategies, and elaboration strategies. School-related indices include students' attitudes toward school, their sense of belonging in school, and indices of teacher support and of disciplinary climate. Box 5.1 describes these scales in more detail.

Classifying countries by students' attitudes toward mathematics, approaches to learning, and school-related indices

Chart A5.1 shows the results of a classification analysis, which grouped countries according to similarities among their averages on the 12 scales. Box 5.2 provides additional information on how the classification analysis was performed. The ordering of groups from top to bottom in the chart is arbitrary and implies no sense of hierarchy.

Box A5.1. Descriptions of indices of students' attitudes towards mathematics, approaches to learning and school-related indices

Attitudes towards mathematics

Students' interest in and enjoyment of mathematics refer to intrinsic motivation, and may affect the intensity and continuity of their engagement in learning situations, their selection of learning strategies and the depth of their understanding.

Instrumental motivation in mathematics refers to the extent to which students are encouraged to learn mathematics by external rewards such as good job prospects, an orientation which can influence both study choices and performance.

Self-concept in mathematics refers to students' beliefs about their own mathematical competence.

Self-efficacy in mathematics refers to the extent to which students believe that they can handle mathematics learning situations effectively and overcoming difficulties, which can affect students' willingness to take on challenging task and persist with it.

Anxiety in mathematics refers to the extent to which students feel helpless and under emotional stress when dealing with mathematics.

Approaches to learning

Memorisation strategies refer to those strategies students use that involve representations of knowledge and procedures stored in memory with little or no further processing.

Elaboration strategies are those strategies in which students connect new material to prior learning, which can result in deeper understanding than through simple memorisation.

Control strategies are those in which students monitor what they are learning, compare it with their goals, and identify what still needs to be learned, which can allow them to adapt their learning to the task at hand.

School-related indices

Students' attitudes towards school refer to the degree to which they believe that school has prepared them for life and work and given them the confidence to make decisions.

Sense of belonging at school refers to students' perceptions about whether school is a place where they feel like an outsider, feel awkward, out-of-place and lonely, or where they feel like they belong and can make friends easily.

Teacher support refers to the individual support students receive from teachers in learning situations. The index was based on students' reports on the degree to which their teachers demonstrate interest and willingness to help their students.

Disciplinary climate refers to the level of disorder and disruption in the classroom. The index was based on students' reports on the degree to which there is noise in the classroom, how quickly they are able to quiet down and get to work, and whether or not other students listen to their teacher.

A5

Chart A5.1. **Classification of countries based on means of students' attitudes toward mathematics, approaches to learning and school-related indices (2003)**

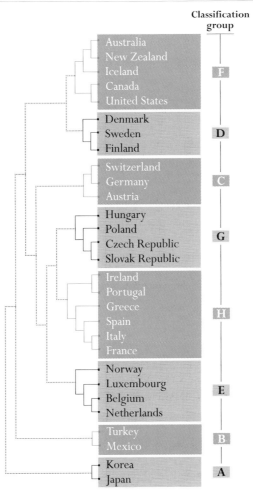

Classification
group

Australia
New Zealand
Iceland   **F**
Canada
United States

Denmark
Sweden   **D**
Finland

Switzerland
Germany   **C**
Austria

Hungary
Poland   **G**
Czech Republic
Slovak Republic

Ireland
Portugal
Greece   **H**
Spain
Italy
France

Norway
Luxembourg   **E**
Belgium
Netherlands

Turkey   **B**
Mexico

Korea   **A**
Japan

Source: OECD PISA 2003 database.
StatLink 🔗 http://dx.doi.org/10.1787/068056433507

The results show that group membership is related to countries' geographical or cultural proximity. For example, two East Asian countries – Japan and Korea – form one group while three of the Nordic countries (Finland, Sweden, and Denmark) form another, and the Central European countries Hungary, Poland, the Czech Republic, and the Slovak Republic form a third group. In these cases, the grouped countries share geographic proximity as well as some commonality in the way the education systems have developed historically. The four Central European countries, for example, share characteristics based on their having developed over the past two decades from centralised socialist states. Western and Southern European countries also cluster together, as do the Benelux countries (with Norway as an anomalous addition to that group).

In the case of the United States, Canada, New Zealand and Australia, which are classified closely, the proximity is not in terms of geography, but language – these countries represent most of the predominantly Anglophone OECD countries that participate in PISA. The group of Austria, Germany and Switzerland shares both geographic and linguistic similarities.

Mexico and Turkey share an economic context that differs significantly from the majority of OECD countries.

To some extent, the group membership may also be influenced by similarities in the way students in certain countries tend to report to self-reported questions on their attitudes.

Box A5.2. How classification analysis was performed

The hierarchical cluster analysis is employed to identify relatively homogeneous groups of countries based on the 12 selected characteristics (see Box A5.1). The algorithm starts with each country in a separate cluster and combines clusters sequentially until only one is left.

Shown above, Chart A5.1, a tree diagram, is used to illustrate the arrangement of the clusters produced by the hierarchical cluster analysis. The axis represents an index of the distances between countries at each point of aggregation. Cutting the tree at a given height will give a clustering at a selected precision. A partition in eight groups was adopted here.

How subgroups are distinct

Table A5.1 provides countries' averages on the 12 scales, which were used in the prior classification analysis, as well as a standardised version of the average scores (*i.e.* Z-scores) for each subgroup. For the analysis presented here, the standardised subgroup averages must be examined.

In the table, subgroups of countries are introduced from top to bottom by the degree of distinctiveness, which is calculated as the mean of the absolute value of the Z-scores. Additionally, values are highlighted in the table when they are greater than 1 or smaller than -1, to indicate that the countries are either on the high or low end of the score distribution for the scale. The table also reports the number of high or low scores as defined by the standardised averages. This provides another indication of the degree of distinctiveness, as the higher the number, the more distinct are the subgroups of countries, as the countries deviate from the average in light of the scales of interest.

Japan and Korea (Group A) form the most distinct subgroup of countries, and are consistently either high or low on all twelve scales. While these are among the best performing education systems in terms of student achievement, students in these countries tend to be more anxious about mathematics and feel more socially isolated than other OECD students (*i.e.* they report relatively negative attitudes towards school and low sense of belonging). They also do not feel positive about mathematics or their mathematical skills, and they rely comparatively little on the systematic learning strategies studied in PISA.

Two other countries form a quite distinct subgroup, Mexico and Turkey (Group B), although the attitudes and characteristics bringing them together are different than in the previous example. Mexican and Turkish students tend to report what are generally considered to be educationally positive and favourable attitudes and approaches. In particular, students report high levels of interest in mathematics, they rely heavily on elaboration strategies for learning, and they report a high level of teacher support. However, their anxiety in mathematics is high compared to other OECD students and their sense of belonging and self-efficacy in mathematics are the second weakest of any of the subgroups of countries, after Japan and Korea.

Austria, Germany, and Switzerland (Group C), as a subgroup, are distinguished by the seemingly favourable social environment of their schools. Students report a relatively strong disciplinary climate and relatively high levels of sense of belonging, as well as positive attitudes towards mathematics such as high levels of self-efficacy and low levels of anxiety. Additionally, students in these countries show common patterns with regard to their preferred approaches to learning (not seen among other subgroups of countries), with a relatively high reliance on control strategies and lesser reliance on memorisation or elaboration strategies.

Compared to these subgroups, the remaining countries are less distinctive. Still, in Denmark, Finland and Sweden (Group D) students report the lowest levels of anxiety in mathematics and they tend to shy away from control strategies (and, to some extent, memorisation strategies) compared to students in other countries. Australia, Canada, Iceland, New Zealand and the United States, (Group F) are somewhat distinct from other subgroups in the relatively high reported levels of teacher support and students' self-concept in mathematics. Students in the Czech Republic, Hungary, Poland and the Slovak Republic (Group G) reported the highest levels of self-efficacy in math. Finally, the subgroup of France, Greece, Ireland, Italy, Portugal and Spain (Group H) was mostly at the average across countries on the 12 scales.

Relating students' attitudes towards mathematics, approaches to learning, and school-related indices with mathematics performance

Tables A5.2a, A5.2b and A5.2c show, for each OECD country, the positive or negative difference in the mathematics score per one-unit change in the index score and whether or not that difference varies from the OECD average. In other words, the data provide an indication of the size of the effect of each of the 12 indices on students' mathematics performance and how that relates to the average effect. For example, in Australia, the mathematics score increases 18.6 points on average for each one-unit increase in the index of students' interest in and enjoyment of mathematics, which is a significantly greater increase than that of the OECD average increase of 11.9 points (at the 95% probability level). In other words, interest in and enjoyment of mathematics has a stronger relationship with performance in Australia than it does in OECD countries generally.

The three tables present each set of indices: attitudes toward mathematics, approaches to learning, and school-related indices. Additionally, the countries are presented by the subgroups identified in the previous analysis. This allows an examination of whether or not the similarities in students' attitudes, approaches and contexts translate into similarities in their effects on mathematics performance.

These tables also provide the general trend of how each of the scales is related to mathematics performance, with the OECD average shown at the bottom of the page. Some of the results are initially counter-intuitive. For example, teacher support, a factor that is generally expected to be positively related to student achievement, is negatively correlated with the mathematics score. However, the change in mathematics score for each unit of increase in the index of teacher support, compared with those for other indices, is small. The use of elaboration strategies and memorisation strategies are also negatively correlated, but again the effect sizes are small.

It is also possible that students who generally are lower performers may be more likely to be choosing these strategies (or, as in the previous example, may be with teachers whose role it is to provide extra support and remediation) and the scales may be sensitive to low performing students. The other indices show the expected directions, with particularly strong relationships between mathematics performance and self-concept in mathematics, self-efficacy in mathematics, anxiety in mathematics and disciplinary climate.

Table A5.2a shows the relationship between students' attitudes towards mathematics and their performance in that subject. In Denmark, Finland and Sweden (Group D), students' attitudes toward mathematics has a strong relationship with students' achievement in mathematics, with above-average positive effects of interest, instrumental motivation and self-concept and an above-average negative effect of anxiety on mathematics performance in all three countries. This is true for the other Nordic countries in PISA 2003 (Norway and Iceland), although in Iceland, the relationship of anxiety with mathematics is similar to that of the OECD average.

Japan and Korea (Group A), on the other hand, have more mixed results across the indices on attitudes. In these two countries, there are above-average positive relationships of interest, instrumental motivation and self-efficacy with mathematics scores. However, anxiety does not have as large a negative effect in these two countries as it does in OECD countries on average.

Similarly, Austria, Germany, and Switzerland (Group C), while internally consistent, also have mixed results across the indices on attitudes. Like Japan and Korea, in these countries, anxiety in mathematics does not have as strong an association with student performance as it does in OECD countries on average. Yet, unlike most other OECD countries, instrumental motivation and self-concept also have a lesser impact on mathematics performance than average, and in Austria and Switzerland, the change in mathematics score related to students' instrumental motivation in mathematics is in the opposite direction (negative) than the OECD average.

With regard to the relationship of attitudes towards mathematics and performance, Mexico and Turkey (Group B) are unique among countries in that their statistics are around the averages, with none of the indices having a relatively strong or weak relationship with mathematics performance compared to other countries.

Table A5.2b shows the relationship between students' approaches to learning and mathematics performance. Japan and Korea (Group A), as well as Finland (Group D) and Norway (Group E), show above-average positive associations between the three indices and students' mathematics performance, indicating the importance of strategic learning techniques for students in these countries. Turkey and Spain (from Groups B and H) also show consistently positive (although generally smaller) associations of all three learning strategies and mathematics performance. In contrast, Austria, Germany and Switzerland (Group C), the Czech and Slovak Republics (Group G), and Belgium and Luxembourg (from Group E) show above-average negative associations between control and, in particular, memorisation strategies and students' performance in mathematics.

Table A5.2c shows the relationship between the selected school-related indices and mathematics performance. Of the school-related indices, disciplinary climate has the largest positive effect on mathematics performance consistently across countries. Among the other school-related indices, the largest positive associations are between students' attitudes toward school and teacher support in the countries in Groups F and D, representing most of the Anglophone and Nordic

A5

countries in the sample. These countries also are similar in the consistently weak associations of sense of belonging and mathematics performance. Germany, Switzerland and Austria (Group C) are similar only in the above-average negative association of teacher support and mathematics performance. In these countries, students with low mathematics scores may be more likely to receive additional support, indicating that these systems may be rich in teacher support for those students who need it.

Definitions and methodologies

PISA was most recently administered in 2006; however, since those data are not yet available, this indicator is based on data from the PISA 2003 survey.

The target population for this indicator was all 15-year-old students (in participating countries) enrolled in educational institutions at the secondary-school level regardless of grade level, type of institution, and part- or full-time enrolment status. Fifteen-year olds were defined as students who were between 15 years and 3 months to 16 years and 2 months at the beginning of the PISA testing period.

Tables A5.2a through A5.2c provide data on the change in a country's mathematics score per unit of the relevant indices. The indices summarise student responses to a series of related questions constructed on the basis of previous research (see Annex A1 of *Learning for Tomorrow's World: First Results from PISA 2003* [OECD 2004a]). The validity of comparisons across countries was explored using structural equation modelling. In describing students in terms of each characteristic (*i.e.* self-concept in mathematics), scales were constructed on which the average OECD student (*i.e.* the student with an average level of self-concept) was given an index value of zero, and about two-thirds of the OECD student population are between the values of -1 and 1 (*i.e.* the index has a standard deviation of 1). Negative values on an index do not necessarily imply that students responded negatively to the underlying questions. Rather, a student with a negative score responded less positively than students on average across OECD countries. Likewise, a student with a positive score responded more positively than the average in the OECD area.

Tables A5.2a, A5.2b and A5.2c also provide an OECD average and an OECD total, per the standard PISA reporting conventions. The OECD average takes the OECD countries as a single entity, to which each country contributes with equal weight. For statistics such as percentages or mean scores, the OECD average corresponds to the arithmetic mean of the respective country statistics. In contrast, for statistics relating to variation, the OECD average may differ from the arithmetic mean of the country statistics because it not only reflects variation within countries, but also variation that lies between countries. The OECD total, rather, takes OECD countries as a single entity, to which each country contributes in proportion to the number of 15-year-olds enrolled in its schools. It illustrates how a country compares with the OECD as a whole and may be used to refer to the stock of human capital in the OECD region. As in the indicator, the average is used when the focus is on comparing performance or other attributes across countries. All averages include data for the United Kingdom, even when the data are not shown in the respective data tables.

The United Kingdom did not reach PISA's unit response rate standard, which precludes its comparison with the other countries on whole population analyses. Estimates for the United Kingdom are still reported in charts and tables dealing with subsets of the population

A5

for the purposes of comparison within the country. When estimates for the United Kingdom are reported, they are reported at the end of charts and tables separate from the estimates of other countries as a cautionary reminder that the estimate may not be as reliable as the estimates of countries that met PISA's unit response rate standard.

Further references

For further information about PISA 2003, see *Learning for Tomorrow's World – First Results from PISA 2003* (OECD, 2004a), and the *PISA 2003 Technical Report* (OECD, 2005b). PISA data are also available on the PISA website: *www.pisa.oecd.org*.

Table A5.1.
Means on students' attitudes towards mathematics, approaches to learning, and school-related indices (2003)

A5

	Classification group	Number of high or low scores	Mean of absolute values of standardised means	Attitudes towards mathematics — Instrumental motivation	Interest in mathematics	Self-concept in mathematics	Self-efficacy in mathematics	Anxiety in mathematics	Approaches to learning — Control strategies	Memorisation strategies	Elaboration strategies	School-related indices — Attitudes toward school	Sense of belonging	Teacher support	Disciplinary climate
Japan	A			-0.66	-0.39	-0.53	-0.53	0.44	-0.54	-0.56	-0.75	-0.50	-0.53	-0.34	0.44
Korea	A			-0.44	-0.12	-0.35	-0.42	0.41	-0.49	-0.35	-0.39	-0.37	-0.39	-0.22	0.12
Average				*-0.55*	*-0.25*	*-0.44*	*-0.47*	*0.43*	*-0.51*	*-0.45*	*-0.57*	*-0.44*	*-0.46*	*-0.28*	*0.28*
Standardised average		12	1.89	*-1.98*	*-1.13*	*-2.52*	*-2.25*	*1.62*	*-1.95*	*-2.17*	*-1.95*	*-2.25*	*-2.02*	*-1.19*	*1.70*
Mexico	B			0.58	0.58	0.17	-0.22	0.47	0.45	0.56	0.85	0.42	0.08	0.48	0.00
Turkey	B			0.23	0.55	0.02	-0.18	0.34	0.26	0.10	0.44	0.13	-0.44	0.41	-0.12
Average				*0.40*	*0.56*	*0.10*	*-0.20*	*0.41*	*0.35*	*0.33*	*0.65*	*0.28*	*-0.18*	*0.45*	*-0.06*
Standardised average		8	1.38	*1.45*	*2.51*	*0.54*	*-0.95*	*1.53*	*1.34*	*1.55*	*2.20*	*1.42*	*-0.81*	*1.90*	*-0.37*
Austria	C			-0.49	-0.28	0.07	0.16	-0.27	0.52	0.06	-0.27	0.12	0.44	-0.39	0.21
Germany	C			-0.04	0.04	0.15	0.15	-0.25	0.38	-0.06	-0.31	-0.08	0.24	-0.29	0.30
Switzerland	C			-0.04	0.12	0.13	0.32	-0.29	0.19	-0.19	-0.06	0.03	0.19	0.01	0.10
Average				*-0.19*	*-0.04*	*0.12*	*0.21*	*-0.27*	*0.37*	*-0.06*	*-0.21*	*0.02*	*0.29*	*-0.22*	*0.21*
Standardised average		5	0.80	*-0.70*	*-0.19*	*0.67*	*1.00*	*-1.02*	*1.38*	*-0.30*	*-0.73*	*0.11*	*1.29*	*-0.96*	*1.25*
Denmark	D			0.37	0.41	0.24	-0.07	-0.46	-0.19	-0.27	0.07	-0.03	0.01	0.14	-0.08
Finland	D			0.06	-0.24	0.01	-0.15	-0.31	-0.48	-0.19	-0.14	0.11	-0.02	0.08	-0.15
Sweden	D			0.02	0.09	0.13	0.03	-0.49	-0.40	-0.08	-0.02	0.02	0.25	0.20	-0.05
Average			0.15	*0.15*	*0.09*	*0.13*	*-0.06*	*-0.42*	*-0.36*	*-0.18*	*-0.03*	*0.03*	*0.08*	*0.14*	*-0.09*
Standardised average		2		*0.54*	*0.38*	*0.71*	*-0.30*	*-1.58*	*-1.36*	*-0.87*	*-0.11*	*0.18*	*0.35*	*0.59*	*-0.55*
Belgium	E			-0.32	-0.17	-0.03	-0.04	0.09	-0.05	-0.09	-0.17	-0.19	-0.28	-0.11	0.04
Luxembourg	E			-0.41	-0.26	0.07	0.10	-0.01	0.08	-0.05	-0.25	-0.23	0.23	-0.30	-0.21
Netherlands	E			-0.26	-0.20	0.00	-0.09	-0.38	-0.27	-0.16	-0.26	-0.19	-0.06	-0.27	-0.13
Norway	E			0.15	-0.17	-0.18	-0.04	-0.05	-0.26	-0.12	-0.16	-0.21	0.24	-0.11	-0.24
Average			0.13	*-0.21*	*-0.20*	*-0.04*	*-0.02*	*-0.09*	*-0.12*	*-0.11*	*-0.21*	*-0.21*	*0.03*	*-0.20*	*-0.13*
Standardised average		1		*-0.76*	*-0.88*	*-0.21*	*-0.10*	*-0.33*	*-0.48*	*-0.51*	*-0.72*	*-1.06*	*0.13*	*-0.85*	*-0.81*
Australia	F			0.23	0.01	0.13	0.10	-0.05	0.01	0.17	0.06	0.25	0.04	0.25	-0.01
Canada	F			0.23	-0.01	0.19	0.25	-0.04	0.06	0.16	0.08	0.06	0.02	0.27	0.02
Iceland	F			0.31	-0.11	0.03	0.04	-0.20	0.00	-0.03	-0.06	0.00	0.16	0.20	-0.15
New Zealand	F			0.29	0.12	0.15	0.01	-0.10	-0.03	0.13	0.13	0.10	-0.01	0.16	-0.17
United States	F			0.17	0.04	0.25	0.27	-0.10	0.01	0.31	0.18	0.09	m	0.34	0.12
Average			0.11	*0.25*	*0.01*	*0.15*	*0.13*	*-0.10*	*0.01*	*0.15*	*0.08*	*0.10*	*0.05*	*0.24*	*-0.04*
Standardised average		1		*0.88*	*0.04*	*0.85*	*0.63*	*-0.37*	*0.03*	*0.69*	*0.26*	*0.51*	*0.23*	*1.04*	*-0.23*
Czech Republic	G			0.01	-0.19	-0.09	0.16	-0.05	0.06	-0.05	0.13	-0.01	-0.27	-0.16	-0.01
Hungary	G			-0.11	-0.21	-0.15	0.36	-0.01	0.06	0.16	-0.10	-0.22	0.08	-0.08	0.17
Poland	G			0.04	0.11	0.03	0.05	0.04	-0.03	0.15	0.25	-0.12	-0.17	-0.18	0.10
Slovak Republic	G			-0.05	0.03	-0.05	0.39	0.04	0.07	0.13	0.38	0.03	-0.16	-0.10	-0.10
Average			0.09	*-0.03*	*-0.06*	*-0.07*	*0.24*	*0.01*	*0.04*	*0.09*	*0.16*	*-0.08*	*-0.13*	*-0.13*	*0.04*
Standardised average		1		*-0.10*	*-0.29*	*-0.39*	*1.12*	*0.03*	*0.14*	*0.44*	*0.56*	*-0.42*	*-0.58*	*-0.56*	*0.24*
France	H			-0.08	0.04	-0.17	-0.01	0.34	0.15	-0.06	-0.10	0.14	-0.18	-0.17	-0.13
Greece	H			-0.05	0.10	0.11	-0.26	0.16	0.27	0.20	0.33	0.08	0.04	-0.06	-0.22
Ireland	H			0.10	-0.05	-0.03	-0.03	0.07	-0.01	0.11	-0.14	0.13	0.08	0.00	0.27
Italy	H			-0.15	0.07	0.00	-0.11	0.29	0.21	0.03	0.04	-0.06	0.05	-0.12	-0.10
Portugal	H			0.27	0.16	-0.18	-0.06	0.15	0.14	-0.11	0.16	0.27	0.09	0.27	0.01
Spain	H			-0.05	-0.07	-0.19	-0.04	0.28	-0.02	0.07	0.09	0.14	0.20	-0.07	-0.04
Average			0.07	*0.01*	*0.04*	*-0.08*	*-0.08*	*0.22*	*0.12*	*0.04*	*0.06*	*0.12*	*0.05*	*-0.02*	*-0.04*
Standardised average		0		*0.02*	*0.19*	*-0.44*	*-0.40*	*0.81*	*0.47*	*0.18*	*0.21*	*0.60*	*0.21*	*-0.11*	*-0.21*
United Kingdom[1]				0.12	0.00	0.11	-0.11	-0.08	-0.11	0.11	0.04	0.12	0.08	0.18	-0.01

Note: Cells shaded in darker blue indicates that the average is at the high or low end of the distribution.
1. Response rate too low to ensure comparability.
Source: OECD PISA 2003.
StatLink ⛭ http://dx.doi.org/10.1787/068056433507

A5

Table A5.2a.
Relationship between students' attitudes towards mathematics and mathematics performance (2003)

	Classification group	Attitudes towards mathematics														
		Change in the mathematics score per unit of the index														
		Interest in and enjoyment of mathematics			Instrumental motivation in mathematics			Self-concept in mathematics			Self-efficacy in mathematics			Anxiety in mathematics		
		Effect	*	S.E.	Effect	*	S.E.	Effect	*	S.E.	Effect	*	S.E.	Effect	*	S.E.
Japan	A	27.6	>	(2.44)	23.9	>	(2.25)	21.2	<	(1.96)	54.9	>	(2.06)	-14.3	>	(2.06)
Korea	A	36.2	>	(1.62)	32.8	>	(1.77)	47.3	>	(1.89)	54.0	>	(1.71)	-24.5	>	(1.66)
Mexico	B	-6.3	<	(2.50)	5.4		(2.44)	24.1	<	(2.42)	30.9	<	(2.20)	-34.0		(2.61)
Turkey	B	16.9		(3.08)	12.9		(2.39)	34.8		(4.23)	48.6		(5.07)	-34.6		(4.01)
Austria	C	8.7		(1.92)	-3.7	<	(1.60)	25.7	<	(1.75)	45.5		(1.80)	-25.1	>	(1.67)
Germany	C	10.2		(1.67)	1.1	<	(1.93)	22.7	<	(1.51)	50.2		(1.86)	-28.1	>	(1.42)
Switzerland	C	10.4		(1.47)	-2.4	<	(1.62)	24.2	<	(1.47)	53.2	>	(2.33)	-28.9	>	(1.73)
Denmark	D	27.7	>	(1.71)	20.9	>	(1.77)	46.5	>	(1.32)	50.8	>	(1.80)	-44.6	<	(1.50)
Finland	D	30.5	>	(1.59)	26.9	>	(1.70)	45.5	>	(1.12)	45.9		(1.41)	-41.9	<	(1.53)
Sweden	D	27.0	>	(1.79)	23.0	>	(2.00)	47.0	>	(1.70)	52.8	>	(1.65)	-42.8	<	(1.69)
Belgium	E	15.0	>	(1.55)	11.0		(1.63)	23.3	<	(1.44)	45.2		(1.52)	-26.1	>	(1.72)
Luxembourg	E	6.7	<	(1.48)	0.0	<	(1.35)	19.1	<	(1.35)	40.5	<	(1.37)	-25.0	>	(1.43)
Netherlands	E	14.3		(2.09)	6.1		(2.00)	22.2	<	(1.75)	44.6		(1.99)	-22.6	>	(2.32)
Norway	E	34.3	>	(1.41)	28.5	>	(1.49)	46.6	>	(1.16)	46.8		(1.49)	-42.1	<	(1.22)
Australia	F	18.6	>	(1.36)	16.9	>	(0.91)	42.3	>	(1.40)	49.6		(1.28)	-37.8		(1.50)
Canada	F	20.3	>	(0.96)	19.8	>	(0.96)	35.9	>	(0.78)	43.8	<	(0.77)	-32.6	>	(0.81)
Iceland	F	24.5	>	(1.44)	17.7	>	(1.72)	39.7	>	(1.15)	40.2	<	(1.33)	-33.4		(1.36)
New Zealand	F	11.4		(1.72)	15.6	>	(1.81)	44.9	>	(1.47)	52.0	>	(1.44)	-48.0	<	(1.56)
United States	F	7.8	<	(1.47)	13.6	>	(1.52)	35.1		(1.54)	46.7		(1.30)	-34.4		(1.52)
Czech Republic	G	22.5	>	(2.22)	10.7		(1.82)	39.8	>	(1.60)	55.5	>	(1.54)	-42.1	<	(1.88)
Hungary	G	10.0		(2.30)	7.9		(1.90)	28.4	<	(1.99)	52.6	>	(1.74)	-33.2		(1.83)
Poland	G	15.6	>	(1.48)	17.0	>	(1.82)	46.0	>	(1.48)	53.3	>	(1.98)	-46.4	<	(1.53)
Slovak Republic	G	12.1		(2.26)	6.3		(1.98)	44.5	>	(1.89)	55.0	>	(1.99)	-44.8	<	(1.71)
France	H	20.9	>	(1.76)	13.7	>	(1.61)	28.3	<	(1.71)	47.4		(1.72)	-25.0	>	(1.68)
Greece	H	23.7	>	(1.88)	14.9	>	(1.76)	42.6	>	(1.88)	45.5		(2.13)	-34.5		(1.75)
Ireland	H	17.4	>	(1.78)	7.7		(1.45)	34.4		(1.77)	47.5		(1.32)	-32.9		(1.65)
Italy	H	10.3		(1.70)	8.5		(1.58)	25.3	<	(1.43)	52.4	>	(2.24)	-33.2		(1.70)
Portugal	H	14.2		(2.20)	17.3	>	(2.04)	36.8	>	(1.53)	55.3	>	(1.92)	-34.2		(1.81)
Spain	H	20.4	>	(1.61)	19.4	>	(1.39)	31.9		(1.61)	42.7	<	(1.46)	-26.7	>	(1.79)
OECD total		*5.1*		*(0.72)*	*3.0*		*(0.75)*	*25.5*		*(0.65)*	*44.4*		*(0.71)*	*-31.9*		*(0.61)*
OECD average		*11.9*		*(0.45)*	*8.5*		*(0.41)*	*32.4*		*(0.37)*	*47.2*		*(0.42)*	*-35.3*		*(0.37)*

Note: * indicates that the effect is statistically significantly greater (>) than that of the OECD average; effect is statistically significantly less (<) than that of the OECD average.
Source: OECD PISA 2003.
StatLink ᔎ http://dx.doi.org/10.1787/068056433507

A5

Table A5.2b.
Relationship between students' approaches to learning and mathematics performance (2003)

	Classification group	Learning approaches								
		Change in mathematics score per unit of the index								
		Control strategies			Memorisation strategies			Elaboration strategies		
		Effect	*	S.E.	Effect	*	S.E.	Effect	*	S.E.
Japan	A	17.2	>	(2.44)	13.9	>	(2.30)	14.4	>	(2.39)
Korea	A	38.0	>	(1.75)	19.6	>	(1.77)	30.0	>	(1.64)
Mexico	B	7.1		(1.77)	2.0	>	(1.42)	-1.0	>	(1.63)
Turkey	B	14.4	>	(2.15)	1.2	>	(2.62)	5.7	>	(2.17)
Austria	C	-4.0	<	(1.47)	-18.5	<	(1.72)	-4.1		(1.59)
Germany	C	-7.3	<	(1.87)	-17.9	<	(1.46)	-5.5		(1.71)
Switzerland	C	-2.6	<	(1.43)	-17.1	<	(1.64)	-5.9		(1.42)
Denmark	D	4.6		(2.23)	9.3	>	(1.79)	10.4	>	(2.13)
Finland	D	11.5	>	(1.42)	6.7	>	(1.53)	16.9	>	(1.52)
Sweden	D	-0.4	<	(1.95)	14.1	>	(1.88)	9.8	>	(2.18)
Belgium	E	-1.7	<	(1.69)	-9.3	<	(1.96)	-10.6	<	(1.92)
Luxembourg	E	-5.4	<	(1.41)	-8.6	<	(1.39)	-7.7		(1.25)
Netherlands	E	-1.2	<	(2.84)	12.8	>	(2.08)	-3.5		(2.43)
Norway	E	14.5	>	(1.59)	22.3	>	(1.48)	8.4	>	(1.46)
Australia	F	15.6	>	(1.14)	9.7	>	(1.29)	-2.1	>	(1.17)
Canada	F	13.2	>	(1.13)	6.2	>	(1.02)	6.2	>	(1.12)
Iceland	F	4.5		(1.66)	-0.7	>	(1.50)	0.1	>	(1.61)
New Zealand	F	11.1	>	(1.85)	4.3	>	(1.96)	-8.2		(2.04)
United States	F	3.4		(1.60)	0.3	>	(1.38)	-7.0		(1.39)
Czech Republic	G	0.4	<	(2.10)	-14.2	<	(2.06)	13.0	>	(1.75)
Hungary	G	-4.4	<	(1.99)	-7.3		(1.88)	-4.9		(2.23)
Poland	G	4.3		(1.88)	-4.5		(1.85)	5.9	>	(1.90)
Slovak Republic	G	-4.7	<	(1.93)	-10.5	<	(1.92)	0.4	>	(1.79)
France	H	7.9		(1.34)	-0.9	>	(1.41)	-1.2	>	(1.69)
Greece	H	6.8		(1.55)	-2.9		(2.09)	8.9	>	(1.82)
Ireland	H	3.9		(1.54)	5.0	>	(1.74)	-3.1		(2.16)
Italy	H	3.6		(1.87)	-11.8	<	(1.97)	-3.9		(1.46)
Portugal	H	18.2	>	(1.79)	-5.4		(1.87)	9.2	>	(2.07)
Spain	H	12.6	>	(1.22)	7.7	>	(1.45)	10.2	>	(1.41)
OECD total		*-0.5*		*(0.73)*	*-7.5*		*(0.72)*	*-11.4*		*(0.76)*
OECD average		*6.42*		*m*	*-4.5*		*(0.41)*	*-5.3*		*(0.43)*

Note: * indicates that the effect is statistically significantly greater (>) than that of the OECD average; effect is statistically significantly less (<) than that of the OECD average.
Source: OECD PISA 2003.
StatLink ⟨⟨⟨⟨ http://dx.doi.org/10.1787/068056433507

A5

Table A5.2c.
Relationship between school-related indices and mathematics performance (2003)

	Classification group	School-related indices											
		Change in mathematics score per unit of the index											
		Attitudes towards school			Students' sense of belonging at school			Teacher support			Disciplinary climate		
		Effect	*	S.E.	Effect	*	S.E.	Effect	*	S.E.	Effect	*	S.E.
Japan	A	2.6		(2.03)	12.9	>	(2.16)	12.9	>	(3.27)	32.7	>	(2.91)
Korea	A	0.2		(1.78)	11.1	>	(2.09)	7.5	>	(2.56)	14.7		(2.17)
Mexico	B	21.4	>	(1.71)	13.3	>	(1.41)	-1.6		(1.41)	18.9		(2.05)
Turkey	B	-3.3		(3.75)	21.0	>	(2.87)	3.8	>	(3.54)	30.0	>	(4.37)
Austria	C	-2.7	<	(1.72)	2.9		(1.64)	-8.4	<	(1.91)	19.3		(2.03)
Germany	C	-9.4	<	(1.98)	-1.4	<	(1.81)	-10.9	<	(1.93)	18.6		(1.73)
Switzerland	C	1.1		(1.95)	8.4	>	(1.90)	-10.3	<	(2.97)	17.3		(2.56)
Denmark	D	7.0	>	(1.78)	3.1		(1.92)	6.7	>	(2.05)	10.4	<	(2.07)
Finland	D	12.5	>	(1.50)	-1.9	<	(1.37)	4.4	>	(1.83)	10.4	<	(1.50)
Sweden	D	14.3	>	(1.65)	0.3	<	(1.57)	4.5	>	(1.81)	15.4		(2.09)
Belgium	E	-4.3	<	(2.16)	6.3		(2.18)	-6.0		(1.61)	23.5	>	(1.57)
Luxembourg	E	-9.2	<	(1.46)	5.9		(1.45)	-9.8	<	(1.30)	13.9	<	(1.40)
Netherlands	E	3.8		(3.05)	7.0		(2.31)	0.3	>	(2.21)	12.4	<	(2.36)
Norway	E	16.3	>	(1.80)	0.1	<	(1.57)	14.0	>	(1.93)	11.8	<	(1.85)
Australia	F	13.8	>	(1.03)	3.1		(1.63)	10.8	>	(1.43)	21.0	>	(1.07)
Canada	F	7.2	>	(1.00)	-1.0	<	(0.85)	6.3	>	(1.08)	17.3		(0.92)
Iceland	F	15.3	>	(1.42)	0.5		(1.55)	9.5	>	(1.87)	12.6	<	(1.71)
New Zealand	F	14.6	>	(1.70)	2.6		(1.51)	3.9	>	(1.62)	17.9		(1.60)
United States	F	6.6	>	(1.39)	m		m	7.9	>	(1.27)	25.8	>	(1.40)
Czech Republic	G	3.6		(1.72)	12.7	>	(1.98)	-5.1		(2.11)	16.7		(2.05)
Hungary	G	-6.5	<	(2.28)	10.0	>	(1.63)	-0.3		(2.14)	20.3		(2.30)
Poland	G	-3.3	<	(1.73)	7.7	>	(1.51)	-2.9		(1.86)	13.5	<	(1.98)
Slovak Republic	G	-10.5	<	(1.51)	3.1		(1.41)	-16.0	<	(1.83)	13.6	<	(1.59)
France	H	6.8	>	(1.69)	1.2		(1.28)	-5.2		(1.93)	12.1	<	(1.83)
Greece	H	-11.4	<	(1.74)	5.8		(1.69)	-6.4		(2.07)	14.1		(2.95)
Ireland	H	6.8	>	(1.53)	-5.2	<	(1.55)	-2.9		(1.81)	15.5		(1.60)
Italy	H	-5.6	<	(1.73)	-3.7	<	(1.92)	-16.3	<	(1.67)	12.5	<	(1.79)
Portugal	H	9.5	>	(1.73)	15.7	>	(1.72)	-5.5		(1.76)	23.7	>	(2.08)
Spain	H	4.2	>	(1.41)	2.4		(1.34)	-1.1	>	(1.55)	16.9		(1.67)
OECD total		*-1.8*		*(0.61)*	*2.0*		*(0.63)*	*-5.9*		*(0.58)*	*23.4*		*(0.65)*
OECD average		*0.9*		*(0.35)*	*3.5*		*(0.38)*	*-4.2*		*(0.36)*	*18.3*		*(0.38)*

OECD countries

Note: * indicates that the effect is statistically significantly greater (>) than that of the OECD average; effect is statistically significantly less (<) than that of the OECD average.
Source: OECD PISA 2003.
StatLink ᴍ͟ꜱ͟ http://dx.doi.org/10.1787/068056433507

WHAT IS THE IMPACT OF IMMIGRANT BACKGROUND ON STUDENT PERFORMANCE?

This indicator compares the performance in mathematics and reading of 15-year-old students with an immigrant background with their native counterparts, using data from the OECD Programme for International Student Assessment 2003 survey. It also looks at the motivation of these students to learn.

Key results

Chart A6.1. **Differences in mathematics performance by immigrant status (2003)**

■ □ Difference in mathematics performance between native and second-generation students
■ ■ Difference in mathematics performance between native and first-generation students

Among the 14 OECD countries with significant immigrant populations, first-generation students lag 48 score points behind their native counterparts on the PISA mathematics scale, equivalent to more than a school year's progress, on average. The performance disadvantage of second-generation students also remains significant, at 40 score points. The disadvantage of students with an immigrant background varies widely across countries, from insignificant amounts in Australia, Canada, New Zealand and Macao-China to more than 90 score points in Belgium and Germany even for second-generation children.

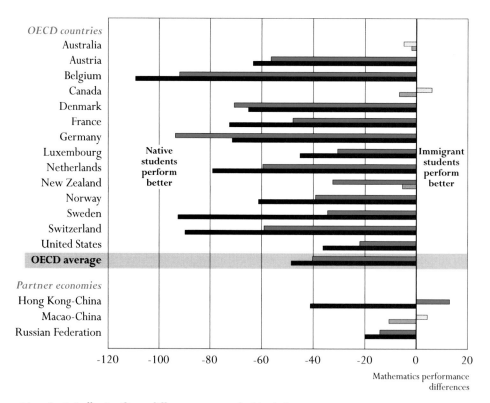

Note: Statistically significant differences are marked in darker tones.
Source: OECD PISA 2003. Table A6.1a.
StatLink ⋙ http://dx.doi.org/10.1787/068061288083

Other highlights of this indicator

- Second-generation students (who were born in the country of the assessment) tend to perform better than their first-generation counterparts (who were born in another country), as one might expect since they did not need to make transitions across systemic, cultural and linguistic borders. However, the gains vary widely across countries. In Canada, Luxembourg, Sweden and Switzerland and the partner economy Hong Kong-China, second-generation students perform significantly better than first-generation students, with the performance gap reduced by 31 score points in Switzerland and 58 score points in Sweden, while in Germany and New Zealand second-generation students born in these countries perform worse than first-generation students.

- The mathematics achievement of the highest performers among students with an immigrant background varies much less across countries than the achievement of the lowest performing students with an immigrant background.

- Despite performing less well on the whole than native students and generally coming from less advantaged families, students who have experienced immigration first-hand tend to report, throughout the OECD area, higher levels of interest and motivation in mathematics.

A6

Policy context

In most OECD countries, policy makers and the general public are paying increasing attention to issues surrounding international migration. In part, this is a consequence of the growth of immigrant inflows that many OECD countries have experienced since the 1980s, whether from globalising economic activities and family reunions in the aftermath of labour migration movements during the 1960s and 1970s, the dissolution of the Eastern Bloc in Europe, or political instability. The issues go well beyond how migration flows can be channelled and managed, and are increasingly related to how the challenges of integration can be addressed effectively – for both the immigrants themselves and the populations in the countries receiving them. Given the pivotal role of education for success in working life, education and training set the stage for the integration of immigrants into labour markets. They can also contribute to overcoming language barriers and facilitate the transmission of the norms and values that provide a basis for social cohesion.

PISA adds a crucial new perspective to the analyses, by assessing the success of 15-year-old students with an immigrant background in school, both in comparison to their native counterparts and in comparison to similar student populations in other countries. The performance disadvantages of students with an immigrant background shown by this indicator lay out major challenges for education systems and these are unlikely to be resolved on their own. On the contrary, given the anticipated effects of population aging and ongoing needs for skilled labour as well as the extent of family reunification, it is likely that migration to OECD countries will remain high on national policy agendas. Education systems, particularly in Europe, will need to deal more effectively with increasing socio-economic and cultural diversity in their student populations and find ways to ensure that children from immigrant backgrounds ultimately enter the labour market with strong foundation skills, as well as with the capacity and motivation to continue learning throughout life.

Evidence and explanations

Among the 14 OECD countries in which students with an immigrant background accounted for more than 3% of 15-year-old students, first-generation students lag 48 score points behind their native counterparts on the PISA mathematics scale, equivalent to more than an average school year's progress (the average performance gain associated with a school year is estimated at 41 score points) (see Chart A6.1). Even after accounting for socio-economic factors such as the occupation and education of their parents, an average disadvantage of 30 score points remains (see *Where Immigrants Succeed: A Comparative Review of Performance and Engagement in PISA 2003* [OECD, 2006b]).

Box A6.1. Terminology used for describing students' immigrant background

Native students: Students with at least one parent born in the country of assessment. Students born in the country who have one foreign-born parent (children of "combined" families) are included in the native category, as previous research indicates that these students perform similarly to native students.

First-generation students: Students born outside of the country of assessment whose parents are also foreign-born.

Second-generation students: Students born in the country of assessment with foreign-born parents.

This suggests that schools and societies face major challenges in bringing the human potential that immigrants bring with them fully to fruition. At the same time, Chart A6.1 shows that the performance disadvantage of students with an immigrant background varies widely across countries, from insignificant amounts in Australia, Canada and New Zealand and the partner economy Macao-China to more than 90 score points in Belgium and Germany even for second-generation children. Further to this, Table A6.1 shows considerable differences in the absolute performance levels of immigrants, with second-generation 15-year-old immigrants in Canada outperforming their German counterparts by 111 score points, a gap that is equivalent to almost three school years. Some of these differences can be explained by socio-economic contextual factors but the residual performance gap that remains after taking such factors into account is sufficiently large to make cross-national analyses a rich source for the search of effective policies for the integration of these students. It should be noted that there is no positive association between the size of these student populations in the countries studied and the size of the performance differences between native students and those with an immigrant background. This finding contradicts the assumption that high levels of immigration will generally impair integration (OECD, 2006b).

Without longitudinal data, it is not possible to assess directly to what extent the observed disadvantages of students with an immigrant background are alleviated over successive generations. However, comparing the performance of students who were born in a different country with students who were themselves born in the country but have foreign-born parents shows important differences (Table A6.1a). In the OECD area as a whole, second-generation students tend to perform better than their first-generation counterparts, as one might expect as they did not need to make transitions across systemic, cultural, and linguistic borders. However, these gains vary widely across countries. In Canada, Luxembourg, Sweden and Switzerland and the partner economy Hong Kong-China, second-generation students perform significantly better than first-generation students, with the performance gap reduced by 31 score points in Switzerland and 58 score points in Sweden. In other countries the performance advantage of second-generation students over first-generation students is much smaller and not statistically significant. Germany and New Zealand even show the opposite pattern, with second-generation students born in these countries performing worse than first-generation students. Given the nature of the PISA data, these patterns may be influenced by differences in the composition of the first and second-generation student populations.

It is noteworthy that the mathematics achievement of the highest performers among students with an immigrant background varies much less across countries than the achievement of the lowest performing students with an immigrant background (see Chart A6.2). Level 2 on the PISA proficiency scale represents the baseline level of mathematics proficiency at which students begin to demonstrate the kind of skills that enable them to actively use mathematics: for example, they are able to use basic algorithms, formulae and procedures, to make literal interpretations and to apply direct reasoning. Students who are classified below Level 2 may thus face considerable challenges in terms of their labour market and earnings prospects, as well as their capacity to participate fully in society. Chart A6.2 compares the distribution across the PISA proficiency levels in mathematics between first-generation and native students. The findings indicate that among native students, only a small percentage fail to reach Level 2, whereas the situation is very different for students with an immigrant background. More than 40% of first-generation students in Belgium, France, Norway and Sweden and more than 30% of first-generation

A6

Chart A6.2. Percentage of students at each level of proficiency on the mathematics scale by immigrant status (2003)

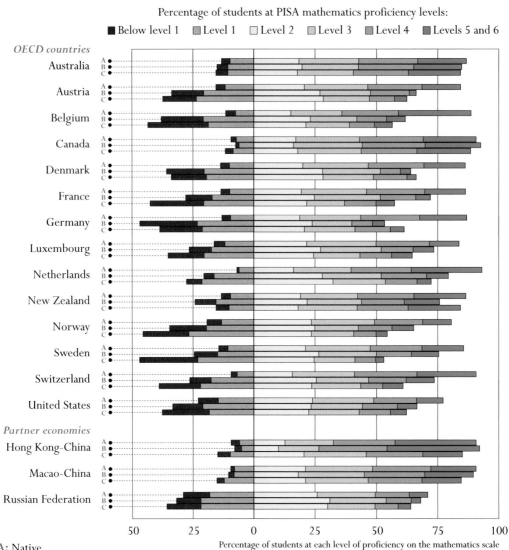

Percentage of students at PISA mathematics proficiency levels:

■ Below level 1   ▨ Level 1   ☐ Level 2   ▨ Level 3   ▨ Level 4   ■ Levels 5 and 6

A: Native
B: Second-generation
C: First-generation
Source: OECD PISA 2003. Tables A6.2a, A6.2b and A6.2c.
StatLink ⧉ http://dx.doi.org/10.1787/068061288083

students in Austria, Denmark, Germany, Luxembourg, Switzerland and the United States and the partner economy the Russian Federation perform below Level 2. In over one-half of the OECD countries compared in this indicator, still more than one-quarter of second-generation students have not acquired the skills to be considered able to actively use mathematics according to the PISA definition. In Germany, 47% of second-generation students perform below Level 2 and in Austria, Belgium, Denmark, France, Luxembourg, Norway, Switzerland and the United States, and the partner economy the Russian Federation, still more than 25% of second-generation students score below Level 2.

A6

A very different picture emerges for Australia and Canada and the partner economies Hong Kong-China and Macao-China. In these countries, the percentage of students performing below Level 2 is comparatively low in all groups, with less than 16% of first-generation, second-generation or native students failing to reach Level 2. The comparatively positive situation of students with an immigrant background in Australia and Canada may, in part, be a result of selective immigration policies resulting in immigrant populations with greater wealth and education. In Hong Kong-China and Macao-China the ethnic background and language between native students and those with an immigrant background is often similar, even if large socio-economic differences exist. However, the bottom line is that these countries have only a relatively small proportion of students at low levels of mathematical literacy.

The trends in reading are similar to those in mathematics. With the exception of the Russian Federation, the percentage of native students who fail to reach Level 2 in reading is less than 20% across all of the countries included in this study. Among students with an immigrant background, however, it is considerably higher (see Tables A6.2d, A6.2e and A6.2f, available on line at [*http://dx.doi.org/10.1787/068061288083*]). In 10 OECD countries – Austria, Belgium, Denmark, France, Germany, Luxembourg, Norway, Sweden, Switzerland and the United States – and in the partner economy the Russian Federation more than 25% of first-generation students fail to reach Level 2. As in mathematics, countries with high percentages of students with an immigrant background below Level 2 in reading may consider introducing support measures particularly geared to the needs of these student groups.

Findings from PISA suggest that students are most likely to initiate high quality learning, using various strategies, if they are well motivated, not anxious about their learning and believe in their own capacities. On the same token, high performance could lead to better motivation and attitudes towards schooling less anxiety. How well do schools and families foster and strengthen positive predispositions to learning among students with an immigrant background and thus contribute to laying a foundation for them to leave school with the motivation and capacity to continue learning throughout life? Chart A6.3 shows that these students report no signs of a lack of instrumental motivation in mathematics (see also Box A5.1 in Indicator A5). Despite performing less well on the whole than native students and generally coming from less advantaged families, students who experience immigration first-hand tend to report, throughout the OECD area, higher levels of instrumental motivation in mathematics than their native and second-generation peers. In fact, in none of the countries studied do students with an immigrant background report lower levels of interest. Much of this difference remains after accounting for socio-economic aspects as well as student performance in mathematics. The consistency of this finding is striking, given the substantial differences between countries in terms of immigration histories, immigrant populations, immigration and integration policies, and the performance of students with immigration background in PISA.

This points to areas where schools and policy makers could develop additional programmes to seek to reduce achievement gaps by using the strong instrumental motivation of students with an immigrant background. Schools and teachers may need to pay additional attention to reducing differences in these essential non-achievement outcomes. This could prove beneficial not only for these students' potential to learn throughout life, but also for helping to increase their level of achievement.

A6

Chart A6.3. Students' instrumental motivation in mathematics by immigrant status (2003)

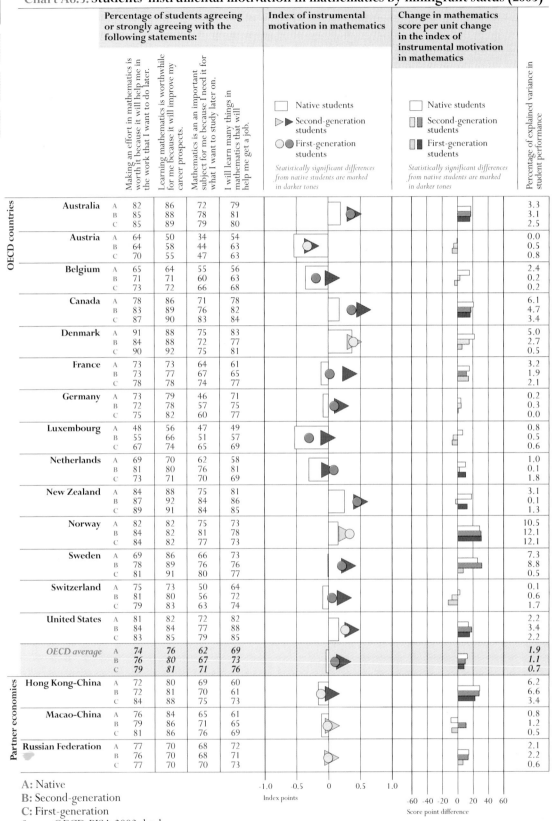

		Percentage of students agreeing or strongly agreeing with the following statements:				Index of instrumental motivation in mathematics	Change in mathematics score per unit change in the index of instrumental motivation in mathematics	Percentage of explained variance in student performance
		Making an effort in mathematics is worth it because it will help me in the work that I want to do later.	Learning mathematics is worthwhile for me because it will improve my career prospects.	Mathematics is an important subject for me because I need it for what I want to study later on.	I will learn many things in mathematics that will help me get a job.			
Australia	A	82	86	72	79			3.3
	B	85	88	78	81			3.1
	C	85	89	79	80			2.5
Austria	A	64	50	34	54			0.0
	B	64	58	44	63			0.5
	C	70	55	47	63			0.8
Belgium	A	65	64	55	56			2.4
	B	71	71	60	63			0.2
	C	73	72	66	68			0.2
Canada	A	78	86	71	78			6.1
	B	83	89	76	82			4.7
	C	87	90	83	84			3.4
Denmark	A	91	88	75	83			5.0
	B	84	88	72	77			2.7
	C	90	92	75	81			0.5
France	A	73	73	64	61			3.2
	B	73	77	67	65			1.9
	C	78	78	74	77			2.1
Germany	A	73	79	46	71			0.2
	B	72	78	57	75			0.3
	C	75	82	60	77			0.0
Luxembourg	A	48	56	47	49			0.8
	B	55	66	51	57			0.5
	C	67	74	65	69			0.6
Netherlands	A	69	70	62	58			1.0
	B	81	80	76	81			0.1
	C	73	71	70	69			1.8
New Zealand	A	84	88	75	81			3.1
	B	87	92	84	86			0.1
	C	89	91	84	85			1.3
Norway	A	82	82	75	73			10.5
	B	84	82	81	78			12.1
	C	84	82	77	73			12.1
Sweden	A	69	86	66	73			7.3
	B	78	89	76	76			8.8
	C	81	91	80	77			0.5
Switzerland	A	75	73	50	64			0.1
	B	81	80	56	72			0.6
	C	79	83	63	74			1.7
United States	A	81	82	72	82			2.2
	B	84	84	77	88			3.4
	C	83	85	79	85			2.2
OECD average	A	*74*	*76*	*62*	*69*			*1.9*
	B	*76*	*80*	*67*	*73*			*1.1*
	C	*79*	*81*	*71*	*76*			*0.7*
Hong Kong-China	A	72	80	69	60			6.2
	B	72	81	70	61			6.6
	C	84	88	75	73			3.4
Macao-China	A	76	84	65	61			0.8
	B	79	86	71	65			1.2
	C	81	86	76	69			0.5
Russian Federation	A	77	70	68	72			2.1
	B	76	70	68	71			2.2
	C	77	70	70	73			0.6

OECD countries — Partner economies

Index of instrumental motivation in mathematics:
- ☐ Native students
- ▷▶ Second-generation students
- ○◐ First-generation students

Statistically significant differences from native students are marked in darker tones

Change in mathematics score per unit change in the index of instrumental motivation in mathematics:
- ☐ Native students
- ▯▮ Second-generation students
- ▮▮ First-generation students

Statistically significant differences from native students are marked in darker tones

Index points scale: -1.0   -0.5   0   0.5   1.0

Score point difference scale: -60 -40 -20 0 20 40 60

A: Native
B: Second-generation
C: First-generation

Source: OECD PISA 2003 database.

StatLink http://dx.doi.org/10.1787/068061288083

In most European countries, students with an immigrant background come from lower level socio-economic backgrounds and their parents often are less educated than native students' parents. This is also the case in the United States and Hong-Kong China. In contrast, the background characteristics of these students and their native counterparts are similar in Australia, Canada and New Zealand, and in the partner economies Macao-China and the Russian Federation. At the country level, there is a relationship between the relative mathematics performance of students with an immigrant background and their relative educational and socio-economic background. However, performance differences remain between these students and native ones in many countries after accounting for these background characteristics. For example, there are still significant performance differences between native and second-generation students in Austria, Belgium, Denmark, France, Germany, Luxembourg, the Netherlands, New Zealand, Norway and Switzerland. This suggests that the relative performance levels of students with an immigrant background cannot solely be attributed to the composition of immigrant populations in terms of their educational and socio-economic background. Students with an immigrant background who do not speak the language of instruction at home tend to be lower performing in mathematics in several countries. Even after accounting for parents' educational and occupational status, the performance gap associated with the language spoken at home remains significant in Belgium, Canada, Germany and the United States, as well as in the partner economies Hong Kong-China, Macao-China and the Russian Federation. Countries with a strong relationship between the language students speak at home and their performance in mathematics may want to consider strengthening language support measures in schools (OECD, 2006b).

Definitions and methodology

PISA was most recently administered in 2006; however, since those data are not yet available, this indicator is based on data from the PISA 2003 survey.

The target population for this indicator was all 15-year old students (in participating countries) enrolled in educational institutions at the secondary-school level regardless of grade level, type of institution, and part- or full-time enrolment status. Fifteen-year olds were defined as students who were between 15 years and 3 months to 16 years and 2 months at the beginning of the PISA testing period. The term "student" is used frequently to denote this target population. Information on students' immigrant background is compiled from students' responses provided in the PISA student questionnaire.

See Box A6.1 above for definitions of the terms "native students", "first-generation students" and "second-generation students".

This indicator includes the 14 OECD countries with significant populations of students with an immigrant background (at least 3% of participating students): Australia, Austria, Belgium, Canada, Denmark, France, Germany, Luxembourg, the Netherlands, New Zealand, Norway, Sweden, Switzerland and the United States. Three partner economies are part of this analysis: Hong Kong-China, Macao-China and the Russian Federation.

The OECD average in this indicator takes the 14 OECD countries as a single entity, to which each country contributes with equal weight. The OECD average corresponds to the arithmetic mean of the respective country statistics.

A6

Further references

For further information about PISA 2003, see *Learning for Tomorrow's World — First Results from PISA 2003* (OECD, 2004a) and the *PISA 2003 Technical Report* (OECD, 2005b). For further information about the expectations and attitudes of students from an immigrant background, see *Where Immigrants Succeed: A Comparative Review of Performance and Engagement in PISA 2003* (OECD, 2006b). PISA data are also available on the PISA website: *www.pisa.oecd.org.*

The following additional material relevant to this indicator is available on line at:

StatLink ⏩ http://dx.doi.org/10.1787/068061288083

- *Table A6.2d. Percentage of native students at each level of proficiency on the reading scale*
- *Table A6.2e. Percentage of second-generation students at each level of proficiency on the reading scale*
- *Table A6.2f. Percentage of first-generation students at each level of proficiency on the reading scale*

Table A6.1a.
Differences in mathematics performance, by immigrant status (2003)

| | Performance on the mathematics scale | | | | | | Difference in the mathematics score | | | | | |
| | Native students | | Second-generation students | | First-generation students | | Second-generation students minus native students | | First-generation students minus native students | | First-generation students minus second-generation students | |
	Mean score	S.E.	Mean score	S.E.	Mean score	S.E.	Difference	S.E.	Difference	S.E.	Difference	S.E.
OECD countries												
Australia	527	(2.1)	522	(4.7)	525	(4.9)	-5	(4.7)	-2	(4.9)	3	(4.8)
Austria	515	(3.3)	459	(8.8)	452	(6.0)	**-56**	(9.3)	**-63**	(6.0)	-7	(9.5)
Belgium	546	(2.5)	454	(7.5)	437	(10.8)	**-92**	(7.6)	**-109**	(10.9)	-17	(12.4)
Canada	537	(1.6)	543	(4.3)	530	(4.7)	6	(4.4)	-7	(4.8)	**-13**	(5.1)
Denmark	520	(2.5)	449	(11.2)	455	(10.1)	**-70**	(11.1)	**-65**	(9.8)	5	(13.5)
France	520	(2.4)	472	(6.1)	448	(15.0)	**-48**	(6.6)	**-72**	(15.0)	-25	(15.5)
Germany	525	(3.5)	432	(9.1)	454	(7.5)	**-93**	(9.6)	**-71**	(7.9)	22	(11.2)
Luxembourg	507	(1.3)	476	(3.3)	462	(3.7)	**-31**	(3.7)	**-45**	(4.1)	**-14**	(5.6)
Netherlands	551	(3.0)	492	(10.3)	472	(8.4)	**-59**	(11.1)	**-79**	(8.8)	-19	(10.8)
New Zealand	528	(2.6)	496	(8.4)	523	(4.9)	**-32**	(9.1)	-5	(5.6)	27	(8.0)
Norway	499	(2.3)	460	(11.7)	438	(9.3)	**-39**	(11.3)	**-61**	(9.4)	-22	(13.8)
Sweden	517	(2.2)	483	(9.8)	425	(9.6)	**-34**	(9.1)	**-92**	(9.7)	**-58**	(10.9)
Switzerland	543	(3.3)	484	(5.0)	453	(6.1)	**-59**	(4.9)	**-89**	(6.0)	**-31**	(6.4)
United States	490	(2.8)	468	(7.6)	453	(7.5)	**-22**	(7.2)	**-36**	(7.5)	-14	(7.4)
OECD average	*523*	*(0.7)*	*483*	*(2.1)*	*475*	*(1.9)*	*-40*	*(2.0)*	*-48*	*(2.1)*	*-8*	*(2.4)*
Partner economies												
Hong Kong-China	557	(4.5)	570	(4.6)	516	(5.3)	13	(4.3)	**-41**	(4.5)	**-54**	(5.2)
Macao-China	528	(5.9)	532	(4.1)	517	(9.2)	4	(7.9)	-11	(10.4)	-15	(10.4)
Russian Federation	472	(4.4)	457	(7.2)	452	(5.9)	-14	(7.2)	**-20**	(5.4)	-6	(8.3)

Note: Differences that are statistically significant are indicated in bold.
Source: OECD PISA 2003.
StatLink ⌗ⅶ🖺 http://dx.doi.org/10.1787/068061288083

Table A6.2a.
Percentage of native students at each level of proficiency on the mathematics scale (2003)

| | Native students - proficiency levels | | | | | | | | | | | |
| | Below Level 1 (below 358 score points) | | Level 1 (from 358 to 420 score points) | | Level 2 (from 421 to 482 score points) | | Level 3 (from 483 to 544 score points) | | Level 4 (from 545 to 606 score points) | | Levels 5 and 6 (above 607 score points) | |
	%	S.E.	%	S.E.	%	S.E.	%	S.E.	%	S.E.	%	S.E.
OECD countries												
Australia	3.7	(0.4)	9.5	(0.5)	18.5	(0.7)	24.4	(0.7)	23.9	(0.6)	20.0	(0.7)
Austria	4.0	(0.7)	11.6	(0.9)	20.6	(1.0)	25.9	(1.3)	21.9	(0.9)	16.0	(1.1)
Belgium	4.0	(0.4)	7.4	(0.5)	15.2	(0.7)	20.8	(0.8)	22.9	(0.7)	29.7	(1.0)
Canada	2.1	(0.3)	7.1	(0.4)	17.3	(0.6)	26.0	(0.8)	25.8	(0.6)	21.7	(0.7)
Denmark	3.8	(0.5)	9.8	(0.7)	20.0	(0.9)	26.6	(0.9)	22.8	(0.9)	17.0	(1.0)
France	3.8	(0.6)	9.7	(0.9)	19.5	(1.0)	26.5	(1.1)	23.7	(1.2)	16.8	(1.0)
Germany	3.6	(0.6)	9.4	(0.8)	18.9	(1.3)	24.8	(1.0)	23.9	(1.1)	19.4	(1.1)
Luxembourg	4.5	(0.5)	11.8	(1.0)	21.6	(1.4)	28.2	(1.0)	21.7	(1.1)	12.2	(0.8)
Netherlands	0.9	(0.3)	6.0	(0.7)	16.3	(1.2)	23.4	(1.2)	24.3	(1.4)	29.0	(1.5)
New Zealand	4.0	(0.5)	9.4	(0.7)	19.0	(0.7)	23.4	(0.9)	22.7	(0.9)	21.5	(0.9)
Norway	6.1	(0.5)	13.2	(0.8)	23.5	(1.1)	25.7	(1.1)	19.6	(1.1)	11.8	(0.7)
Sweden	3.8	(0.4)	10.5	(0.6)	21.2	(0.9)	26.2	(0.9)	21.1	(0.9)	17.2	(0.8)
Switzerland	2.6	(0.4)	6.7	(0.6)	15.8	(0.8)	25.3	(1.1)	25.3	(0.8)	24.2	(1.6)
United States	8.4	(0.7)	14.5	(0.9)	24.0	(0.8)	24.8	(0.9)	17.5	(0.8)	10.9	(0.8)
Partner economies												
Hong Kong-China	3.5	(0.8)	5.8	(0.8)	12.8	(1.0)	19.6	(1.4)	25.0	(1.4)	33.2	(1.8)
Macao-China	1.5	(0.9)	7.8	(3.2)	21.1	(4.1)	27.3	(3.6)	23.8	(3.6)	18.5	(2.6)
Russian Federation	10.9	(1.1)	18.2	(1.2)	25.9	(1.1)	23.6	(1.0)	13.9	(1.0)	7.5	(0.8)

Source: OECD PISA 2003.
StatLink ⌗ⅶ🖺 http://dx.doi.org/10.1787/068061288083

A6

Table A6.2b.
Percentage of second-generation students at each level of proficiency on the mathematics scale (2003)

| | Second-generation students - proficiency levels | | | | | | | | | | |
| | Below Level 1 (below 358 score points) | | Level 1 (from 358 to 420 score points) | | Level 2 (from 421 to 482 score points) | | Level 3 (from 483 to 544 score points) | | Level 4 (from 545 to 606 score points) | | Levels 5 and 6 (above 607 score points) | |
	%	S.E.	%	S.E.	%	S.E.	%	S.E.	%	S.E.	%	S.E.
Australia	4.7	(1.0)	10.4	(1.0)	19.7	(1.6)	23.1	(2.0)	22.4	(2.3)	19.7	(2.0)
Austria	13.2	(3.4)	20.6	(3.6)	27.0	(3.9)	20.6	(3.5)	15.7	(3.6)	2.9	(1.5)
Belgium	17.4	(2.5)	20.7	(2.0)	23.1	(2.4)	19.0	(3.1)	11.9	(2.4)	7.8	(2.0)
Canada	1.4	(0.6)	5.9	(1.0)	16.3	(1.7)	28.0	(2.3)	25.5	(2.3)	22.9	(9.0)
Denmark	15.7	(3.9)	20.4	(4.6)	28.0	(6.9)	23.5	(6.7)	8.2	(3.6)	4.2	(2.6)
France	10.9	(2.3)	17.1	(2.3)	24.8	(3.5)	26.7	(2.8)	14.5	(2.6)	5.9	(2.3)
Germany	23.5	(4.2)	23.3	(3.3)	23.8	(3.4)	16.3	(2.7)	8.4	(2.3)	4.8	(1.4)
Luxembourg	9.3	(1.3)	17.4	(2.1)	27.3	(2.3)	24.5	(2.0)	13.1	(1.7)	8.5	(1.1)
Netherlands	4.2	(1.5)	16.4	(4.2)	27.9	(4.3)	23.9	(4.2)	18.6	(3.2)	9.0	(2.6)
New Zealand	8.7	(3.3)	15.6	(3.1)	21.8	(3.4)	22.2	(3.1)	17.4	(2.7)	14.4	(2.7)
Norway	15.2	(4.9)	19.5	(4.8)	25.0	(7.9)	17.7	(5.8)	13.6	(4.2)	9.0	(3.6)
Sweden	9.6	(2.4)	14.8	(3.4)	26.5	(3.2)	23.5	(4.9)	14.4	(3.7)	11.2	(3.3)
Switzerland	8.8	(1.6)	17.6	(2.3)	25.6	(2.7)	21.3	(2.4)	15.3	(1.7)	11.4	(2.3)
United States	12.5	(2.5)	21.0	(3.0)	23.3	(2.3)	21.0	(2.4)	14.2	(2.2)	8.0	(2.0)
Hong Kong-China	2.9	(0.8)	4.9	(0.9)	10.2	(1.4)	16.3	(1.5)	27.8	(1.9)	37.9	(2.2)
Macao-China	2.4	(0.7)	7.9	(1.2)	18.2	(1.8)	26.9	(2.4)	24.6	(2.2)	20.0	(2.1)
Russian Federation	10.0	(2.4)	21.9	(3.1)	31.0	(4.1)	22.8	(3.7)	10.3	(2.5)	4.0	(2.0)

Source: OECD PISA 2003.
StatLink ⟐ http://dx.doi.org/10.1787/068061288083

Table A6.2c.
Percentage of first-generation students at each level of proficiency on the mathematics scale (2003)

| | First-generation students - proficiency levels | | | | | | | | | | |
| | Below Level 1 (below 358 score points) | | Level 1 (from 358 to 420 score points) | | Level 2 (from 421 to 482 score points) | | Level 3 (from 483 to 544 score points) | | Level 4 (from 545 to 606 score points) | | Levels 5 and 6 (above 606 score points) | |
	%	S.E.	%	S.E.	%	S.E.	%	S.E.	%	S.E.	%	S.E.
Australia	5.1	(1.0)	10.5	(1.5)	17.9	(1.5)	22.7	(1.9)	22.4	(2.0)	21.5	(2.0)
Austria	14.1	(2.4)	23.6	(3.9)	28.4	(3.2)	18.7	(2.2)	10.2	(1.8)	5.1	(1.4)
Belgium	25.0	(4.6)	18.6	(2.7)	21.2	(3.0)	17.9	(2.7)	10.0	(2.1)	7.3	(1.6)
Canada	3.3	(0.7)	8.3	(1.4)	18.0	(2.4)	25.7	(2.2)	22.8	(2.0)	22.0	(2.1)
Denmark	14.4	(4.3)	19.4	(4.7)	28.2	(4.5)	20.5	(4.4)	13.6	(3.8)	3.8	(2.3)
France	22.0	(5.3)	20.6	(4.1)	21.7	(4.2)	15.3	(3.7)	12.8	(3.9)	7.5	(2.7)
Germany	17.5	(2.8)	21.3	(3.4)	20.7	(2.9)	20.5	(2.4)	14.4	(2.7)	5.6	(2.0)
Luxembourg	15.0	(1.7)	20.4	(2.1)	24.4	(2.0)	18.9	(1.7)	12.9	(1.6)	8.5	(1.4)
Netherlands	6.3	(2.1)	21.4	(4.8)	32.2	(5.6)	21.3	(5.0)	12.9	(4.2)	5.8	(2.3)
New Zealand	5.5	(1.3)	10.0	(1.9)	18.2	(3.1)	24.1	(2.8)	20.7	(2.1)	21.6	(1.9)
Norway	18.9	(4.3)	26.8	(5.1)	23.5	(4.2)	17.3	(4.5)	8.9	(4.3)	4.6	(2.2)
Sweden	24.0	(4.2)	23.1	(3.9)	24.7	(4.2)	16.5	(2.7)	8.4	(2.4)	3.3	(1.5)
Switzerland	17.2	(2.1)	21.9	(2.4)	23.7	(2.7)	20.0	(2.0)	8.8	(1.3)	8.4	(1.7)
United States	19.5	(3.4)	18.3	(2.4)	22.4	(4.0)	20.6	(3.3)	12.7	(2.5)	6.5	(1.6)
Hong Kong-China	5.2	(1.3)	9.6	(1.3)	20.5	(2.3)	25.4	(2.5)	23.0	(2.2)	16.3	(1.6)
Macao-China	3.2	(1.8)	12.1	(4.0)	21.2	(4.0)	25.5	(4.2)	21.9	(3.8)	16.1	(3.7)
Russian Federation	14.1	(2.5)	21.9	(3.2)	30.1	(3.0)	19.3	(2.1)	9.5	(1.8)	5.2	(1.5)

Source: OECD PISA 2003.
StatLink ⟐ http://dx.doi.org/10.1787/068061288083

Table A6.3.
Index of instrumental motivation in mathematics and student performance on the mathematics scale (2003)
Results based on students' self-reports

		Index of instrumental motivation in mathematics						Change in the mathematics score per unit of the index of instrumental motivation in mathematics									
		Native students		Second-generation students		First-generation students		Native students		Explained variance in student performance (r-squared x 100)	Second-generation students		Explained variance in student performance (r-squared x 100)	First-generation students		Explained variance in student performance (r-squared x 100)
		Mean index	S.E.	Mean index	S.E.	Mean index	S.E.	Effect	S.E.	%	Effect	S.E.	%	Effect	S.E.	%
OECD countries	Australia	0.19	(0.02)	**0.35**	(0.04)	**0.37**	(0.03)	**17.4**	(1.2)	3.3	**17.4**	(3.3)	3.1	**16.3**	(2.8)	2.5
	Austria	-0.53	(0.03)	-0.32	(0.10)	**-0.29**	(0.07)	-0.6	(1.7)	0.0	-4.9	(7.1)	0.5	-7.1	(4.5)	0.8
	Belgium	-0.35	(0.02)	**-0.19**	(0.07)	0.03	(0.06)	**15.8**	(1.6)	2.4	3.2	(6.3)	0.2	-4.0	(5.6)	0.2
	Canada	0.17	(0.01)	**0.36**	(0.05)	**0.52**	(0.04)	**20.8**	(1.1)	6.1	**17.6**	(3.2)	4.7	**16.6**	(3.4)	3.4
	Denmark	0.37	(0.02)	0.39	(0.09)	0.37	(0.10)	**22.2**	(1.7)	5.0	15.1	(10.5)	2.7	5.9	(9.2)	0.5
	France	-0.11	(0.02)	**0.02**	(0.05)	**0.30**	(0.10)	**15.5**	(1.6)	3.2	**11.4**	(3.8)	1.9	14.4	(10.9)	2.1
	Germany	-0.08	(0.02)	**0.09**	(0.06)	**0.17**	(0.06)	**4.4**	(2.2)	0.2	4.6	(5.8)	0.3	0.7	(6.3)	0.0
	Luxembourg	-0.52	(0.02)	**-0.30**	(0.05)	-0.04	(0.05)	**6.6**	(1.9)	0.8	-5.9	(3.5)	0.5	-7.2	(3.8)	0.6
	Netherlands	-0.30	(0.02)	0.08	(0.07)	-0.03	(0.09)	**10.3**	(1.9)	1.0	2.2	(8.5)	0.1	10.7	(7.6)	1.8
	New Zealand	0.25	(0.02)	**0.45**	(0.06)	**0.47**	(0.04)	**18.3**	(2.1)	3.1	-2.8	(6.9)	0.1	**12.5**	(5.1)	1.3
	Norway	0.15	(0.02)	0.33	(0.12)	0.24	(0.09)	**28.8**	(1.5)	10.5	**30.5**	(10.2)	12.1	**30.9**	(7.9)	12.1
	Sweden	-0.01	(0.02)	**0.21**	(0.07)	**0.28**	(0.04)	**26.1**	(1.8)	7.3	**31.5**	(8.8)	8.8	7.2	(7.6)	0.5
	Switzerland	-0.09	(0.02)	**0.05**	(0.04)	**0.21**	(0.05)	2.8	(1.8)	0.1	-7.6	(4.0)	0.6	**-12.5**	(4.2)	1.7
	United States	0.16	(0.02)	0.26	(0.05)	**0.33**	(0.06)	**13.8**	(1.7)	2.2	**18.2**	(5.0)	3.4	**15.7**	(6.4)	2.2
	OECD average	*-0.04*	*(0.01)*	*0.10*	*(0.02)*	*0.20*	*(0.02)*	*12.4*	*(0.5)*	*1.9*	*9.6*	*(1.2)*	*1.1*	*8.2*	*(1.6)*	*0.7*
Partner economies	Hong Kong-China	-0.16	(0.02)	-0.12	(0.03)	0.02	(0.03)	**28.7**	(2.3)	6.2	**27.6**	(4.0)	6.6	**22.5**	(5.2)	3.4
	Macao-China	-0.11	(0.05)	-0.02	(0.04)	0.02	(0.06)	-9.1	(7.5)	0.8	**10.7**	(4.6)	1.2	-8.0	(10.8)	0.5
	Russian Federation	0.00	(0.02)	-0.01	(0.05)	0.01	(0.06)	**14.4**	(1.6)	2.1	**13.4**	(5.2)	2.2	6.8	(4.7)	0.6

		Regression estimate of the index of instrumental motivation in mathematics							
		Accounting for ESCS				Accounting for mathematics performance			
		Second-generation students		First-generation students		Second-generation students		First-generation students	
		Coef.	S.E.	Coef.	S.E.	Coef.	S.E.	Coef.	S.E.
OECD countries	Australia	**0.18**	(0.04)	**0.19**	(0.03)	**0.17**	(0.04)	**0.19**	(0.03)
	Austria	**0.14**	(0.10)	**0.16**	(0.07)	**0.20**	(0.10)	**0.22**	(0.08)
	Belgium	**0.24**	(0.07)	**0.43**	(0.07)	**0.29**	(0.08)	**0.51**	(0.07)
	Canada	**0.19**	(0.05)	**0.33**	(0.04)	**0.17**	(0.05)	**0.36**	(0.04)
	Denmark	0.12	(0.09)	0.06	(0.10)	0.18	(0.10)	0.14	(0.10)
	France	**0.19**	(0.06)	**0.48**	(0.11)	**0.23**	(0.06)	**0.55**	(0.12)
	Germany	**0.16**	(0.06)	**0.24**	(0.07)	**0.22**	(0.07)	**0.29**	(0.07)
	Luxembourg	**0.21**	(0.06)	**0.48**	(0.06)	**0.24**	(0.05)	**0.51**	(0.05)
	Netherlands	**0.42**	(0.07)	**0.30**	(0.09)	**0.44**	(0.07)	**0.36**	(0.09)
	New Zealand	**0.24**	(0.07)	**0.20**	(0.04)	**0.25**	(0.07)	**0.22**	(0.04)
	Norway	**0.27**	(0.12)	**0.25**	(0.07)	**0.32**	(0.11)	**0.32**	(0.08)
	Sweden	**0.30**	(0.08)	**0.39**	(0.05)	**0.31**	(0.07)	**0.53**	(0.05)
	Switzerland	**0.10**	(0.05)	**0.25**	(0.05)	**0.15**	(0.05)	**0.31**	(0.05)
	United States	**0.14**	(0.05)	**0.21**	(0.06)	**0.14**	(0.05)	**0.23**	(0.06)
	OECD average	*0.29*	*(0.02)*	*0.28*	*(0.04)*	*0.20*	*(0.02)*	*0.31*	*(0.02)*
Partner economies	Hong Kong-China	**0.07**	(0.03)	**0.22**	(0.03)	0.00	(0.03)	**0.26**	(0.03)
	Macao-China	0.09	(0.07)	0.10	(0.08)	0.09	(0.06)	0.13	(0.08)
	Russian Federation	-0.01	(0.06)	0.02	(0.06)	0.01	(0.06)	0.05	(0.06)

Note: Statistically significant values are indicated in bold.
Source: OECD PISA 2003.
StatLink ⌨ http://dx.doi.org/10.1787/068061288083

DOES THE SOCIO-ECONOMIC STATUS OF THEIR PARENTS AFFECT STUDENTS' PARTICIPATION IN HIGHER EDUCATION?

This indicator examines the socio-economic status of students enrolled in higher education, an important gauge of access to higher education for all. International comparable data on the socio-economic status of students in higher education is not widely available and this indicator is a first attempt to illustrate the analytical potential that would be offered by better data on this issue. It takes a close look at data from ten OECD countries, examining the occupational status (white collar or blue collar) of students' fathers and the fathers' educational background and also considers data from the OECD Programme for International Student Assessment (PISA) 2000 survey.

Key results

Chart A7.1. **Occupational status of students' fathers**

This chart depicts the proportion of higher education students' fathers compared with the proportion of men of corresponding age (40-to-60-year-olds) from a blue-collar background, in %.

■ Students' father (left-hand scale)
■ Men in same age group (left-hand scale)
▲ Odds-ratio (right-hand scale)

There are large differences between countries in how well they succeed in having students from a blue-collar background participate in higher education. Ireland and Spain stand out as providing the most equitable access to higher education, whereas in Austria, France, Germany and Portugal students from a blue-collar background are about one-half as likely to be in higher education as compared with what their proportion in the population would suggest.

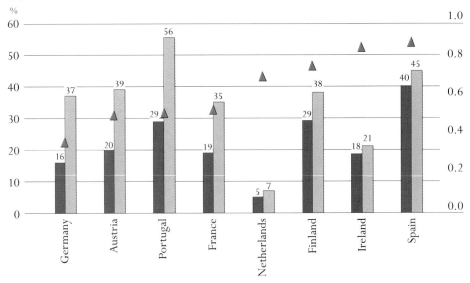

Source: EUROSTUDENT 2005.
StatLink http://dx.doi.org/10.1787/068114616808

▪ When measuring the socio-economic status of students in higher education by their fathers' educational background large differences between countries emerge. In many countries, students are substantially more likely to be in higher education if their fathers completed higher education. Students from such a background are more than twice as likely to be in higher education in Austria, France, Germany, Portugal and the United Kingdom than are students whose fathers did not complete higher education. In Ireland and Spain this ratio drops to 1.1 and 1.5, respectively.

▪ Among the countries providing information on the socio-economic status of students in higher education it appears that inequalities in previous schooling are reflected in the intake of students from less advantaged backgrounds. Countries providing more equitable access to higher education – such as Finland, Ireland and Spain – were also the countries with the most equal between-school performances in PISA 2000.

A7

Policy context

The pool of available workers with sufficient education and skills will be increasingly important for countries in securing innovation and future growth. Few countries can afford to rely only on families rich in wealth and/or human capital to provide society with higher educated individuals. The transfer of low skill jobs to countries with substantially lower cost structures further suggests that having a large fraction of the workforce with skills too low for them to be able to compete for jobs on the international arena will lead to an increasing social burden and deepening inequalities.

The socio-economic status of students in higher education is one way of examining to what extent countries are using their full potential in generating future human capital. A key issue for educational systems is to provide equal opportunity to education for all in the society, regardless of the socio-economic status. Levelling the playing field between affluent and less affluent students is not only a matter of equality, but more importantly it is also a way of increasing the recruiting ground for high skilled jobs and of increasing the overall labour competitiveness.

Expanding higher education depends on a corresponding quality in outputs of schools. Findings from the PISA 2000 survey suggests that in most countries performance is linked to students' socio-economic status and it thus appears that interventions are warranted at an earlier stage (primary and lower secondary education) to correct these disadvantages. Successful completion rates of upper secondary education by students with lower socio-economic status is another important threshold that needs to be considered in understanding potential skewed intakes to higher education.

Evidence and explanations

Chart A7.1 above shows substantial differences between countries in the socio-economic composition of the student body in higher education. Note that students in higher education are defined as those students attending ISCED level 5B, 5A, and 6 courses. At 40%, Spain has the largest proportion of students with fathers who have blue-collar occupations, followed by Finland and Portugal at 29%. For the remaining six countries covered in this indicator, students with fathers who have blue-collar occupations comprise 20% or less of the student body. The overall intake of students from such backgrounds is dependent on the composition of blue-collar jobs as a whole within countries and as such the relation between the two country bars shown in Chart A7.1 is more informative about the socio-economic status of the student body. This relation is illustrated by the odds-ratio in the chart. With the exception of Ireland and Spain, countries still recruit proportionally more students to higher education whose fathers' have white-collar occupations.

The proportion of students in higher education with fathers having completed higher education provides another angle on the same topic. Chart A7.2a shows the proportion of students' fathers with higher education and the corresponding proportion of men with higher education in the same age group as students' fathers. Finland, France, the Netherlands and the United Kingdom have the largest intake of students with fathers holding a higher education degree, whereas Ireland and Italy have the lowest intake from this group. This circumstance reflects to some extent the attainment levels in different countries and to have a better view of the social selectivity in higher education the attainment level of men in the same age group as students' fathers need to be taken into account. The ratio of the proportion of students' fathers with higher education to

Chart A7.2a. **Educational status of students' fathers**

Proportion of students' fathers with higher education compared with the proportion of men of corresponding age group as students' fathers (40-to-60-year-olds) with higher education

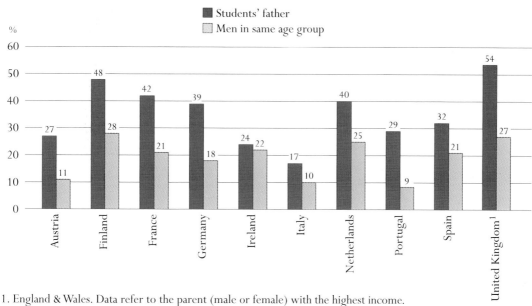

1. England & Wales. Data refer to the parent (male or female) with the highest income.
Source: EUROSTUDENT 2005.
StatLink ⬛⬛ http://dx.doi.org/10.1787/068114616808

the proportion of men of the corresponding age group with higher education is shown in the second chart.

For all ten countries, more students are recruited from backgrounds where their father has a higher level of education than is warranted by the percentage of such families in the population. There are substantial differences between countries on this socio-economic status indicator as well. The strongest selectivity into higher education is found in Portugal, with a ratio of 3.2. In Austria, France, Germany and the United Kingdom students are about twice as likely to be in higher education if their fathers hold a university degree as compared with what their proportion in the population would suggest. Ireland stands out with a ratio (1.1) almost matching that of the general population.

In most countries, there is a strong socio-economic selection into higher education where students from homes with higher educational background are overrepresented and students from a blue-collar background are underrepresented (in many cases severely so). Some countries appear to do better in this respect, and in this relatively confined sample of countries, Ireland and Spain perform substantially better in terms of providing higher education for all, irrespective of students' background.

Differences between countries in duration of higher degree programs, the type of degree students pursue and the existence of non-university institutions all play a role in explaining participation in higher education by students from less advantaged backgrounds. Students from lower educational family backgrounds are more frequently enrolled in non-university institutions and this might, to some extent, explain differences in the socio-economic status of students between countries,

A7

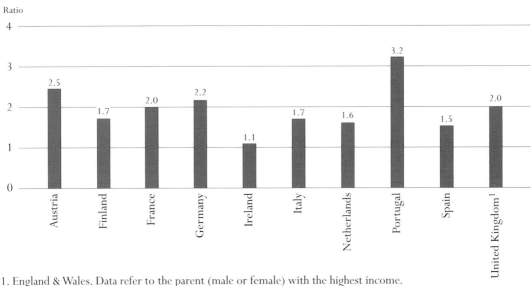

Chart A7.2b. Educational status of students' fathers
Ratio of the proportion of students' fathers with higher education to the proportion of men of the corresponding age group as students' fathers (40-to-60-year-olds) with higher education

1. England & Wales. Data refer to the parent (male or female) with the highest income.
Source: EUROSTUDENT 2005.
StatLink ⬛⬛⬛ http://dx.doi.org/10.1787/068114616808

as not all countries provide this opportunity in higher education. Countries that have expanded their tertiary education in recent years will also, by default, have a higher intake of students from less advantaged backgrounds.

Beside these and other factors, there are indications that previous schooling plays an important role in building the ground for equal opportunities in higher education. Not surprisingly, inequalities in the performance of students in the PISA survey (15-year-olds) are also carried forward to higher education. Measures such as the PISA index of economic, social and cultural status (ESCS) of students and variation of PISA scores related to students' fathers educational background are linked to the intake of students from less affluent backgrounds. The more prominent link, however, appears to be related to inequalities between schools and the extent to which education systems are stratified.

Chart A7.3 shows the relation between the ratio of students from blue-collar backgrounds (from chart A7.1) and the between-school variance in mathematic performance in PISA 2000. For the dark-blue bar, a ratio closer to 1 indicates an intake of students from blue-collar background in line with the population as a whole. The light-blue bar shows between school variance in PISA. The lower the between-school variance, the more equal is the school system in terms of providing similar quality of education irrespective of schools attended by the students. Ranking countries on equal opportunities in higher education largely resembles the ranking of countries with respect to providing equal education between schools. Among the countries for which data is available on the socio-economic status of students in higher education, it thus appears that providing an equitable distribution of learning outcomes and opportunities at school is important in order to have more students from less affluent backgrounds participating in higher education.

Chart A7.3. **Proportion of students in higher education (2003-2005) from a blue-collar background and between-school variance in PISA 2000**

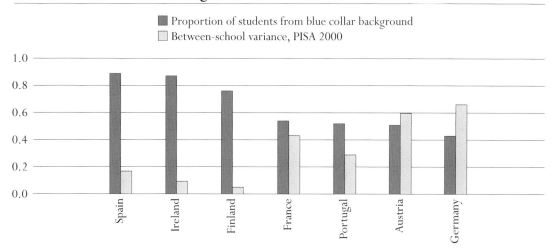

Note: The first bar shows the ratio of students with fathers from a blue collar background compared with men of corresponding age group (40-to-60-year-olds) in blue collar occupations. The second bar shows the between school variance in mathematics from PISA 2000 survey.
Source: OECD PISA 2000 survey, EUROSTUDENT 2005.
StatLink 🔗 http://dx.doi.org/10.1787/068114616808

International comparable data on the socio-economic status of students in higher education is at present reported only in a limited way. More information and better country coverage is required for a better understanding of what policies might work and when actions need to be taken for improving the prospect of having more students from disadvantaged backgrounds in higher education. In the present sample, there is a fairly strong ranking linking inequalities between schools in lower secondary education and inequalities in higher education. With better country coverage and with data over time considerably more could be done in understanding what the main obstacles are in having a more equal distribution of students in higher education. The economic motivation for recruiting more students from less affluent homes is in place and better information on student background is essential to respond to the question how to best achieve this objective.

Definitions and methodologies

The participating countries survey their students using the EUROSTUDENT core questionnaire within a specific time frame. In many cases, these questions are integrated into larger national surveys. Most countries have included students attending ISCED 5B and 5A programmes, exceptions are Austria, Germany, Italy, and Spain where only students in ISCED 5A were surveyed, and Portugal where students in 5A, 5B, and 6 level of education were surveyed. That some countries included ISCED 5B and 6 levels of education whereas other countries did not, might to some extent distort the comparability. The definition used in EUROSTUDENT for blue-collar background and higher education varies between countries but is harmonized within each country so that ratios will provide consistent estimates. Note also that the corresponding age group as students' fathers with higher education is 40-to-64-year-olds in Italy and that the corresponding age group as students' fathers in blue-collar occupations is defined in Ireland as "fathers of children who are 15 years old or younger".

A7

The number of responses varied between 994 students in Latvia to 25 385 students in France, with a response rate between 30% (Germany) and 100% (Spain, Portugal) depending on survey method used. Most countries used a randomized design (stratified, quota) in sampling the students. However, the survey method varied: a postal questionnaire was used in four countries; an online survey in two countries; telephone interviews in one country; face-to-face interviews in three countries; and classroom questionnaires in two countries.

Further references

This indicator draws on data collected as part of the EUROSTUDENT project (*http://www. eurostudent.eu*) and published in the *EUROSTUDENT Report 2005: Social and Economic Conditions of Student Life in Europe 2005*, available on the EUROSTUDENT website.

HOW DOES PARTICIPATION IN EDUCATION AFFECT PARTICIPATION IN THE LABOUR MARKET?

This indicator examines relationships between educational attainment and labour force status, for both males and females, and considers changes in these relationships over time.

Key results

Chart A8.1. **Employment rates by educational attainment (2005)**

This chart shows the percentage of the 25-to-64-year-old population that is employed.

▢ Below upper secondary
▣ Upper secondary and post-secondary non-tertiary

Compared to people who have not completed upper secondary education, people who have completed upper secondary education are much more likely to be in work, but the employment advantage of upper secondary attainment varies across countries.

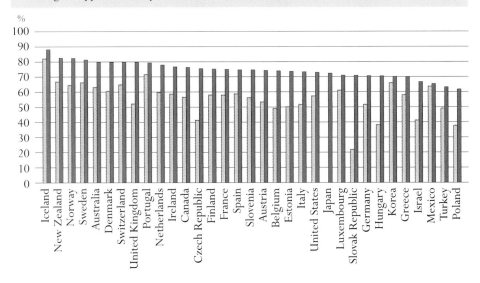

Countries are ranked in descending order of the employment rates in upper secondary and post-secondary non-tertiary education.
Source: OECD. Table A8.3. See Annex 3 for notes (www.oecd.org/edu/eag2007).
StatLink ⫶⫶⫶ http://dx.doi.org/10.1787/068152681851

- Employment rates rise with educational attainment in most OECD countries. With few exceptions, the employment rate for graduates of tertiary education is markedly higher than the rate for upper secondary graduates. For males, the gap is particularly wide between upper secondary graduates and those without an upper secondary qualification.

- Higher educated individuals also face a more stable labour market than lower educated individuals. In almost all OECD countries, tertiary-educated adults have had substantially less variation in unemployment rates compared with lower secondary educated adults. This advantage appears to be particularly large in the Czech Republic, Germany, Ireland, Norway and the Slovak Republic.

- Those with low educational attainment are both less likely to be labour force participants and more likely to be unemployed. Unemployment rates fall with higher educational attainment. The greatest gender differences in unemployment rates are seen among adults with lower levels of education (Chart A8.3).

- Differences in employment rates between males and females are also wider among less educated groups. The chance of being in employment is 23 percentage points higher for males than for females among those without upper secondary qualifications, falling to 10 points for the most highly qualified.

A8

Policy content

The economies and labour markets of OECD countries depend upon a stable supply of well-educated workers to further their economic development. As levels of skill tend to rise with educational attainment, the costs incurred also rise when those with higher levels of education do not work. As populations in OECD countries age, higher levels of education and longer participation in employment can lower dependency ratios and help to alleviate the burden of financing public pensions.

Employment rates normally rise with educational attainment. This is principally due to the larger investment in human capital made by higher-educated individuals and the need for these individuals to recoup this investment. However, between countries variation in employment rates often reflect cultural differences and, most notably, differences in the labour participation rates among female workers. Similarly, unemployment rates are generally lower for higher-educated individuals, but this is typically because higher educational attainment makes an individual more attractive in the labour market. Unemployment rates thus include information on the individual's desire to work, as well as on the attractiveness of the individual for potential employers.

In this sense, employment rates are more tied to the labour supply while unemployment rates are more tied to the labour demand. Time series on both measures thus carries important information for policy makers about the supply, and potential supply, of skills to the labour market and the demand for these skills by employers.

Evidence and explanations

Employment

Variation among countries in employment among females is a primary factor in the differences in overall employment rates. The seven countries with the highest overall rate of employment for individuals aged 25 to 64 – Denmark, Iceland, New Zealand, Norway, Sweden, Switzerland and the United Kingdom – also have among the highest overall rate of employment for females. The overall employment rate for males aged 25 to 64 ranges from 77% or less in Belgium, Finland, France, Germany, Hungary, Italy, Poland, and the Slovak Republic to above 85% in Iceland, Japan, Korea, New Zealand, Mexico and Switzerland (Table A8.1a). By contrast, employment rates among females range from 55% or less in Greece, Italy, Mexico, Poland, Spain and Turkey, to 77% and more in Iceland, Norway and Sweden, reflecting different cultural and social patterns.

Employment rates for graduates of tertiary education are markedly higher – around 9 percentage points on average for OECD countries – than that for upper secondary graduates. For 2005, the difference ranges from a few percentage points to 12 percentage points or more in Germany, Greece, Hungary, Luxembourg, Mexico, Poland, the Slovak Republic and Turkey (Table A8.3a). While there have been some large changes over time in the employment rates of educational groups within countries, the OECD averages for lower secondary, upper secondary and tertiary educated adults have been rather stable over last decade.

The gap in employment rates of males aged 25 to 64 years is particularly wide between upper secondary graduates and those who have not completed an upper secondary qualification. The extreme cases are the Czech Republic, Hungary and the Slovak Republic, where rates of employment for males with an upper secondary level of education are at least 30 percentage points higher than

Chart A8.2. **Employment rates, by educational attainment (2005)**

Percentage of the 25-to-64-year-old population that is employed

□ Males   ■ Females

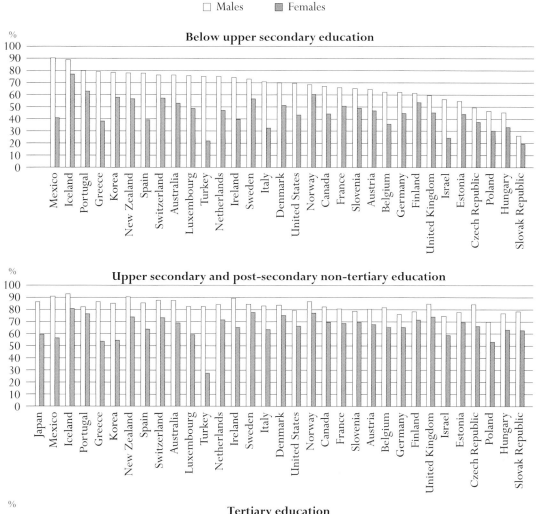

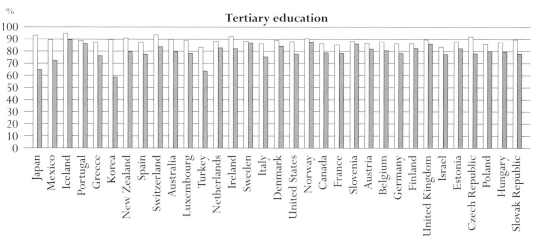

Countries are ranked in descending order of the employment rate of males having attained less than upper secondary education.
Source: OECD. Table A8.3b and A8.3c. See Annex 3 for notes (*www.oecd.org/edu/eag2007*).
StatLink ⬛⬛ http://dx.doi.org/10.1787/068152681851

for a male without such attainment. The gap in employment rates between males with and without upper secondary attainment is 7 percentage points or less in Iceland, Korea, Luxembourg, Mexico and Portugal (Chart A8.2 and Table A3b).

In 2005, employment rates for females aged 25 to 64 show more substantial differences, not only between those with below upper secondary and those with upper secondary attainment (15 percentage points or more in 24 out of the 29 OECD countries for which data were available), but also between those with upper secondary and those with tertiary attainment (10 percentage points or more in 20 countries).

Employment rates for females with lower secondary attainment are particularly low, averaging 49% across all OECD countries and standing at 35% or below in Hungary, Poland, the Slovak Republic and Turkey and the partner economies Chile and Israel. Employment rates for females with tertiary-type A attainment equal or exceed 75 % everywhere except Japan, Korea, Mexico and Turkey, but remain below those of males in all countries (Table A8.1a).

On average among OECD countries, at successively higher levels of educational attainment, the difference between the employment rates of males and females decreases significantly: from 23 percentage points at the below upper secondary level to 10 percentage points at the tertiary level (Tables A8.3b and A8.3c).

Unemployment rates fall with higher educational attainment

The employment prospects of individuals with varying levels of educational attainment depend largely on the requirements of labour markets and on the supply of workers with different skills. Unemployment rates thus provide a signal of the match between what is produced in the education system and the demand for these skills in the labour market. Those with low educational qualifications are at particular risk of economic marginalisation since they are both less likely to be labour force participants and more likely to be without a job even if they are actively seeking one.

Among OECD countries, an upper-secondary level of education is typically considered to be the minimum level needed to obtain a satisfactory, competitive, position in the labour market. On average, the rate of unemployment among individuals with an upper secondary education is 5 percentage points lower than among individuals who only have not completed upper secondary education (Table A8.4a). Depending on industry composition and levels of economic development, the unemployment risk associated with non-attainment of the upper secondary level varies among countries, being particularly large (at over 10%) in the Czech Republic, Poland, and especially high in the Slovak Republic (36.5%). In only four countries is a lack of upper secondary education not associated with a higher unemployment risk: Greece, Korea, Mexico and Turkey. The unemployment rate for below upper secondary level of education is even lower than for upper.

On average in OECD countries, male labour force participants aged 25 to 64 and with education below the upper secondary level are more than twice as likely to be unemployed as their counterparts who have completed upper secondary education, reflecting the role of upper secondary education as a minimum requirement to meet skills demands in the labour market in most countries (Table A8.4a). The negative association between unemployment rates and educational attainment

Chart A8.3. **Differences between unemployment rates of females and males, by level of educational attainment**

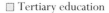

☐ Tertiary education

▨ Upper secondary and post-secondary non-tertiary education

■ Below upper secondary education

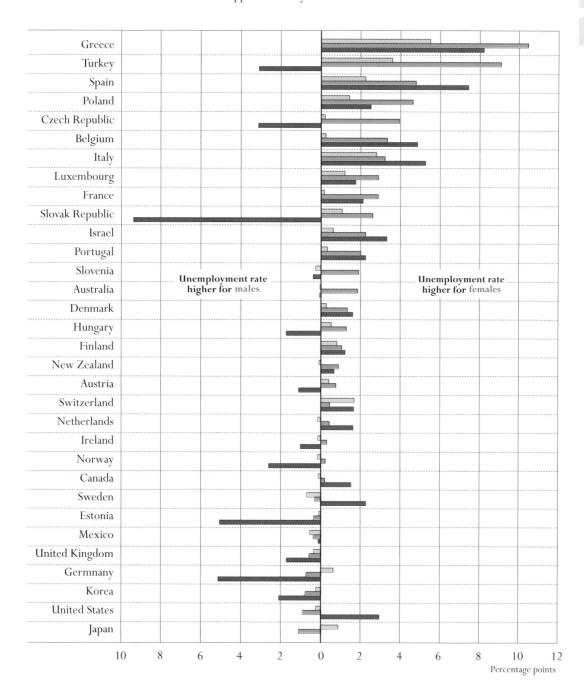

Countries are ranked in descending order of the difference in unemployment rates of females and males who have completed upper secondary or post-secondary non-tertiary education.

Source: OECD. Table A8.4. See Annex 3 for notes (*www.oecd.org/edu/eag2007*).

StatLink ᵐˢᵖ http://dx.doi.org/10.1787/068152681851

is similar among females. Differences in unemployment rates among males and females generally decrease with educational attainment. Among tertiary educated females, unemployment rates are above two percentage points only in Greece, Italy, Spain, and Turkey. In 12 OECD countries and 2 partner economies, unemployment rates for males with below upper secondary education are higher than those for females (Chart A8.3, Tables A8.4b and A8.4c).

The changes in unemployment

Between 1995 and 2005, on average across OECD countries, the unemployment rates for those with upper secondary education decreased by almost 1.5 percentage points. Among the 15 countries that experienced this decrease, Australia, Canada, Denmark, Finland, France, Ireland, Italy, Mexico, Netherlands, New Zealand, Spain and the United Kingdom also decreased the unemployment rates for those with education below the upper secondary level and for those with tertiary education. Although the difference between the unemployment rate among individuals with upper secondary and tertiary levels of education has been stable over the past ten years, achieving an upper secondary education makes less of a difference in the labour market than the achievement of tertiary education since the tertiary-level unemployment rate is almost – except Italy and Mexico – always lower than the upper secondary level rate (Table A8.4a).

The difference in unemployment rates between those with an upper secondary education and those with tertiary education has decreased marginally, from 2.8% to 2.2% during the period 1995 to 2005. In contrast, the difference between upper secondary and lower secondary unemployment rates increased from 3.4% to 5.0% during the same period. Considering the substantial expansion of upper secondary and tertiary attainment levels in most countries during this period, these time series suggest that these increases have been matched by a demand for higher skills in most countries. That it is increasingly difficult for those with a lower secondary education to find employment also suggests that the number of jobs at this level of education is decreasing in most labour markets.

Achieving tertiary education not only means that individuals are more likely to find a job, but also that tertiary educated individuals experience substantially less variation in their employments compared with lower educated individuals, as shown by the trend data in Table A8.4a. The variation in unemployment over the period 1991 to 2005 is higher for lower secondary educated individuals than for tertiary educated individuals in all OECD countries except Turkey where lower and higher educated have experience similar fluctuation in unemployment rates during this period. The advantage of a more stable position in the labour market appears to be particularly large in the Czech Republic, Germany, Ireland, Norway and the Slovak Republic for individuals with tertiary education as unemployment rates varies substantially less in these countries.

Definition and methodologies

Under the auspices of the International Labour Organisation (ILO) and the conferences of labour statisticians, concepts and definitions to measure labour force participation were progressively established and are now used as a common reference (see the "Resolution Concerning Statistics of the Economically Active Population, Employment, Unemployment and Underemployment" (1982), adopted by the 13th International Conference of Labour Statisticians). The employment rate refers to the number of persons in employment as a percentage of the population of working age. Unemployment rates refer to unemployed persons as a percentage of the civilian labour force.

A8

The unemployed are defined as individuals who are, during the survey reference week, without work, actively seeking employment and currently available to start work. The employed are defined as those who during the survey reference week: *i)* work for pay (employees) or profit (self-employed and unpaid family workers) for at least one hour; or *ii)* have a job but are temporarily not at work (through injury, illness, holiday, strike or lock-out, educational or training leave, maternity or parental leave, etc.).

Further references

The following additional material relevant to this indicator is available on line at:

StatLink ⬛📊 http://dx.doi.org/10.1787/068152681851

- *Employment rates and educational attainment:*
  Table A8.1b: Total adult population

- *Unemployment rates and educational attainment:*
  Table A8.2b: Total adult population
- *Trends in employment rates by educational attainment, by gender*
  Table A8.3b: Males
  Table A8.3c: Females

- *Trends in unemployment rates by educational attainment, by gender*
  Table A8.4b: Males
  Table A8.4c: Females

A8

Table A8.1a.
Employment rates and educational attainment, by gender (2005)
Number of 25-to-64-year-olds in employment as a percentage of the population aged 25 to 64, by level of education attained and gender

				Upper secondary education				Tertiary education		
		Pre-primary and primary education	Lower secondary education	ISCED 3C short	ISCED 3C long/3B	ISCED 3A	Post-secondary non-tertiary education	Type B	Type A and advanced research programmes	All levels of education
		(1)	(2)	(3)	(4)	(5)	(6)	(7)	(8)	(9)
Australia	Males	64	81	a	a	87	90	89	90	85
	Females	36	58	a	a	68	78	75	82	66
Austria	Males	x(2)	65	a	80	77	85	85	89	79
	Females	x(2)	47	a	66	65	78	81	82	65
Belgium	Males	49	72	a	82	81	87	87	89	77
	Females	25	46	a	60	67	73	80	82	60
Canada	Males	56	72	a	x(5)	82	84	87	86	82
	Females	32	51	a	x(5)	69	72	78	80	71
Czech Republic	Males	c	51	a	82	88	x(5)	x(8)	92	83
	Females	c	38	a	61	71	x(5)	x(8)	78	64
Denmark	Males	55	71	82	84	75	94	89	89	83
	Females	42	52	71	76	66	100	81	85	74
Finland	Males	54	71	a	a	78	89	84	88	77
	Females	46	62	a	a	71	95	81	83	72
France	Males	52	75	a	81	81	70	88	84	77
	Females	41	59	a	67	71	66	81	76	65
Germany	Males	52	65	a	76	61	83	84	88	77
	Females	32	47	a	65	52	74	77	79	64
Greece	Males	76	86	85	91	86	88	85	88	84
	Females	36	45	54	57	50	66	74	77	52
Hungary	Males	18	48	a	76	79	84	81	88	72
	Females	7	35	a	59	66	66	89	79	58
Iceland	Males	82	90	92	95	84	94	93	95	92
	Females	79	77	83	84	74	96	92	89	82
Ireland	Males	63	85	78	a	89	90	92	92	84
	Females	31	48	52	a	63	69	78	85	62
Italy	Males	52	78	79	84	83	87	81	86	77
	Females	18	43	51	60	64	70	70	75	50
Japan	Males	x(5)	x(5)	x(5)	x(5)	86	a	93	93	89
	Females	x(5)	x(5)	x(5)	x(5)	59	a	64	66	61
Korea	Males	75	81	a	x(5)	85	a	89	90	86
	Females	57	59	a	x(5)	54	a	59	58	57
Luxembourg	Males	71	85	84	81	84	83	85	90	83
	Females	50	47	54	51	66	74	78	78	60
Mexico	Males	89	93	a	91	x(2)	a	93	89	90
	Females	37	48	a	56	x(2)	a	76	72	46
Netherlands	Males	62	80	x(4)	80	87	81	87	88	83
	Females	34	52	x(4)	67	74	74	82	83	67
New Zealand	Males	x(2)	78	a	91	89	92	92	91	88
	Females	x(2)	57	a	75	72	76	78	80	72
Norway	Males	c	69	a	88	84	86	95	90	84
	Females	c	61	a	77	76	84	89	87	77

Source: OECD. See Annex 3 for a description of ISCED-97 levels, ISCED-97 country mappings and national data sources (*www.oecd.org/edu/eag2007*).
Please refer to the Reader's Guide for information concerning the symbols replacing missing data.
StatLink ⫷⫸ http://dx.doi.org/10.1787/068152681851

A8

Table A8.1a. *(continued)*
Employment rates and educational attainment, by gender (2005)
Number of 25-to-64-year-olds in employment as a percentage of the population aged 25 to 64, by level of education attained and gender

| | | Pre-primary and primary education | Lower secondary education | Upper secondary education | | | Post-secondary non-tertiary education | Tertiary education | | All levels of education |
				ISCED 3C short	ISCED 3C long/3B	ISCED 3A		Type B	Type A and advanced research programmes	
		(1)	(2)	(3)	(4)	(5)	(6)	(7)	(8)	(9)
Poland	Males	x(2)	47	67	a	74	77	x(8)	86	69
	Females	x(2)	30	46	a	57	64	x(8)	80	55
Portugal	Males	78	85	x(5)	x(5)	82	83	x(8)	89	81
	Females	60	74	x(5)	x(5)	77	69	x(8)	86	68
Slovak Republic	Males	c	28	x(4)	73	85	x	83	90	75
	Females	c	20	x(4)	56	67	x	75	78	57
Spain	Males	70	85	a	88	84	87	88	87	82
	Females	31	48	a	63	64	74	73	79	55
Sweden	Males	63	80	a	x(5)	85	84	84	89	83
	Females	46	64	a	x(5)	78	75	86	87	78
Switzerland	Males	74	77	82	88	83	88	94	93	89
	Females	51	59	65	74	73	82	87	82	73
Turkey	Males	75	78	a	84	82	a	x(8)	83	78
	Females	22	19	a	29	26	a	x(8)	64	26
United Kingdom	Males	c	60	83	84	88	a	88	90	83
	Females	c	45	70	75	80	a	85	87	73
United States	Males	70	69	x(5)	x(5)	79	x(5)	85	89	81
	Females	39	46	x(5)	x(5)	66	x(5)	77	78	68
OECD average	*Males*	*64*	*73*		*84*	*82*	*86*	*88*	*89*	*82*
	Females	*39*	*49*		*64*	*66*	*76*	*79*	*79*	*63*
EU19 average	*Males*	*58*	*69*		*82*	*81*	*85*	*86*	*89*	*79*
	Females	*36*	*47*		*63*	*67*	*74*	*79*	*81*	*63*
Chile[1]	Males	24	63	x(5)	x(5)	72	a	81	84	74
	Females	9	27	x(5)	x(5)	60	a	69	80	61
Estonia	Males	16	59	a	64	82	73	86	89	78
	Females	26	45	a	66	68	76	78	85	72
Israel	Males	x(2)	56	a	x(5)	75	a	81	85	74
	Females	x(2)	24	a	x(5)	59	a	71	81	61
Slovenia	Males	44	69	a	77	81	a	84	92	78
	Females	26	52	a	67	71	a	82	90	69

Note: Due to incomplete data, some averages have not been calculated.
1. Year of reference 2004.
Source: OECD. See Annex 3 for a description of ISCED-97 levels, ISCED-97 country mappings and national data sources (*www.oecd.org/edu/eag2007*).
Please refer to the Reader's Guide for information concerning the symbols replacing missing data.
StatLink ⌐▨⌐ http://dx.doi.org/10.1787/068152681851

A8

Table A8.2a.
Unemployment rates and educational attainment, by gender (2005)
Number of 25-to-64-year-olds in unemployment as a percentage of the labour force aged 25 to 64, by level of education attained and gender

		Pre-primary and primary education	Lower secondary education	Upper secondary education			Post-secondary non-tertiary education	Tertiary education		All levels of education
				ISCED 3C short	ISCED 3C long/3B	ISCED 3A		Type B	Type A and advanced research programmes	
		(1)	(2)	(3)	(4)	(5)	(6)	(7)	(8)	(9)
Australia	Males	7.4	6.0	a	a	2.7	3.6	2.9	2.4	3.7
	Females	9.2	5.7	a	a	4.6	4.5	2.9	2.3	4.3
Austria	Males	x(2)	9.2	a	3.6	c	c	c	3.1	4.0
	Females	x(2)	8.1	a	4.4	c	c	c	c	4.7
Belgium	Males	14.9	8.2	a	7.0	5.0	c	3.3	3.9	6.3
	Females	18.5	13.7	a	12.1	7.4	8.8	3.6	4.3	8.2
Canada	Males	10.8	8.6	a	x(5)	5.9	5.6	4.9	4.5	5.8
	Females	13.7	9.7	a	x(5)	6.0	6.1	4.7	4.4	5.7
Czech Republic	Males	c	26.4	a	5.5	2.8	x(8)	x(8)	1.9	5.2
	Females	c	23.0	a	12.1	5.5	x(8)	x(8)	2.1	9.0
Denmark	Males	c	5.9	c	3.4	c	c	2.9	3.8	3.9
	Females	c	7.6	c	4.7	5.8	c	5.3	3.5	4.8
Finland	Males	8.4	11.9	a	a	6.9	c	4.4	3.7	6.6
	Females	11.4	11.5	a	a	8.0	c	5.1	4.4	7.1
France	Males	12.8	10.7	a	5.6	7.7	6.8	5.3	6.3	7.5
	Females	13.3	13.7	a	9.3	8.0	20.4	5.4	6.6	9.4
Germany	Males	29.2	21.3	a	11.9	11.0	7.2	5.7	5.0	10.9
	Females	25.4	16.4	a	11.3	10.0	6.5	6.1	5.7	10.6
Greece	Males	4.8	6.0	c	c	3.8	6.5	4.4	4.6	4.9
	Females	12.2	16.8	c	23.2	14.0	16.7	10.3	9.9	13.2
Hungary	Males	c	12.5	a	6.5	3.8	c	c	2.0	5.8
	Females	c	11.2	a	9.1	5.4	c	c	2.6	6.5
Iceland	Males	c	c	c	c	c	c	c	c	1.5
	Females	c	c	c	c	c	c	c	c	1.8
Ireland	Males	8.2	5.0	c	a	3.0	2.8	c	1.9	3.9
	Females	5.5	5.2	c	a	3.1	3.7	c	1.7	3.2
Italy	Males	7.9	5.5	7.8	3.0	3.9	6.2	7.4	4.2	4.9
	Females	11.9	11.0	15.9	7.0	6.6	11.6	9.5	7.0	8.4
Japan	Males	x(5)	x(5)	x(5)	x(5)	5.4	a	3.5	2.5	4.3
	Females	x(5)	x(5)	x(5)	x(5)	4.3	a	3.9	3.0	4.1
Korea	Males	3.9	4.0	a	x(5)	4.1	a	4.3	2.6	3.6
	Females	1.9	1.9	a	x(5)	3.3	a	3.7	2.3	2.7
Luxembourg	Males	4.3	c	c	c	3.1	c	c	2.4	2.9
	Females	5.7	c	c	7.7	3.1	c	c	5.0	5.0
Mexico	Males	2.3	2.8	a	3.5	a	a	2.6	4.0	2.8
	Females	1.9	3.2	a	3.1	a	a	1.7	3.5	2.6
Netherlands	Males	8.0	4.3	x(4)	4.7	3.4	3.9	2.3	2.9	3.9
	Females	8.9	6.2	x(4)	4.5	4.3	3.9	c	2.8	4.4
New Zealand	Males	x(2)	3.5	a	1.9	2.1	2.2	c	2.0	2.3
	Females	x(2)	4.2	a	3.1	2.3	3.6	1.6	2.0	2.8
Norway	Males	c	8.5	a	2.1	c	c	c	2.4	3.7
	Females	c	6.2	a	2.7	c	c	c	2.2	3.3

Note: c too small sample to provide reliable estimates.
Source: OECD. See Annex 3 for a description of ISCED-97 levels, ISCED-97 country mappings and national data sources (*www.oecd.org/edu/eag2007*).
Please refer to the Reader's Guide for information concerning the symbols replacing missing data.
StatLink ⫶ᵐ⫶sᴸ http://dx.doi.org/10.1787/068152681851

Table A8.2a. *(continued)*
Unemployment rates and educational attainment, by gender (2005)
Number of 25-to-64-year-olds in unemployment as a percentage of the labour force aged 25 to 64, by level of education attained and gender

| | | Pre-primary and primary education | Lower secondary education | Upper secondary education | | | Post-secondary non-tertiary education | Tertiary education | | All levels of education |
| | | | | ISCED 3C short | ISCED 3C long/3B | ISCED 3A | | Type B | Type A and advanced research programmes | |
		(1)	(2)	(3)	(4)	(5)	(6)	(7)	(8)	(9)
Poland	Males	x(2)	26.0	17.1	a	11.1	11.0	x(8)	5.4	14.3
	Females	x(2)	28.5	24.6	a	16.6	12.7	x(8)	6.8	17.1
Portugal	Males	6.5	6.8	x(5)	x(5)	5.6	c	x(8)	5.2	6.3
	Females	8.6	9.5	x(5)	x(5)	7.5	c	x(8)	5.5	8.0
Slovak Republic	Males	85.0	52.7	x(4)	15.8	6.5	a	c	3.9	13.2
	Females	94.6	43.0	x(4)	19.6	10.8	a	c	4.5	15.7
Spain	Males	7.7	6.0	c	4.8	5.4	c	4.7	5.4	5.8
	Females	13.9	14.3	c	12.1	8.8	c	9.2	6.9	10.6
Sweden	Males	9.1	6.9	a	x(5)	6.0	7.0	5.8	4.6	6.0
	Females	11.0	9.4	a	x(5)	5.5	8.5	3.7	4.5	5.7
Switzerland	Males	c	6.9	c	3.2	c	c	c	2.5	3.3
	Females	11.2	7.7	c	3.7	5.3	c	c	4.4	4.5
Turkey	Males	9.4	9.2	a	7.0	8.2	x(8)	x(8)	5.8	8.5
	Females	5.6	13.5	a	15.5	17.5	x(8)	x(8)	9.4	8.5
United Kingdom	Males	x(2)	7.4	4.0	3.5	2.0	a	1.5	2.2	3.6
	Females	x(2)	5.7	3.4	2.5	1.6	a	1.5	1.8	3.1
United States	Males	6.8	8.7	x(5)	x(5)	5.5	x(5)	3.7	2.5	4.7
	Females	9.0	11.8	x(5)	x(5)	4.6	x(5)	3.4	2.2	4.2
OECD average	*Males*	*13.0*	*10.8*		*5.5*	*5.2*		*4.1*	*3.6*	*5.5*
	Females	*14.7*	*11.8*		*8.8*	*6.9*		*4.8*	*4.3*	*6.6*
EU19 average	*Males*	*15.9*	*12.9*		*6.3*	*5.4*		*4.4*	*3.8*	*6.3*
	Females	*18.5*	*14.2*		*10.0*	*7.3*		*6.0*	*4.7*	*8.1*
Chile[1]	Males	5.8	6.9	x(5)	x(5)	6.8	a	12.6	6.0	6.6
	Females	6.1	8.9	x(5)	x(5)	9.2	a	10.7	7.1	8.4
Estonia	Males	c	12.8	a	10.4	7.6	14.2	c	4.4	7.8
	Females	c	10.2	a	c	8.9	6.1	5.0	3.1	6.4
Israel	Males	x(2)	13.1	a	a	8.5	a	6.6	3.9	7.6
	Females	x(2)	16.4	a	a	10.8	a	6.6	4.8	8.1
Slovenia	Males	8.5	8.9	a	5.5	4.2	a	3.2	3.0	5.1
	Females	16.2	8.0	a	7.3	6.5	a	3.3	2.5	6.0

Note: c too small sample to provide reliable estimates. Due to incomplete data, some averages have not been calculated.
1. Year of reference 2004.
Source: OECD. See Annex 3 for a description of ISCED-97 levels, ISCED-97 country mappings and national data sources (*www.oecd.org/edu/eag2007*).
Please refer to the Reader's Guide for information concerning the symbols replacing missing data.
StatLink ⌐┐┌┌ http://dx.doi.org/10.1787/068152681851

A8

Table A8.3a.
Trends in employment rates, by educational attainment (1991-2005)
Number of 25-to-64-year-olds in employment as a percentage of the population aged 25 to 64, by level of educational attainment

		1991	1995	1998	1999	2000	2001	2002	2003	2004	2005
Australia	Below upper secondary	54	60	59	59	61	60	60	61	61	63
	Upper secondary and post-secondary non-tertiary	71	75	76	76	77	78	78	79	79	80
	Tertiary education	81	83	84	82	83	83	83	83	83	84
Austria	Below upper secondary	52	56	53	53	54	54	55	55	52	53
	Upper secondary and post-secondary non-tertiary	73	77	75	76	75	75	75	75	74	74
	Tertiary education	88	88	86	87	87	86	86	85	82	85
Belgium	Below upper secondary	49	47	47	49	51	49	49	49	49	49
	Upper secondary and post-secondary non-tertiary	75	72	72	75	75	74	74	73	73	74
	Tertiary education	85	84	84	85	85	84	84	84	84	84
Canada	Below upper secondary	55	52	53	54	55	54	55	56	57	56
	Upper secondary and post-secondary non-tertiary	75	73	74	75	76	75	76	76	77	76
	Tertiary education	83	82	82	82	83	82	82	82	82	82
Czech Republic	Below upper secondary	m	56	50	47	47	47	45	44	42	41
	Upper secondary and post-secondary non-tertiary	m	82	78	76	76	76	76	75	75	75
	Tertiary education	m	92	89	87	87	88	87	86	86	86
Denmark	Below upper secondary	62	61	61	62	62	61	61	61	60	60
	Upper secondary and post-secondary non-tertiary	81	76	79	81	81	81	80	80	80	80
	Tertiary education	89	89	87	88	89	87	86	85	86	86
Finland	Below upper secondary	64	54	56	59	57	58	58	58	57	58
	Upper secondary and post-secondary non-tertiary	78	70	73	74	75	75	74	73	74	75
	Tertiary education	88	81	83	85	84	85	85	85	84	84
France	Below upper secondary	58	57	56	56	57	58	58	58	58	58
	Upper secondary and post-secondary non-tertiary	78	76	75	75	76	77	77	76	75	75
	Tertiary education	85	82	82	82	83	84	83	82	82	82
Germany	Below upper secondary	51	49	46	49	51	52	51	50	49	52
	Upper secondary and post-secondary non-tertiary	74	71	68	70	70	71	70	70	69	71
	Tertiary education	86	84	82	83	83	83	84	83	83	83
Greece	Below upper secondary	m	56	57	56	57	57	57	59	57	58
	Upper secondary and post-secondary non-tertiary	m	62	66	66	66	66	67	68	69	70
	Tertiary education	m	79	81	81	81	80	81	82	82	82
Hungary	Below upper secondary	m	m	36	36	36	37	37	37	37	38
	Upper secondary and post-secondary non-tertiary	m	m	71	72	72	72	72	71	71	70
	Tertiary education	m	m	81	82	82	83	82	83	83	83
Iceland	Below upper secondary	m	m	85	86	87	87	86	82	81	82
	Upper secondary and post-secondary non-tertiary	m	m	89	91	89	89	89	89	87	88
	Tertiary education	m	m	95	95	95	95	95	93	92	92
Ireland	Below upper secondary	46	49	53	54	60	57	57	57	57	58
	Upper secondary and post-secondary non-tertiary	63	67	72	75	77	77	77	76	76	77
	Tertiary education	81	83	85	87	87	87	86	86	86	87
Italy	Below upper secondary	54	49	47	48	48	49	50	51	52	52
	Upper secondary and post-secondary non-tertiary	74	70	70	70	71	72	72	72	73	73
	Tertiary education	87	81	81	81	81	82	82	82	81	80
Japan	Below upper secondary	m	m	69	68	67	68	67	67	m	m
	Upper secondary and post-secondary non-tertiary	m	m	76	74	74	74	74	74	72	72
	Tertiary education	m	m	79	79	79	80	79	79	79	79
Korea	Below upper secondary	70	71	66	67	68	68	68	67	66	66
	Upper secondary and post-secondary non-tertiary	70	71	66	66	69	69	70	70	70	70
	Tertiary education	80	80	76	75	75	76	76	76	77	77
Luxembourg	Below upper secondary	m	m	m	55	58	58	59	59	59	61
	Upper secondary and post-secondary non-tertiary	m	m	m	73	73	74	74	71	69	71
	Tertiary education	m	m	m	85	84	86	85	82	84	84
Mexico	Below upper secondary	m	60	64	64	63	63	64	63	65	63
	Upper secondary and post-secondary non-tertiary	m	63	64	62	66	64	63	63	64	65
	Tertiary education	m	82	84	83	83	81	82	82	82	82

Source: OECD. See Annex 3 for notes (*www.oecd.org/edu/eag2007*).
Please refer to the Reader's Guide for information concerning the symbols replacing missing data.
StatLink ⦿⦿ http://dx.doi.org/10.1787/068152681851

Table A8.3a. *(continued)*

Trends in employment rates, by educational attainment (1991-2005)

Number of 25-to-64-year-olds in employment as a percentage of the population aged 25 to 64, by level of educational attainment

			1991	1995	1998	1999	2000	2001	2002	2003	2004	2005
OECD countries	**Netherlands**	Below upper secondary	50	52	55	57	58	59	61	59	59	60
		Upper secondary and post-secondary non-tertiary	73	74	77	78	79	80	80	79	78	78
		Tertiary education	85	83	85	87	86	86	86	86	85	86
	New Zealand	Below upper secondary	57	58	59	60	61	62	64	63	65	67
		Upper secondary and post-secondary non-tertiary	73	80	79	80	80	81	81	82	82	83
		Tertiary education	80	82	80	81	81	82	82	81	84	84
	Norway	Below upper secondary	62	61	68	67	65	63	64	64	62	64
		Upper secondary and post-secondary non-tertiary	80	80	84	83	83	83	81	80	79	82
		Tertiary education	90	89	90	90	90	90	89	89	89	89
	Poland	Below upper secondary	m	50	49	47	43	41	39	38	37	38
		Upper secondary and post-secondary non-tertiary	m	70	71	70	67	65	62	62	61	62
		Tertiary education	m	85	87	87	85	84	83	83	82	83
	Portugal	Below upper secondary	62	67	72	72	73	73	73	72	72	71
		Upper secondary and post-secondary non-tertiary	84	77	80	82	83	83	82	82	80	79
		Tertiary education	92	89	89	90	91	91	88	87	88	87
	Slovak Republic	Below upper secondary	m	39	37	33	31	30	28	29	22	22
		Upper secondary and post-secondary non-tertiary	m	75	75	72	71	70	70	71	70	71
		Tertiary education	m	88	89	87	86	87	87	87	84	84
	Spain	Below upper secondary	49	46	49	51	54	55	56	57	57	59
		Upper secondary and post-secondary non-tertiary	72	65	67	70	72	72	72	72	73	75
		Tertiary education	79	75	76	78	80	81	81	82	82	82
	Sweden	Below upper secondary	83	78	66	66	68	69	68	68	67	66
		Upper secondary and post-secondary non-tertiary	91	84	79	80	82	82	82	81	81	81
		Tertiary education	94	89	85	86	87	87	86	86	85	87
	Switzerland	Below upper secondary	78	67	69	69	66	69	68	66	65	65
		Upper secondary and post-secondary non-tertiary	80	80	81	81	82	81	81	80	80	80
		Tertiary education	92	90	90	91	91	91	91	90	90	90
	Turkey	Below upper secondary	60	64	57	56	53	52	50	49	50	49
		Upper secondary and post-secondary non-tertiary	67	63	66	64	64	62	62	61	62	63
		Tertiary education	87	74	81	79	78	78	76	75	75	76
	United Kingdom	Below upper secondary	61	55	53	53	54	54	53	54	53	52
		Upper secondary and post-secondary non-tertiary	78	77	79	79	79	79	79	80	79	80
		Tertiary education	86	86	87	88	88	88	88	88	88	88
	United States	Below upper secondary	52	54	58	58	58	58	57	58	57	57
		Upper secondary and post-secondary non-tertiary	74	75	76	76	77	76	74	73	73	73
		Tertiary education	85	86	85	85	85	84	83	82	82	82
	OECD average	***Below upper secondary***		*57*	*57*	*57*	*57*	*57*	*57*	*57*	*56*	*56*
		Upper secondary and post-secondary non-tertiary		*73*	*74*	*75*	*75*	*75*	*75*	*74*	*74*	*75*
		Tertiary education		*84*	*84*	*85*	*85*	*85*	*84*	*84*	*84*	*84*
	EU19 average	***Below upper secondary***		*54*	*52*	*53*	*53*	*54*	*53*	*53*	*52*	*53*
		Upper secondary and post-secondary non-tertiary		*73*	*74*	*74*	*75*	*75*	*74*	*74*	*74*	*74*
		Tertiary education		*85*	*85*	*85*	*85*	*85*	*85*	*84*	*84*	*84*
Partner economies	**Estonia**	Below upper secondary	m	m	m	m	m	m	44	49	51	50
		Upper secondary and post-secondary non-tertiary	m	m	m	m	m	m	72	73	73	74
		tertiary education	m	m	m	m	m	m	82	80	82	84
	Israel	Below upper secondary	m	m	m	m	m	m	43	43	40	41
		Upper secondary and post-secondary non-tertiary	m	m	m	m	m	m	67	66	66	67
		tertiary education	m	m	m	m	m	m	79	79	79	80
	Slovenia	Below upper secondary	m	m	m	m	m	m	56	54	56	56
		Upper secondary and post-secondary non-tertiary	m	m	m	m	m	m	74	73	74	75
		tertiary education	m	m	m	m	m	m	86	86	87	87

Note: Due to incomplete data, some averages have not been calculated.

Source: OECD. See Annex 3 for notes (*www.oecd.org/edu/eag2007*).

Please refer to the Reader's Guide for information concerning the symbols replacing missing data.

StatLink http://dx.doi.org/10.1787/068152681851

A8

Table A8.4a.
Trends in unemployment rates by educational attainment (1991-2005)
Number of 25-to-64-year-olds in unemployment as a percentage of the labour force aged 25 to 64, by level of educational attainment

		1991	1995	1998	1999	2000	2001	2002	2003	2004	2005
Australia	Below upper secondary	9.2	8.7	9.0	8.4	7.5	7.6	7.5	7.0	6.2	6.3
	Upper secondary and post-secondary non-tertiary	6.8	6.2	5.8	5.1	4.5	4.7	4.3	4.3	3.9	3.4
	Tertiary education	3.9	4.0	3.3	3.4	3.6	3.1	3.3	3.0	2.8	2.5
Austria	Below upper secondary	4.8	5.7	6.9	6.1	6.3	6.4	6.9	7.9	7.8	8.6
	Upper secondary and post-secondary non-tertiary	3.1	2.9	3.6	3.2	3.0	3.0	3.4	3.4	3.8	3.9
	Tertiary education	1.5	2.0	2.0	1.9	1.6	1.5	1.9	2.0	2.9	2.6
Belgium	Below upper secondary	11.8	13.4	13.1	12.0	9.8	8.5	10.3	10.7	11.7	12.4
	Upper secondary and post-secondary non-tertiary	4.2	7.5	7.4	6.6	5.3	5.5	6.0	6.7	6.9	6.9
	Tertiary education	2.0	3.6	3.2	3.1	2.7	2.7	3.5	3.5	3.9	3.7
Canada	Below upper secondary	13.8	13.3	11.9	10.8	10.2	10.5	11.0	10.9	10.2	9.8
	Upper secondary and post-secondary non-tertiary	9.0	8.9	7.5	6.7	5.9	6.3	6.7	6.5	6.2	5.9
	Tertiary education	5.8	5.6	4.7	4.5	4.1	4.7	5.1	5.2	4.8	4.6
Czech Republic	Below upper secondary	m	7.7	14.5	18.8	19.3	19.2	18.8	19.8	23.0	24.4
	Upper secondary and post-secondary non-tertiary	m	2.1	4.6	6.5	6.7	6.2	5.6	6.1	6.4	6.2
	Tertiary education	m	0.7	1.9	2.6	2.5	2.0	1.8	2.0	2.0	2.0
Denmark	Below upper secondary	14.2	14.6	7.0	7.0	6.9	(6)	6.4	7.2	8.6	6.8
	Upper secondary and post-secondary non-tertiary	9.1	9.9	4.6	4.1	3.9	3.7	3.7	4.4	4.8	4.0
	Tertiary education	4.9	4.6	3.3	3.0	3.0	3.6	3.9	4.7	4.4	3.7
Finland	Below upper secondary	8.6	21.6	13.8	13.1	12.1	11.4	12.2	11.1	11.3	10.7
	Upper secondary and post-secondary non-tertiary	7.3	16.7	10.6	9.5	8.9	8.5	8.8	9.2	7.9	7.4
	Tertiary education	3.4	9.1	5.8	4.7	4.7	4.4	4.5	4.3	4.5	4.4
France	Below upper secondary	10.6	13.7	14.9	15.3	13.9	11.9	11.8	12.1	12.1	12.4
	Upper secondary and post-secondary non-tertiary	6.6	9.0	9.6	9.2	7.9	6.9	6.8	7.4	7.5	7.3
	Tertiary education	3.7	6.5	6.6	6.1	5.1	4.8	5.2	6.0	6.1	6.0
Germany	Below upper secondary	7.4	13.3	16.5	15.6	13.7	13.5	15.3	18.0	20.4	20.2
	Upper secondary and post-secondary non-tertiary	4.7	7.9	10.3	8.6	7.8	8.2	9.0	10.2	11.2	11.0
	Tertiary education	3.2	4.9	5.5	4.9	4.0	4.2	4.5	5.2	5.6	5.5
Greece	Below upper secondary	m	6.3	7.5	8.5	7.9	7.6	7.4	6.9	8.4	8.2
	Upper secondary and post-secondary non-tertiary	m	9.0	10.4	11.0	11.1	10.1	9.9	9.5	9.6	9.2
	Tertiary education	m	8.1	6.3	7.8	7.4	6.9	6.7	6.1	7.2	7.0
Hungary	Below upper secondary	m	m	11.4	11.1	9.9	10.0	10.5	10.6	10.8	12.4
	Upper secondary and post-secondary non-tertiary	m	m	6.2	5.8	5.3	4.6	4.4	4.8	5.0	6.0
	Tertiary education	m	m	1.7	1.4	1.3	1.2	1.5	1.4	1.9	2.3
Iceland	Below upper secondary	m	m	3.4	2.3	2.5	2.4	3.1	3.7	2.8	c
	Upper secondary and post-secondary non-tertiary	m	m	c	c	c	c	2.4	c	c	c
	Tertiary education	m	m	c	c	c	c	c	c	c	c
Ireland	Below upper secondary	20.3	16.4	11.6	9.2	5.9	5.5	5.9	6.3	6.1	6.0
	Upper secondary and post-secondary non-tertiary	7.3	7.6	4.5	3.5	2.3	2.4	2.8	2.9	3.0	3.1
	Tertiary education	4.1	4.2	3.0	1.7	1.6	1.8	2.2	2.6	2.2	2.0
Italy	Below upper secondary	5.7	9.1	10.8	10.6	10.0	9.1	9.0	8.8	8.1	7.7
	Upper secondary and post-secondary non-tertiary	7.2	7.9	8.2	8.0	7.4	6.8	6.4	6.1	5.6	5.3
	Tertiary education	5.0	7.3	6.9	6.9	5.9	5.3	5.3	5.3	5.3	5.7
Japan	Below upper secondary	m	m	4.3	5.6	6.0	5.9	6.6	6.7	m	m
	Upper secondary and post-secondary non-tertiary	m	m	3.3	4.4	4.7	4.8	5.3	5.4	5.1	4.9
	Tertiary education	m	m	2.6	3.3	3.5	3.1	3.8	3.7	3.4	3.1
Korea	Below upper secondary	0.9	1.0	6.0	5.4	3.7	3.1	2.2	2.2	2.6	2.9
	Upper secondary and post-secondary non-tertiary	1.9	1.6	6.8	6.4	4.1	3.6	3.0	3.3	3.5	3.8
	Tertiary education	2.7	2.0	4.9	4.7	3.6	3.5	3.2	3.1	2.9	2.9
Luxembourg	Below upper secondary	m	m	m	3.7	3.1	1.8	3.8	3.5	5.4	5.0
	Upper secondary and post-secondary non-tertiary	m	m	m	1.1	1.6	1.1	1.2	2.6	4.3	3.5
	Tertiary education	m	m	m	c	c	c	1.8	4.0	3.2	3.2
Mexico	Below upper secondary	m	4.2	1.9	1.4	1.3	1.4	1.5	1.6	1.9	2.5
	Upper secondary and post-secondary non-tertiary	m	5.2	2.6	1.9	1.6	1.7	1.8	1.9	2.8	3.2
	Tertiary education	m	4.7	2.5	2.9	2.0	2.2	2.5	2.6	3.0	3.7

Note: c too small sample to provide reliable estimates.
Source: OECD. See Annex 3 for notes (*www.oecd.org / edu / eag2007*).
Please refer to the Reader's Guide for information concerning the symbols replacing missing data.
StatLink ⏤ http://dx.doi.org/10.1787/068152681851

Table A8.4a. *(continued)*
Trends in unemployment rates by educational attainment (1991–2005)
Number of 25-to-64-year-olds in unemployment as a percentage of the labour force aged 25 to 64, by level of educational attainment

			1991	1995	1998	1999	2000	2001	2002	2003	2004	2005
OECD countries	**Netherlands**	Below upper secondary	8.6	7.9	0.9	4.9	3.9	2.9	3.0	4.5	5.5	5.8
		Upper secondary and post-secondary non-tertiary	4.6	4.8	1.7	2.4	2.3	1.6	2.0	2.8	3.8	4.1
		Tertiary education	1.5	4.1	c	1.7	1.9	1.2	2.1	2.5	2.8	2.8
	New Zealand	Below upper secondary	12.5	8.2	10.5	8.8	7.8	6.7	5.6	4.9	4.2	3.8
		Upper secondary and post-secondary non-tertiary	7.3	3.3	4.7	4.6	3.5	3.2	3.3	2.9	2.4	2.4
		Tertiary education	4.8	3.2	4.5	4.0	3.6	3.2	3.4	3.5	2.4	1.9
	Norway	Below upper secondary	6.7	6.5	2.9	2.5	2.2	3.4	3.4	3.9	4.0	7.3
		Upper secondary and post-secondary non-tertiary	4.4	4.0	2.4	2.5	2.6	2.7	2.9	3.6	3.8	2.6
		Tertiary education	2.0	2.4	1.5	1.4	1.9	1.7	2.1	2.5	2.4	2.1
	Poland	Below upper secondary	m	13.9	13.9	16.4	20.6	22.6	25.2	25.9	27.8	27.1
		Upper secondary and post-secondary non-tertiary	m	11.1	9.1	10.7	13.9	15.9	17.8	17.8	17.4	16.6
		Tertiary education	m	2.8	2.5	3.1	4.3	5.0	6.3	6.6	6.2	6.2
	Portugal	Below upper secondary	5.3	6.2	4.4	4.0	3.6	3.6	4.4	5.7	6.4	7.5
		Upper secondary and post-secondary non-tertiary	4.5	6.4	5.1	4.4	3.5	3.3	4.3	5.1	5.6	6.7
		Tertiary education	c	3.2	2.8	3.0	2.7	2.8	3.9	4.9	4.4	5.4
	Slovak Republic	Below upper secondary	m	24.0	24.3	30.3	36.3	38.7	42.3	44.9	47.7	49.2
		Upper secondary and post-secondary non-tertiary	m	9.6	8.8	11.9	14.3	14.8	14.2	13.5	14.6	12.7
		Tertiary education	m	2.7	3.3	4.0	4.6	4.2	3.6	3.7	4.8	4.4
	Spain	Below upper secondary	13.7	20.6	17.1	14.7	13.7	10.2	11.2	11.2	11.0	9.3
		Upper secondary and post-secondary non-tertiary	12.2	18.5	15.3	12.9	11.0	8.4	9.5	9.5	9.5	7.3
		Tertiary education	9.3	14.5	13.1	11.1	9.5	6.9	7.7	7.7	7.3	6.2
	Sweden	Below upper secondary	2.6	10.1	10.4	9.0	8.0	5.9	5.8	6.1	6.5	8.5
		Upper secondary and post-secondary non-tertiary	2.3	8.7	7.8	6.5	5.3	4.6	4.6	5.2	5.8	6.0
		Tertiary education	1.1	4.5	4.4	3.9	3.0	2.6	3.0	3.9	4.3	4.5
	Switzerland	Below upper secondary	1.2	5.8	5.6	5.0	5.0	3.7	4.6	6.1	7.3	7.7
		Upper secondary and post-secondary non-tertiary	1.5	2.8	2.8	2.3	2.0	2.0	2.4	3.2	3.8	3.7
		Tertiary education	1.3	c	2.8	1.7	1.3	1.3	2.2	2.9	2.8	2.7
	Turkey	Below upper secondary	5.7	4.8	4.4	5.3	4.6	6.7	8.5	8.8	8.1	8.7
		Upper secondary and post-secondary non-tertiary	7.2	6.9	6.6	8.2	5.5	7.4	8.7	7.8	10.1	9.2
		Tertiary education	3.1	3.3	4.8	5.1	3.9	4.7	7.5	6.9	8.2	6.9
	United Kingdom	Below upper secondary	10.4	12.8	10.5	10.0	8.9	7.6	8.5	6.9	6.5	6.6
		Upper secondary and post-secondary non-tertiary	6.5	7.5	5.0	4.9	4.6	3.9	4.1	3.9	3.7	3.2
		Tertiary education	3.3	3.7	2.6	2.7	2.1	2.0	2.4	2.4	2.3	2.0
	United States	Below upper secondary	12.3	10.0	8.5	7.7	7.9	8.1	10.2	9.9	10.5	9.0
		Upper secondary and post-secondary non-tertiary	6.5	5.0	4.5	3.7	3.6	3.8	5.7	6.1	5.6	5.1
		Tertiary education	2.9	2.7	2.1	2.1	1.8	2.1	3.0	3.4	3.3	2.6
	OECD average	*Below upper secondary*		*11*	*10*	*9*	*9*	*9*	*9*	*10*	*10*	*11*
		Upper secondary and post-secondary non-tertiary		*7*	*6*	*6*	*6*	*6*	*6*	*6*	*6*	*6*
		Tertiary education		*5*	*4*	*4*	*3*	*3*	*4*	*4*	*4*	*4*
	EU19 average	*Below upper secondary*		*13*	*12*	*12*	*11*	*11*	*12*	*12*	*13*	*13*
		Upper secondary and post-secondary non-tertiary		*9*	*7*	*7*	*7*	*6*	*7*	*7*	*7*	*7*
		Tertiary education		*5*	*4*	*4*	*4*	*4*	*4*	*4*	*4*	*4*
Partner economies	**Estonia**	Below upper secondary	m	m	m	m	m	m	19.0	14.8	15.4	13.0
		Upper secondary and post-secondary non-tertiary	m	m	m	m	m	m	10.5	9.5	9.5	8.4
		tertiary education	m	m	m	m	m	m	5.8	6.5	5.0	3.8
	Israel	Below upper secondary	m	m	m	m	m	m	14.0	15.2	15.6	14.0
		Upper secondary and post-secondary non-tertiary	m	m	m	m	m	m	9.8	10.3	10.6	9.5
		Tertiary education	m	m	m	m	m	m	6.4	6.4	6.1	5.1
	Slovenia	Below upper secondary	m	m	m	m	m	m	8.4	8.7	8.4	8.7
		Upper secondary and post-secondary non-tertiary	m	m	m	m	m	m	5.2	5.5	5.3	5.7
		tertiary education	m	m	m	m	m	m	2.3	3.0	2.8	3.0

Note: c too small sample to provide reliable estimates. Due to incomplete data, some averages have not been calculated.
Source: OECD. See Annex 3 for notes (www.oecd.org / edu / eag2007).
Please refer to the Reader's Guide for information concerning the symbols replacing missing data.
StatLink ⫘⫘ http://dx.doi.org/10.1787/068152681851

WHAT ARE THE ECONOMIC BENEFITS OF EDUCATION?

This indicator examines the relative earnings of workers with different levels of educational attainment of 25 OECD countries and the partner economy Israel. This indicator also presents data that describe the distribution of pre-tax earnings (see Annex 3 for notes) within five ISCED levels of educational attainment to help show how returns to education vary within countries among individuals with comparable levels of educational attainment. The financial returns to educational attainment are calculated for investments undertaken as a part of initial education, as well as for the case of a hypothetical 40-year-old who decides to return to education in mid-career. For the first time, this indicator presents new estimates of the rate of return for an individual investing in upper secondary education instead of working for the minimum wage with a lower secondary level of education.

Key results

Chart A9.1. Private internal rates of return for an individual obtaining an upper secondary or post-secondary non-tertiary education, ISCED 3/4 and for an individual obtaining a university-level degree, ISCED 5/6 (2003)

☐ Private internal rates of return for an individual immediately acuiring the next level of education: an upper secondary or post-secondary non-tertiary education, ISCED 3/4

▲ Private internal rates of return for an individual immediately acuiring the next level of education: a tertiary level degree, ISCED 5/6

In all countries, for males and females, private internal rates of return exceed 4.5% on an investment in upper secondary education (completed immediately following initial education). Private internal rates of return are, on average, higher for investment in upper secondary or post-secondary non-tertiary education than for tertiary education. Attaining higher levels of education can be viewed as an economic investment in which there are costs paid by the individual (including reductions in earnings while receiving education) that typically result in higher earnings over the individual's lifetime. In this context, the investment in obtaining a tertiary degree, when undertaken as part of initial education, can produce private annual returns as high as 22.6%, with all countries showing a rate of return above 8%.

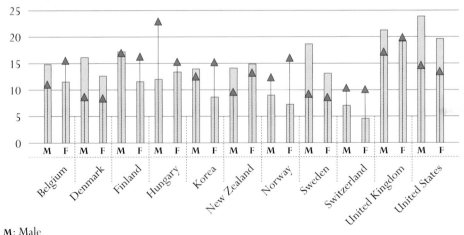

M: Male
F: Female
Source: OECD. Tables A9.5 and A9.6. See Annex 3 for notes (*www.oecd.org/edu/eag2007*).
StatLink ᵐˢᴸ http://dx.doi.org/10.1787/068170623457

Other highlights of this indicator

- Earnings increase with each level of education. Those who have attained upper secondary, post-secondary non-tertiary or tertiary education enjoy substantial earnings advantages compared with those of the same gender who have not completed upper secondary education. Across all countries, individuals with tertiary-type A and advanced research education had earnings that were at least 50% higher than individuals whose highest level of educational attainment was below upper secondary level of education (Chart A9.4).

- In all countries, females earn less than males with similar levels of educational attainment (Table A9.3). For a given level of educational attainment, they typically earn between 50 and 80% of what males earn.

- Countries differ significantly in the dispersion of earnings among individuals with similar levels of educational attainment. Although individuals with higher levels of education are more likely to be in the highest earnings group, this is not always the case. The proportion of individuals with the highest educational attainment (tertiary-type A and advanced research programmes) in the lowest earning category (at or below half of the median) vary from 0 to 19.6%, in Portugal and Canada, respectively. Countries also differ in the relative share of men and women in the upper and lower categories of earnings.

- In all countries, it is profitable for a 40-year-old to return to education mid-career and obtain a tertiary degree. This applies to both males and females. The rate of return when the individual, at age 40, begins the next level of higher education in full-time university studies varies between 6.5% for males in New Zealand and 28.2% for females in Belgium.

A9

Policy context

One way in which markets provide incentives for individuals to develop and maintain appropriate skills is through wage differentials – in particular through the enhanced earnings awarded to persons with higher levels of education. At the same time, education involves costs that must be balanced against these higher earnings. This indicator examines relative earnings associated with different levels of education, the variation in these earnings and the estimated rates of return to individuals making investments to obtain higher levels of education.

The dispersion of earnings is also relevant for policies that support attainment of higher levels of education. Evidence suggests that some individuals may be receiving relatively low returns to investments in education, that is, they earn relatively low wages even though they have relatively high levels of educational attainment. Policy makers may wish to examine characteristics of the education programmes which appear to have low rates of return for some people or to examine the characteristics of the individuals in these programmes, such as their gender or occupation.

Evidence and explanations

Education and earnings

Earnings differentials according to educational attainment

A key measure of the financial incentive available for an individual to invest in further education, earnings differentials may also reflect differences in the supply of educational programmes at different levels (or barriers to access to those programmes). The earnings benefit of completing tertiary education can be seen by comparing the average annual earnings of those who graduate from tertiary education with the average annual earnings of upper secondary or post-secondary non-tertiary graduates. The earnings disadvantage from not completing upper secondary education is apparent from a similar comparison of average earnings. Variations in relative earnings (before taxes) among countries reflect a number of factors, including the demand for skills in the labour market, minimum wage legislation, the strength of unions, the coverage of collective bargaining agreements, the supply of workers at the various levels of educational attainment, the range of work experience of workers with high and low levels of educational attainment, the distribution of employment among occupations and, last but not least, the relative incidence of part-time and seasonal work.

Chart A9.2 shows a strong positive relationship between educational attainment and average earnings. In all countries, graduates of tertiary-level education earn substantially more than upper secondary and post-secondary non-tertiary graduates. Earnings differentials between those who have tertiary education – especially those with a tertiary-type A level of attainment – and those who have upper secondary education are generally more pronounced than the differentials between upper secondary and lower secondary or below, suggesting that in many countries upper secondary (and, with a small number of exceptions, post-secondary non-tertiary) education forms a break-point beyond which additional education attracts a particularly high premium. Table A9.1a shows that the earnings premium for 25-to-64-year-olds with tertiary-level education, relative to upper secondary education, ranges from 26% in Denmark (2004) to 115% in Hungary (2005).

The earnings data shown in this indicator differ across countries in a number of ways. The results should therefore be interpreted with caution. In particular, in countries reporting annual earnings, differences in the incidence of seasonal work among individuals with different levels of educational attainment will have an effect on relative earnings that is not reflected in the data for countries reporting weekly or monthly earnings (see the Definitions and methodologies section below).

Chart A9.2. Relative earnings from employment (2005 or latest available year)

By level of educational attainment and gender for 25-to-64-years-olds
(upper secondary and post-secondary non-tertiary education = 100)

■ Below upper secondary
■ Tertiary-type B education
□ Tertiary-type A and advanced research programmes

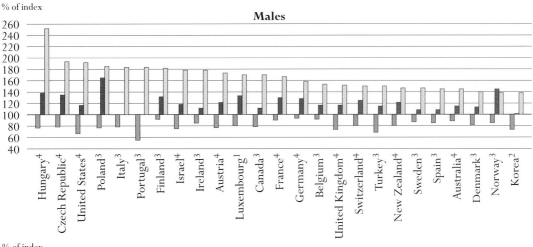

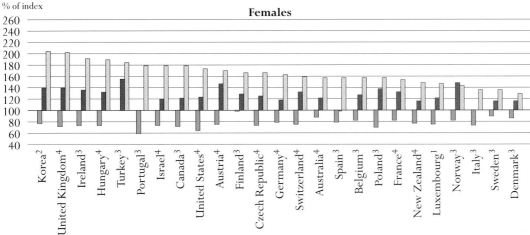

1. Year of reference 2002.
2. Year of reference 2003.
3. Year of reference 2004.
4. Year of reference 2005.

Countries are ranked in descending order of the relative earnings of the population with a tertiary-type A level of educational attainment.

Source: OECD. Table A9.1a. See Annex 3 for notes (*www.oecd.org/edu/eag2007*).

StatLink ᵐˢᴾ http://dx.doi.org/10.1787/068170623457

Education and gender disparity in earnings

For 25-to-64-year-olds, financial rewards from tertiary education benefit females more than males in Australia, Austria, Canada, Ireland, Korea, the Netherlands, Norway, Spain, Switzerland, Turkey and the United Kingdom. The reverse is true in the remaining countries, with the exception of Belgium and Germany, where – relative to upper secondary education – the earnings of males and females are equally enhanced by tertiary education (Table A9.1a).

Both males and females with upper secondary, post-secondary non-tertiary or tertiary attainment have substantial earnings advantages (compared with those of the same gender who do not complete upper secondary education), but earnings differentials between males and females with the same educational attainment remain substantial. In all countries, and at all levels of educational attainment, females in the 30-to-44-year-old age group earn less than their male counterparts (Chart A9.3 and Table A9.1b). When all levels of education are taken together (*i.e.* total earnings are divided by the total number of income earners, by gender), average earnings of females between the ages of 30 and 44 range from 51% of those of males, in Korea, to 84% in Luxembourg (Chart A9.3 and Table A9.1b).

Chart A9.3. Differences in earnings between females and males (2005 or latest available year)

Average female earnings as a percentage of male earnings (30-to-44-year-old age group), by level of educational attainment

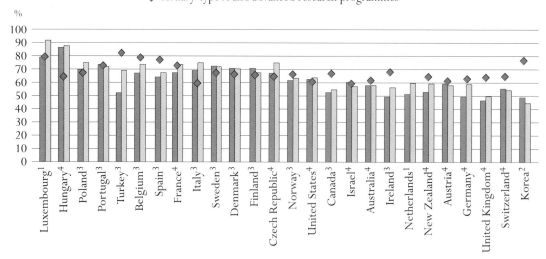

1. Year of reference 2002.
2. Year of reference 2003.
3. Year of reference 2004.
4. Year of reference 2005.
Notes: Data on earnings for individuals in part-time work are excluded for the Czech Republic, Hungary, Luxembourg and Poland, while data on part-year earnings are excluded for Hungary, Luxembourg and Poland.
Source: OECD. Table A9.1b. See Annex 3 for notes (*www.oecd.org/edu/eag2007*).
StatLink ⟐⟐⟐ http://dx.doi.org/10.1787/068170623457

The relative differential between men and women must be treated with caution, however, since in most countries earnings data include part-time work. Part-time work is often a major characteristic of women's employment and its prevalence is likely to vary a lot from one country to another. In Luxembourg, Hungary and Poland, those with part-time work and part-year earnings are excluded from the calculations. Earnings of females between the ages of 30 and 44 reach 84, 83 and 81% of those of males, respectively.

The gap in earnings between males and females presented in Chart A9.3 is explained in part by different choices of career and occupation, differences in the amount of time that males and females spend in the labour force, and the relatively high incidence of part-time work among females.

The distribution of earnings within levels of educational attainment

Data on the distribution of the share of individuals with a given level of educational attainment in different earnings groups can be used to describe how tightly earnings are distributed around the country median.

Tables A9.4a, A9.4b and A9.4c show the distributions of earnings among 25-to-64-year-olds for 25 OECD countries and the partner economy Israel. Distributions are given for the combined male and female populations, as well as for males and females separately. There are five categories of the earnings distribution, ranging from "At or below one-half of the median" to "More than twice the median". For example, in Table A9.4a, for Australia, the figure of 24.3% is found in the row "Below upper secondary" under the column "At or below one-half of the median". This means that 24.3% of Australians who are between the ages of 25 and 64 and whose highest educational attainment is below the upper secondary level have pre-tax earnings at or below one-half of the median earnings of all Australian 25-to-64-year-olds who had earnings from work during the reference period of the national survey. Tables A9.4b and A9.4c also present earnings distributions among males and females relative to the median of the entire adult population with earnings from work.

Indicators based on average earnings do not consider the range of earnings that individuals with a given level of educational attainment experience. Some individuals with high levels of educational attainment may have relatively low levels of earnings and individuals with low levels of education may have high levels of earnings. This variation may reflect differences in the returns to education across individuals and may be of concern to policy makers if they indicate that the labour market signals individuals receive as they consider investment in education are not clear.

The data show that in most countries the share of individuals in the lowest earnings categories falls as the level of educational attainment rises. This result is another way of viewing the well-established positive relationship between earnings and educational attainment. However, it is notable that even at higher levels of education there are individuals in the lower earnings categories, indicating that they have experienced a relatively low rate of return to education.

Still, countries differ significantly in the dispersion of earnings. For instance, Table A9.4a shows that in most countries the largest proportion of the population has earnings above one-half of the median but less than 1.5 times the median. Yet this percentage ranges from less than 45% in

Canada to more than 80% in Belgium. Across all levels of education, countries such as Belgium, the Czech Republic, Luxembourg and Portugal have no or relatively few individuals with earnings either at or below one-half the median. Conversely, while across all countries almost 22%, on average, of individuals between the ages of 25 and 64 have earnings above 1.5 times the median, this population share is as low as 14.1% in Belgium.

Countries also differ significantly in the gender distribution of individuals in the lowest earnings group. For example, taking into account all levels of educational attainment, Hungary is the only country in which the percentage of females in the lowest earnings category is smaller than the percentage of males in the same category. At the opposite end of the spectrum, the percentage of females in the highest earnings category is smaller than that of males in all countries. This is particularly marked in Switzerland, with 13% of males in the highest earnings category versus 2% of females and 4% of males in the lowest earnings category compared to 35% of females (Chart A9.5).

The interpretation of earnings dispersion data

A wide range of factors – from differences in institutional arrangements to variation in individual abilities – is likely to determine the extent of earnings dispersion among individuals of similar educational attainment. At an institutional level, countries in which wage setting is more centralised would tend to see lower earnings dispersion, owing to a degree of convergence between occupational status and educational attainment. More broadly, earnings dispersions also reflect the fact that educational attainment cannot be fully equated with proficiency and skills: skills other than those indicated by educational attainment, as well as experience, are rewarded in the labour market. Differences in the scale and operation of training systems for adult learners also influence national patterns of earnings dispersion, as do non-skills-related recruitment considerations – such as gender, race or age discrimination (and consequently the relative effectiveness of national legislative frameworks in countering such problems). Finally, note that in Belgium earnings are centred on the median; this is probably in part because Belgian earnings data are net of income tax.

However, the data do show that in all countries, earnings dispersion falls as educational attainment rises. This trend has many possible interpretations, including that greater educational attainment could be providing more information on an individual's skills to potential employers, resulting in a closer link between education and wages.

More generally, the data point to gaps in the understanding of earnings determination. Research in the United States has shown that for individuals of the same race and sex, over one-half of the variance in earnings is not explained by quantifiable factors such as a person's years of schooling, age, duration of labour market experience, or indeed the schooling, occupation and income of their parents. Some research on the determinants of earnings has highlighted the importance that employers give to so-called non-cognitive skills – such as persistence, reliability and self-discipline – as well as raising questions for policy-oriented research on the role of education systems, and particularly early childhood education, in developing and signalling such skills (see the Definitions and methodologies section below).

Chart A9.4. Share of 25-to-64-year-olds in earnings categories by level of educational attainment (2005 or latest available year)

A9

- Below upper secondary
- Upper secondary and post-secondary non tertiary
- Tertiary-type A and advanced research programmes
- Tertiary-type B education

With earnings one half of the country median or less

With earnings twice the country median or more

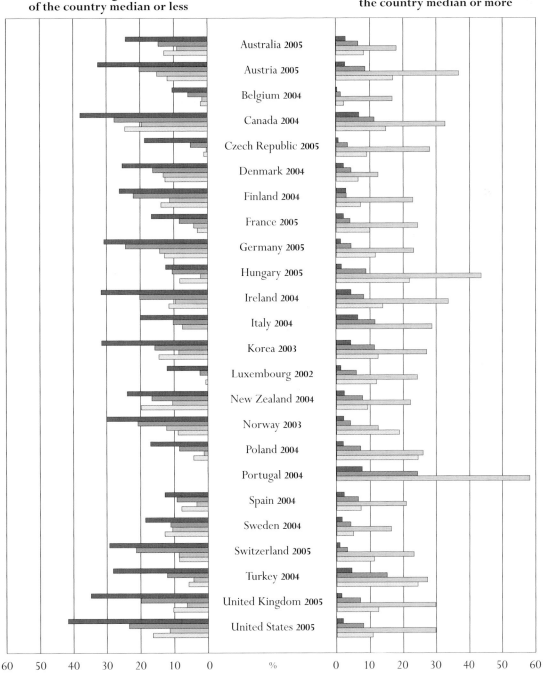

Australia 2005	
Austria 2005	
Belgium 2004	
Canada 2004	
Czech Republic 2005	
Denmark 2004	
Finland 2004	
France 2005	
Germany 2005	
Hungary 2005	
Ireland 2004	
Italy 2004	
Korea 2003	
Luxembourg 2002	
New Zealand 2004	
Norway 2003	
Poland 2004	
Portugal 2004	
Spain 2004	
Sweden 2004	
Switzerland 2005	
Turkey 2004	
United Kingdom 2005	
United States 2005	

60 50 40 30 20 10 0   %   0 10 20 30 40 50 60

Source: OECD. Table A9.4a. See Annex 3 for notes (*www.oecd.org/edu/eag2007*).

StatLink ᴍᵫ᠊ᔕᒪ http://dx.doi.org/10.1787/068170623457

A9

Chart A9.5. Share of 25-to-64-year-olds in earnings categories by level of educational attainment and gender (2005 or latest available year)

☐ Males ■ Females

ISCED Levels 0/1/2
ISCED Levels 3/4
ISCED Levels 5B/5A/6

**With earnings half
of the country median or less**

**With earnings twice
the country median or more**

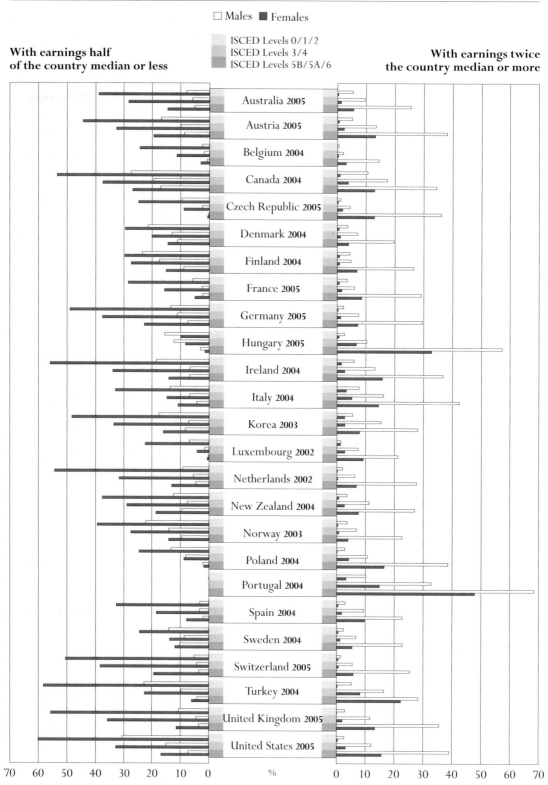

Australia 2005
Austria 2005
Belgium 2004
Canada 2004
Czech Republic 2005
Denmark 2004
Finland 2004
France 2005
Germany 2005
Hungary 2005
Ireland 2004
Italy 2004
Korea 2003
Luxembourg 2002
Netherlands 2002
New Zealand 2004
Norway 2003
Poland 2004
Portugal 2004
Spain 2004
Sweden 2004
Switzerland 2005
Turkey 2004
United Kingdom 2005
United States 2005

70 60 50 40 30 20 10 0   %   0 10 20 30 40 50 60 70

Source: OECD. Table A9.4b, Table A9.4c. See Annex 3 for notes (*www.oecd.org/edu/eag2007*).
StatLink ⌨️💷 http://dx.doi.org/10.1787/068170623457

A9

Box A9.1. Variations in earnings by disciplines – the example of Canada

Though indicators present a single estimate for returns to a particular level of education, the variations and explanations behind such indicators are great. This box explores these variations for Canada. Data from three different cohorts of tertiary-type B graduates (1990, 1995 and 2000, along with earnings two years after graduation) suggest that earnings vary by discipline as well as by gender. The chart below shows that median earnings in 2002 (in 1997 constant Canadian dollars) for graduates from 2000 can be as high as $32 911 for male health graduates and as low $22 604 for women graduates of education. By reviewing the earnings of three different cohorts of graduates, the impact of labour market demands over a ten-year period can be shown. Gains over the period were evident for men and women who were graduates in fine arts, but they had the lowest median earnings. Those with degrees in health fields lost ground, however, although they had higher earnings than most other graduates. In general, women graduates earn slightly less compared to men with degrees in the same discipline.

Median earnings for three cohorts of tertiary-type B male and female graduates by discipline (1990, 1995, 2000)

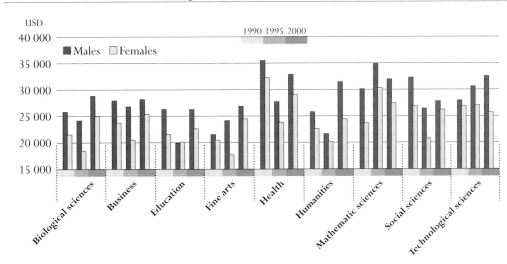

Source: Drewes, Torben (2006), *Returns to College Education: Evidence from the 1990, 1995, and 2000 National Graduates Surveys*, Learning Research Series, Human Resources and Social Development Canada.

Information on variation in earnings by disciplines is important information for students and other stakeholders, as well as an essential way of analysing how different disciplinary fields contribute to the economy. Similarly, accessing data over time on earnings by levels of education provides further information about the match between supply and demand. In addition, the analytical possibilities and the policy implications that can be drawn from trend data by fields of study are substantial. International comparable data would provide additional analytical potentials by connecting country specific and global trends. The Canadian illustration thus serves as an example to strive for in international data collections.

For more information, see:
http://www.hrsdc.gc.ca/en/cs/sp/hrsdc/lp/publications/sp-654-09-06/SP-654-09-06E.pdf

Rates of return to investment in education

The impact of education on earnings can be evaluated in the framework of investment analysis in which an individual incurs costs of getting an education (direct costs such as tuition while in school and indirect costs such as foregone earnings while in school). The effectiveness of this investment can be assessed by estimating the economic rate of return to the investment, which measures the degree to which the costs of attaining higher levels of education are translated into higher levels of earnings. The measure of return used here is the internal rate of return, which is effectively an interest rate that measures the economic return to an investment. This rate equates the costs required to attain the next highest level of education with the present value of a lifetime stream of additional earnings associated with the higher level of attainment. This indicator is analysed from two different points of view: rates of return to the individual (Tables A9.5 and A9.6), which reflect only the individual's earnings and costs, and rates of return to government (Tables A9.7 and A9.8). The return to government includes higher income tax and social contributions collected, as well as costs borne by the government. These private and public returns are calculated for 11 OECD countries.

Internal rates of return are computed for the attainment of two different levels of education: upper secondary education or post-secondary non-tertiary education, following from a lower secondary level of attainment (Tables A9.5 and A9.7); and tertiary education, following from an upper secondary or post-secondary non-tertiary level of educational attainment (Tables A9.6 and A9.8). Unlike the results presented in *Education at a Glance 2006* (OECD, 2006a), this year this indicator presents internal rates of return for obtaining upper secondary education or post-secondary non-tertiary education, following from a lower secondary level of attainment and based on the assumption that foregone earnings are fixed at the level of the minimum wage (when no national minimum wage was available, the wage was selected among wages determined in collective agreements). This implies that while in school obtaining an upper secondary level of education, the individual receives no earnings, compared with an individual at lower secondary level of education who receives the minimum wage or equivalent.

Internal rates of return are computed for two different periods in the individual's lifetime: immediately following initial education, and at the age of 40. In the latter, forgone earnings depends upon average earnings at the lower level of education and social benefits varying accross countries.

In addition, when calculating the internal rate of return at the age of 40, the analysis explores the impact on rates of return – for individuals and government – of the costs of education.

All results are presented separately for males and females.

Private internal rates of return to investment in education

The private internal rate of return for the individual is estimated on the basis of the additions to after-tax earnings that result from a higher level of educational attainment, net of the additional private costs (private expenditures and foregone earnings) that attaining this higher level of education requires. In general, the living expenses of students (cost of housing, meals, clothing, recreation, etc.) are excluded from these private expenditures.

Estimates of private rates of return for an individual who has invested in obtaining upper secondary or post-secondary non-tertiary education from an original lower secondary level of education are presented in Table A9.5. Estimates for an individual who has invested in obtaining a tertiary-level education, up to the attainment of an advanced research qualification starting from an upper secondary level of education are presented in Table A9.6.

Private rates of return were calculated for the following two scenarios:

1. The individual has continued directly to the next highest level of education before entering the labour market.

2. Attaining the next highest level of education has been postponed until the age of 40, when education is resumed on a full-time basis. Two cases are examined in this scenario: *i)* the individual bears the direct costs of tuition (as reported by national education authorities) and foregoes earnings (net of taxes) while studying; and *ii)* the individual bears no direct tuition costs, but again bears the cost of foregoing earnings.

The results show that for males, in all countries except Hungary, Norway and Switzerland, the rates of return to the attainment of upper secondary or post-secondary non-tertiary education exceed those for tertiary education.

At the upper secondary level, the private internal rate of return shows greater variability than at tertiary level, while the former varies from 4.6 to 24%, the latter is not below 8% (Table A9.5, A9.6). Private rates of return at the upper secondary level are seen to be higher for females than males in two countries: Hungary and New Zealand, and in five countries at the tertiary level: Belgium, Korea, New Zealand, Norway and the United Kingdom.

The results also show that when an individual attains the next higher level of education at age 40, private rates of return to tertiary education are generally higher than those for the achievement of upper secondary education, except in Denmark, New Zealand and the United States. At the tertiary level, the additional incentive created by eliminating tuition costs tends to be weak. At the upper secondary level, eliminating tuition costs results on average in 0.4 of a percentage point increase in the private rate of return for males and a 1.0 percentage point increase for females. At the tertiary level, eliminating tuition costs increases the private rate of return by 0.9 percentage points for males and 1.7 percentage points for females. Nevertheless, while in countries such as Denmark, Finland and Norway the impact on private rates of return from eliminating the student's tertiary-level tuition costs is small, the impact is significantly larger in Belgium, Hungary, Korea, the United Kingdom and the United States.

Public internal rates of return to investment in education

The public internal rate of return is one way of examining the effect on public-sector accounts of individuals' choices to invest in education and the effect of the different policy settings that affect these investments. For the public sector, the costs of education include direct expenditures on educational institutions (such as direct payment of teachers' salaries, direct payments for the construction of school buildings, and buying textbooks, etc.) and public private transfers (such as public subsidies to households for scholarships and other grants and to other private entities for the provision of training at the workplace, etc.). The public costs of education also include income tax revenues on students' foregone earnings. The benefits include increased revenues from income taxes on higher wages, plus social insurance payments. In practice, the achievement of higher levels of education will give rise to a complex set of fiscal effects on the benefit side, beyond the effects of

A9

wage and government payments-based revenue growth. For instance, better educated individuals generally experience superior health status, lowering public expenditure on the provision of health care. And, for some individuals, achieving higher levels of educational attainment may lower the likelihood of committing certain types of crime (see Indicator A10 in *Education at a Glance 2006*); this in turn reduces public expenditure. However, tax and expenditure data on such indirect effects of education are not readily available for inclusion in these rate-of-return calculations.

Estimates of public rates of return are shown in Tables A9.7 and A9.8. Table A9.7 presents public rates of return for an individual who has invested in obtaining upper secondary or post-secondary non-tertiary education (ISCED level 3/4), from an original lower secondary level of education. This estimate depends on the same assumption made for the private rate of return, *i.e.* an individual with a lower secondary level of education who earns the minimum wage or equivalent. Table A9.8 concerns an individual who has invested in obtaining a tertiary-level education, up to the attainment of an advanced research qualification (ISCED level 5(A, B)/6), starting from an upper secondary or post-secondary non-tertiary level of education (ISCED level 3/4).

As with the estimation of private rates of return, the calculation considered two scenarios:

1. Following initial education, the individual has continued directly to the next highest level of education, before entering the labour market.

2. Attaining the next highest level of education has been postponed until the age of 40, when education is resumed on a full-time basis. Two cases are examined in this scenario: *i)* the individual bears the direct costs of tuition (as reported by national education authorities) and foregoes earnings (net of taxes) while studying; and *ii)* the individual bears no direct tuition costs, but again bears the cost of foregoing earnings.

The results show that, for the achievement of the tertiary level of attainment during initial education, the public rate of return is in all cases lower than the private rate of return (except for Belgium, Korea and, for males, New Zealand). When the individual goes back to full-time education in mid-career, and bears the direct costs of tuition and foregone earnings, public rates of return for completing tertiary education are lower than private rates of return in all countries (Table A9.8). These low rates are driven by a number of factors including the high costs of providing education and high losses in tax receipts (when the individual in study foregoes earnings) relative to tax revenues (when the individual returns to work).

The results show that, for upper secondary education, the effect of the public sector bearing the individual's tuition costs is to lower the public rate of return by an average of 0.2 percentage points for males and 0.3 percentage points for females (Table A9.7). At the tertiary level, the average effect is to lower the public rate of return by about 0.7 of a percentage point for males and 1 percentage point for females. The magnitude of this decline in the public rate of return in the United States is noteworthy – 2.3 percentage points for males and 2.8 percentage points for females (Table A9.8) – which is partially explained by the high private contributions to the costs of tertiary education in the United States.

The interpretation of internal rates of return

For those who acquire upper secondary or tertiary education, high private internal rates of return in most countries (though not in all) indicate that human capital investment appears to be an attractive way for the average person to build wealth. Furthermore, and with some exceptions, policies that reduce or eliminate the direct costs of education are seen to have only a modest impact on individuals' decisions to invest in mid-career learning.

In many cases, the reported private internal rates of return are above – and in a number of countries significantly above – the risk-free real interest rate, which is typically measured with reference to rates applying on long-term government bonds. However, returns on human capital accumulation are not risk-free, as indicated by the wide distribution of earnings among the better educated. Moreover, not everyone who invests in a course of education actually completes the course. Rates of return will be low, and possibly negative, for individuals who drop out. Therefore, individuals contemplating an investment in education are likely to require a compensating risk premium. However, in a number of countries, the size of the premium of the internal rates of return over the real interest rate is higher than would seem to be warranted by considerations of risk alone. If returns to this form of investment are high, relative to investments of similar risk, there is some obstacle to individuals making the investment. High risk-adjusted private rates of return provide initial grounds for policy intervention to alleviate the relevant constraints.

For one, high rates of return indicate a shortage of better-educated workers, driving up earnings for these workers. Such a situation might be temporary, with high returns to education eventually generating enough supply response to push the rates into line with returns to other productive assets. However, the speed of adjustment would depend largely on the capacity of the education system to respond to the derived increase in demand and the capacity of the labour market to absorb the changing relative supplies of labour. The rebalancing mechanism could be accelerated by making better information about the returns to different courses of study available to students, helping them to make more informed choices.

Part of the high returns may also be compatible with market stability. According to this interpretation, the high internal rates of return would partly reflect economic rents on a scarce resource, namely ability and motivation. If the returns to education at the margin are lower, the case for public intervention to stimulate human capital accumulation is lessened if the quality of the marginal student cannot be improved. However, to the extent that the education system can improve both cognitive and non-cognitive skills of young people, education policy can make a significant contribution to efficiency and equity in the long run. The results from the OECD Programme for International Student Assessment (PISA) suggest that some countries succeed much better than others in securing high and equitable educational performances at the age of 15 years.

Internal rates of return to investment in education can also be viewed from a societal perspective. Such a perspective would combine both the private and public costs and benefits of additional education. For instance, the social cost of education would include foregone production of output during study periods as well as the full cost of providing education, rather than just the cost borne by the individual. A social rate of return should also include a range of possible indirect benefits of education, which also have economic repercussions, such as better health, more social cohesion and more informed and effective citizens. While data on social costs are available for most OECD countries, information on the full range of social benefits is less readily available. Indeed, for a number of possible external factors associated with education, current understanding of the nature and size of the effects is incomplete.

It is important to consider some of the broad conceptual limitations to estimating internal rates of return in the manner done here:

- The data reported are accounting rates of return only. The results would no doubt differ from econometric estimates that would rely, for example, on an earnings function approach, rather than on a lifetime stream of earnings derived from average empirical earnings.

- Estimates relate to levels of formal educational attainment only. They do not reflect the effects of learning outside of formal education.

- The approach used here estimates future earnings for individuals with different levels of educational attainment based on knowledge of how average gross earnings in the present vary by level of attainment and age. However, the relationship between different levels of educational attainment and earnings may not be the same in the future as it is today. Technological, economic and social change could all alter how wage levels relate to the level of educational attainment.

- As with the discussion of the interpretation of earnings dispersion data, differences in internal rates of return across countries in part reflect different institutional and non-market conditions that bear on earnings. Institutional settings that limit flexibility in relative earnings are a case in point.

- Estimates are based on average pre-tax earnings for persons at different levels of educational attainment. However, at a given level of educational attainment, individuals who have chosen different courses of study or who come from different social groups may register different rates of return.

- In estimating benefits, the effect of education in increasing the likelihood of employment is taken into account. However, this also makes the estimate sensitive to the stage in the economic cycle when the data were collected.

The rate-of-return calculations also involve a number of restrictive assumptions necessary for international comparability. In particular, it was not possible to include the effects on public accounts of changes in social transfer payments resulting from changes in wages. This is largely because the rules that govern eligibility for a broad range of social entitlements vary greatly across countries as well as by marital or civic status (and sometimes other criteria). Consequently, to ensure comparability, the rates of return have been calculated on the assumption that the individual in question is single and childless.

The above analyses could be extended in a number of ways, subject to data availability. In particular, more differentiated and comparable data relative to costs per student and a range of social transfer payments would be useful. Estimating changes in value added tax receipts resulting from the increased earnings acquired through obtaining higher levels of education would also contribute to a more complete assessment of impact on public accounts. The calculations do not consider that those with high earnings can often generate higher levels of income after age 64 as a consequence of their having superior pension arrangements.

Definitions and methodologies

Earnings data in Table A9.1a are based on an annual reference period in Austria, Canada, the Czech Republic, Denmark, Finland, Ireland, Italy, Korea, Luxembourg, Norway, Portugal, Spain, Sweden, Turkey and the United States. Earnings are reported weekly in Australia, New Zealand and the United Kingdom, and monthly in Belgium, France, Germany, Hungary, Poland and

Switzerland, and the partner economy Israel. Data on earnings are before income tax, while earnings for Belgium, Korea and Turkey are net of income tax. Data on earnings for individuals in part-time work are excluded for the Czech Republic, Hungary, Luxembourg and Poland, while data on part-year earnings are excluded for Hungary, Luxembourg and Poland.

The research regarding earnings determination in the United States is described in Bowles and Gintis (2000).

Earnings assumptions were made in calculating rates of return.

For the individual who decides to attain upper secondary education as part of his or her original education, the assumptions concerned the estimated level of foregone earnings fixed at the minimum wage (when no national minimum wage was available, the wage has been selected among wages determined in collective agreements). This assumption aims at counterbalancing the excessively low recorded earnings for 15-to-24-year-olds with lower secondary education, which caused excessively high estimates in earlier editions of *Education at a Glance*.

For the individual who decides to return to education in mid-career, the assumptions concerned the immediate earnings increase (10% relative to the level of earnings at the previous level of educational attainment) and the time required for convergence with the average wage of individuals already holding the next highest level of educational qualification (two years). These assumptions are somewhat *ad hoc*. Empirical evidence on the earnings of adults who return to work following part-time or full-time studies is scarce, especially for individuals attaining an upper secondary qualification. However, Canadian data indicate a convergence period of just two years for 30-to-49-year-olds who obtain a university degree, with a still shorter catch-up time for those who obtain a tertiary degree. It should be noted, nevertheless, that the Canadian data are derived from a small sample of individuals and do not control for the fact that those who invested in education may differ in important ways – such as motivation and inherent ability – by comparison with those who did not.

For the methods employed for the calculation of the rates of return in Tables A9.5 to A9.8, see Annex 3 at *www.oecd.org/edu/eag2007*.

Further references

The following additional material relevant to this indicator is available on line at:
StatLink ᗰᔕᒪ http://dx.doi.org/10.1787/068170623457

- *Table A9.2b Trends in relative earnings: male population (1997-2005)*
- *Table A9.2c Trends in relative earnings: female population (1997-2005)*
- *Table A9.4b Distribution of 25-to-64-year-old males by level of earnings and educational attainment (2005 or latest available year)*
- *Table A9.4c Distribution of 25-to-64-year-old females by level of earnings and educational attainment (2005 or latest available year)*

A9

Table A9.1a.

Relative earnings of the population with income from employment (2005 or latest available year)

By level of educational attainment and gender for 25-to-64-year-olds and 30-to-44-year-olds (upper secondary and post-secondary non-tertiary education = 100)

			Below upper secondary education		Post-secondary non-tertiary education		Tertiary-type B education		Tertiary-type A and advanced research programmes		All tertiary education	
			25-64	30-44	25-64	30-44	25-64	30-44	25-64	30-44	25-64	30-44
Australia	2005	Men	86	88	105	111	115	117	143	150	136	141
		Women	86	88	104	103	120	128	156	156	146	149
		M+W	81	83	96	99	110	113	139	141	131	134
Austria	2005	Men	76	73	131	136	122	119	173	164	149	144
		Women	74	75	122	119	145	132	168	170	156	151
		M+W	71	69	121	122	129	123	174	170	152	148
Belgium	2004	Men	91	93	100	103	117	120	153	151	137	137
		Women	82	84	106	110	127	127	155	160	137	139
		M+W	90	92	102	104	116	118	155	154	134	134
Canada	2004	Men	79	78	103	105	111	107	169	157	140	132
		Women	70	74	96	98	120	125	176	186	146	155
		M+W	78	78	102	104	110	108	168	161	138	134
Czech Republic	2005	Men	79	82	m	m	135	148	193	201	190	199
		Women	72	74	m	m	125	136	165	171	161	169
		M+W	72	76	m	m	125	139	185	194	181	191
Denmark	2004	Men	82	79	97	92	113	112	141	134	133	128
		Women	85	80	96	96	115	115	128	124	126	123
		M+W	82	80	103	98	115	116	129	124	126	122
Finland	2004	Men	91	88	m	m	131	125	180	168	161	150
		Women	97	92	m	m	129	125	165	160	146	141
		M+W	94	91	m	m	123	115	171	159	149	138
France	2005	Men	90	89	m	m	129	134	167	166	152	152
		Women	81	81	m	m	130	134	152	161	142	149
		M+W	86	87	m	m	125	131	157	161	144	148
Germany	2005	Men	93	95	114	117	128	126	159	152	151	144
		Women	77	80	117	117	117	113	161	160	151	149
		M+W	88	86	111	111	132	130	164	157	156	150
Hungary	2005	Men	76	76	127	127	138	144	253	269	253	268
		Women	72	75	117	117	131	134	188	194	188	194
		M+W	73	75	121	120	131	133	216	225	215	225
Ireland	2004	Men	83	87	104	107	111	114	178	167	157	150
		Women	72	76	101	101	134	132	190	199	170	175
		M+W	86	90	104	102	119	119	186	179	164	159
Italy	2004	Men	78	79	m	m	m	m	183	163	183	163
		Women	73	74	m	m	m	m	134	128	134	128
		M+W	79	81	m	m	m	m	160	143	160	143
Korea	2003	Men	73	83	m	m	103	109	138	132	127	125
		Women	75	91	m	m	138	146	201	227	176	195
		M+W	67	77	m	m	111	122	156	161	141	148
Luxembourg	2002	Men	79	78	114	137	132	139	170	176	149	156
		Women	74	67	120	129	120	125	145	150	131	137
		M+W	78	76	117	120	129	136	165	171	145	152
Netherlands	2002	Men	84	84	m	m	m	m	m	m	143	141
		Women	72	72	m	m	m	m	m	m	155	156
		M+W	84	84	m	m	m	m	m	m	148	147

Source: OECD. See Annex 3 for notes (*www.oecd.org/edu/eag2007*).

Please refer to the Reader's Guide for information concerning the symbols replacing missing data.

StatLink ⟲▣ http://dx.doi.org/10.1787/068170623457

Table A9.1a. *(continued)*
Relative earnings of the population with income from employment (2005 or latest available year)
By level of educational attainment and gender for 25-to-64-year-olds and 30-to-44-year-olds (upper secondary and post-secondary non-tertiary education = 100)

				Below upper secondary education		Post-secondary non-tertiary education		Tertiary-type B education		Tertiary-type A and advanced research programmes		All tertiary education	
				25-64	30-44	25-64	30-44	25-64	30-44	25-64	30-44	25-64	30-44
New Zealand	2005	Men		79	81	107	109	122	110	146	139	140	133
		Women		77	73	105	103	115	113	147	149	135	137
		M+W		78	79	105	106	108	102	144	141	132	131
Norway	2004	Men		84	88	118	113	143	143	139	137	140	138
		Women		82	86	121	116	148	151	141	142	142	143
		M+W		84	88	125	120	154	146	135	133	136	134
Poland	2004	Men		77	76	107	110	164	175	184	186	179	183
		Women		68	71	102	103	136	150	155	164	151	162
		M+W		78	80	99	100	154	166	166	170	163	169
Portugal	2004	Men		54	60	m	m	m	m	182	180	182	180
		Women		58	61	m	m	m	m	177	180	177	180
		M+W		57	62	m	m	m	m	179	179	179	179
Spain	2004	Men		84	83	83	87	107	105	144	141	132	128
		Women		78	79	95	62	97	100	156	158	141	144
		M+W		85	84	89	96	104	105	144	141	132	130
Sweden	2004	Men		85	81	121	124	107	106	145	140	135	132
		Women		87	82	105	107	114	106	133	129	127	122
		M+W		87	82	120	121	105	100	137	131	127	122
Switzerland	2005	Men		79	79	109	106	123	122	149	145	140	137
		Women		75	81	112	110	131	140	158	170	149	161
		M+W		76	80	109	108	139	142	164	165	156	157
Turkey	2004	Men		67	64	m	m	115	110	149	145	139	133
		Women		46	48	m	m	154	174	183	169	164	167
		M+W		65	63	m	m	121	119	152	143	141	135
United Kingdom	2005	Men		72	70	m	m	117	118	152	161	142	148
		Women		70	65	m	m	137	136	200	203	180	181
		M+W		69	71	m	m	123	124	169	177	155	161
United States	2005	Men		64	65	113	112	117	115	192	193	183	183
		Women		63	63	109	111	122	119	173	180	167	172
		M+W		67	67	110	110	117	114	183	183	175	175
Israel	2005	Men		74	62	107	112	119	113	179	185	159	162
		Women		72	66	120	122	119	119	177	188	157	165
		M+W		79	71	104	105	113	109	169	178	151	156

Left margin: OECD countries (New Zealand through United States); Partner economy (Israel).

Source: OECD. See Annex 3 for notes (*www.oecd.org/edu/eag2007*).
Please refer to the Reader's Guide for information concerning the symbols replacing missing data.
StatLink ᔟ᎙᏿ http://dx.doi.org/10.1787/068170623457

A9

Table A9.1b.
Differences in earnings between females and males (2005 or latest available year)
Average annual earnings of females as a percentage of males by level of educational attainment of 30-to-44-year-olds and 55-to-64-year-olds

		Below upper secondary education		Upper secondary and post-secondary non-tertiary education		Tertiary-type B education		Tertiary-type A and advanced research programmes		All levels of education	
		30-44	55-64	30-44	55-64	30-44	55-64	30-44	55-64	30-44	55-64
Australia	2005	58	59	58	56	64	62	61	60	62	59
Austria	2005	59	54	58	55	64	99	60	64	57	53
Belgium	2004	67	67	74	65	78	79	78	84	76	67
Canada	2004	53	50	55	56	64	55	65	57	63	54
Czech Republic	2005	67	78	75	90	69	79	64	74	69	81
Denmark	2004	71	70	70	72	72	71	65	64	72	69
Finland	2004	71	78	68	78	67	74	65	71	70	73
France	2005	67	65	74	71	74	62	72	64	74	62
Germany	2005	49	50	58	50	52	52	62	62	57	53
Hungary	2005	87	86	87	102	81	107	63	77	83	84
Ireland	2004	49	56	56	63	65	57	67	52	62	58
Italy	2004	69	76	75	70	m	m	59	55	74	70
Korea	2003	49	45	44	52	59	107	76	62	51	37
Luxembourg	2002	79	83	92	71	83	105	78	131	84	56
Netherlands	2002	51	47	60	47	m	m	m	m	62	50
New Zealand	2005	53	60	59	71	61	54	64	65	61	65
Norway	2004	61	63	63	65	66	69	65	63	66	63
Poland	2004	70	72	75	95	64	76	66	74	81	87
Portugal	2004	73	96	72	130	m	m	72	193	78	114
Spain	2004	64	57	68	67	64	56	76	74	75	65
Sweden	2004	73	76	72	73	72	77	66	68	72	74
Switzerland	2005	55	46	54	52	62	53	64	53	54	47
Turkey	2004	52	38	69	113	109	m	81	176	78	85
United Kingdom	2005	47	49	50	56	57	59	63	71	56	54
United States	2005	62	54	64	62	66	67	60	58	65	58
Israel	2005	61	48	57	56	60	51	58	58	62	58

Source: OECD. See Annex 3 for notes (*www.oecd.org/edu/eag2007*).
Please refer to the Reader's Guide for information concerning the symbols replacing missing data.
StatLink ⟪≣⟫ http://dx.doi.org/10.1787/068170623457

Table A9.2a.
Trends in relative earnings: adult population (1997-2005)
By educational attainment, for 25-to-64-year-olds (upper secondary and post-secondary non-tertiary education = 100)

A9

		1997	1998	1999	2000	2001	2002	2003	2004	2005
Australia	Below upper secondary	79	m	80	m	77	m	m	m	81
	Tertiary	124	m	134	m	133	m	m	m	131
Austria	Below upper secondary	m	m	m	m	m	m	m	m	71
	Tertiary	m	m	m	m	m	m	m	m	152
Belgium	Below upper secondary	m	m	m	92	m	91	89	90	m
	Tertiary	m	m	m	128	m	132	130	134	m
Canada	Below upper secondary	m	77	79	79	76	77	78	78	m
	Tertiary	m	141	141	145	146	139	140	138	m
Czech Republic	Below upper secondary	68	68	68	m	m	m	m	73	72
	Tertiary	179	179	179	m	m	m	m	182	181
Denmark	Below upper secondary	85	86	86	m	87	88	82	82	m
	Tertiary	123	124	124	m	124	124	127	126	m
Finland	Below upper secondary	97	96	96	m	95	95	94	94	m
	Tertiary	148	148	153	m	150	150	148	149	m
France	Below upper secondary	84	84	84	m	m	84	84	85	86
	Tertiary	149	150	150	m	m	152	146	147	144
Germany	Below upper secondary	81	78	79	75	m	77	87	88	88
	Tertiary	133	130	135	143	m	143	153	153	156
Hungary	Below upper secondary	68	68	70	71	71	74	74	73	73
	Tertiary	179	184	200	194	194	205	219	217	215
Ireland	Below upper secondary	75	79	m	89	m	76	m	86	m
	Tertiary	146	142	m	153	m	144	m	164	m
Italy	Below upper secondary	m	58	m	78	m	78	m	79	m
	Tertiary	m	127	m	138	m	153	m	160	m
Korea	Below upper secondary	m	78	m	m	m	m	67	m	m
	Tertiary	m	135	m	m	m	m	141	m	m
Luxembourg	Below upper secondary	m	m	m	m	m	78	m	m	m
	Tertiary	m	m	m	m	m	145	m	m	m
Netherlands	Below upper secondary	83	m	m	m	m	84	m	m	m
	Tertiary	141	m	m	m	m	148	m	m	m
New Zealand	Below upper secondary	77	76	76	74	74	m	76	75	78
	Tertiary	148	136	139	133	133	m	126	129	132
Norway	Below upper secondary	85	84	84	m	m	84	80	84	m
	Tertiary	138	132	133	m	m	135	126	136	m
Poland	Below upper secondary	m	m	m	m	m	m	m	78	m
	Tertiary	m	m	m	m	m	m	m	163	m
Portugal	Below upper secondary	62	62	62	m	m	m	m	57	m
	Tertiary	176	177	178	m	m	m	m	179	m
Spain	Below upper secondary	76	80	m	m	78	m	m	85	m
	Tertiary	149	144	m	m	129	m	m	132	m
Sweden	Below upper secondary	90	89	89	m	86	87	87	87	m
	Tertiary	129	130	131	m	131	130	128	127	m
Switzerland	Below upper secondary	74	75	76	78		77	75	74	76
	Tertiary	152	153	151	157		156	156	164	156
Turkey	Below upper secondary	m	m	m	m	m	m	m	65	m
	Tertiary	m	m	m	m	m	m	m	141	m
United Kingdom	Below upper secondary	64	65	65	67	67	91	69	67	69
	Tertiary	153	157	159	159	159	m	162	158	155
United States	Below upper secondary	70	67	65	65	m	66	66	65	67
	Tertiary	168	173	166	172	m	172	172	172	175
Israel	Below upper secondary	m	m	m	m	m	m	m	m	79
	Tertiary	m	m	m	m	m	m	m	m	151

(OECD countries: Australia through United States. Partner economy: Israel.)

Source: OECD. See Annex 3 for notes (*www.oecd.org/edu/eag2007*).
Please refer to the Reader's Guide for information concerning the symbols replacing missing data.
StatLink ᔼᒻᐳ http://dx.doi.org/10.1787/068170623457

A9

Table A9.3.
Trends in differences in earnings between females and males (1997-2005)
Average annual earnings of females as a percentage of males by level of educational attainment of 25-to-64-year-olds

		1997	1998	1999	2000	2001	2002	2003	2004	2005
Australia	Below upper secondary	60	m	66	m	62	m	m	m	61
	Upper secondary and post-secondary non tertiary	62	m	64	m	62	m	m	m	60
	Tertiary	62	m	67	m	63	m	m	m	65
Austria	Below upper secondary	m	m	m	m	m	m	m	m	57
	Upper secondary and post-secondary non tertiary	m	m	m	m	m	m	m	m	60
	Tertiary	m	m	m	m	m	m	m	m	62
Belgium	Below upper secondary	m	m	m	64	m	65	66	66	m
	Upper secondary and post-secondary non tertiary	m	m	m	72	m	72	74	74	m
	Tertiary	m	m	m	74	m	76	74	74	m
Canada	Below upper secondary	m	52	51	52	51	50	52	52	m
	Upper secondary and post-secondary non tertiary	m	59	60	60	59	61	60	59	m
	Tertiary	m	61	60	58	58	60	61	61	m
Czech Republic	Below upper secondary	66	66	66	m	m	m	m	74	74
	Upper secondary and post-secondary non tertiary	69	69	69	m	m	m	m	80	80
	Tertiary	66	65	65	m	m	m	m	67	68
Denmark	Below upper secondary	73	73	73	m	74	75	73	74	m
	Upper secondary and post-secondary non tertiary	72	71	71	m	71	73	71	71	m
	Tertiary	68	66	66	m	67	68	67	67	m
Finland	Below upper secondary	78	77	77	m	76	76	76	76	m
	Upper secondary and post-secondary non tertiary	74	72	72	m	71	72	72	72	m
	Tertiary	66	65	62	m	63	64	66	65	m
France	Below upper secondary	68	68	68	m	m	68	68	68	68
	Upper secondary and post-secondary non tertiary	75	75	75	m	m	75	75	74	75
	Tertiary	69	69	69	m	m	69	72	70	70
Germany	Below upper secondary	63	74	70	56	m	53	54	54	52
	Upper secondary and post-secondary non tertiary	64	67	68	63	m	61	60	60	62
	Tertiary	63	68	60	61	m	60	58	60	62
Hungary	Below upper secondary	79	80	84	83	83	85	89	89	88
	Upper secondary and post-secondary non tertiary	88	86	89	88	88	93	95	96	93
	Tertiary	64	63	62	62	62	67	71	72	69
Ireland	Below upper secondary	46	48	m	46	m	48	m	49	
	Upper secondary and post-secondary non tertiary	59	63	m	60	m	57	m	56	m
	Tertiary	70	70	m	71	m	62	m	61	m
Italy	Below upper secondary	m	70	m	76	m	70	m	69	m
	Upper secondary and post-secondary non tertiary	m	62	m	65	m	66	m	74	m
	Tertiary	m	52	m	62	m	60	m	54	m
Korea	Below upper secondary	m	56	m	m	m	m	48	m	m
	Upper secondary and post-secondary non tertiary	m	70	m	m	m	m	47	m	m
	Tertiary	m	75	m	m	m	m	65	m	m
Luxembourg	Below upper secondary	m	m	m	m	m	80	m	m	m
	Upper secondary and post-secondary non tertiary	m	m	m	m	m	86	m	m	m
	Tertiary	m	m	m	m	m	75	m	m	m
Netherlands	Below upper secondary	46	m	m	m	m	49	m	m	m
	Upper secondary and post-secondary non tertiary	56	m	m	m	m	58	m	m	m
	Tertiary	57	m	m	m	m	62	m	m	m

Note: Data on earnings for individuals in part-time work are excluded for the Czech Republic, Hungary, Luxembourg, Poland and Portugal, while data on part-year earnings are excluded for Belgium, Hungary, Luxembourg, Poland and Portugal.
Source: OECD. See Annex 3 for notes (*www.oecd.org/edu/eag2007*).
Please refer to the Reader's Guide for information concerning the symbols replacing missing data.
StatLink ⟶ http://dx.doi.org/10.1787/068170623457

A9

Table A9.3. *(continued)*
Trends in differences in earnings between females and males (1997-2005)
Average annual earnings of females as a percentage of males by level of educational attainment of 25-to-64-year-olds

		1997	1998	1999	2000	2001	2002	2003	2004	2005
New Zealand	Below upper secondary	52	61	65	61	61	m	65	66	61
	Upper secondary and post-secondary non tertiary	62	63	67	64	64	m	63	63	62
	Tertiary	60	59	61	67	67	m	62	62	60
Norway	Below upper secondary	60	60	61	m	m	61	63	63	m
	Upper secondary and post-secondary non tertiary	61	61	62	m	m	63	66	64	m
	Tertiary	63	62	62	m	m	64	66	65	m
Poland	Below upper secondary	m	m	m	m	m	m	m	71	m
	Upper secondary and post-secondary non tertiary	m	m	m	m	m	m	m	81	m
	Tertiary	m	m	m	m	m	m	m	68	m
Portugal	Below upper secondary	72	71	71	m	m	m	m	74	m
	Upper secondary and post-secondary non tertiary	69	69	69	m	m	m	m	69	m
	Tertiary	66	66	65	m	m	m	m	67	m
Spain	Below upper secondary	60	61	m	m	58	m	m	63	m
	Upper secondary and post-secondary non tertiary	72	76	m	m	71	m	m	68	m
	Tertiary	68	69	m	m	64	m	m	73	m
Sweden	Below upper secondary	73	74	74	m	74	74	75	75	m
	Upper secondary and post-secondary non tertiary	72	72	73	m	71	72	73	73	m
	Tertiary	67	66	67	m	65	67	68	69	m
Switzerland	Below upper secondary	51	51	53	51	m	51	52	54	53
	Upper secondary and post-secondary non tertiary	55	57	58	57	m	53	54	52	56
	Tertiary	60	61	62	62	m	59	60	58	60
Turkey	Below upper secondary	m	m	m	m	m	m	m	52	m
	Upper secondary and post-secondary non tertiary	m	m	m	m	m	m	m	75	m
	Tertiary	m	m	m	m	m	m	m	89	m
United Kingdom	Below upper secondary	47	50	51	50	50	m	52	52	50
	Upper secondary and post-secondary non tertiary	53	53	53	52	52	m	54	53	52
	Tertiary	60	62	63	64	64	m	64	63	66
United States	Below upper secondary	53	60	59	59	m	63	67	63	63
	Upper secondary and post-secondary non tertiary	59	62	61	60	m	63	64	63	65
	Tertiary	59	58	59	56	m	58	61	59	59
Israel	Below upper secondary	m	m	m	m	m	m	m	m	57
	Upper secondary and post-secondary non tertiary	m	m	m	m	m	m	m	m	59
	Tertiary	m	m	m	m	m	m	m	m	58

(Left margin labels: OECD countries; Partner economy)

Note: Data on earnings for individuals in part-time work are excluded for the Czech Republic, Hungary, Luxembourg, Poland and Portugal, while data on part-year earnings are excluded for Belgium, Hungary, Luxembourg, Poland and Portugal.
Source: OECD. See Annex 3 for notes (*www.oecd.org/edu/eag2007*).
Please refer to the Reader's Guide for information concerning the symbols replacing missing data.
StatLink ⊞ॼ⅃ http://dx.doi.org/10.1787/068170623457

A9

Table A9.4a.
Distribution of the 25-to-64-year-old population by level of earnings and educational attainment
(2005 or latest available year)

			Level of earnings					
			At or below half of the median	More than half the median but at or below the median	More than the median but at or below 1.5 times the median	More than 1.5 times the median but at or below 2.0 times the median	More than 2 times the median	All categories
			%	%	%	%	%	%
Australia	2005	Below upper secondary	24.3	46.3	21.1	5.6	2.8	100
		Upper secondary and post-secondary non-tertiary	14.5	39.2	29.9	10.0	6.4	100
		Tertiary-type B education	12.9	32.6	35.2	11.3	8.0	100
		Tertiary-type A and advanced research programmes	9.1	20.5	33.1	19.5	17.9	100
		All levels of education	15.5	35.1	28.9	11.6	8.9	100
Austria	2005	Below upper secondary	32.6	41.0	18.9	4.9	2.6	100
		Upper secondary and post-secondary non-tertiary	20.2	30.6	29.2	11.6	8.5	100
		Tertiary-type B education	11.9	17.1	30.3	23.8	16.8	100
		Tertiary-type A and advanced research programmes	15.0	13.4	15.7	19.3	36.6	100
		All levels of education	20.8	29.2	26.5	12.5	11.1	100
Belgium	2004	Below upper secondary	10.5	58.0	27.9	3.3	0.3	100
		Upper secondary and post-secondary non-tertiary	5.8	52.8	33.8	6.3	1.4	100
		Tertiary-type B education	2.1	35.3	48.4	12.0	2.2	100
		Tertiary-type A and advanced research programmes	1.6	17.8	37.3	26.7	16.7	100
		All levels of education	5.5	44.5	35.9	10.2	3.9	100
Canada	2004	Below upper secondary	37.9	29.6	16.9	8.9	6.7	100
		Upper secondary and post-secondary non-tertiary	27.6	26.5	23.0	11.6	11.2	100
		Tertiary-type B education	24.4	23.0	23.2	14.6	14.8	100
		Tertiary-type A and advanced research programmes	19.6	14.7	17.2	15.8	32.6	100
		All levels of education	26.5	23.4	20.8	13.0	16.3	100
Czech Republic	2005	Below upper secondary	18.7	65.3	13.7	1.7	0.7	100
		Upper secondary and post-secondary non-tertiary	5.1	49.8	34.1	7.7	3.3	100
		Tertiary-type B education	1.1	33.5	43.8	12.7	9.0	100
		Tertiary-type A and advanced research programmes	0.3	10.5	39.2	21.9	28.0	100
		All levels of education	5.4	44.6	33.3	9.6	7.2	100
Denmark	2004	Below upper secondary	25.3	41.3	26.9	4.4	2.2	100
		Upper secondary and post-secondary non-tertiary	16.2	35.8	35.8	7.8	4.3	100
		Tertiary-type B education	12.6	23.4	43.5	14.0	6.4	100
		Tertiary-type A and advanced research programmes	13.2	20.3	38.8	15.4	12.3	100
		All levels of education	17.6	32.4	34.8	9.2	5.9	100
Finland	2004	Below upper secondary	26.2	36.7	27.4	6.8	2.8	100
		Upper secondary and post-secondary non-tertiary	22.1	36.4	30.9	7.8	2.9	100
		Tertiary-type B education	13.8	27.2	39.6	12.3	7.1	100
		Tertiary-type A and advanced research programmes	11.3	16.4	27.4	22.1	22.8	100
		All levels of education	19.2	30.8	31.1	11.3	7.7	100
France	2005	Below upper secondary	16.6	51.8	23.9	5.5	2.2	100
		Upper secondary and post-secondary non-tertiary	8.4	46.1	32.7	8.8	4.0	100
		Tertiary-type B education	3.1	28.8	40.9	17.3	9.9	100
		Tertiary-type A and advanced research programmes	4.1	17.4	33.7	20.5	24.3	100
		All levels of education	9.4	40.9	31.3	10.8	7.5	100
Germany	2005	Below upper secondary	30.8	32.7	28.2	7.0	1.3	100
		Upper secondary and post-secondary non-tertiary	24.4	33.9	29.0	8.3	4.3	100
		Tertiary-type B education	12.8	25.4	32.3	18.0	11.5	100
		Tertiary-type A and advanced research programmes	14.2	17.1	24.9	20.7	23.0	100
		All levels of education	21.5	28.5	28.1	12.3	9.6	100

Source: OECD. See Annex 3 for notes (*www.oecd.org/edu/eag2007*).
Please refer to the Reader's Guide for information concerning the symbols replacing missing data.
StatLink http://dx.doi.org/10.1787/068170623457

A9

Table A9.4a. *(continued-1)*
Distribution of the 25-to-64-year-old population by level of earnings and educational attainment
(2005 or latest available year)

			Level of earnings					
			At or below half of the median	More than half the median but at or below the median	More than the median but at or below 1.5 times the median	More than 1.5 times the median but at or below 2.0 times the median	More than 2 times the median	All categories
			%	%	%	%	%	%
Hungary	2005	Below upper secondary	12.5	67.0	16.1	3.0	1.5	100
		Upper secondary and post-secondary non-tertiary	10.5	43.8	26.7	10.3	8.7	100
		Tertiary-type B education	8.3	29.4	30.0	10.6	21.8	100
		Tertiary-type A and advanced research programmes	2.1	6.7	23.4	24.4	43.5	100
		All levels of education	9.0	39.6	24.1	12.2	15.2	100
Ireland	2004	Below upper secondary	31.7	33.9	21.9	8.2	4.3	100
		Upper secondary and post-secondary non-tertiary	20.2	33.7	25.6	12.4	8.0	100
		Tertiary-type B education	11.5	30.1	29.0	15.6	13.8	100
		Tertiary-type A and advanced research programmes	9.6	14.9	19.3	22.7	33.5	100
		All levels of education	20.8	29.2	23.3	13.5	13.1	100
Italy	2004	Below upper secondary	20.0	44.2	24.0	5.5	6.2	100
		Upper secondary and post-secondary non-tertiary	10.3	33.6	34.1	10.7	11.4	100
		Tertiary-type B education	m	m	m	m	m	m
		Tertiary-type A and advanced research programmes	7.5	17.7	31.0	15.2	28.6	100
		All levels of education	14.0	36.0	29.4	9.1	11.5	100
Korea	2003	Below upper secondary	31.5	42.8	19.0	2.5	4.2	100
		Upper secondary and post-secondary non-tertiary	15.7	34.9	29.6	8.6	11.2	100
		Tertiary-type B education	14.5	30.8	31.0	11.3	12.4	100
		Tertiary-type A and advanced research programmes	8.6	17.5	29.7	17.1	27.0	100
		All levels of education	17.8	32.1	27.1	9.5	13.5	100
Luxembourg	2002	Below upper secondary	12.1	60.1	21.6	4.9	1.3	100
		Upper secondary and post-secondary non-tertiary	2.3	52.2	28.0	11.7	5.8	100
		Tertiary-type B education	0.6	28.6	41.7	17.2	11.8	100
		Tertiary-type A and advanced research programmes	0.0	14.4	36.6	24.9	24.1	100
		All levels of education	3.5	45.4	30.0	13.0	8.2	100
Netherlands	2002	Below upper secondary	26.9	37.9	29.0	5.0	1.3	100
		Upper secondary and post-secondary non-tertiary	17.4	36.5	33.2	9.3	3.6	100
		All tertiary education	8.3	20.8	30.5	21.9	18.6	100
		All levels of education	17.4	32.6	31.3	11.6	7.1	100
New Zealand	2005	Below upper secondary	22.9	48.4	20.8	5.4	2.5	100
		Upper secondary and post-secondary non-tertiary	17.4	34.1	28.8	11.5	8.2	100
		Tertiary-type B education	16.9	29.3	30.8	11.2	11.7	100
		Tertiary-type A and advanced research programmes	11.5	21.9	26.9	19.4	20.3	100
		All levels of education	17.0	33.5	27.2	12.1	10.2	100
Norway	2004	Below upper secondary	30.1	37.1	25.5	5.1	2.2	100
		Upper secondary and post-secondary non-tertiary	20.4	35.4	32.2	8.1	4.0	100
		Tertiary-type B education	8.7	15.3	34.7	22.8	18.4	100
		Tertiary-type A and advanced research programmes	12.3	22.0	40.1	13.5	12.1	100
		All levels of education	19.0	31.0	33.7	9.7	6.6	100
Poland	2004	Below upper secondary	17.0	54.4	21.0	5.7	1.9	100
		Upper secondary and post-secondary non-tertiary	8.5	44.7	29.1	10.7	7.0	100
		Tertiary-type B education	4.2	27.9	28.0	15.6	24.3	100
		Tertiary-type A and advanced research programmes	1.2	16.6	35.6	20.8	25.8	100
		All levels of education	9.6	41.0	27.6	11.4	10.4	100

OECD countries

Source: OECD. See Annex 3 for notes (*www.oecd.org/edu/eag2007*).
Please refer to the Reader's Guide for information concerning the symbols replacing missing data.
StatLink ﹏ http://dx.doi.org/10.1787/068170623457

A9

Table A9.4a. *(continued-2)*
Distribution of the 25-to-64-year-old population by level of earnings and educational attainment
(2005 or latest available year)

				Level of earnings					
			At or below half of the median	More than half the median but at or below the median	More than the median but at or below 1.5 times the median	More than 1.5 times the median but at or below 2.0 times the median	More than 2 times the median	All categories
			%	%	%	%	%	%
Portugal	2004	Below upper secondary	0.0	61.6	23.2	7.7	7.5	100
		Upper secondary and post-secondary non-tertiary	0.0	32.9	27.8	15.1	24.2	100
		Tertiary-type B education	m	m	m	m	m	m
		Tertiary-type A and advanced research programmes	0.0	7.1	16.5	18.3	58.2	100
		All levels of education	0.0	50.0	23.2	10.3	16.5	100
Spain	2004	Below upper secondary	12.8	50.8	29.0	5.2	2.2	100
		Upper secondary and post-secondary non-tertiary	9.3	42.6	31.6	10.2	6.3	100
		Tertiary-type B education	7.8	43.8	30.6	10.6	7.1	100
		Tertiary-type A and advanced research programmes	3.3	22.8	33.2	19.9	20.7	100
		All levels of education	9.1	41.0	30.9	10.7	8.4	100
Sweden	2004	Below upper secondary	18.6	44.0	31.1	4.8	1.6	100
		Upper secondary and post-secondary non-tertiary	11.1	41.9	34.9	8.0	4.1	100
		Tertiary-type B education	12.9	31.1	39.8	11.4	4.9	100
		Tertiary-type A and advanced research programmes	10.6	21.5	36.4	15.3	16.3	100
		All levels of education	12.8	37.2	34.8	9.1	6.1	100
Switzerland	2005	Below upper secondary	29.2	51.7	16.9	1.3	0.9	100
		Upper secondary and post-secondary non-tertiary	21.3	35.4	32.3	7.9	3.1	100
		Tertiary-type B education	8.6	20.5	39.7	20.0	11.2	100
		Tertiary-type A and advanced research programmes	8.7	19.0	25.9	23.4	23.0	100
		All levels of education	18.0	31.8	30.2	12.0	8.1	100
Turkey	2004	Below upper secondary	28.2	39.5	20.2	7.7	4.4	100
		Upper secondary and post-secondary non-tertiary	12.1	26.1	29.6	17.1	15.0	100
		Tertiary-type B education	5.8	11.8	25.4	32.8	24.2	100
		Tertiary-type A and advanced research programmes	4.3	9.6	27.8	31.0	27.2	100
United Kingdom	2005	Below upper secondary	34.9	46.0	14.3	3.4	1.4	100
		Upper secondary and post-secondary non-tertiary	20.0	38.8	23.9	10.5	6.9	100
		Tertiary-type B education	10.3	28.0	28.8	20.4	12.5	100
		Tertiary-type A and advanced research programmes	6.3	15.4	23.4	25.2	29.7	100
		All levels of education	17.3	33.1	23.3	14.1	12.2	100
United States	2005	Below upper secondary	41.7	40.4	12.2	3.9	1.8	100
		Upper secondary and post-secondary non-tertiary	23.5	36.2	21.3	11.3	7.8	100
		Tertiary-type B education	16.4	31.0	25.2	16.7	10.7	100
		Tertiary-type A and advanced research programmes	11.4	19.2	21.4	18.3	29.7	100
		All levels of education	20.3	29.9	20.7	13.5	15.7	100
Partner economy **Israel**	2005	Below upper secondary	22.4	54.4	16.4	3.7	3.1	100
		Upper secondary and post-secondary non-tertiary	16.7	43.1	22.6	8.7	9.0	100
		Tertiary-type B education	16.3	36.6	23.0	10.3	13.8	100
		Tertiary-type A and advanced research programmes	10.5	24.9	20.5	13.1	31.1	100
		All levels of education	14.6	35.4	21.4	10.4	18.2	100

Source: OECD. See Annex 3 for notes (*www.oecd.org/edu/eag2007*).
Please refer to the Reader's Guide for information concerning the symbols replacing missing data.
StatLink ᛜᔖ http://dx.doi.org/10.1787/068170623457

Table A9.5.
Private internal rates of return for an individual obtaining an upper secondary or post-secondary non-tertiary education, ISCED 3/4 (2003)
Assuming that all individual after lower secondary level of education will receive the minimum wage

	Rate of return when the individual immediately acquires the next higher level of education		Rate of return when the individual, at age 40, begins the next higher level of education in full time studies, and the individual bears:			
			Direct costs and foregone earnings		No direct costs but foregone earnings	
	Males %	Females %	Males %	Females %	Males %	Females %
Belgium	14.8	11.6	9.0	24.4	9.3	25.8
Denmark	16.2	12.7	12.8	12.9	13.0	13.1
Finland	17.3	11.6	-0.5	2.6	-0.5	2.7
Hungary	12.0	13.4	11.4	13.7	11.7	14.1
Korea	14.0	8.6	13.2	12.2	13.6	13.1
New Zealand	14.1	14.9	10.3	7.3	10.7	7.8
Norway	9.0	7.3	9.3	10.8	9.7	11.9
Sweden	18.7	13.1	7.7	5.4	7.7	5.4
Switzerland	7.0	4.6	10.2	10.2	12.1	15.6
United Kingdom	21.3	19.2	8.2	9.0	8.6	9.8
United States	23.9	19.7	20.9	18.7	21.4	19.3

Note: Negative benefits occur when excessively high forgone earnings cause excessively low estimates.
Source: OECD. See Annex 3 for notes (*www.oecd.org/edu/eag2007*).
StatLink ⌗ http://dx.doi.org/10.1787/068170623457

Table A9.6.
Private internal rates of return for an individual obtaining a university-level degree, ISCED 5/6 (2003)

	Rate of return when the individual immediately acquires the next higher level of education		Rate of return when the individual, at age 40, begins the next higher level of education in full time studies, and the individual bears:			
			Direct costs and foregone earnings		No direct costs but foregone earnings	
	Males %	Females %	Males %	Females %	Males %	Females %
Belgium	10.7	15.2	20.0	28.2	21.1	32.2
Denmark	8.3	8.1	12.4	10.2	12.5	10.5
Finland	16.7	16.0	16.2	13.2	16.4	13.4
Hungary	22.6	15.0	25.1	19.4	27.8	22.0
Korea	12.2	14.9	15.0	27.7	15.9	31.1
New Zealand	9.3	12.9	6.5	7.5	7.2	8.8
Norway	12.1	15.7	15.6	15.9	15.8	16.2
Sweden	8.9	8.2	10.4	8.2	10.8	8.7
Switzerland	10.0	9.8	10.9	20.6	11.3	22.2
United Kingdom	16.8	19.6	11.4	14.9	12.5	16.8
United States	14.3	13.1	12.9	9.7	15.1	13.0

Source: OECD. See Annex 3 for notes (*www.oecd.org/edu/eag2007*).
StatLink ⌗ http://dx.doi.org/10.1787/068170623457

A9

Table A9.7.
**Public internal rates of return for an individual obtaining an upper secondary
or post-secondary non-tertiary education, ISCED 3/4 (2003)**
Assuming that all individual after lower secondary level of education will receive the minimum wage

	Rate of return when the individual immediately acquires the next higher level of education		Rate of return when the individual, at age 40, begins the next higher level of education in full time studies, and the individual bears:			
			Direct costs and foregone earnings		No direct costs but foregone earnings	
	Males %	Females %	Males %	Females %	Males %	Females %
Belgium	11.4	9.4	2.2	6.4	2.1	6.2
Denmark	11.1	8.5	2.1	1.9	2.1	1.9
Finland	8.2	4.7	-9.2	-2.6	-9.2	-2.6
Hungary	8.3	8.9	3.3	5.9	3.2	5.7
Korea	6.7	3.0	3.2	3.7	2.6	3.0
New Zealand	8.3	5.2	3.0	-2.2	2.7	-2.4
Norway	5.5	3.5	0.4	-0.2	0.2	-0.4
Sweden	10.4	6.9	-0.2	-0.1	-0.2	-0.1
Switzerland	1.7	2.4	-4.1	-3.1	-4.6	-3.7
United Kingdom	13.4	10.6	4.8	4.1	4.3	3.4
United States	12.5	9.7	14.2	13.1	13.7	12.5

OECD countries

Note: Negative benefits occur when excessively high forgone earnings cause excessively low estimates.
Source: OECD. See Annex 3 for notes (*www.oecd.org/edu/eag2007*).
StatLink ▄ɪ§▄ http://dx.doi.org/10.1787/068170623457

Table A9.8.
Public internal rates of return for an individual obtaining a university-level degree, ISCED 5/6 (2003)

	Rate of return when the individual immediately acquires the next higher level of education		Rate of return when the individual, at age 40, begins the next higher level of education in full time studies, and the individual bears:			
			Direct costs and foregone earnings		No direct costs but foregone earnings	
	Males %	Females %	Males %	Females %	Males %	Females %
Belgium	12.2	17.9	10.6	9.4	10.3	9.0
Denmark	7.8	6.9	3.4	1.0	3.3	0.9
Finland	13.6	11.3	10.7	8.7	10.6	8.6
Hungary	18.8	13.1	14.8	10.3	13.6	9.2
Korea	14.2	16.8	7.4	17.2	5.9	13.1
New Zealand	9.9	9.9	2.4	2.1	1.7	1.2
Norway	9.5	9.9	4.3	4.5	4.3	4.5
Sweden	7.5	6.3	3.6	1.8	3.4	1.6
Switzerland	6.3	5.8	-0.1	-0.7	-0.2	-0.9
United Kingdom	13.7	16.1	6.4	8.4	5.6	7.1
United States	14.1	13.0	9.6	6.0	7.3	3.2

OECD countries

Source: OECD. See Annex 3 for notes (*www.oecd.org/edu/eag2007*).
StatLink ▄ɪ§▄ http://dx.doi.org/10.1787/068170623457

Chapter

B

FINANCIAL AND HUMAN RESOURCES INVESTED IN EDUCATION

Classification of educational expenditure

Educational expenditure in this chapter are classified through three dimensions:

- The first dimension – represented by the horizontal axis in the diagram below – relates to the location where spending occurs. Spending on schools and universities, education ministries and other agencies directly involved in providing and supporting education is one component of this dimension. Spending on education outside these institutions is another.

- The second dimension – represented by the vertical axis in the diagram below – classifies the goods and services that are purchased. Not all expenditure on educational institutions can be classified as direct educational or instructional expenditure. Educational institutions in many OECD countries offer various ancillary services – such as meals, transports, housing, etc. – in addition to teaching services to support students and their families. At the tertiary level spending on research and development can be significant. Not all spending on educational goods and services occurs within educational institutions. For example, families may purchase textbooks and materials themselves or seek private tutoring for their children.

- The third dimension – represented by the colours in the diagram below – distinguishes among the sources from which funding originates. These include the public sector and international agencies (indicated by the light blue colour), and households and other private entities (indicated by the medium-blue colour). Where private expenditure on education is subsidised by public funds, this is indicated by cells in the dark blue colour.

▫ Public sources of funds	▪ Private sources of funds	▪ Private funds publicly subsidised

	Spending on educational institutions (*e.g.* schools, universities, educational administration and student welfare services)	Spending on education outside educational institutions (*e.g.* private purchases of educational goods and services, including private tutoring)
Spending on educational core services	*e.g.* public spending on instructional services in educational institutions	*e.g.* subsidised private spending on books
	e.g. subsidised private spending on instructional services in educational institutions	*e.g.* private spending on books and other school materials or private tutoring
	e.g. private spending on tuition fees	
Spending on research and development	*e.g.* public spending on university research	
	e.g. funds from private industry for research and development in educational institutions	
Spending on educational services other than instruction	*e.g.* public spending on ancillary services such as meals, transport to schools, or housing on the campus	*e.g.* subsidised private spending on student living costs or reduced prices for transport
	e.g. private spending on fees for ancillary services	*e.g.* private spending on student living costs or transport

Coverage diagrams

For Indicators **B1, B2** and **B3**

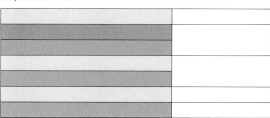

For Indicators **B4** and **B5**

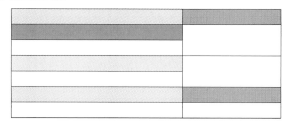

For Indicator **B6**

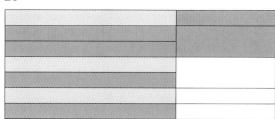

HOW MUCH IS SPENT PER STUDENT?

This indicator provides an assessment of the investment made in each student. Expenditure per student is largely influenced by teacher salaries (see Indicators B6 and D3), pension systems, instructional and teaching hours (see Indicators D1 and D4), teaching materials and facilities, the programme orientation provided to pupils/students (see Indicator C2) and the number of students enrolled in the education system (see Indicator C1). Policies put in place to attract new teachers or to reduce average class size or staffing patterns (see Indicator D2) have also contributed to changes over the time in expenditure per student.

Key results

Chart B1.1. **Annual expenditure on educational institutions per student in primary through tertiary education (2004)**

Expenditure on educational institutions per student gives a measure of unit costs in formal education. This chart expresses annual expenditure on educational institutions per student in equivalent USD converted using purchasing power parities, based on full-time equivalents.

OECD countries as a whole spend USD 7 572 per student annually between primary and tertiary education, that is – USD 5 331 per primary student, USD 7 163 per secondary student and USD 14 027 per tertiary student, but these averages mask a broad range of expenditure across countries. As represented by the simple average across all OECD countries, countries spend twice as much per student at the tertiary level than at the primary level.

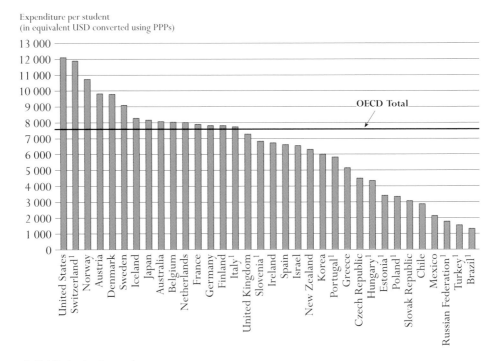

Expenditure per student
(in equivalent USD converted using PPPs)

1. Public institutions only.
Countries are ranked in descending order of expenditure on educational institutions per student.
Source: OECD. Tables B1.1a. See Annex 3 for notes (*www.oecd.org/edu/eag2007*).
StatLink ⌨ http://dx.doi.org/10.1787/068176572003

Other highlights of this indicator

▪ Excluding R&D activities and ancillary services, expenditure on educational core services in tertiary institutions represents on average USD 7 664 and ranges from USD 4 500 or below in Greece, Italy, Poland and Turkey to more than USD 9 000 in Australia, Austria, Denmark, Norway, Switzerland and the United States.

▪ OECD countries spend on average USD 81 485 per student over the theoretical duration of primary and secondary studies. The cumulative expenditure for each primary and secondary student ranges from less than USD 40 000 in Mexico, Poland, the Slovak Republic and Turkey, and the partner economies Brazil, Chile, Estonia and the Russian Federation, to USD 100 000 or more in Austria, Denmark, Iceland, Luxembourg, Norway, Switzerland and the United States.

▪ Lower unit expenditure does not necessarily lead to lower achievement and it would be misleading to equate lower unit expenditure generally with lower quality of educational services. For example, the cumulative expenditure of Korea and the Netherlands is below the OECD average and yet both are among the best-performing countries in the PISA 2003 survey.

▪ Countries with low levels of expenditure per student can nevertheless show distributions of investment relative to GDP per capita similar to those countries with high levels of spending per student. For example, Hungary, Korea, Poland and Portugal, and the partner economy Estonia – countries with expenditure per student and GDP per capita below the OECD average at primary, secondary and post-secondary non-tertiary level of education – spend a higher proportion of money per student relative to GDP per capita than the OECD average.

▪ Expenditure on education tends to rise over time in real terms, as teachers' pay (the main component of costs) rises in line with general earnings. On the one hand, rising unit costs that are not paralleled by increasing outcomes raise the spectre of falling productivity levels in education. This differs considerably across educational sectors. Expenditure per student at primary, secondary and post-secondary non-tertiary levels increased by 50% or more between 1995 and 2004 in Greece, Hungary, Ireland, Poland, Portugal, the Slovak Republic and Turkey, and the partner economy Chile. On the other hand, spending per student at the tertiary level has in some cases fallen, as expenditure does not keep up with expanding student numbers.

Policy context

Annual and cumulative expenditure on education per student in absolute terms and relative to GDP per capita

B1

Effective schools require the right combination of trained and talented personnel, adequate facilities, and motivated students ready to learn. The demand for high-quality education, which can translate into higher costs per student, must be balanced against placing undue burden on taxpayers.

As a result, the question of whether the resources devoted to education yield adequate returns to the investments made figures prominently in the public debate. Although it is difficult to assess the optimal volume of resources required to prepare each student for life and work in modern societies, international comparisons of spending on education per student can provide a starting point for evaluating the effectiveness of different models of educational provision.

Trends in the development of expenditure on education per student

Policy makers must balance the importance of improving the quality of educational services with the desirability of expanding access to educational opportunities, notably at the tertiary level. The comparative review of how trends in educational expenditure per student have evolved shows that in many OECD countries the expansion of enrolments, particularly in tertiary education, has not always been paralleled by changes in educational investment.

In addition, decisions on the allocation of funds among the various levels of education are also important. For example, some OECD countries emphasise broad access to higher education and some invest in near-universal education for children as young as 3 or 4 years old.

Evidence and explanations

What this indicator covers and what it does not cover

The indicator shows direct public and private expenditure on educational institutions in relation to the number of full-time equivalent students enrolled in these institutions.

Public subsidies for students' living expenses have been excluded to ensure international comparability of the data. Expenditure data for students in private educational institutions are not available for certain OECD countries, and some other countries do not provide complete data on independent private institutions. Where this is the case, only the expenditure on public and government-dependent private institutions has been taken into account. Note that variation in expenditure on education per student may reflect not only variation in the material resources provided to students (*e.g.* variations in the ratio of students to teaching staff) but also variation in relative salary and price levels.

At the primary and secondary levels, educational expenditure is dominated by spending on instructional services; at the tertiary level, other services – particularly those related to R&D activities or ancillary services – can account for a significant proportion of educational spending. Indicator B6 provides further information on how spending is distributed by different types of services provided.

B1

Chart B1.2. **Annual expenditure on educational institutions per student for all services, by level of education (2004)**

In equivalent USD converted using PPPs, based on full-time equivalents

Expenditure per student
(equivalent USD converted using PPPs)

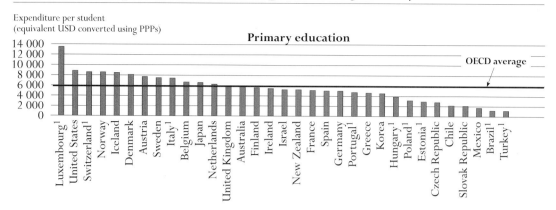

Primary education

OECD average

■ Secondary education   ◇ Lower secondary education   ◆ Upper secondary education

Expenditure per student
(equivalent USD converted using PPPs)

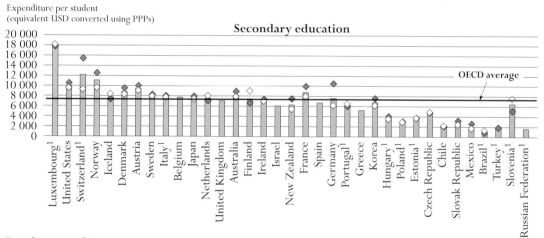

Secondary education

OECD average

Expenditure per student
(equivalent USD converted using PPPs)

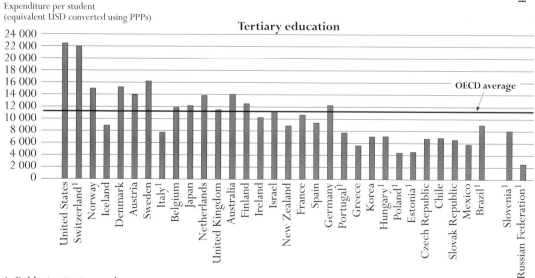

Tertiary education

OECD average

1. Public institutions only.
Countries are ranked in descending order of expenditure per student in primary education.
Source: OECD. Table B1.1a. See Annex 3 for notes (*www.oecd.org/edu/eag2007*).

StatLink ᗑᒕ http://dx.doi.org/10.1787/068176572003

Expenditure on education per student in equivalent USD

B1

Annual expenditure per student on educational institutions from primary through tertiary education provides an assessment of the investment made in each student. OECD countries as a whole spend on average USD 7 572 per student annually for students enrolled in primary through tertiary education. In 11 out of 34 OECD countries and partner economies, spending on education falls between USD 6 000 and 8 000 per student. Spending on education at these levels ranges from USD 4 000 per student or less in Mexico, Poland, the Slovak Republic and Turkey, and the partner economies Brazil, Chile, Estonia and the Russian Federation, to more than USD 9 000 per student in Austria, Denmark, Norway, Sweden, Switzerland and the United States (Table B1.1a). The drivers of expenditure per student vary across countries: among the five countries with the highest expenditure per student enrolled in primary through tertiary education, Switzerland is one of the countries with the highest teachers' salaries at the secondary level (see Indicator D3), the United States is one of the countries with the highest level of private expenditure at tertiary level of education whereas Austria, Denmark and Norway are among the countries with the lowest student to teaching staff ratio (see Indicator D2).

Even if overall spending per student is similar in some OECD countries, the ways in which resources are allocated across the different levels of education vary widely. OECD countries as a whole spend USD 5 331 per student at the primary level, USD 7 163 per student at the secondary level and USD 14 027 per student at the tertiary level. At the tertiary level, these totals are influenced by high expenditure in a few large OECD countries, most notably the United States. Spending on education per student in a typical OECD country (as represented by the simple mean across all OECD countries) amounts to USD 5 832 at the primary level, USD 7 276 at the secondary level and USD 11 100 at the tertiary level (Table B1.1a and Chart B1.2).

These averages mask a broad range of expenditure on education per student across OECD countries and partner economies. At the primary level, expenditure on educational institutions ranges from less than USD 1 200 per student in Turkey and the partner economy Brazil to USD 13 458 per student in Luxembourg. Differences among OECD countries are even greater at the secondary level, where spending on education per student varies by a factor of 15, from USD 1 033 in Brazil to USD 17 876 in Luxembourg. Expenditure on education per tertiary student ranges from USD 2 562 in the Russian Federation to more than USD 21 000 in Switzerland and the United States (Table B1.1a and Chart B1.2).

These comparisons are based on purchasing power parities for GDP, not on market exchange rates. They therefore reflect the amount of a national currency required to produce the same basket of goods and services in a given country as that produced by the USD in the United States.

Expenditure on educational core services per student

On average, OECD countries for which data are available spend USD 5 745 on core educational services at primary, secondary and post secondary non-tertiary levels, which corresponds to 86% of the total expenditure per student at these levels. In 16 out of the 26 OECD countries and partner economies with available data, ancillary services provided by primary, secondary and post-secondary non-tertiary institutions account for less than 5% of the total expenditure per student. This proportion exceeds 10% of the total expenditure per student in a small group of countries including Finland, France, Hungary, the Slovak Republic and Sweden.

Chart B1.3. Annual expenditure on educational institutions per student relative to GDP per capita, by service category and level of education (2004)

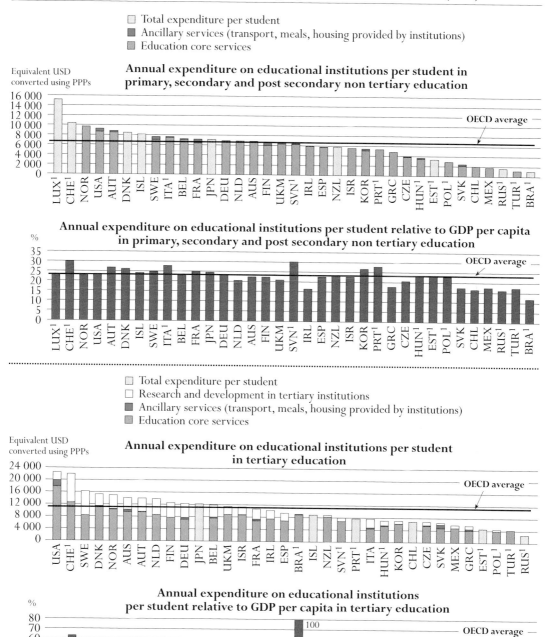

☐ Total expenditure per student
■ Ancillary services (transport, meals, housing provided by institutions)
■ Education core services

Equivalent USD converted using PPPs

Annual expenditure on educational institutions per student in primary, secondary and post secondary non tertiary education

Annual expenditure on educational institutions per student relative to GDP per capita in primary, secondary and post secondary non tertiary education

☐ Total expenditure per student
☐ Research and development in tertiary institutions
■ Ancillary services (transport, meals, housing provided by institutions)
■ Education core services

Equivalent USD converted using PPPs

Annual expenditure on educational institutions per student in tertiary education

Annual expenditure on educational institutions per student relative to GDP per capita in tertiary education

Note: Please refer to the Reader's Guide for the list of country codes used in this chart.
1. Public institutions only.
Countries are ranked in descending order of expenditure per student for all services.
Source: OECD. Tables B1.1b and B1.4. See Annex 3 for notes (*www.oecd.org/edu/eag2007*).
StatLink ⓘ http://dx.doi.org/10.1787/068176572003

More differences in expenditure per student on core educational services compared to total expenditure are observed at the tertiary level. OECD countries in which most R&D is performed by tertiary educational institutions tend to report higher expenditure per tertiary student than countries in which a large part of R&D is performed in other public institutions or by industry. Excluding R&D activities and ancillary services, expenditure on core educational services in tertiary institutions represents, on average, USD 7 664 and ranges from USD 4 500 or below in Greece, Italy, Poland and Turkey to more than USD 9 000 in Australia, Austria, Denmark, Norway, Switzerland and the United States (Table B1.1b).

On average, expenditure on R&D and ancillary services at the tertiary level represents respectively 29 and 4% of all tertiary expenditure per student. In 8 out of 27 OECD countries and partner economies for which tertiary expenditure is available for every service category – Belgium, Finland, France, Germany, Italy, the Netherlands, Sweden and Switzerland – R&D expenditure and ancillary services in tertiary institutions represents 35% or more of total tertiary expenditure per student. On a per student basis this can translate into significant amounts, as in Finland, Germany, the Netherlands, Norway, Sweden, Switzerland and the United States, expenditure for R&D and ancillary services in tertiary institutions amounts to more than USD 4 500 per student (Chart B1.3 and Table B1.1b).

Differences in educational expenditure per student between levels of education

Expenditure on education per student exhibits a common pattern throughout OECD countries: in each OECD country, spending rises sharply from primary to tertiary education. This pattern can be understood by looking at the main determinants of expenditure, particularly the location and mode of educational provision. The vast majority of education still takes place in traditional school settings with (generally) similar organisation, curriculum, teaching style and management. These shared features are likely to lead to similar patterns of unit expenditure.

Comparisons of the distribution of expenditure between levels of education indicate the relative emphasis placed on education at different levels in various OECD countries, as well as of the relative costs of providing education at those levels.

Although expenditure on education per student rises with the level of education (from primary to tertiary) in almost all OECD countries and partner economies, the relative sizes of the differentials vary markedly among countries (Chart B1.4). At the secondary level, expenditure on education per student is, on average, 1.2 times that at the primary level, and the difference exceeds 1.5 in the Czech Republic, France, Germany, Korea and Turkey. These five OECD countries have similar patterns with a significant increase of the number of instructional hours received by the students between primary and secondary education combined to a decrease compared to the OECD average in the number of teaching hours given by teachers between these two levels of education (see Indicators D1 and D4).

OECD countries spend, on average, 2.0 times as much on education per student at the tertiary level than at the primary level, but spending patterns vary widely among countries. For example, whereas Greece, Iceland, Italy and Poland only spend between 1.1 and 1.5 times as much on a student in tertiary education as on a student in primary education, Mexico, the Slovak Republic and Turkey, and the partner economies Brazil and Chile, spend more than 3.0 times on a student at the tertiary level (Chart B1.4).

B1

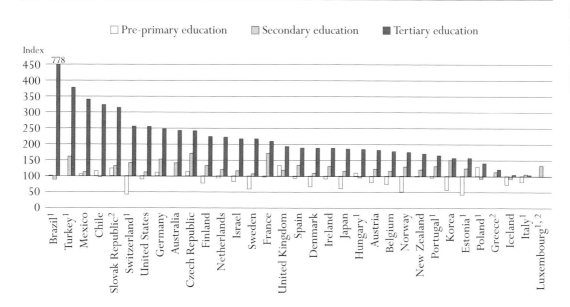

Chart B1.4. Expenditure on educational institutions per student at various levels of education for all services relative to primary education (2004)
Primary education = 100

□ Pre-primary education   ▨ Secondary education   ■ Tertiary education

Note: A ratio of 300 for tertiary education means that expenditure on educational institutions per tertiary student is three times the expenditure on educational institutions per primary student. A ratio of 50 for pre-primary education means that expenditure on educational institutions per pre-primary student is half the expenditure on educational institutions per primary student.
1. Public institutions only.
2. Some levels of education are included with others. Refer to "x" code in Table B1.1a for details.
Countries are ranked in descending order of expenditure on educational institutions per student in tertiary education relative to primary education.
Source: OECD. Table B1.1a. See Annex 3 for notes (*www.oecd.org/edu/eag2007*).
StatLink ᠗ᡋ᠊᠊ http://dx.doi.org/10.1787/068176572003

Distribution of expenditure on educational institutions relative to number of students enrolled

The money invested in the education systems of OECD countries can be compared to the proportion of students enrolled at each level of education. Table B1.2 shows the relationship between the two and analyses the different strategies put in place by countries to allocate the expenditure between the levels of education.

On average among the 26 OECD countries for which data are available, two-thirds of all expenditure on educational institutions is allocated to primary, secondary and post-secondary non-tertiary education while around three-quarters of students are enrolled at this level of education. The difference between the two figures exceeds 10 percentage points in Hungary, Japan, Mexico, the Slovak Republic and the United States, and the partner economies Brazil, Chile and Israel (Table B1.2).

Compared to primary, secondary and post-secondary non-tertiary education, there are significant differences between the proportion of money invested and the proportion of students enrolled in tertiary education. On average among the 26 OECD countries for which data are available, 24% of all expenditure on educational institutions is allocated to tertiary education, whereas only 15% of students are enrolled in tertiary education. The difference between the two proportions in tertiary education ranges from below 7 percentage points in France, Greece, Iceland, Italy, Korea, New Zealand, Poland, Portugal and the United Kingdom, and the partner economies Estonia and Slovenia, to more than 14 percentage points in the United States, and the partner economies Brazil and Chile (Table B1.2).

Educational expenditure per student over the theoretical duration of primary and secondary education

OECD countries spend on average USD 81 485 per student over the theoretical duration of primary and secondary studies. Although the theoretical duration of primary and secondary studies is quite similar – between 12 and 13 years in 30 out of 36 OECD countries and partner economies – the cumulative expenditure per student varies considerably. The cumulative expenditure for each primary and secondary student ranges from less than USD 40 000 in Mexico, Poland, the Slovak Republic and Turkey, and the partner economies Brazil, Chile, Estonia and the Russian Federation, to USD 100 000 or more in Austria, Denmark, Iceland, Luxembourg, Norway, Switzerland and the United States (Table B1.3a and Chart B1.5a).

Lower unit expenditure does not necessarily produce lower achievement and it would be misleading to equate lower unit expenditure generally with lower quality of educational services. Cumulative spending per student between primary and secondary education is moderate in Korea and the Netherlands and yet both were among the best-performing countries in PISA 2003 survey. In contrast, spending per student is USD 100 000 or more in Italy and the United States, while both performed below average in the PISA 2003 survey.

Educational expenditure per student over the average duration of tertiary studies

Both the typical duration and the intensity of tertiary education vary among OECD countries. Therefore, the differences among countries in annual expenditure on educational services per student (as shown in Chart B1.2) do not necessarily reflect the variation in the total cost of educating the typical tertiary student.

Today, students can choose from a range of institutions and enrolment options to find the best fit for their degree objectives, abilities and personal interests. Many students enrol on a part-time basis while others work while studying or attend more than one institution before graduating. These varying enrolment patterns can affect the interpretation of expenditure on education per student.

In particular, comparatively low annual expenditure on education per student can result in comparatively high overall costs of tertiary education if the typical duration of tertiary studies is long. Chart B1.5b shows the average expenditure incurred per student throughout the course of tertiary studies. The figures account for all students for whom expenditure is incurred, including those who do not finish their studies. Although the calculations are based on a number of simplified assumptions and therefore should be treated with some caution (see Annex 3 at *www.oecd.org/edu/eag2007*), some striking shifts in the rank order of OECD countries and partner economies between the annual and aggregate expenditure can be noted.

For example, annual spending per tertiary student in Japan is about the same as in Germany: USD 12 193 in Japan compared with USD 12 255 in Germany (Table B1.1a). But because of differences in the tertiary degree structure (see Indicator A2), the average duration of tertiary studies is a little bit more than one year longer in Germany than in Japan (5.4 years in Germany, compared with 4.1 years in Japan). As a consequence, the cumulative expenditure for each tertiary student is almost USD 15 000 lower in Japan than in Germany: USD 49 624 compared with USD 65 733 (Chart B1.5b and Table B1.3b).

The total cost of tertiary-type A studies in Switzerland (USD 127 568) is more than twice as high as in the other reporting countries, except Austria, Germany and the Netherlands (Table B1.3b). These differences must, of course, be interpreted in light of differences in national degree structures, as well as possible differences among OECD countries in the academic level of the qualifications of students leaving university. While similar trends are observed in tertiary-type B studies, the total cost of these studies tends to be much lower than those of tertiary-type A programmes, largely because of their shorter duration.

Chart B1.5a. Cumulative expenditure on educational institutions per student over the theoretical duration of primary and secondary studies (2004)

Annual expenditure on educational institutions per student multiplied by the theoretical duration of studies, in equivalent USD converted using PPPs

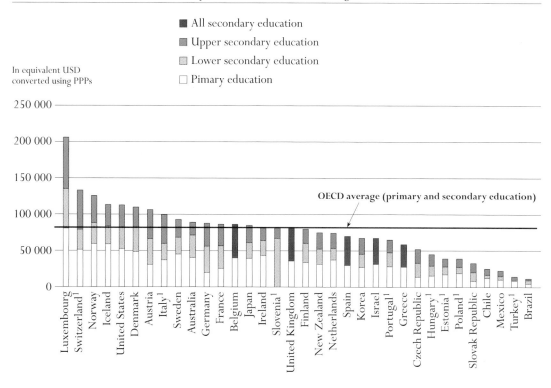

1. Public institutions only.
Countries are ranked in descending order of the total expenditure on educational institutions per student over the theoretical duration of primary and secondary studies.
Source: OECD. Table B1.3a. See Annex 3 for notes (*www.oecd.org/edu/eag2007*).
StatLink ⟪⟫ http://dx.doi.org/10.1787/068176572003

Chart B1.5b. Cumulative expenditure on educational institutions per student over the average duration of tertiary studies (2004)

Annual expenditure on educational institutions per student multiplied by the average duration of studies, in equivalent USD converted using PPPs

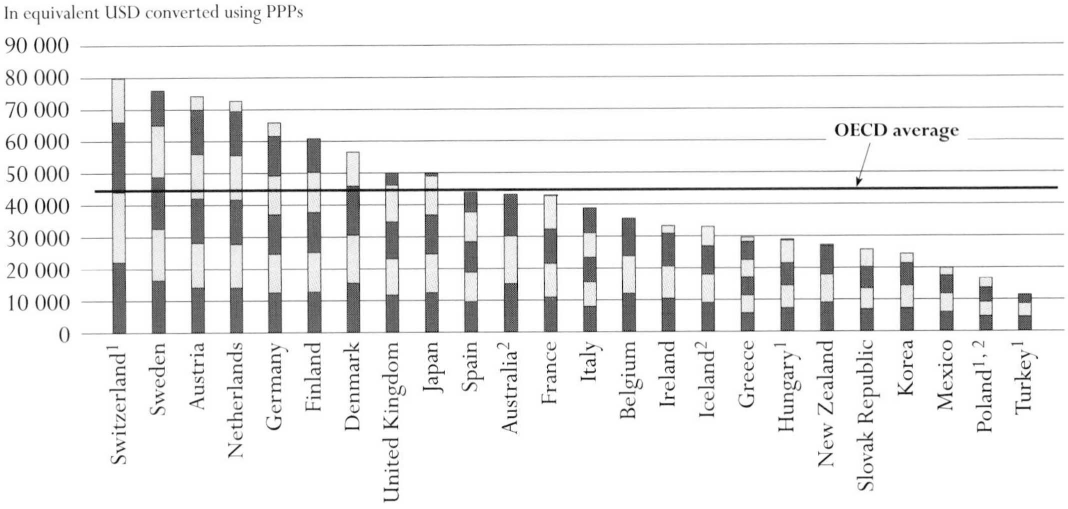

Note: Each segment of the bar represents the annual expenditure on educational institutions per student.The number of segments represents the number of years a student remains on average in tertiary education.

1. Public institutions only.
2. Tertiary-type A and advanced research programmes only.

Countries are ranked in descending order of the total expenditure on educational institutions per student over the average duration of tertiary studies.

Source: OECD. Table B1.3b. See Annex 3 for notes (*www.oecd.org/edu/eag2007*).

StatLink http://dx.doi.org/10.1787/068176572003

Educational expenditure per student in relation to GDP per capita

Expenditure on education per student relative to GDP per capita is a unit spending measure that takes OECD countries' relative wealth into account. Since education is universal at lower levels, spending on education per student at the lower levels of education relative to GDP per capita can be interpreted as the resources spent on young people relative to a country's ability to pay. At higher levels of education, this measure is affected by a combination of national income, spending and enrolment rates. At the tertiary level, for example, OECD countries can be relatively high on this measure if a large proportion of their wealth is spent on educating a relatively small number of students.

The relationship between GDP per capita and expenditure per student is complex. Chart B1.6 shows the co-existence of two different relationships between two distinct groups of countries (see the ovals in Chart B1.6). Countries with a GDP per capita equivalent to less than USD 27 500 demonstrate a clear positive relationship between spending on education per student and GDP per capita at primary and secondary levels of education (the Czech Republic, Hungary, Korea, Mexico, New Zealand, Poland, Portugal, the Slovak Republic, Spain and Turkey, and the partner economies Brazil, Chile, Estonia, Israel, the Russian Federation and Slovenia). Poorer OECD countries tend to spend less per student than richer OECD countries.

B1

Chart B1.6. Annual expenditure on educational institutions per student relative to GDP per capita (2004)

In equivalent USD converted using PPPs, by level of education

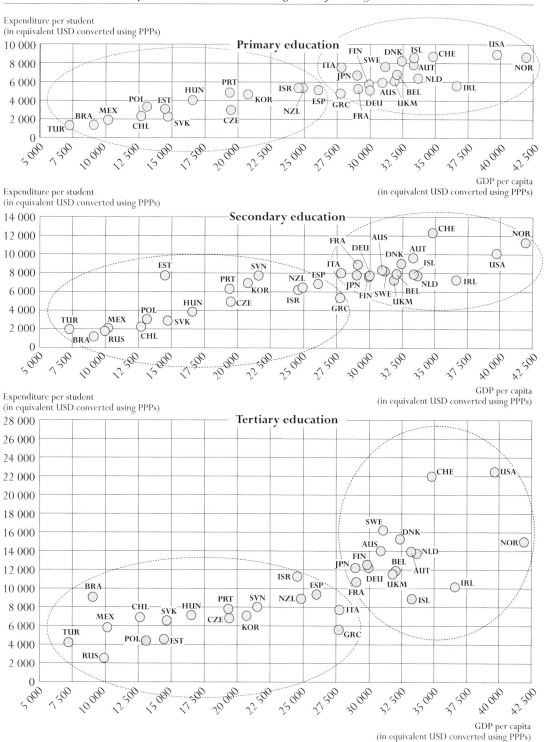

By contrast, there is a considerable variation in spending on education per student among OECD countries with a GDP per capita greater than USD 27 500 (see the ovals in Chart B1.6). Finland, France and Japan, for example, are countries with similar levels of GDP per capita that spend very different proportions of their GDP per capita on both the secondary and tertiary levels of education. Thus, the proportion of GDP per capita spent per secondary student in Finland and Japan at 25 and 26 %, respectively, are at the level of the OECD average, while for France (at 30%) the proportion is above average. However, France spends 37% of GDP per capita per tertiary student, whereas Finland and Japan spend both 42%, (Table B1.4 and Chart B1.3).

Expenditure on education per student averages 20% of GDP per capita at the primary level, 25% at the secondary level and 40% at the tertiary level (Table B1.4). Countries with low levels of expenditure per student can nevertheless show distributions of investment relative to GDP per capita which are similar to countries with a high level of spending per student. For example, Hungary, Korea, Poland and Portugal and the partner economy Estonia – countries with expenditure per student and GDP per capita below the OECD average at primary, secondary and post-secondary non-tertiary level of education – spend more per student relative to GDP per capita than the OECD average. Similarly, Mexico, Sweden, Turkey and the United States and the partner economy Chile spend more than 50% of GDP per capita on each tertiary-level student; this is among the highest proportions after Switzerland, which spend 63% of GDP per capita on each tertiary-level student. Brazil has the highest proportion, with 100% of GDP per capita spent per each tertiary-level student. However, this high level of expenditure is allocated to a small number of students because only 3% of the students enrolled in all levels of education combined are enrolled at the tertiary level in Brazil (Tables B1.2 and B1.4 and Chart B1.3).

Change in expenditure on education per student between 1995 and 2004

The number of young people in a population influences both the enrolment rate and the amount of resources and organisational effort which a country must invest in its education system. The size of the youth population in a given country shapes the potential demand for initial education and training. The higher the number of young people, the greater the potential demand for educational services. Table B1.5 and Chart B1.7 show, in absolute terms and at 2004 constant prices, the effects of changes in enrolment and total expenditure between 1995 and 2004 on educational expenditure per student.

Expenditure per primary, secondary and post-secondary non-tertiary student increased in every country between 1995 and 2004. In 18 out of the 25 OECD countries and partner economies for which data are available, changes exceed 20% between 1995 and 2004 and this increase is of 50% or more in a group of countries including Greece, Hungary, Ireland, Poland, Portugal, the Slovak Republic and Turkey, and the partner economy Chile. All the countries with the highest increases present similar patterns with a level of expenditure per primary, secondary and post-secondary non-tertiary student below the OECD average in 2004 combined for all of them (except Turkey and the partner economy Chile) to a decrease in the number of students enrolled in primary, secondary and post-secondary non-tertiary education between 1995 and 2004. The only countries where the increase in expenditure on education per primary, secondary and post-secondary non-tertiary student is 10% or below for the same period are Germany, Italy, Norway and Switzerland, and the partner economy Israel (Table B1.5 and Chart B1.7).

B1

Chart B1.7. Changes in the number of students as well as changes in expenditure on educational institutions per student, by level of education (1995, 2004)

Index of change between 1995 and 2004 (1995=100, 2004 constant prices)

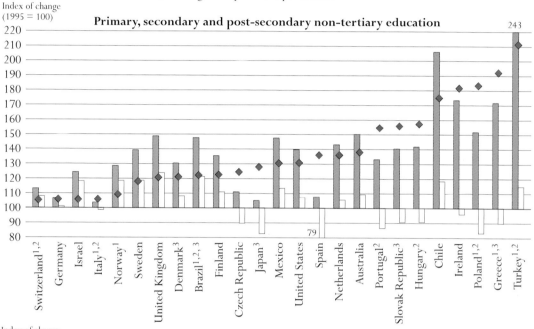

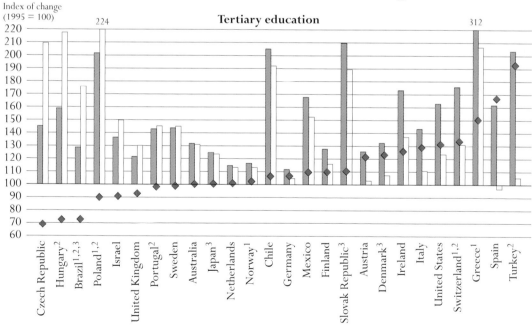

1. Public expenditure only.

2. Public institutions only.

3. Some levels of education are included with others. Refer to "x"code in Table B1.1a for details.

Countries are ranked in ascending order of change in expenditure on educational institutions per student.

Source: OECD. Table B1.5. See Annex 3 for notes (*www.oecd.org/edu/eag2007*).

StatLink ⌘S⌐ http://dx.doi.org/10.1787/068176572003

Although institutional arrangements are often slow in adapting to changing demographic conditions, changes in enrolments do not seem to have been the main factor driving changes in expenditure per primary, secondary and post-secondary non-tertiary student. The Czech Republic, Greece, Hungary, Japan, Poland, Portugal and Spain are exceptions to this pattern, where a drop of more than 10% in enrolments contributed to a significant increase in spending on education per student. In the case of Japan and Spain, the enrolment decline was concomitant with a slight rise in expenditure on education; in Greece, Poland and Portugal, it came at the same time as a sharp spending increase (Table B1.5 and Chart B1.7).

Other patterns are found in Finland, Mexico, Norway, Sweden, Turkey and the United Kingdom, and the partner economies Brazil, Chile and Israel: the nine countries with the highest percent increase in the number of primary, secondary and post-secondary non-tertiary students between 1995 and 2004. In Finland, Mexico, Norway, Sweden, Turkey and the United Kingdom, and the partner economies Brazil and Chile, increases in expenditure outpaced rising enrolments, leading to an increase in expenditure per student whereas in the partner economy Israel, an increase in student numbers was counterbalanced by a similar increase in educational spending (Table B1.5 and Chart B1.7).

The pattern is different at the tertiary level of education. Out of the 26 OECD countries and partner economies for which data are available, the Czech Republic, Hungary, Poland, Portugal, Sweden and the United Kingdom, and in the partner economies Brazil and Israel show expenditure on tertiary education per student declining between 1995 and 2004. In all of these countries, this decline was mainly the result of a rapid increase (30% or more) in the number of tertiary students during the same period (Chart B1.7). However, expenditure per student at the tertiary level rose significantly in Greece, Ireland, Mexico, the Slovak Republic and Switzerland, and the partner economy Chile, despite a significant growth in enrolment of 107, 37, 53, 90, 31 and 92%, respectively. Austria, Denmark, Germany, Spain and Turkey were the only countries in which the number of tertiary students increased by less than 10% (Table B1.5 and Chart B1.7).

Definitions and methodologies

Data refer to the financial year 2004 and are based on the UOE data collection on education statistics administered by the OECD in 2006 (for details see Annex 3 at *www.oecd.org/edu/eag2007*). Expenditure on education per student at a particular level of education is calculated by dividing the total expenditure on educational institutions at that level by the corresponding full-time equivalent enrolment. Only those educational institutions and programmes for which both enrolment and expenditure data are available are taken into account. Expenditure in national currency is converted into equivalent USD by dividing the national currency figure by the purchasing power parity (PPP) index for GDP. The PPP exchange rate is used because the market exchange rate is affected by many factors (interest rates, trade policies, expectations of economic growth, etc.) that have little to do with current relative domestic purchasing power in different OECD countries (Annex 2 gives further details).

The OECD average is calculated as the simple average over all OECD countries for which data are available. The OECD total reflects the value of the indicator if the OECD region is considered as a whole (see the Reader's Guide for details).

Table B1.5 shows the changes in expenditure on educational institutions per student between the financial years 1995 and 2004. OECD countries were asked to collect the 1995 data according to the definitions and the coverage of UOE 2006 data collection. All expenditure data, as well as the GDP for 1995, are adjusted to 2004 prices using the GDP price deflator.

Expenditure on education per student relative to GDP per capita is calculated by expressing expenditure on education per student in units of national currency as a percentage of GDP per capita, also in national currency. In cases where the educational expenditure data and the GDP data pertain to different reference periods, the expenditure data are adjusted to the same reference period as the GDP data, using inflation rates for the OECD country in question (see Annex 2).

Expected expenditure over the average duration of tertiary studies (Table B1.3b) is calculated by multiplying current annual expenditure by the typical duration of tertiary studies. The methodology used for the estimation of the typical duration of tertiary studies is described in Annex 3 (*www.oecd.org/edu/eag2007*). For the estimation of the duration of tertiary education, data are based on a special survey carried out in OECD countries in 2005.

The ranking of OECD countries by annual expenditure on educational services per student is affected by differences in how countries define full-time, part-time and full-time equivalent enrolment. Some OECD countries count every participant at the tertiary level as a full-time student while others determine a student's intensity of participation by the credits which he or she obtains for successful completion of specific course units during a specified reference period. OECD countries that can accurately account for part-time enrolment will have higher expenditure per full-time equivalent student than OECD countries that cannot differentiate between different modes of student attendance.

Note that data appearing in earlier editions of this publication may not always be comparable to data shown in the 2007 edition due to changes in definitions and coverage that were made as a result of the OECD expenditure comparability study (see Annex 3 at *www.oecd.org/edu/eag2007* for details on changes).

Further references

The following additional material relevant to this indicator is available on line at:

StatLink ⫘ http://dx.doi.org/10.1787/068176572003

• *Table B1.1c Annual expenditure on educational institutions per student for core services (2004)*

B1

Table B1.1a.
Annual expenditure on educational institutions per student for all services (2004)
In equivalent USD converted using PPPs for GDP, by level of education, based on full-time equivalents

		Pre-primary education (for children 3 years and older)	Primary education	Secondary education			Post-secondary non-tertiary education	Tertiary education (including R&D activities)			All tertiary education excluding R&D activities	Primary to tertiary education
				Lower secondary education	Upper secondary education	All secondary education		Tertiary-type B education	Tertiary-type A & advanced research programmes	All tertiary education		
		(1)	(2)	(3)	(4)	(5)	(6)	(7)	(8)	(9)	(10)	(11)
OECD countries	Australia	m	5 776	7 747	8 853	8 160	7 969	8 425	15 000	14 036	10 250	8 053
	Austria	6 106	7 669	8 969	9 962	9 446	x(4)	10 072	14 281	13 959	9 595	9 803
	Belgium	4 915	6 636	x(5)	x(5)	7 751	x(5)	x(9)	x(9)	11 842	7 920	8 019
	Canada	m	m	m	m	m	m	m	m	m	m	m
	Czech Republic	3 178	2 791	4 769	4 790	4 779	2 191	3 273	7 142	6 752	5 711	4 484
	Denmark	5 323	8 081	8 224	9 466	8 849	x(4, 9)	x(9)	x(9)	15 225	11 387	9 766
	Finland	4 282	5 581	8 918	6 555	7 441	x(5)	8 729	12 507	12 505	7 697	7 798
	France	4 938	5 082	7 837	9 883	8 737	4 081	9 113	11 195	10 668	7 372	7 880
	Germany	5 489	4 948	6 082	10 459	7 576	10 573	6 413	13 218	12 255	7 724	7 802
	Greece	x(2)	4 595	x(5)	x(5)	5 213	5 688	2 549	7 199	5 593	4 521	5 135
	Hungary[1]	4 231	3 841	3 433	3 968	3 692	6 351	5 089	7 198	7 095	5 607	4 326
	Iceland	6 114	8 434	8 284	7 330	7 721	x(4, 9)	x(9)	x(9)	8 881	m	8 264
	Ireland	4 948	5 422	6 943	7 309	7 110	5 169	x(9)	x(9)	10 211	7 445	6 713
	Italy[1]	5 971	7 390	7 657	7 971	7 843	m	8 378	7 716	7 723	4 812	7 723
	Japan	3 945	6 551	7 325	7 883	7 615	x(4, 9)	7 619	13 777	12 193	m	8 148
	Korea	2 520	4 490	6 057	7 485	6 761	a	4 263	8 600	7 068	6 154	5 994
	Luxembourg[1]	x(2)	13 458	18 036	17 731	17 876	m	m	m	m	m	m
	Mexico	1 794	1 694	1 602	2 564	1 922	a	x(9)	x(9)	5 778	4 834	2 128
	Netherlands	5 807	6 222	7 948	7 037	7 541	6 624	a	13 846	13 846	8 637	7 999
	New Zealand	5 112	5 190	5 334	7 424	6 299	5 412	5 791	9 834	8 866	8 240	6 298
	Norway	4 327	8 533	9 476	12 498	11 109	x(5)	x(9)	x(9)	14 997	10 449	10 721
	Poland[1]	4 045	3 130	2 822	2 949	2 889	3 147	2 756	4 471	4 412	3 893	3 323
	Portugal[1]	4 461	4 681	6 359	5 962	6 168	m	x(9)	x(9)	7 741	m	5 809
	Slovak Republic	2 575	2 073	2 389	3 155	2 744	x(4)	x(4)	6 535	6 535	5 940	3 058
	Spain	4 617	4 965	x(5)	x(5)	6 701	a	8 363	9 582	9 378	6 853	6 599
	Sweden	4 417	7 469	7 836	8 218	8 039	3 437	x(9)	x(9)	16 218	8 355	9 085
	Switzerland[1]	3 581	8 570	9 197	15 368	12 176	8 401	5 971	23 395	21 966	12 515	11 883
	Turkey[1]	m	1 120	a	1 808	1 808	a	x(9)	x(9)	m	4 231	1 527
	United Kingdom	7 924	5 941	x(5)	x(5)	7 090	x(5)	x(9)	x(9)	11 484	8 792	7 270
	United States	7 896	8 805	9 490	10 468	9 938	m	x(9)	x(9)	22 476	19 842	12 092
	OECD average	*4 741*	*5 832*	*6 909*	*7 884*	*7 276*	*4 315*	~	~	*11 100*	*7 951*	*7 061*
	OECD total	*5 117*	*5 331*	~	~	*7 163*	~	~	~	*14 027*	*11 443*	*7 572*
	EU19 average	*4 896*	*5 788*	*7 215*	*7 694*	*7 236*	*4 726*	~	~	*10 191*	*7 192*	*6 811*
Partner economies	Brazil[1]	1 171	1 159	1 172	801	1 033	a	x(4)	9 019	9 019	8 903	1 303
	Chile[2]	2 460	2 120	2 106	2 062	2 077	a	4 371	8 090	6 873	m	2 864
	Estonia[1]	1 186	2 894	3 579	3 670	3 623	3 717	4 194	n	4 552	m	3 402
	Israel	4 278	5 192	x(5)	x(5)	6 066	4 272	8 673	11 922	11 289	8 771	6 540
	Russian Fed.[1]	m	x(5)	x(5)	x(5)	1 615	x(5)	1 863	2 840	2 562	m	1 775
	Slovenia[1]	6 369	x(3)	7 428	5 062	6 525	x(4)	x(9)	x(9)	8 011	6 866	6 824

1. Public institutions only.
2. Year of reference 2005.
Source: OECD. See Annex 3 for notes (*www.oecd.org/edu/eag2007*).
Please refer to the Reader's Guide for information concerning the symbols replacing missing data.
StatLink http://dx.doi.org/10.1787/068176572003

Table B1.1b.
Annual expenditure per student on core services, ancillary services and R&D (2004)
In equivalent USD converted using PPPs for GDP, by level of education and type of service, based on full-time equivalents

	Primary, secondary and post-secondary non-tertiary education			Tertiary education			
	Educational core services	Ancillary services (transport, meals, housing provided by institutions)	Total	Educational core services	Ancillary services (transport, meals, housing provided by institutions)	R & D	Total
	(1)	(2)	(3)	(4)	(5)	(6)	(7)
Australia	6 626	285	**6 911**	9 543	707	3 786	**14 036**
Austria	8 516	422	**8 938**	9 493	102	4 364	**13 959**
Belgium	7 031	279	**7 310**	7 596	324	3 922	**11 842**
Canada	m	m	**m**	m	m	m	**m**
Czech Republic	3 822	208	**4 030**	5 490	222	1 041	**6 752**
Denmark[1]	8 492	a	**8 492**	11 387	a	3 838	**15 225**
Finland	5 963	697	**6 660**	7 696	n	4 808	**12 505**
France	6 361	901	**7 262**	6 770	602	3 296	**10 668**
Germany	6 828	155	**6 983**	7 132	591	4 531	**12 255**
Greece[1]	4 855	76	**4 931**	4 072	448	1 072	**5 593**
Hungary[2]	3 436	397	**3 833**	5 313	294	1 488	**7 095**
Iceland[1]	x(3)	x(3)	**8 138**	x(7)	x(7)	x(7)	**8 881**
Ireland	5 902	131	**6 034**	7 445	x(7)	2 766	**10 211**
Italy[2]	7 434	307	**7 741**	4 498	314	2 912	**7 723**
Japan[1]	x(3)	x(3)	**7 105**	x(7)	x(7)	x(7)	**12 193**
Korea	5 079	471	**5 550**	6 105	49	913	**7 068**
Luxembourg[1,2]	x(3)	x(3)	**15 157**	m	m	m	**m**
Mexico	1 789	m	**1 789**	4 834	m	944	**5 778**
Netherlands	6 841	73	**6 914**	8 634	3	5 210	**13 846**
New Zealand	x(3)	x(3)	**5 815**	8 240	x(7)	627	**8 866**
Norway	9 670	101	**9 772**	10 265	184	4 548	**14 997**
Poland[2]	2 914	84	**2 998**	3 891	2	519	**4 412**
Portugal[2]	5 362	37	**5 400**	x(7)	x(7)	x(7)	**7 741**
Slovak Republic[1]	2 120	442	**2 562**	4 781	1 160	594	**6 535**
Spain	5 683	209	**5 892**	6 853	m	2 525	**9 378**
Sweden	7 001	743	**7 744**	8 355	n	7 863	**16 218**
Switzerland[2]	x(3)	x(3)	**10 378**	12 515	x(4)	9 451	**21 966**
Turkey[2]	1 183	79	**1 262**	4 170	x(4)	m	**m**
United Kingdom	6 323	333	**6 656**	8 792	m	2 693	**11 484**
United States	8 640	729	**9 368**	17 738	2 104	2 634	**22 476**
OECD average	*5 745*	*311*	*6 608*	*7 664*	*395*	*3 181*	*11 100*
EU19 average	*5 827*	*305*	*6 607*	*6 953*	*290*	*3 144*	*10 191*
Brazil[1,2]	x(3)	x(3)	**1 087**	8 903	x(4)	116	**9 019**
Chile[3]	2 013	86	**2 099**	x(7)	x(7)	x(7)	**6 873**
Estonia[2]	x(3)	x(3)	**3 340**	x(7)	x(7)	n	**4 552**
Israel	5 542	22	**5 564**	8 658	113	2 517	**11 289**
Russian Federation[2]	x(3)	x(3)	**1 615**	x(7)	x(7)	x(7)	**2 562**
Slovenia[2]	6 258	267	**6 525**	6 851	15	1 145	**8 011**

OECD countries / Partner economies

1. Some levels of education are included with others. Refer to "x" code in Table B1.1a for details.
2. Public institutions only.
3. Year of reference 2005.
Source: OECD. See Annex 3 for notes (*www.oecd.org/edu/eag2007*).
Please refer to the Reader's Guide for information concerning the symbols replacing missing data.
StatLink ⟐⟐ http://dx.doi.org/10.1787/068176572003

B1

Table B1.2.

Distribution of expenditure (as a percentage) on educational institutions compared to number of students enrolled at each level of education (2004)

This table shows the distribution of educational expenditure and of students across levels of education. The number of students is adjusted to the financial year, e.g. when reading the first and second columns, in the Czech Republic, 9.5 % of all expenditure on educational institutions is allocated to pre-primary education whereas 13.3 % of pupils/students are enrolled at this level of education.

		Pre-primary education (for children 3 years and older)		Primary, secondary and post-secondary non-tertiary education		All tertiary education		Not allocated by level		All levels of education	
		Proportion of expenditure on educational institutions	Proportion of students enrolled, based on full-time equivalents	Proportion of expenditure on educational institutions	Proportion of students enrolled, based on full-time equivalents	Proportion of expenditure on educational institutions	Proportion of students enrolled, based on full-time equivalents	Proportion of expenditure on educational institutions	Proportion of students enrolled, based on full-time equivalents	Proportion of expenditure on educational institutions	Proportion of students enrolled, based on full-time equivalents
		(1)		(2)		(3)		(4)		(5)	
OECD countries	Australia	m	2.9	m	81.5	m	15.5	m	0.1	m	100
	Austria	8.6	13.2	68.4	71.9	22.4	15.0	a	a	100	100
	Belgium	9.8	15.3	67.9	71.4	20.4	13.2	2.0	n	100	100
	Canada	m	m	m	m	m	m	m	m	m	m
	Czech Republic	9.5	13.3	65.7	72.2	22.1	14.5	2.7	n	100	100
	Denmark[1]	12.0	20.5	60.3	64.5	25.2	15.0	2.5	n	100	100
	Finland	6.2	10.8	64.5	71.8	29.3	17.4	n	n	100	100
	France	11.6	17.3	66.7	67.7	21.7	15.0	n	n	100	100
	Germany	9.6	13.4	66.7	73.1	21.5	13.4	2.1	0.1	100	100
	Greece	x(2)	x(2)	64.7	71.2	32.6	28.8	2.7	n	100	100
	Hungary[2]	15.4	16.4	60.4	71.0	19.9	12.7	4.3	n	100	100
	Iceland[1]	9.2	12.8	68.3	73.7	14.6	13.5	7.9	n	100	100
	Ireland	0.1	0.1	74.3	82.6	25.7	17.3	n	n	100	100
	Italy[2]	9.3	11.7	71.7	69.6	19.0	18.7	n	n	100	100
	Japan[1]	4.0	8.4	61.7	71.9	27.3	18.6	6.9	1.1	100	100
	Korea	1.9	4.7	61.3	67.4	32.2	27.9	4.5	n	100	100
	Luxembourg	m	m	m	m	m	m	m	m	m	m
	Mexico	10.3	12.3	67.0	80.2	20.1	7.5	2.6	n	100	100
	Netherlands	7.4	9.9	67.5	76.0	25.1	14.1	n	n	100	100
	New Zealand	4.8	6.0	72.8	79.1	20.9	14.9	1.5	n	100	100
	Norway	4.8	11.5	68.4	72.2	23.3	16.0	3.5	n	100	100
	Poland[2]	11.0	9.2	66.7	75.4	22.2	15.3	n	n	100	100
	Portugal[2]	5.9	7.8	69.2	76.2	21.1	16.1	3.9	n	100	100
	Slovak Republic[1]	10.5	12.6	63.5	76.5	23.1	10.9	3.0	n	100	100
	Spain	12.4	16.8	62.4	66.3	25.2	16.9	n	n	100	100
	Sweden	7.8	14.7	66.2	71.8	26.1	13.5	n	n	100	100
	Switzerland[2]	3.8	10.6	69.0	77.8	25.5	11.6	1.7	n	100	100
	Turkey[2]	m	1.6	m	89.6	m	8.8	n	n	m	100
	United Kingdom	6.2	4.3	75.0	83.5	18.9	12.2	n	a	100	100
	United States	5.8	8.7	57.8	72.4	36.4	19.0	n	n	100	100
	OECD average	*7.9*	*10.6*	*66.5*	*74.2*	*23.9*	*15.5*	*1.9*	*n*	*100*	*100*
Partner economies	Brazil[1,2]	9.0	9.9	73.7	87.5	17.2	2.6	n	n	100	100
	Chile[3]	7.6	8.8	56.8	76.6	35.5	14.6	n	n	100	100
	Estonia[2]	7.6	19.2	85.4	76.7	6.3	4.1	0.7	n	100	100
	Israel	10.3	16.0	56.1	68.0	23.4	14.0	10.2	1.9	100	100
	Russian Federation[2]	15.2	m	56.5	m	18.3	m	10.0	n	100	m
	Slovenia[2]	9.8	10.4	68.9	71.6	21.3	18.0	n	n	100	100

1. Some levels of education are included with others. Refer to "x" code in Table B1.1a for details.
2. Public institutions only.
3. Year of reference 2005.
Source: OECD. See Annex 3 for notes (*www.oecd.org/edu/eag2007*).
Please refer to the Reader's Guide for information concerning the symbols replacing missing data.
StatLink ᔖᔲᔲ http://dx.doi.org/10.1787/068176572003

Table B1.3a.
Cumulative expenditure on educational institutions per student for all services over the theoretical duration of primary and secondary studies (2004)
In equivalent USD converted using PPPs for GDP, by level of education

	Average theoretical duration of primary and secondary studies (in years)				Cumulative expenditure per student over the theoretical duration of primary and secondary studies (in USD)				
	Primary education	Lower secondary	Upper secondary education	Total primary and secondary education	Primary education	Lower secondary	Upper secondary education	All secondary education	Total primary and secondary education
	(1)	(2)	(3)	(4)	(5)	(6)	(7)	(8)	(9)
Australia	7.0	4.0	2.0	**13.0**	40 434	30 988	17 706	48 694	**89 128**
Austria	4.0	4.0	4.0	**12.0**	30 674	35 875	39 848	75 723	**106 397**
Belgium	6.0	2.0	4.0	**12.0**	39 813	x(8)	x(8)	46 508	**86 321**
Canada	6.0	3.0	3.0	**12.0**	m	m	m	m	**m**
Czech Republic	5.0	4.0	4.0	**13.0**	13 957	19 076	19 159	38 234	**52 191**
Denmark	6.0	4.0	3.0	**13.0**	48 485	32 895	28 398	61 292	**109 778**
Finland	6.0	3.0	3.0	**12.0**	33 484	26 753	19 664	46 417	**79 901**
France	5.0	4.0	3.0	**12.0**	25 410	31 348	29 649	60 996	**86 406**
Germany	4.0	6.0	3.0	**13.0**	19 792	36 491	31 377	67 868	**87 660**
Greece	6.0	3.0	3.0	**12.0**	27 570	x(8)	x(8)	31 280	**58 850**
Hungary[1]	4.0	4.0	4.0	**12.0**	15 365	13 731	15 873	29 604	**44 969**
Iceland	7.0	3.0	4.0	**14.0**	59 041	24 852	29 321	54 173	**113 214**
Ireland	8.0	3.0	2.5	**13.5**	43 378	20 828	18 273	39 102	**82 479**
Italy[1]	5.0	3.0	5.0	**13.0**	36 951	22 970	39 857	62 827	**99 778**
Japan	6.0	3.0	3.0	**12.0**	39 308	21 974	23 648	45 623	**84 931**
Korea	6.0	3.0	3.0	**12.0**	26 942	18 171	22 455	40 626	**67 568**
Luxembourg[1]	6.0	3.0	4.0	**13.0**	80 748	54 109	70 924	125 033	**205 781**
Mexico	6.0	3.0	3.0	**12.0**	10 166	4 805	7 692	12 496	**22 662**
Netherlands	6.0	2.0	3.0	**11.0**	37 332	15 895	21 112	37 008	**74 340**
New Zealand	6.0	4.0	3.0	**13.0**	31 140	21 334	22 271	43 606	**74 746**
Norway	7.0	3.0	3.0	**13.0**	59 729	28 427	37 493	65 921	**125 650**
Poland[1]	6.0	3.0	4.0	**13.0**	18 783	8 467	11 797	20 264	**39 047**
Portugal[1]	6.0	3.0	3.0	**12.0**	28 088	19 076	17 887	36 963	**65 051**
Slovak Republic	4.0	5.0	4.0	**13.0**	8 294	11 943	12 620	24 563	**32 857**
Spain	6.0	4.0	2.0	**12.0**	29 787	x(8)	x(8)	40 206	**69 994**
Sweden	6.0	3.0	3.0	**12.0**	44 817	23 509	24 653	48 162	**92 979**
Switzerland[1]	6.0	3.0	3.5	**12.5**	51 420	27 590	53 788	81 378	**132 798**
Turkey[1]	8.0	a	3.0	**11.0**	8 961	a	5 423	5 423	**14 384**
United Kingdom	6.0	3.0	3.5	**12.5**	35 646	x(8)	x(8)	46 086	**81 732**
United States	6.0	3.0	3.0	**12.0**	52 833	28 470	31 403	59 872	**112 705**
OECD average	*5.9*	*3.3*	*3.3*	*12.4*	*33 768*	*~*	*~*	*47 717*	*81 485*
Brazil[1]	4.0	4.0	3.0	**11.0**	4 636	4 687	2 404	7 091	**11 727**
Chile[2]	6.0	2.0	4.0	**12.0**	12 722	4 211	8 248	12 459	**25 182**
Estonia[1]	6.0	3.0	3.0	**12.0**	17 363	10 736	11 009	21 746	**39 108**
Israel	6.0	3.0	3.0	**12.0**	31 152	x(8)	x(8)	36 396	**67 548**
Russian Federation[1]	4.0	5.0	2.0	**11.0**	x(9)	x(9)	x(9)	x(9)	**17 763**
Slovenia[1]	6.0	3.0	3.0	**12.0**	x(6)	66 854	15 187	82 041	**82 041**

OECD countries (left vertical label for the upper group)
Partner economies (left vertical label for the lower group)

1. Public institutions only.
2. Year of reference 2005.
Source: OECD. See Annex 3 for notes (*www.oecd.org/edu/eag2007*).
Please refer to the Reader's Guide for information concerning the symbols replacing missing data.
StatLink http://dx.doi.org/10.1787/068176572003

B1

Table B1.3b.
Cumulative expenditure on educational institutions per student for all services
over the average duration of tertiary studies (2004)
In equivalent USD converted using PPPs for GDP, by type of programme

	Method[1]	Average duration of tertiary studies (in years)			Cumulative expenditure per student over the average duration of tertiary studies (in USD)		
		Tertiary-type B education	Tertiary-type A and advanced research programmes	All tertiary education	Tertiary-type B education	Tertiary-type A and advanced research programmes	All tertiary education
		(1)	(2)	(3)	(4)	(5)	(6)
Australia	CM	m	2.87	m	m	43 050	m
Austria	CM	2.78	5.60	5.30	28 001	79 971	73 984
Belgium	CM	2.41	3.67	2.99	x(6)	x(6)	35 406
Canada		m	m	m	m	m	m
Czech Republic		m	m	m	m	m	m
Denmark	AF	2.10	3.84	3.70	x(6)	x(6)	56 333
Finland	CM	a	4.85	4.85	a	60 659	60 659
France[2]	CM	3.00	4.74	4.02	27 340	53 062	42 885
Germany	CM	2.37	6.57	5.36	15 205	86 815	65 733
Greece	CM	5.00	5.26	5.25	12 745	37 869	29 362
Hungary[3]	CM	2.00	4.05	4.05	10 178	29 153	28 736
Iceland	CM	x(3)	x(3)	3.69	x(6)	x(6)	32 770
Ireland	CM	2.21	4.02	3.24	x(6)	x(6)	33 083
Italy	AF	m	5.14	5.01	m	39 658	38 694
Japan	CM	2.11	4.51	4.07	16 077	62 132	49 624
Korea	CM	2.07	4.22	3.43	8 825	36 291	24 242
Luxembourg		m	m	m	m	m	m
Mexico	AF	x(3)	3.42	3.42	x(6)	x(6)	19 762
Netherlands	CM	a	5.24	5.24	a	72 555	72 555
New Zealand	CM	1.87	3.68	3.05	10 829	36 188	27 042
Norway	CM	m	m	m	m	m	m
Poland[3]	CM	m	3.68	m	m	16 453	m
Portugal		m	m	m	m	m	m
Slovak Republic	AF	2.47	3.90	3.82	x(6)	x(6)	25 485
Spain	CM	2.15	5.54	4.66	17 980	53 084	43 700
Sweden	CM	2.26	4.93	4.68	x(6)	x(6)	75 901
Switzerland[3]	CM	2.19	5.45	3.62	13 057	127 568	79 611
Turkey[3]	CM	2.73	2.37	2.65	x(6)	x(6)	11 229
United Kingdom[2]	CM	3.52	5.86	4.34	x(6)	x(6)	49 873
United States		m	m	m	m	m	m
OECD average		*2.28*	*4.50*	*4.11*	*~*	*~*	*44 394*

1. Either the chain method (CM) or an approximation formula (AF) was used to estimate the duration of tertiary studies.
2. Average duration of tertiary studies is estimated based on national data.
3. Public institutions only.
Source: OECD. See Annex 3 for notes (*www.oecd.org/edu/eag2007*).
Please refer to the Reader's Guide for information concerning the symbols replacing missing data.
StatLink ᵐˢᴾ http://dx.doi.org/10.1787/068176572003

Table B1.4.
Annual expenditure on educational institutions per student for all services relative to GDP per capita (2004)
By level of education, based on full-time equivalents

| | Pre-primary education (for children 3 years and older) | Primary education | Secondary education | | | Post-secondary non-tertiary education | Tertiary education (including R&D activities) | | | All tertiary education excluding R&D activities | Primary to tertiary education |
| | | | Lower secondary education | Upper secondary education | All secondary education | | Tertiary-type B education | Tertiary-type A and advanced research programmes | All tertiary education | | |
	(1)	(2)	(3)	(4)	(5)	(6)	(7)	(8)	(9)	(10)	(11)
Australia	m	19	25	29	26	26	27	49	45	33	26
Austria	18	23	27	30	28	x(4)	30	43	42	29	29
Belgium	15	21	x(5)	x(5)	24	x(5)	x(9)	x(9)	37	25	25
Canada	m	m	m	m	m	m	m	m	m	m	m
Czech Rep.	16	14	25	25	25	11	17	37	35	29	23
Denmark	16	25	25	29	27	x(4, 9)	x(9)	x(9)	47	35	30
Finland	14	19	30	22	25	x(5)	29	42	42	26	26
France	17	18	27	34	30	14	31	39	37	25	27
Germany	18	17	20	35	25	35	21	44	41	26	26
Greece	x(2)	17	x(5)	x(5)	19	21	9	26	20	16	19
Hungary[1]	26	23	21	24	22	38	31	44	43	34	26
Iceland	18	25	25	22	23	x(4, 9)	x(9)	x(9)	27	m	25
Ireland	14	15	19	20	19	14	x(9)	x(9)	28	20	18
Italy[1]	22	27	28	29	28	m	30	28	28	17	28
Japan	14	23	25	27	26	x(4, 9)	26	48	42	m	28
Korea	12	22	29	36	33	a	21	42	34	30	29
Luxembourg[1]	x(2)	21	28	27	28	x(5)	m	m	m	m	m
Mexico	18	17	16	25	19	a	x(9)	x(9)	57	48	21
Netherlands	17	19	24	21	22	20	a	41	41	26	24
New Zealand	21	21	21	30	25	22	23	40	36	33	25
Norway	10	20	23	30	27	x(5)	x(9)	x(9)	36	25	26
Poland[1]	31	24	22	23	22	24	27	34	34	30	25
Portugal[1]	23	24	33	31	32	m	x(9)	x(9)	40	m	30
Slovak Rep.	18	14	16	22	19	x(4)	x(4)	45	45	41	21
Spain	18	19	x(5)	x(5)	26	a	32	37	36	26	25
Sweden	14	24	25	26	26	11	x(9)	x(9)	52	27	29
Switzerland[1]	10	25	26	44	35	24	17	67	63	36	34
Turkey[1]	m	16	a	25	25	a	x(9)	x(9)	m	59	21
United Kingdom	25	19	x(5)	x(5)	22	x(5)	x(9)	x(9)	36	28	23
United States	20	22	24	26	25	m	x(9)	x(9)	57	50	30
OECD average	*18*	*20*	*23*	*28*	*25*	*16*	*23*	*41*	*40*	*31*	*26*
EU19 average	*17*	*19*	*23*	*27*	*25*	*13*	*25*	*40*	*38*	*31*	*25*
Brazil[1]	13	13	13	9	11	a	x(4)	100	100	98	14
Chile[2]	19	17	17	16	16	a	35	64	54	m	23
Estonia[1]	8	20	25	25	25	26	29	n	32	m	24
Israel	17	21	x(5)	x(5)	25	17	35	49	46	36	27
Russian Fed.[1]	m	x(5)	x(5)	x(5)	16	x(5)	19	29	26	m	18
Slovenia[1]	30	x(3)	34	24	30	x(4)	x(9)	x(9)	37	32	32

The left margin labels "OECD countries" apply to the top group and "Partner economies" to Brazil, Chile, Estonia, Israel, Russian Fed., Slovenia.

1. Public institutions only.
2. Year of reference 2005.
Source: OECD. See Annex 3 for notes (*www.oecd.org/edu/eag2007*).
Please refer to the Reader's Guide for information concerning the symbols replacing missing data.
StatLink http://dx.doi.org/10.1787/068176572003

Table B1.5.
**Change in expenditure on educational institutions for all services per student relative to different factors,
by level of education (1995, 2004)**
Index of change between 1995 and 2004 (GDP deflator 1995=100, 2004 constant prices)

	Primary, secondary and post-secondary non-tertiary education				Tertiary education		
	Change in expenditure	Change in the number of students	Change in expenditure per student		Change in expenditure	Change in the number of students	Change in expenditure per student
Australia	150	109	138	Australia	132	131	101
Austria	108	m	m	Austria	126	103	122
Belgium	m	m	m	Belgium	m	m	m
Canada	m	m	m	Canada	m	m	m
Czech Republic	111	89	124	Czech Republic	145	210	69
Denmark[1]	130	108	121	Denmark[1]	133	107	123
Finland	135	111	122	Finland	128	116	110
France	m	m	m	France	m	m	m
Germany	106	101	105	Germany	112	105	107
Greece[1,2]	172	90	192	Greece[2]	312	207	151
Hungary[3]	142	90	157	Hungary[3]	159	218	73
Iceland	m	m	m	Iceland	m	m	m
Ireland	174	96	181	Ireland	174	137	126
Italy[2,3]	104	98	105	Italy	144	111	130
Japan[1]	105	82	127	Japan[1]	125	124	101
Korea	m	91	m	Korea	m	150	m
Luxembourg	m	m	m	Luxembourg	m	m	m
Mexico	147	114	130	Mexico	168	153	110
Netherlands	143	106	136	Netherlands	115	113	101
New Zealand[2]	162	m	m	New Zealand[2]	109	m	m
Norway[2]	129	118	109	Norway[2]	117	113	103
Poland[2,3]	152	83	183	Poland[2,3]	202	224	90
Portugal[3]	133	86	154	Portugal[3]	143	146	98
Slovak Republic[1]	140	90	155	Slovak Republic[1]	210	190	111
Spain	107	79	136	Spain	162	97	167
Sweden	139	119	117	Sweden	144	145	99
Switzerland[2,3]	113	108	105	Switzerland[2,3]	176	131	134
Turkey[2,3]	243	115	211	Turkey[3]	191	106	181
United Kingdom	149	124	120	United Kingdom	122	130	93
United States	140	107	130	United States	163	124	132
OECD average	*139*	*101*	*138*		*155*	*141*	*109*
EU19 average	*134*	*98*	*137*		*158*	*148*	*107*
Brazil[1,2,3]	148	123	122	Brazil[1,2,3]	129	176	73
Chile[4]	207	118	175	Chile[4]	206	192	107
Estonia	m	m	m	Estonia	m	m	m
Israel	124	118	105	Israel	137	150	91
Russian Federation	m	m	m	Russian Federation	m	m	m
Slovenia	m	m	m	Slovenia	m	m	m

1. Some levels of education are included with others. Refer to "x" code in Table B1.1a for details.
2. Public expenditure only.
3. Public institutions only.
4. Year of reference 2005.
Source: OECD. See Annex 3 for notes (*www.oecd.org/edu/eag2007*).
Please refer to the Reader's Guide for information concerning the symbols replacing missing data.
StatLink ⬛🗐 http://dx.doi.org/10.1787/068176572003

WHAT PROPORTION OF NATIONAL WEALTH IS SPENT ON EDUCATION?

Education expenditure as a percentage of GDP shows how a country prioritises education in relation to its overall allocation of resources. Tuition fees and investment in education from private entities other than households (see Indicator B5) have a strong impact on differences in the overall amount of financial resources that OECD countries devote to their education systems, especially at the tertiary level.

Key results

Chart B2.1. **Expenditure on educational institutions as a percentage of GDP for all levels of education (1995, 2004)**

This chart measures educational investment through the share of national income that each country devotes to spending on educational institutions in 1995 and 2004. It captures both direct and indirect expenditure on educational institutions from both public and private sources of funds.

☐ 2004   ◆ 1995

OECD countries spend 6.2% of their collective GDP on educational institutions. The increase in spending on education between 1995 and 2004 fell behind the growth in national income in one-third of the 24 OECD countries and partner economies for which data are available.

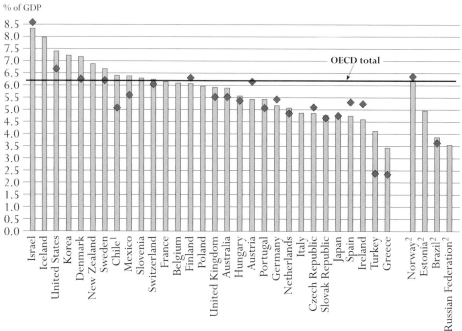

1. Years of reference 2005 and 1995.
2. Expenditure from public sources only.
Countries are ranked in descending order of total expenditure from both public and private sources on educational institutions in 2004.
Source: OECD. Table B2.1. See Annex 3 for notes (*www.oecd.org/edu/eag2007*).
StatLink ⇒ http://dx.doi.org/10.1787/068186423156

Other highlights of this indicator

- Around two-thirds of expenditure on educational institutions, or 3.8% of the combined GDP in the OECD area, are devoted to primary, secondary and post-secondary non-tertiary education. Iceland and New Zealand, and, to a lesser extent, Sweden and Switzerland, spend more than twice the level of expenditure compared to their GDP than Greece.

- Tertiary education accounts for more than one-quarter of the combined OECD expenditure on educational institutions (1.9% of the combined GDP).

- Korea and the United States spend 2.3 and 2.9% of their GDP, respectively, on tertiary institutions. These two countries, along with the partner economy Chile (2.0%), show the highest proportions of private expenditure at the tertiary level of education. Compared to GDP, the United States spends on tertiary education up to three times more than Italy, Portugal and Turkey and partner economy Estonia, and four times more than partner economies Brazil and the Russian Federation.

- More people are completing upper secondary and tertiary education than ever before, and in many countries the expansion has been accompanied by massive financial investments. Between 1995 and 2004 and for all levels of education combined, expenditure on educational institutions increased in the 24 countries with comparable data for the period. The increase was, on average, 42% in OECD countries. The increase is usually larger for tertiary education than for primary to post-secondary non-tertiary levels of education combined.

- At the tertiary level of education, the increase of expenditure over the period 1995-2004 was more pronounced from 2000 onward than before 2000 in nearly one-half of OECD countries. Between 2000 and 2004, expenditure increased by more than 30 percentage points in the Czech Republic, Greece, Mexico, Poland, the Slovak Republic and Switzerland and the partner economy Chile.

- The size of the school-age population shapes the potential demand for initial education and training and therefore affects expenditure on educational institutions. Thus, countries with more than 25% of their population enrolled in education have an above OECD average proportion of their GDP devoted to education. On the contrary, countries with less than 20% of their population enrolled in education have a below OECD average proportion of their GDP devoted to education.

Policy context

This indicator provides a measure of the relative proportion of a nation's wealth that is invested in educational institutions. Expenditure on education is an investment that can help foster economic growth, enhance productivity, contribute to personal and social development, and reduce social inequality. Relative to gross domestic product, expenditure on education shows the priority given to education by each country in terms of allocating its overall resources. The proportion of total financial resources devoted to education is one of the key choices made in each OECD country. This is an aggregate choice made by government, enterprise and individual students and their families and is partially driven by the importance of the school-age population in the country and enrolment in education. If the social and private returns on investment in education are sufficiently large, there is an incentive for enrolment to expand and total investment to increase.

The indicator also includes a comparative review of changes in educational investment over time. In deciding how much is allocated to education, governments must assess demands for increased spending in areas such as teachers' salaries and educational facilities. This indicator can provide a point of reference as it shows how the volume of educational spending, relative to the size of national wealth and in absolute terms, has evolved over time in various OECD countries.

Evidence and explanations

What this indicator does and does not cover

This indicator covers expenditure on schools, universities and other public and private institutions involved in delivering or supporting educational services. Expenditure on institutions is not limited to expenditure on instructional services but also includes public and private expenditure on ancillary services for students and families (such as housing and transportation services), where these services are provided through educational institutions. Spending on research and development can also be significant in tertiary education and is included in this indicator, to the extent that the research is performed by educational institutions.

Not all spending on educational goods and services occurs within educational institutions. For example, families may purchase textbooks and materials commercially or seek private tutoring for their children outside educational institutions. At the tertiary level, student living costs and forgone earnings can also account for a significant proportion of the costs of education. All such expenditure outside educational institutions is excluded from this indicator, even if it is publicly subsidised. Public subsidies for educational expenditure outside institutions are discussed in Indicators B4 and B5.

Overall investment relative to GDP

All OECD countries invest a substantial proportion of national resources in education. Taking into account both public and private sources of funds, OECD countries as a whole spend 6.2% of their collective GDP on educational institutions at the pre-primary, primary, secondary and tertiary levels. Under current conditions of tight constraints on public budgets, such a large spending item is subject to close scrutiny by governments looking for ways to reduce or limit the growth of expenditure.

The highest spending on educational institutions can be observed in Denmark, Iceland, Korea and the United States, and the partner economy Israel, with at least 7% of GDP accounted for by public and private spending on educational institutions, followed by New Zealand, and Sweden with more than 6.5%. Eight out of 28 OECD countries for which data are available as well as three partner economies, however, spend less than 5% of GDP on educational institutions, and in Greece and Turkey, as well as in the partner economies Brazil and the Russian Federation, this figure is only between 3.4 and 4.1% (Table B2.1).

Expenditure on educational institutions by level of education

Differences in spending on educational institutions are most striking at the pre-primary level of education. Here, spending ranges from 0.1% of GDP in Australia and Korea to 0.8% or more in Denmark and Hungary, and the partner economy Israel (Table B2.2). Differences at the pre-primary level can be explained mainly by participation rates among younger children (see Indicator C1),

Chart B2.2. Expenditure on educational institutions as a percentage of GDP (2004)

From public and private sources, by level of education, source of funds and year

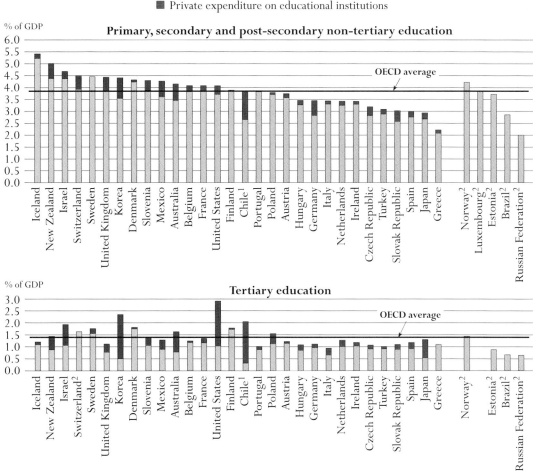

1. Year of reference 2005.
2. Public expenditure only.
Countries are ranked in descending order of expenditure from both public and private sources on educational institutions in primary, secondary and post-secondary non-tertiary education.
Source: OECD. Table B2.4. See Annex 3 for notes (*www.oecd.org/edu/eag2007*).
StatLink http://dx.doi.org/10.1787/068186423156

but are also sometimes a result of the extent to which private early childhood education is covered by this indicator. In Ireland, for example, the majority of early childhood education is delivered in private institutions that are not yet covered in the Irish data collection. Moreover, high-quality early childhood education and care are not only provided by the educational institutions covered by this indicator but often also in more informal settings. Inferences on access to and quality of early childhood education and care should therefore be made with caution.

On average, among OECD countries, around two-thirds of expenditure on educational institutions is devoted to primary, secondary and post-secondary non-tertiary education. Because enrolment in primary and lower secondary education is almost universal in OECD countries, and participation rates in upper secondary education are high (see Indicators C1 and C2), these levels account for the bulk of expenditure on educational institutions: 3.8% of the combined OECD GDP (Chart B2.2). At the same time, significantly higher spending on education per student at the upper secondary and tertiary levels causes the overall investment in these levels to be higher than enrolment numbers alone would suggest.

More than one-quarter of combined OECD expenditure on educational institutions is accounted for by tertiary education. At this level of education, pathways available to students, programme durations and the organisation of teaching vary greatly among OECD countries, leading to greater differences in the level of expenditure allocated to tertiary education. On the one hand, Korea and the United States spend 2.3 and 2.9%, respectively, of their GDP on tertiary institutions and these two countries (with partner economy Chile) are also those with the highest proportion of private expenditure on tertiary education. Denmark, Finland and Sweden, as well as the partner economy Israel, also show high levels of spending, with 1.8% or more of GDP devoted to tertiary institutions. On the other hand, the proportion of GDP spent on tertiary institutions in Belgium, France, Iceland, Mexico, Portugal and the United Kingdom is below the OECD average and these countries are among the OECD countries where the proportion of GDP spent on primary, secondary and post-secondary non-tertiary education is above the OECD average (Chart B2.2). In Switzerland, a moderate proportion of GDP spent on tertiary institutions translates to one of the highest levels of spending per tertiary student, due to a comparatively low tertiary enrolment rate and a high GDP (Tables B2.1 and B1.2).

Relationship between national expenditure on education and demographic pattern

The amount of national resources devoted to education depends on a number of interrelated factors of supply and demand, such as the demographic structure of the population, enrolment rates, income per capita, national levels of teachers' salaries, and the organisation and delivery of instruction. For example, OECD countries with high spending levels may be enrolling larger numbers of students, while countries with low spending levels may either be limiting access to higher levels of education or delivering educational services in a particularly efficient manner. The distribution of enrolment among sectors and fields of study may also differ, as may the duration of studies and the scale and organisation of related educational research. Finally, large differences in GDP among OECD countries imply that similar percentages of GDP spent on education can translate into very different absolute amounts per student (see Indicator B1).

Chart B2.3. Expenditure on educational institutions as a percentage of GDP and total enrolment in education as a percentage of total population (2004)

For all levels of education combined, based on full-time equivalents

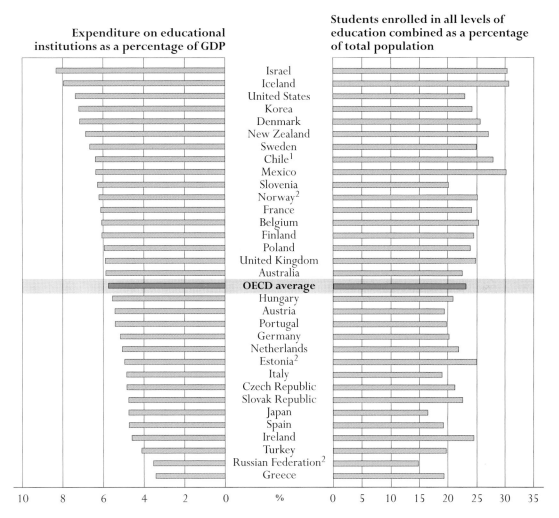

Expenditure on educational institutions as a percentage of GDP

Students enrolled in all levels of education combined as a percentage of total population

Israel
Iceland
United States
Korea
Denmark
New Zealand
Sweden
Chile[1]
Mexico
Slovenia
Norway[2]
France
Belgium
Finland
Poland
United Kingdom
Australia
OECD average
Hungary
Austria
Portugal
Germany
Netherlands
Estonia[2]
Italy
Czech Republic
Slovak Republic
Japan
Spain
Ireland
Turkey
Russian Federation[2]
Greece

1. Year of reference 2005.
2. Expenditure from public sources only.
Countries are ranked in descending order of total expenditure on educational institutions as a percentage of GDP.
Source: OECD. Table B2.1 and Annex 2. See Annex 3 for notes (*www.oecd.org/edu/eag2007*).
StatLink ᴍ᷿ᵴ⃞ http://dx.doi.org/10.1787/068186423156

The size of the school-age population in a particular country shapes the potential demand for initial education and training. The larger the number of young people, the greater the potential demand for educational services. Among OECD countries of comparable national income, a country with a relatively large youth population will have to spend a higher percentage of its GDP on education so that each young person in that country has the opportunity to receive the same quantity of education as young people in other OECD countries, based on the assumption that the cost for teachers and facilities are comparable in these countries. Conversely, but based on the same assumption, if the youth population is relatively small, the same country will be required to spend less of its wealth on education in order to achieve similar results.

B2

Comparing expenditure on educational institutions as a percentage of GDP to the proportion of the population enrolled in education shows in general that countries with a proportion of their population enrolled in formal education above 25% (such as Belgium, Denmark, Iceland, Mexico, Norway and New Zealand and the partner economies Chile and Israel) are also countries with above OECD average expenditure on education as a percentage of GDP (Chart B2.3). On the contrary, in Austria, Italy, Japan, Greece, Portugal, Spain and Turkey, and the partner economy the Russian Federation, students enrolled in formal education represent the lowest proportions the population (less than 20%) and these countries have expenditure on education below the OECD average. Some of these countries also have the lowest shares of GDP devoted to education among OECD countries and partner economies.

Nevertheless, the proportion of the school-age population is not the sole factor influencing expenditure. Countries with similar proportions of the population in education may spend different shares of their GDP, according to the level of priority given to the education sector, or the ways education expenditure are distributed between the different levels of education. For example, the proportion of the population enrolled in education are quite similar in Mexico and the partner economy Israel (30.2 and 30.3% of the population), but Mexico spends nearly 2 percentage points less of its GDP on education than does Israel. However, countries spending similar proportion of their GDP on education do not necessarily have the same proportion of their population enrolled in education. For example, the Slovak Republic and Japan spend 4.8% of their GDP on education, but students represent about 17% of the population in Japan against 23% of the population in the Slovak Republic. Differences in expenditure per student may explain this variation (see Table B1.1a).

Changes in overall educational spending between 1995 and 2004

More people are completing upper secondary and tertiary education than ever before (see Indicator A1), and in many countries, this expansion has been accompanied by massive financial investment. In the 26 OECD countries and partner economies for which comparable trend data are available for all levels of education combined, public and private investment in education increased in all countries by at least 7% between 1995 and 2004 in real terms and increased on average by 42% in OECD countries. Australia, Denmark, Finland, Hungary, the Netherlands, Norway, Portugal, the Slovak Republic, Sweden, the United Kingdom and the United States, and the partner economy Brazil, increased expenditure on education by 30 to 50% while Greece, Ireland, Mexico, New Zealand, Poland and Turkey, and the partner economy Chile, increased spending by more than 50% (Table B2.3).

Countries vary in the levels of education at which spending has increased over the period 1995 to 2004, but in most countries, expenditure in tertiary education increased in higher proportions compared to primary, secondary and post-secondary non-tertiary education. In the Czech Republic, Greece, Italy, Japan, Mexico, Poland, the Slovak Republic, Spain, Switzerland and the United States, increases in spending on tertiary education surpassed increases at the primary, secondary and post-secondary non-tertiary levels by 20 percentage points or more. Denmark, Finland, Germany, Ireland, Sweden, as well as partner economy Chile, invested additional resources in similar proportions in primary, secondary and post-secondary non-tertiary and tertiary education combined. Conversely, Australia, the Netherlands, New Zealand, Norway, Turkey and the United Kingdom and partner economy Brazil invested most of the increases

B2

(in relative terms) between 1995 and 2004 in primary, secondary and post-secondary non-tertiary education (Table B2.3).

During the period 1995 to 2004, the variation of expenditure on educational institutions was not necessarily constant over time – whether for all levels of education combined or for each level of education considered separately. Across OECD countries, the increase of expenditure for all levels of education combined is greater before 2000 than from 2000 in nearly one-half of the countries with available data. This does not solely result from the difference in the length of time over which the variation is measured, as in three-quarters of these countries, the average annual variation is larger over the period 1995 to 2000 than over the period 2000 to 2004. This slower growth of expenditure for 2000 to 2004 is particularly marked in Portugal and Turkey and in the partner economy Chile. The reverse pattern is true for the Czech Republic, Hungary, Norway, the Slovak Republic and the United Kingdom (Table B2.3; Chart B2.4c available on line at *http://dx.doi.org/10.1787/068186423156*).

Over the period 1995 to 2004, spending on the various levels of education evolved quite differently. Expenditure on primary to post-secondary non-tertiary education follow the same trends as for all levels of education combined. The slower growth of expenditure for 2000 to 2004 is particularly marked in Greece and Portugal, and in the partner economy Chile, whereas the reverse pattern is true in the Czech Republic, Hungary, Ireland and the Slovak Republic (Table B2.3 and Chart B2.4a).

Chart B2.4a. Change in expenditure on educational institutions between 1995 and 2004 for primary, secondary and post-secondary non tertiary education
(1995=100, constant prices)

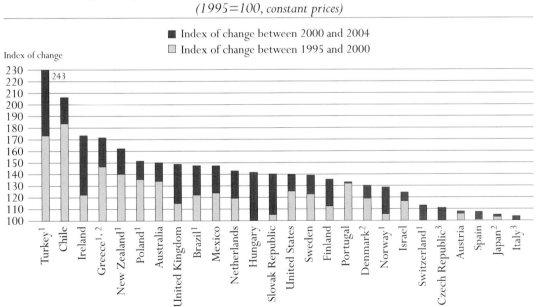

1. Public expenditure only.
2. Some levels of education are included with others. Refer to "x" code in Table B1.1b for details.
3. Expenditure on educational institutions decreased between 1995 and 2000 but have increased over the period 1995-2004.
Countries are ranked in descending order of change between 1995 and 2004 in total expenditure from both public and private sources on educational institutions.
Source: OECD. Table B2.3. See Annex 3 for notes (*www.oecd.org/edu/eag2007*).
StatLink ᴬᴵˢᴾ http://dx.doi.org/10.1787/068186423156

At the tertiary level, however, the increase is more pronounced from 2000 than before 2000 in one-half of the countries (even if based on the average annual variation). The increase of expenditure is more marked from 2000 than before 2000 particularly in the Austria, the Czech Republic, Greece, Norway, Poland, and the Slovak Republic. On the contrary, the increase of expenditure from 2000 is significantly smaller than from before 2000 in Ireland, Portugal, Turkey and the United States, as well as in partner economies Brazil, Chile and Israel (Table B2.3 and Chart B2.4b).

Chart B2.4b. Change in expenditure on educational institutions between 1995 and 2004 for tertiary education
(1995=100, constant prices)

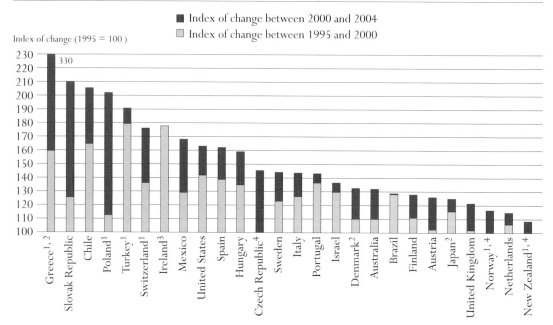

■ Index of change between 2000 and 2004
□ Index of change between 1995 and 2000

Index of change (1995 = 100)

1. Public expenditure only.
2. Some levels of education are included with others. Refer to "x" code in Table B1.1b for details.
3. Expenditure on educational institutions decreased by 4 percentage points between 2000 and 2004.
4. Expenditure on educational institutions decreased between 1995 and 2000 but have increased over the period 1995-2004.
Countries are ranked in descending order of change between 1995 and 2004 in total expenditure from both public and private sources on educational institutions.
Source: OECD. Table B2.3. See Annex 3 for notes (*www.oecd.org/edu/eag2007*).
StatLink ⬛⬛⬛ http://dx.doi.org/10.1787/068186423156

However, to make a sound interpretation, these variations over time should be viewed in light of the trends in national income. The increase in spending on education between 1995 and 2004 tended to fall behind the growth in national income in a third of the 26 OECD countries and partner economies for which data are available. The most notable differences are observed in Austria, Ireland and Spain, where the proportion of GDP spent on education decreased by 0.5 or more percentage points between 1995 and 2004 (Table B2.1). In Ireland, the strong growth of GDP hides a significant increase in spending on educational institutions when spending on education is considered as a proportion of GDP, while education in the Czech Republic did not benefit

B2

significantly from growth in GDP. Both countries were already among the OECD countries spending a lower proportion of GDP on education in 1995 and have now fallen further behind (Table B2.1, Table B2.3 and Annex 2, and Chart B2.5 available on line). By contrast, the proportion of GDP spent on education increased by 0.8 percentage points or more between 1995 and 2004 in Denmark, Greece, Mexico, Turkey and the United States, and the partner economy Chile: six countries that significantly increased their investment at the tertiary level between 1995 and 2004 (Tables B2.1 and B2.3).

Expenditure on educational institutions by source of funding

Increased expenditure on education in order to sustain growth in enrolment implies a heavier financial burden for society as a whole, but this burden does not rest only on public funding.

On average, from the 6.2% of the combined GDP in the OECD area devoted to education, more than three-quarters of expenditure come from public sources (Table B2.4). The majority of the funding is from public sources in all countries and public expenditure may constitute nearly the sole source of funding in Norway. However, the breakdown of educational expenditure by source of funding and by level of education shows more differences between countries (see Indicator B3).

Definitions and methodologies

Data refer to the financial year 2004 and are based on the UOE data collection on education statistics administered by the OECD in 2006 (for details see Annex 3 at *www.oecd.org/edu/eag2007*). Expenditure on educational institutions, as covered by this indicator, includes expenditure on both instructional and non-instructional educational institutions. Instructional educational institutions are educational institutions which directly provide instructional programmes (*i.e.* teaching) to individuals in an organised group setting or through distance education. Business enterprises or other institutions providing short-term courses of training or instruction to individuals on a one-to-one basis are not included. Non-instructional educational institutions provide administrative, advisory or professional services to other educational institutions, although they do not enrol students themselves. Examples include national, state and provincial ministries or departments of education; other bodies that administer education at various levels of government or analogous bodies in the private sector: and organisations that provide such education-related services as vocational or psychological counselling, placement, testing, financial aid to students, curriculum development, educational research, building operations and maintenance services, transportation of students, and student meals and housing.

This broad definition of institutions ensures that expenditure on services, which are provided in some OECD countries by schools and universities and in others by agencies other than schools, are covered on a comparable basis.

The distinction by source of funds is based on the initial source of funds and does not reflect subsequent public-to-private or private-to-public transfers. For this reason, subsidies to households and other entities, such as subsidies for tuition fees and other payments to educational institutions, are included in public expenditure in this indicator. Payments from households and other private entities to educational institutions include tuition and other fees, net of offsetting public subsidies. A detailed discussion of public subsidies can be found in Indicator B5.

B2

The OECD average is calculated as the simple average of all OECD countries for which data are available. The OECD total reflects the value of the indicator if the OECD region is considered as a whole (see the Reader's Guide for details).

Tables B2.1 and B2.3 show expenditure on educational institutions for the financial year 1995 and also for financial years 2000 to 2004 for Table B2.3. The data on expenditure for 1995 were obtained by a special survey in 2002 and updated in 2006; expenditure for 1995 was adjusted to methods and definitions used in the 2006 UOE data collection.

Data for 1995 are expressed in 2004 price levels. Charts B2.1, B2.4a and B2.4b and Tables B2.1 and B2.3 present an index of change in expenditure on institutions and GDP between 1995 and 2004. All expenditure, as well as 1995 GDP, is adjusted to 2004 prices using the GDP deflator.

For comparisons over time, the OECD average accounts only for those OECD countries for which data are available for all reported reference years.

Note that data appearing in earlier editions of this publication may not always be comparable to data shown in the 2007 edition due to changes in definitions and coverage that were made as a result of the OECD expenditure comparability study (for details on changes, see Annex 3 at *www.oecd.org/edu/eag2007*).

Further references

The following additional information relevant to this indicator is available on line at:
StatLink ᠊ᠠᠯᡓᢁ http://dx.doi.org/10.1787/068186423156

- *Chart B2.4c. Change in expenditure on educational institutions between 1995 and 2004 for all levels of education combined*
- *Chart B2.5. Changes in expenditure on educational institutions and changes in GDP (1995, 2004)*

Table B2.1.
Expenditure on educational institutions as a percentage of GDP, by levels of education (1995, 2000, 2004)
From public and private sources, by year

		2004			2000			1995	
	Primary, secondary and post-secondary non-tertiary education	Tertiary education	Total all levels of education	Primary, secondary and post-secondary non-tertiary education	Tertiary education	Total all levels of education	Primary, secondary and post-secondary non-tertiary education	Tertiary education	Total all levels of education
OECD countries									
Australia	4.2	1.6	**5.9**	4.2	1.5	**5.6**	3.7	1.7	**5.5**
Austria	3.7	1.2	**5.4**	3.9	1.0	**5.5**	4.2	1.2	**6.1**
Belgium	4.1	1.2	**6.1**	4.1	1.3	**6.1**	m	m	**m**
Canada	m	m	**m**	3.3	2.3	**5.9**	4.5	2.3	**7.0**
Czech Republic	3.2	1.1	**4.9**	2.8	0.8	**4.2**	3.5	0.9	**5.1**
Denmark	4.3	1.8	**7.2**	4.1	1.6	**6.6**	4.0	1.6	**6.2**
Finland	3.9	1.8	**6.1**	3.6	1.7	**5.6**	4.0	1.9	**6.3**
France	4.1	1.3	**6.1**	m	m	**m**	m	m	**m**
Germany	3.5	1.1	**5.2**	m	m	**m**	3.7	1.1	**5.4**
Greece	2.2	1.1	**3.4**	2.3	0.7	**3.1**	1.8	0.5	**2.3**
Hungary	3.5	1.1	**5.6**	2.9	1.1	**4.9**	3.5	1.0	**5.3**
Iceland	5.4	1.2	**8.0**	4.7	0.9	**6.1**	m	m	**m**
Ireland	3.4	1.2	**4.6**	2.9	1.5	**4.5**	3.8	1.3	**5.2**
Italy	3.4	0.9	**4.9**	3.2	0.9	**4.8**	m	0.7	**m**
Japan	2.9	1.3	**4.8**	3.0	1.3	**4.8**	3.1	1.1	**4.7**
Korea	4.4	2.3	**7.2**	4.0	2.6	**7.1**	m	m	**m**
Luxembourg[1]	3.8	m	**m**	m	m	**m**	m	m	**m**
Mexico	4.3	1.3	**6.4**	3.8	1.1	**5.5**	4.0	1.1	**5.6**
Netherlands	3.4	1.3	**5.1**	3.0	1.2	**4.5**	3.0	1.4	**4.8**
New Zealand	5.0	1.4	**6.9**	m	m	**m**	m	m	**m**
Norway[1]	4.2	1.4	**6.2**	3.8	1.3	**5.4**	4.3	1.7	**6.3**
Poland	3.8	1.5	**6.0**	3.9	1.1	**5.6**	m	m	**m**
Portugal	3.8	1.0	**5.4**	3.9	1.0	**5.4**	3.6	0.9	**5.0**
Slovak Republic	3.0	1.1	**4.8**	2.7	0.8	**4.0**	3.0	0.7	**4.6**
Spain	3.0	1.2	**4.7**	3.2	1.1	**4.8**	3.8	1.0	**5.3**
Sweden	4.5	1.8	**6.7**	4.3	1.6	**6.4**	4.1	1.6	**6.2**
Switzerland	4.5	1.6	**6.2**	4.1	1.1	**5.8**	4.6	0.9	**6.0**
Turkey	3.1	1.0	**4.1**	2.4	1.0	**3.4**	1.7	0.7	**2.4**
United Kingdom	4.4	1.1	**5.9**	3.6	1.0	**5.0**	3.9	1.2	**5.5**
United States	4.1	2.9	**7.4**	3.9	2.7	**7.0**	3.9	2.4	**6.6**
OECD average	*3.8*	*1.4*	*5.8*	*~*	*~*	*~*	*~*	*~*	*~*
OECD total	*3.8*	*1.9*	*6.2*	*~*	*~*	*~*	*~*	*~*	*~*
EU19 average	*3.6*	*1.3*	*5.4*	*~*	*~*	*~*	*~*	*~*	*~*
OECD mean for countries with 1995, 2000 and 2004 data (20 countries)	*3.7*	*1.4*	*5.5*	*3.4*	*1.3*	*5.1*	*3.6*	*1.2*	*5.3*
Partner economies									
Brazil[1]	2.9	0.7	**3.9**	2.8	0.7	**3.8**	2.5	0.7	**3.6**
Chile[2]	3.8	2.0	**6.4**	4.3	2.2	**6.9**	3.1	1.7	**5.1**
Estonia[1]	3.7	0.9	**4.9**	m	m	**m**	m	m	**m**
Israel	4.7	1.9	**8.3**	4.6	1.9	**8.1**	5.0	1.9	**8.6**
Russian Federation[1]	2.0	0.7	**3.6**	1.7	0.5	**2.9**	m	m	**m**
Slovenia	4.3	1.4	**6.3**	m	m	**m**	m	m	**m**

1. Expenditure from public sources only.
2. Year of reference 2005.
Source: OECD. See Annex 3 for notes (*www.oecd.org/edu/eag2007*).
Please refer to the Reader's Guide for information concerning the symbols replacing missing data.
StatLink ⬛ᵐˢ┗ http://dx.doi.org/10.1787/068186423156

B₂

Table B2.2.
Expenditure on educational institutions as a percentage of GDP, by level of education (2004)
From public and private sources[1]

	Pre-primary education (for children 3 years and older)	Primary, secondary and post-secondary non-tertiary education				Tertiary education			All levels of education combined (including undistributed programmes)
		All primary, secondary and post-secondary non-tertiary education	Primary & lower secondary education	Upper secondary education	Post-secondary non-tertiary education	All tertiary education	Tertiary-type B education	Tertiary-type A education and advanced research programmes	
	(1)	(2)	(3)	(4)	(5)	(6)	(7)	(8)	(9)
Australia	0.1	4.2	3.2	0.9	0.1	1.6	0.1	1.5	5.9
Austria	0.5	3.7	2.4	1.4	n	1.2	0.1	1.2	5.4
Belgium[2]	0.6	4.1	1.5	2.7	x(4)	1.2	x(6)	x(6)	6.1
Canada	m	m	m	m	m	m	m	m	m
Czech Republic	0.5	3.2	1.9	1.2	0.1	1.1	0.1	1.0	4.9
Denmark	0.9	4.3	3.0	1.3	x(4, 6)	1.8	x(6)	x(6)	7.2
Finland	0.4	3.9	2.5	1.4	x(4)	1.8	n	1.8	6.1
France	0.7	4.1	2.6	1.5	n	1.3	0.3	1.1	6.1
Germany	0.5	3.5	2.0	1.2	0.2	1.1	0.1	1.0	5.2
Greece[2]	x(3)	2.2	1.0	1.2	0.1	1.1	0.2	0.9	3.4
Hungary	0.8	3.5	2.1	1.2	0.2	1.1	n	1.0	5.6
Iceland	0.7	5.4	3.8	x(2)	x(2)	1.2	x(6)	x(6)	8.0
Ireland	n	3.4	2.5	0.7	0.2	1.2	x(6)	x(6)	4.6
Italy	0.5	3.4	2.1	1.3	0.1	0.9	n	0.9	4.9
Japan	0.2	2.9	2.1	0.9	x(4, 6)	1.3	0.2	1.1	4.8
Korea	0.1	4.4	3.0	1.4	a	2.3	0.5	1.8	7.2
Luxembourg[3]	x(2)	3.8	2.9	0.9	m	m	m	m	m
Mexico	0.7	4.3	3.4	0.8	a	1.3	x(6)	x(6)	6.4
Netherlands	0.4	3.4	2.6	0.8	n	1.3	a	1.3	5.1
New Zealand	0.3	5.0	3.2	1.6	0.2	1.4	0.2	1.2	6.9
Norway[3]	0.3	4.2	2.8	1.4	x(4)	1.4	x(6)	x(6)	6.2
Poland	0.6	3.8	2.7	1.1	0.1	1.5	n	1.5	6.0
Portugal	0.4	3.8	2.8	1.0	m	1.0	0.3	0.7	5.4
Slovak Republic	0.5	3.0	1.8	1.3	x(4)	1.1	x(4)	1.1	4.8
Spain	0.6	3.0	3.0	x(3)	a	1.2	x(6)	x(6)	4.7
Sweden	0.5	4.5	3.1	1.3	n	1.8	x(6)	x(6)	6.7
Switzerland[3]	0.2	4.5	2.8	1.7	0.1	1.6	n	1.6	6.2
Turkey	m	3.1	2.2	0.9	a	1.0	x(6)	x(6)	4.1
United Kingdom[2]	0.4	4.4	1.5	2.9	x(4)	1.1	x(6)	x(6)	5.9
United States	0.4	4.1	3.0	1.0	m	2.9	x(6)	x(6)	7.4
OECD average	*0.5*	*3.8*	*2.5*	*1.3*	*0.1*	*1.4*	*0.1*	*1.2*	*5.8*
OECD total	*0.4*	*3.8*	*2.6*	*1.2*	*0.1*	*1.9*	*0.2*	*1.2*	*6.2*
EU19 average	*0.5*	*3.6*	*2.3*	*1.4*	*0.1*	*1.3*	*0.1*	*1.1*	*5.4*
Brazil[3]	0.3	2.9	2.4	0.5	a	0.7	x(4)	0.7	3.9
Chile[4]	0.5	3.8	2.5	1.3	a	2.0	0.4	1.6	6.4
Estonia[3]	0.3	3.7	2.4	1.1	0.2	0.9	0.3	0.6	4.9
Israel[2]	0.9	4.7	2.5	2.2	n	1.9	0.4	1.5	8.3
Russian Federation[3]	0.5	2.0	x(2)	x(2)	x(2)	0.7	0.1	0.5	3.6
Slovenia	0.6	4.3	3.0	1.3	x(4)	1.4	x(6)	x(6)	6.3

1. Including international sources.
2. Column 3 only refers to primary education and column 4 refers to all secondary education.
3. Public expenditure only (for Switzerland, in tertiary education only).
4. Year of reference 2005.
Source: OECD. See Annex 3 for notes *(www.oecd.org/edu/eag2007).*
Please refer to the Reader's Guide for information concerning the symbols replacing missing data.
StatLink ⏣ http://dx.doi.org/10.1787/068186423156

Table B2.3.

Change in expenditure on educational institutions (1995, 2000, 2001, 2002, 2003, 2004)

Index of change between 1995 and 2004 in expenditure on educational institutions from public and private sources, by level of education [GDP deflator (1995=100), constant price]

		All levels of education						Primary, secondary and post-secondary non-tertiary education						Tertiary education					
		1995	2000	2001	2002	2003	2004	1995	2000	2001	2002	2003	2004	1995	2000	2001	2002	2003	2004
		(1)	(2)	(3)	(4)	(5)	(6)	(7)	(8)	(9)	(10)	(11)	(12)	(13)	(14)	(15)	(16)	(17)	(18)
OECD countries	Australia	100	127	133	137	141	145	100	134	141	143	148	150	100	110	113	122	125	132
	Austria	100	103	105	106	107	108	100	106	103	104	108	108	100	102	117	111	115	126
	Belgium	m	m	m	m	m	m	m	m	m	m	m	m	m	m	m	m	m	m
	Canada[1]	100	108	111	114	m	m	100	95	95	106	m	m	100	134	141	142	m	m
	Czech Republic	100	89	93	96	107	116	100	86	90	92	102	111	100	99	107	116	138	145
	Denmark[1]	100	123	131	132	132	138	100	119	125	123	125	130	100	110	129	135	125	133
	Finland	100	113	117	122	129	134	100	112	117	123	131	135	100	111	112	116	121	128
	France[2]	100	110	111	111	m	m	100	110	111	111	m	m	100	110	110	111	m	m
	Germany	100	m	m	m	110	109	100	m	m	m	107	106	100	m	m	m	114	112
	Greece[1, 3]	100	155	166	176	200	208	100	147	137	145	161	172	100	160	217	246	310	312
	Hungary	100	111	119	134	155	150	100	100	107	121	143	142	100	135	145	162	185	159
	Iceland	m	m	m	m	m	m	m	m	m	m	m	m	m	m	m	m	m	m
	Ireland	100	137	142	148	159	171	100	122	134	141	157	174	100	178	167	167	162	174
	Italy	100	103	113	107	109	107	100	95	110	103	107	104	100	126	135	139	136	144
	Japan[1]	100	107	108	109	112	111	100	103	104	106	106	105	100	116	115	118	124	125
	Korea	m	m	m	m	m	m	m	m	m	m	m	m	m	m	m	m	m	m
	Luxembourg	m	m	m	m	m	m	m	m	m	m	m	m	m	m	m	m	m	m
	Mexico	100	129	138	148	162	159	100	124	137	135	149	147	100	129	123	172	167	168
	Netherlands	100	115	121	126	129	134	100	119	127	134	138	143	100	106	109	107	111	115
	New Zealand[3]	100	133	133	143	152	154	100	140	140	149	159	162	100	96	100	107	112	109
	Norway[3]	100	103	116	126	136	134	100	106	110	122	132	129	100	94	98	110	115	117
	Poland[3]	100	125	134	136	142	151	100	136	147	145	149	152	100	113	132	166	170	202
	Portugal	100	130	138	137	139	136	100	132	139	139	136	133	100	136	147	137	150	143
	Slovak Republic[1]	100	105	109	116	136	146	100	105	107	116	134	140	100	126	148	149	167	210
	Spain	100	110	113	115	119	124	100	101	101	102	104	107	100	139	147	151	158	162
	Sweden	100	123	124	135	137	139	100	123	123	133	135	139	100	123	126	135	141	144
	Switzerland[3]	100	106	112	118	120	116	100	100	105	109	109	113	100	136	153	167	177	176
	Turkey[3]	100	175	167	176	196	229	100	174	166	171	194	243	100	179	170	191	202	191
	United Kingdom	100	112	120	131	139	139	100	115	123	136	149	149	100	102	109	118	120	122
	United States	100	131	130	135	143	148	100	125	132	136	139	140	100	142	127	133	150	163
	OECD average	*100*	*119*	*124*	*129*	*138*	*142*	*100*	*117*	*121*	*126*	*134*	*139*	*100*	*124*	*132*	*141*	*150*	*155*
	EU19 average	*100*	*117*	*122*	*127*	*134*	*138*	*100*	*114*	*119*	*123*	*130*	*134*	*100*	*124*	*135*	*142*	*152*	*158*
Partner economies	Brazil[1, 3]	100	121	122	123	136	140	100	122	125	125	142	148	100	128	128	131	140	129
	Chile[4]	100	178	m	201	206	211	100	184	m	206	210	207	100	165	m	186	193	206
	Estonia	m	m	m	m	m	m	m	m	m	m	m	m	m	m	m	m	m	m
	Israel	100	119	125	127	125	129	100	117	123	126	121	124	100	130	132	131	133	137
	Russian Federation	m	m	m	m	m	m	m	m	m	m	m	m	m	m	m	m	m	m
	Slovenia	m	m	m	m	m	m	m	m	m	m	m	m	m	m	m	m	m	m

1. Some levels of education are included with others. Refer to "x"code in Table B1.1b for details.
2. Excluding over sea departments (DOM).
3. Public expenditure only.
4. Year of reference 2005 instead of 2004.

Source: OECD. See Annex 3 for notes (*www.oecd.org/edu/eag2007*).

Please refer to the Reader's Guide for information concerning the symbols replacing missing data.

StatLink http://dx.doi.org/10.1787/068186423156

B2

Table B2.4.
Expenditure on educational institutions as a percentage of GDP, by source of fund and level of education (2004)
From public and private sources of fund

	Primary, secondary and post-secondary non-tertiary education			Tertiary education			Total all levels of education		
	Public[1]	Private[2]	Total	Public[1]	Private[2]	Total	Public[1]	Private[2]	Total
Australia	3.5	0.7	**4.2**	0.8	0.8	**1.6**	4.3	1.6	**5.9**
Austria	3.6	0.2	**3.7**	1.1	0.1	**1.2**	5.0	0.4	**5.4**
Belgium	4.0	0.2	**4.1**	1.2	0.1	**1.2**	5.8	0.2	**6.1**
Canada	m	m	**m**	m	m	**m**	m	m	**m**
Czech Republic	2.8	0.4	**3.2**	0.9	0.2	**1.1**	4.2	0.6	**4.9**
Denmark[3]	4.2	0.1	**4.3**	1.8	0.1	**1.8**	6.9	0.3	**7.2**
Finland	3.9	n	**3.9**	1.7	0.1	**1.8**	6.0	0.1	**6.1**
France	3.9	0.2	**4.1**	1.2	0.2	**1.3**	5.7	0.4	**6.1**
Germany	2.8	0.6	**3.5**	1.0	0.1	**1.1**	4.3	0.9	**5.2**
Greece[3]	2.1	0.1	**2.2**	1.1	n	**1.1**	3.3	0.2	**3.4**
Hungary	3.3	0.2	**3.5**	0.9	0.2	**1.1**	5.1	0.5	**5.6**
Iceland[3]	5.2	0.2	**5.4**	1.1	0.1	**1.2**	7.2	0.7	**8.0**
Ireland	3.3	0.1	**3.4**	1.0	0.1	**1.2**	4.3	0.3	**4.6**
Italy	3.3	0.1	**3.4**	0.7	0.3	**0.9**	4.4	0.5	**4.9**
Japan[3]	2.7	0.3	**2.9**	0.5	0.8	**1.3**	3.5	1.2	**4.8**
Korea	3.5	0.9	**4.4**	0.5	1.8	**2.3**	4.4	2.8	**7.2**
Luxembourg[3]	3.8	m	**m**	m	m	**m**	m	m	**m**
Mexico	3.6	0.7	**4.3**	0.9	0.4	**1.3**	5.2	1.2	**6.4**
Netherlands	3.3	0.2	**3.4**	1.0	0.3	**1.3**	4.6	0.5	**5.1**
New Zealand	4.4	0.6	**5.0**	0.9	0.6	**1.4**	5.6	1.3	**6.9**
Norway	4.2	m	**m**	1.4	m	**m**	6.2	m	**m**
Poland	3.7	0.1	**3.8**	1.1	0.4	**1.5**	5.4	0.6	**6.0**
Portugal	3.8	n	**3.8**	0.9	0.1	**1.0**	5.3	0.1	**5.4**
Slovak Republic[3]	2.6	0.5	**3.0**	0.9	0.2	**1.1**	4.0	0.8	**4.8**
Spain	2.8	0.2	**3.0**	0.9	0.3	**1.2**	4.2	0.6	**4.7**
Sweden	4.5	n	**4.5**	1.6	0.2	**1.8**	6.5	0.2	**6.7**
Switzerland	3.9	0.6	**4.5**	1.6	m	**m**	5.9	m	**m**
Turkey	2.9	0.2	**3.1**	0.9	0.1	**1.0**	3.8	0.3	**4.1**
United Kingdom	3.8	0.6	**4.4**	0.8	0.3	**1.1**	5.0	1.0	**5.9**
United States	3.7	0.4	**4.1**	1.0	1.9	**2.9**	5.1	2.3	**7.4**
OECD average	*3.6*	*0.3*	*3.8*	*1.0*	*0.4*	*1.4*	*5.0*	*0.7*	*5.7*
OECD total	*3.4*	*0.4*	*3.8*	*0.9*	*1.0*	*1.9*	*4.7*	*1.4*	*6.2*
EU19 average	*3.4*	*0.2*	*3.6*	*1.1*	*0.2*	*1.3*	*5.0*	*0.5*	*5.4*
Brazil[3]	2.9	m	**m**	0.7	m	**m**	3.9	m	**m**
Chile[4]	2.7	1.2	**3.8**	0.3	1.7	**2.0**	3.3	3.1	**6.4**
Estonia	3.7	m	**m**	0.9	m	**m**	4.9	m	**m**
Israel	4.4	0.3	**4.7**	1.1	0.9	**1.9**	6.6	1.8	**8.3**
Russian Federation	2.0	m	**m**	0.7	m	**m**	3.6	m	**m**
Slovenia	3.9	0.4	**4.3**	1.1	0.3	**1.4**	5.4	0.9	**6.3**

(Left margin labels: OECD countries; Partner economies)

1. Including public subsidies to households for educational institutions, as well as direct expenditure on educational institutions from international sources.
2. Net of public subsidies attributable for educational institutions.
3. Some levels of education are included with others. Refer to "x"code in table B1.1a for details.
4. Year of reference 2005.
Source: OECD. See Annex 3 for notes *(www.oecd.org/edu/eag2007).*
Please refer to the Reader's Guide for information concerning the symbols replacing missing data.
StatLink ᴍˢᴸ http://dx.doi.org/10.1787/068186423156

HOW MUCH PUBLIC AND PRIVATE INVESTMENT IS THERE IN EDUCATION?

This indicator examines the proportion of public and private funding allocated to educational institutions for each level of education. It also provides the breakdown of private funding between household expenditure and expenditure from private entities other than households. This indicator sheds some light on the widely debated issue of how the financing of educational institutions should be shared between public entities and private ones, particularly those at the tertiary level.

Key results

Chart B3.1. Share of private expenditure on educational institutions (2004)

The chart shows private spending on educational institutions as a percentage of total spending on educational institutions. This includes all money transferred to such institutions through private sources, including public funding via subsidies to households, private fees for educational services or other private spending (e.g. on accommodation) that passes through the institution.

☐ Primary, secondary and post-secondary non-tertiary education
■ Tertiary education

On average over 90% of primary and secondary education in OECD countries, and nowhere less than 80% (except in Korea and in the partner economy Chile), is paid for publicly. However, in tertiary education the proportion funded privately varies widely, from less than 5% in Denmark, Finland and Greece, to more than 50% in Australia, Japan and the United States and in partner economy Israel, and to above 75% in Korea and in the partner economy Chile.

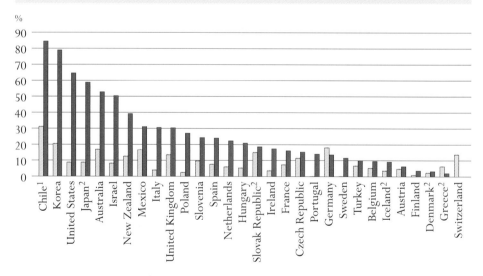

1. Year of reference 2005.
2. Some levels of education are included with others. Refer to "x" code in Table B1.1b for details.
Countries are ranked in descending order of the share of private expenditure on educational institutions for tertiary education.
Source: OECD. Tables B3.2a and B3.2b. See Annex 3 for notes (*www.oecd.org/edu/eag2007*).
StatLink ⫗ http://dx.doi.org/10.1787/068188403262

Other highlights of this indicator

- In all countries for which comparable data are available, for all levels of education combined, public funding increased between 1995 and 2004. However, private spending increased even more in nearly three-quarters of these countries. Nevertheless, in 2004, on average 87% of expenditure, for all levels of education combined, was still from public sources.

- The share of tertiary spending from private sources rose substantially in some countries between 1995 and 2004, but this was not the case at other levels of education.

- On average among the 18 OECD countries for which trend data are available, the share of public funding in tertiary institutions decreased slightly between 1995 and 2000, as well as every year between 2001 and 2004. However in general the increase of private investment has not displaced public financing, but rather complemented it.

- The share of public funding at the tertiary level in OECD countries represents on average 76% in 2004.

- Compared to other levels of education, tertiary institutions and to a lesser extent pre-primary institutions obtain the largest proportions of funds from private sources: respectively, 24 and 20% of funds at these levels come from private sources.

- In tertiary education, households cover the majority of all private expenditure in all countries with available data except Greece, Hungary and Sweden. Private expenditure from other entities than households is still significant, representing 10% or more in Australia, Hungary, Italy, Korea, the Netherlands, Sweden, the United Kingdom and the United States, and the partner economy Israel.

Policy context

Cost-sharing between participants in the education system and society as a whole is an issue under discussion in many OECD countries. This question is especially relevant for pre-primary and tertiary education, where full or nearly full public funding is less common.

As new client groups participate in a wider range of educational programmes and choose among more opportunities from increasing numbers of providers, governments are forging new partnerships to mobilise the necessary resources to pay for education and to share costs and benefits more equitably.

As a result, public funding is more often seen as providing only a part (although a very important part) of investment in education and the role of private sources has become more important. Some stakeholders are concerned that this balance should not become so tilted as to discourage potential students. Thus, changes in a country's public/private funding shares can provide important context for changing patterns and levels of participation within its educational system.

Evidence and explanations

What this indicator does and does not cover

Governments can spend public funds directly on educational institutions or use them to provide subsidies to private entities for the purpose of education. When reporting on the public and private proportions of educational expenditure, it is therefore important to distinguish between the initial sources of funds and the final direct purchasers of educational goods and services.

Initial public spending includes both direct public expenditure on educational institutions and transfers to the private sector. To gauge the level of public expenditure, it is necessary to add together the components showing direct public expenditure on educational institutions and public subsidies for education. Initial private spending includes tuition fees and other student or household payments to educational institutions, less the portion of such payments offset by public subsidies.

The final public and private proportions are the percentages of educational funds spent directly by public and private purchasers of educational services. Final public spending includes direct public purchases of educational resources and payments to educational institutions and other private entities. Final private spending includes tuition fees and other private payments to educational institutions.

Not all spending on instructional goods and services occurs within educational institutions. For example, families may purchase textbooks and materials commercially or seek private tutoring for their children outside educational institutions. At the tertiary level, student living costs and forgone earnings can also account for a significant proportion of the costs of education. All such expenditure outside educational institutions, even if it is publicly subsidised, is excluded from this indicator. Public subsidies for educational expenditure outside institutions are discussed in Indicators B4 and B5.

B3

Public and private expenditure on educational institutions at all levels of education

Educational institutions are still mainly publicly funded, although there is a substantial and growing degree of private funding at the tertiary level of education. On average across OECD countries, 87% of all funds for educational institutions come directly from public sources. In addition, 0.6% is channelled to institutions via public subsidies to households (Table B3.1).

In all the OECD countries for which comparable data are available, private funding represents 13% of all funds on average. This proportion varies widely among countries and only nine OECD countries and three partner economies report a share of private funding above the OECD average. Nevertheless, in Australia, Japan and the United States, as well as in partner economy Israel, private funds constitute around one-quarter of all educational expenditure and exceed 39% in Korea and the partner economy Chile (Table B3.1).

In all countries for which comparable data are available, for all levels of education combined, public funding increased between 1995 and 2004. However, private spending increased even more in nearly three-quarters of these countries. The decrease in the share of public funding was more than 5 percentage points only in Australia and the Slovak Republic. It is notable that decreases in the share of public expenditure in regard to total expenditure on educational institutions and, consequently increases in the share of private expenditure, have not generally gone hand in hand with cuts (in real terms) in public expenditure on education (Table B3.1). In fact, many OECD countries with the highest growth in private spending have also shown the highest increase in public funding of education. This indicates that an increase in private spending tends not to replace public investment but to complement it.

However, the share of private expenditure on education and how this varies among countries depends on the level of education: pre-primary, primary, secondary, post-secondary non-tertiary or tertiary.

Public and private expenditure on educational institutions in pre-primary, primary, secondary and post-secondary non-tertiary education

Investment in early childhood education is of key importance in order to build a strong foundation for lifelong learning and to ensure equitable access to learning opportunities later in school. In pre-primary education, the private share of total payments to educational institutions is more important than for all levels of education combined and represents on average 20%, but this proportion is very uneven between countries, ranging from 5% or less in France, the Netherlands and Sweden, to well over 25% in Australia, Austria, Germany, Iceland and New Zealand and the partner economy Chile, to 50% in Japan, and over 60% in Korea (Table B3.2a). Except in Austria and the Netherlands, the major part of private funding is covered by households.

Public funding dominates the primary, secondary and post-secondary non-tertiary levels of education in OECD countries and partner economies and among OECD countries reaches 92% on average. Nevertheless, the proportions of private funding exceed 10% in Australia, the Czech Republic, Germany, Korea, Mexico, New Zealand, the Slovak Republic, Switzerland and the United Kingdom, and the partner economy Chile (Table B3.2a and Chart B3.2). The importance of public funding may result from the fact that primary, secondary and post-secondary non-tertiary education are usually perceived as a public good with mainly public returns. In most

B3

Chart B3.2. Distribution of public and private expenditure on educational institutions (2004)

By level of education

■ All private sources, including subsidies for payments to educational institutions received from public sources
□ Expenditure of other private entities
■ Household expenditure
▨ Public expenditure on educational institutions

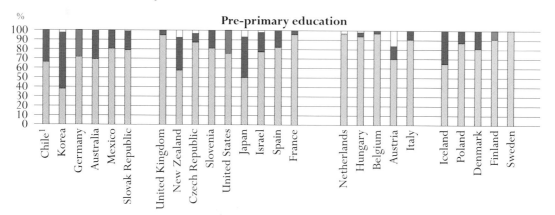

Pre-primary education

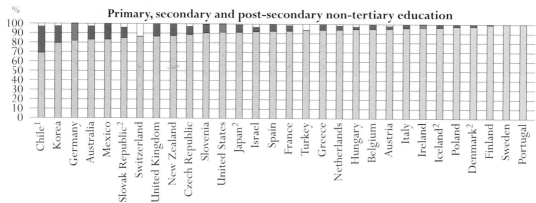

Primary, secondary and post-secondary non-tertiary education

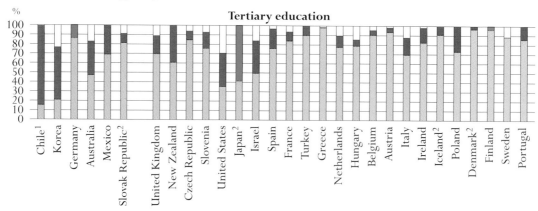

Tertiary education

1. Year of reference 2005.
2. Some levels of education are included with others. Refer to "x" code in Table B1.1b for details.
Countries are ranked in ascending order of the share of public expenditure on educational institutions in primary, secondary and post-secondary non-tertiary education.
Source: OECD. Tables B3.2a and B3.2b. See Annex 3 for notes (www.oecd.org/edu/eag2007).
StatLink ⫘▨▤ http://dx.doi.org/10.1787/068188403262

B3

countries, at the primary, secondary and post-secondary non-tertiary level, the share of private expenditure results from household expenditure and comprises mainly expenditure on tuition. In Germany and Switzerland, however, most private expenditure is accounted for by contributions from the business sector to the dual system of apprenticeship at the upper secondary and post-secondary non-tertiary levels.

Between 1995 and 2004, among the 20 OECD countries and partner economies with comparable data available, there was a small decrease in the share of public funding at primary, secondary and post-secondary non-tertiary levels in two-thirds of countries. Twelve countries recorded shifts from public to private funding, but the increase in the private share is about 2 percentage points or more only in Australia (14.5 to 16.8%), the Czech Republic (9.1 to 11.4%), the Slovak Republic (from 0.9 to 14.9%), Switzerland (10.9 to 13.6%) and the United Kingdom (from 11.5 to 13.4%), as well as in the partner economy Chile (from 28.2 to 31.1%). Funding shifts in the opposite direction, towards public funding, are notable in the other one-third of countries; the share of public funding increased by 3 percentage points or more in Hungary (from 91.7 to 94.7%) and Spain (87.6 to 92.5%) (Chart B3.3 and Table B3.2a).

Whatever the variation of the share of public funding at primary, secondary and post-secondary non-tertiary levels between 1995 and 2004, public educational expenditure increased in all countries with comparable data over this period. Contrary to the general picture given when all levels of education are combined, the increase in public expenditure does go along with a decrease of private expenditure in some countries (Hungary, Spain and Sweden). However, it is only in Spain that this may result in a decrease of total educational expenditure compared to GDP (see Table B2.1).

Public and private expenditure on educational institutions in tertiary institutions

In all OECD countries and partner economies except Germany and Greece, the private proportion of educational expenditure is far higher at the tertiary level than at the primary, secondary and post-secondary non-tertiary levels and represents on average nearly one-quarter of total expenditure on educational institutions at this level. At the tertiary level, the high private returns in the form of better employment and income opportunities (see Indicator A9) suggest that a greater contribution by individuals to the costs of tertiary education may be justified, provided, of course, that governments can ensure that funding is accessible to students irrespective of their economic background (see Indicator B5).

The proportion of expenditure on tertiary institutions covered by individuals, businesses and other private sources, including subsidised private payments, ranges from less than 5% in Denmark, Finland and Greece, to more than 50% in Australia, Japan and the United States and in the partner economy Israel and over 75% in Korea and the partner economy Chile (Chart B3.2 and Table B3.2b). In Korea, around 80% of tertiary students are enrolled in private universities, where more than 70% of budgets are derived from tuition fees. The contribution of private entities other than households to the financing of educational institutions is on average higher for tertiary education than for other levels of education. In one-quarter of OECD countries and partner economies – Australia, Hungary, Italy, Korea, the Netherlands, Sweden, the United Kingdom and the United States, and the partner economy Israel – the proportion of expenditure on tertiary institutions covered by private entities other than households represents 10% or more.

B3

Chart B3.3. Share of private expenditure on educational institutions (1995, 2004)

Percentage

□ 1995   ◆ 2004

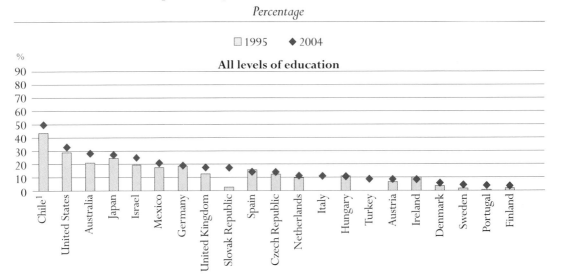

All levels of education

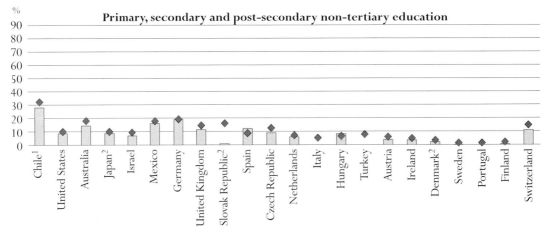

Primary, secondary and post-secondary non-tertiary education

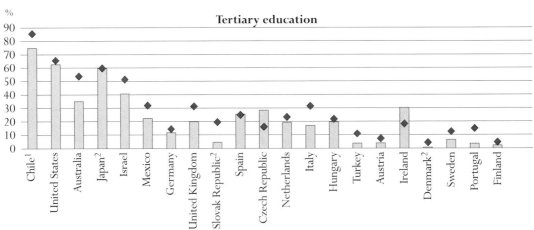

Tertiary education

1. Year of reference 2005.
2. Some levels of education are included with others. Refer to "x" code in Table B1.1b for details.
Countries are ranked in descending order of the share of private expenditure on educational institutions in 2004 for all levels of education.
Source: OECD. Tables B3.1, B3.2a and B3.2b. See Annex 3 for notes (*www.oecd.org/edu/eag2007*).
StatLink ⟨⟩ http://dx.doi.org/10.1787/068188403262

In many OECD countries, the growth in tertiary participation (see Indicator C2) represents a response to heavy demand, both individual and social. Just as many tertiary structures and programmes were designed for a different era, so too were its funding mechanisms. The share of public funding at the tertiary level represents on average in OECD countries 76% in 2004. On average among the 18 OECD countries for which trend data are available, the share of public funding in tertiary institutions slightly decreased between 1995 and 2000 and every year between 2001 and 2004 (Table B3.3).

In more than one-half of the OECD countries and partner economies with comparable data in 1995 and 2004, the private share increased by 3 percentage points or more. This increase exceeds 9 percentage points in Australia, Italy, Portugal, the Slovak Republic and the United Kingdom, as well as the partner economies Chile and Israel. However, only the Czech Republic and Ireland – and to a lesser extent Spain – show a significant decrease in the private share allocated to tertiary educational institutions (Table B3.2b and Chart B3.3). In Australia, the main reason for the increase in the private share of spending on tertiary institutions between 1995 and 2004 was changes to the Higher Education Contribution Scheme (HECS) that took place in 1997. The changes in HECS were part of a reform process aimed at providing more funds for higher education, partly through increased student/former student contributions. Thus, Australian figures on the public expenditure on educational institutions exclude HECS/HELP outlays. Public outlays on HECS/HELP by the Commonwealth government on behalf of students are treated as government loans or subsidies to households. Funds received by tertiary-type A institutions are treated as private payments from students (see Indicator B5).

The amounts paid by students and their families to cover tuition fees and other education-related expenditures differ among OECD countries according to taxation and spending policies, and the willingness of governments to support students (see Indicator B5). This willingness is influenced by students' enrolment status (full-time or part-time), age and residency (whether they are living at home). To some extent, however, the guidelines used in establishing eligibility for these subsidies are breaking down. Mature students, whose numbers are increasing, are more likely to have established their own households and to prefer part-time or distance learning to full-time, on-campus study.

Rises in private educational expenditure have generally gone hand in hand with rises (in real terms) in public expenditure on education at the tertiary level, as for educational expenditure when all levels of education are combined. Public investment in tertiary education has increased in all OECD countries and partner economies (except Australia) for which 1995 to 2004 data are available, regardless of changes in private spending (see Table B3.1). The only exception to this is Australia (see explanation on HECS above), where the shift towards private expenditure at tertiary level has been accompanied both by a small fall in the level of public expenditure in real terms and also by a significant increase of public subsidies provided to tertiary students.

Definitions and methodologies

Data refer to the financial year 2004 and are based on the UOE data collection on education statistics administered by the OECD in 2006 (for details see Annex 3 at *www.oecd.org/edu/eag2007*).

The public and private proportions of expenditure on educational institutions are the percentages of total spending originating in, or generated by, the public and private sectors. Private spending includes all direct expenditure on educational institutions, whether partially covered by public subsidies or not. Public subsidies attributable to households, included in private spending, are shown separately.

A portion of the budgets of educational institutions is related to ancillary services offered to students, including student welfare services (student meals, housing and transportation). Part of the cost for these services is covered by fees collected from students and is included in the indicator.

Other private entities include private businesses and non-profit organisations, including religious organisations, charitable organisations, and business and labour associations. Expenditure by private companies on the work-based element of school and work-based training of apprentices and students are also taken into account.

The data on expenditure for 1995 were obtained by a special survey updated in 2006 in which expenditure for 1995 was adjusted to methods and definitions used in the current UOE data collection.

Note that data appearing in earlier editions of this publication may not always be comparable to data shown in the 2007 edition due to changes in definitions and coverage that were made as a result of the OECD expenditure comparability study (for details on changes, see Annex 3 at *www.oecd.org/edu/eag2007*).

Table B3.1.
Relative proportions of public and private expenditure on educational institutions for all levels of education (1995, 2004)
Distribution of public and private sources of funds for educational institutions after transfers from public sources, by year

		2004					1995				Index of change between 1995 and 2004 in expenditure on educational institutions	
		Private sources					Private sources					
	Public sources	Household expenditure	Expenditure of other private entities	All private sources[1]	Private: of which, subsidised	Public sources	Household expenditure	Expenditure of other private entities	All private sources[1]	Private: of which, subsidised	Public sources	All private sources[1]
	(1)	(2)	(3)	(4)	(5)	(6)	(7)	(8)	(9)	(10)	(11)	(12)
Australia	73.0	20.3	6.7	27.0	0.2	78.9	13.7	7.4	21.1	0.5	134	185
Austria	92.8	4.1	3.2	7.2	2.1	93.4	3.4	3.2	6.6	1.5	107	118
Belgium	94.3	4.8	0.9	5.7	1.8	m	m	m	m	m	m	m
Canada	m	m	m	m	m	81.2	7.7	11.1	18.8	m	m	m
Czech Republic	87.3	9.1	3.6	12.7	m	87.5	x(9)	x(9)	12.5	6.2	115	118
Denmark	95.6	4.4	n	4.4	m	96.5	3.5	n	3.5	n	136	175
Finland	97.9	x(4)	x(4)	2.1	n	98.1	x(9)	x(9)	1.9	n	134	153
France	91.2	6.5	2.3	8.8	1.6	m	m	m	m	m	m	m
Germany	82.3	x(4)	x(4)	17.7	n	82.3	x(9)	x(9)	17.7	a	109	109
Greece	95.3	4.2	0.5	4.7	m	m	m	m	m	m	208	m
Hungary	90.7	3.6	5.7	9.3	n	89.0	5.0	6.0	11.0	n	153	127
Iceland	90.6	9.4	m	9.4	m	m	m	m	m	m	m	m
Ireland	92.9	6.6	0.5	7.1	m	89.8	9.7	0.5	10.2	m	178	119
Italy	90.4	7.2	2.4	9.6	n	m	m	m	m	m	107	m
Japan	74.2	23.2	2.6	25.8	m	75.5	22.6	1.9	24.5	m	109	117
Korea	60.5	30.1	9.4	39.5	0.9	m	m	m	m	m	m	m
Luxembourg	m	m	m	m	m	m	m	m	m	m	m	m
Mexico	80.5	19.3	0.2	19.5	1.0	82.6	17.4	m	17.4	m	155	178
Netherlands	90.1	5.9	4.0	9.9	0.9	90.2	6.4	3.4	9.8	1.8	134	135
New Zealand	80.7	18.8	0.5	19.3	m	m	m	m	m	m	154	m
Norway	m	m	m	m	m	94.1	x(9)	x(9)	5.9	n	134	m
Poland	90.1	9.9	m	9.9	m	m	m	m	m	a	151	m
Portugal	97.5	2.5	m	2.5	m	99.4	0.6	m	0.6	m	131	508
Slovak Republic	84.0	11.2	4.8	16.0	a	97.2	1.8	0.8	2.8	m	125	842
Spain	87.1	12.1	0.8	12.9	0.5	84.2	x(9)	x(9)	15.8	0.4	129	102
Sweden	97.0	0.1	2.9	3.0	a	98.3	0.1	1.6	1.7	m	137	244
Switzerland	m	m	m	m	m	m	m	m	m	m	116	m
Turkey	92.6	2.6	4.8	7.4	a	m	m	m	m	m	229	m
United Kingdom	83.9	14.0	2.1	16.1	n	87.3	x(9)	x(9)	12.7	n	134	177
United States	68.4	20.0	11.6	31.6	m	71.0	x(9)	x(9)	29.0	m	143	162
OECD average	*87.0*	*~*	*~*	*13.0*	*0.6*	*~*	*~*	*~*	*~*	*~*	*140*	*210*
EU19 average	*91.1*	*~*	*~*	*8.9*	*0.6*	*~*	*~*	*~*	*~*	*~*	*137*	*225*
Brazil	m	m	m	m	m	m	m	m	m	m	140	m
Chile[2]	51.6	46.2	2.2	48.4	0.8	56.4	42.4	1.2	43.6	m	193	234
Estonia	m	m	m	m	n	m	m	m	m	m	m	m
Israel	76.4	16.7	6.9	23.6	2.2	80.5	13.0	6.4	19.5	1.3	122	156
Russian Fed.	m	m	m	m	a	m	m	m	m	m	m	m
Slovenia	86.3	11.8	1.9	13.7	0.6	m	m	m	m	m	m	m

OECD countries (left margin) / *Partner economies* (left margin)

1. Including subsidies attributable to payments to educational institutions received from public sources.
2. Year of reference 2005.

Source: OECD. See Annex 3 for notes (*www.oecd.org/edu/eag2007*).

Please refer to the Reader's Guide for information concerning the symbols replacing missing data.

StatLink ᵒᵐˢᴸ http://dx.doi.org/10.1787/068188403262

B3

Table B3.2a.
Relative proportions of public and private expenditure on educational institutions, as a percentage, by level of education (1995, 2004)
Distribution of public and private sources of funds for educational institutions after transfers from public sources, by year

	Pre-primary education (for children 3 years and older) 2004					Primary, secondary and post-secondary non-tertiary education					2004		1995	Index of change between 1995 and 2004 in expenditure on educational institutions	
	Public sources	Household expenditure	Expenditure of other private entities	All private sources[1]	Private: of which subsidised	Public sources	Household expenditure	Expenditure of other private entities	All private sources[1]	Private: of which subsidised	Public sources	All private sources[1]	Private: of which subsidised	Public sources	All private sources[1]
	(1)	(2)	(3)	(4)	(5)	(6)	(7)	(8)	(9)	(10)	(11)	(12)	(13)	(14)	(15)
Australia	69.3	30.0	0.7	30.7	n	83.2	14.1	2.7	16.8	n	85.5	14.5	0.7	146	174
Austria	70.0	13.9	16.1	30.0	14.4	95.3	2.6	2.1	4.7	0.6	96.2	3.8	0.6	107	132
Belgium	97.1	2.9	m	m	0.3	94.9	5.1	m	m	1.2	m	m	m	m	m
Canada	x(6)	x(7)	x(8)	x(9)	x(6)	m	m	m	m	x(6)	92.8	7.2	x(11)	m	m
Czech Republic	87.3	9.3	3.3	12.7	m	88.6	8.6	2.8	11.4	m	90.9	9.1	6.8	108	139
Denmark[2]	81.1	18.9	m	18.9	m	97.8	2.2	m	2.2	m	97.8	2.2	n	130	127
Finland	91.1	x(4)	x(4)	8.9	n	99.2	x(9)	x(9)	0.8	n	99.5	0.5	n	135	200
France	95.8	4.2	n	4.2	n	92.7	5.9	1.4	7.3	1.7	m	m	m	m	m
Germany	71.8	x(4)	x(4)	28.2	n	81.9	x(9)	x(9)	18.1	n	81.0	19.0	a	108	101
Greece	x(6)	x(7)	x(8)	x(9)	m	93.8	6.2	n	6.2	m	m	m	m	172	m
Hungary	93.9	4.3	1.8	6.1	n	94.7	2.7	2.6	5.3	n	91.7	8.3	n	147	90
Iceland[2]	64.9	35.1	m	35.1	n	96.5	3.5	m	3.5	n	m	m	m	m	m
Ireland	m	m	m	m	m	96.4	x(9)	x(9)	3.6	n	96.5	3.5	m	174	177
Italy	90.8	9.2	m	9.2	0.4	96.1	3.9	0.1	3.9	n	m	m	m	104	m
Japan[2]	50.0	43.1	6.8	50.0	a	91.3	7.7	1.0	8.7	n	91.2	8.8	m	105	104
Korea	37.9	59.6	2.5	62.1	6.0	79.5	17.8	2.7	20.5	0.8	m	m	m	m	m
Luxembourg	m	m	m	m	m	m	m	m	m	m	m	m	m	m	m
Mexico	80.5	19.4	0.1	19.5	0.2	83.4	16.5	0.1	16.6	1.1	83.8	16.2	m	147	151
Netherlands	96.2	0.6	3.1	3.8	a	94.1	4.3	1.7	5.9	0.9	93.9	6.1	1.4	143	138
New Zealand	57.6	34.9	7.5	42.4	m	87.5	12.2	0.2	12.5	m	m	m	m	162	m
Norway	86.3	13.7	m	13.7	n	m	m	m	m	m	99.0	1.0	x(11)	129	m
Poland	87.1	12.9	m	12.9	n	97.6	2.4	m	2.4	m	m	m	m	152	m
Portugal	m	m	m	m	m	99.9	0.1	m	0.1	m	100.0	n	m	133	207
Slovak Republic[2]	79.0	19.9	1.1	21.0	a	85.1	10.8	4.1	14.9	a	99.1	0.9	m	120	2445
Spain	82.5	17.5	m	17.5	n	92.5	7.5	m	7.5	n	87.6	12.4	m	113	65
Sweden	100.0	n	n	n	n	99.9	0.1	a	0.1	a	99.8	0.2	m	139	80
Switzerland	m	m	m	m	m	86.4	n	13.6	13.6	0.8	89.1	10.9	1.1	113	m
Turkey	m	m	m	m	m	93.4	0.2	6.4	6.6	a	m	m	m	243	m
United Kingdom	94.9	5.1	n	5.1	a	86.6	13.4	n	13.4	m	88.5	11.5	m	146	174
United States	75.4	x(4)	x(4)	24.6	a	91.3	x(9)	x(9)	8.7	a	91.3	8.7	m	140	140
OECD average	*80.0*	*~*	*~*	*20.0*	*1.1*	*91.8*	*~*	*~*	*8.3*	*0.4*	*~*	*~*	*~*	*138*	*273*
EU19 average	*87.9*	*~*	*~*	*12.1*	*1.7*	*93.7*	*~*	*~*	*6.3*	*0.4*	*~*	*~*	*~*	*141*	*356*
Brazil	m	m	m	m	m	m	m	m	m	m	m	m	m	148	m
Chile[3]	66.2	33.7	0.1	33.8	m	68.9	28.0	3.1	31.1	m	71.8	28.2	m	198	227
Estonia	m	m	m	m	m	m	m	m	m	n	m	m	m	m	m
Israel	77.2	20.7	2.1	22.8	n	91.9	4.9	3.2	8.1	1.4	93.1	6.9	0.8	123	145
Russian Federation	m	m	m	m	a	m	m	m	m	m	m	m	m	m	m
Slovenia	81.1	18.9	0.1	18.9	n	90.4	9.0	0.5	9.6	0.8	m	m	m	m	m

OECD countries (left margin label)
Partner economies (left margin label)

1. Including subsidies attributable to payments to educational institutions received from public sources. To calculate private funds net of subsidies, subtract public subsidies (columns 5, 10, 15) from private funds (columns 4, 9, 14). To calculate total public funds, including public subsidies, add public subsidies (columns 5, 10, 15) to direct public funds (columns 1, 6, 11).
2. Some levels of education are included with others. Refer to "x" code in Table B1.1a for details.
3. Year of reference 2005.
Source: OECD. See Annex 3 for notes (*www.oecd.org/edu/eag2007*).
Please refer to the Reader's Guide for information concerning the symbols replacing missing data.
StatLink ⫘⫘ http://dx.doi.org/10.1787/068188403262

B3

Table B3.2b.

Relative proportions of public and private expenditure on educational institutions, as a percentage, for tertiary education (1995, 2004)

Distribution of public and private sources of funds for educational institutions after transfers from public sources, by year

	Tertiary education								Index of change between 1995 and 2004 in expenditure on educational institutions	
	2004					1995				
		Private sources								
	Public sources	Household expenditure	Expenditure of other private entities	All private sources[1]	Private: of which subsidised	Public sources	All private sources[1]	Private: of which subsidised	Public sources	All private sources[1]
	(1)	(2)	(3)	(4)	(5)	(6)	(7)	(8)	(9)	(10)
Australia	47.2	35.6	17.2	52.8	0.8	64.8	35.2	n	96	198
Austria	93.7	4.8	1.6	6.3	2.0	96.1	3.9	5.1	123	205
Belgium	90.4	5.1	4.5	9.6	4.7	m	m	m	m	m
Canada	m	m	m	m	m	56.6	43.4	22.3	m	m
Czech Republic	84.7	9.2	6.1	15.3	m	71.5	28.5	8.7	170	77
Denmark[2]	96.7	3.3	n	3.3	a	99.4	0.6	n	129	733
Finland	96.3	x(4)	x(4)	3.7	n	97.8	2.2	n	126	208
France	83.9	9.8	6.4	16.1	2.2	m	m	m	m	m
Germany	86.4	x(4)	x(4)	13.6	n	88.6	11.4	a	109	133
Greece	97.9	0.4	1.7	2.1	m	m	m	m	312	m
Hungary	79.0	6.6	14.4	21.0	n	80.3	19.7	n	157	169
Iceland[2]	90.9	9.1	m	9.1	m	m	m	m	m	m
Ireland	82.6	15.6	1.8	17.4	4.4	69.7	30.3	m	208	101
Italy	69.4	18.4	12.2	30.6	4.6	82.9	17.1	0.1	119	254
Japan[2]	41.2	x(4)	x(4)	58.8	m	40.2	59.8	m	128	123
Korea	21.0	55.6	23.3	79.0	0.3	m	m	m	m	m
Luxembourg	m	m	m	m	m	m	m	m	m	m
Mexico	68.9	30.6	0.5	31.1	0.8	77.4	22.6	m	150	231
Netherlands	77.6	12.0	10.4	22.4	1.4	80.6	19.4	2.5	111	133
New Zealand	60.8	39.2	m	39.2	m	m	m	m	109	m
Norway	m	m	m	m	m	93.7	6.3	n	117	m
Poland	72.9	27.1	m	m	m	m	m	m	202	m
Portugal	86.0	14.0	m	14.0	m	96.5	3.5	m	116	522
Slovak Republic[2]	81.3	9.7	9.0	18.7	a	95.4	4.6	m	178	850
Spain	75.9	20.8	3.3	24.1	1.9	74.4	25.6	2.0	165	153
Sweden	88.4	n	11.6	11.6	a	93.6	6.4	a	134	254
Switzerland	m	m	m	m	m	m	m	m	176	m
Turkey	90.0	10.0	m	10.0	a	96.3	3.7	0.7	191	548
United Kingdom	69.6	19.4	11.1	30.4	n	80.0	20.0	n	106	185
United States	35.4	35.1	29.5	64.6	m	37.4	62.6	m	154	168
OECD average	*75.7*	~	~	*24.3*	*1.3*	~	~		*149*	*276*
EU19 average	*84.0*	~	~	*16.0*	*1.0*	~	~		*154*	*284*
Brazil	m	m	m	m	m	m	m	m	129	m
Chile[3]	15.5	83.7	0.9	84.5	2.5	25.1	74.9	m	127	232
Estonia	m	m	m	m	n	m	m	m	m	m
Israel	49.6	34.4	16.1	50.4	5.4	59.2	40.8	3.0	114	169
Russian Federation	m	m	m	m	m	m	m	m	m	m
Slovenia	75.7	17.3	7.1	24.3	n	m	m	m	m	m

1. Including subsidies attributable to payments to educational institutions received from public sources. To calculate private funds net of subsidies, subtract public subsidies (columns 5, 10) from private funds (columns 4, 9). To calculate total public funds, including public subsidies, add public subsidies (columns 5, 10) to direct public funds (columns 1, 6).

2. Some levels of education are included with others. Refer to "x" code in Table B1.1a for details.

3. Year of reference 2005.

Source: OECD. See Annex 3 for notes (www.oecd.org/edu/eag2007).

Please refer to the Reader's Guide for information concerning the symbols replacing missing data.

StatLink ⌷⌷⌷ http://dx.doi.org/10.1787/068188403262

B3

Table B3.3.
Trends in relative proportions of public expenditure[1] on educational institutions and index of change
between 1995 and 2004 (1995=100, constant prices), for tertiary education (1995, 2000, 2001, 2002, 2003, 2004)

	Share of public expenditure on educational institutions (%)						Index of change between 1995 and 2004 in public expenditure on educational institutions (1995=100)					
	1995	2000	2001	2002	2003	2004	1995	2000	2001	2002	2003	2004
Australia	64.8	51.0	51.3	48.7	48.0	47.2	100	87	89	91	92	96
Austria	96.1	96.3	94.6	91.6	92.7	93.7	100	103	115	106	111	123
Belgium	m	91.5	89.5	86.1	86.7	90.4	m	m	m	m	m	m
Canada	56.6	61.0	58.6	56.4	m	m	100	144	146	141	m	m
Czech Republic	71.5	85.4	85.3	87.5	83.3	84.7	100	116	126	141	160	170
Denmark	99.4	97.6	97.8	97.9	96.7	96.7	100	108	127	133	122	129
Finland	97.8	97.2	96.5	96.3	96.4	96.3	100	110	111	115	120	126
France	m	m	m	m	m	m	m	m	m	m	m	m
Germany	88.6	m	m	m	87.0	86.4	100	m	m	m	111	109
Greece	m	99.7	99.6	99.6	97.9	97.9	100	160	217	246	310	312
Hungary	80.3	76.7	77.6	78.7	78.5	79.0	100	129	140	159	180	157
Iceland	m	94.9	95.0	95.6	88.7	90.9	m	m	m	m	m	m
Ireland	69.7	79.2	84.7	85.8	83.8	82.6	100	204	204	210	198	208
Italy	82.9	77.5	77.8	78.6	72.1	69.4	100	118	126	131	118	119
Japan	40.2	43.6	41.6	40.2	41.1	41.2	100	126	120	118	127	128
Korea	m	23.3	15.9	14.9	23.2	21.0	m	m	m	m	m	m
Luxembourg	m	m	m	m	m	m	m	m	m	m	m	m
Mexico	77.4	79.4	70.4	71.0	69.1	68.9	100	133	112	158	149	150
Netherlands	80.6	78.2	78.2	78.8	78.6	77.6	100	103	106	108	108	111
New Zealand	m	m	m	62.5	61.5	60.8	100	96	100	107	112	109
Norway	93.7	96.3	m	96.3	96.7	m	100	94	98	110	115	117
Poland	m	66.6	66.9	69.7	69.0	72.9	100	113	132	166	170	202
Portugal	96.5	92.5	92.3	91.3	91.5	86.0	100	131	141	130	143	116
Slovak Republic	95.4	91.2	93.3	85.2	86.2	81.3	100	119	130	132	150	178
Spain	74.4	74.4	75.5	76.3	76.9	75.9	100	139	149	155	163	165
Sweden	93.6	91.3	91.0	90.0	89.0	88.4	100	118	121	128	132	134
Switzerland	m	m	m	m	m	m	100	136	153	167	177	176
Turkey	96.3	95.4	94.6	90.1	95.2	90.0	100	179	170	191	202	191
United Kingdom	80.0	67.7	71.0	72.0	70.2	69.6	100	86	97	106	106	106
United States	37.4	31.1	38.1	39.5	38.3	35.4	100	118	129	141	153	154
OECD average	*79.9*	*77.6*	*76.5*	*76.2*	*76.9*	*75.4*	*100*	*124*	*132*	*141*	*147*	*149*
OECD average (for countries with data available for all reference years)	*79.8*	*78.1*	*78.4*	*77.7*	*77.1*	*76.1*	*100*	*123*	*132*	*141*	*149*	*153*
EU19 average (for countries with data available for all reference years)	*85.9*	*85.0*	*85.8*	*85.4*	*84.3*	*83.2*	*100*	*124*	*138*	*144*	*153*	*157*
Brazil	m	m	m	m	m	m	100	128	128	131	140	129
Chile	25.1	19.5	m	19.3	17.0	15.5	100	128	m	143	131	127
Estonia	m	m	m	m	m	m	m	m	m	m	m	m
Israel	59.2	56.5	56.8	53.4	59.3	49.6	100	124	127	118	133	114
Russian Federation	m	m	m	m	m	m	m	m	m	m	m	m
Slovenia	m	m	m	m	m	75.7	m	m	m	m	m	m

1. Public expenditure on educational institutions excludes international funds.
Source: OECD. See Annex 3 for notes (www.oecd.org/edu/eag2007).
Please refer to the Reader's Guide for information concerning the symbols replacing missing data.
StatLink ⟪ヨ⟫ http://dx.doi.org/10.1787/068188403262

WHAT IS THE TOTAL PUBLIC SPENDING ON EDUCATION?

Public expenditure on education as a percentage of total public expenditure indicates the value placed on education relative to that of other public investments such as health care, social security, defence and security. It provides an important context for the other indicators on expenditure, particularly for Indicator B3 (the public and private shares of educational expenditure), as well as quantification of an important policy lever in its own right.

Key results

Chart B4.1. **Total public expenditure on education as a percentage of total public expenditure (1995, 2004)**

The chart shows direct public expenditure on educational institutions plus public subsidies to households (including subsidies for living costs) and other private entities, as a percentage of total public expenditure, by year. This must be interpreted in the context of public sectors that differ in the size and breadth of responsibility from country to country.

◼ 2004   ○ 1995

On average, OECD countries devote 13.4% of total public expenditure to educational institutions, but the values for individual countries range from 10% or below in the Czech Republic, Germany, Greece, Italy and Japan to more than 20% in Mexico and New Zealand.

% of total public expenditure

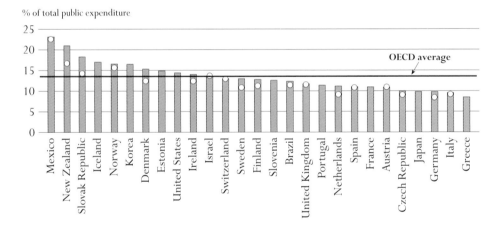

Countries are ranked in descending order of total public expenditure on education at all levels of education as a percentage of total public expenditure in 2004.
Source: OECD. Table B4.1. See Annex 3 for notes (*www.oecd.org/edu/eag2007*).
StatLink ⫘ http://dx.doi.org/10.1787/068247218642

Other highlights of this indicator

- Public funding of education is a social priority, even in OECD countries with little public involvement in other areas.

- In OECD countries, public funding of primary, secondary and post-secondary non-tertiary education is on average about three times that of tertiary education, mainly due to largely universal enrolment rates but also because the private share in expenditure tends to be higher at the tertiary level. This ratio varies by country from less than double in Denmark, Finland, Greece and Norway to nearly six times in Korea. The latter figure is indicative of the relatively high proportion of private funds that go into tertiary education in Korea.

- Between 1995 and 2004, public budgets as a percentage of GDP tended to increase slightly. Education took a growing share of total public expenditure in most countries, and it did also on average grow as fast as GDP. In Denmark, the Netherlands, New Zealand, the Slovak Republic and Sweden, there have been particularly significant shifts in public funding in favour of education.

- On average among OECD countries, 85% of public expenditure on education is transferred to public institutions. In two-thirds of the OECD countries, as well as in the partner economies Brazil, Estonia and Slovenia, the share of public expenditure on education transferred to public institutions exceeds 80%. The share of public expenditure transferred to the private sector is larger at the tertiary level than at primary to post-secondary non-tertiary levels and reaches 26% on average among OECD countries with available data.

Policy context

If the public benefits from a particular service are greater than the private benefits, then markets alone may fail to provide these services adequately and governments may need to become involved. Education is one area where all governments intervene to fund or direct the provision of services. As there is no guarantee that markets will provide equal access to educational opportunities, government funding of educational services ensures that education is not beyond the reach of some members of society.

This indicator focuses on public expenditure on education but also evaluates how public expenditure has changed over time in absolute terms and relative to total governmental spending. Since the second half of the 1990s, most OECD countries have made serious efforts to consolidate public budgets. Education has had to compete with a wide range of other areas covered in government budgets for public financial support. To examine this evolution, the indicator evaluates the change in educational expenditure in absolute terms and relative to changes in the size of public budgets.

Evidence and explanations

What this indicator does and does not cover

This indicator shows total public expenditure on education, which includes direct public expenditure on educational institutions as well as public subsidies to households (*e.g.* scholarships and loans to students for tuition fees and student living costs) and to other private entities for education (*e.g.* subsidies to companies or labour organisations that operate apprenticeship programmes). Unlike the preceding indicators, this indicator also includes public subsidies that are not attributable to household payments for educational institutions, such as subsidies for student living costs.

OECD countries differ in the ways in which they use public money for education. Public funds may flow directly to schools or may be channelled to institutions via government programmes or via households; they may also be restricted to the purchase of educational services or be used to support student living costs.

Total public expenditure on all services, excluding education, includes expenditure on debt servicing (*e.g.* interest payments) that are not included in public expenditure on education. The reason for this exclusion is that some countries cannot separate interest payment outlays for education from those for other services. This means that public expenditure on education as a percentage of total public expenditure can be underestimated in countries where interest payments represent a high proportion of total public expenditure on all services.

It is important to examine public investment in education in conjunction with private investment, as shown in Indicator B3, in order to get a total picture of investment in education.

Overall level of public resources invested in education

On average, OECD countries devoted 13.4% of total public expenditure to education in 2004. However, the values for individual countries range from 10% or below in the Czech Republic, Germany, Greece, Italy and Japan, to more than 20% in Mexico and New Zealand (Chart B4.1). As in the case of spending on education in relation to GDP per capita, these values must be interpreted in the context of student demography and enrolment rates.

The public-sector proportion of funding of the different levels of education varies widely among OECD countries. In 2004, OECD countries and partner economies spent between 5.3% (Greece) and 16.1% (Mexico) of total public expenditure on primary, secondary and post-secondary non-tertiary education, and between 1.6% (Italy) and 5.3% (Norway) on tertiary education. On average in OECD countries, public funding of primary, secondary and post-secondary non-tertiary education is nearly three times that of tertiary education, mainly due to enrolment rates (see Indicator C1) or because the private share in expenditure tends to be higher at the tertiary level. This ratio varies by country from less than two times in Denmark, Finland, Greece and Norway to as high as six times in Korea. The latter figure is indicative of the relatively high proportion of private funds that go into tertiary education in Korea (Table B4.1).

Public funding of education is a social priority, even in OECD countries with little public involvement in other areas. When public expenditure on education is examined as a proportion of total public spending, the relative sizes of public budgets (as measured by public spending in relation to GDP) must be taken into account.

Across OECD countries, when the size of public budgets relative to GDP is compared with the proportion of public spending committed to education, it is evident that even in countries with relatively low rates of public spending, education is awarded a very high level of priority. For instance, the share of public spending that goes to education in Korea, Mexico, New Zealand and the United States is among the highest of OECD countries (Chart B4.1), yet total public spending accounts for a relatively low proportion of GDP in these countries (Chart B4.2).

Although the overall pattern is not clear, there is some evidence to suggest that countries with high rates of public spending spend proportionately less on education; only one of the top ten countries for public spending on public services overall – Denmark – is among the top ten public spenders on education (Charts B4.1 and B4.2).

Chart B4.2. **Total public expenditure on all services as a percentage of GDP (1995, 2004)**

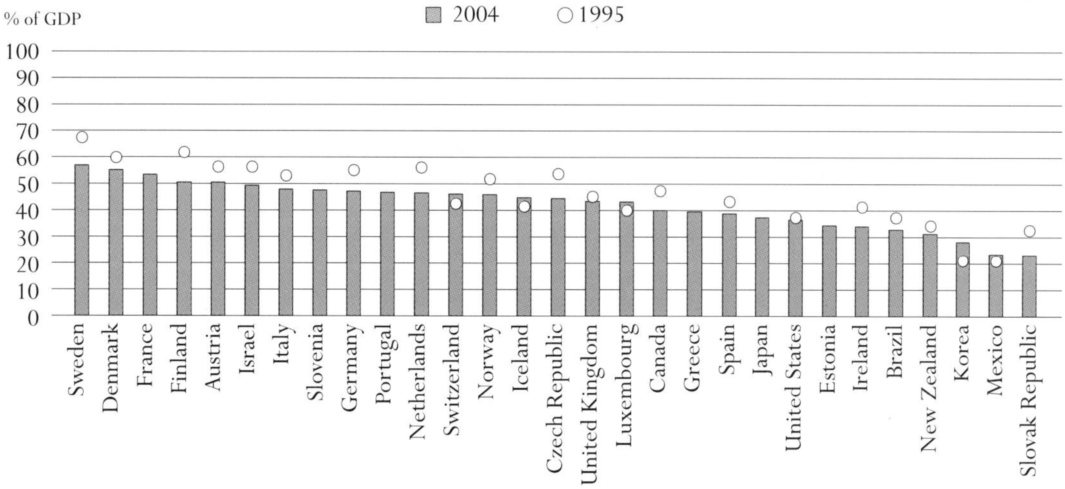

% of GDP   ■ 2004   ○ 1995

Note: This chart represents public expenditure on all services and not simply public expenditure on education.
Countries are ranked in descending order of total public expenditure as a percentage of GDP in 2004.
Source: OECD. Annex 2. See Annex 3 for notes (*www.oecd.org/edu/eag2007*).
StatLink ⫘ http://dx.doi.org/10.1787/068247218642

B4

Typically, from 1995 to 2004, public expenditure on education grew faster than total public spending, and as fast as national income: the average proportion of public expenditure spent on education increased in 16 of the 18 countries with comparable data in both 1995 and 2004 and, simultaneously, on average in these 18 countries, public expenditure on education as a percentage of GDP increased slightly. The process of budget consolidation puts pressure on education along with every other service. Nevertheless, with the exception of the partner economy Israel, spending on education grew at least as fast as spending in other public areas between 1995 and 2004; on average, the proportion of public budgets spent on education in OECD countries grew from 12.3% in 1995 to 13.4% in 2004. The figures suggest that the greatest relative increases in the share of public expenditure on education during this period took place in Denmark (increasing from 12.2 to 15.3%), the Netherlands (from 9.0 to 11.1%), New Zealand (16.5 to 21.0%), the Slovak Republic (14.1 to 18.2%) and Sweden (10.7 to 12.9%).

Distribution of public expenditure to the public and private sectors

The vast majority of public funds on education are directed at public institutions: an average of 85% of public expenditure is transferred to public institutions among OECD countries. In two-thirds of the OECD countries, as well as in the partner economies Brazil, Estonia and Slovenia, the share of public expenditure on education transferred to public institutions exceeds 80%. However, significant public funds are transferred to private institutions or given directly to households to spend in the institution of their choice in a number of countries: more than 20% of public expenditure is distributed (directly or indirectly) to the private sector in Belgium, Denmark, New Zealand, Norway and the United Kingdom and in the partner economies Chile and Israel. In Belgium, the majority of public funds goes to government-dependent institutions that are managed by private bodies but that otherwise operate under the aegis of the regular education system (Table B4.2).

On average among OECD countries, at the primary, secondary and post-secondary non-tertiary levels, nearly 12% of public funding designated for educational institutions is spent in privately managed institutions. Belgium is the only country where the majority of funds goes to privately managed institutions, but in the partner economy Chile a large part of public funds (40%) also goes to the privately managed institutions. Public funding transfers to private households and other private entities are generally not a significant feature at primary, secondary and post-secondary non-tertiary levels. On average among OECD countries, these transfers represent 3.6% of public expenditure on education and exceed 10% only in Denmark.

At the tertiary level, on average among OECD countries, the majority of public funds are still directed at public institutions, but the share of public expenditure transferred to the private sector is larger than at primary to post-secondary non-tertiary level and reaches 26% on average among countries with available data. There are, however, substantial variations among countries in the share of public expenditure devoted to the private sector. In Belgium and the United Kingdom (where there are no public tertiary institutions), as well as the partner economies Chile, Estonia and Israel, public expenditure is mainly devoted to privately managed institutions. The share of public expenditure indirectly transferred to the private sector is larger at the tertiary level than below as it is more typical for households/students to receive some transfers of public funding at the tertiary level than at other levels. On average, 18% of public funding is indirectly transferred to the private sector at the tertiary level. These transfers result partly from financial aid attributed to tertiary students through scholarships, grants and loans (see Indicator B5). The proportion of public expenditure indirectly transferred to the private sector exceeds 30% in Australia, Denmark, New Zealand and Norway and, among partner economies, in Chile.

Definitions and methodologies

Data refer to the financial year 2004 and are based on the UOE data collection on education statistics administered by the OECD in 2006 (for details see Annex 3 at *www.oecd.org/edu/ eag2007*). Educational expenditure is expressed as a percentage of a country's total public sector expenditure and as a percentage of GDP. Public educational expenditure includes expenditure on educational institutions and subsidies for students' living costs and for other private expenditure outside institutions. Public expenditure on education includes expenditure by all public entities, including ministries other than the ministry of education, local and regional governments and other public agencies.

Total public expenditure, also referred to as total public spending, corresponds to the non-repayable current and capital expenditure of all levels of government: central, regional and local. Current expenditure includes final consumption expenditure, property income paid, subsidies and other current transfers (*e.g.* social security, social assistance, pensions and other welfare benefits). Figures for total public expenditure have been taken from the OECD National Accounts Database (see Annex 2) and use the System of National Accounts 1993.

The glossary at *www.oecd.org/edu/eag2007* gives a definition of public, government-dependent private and independent private institutions.

Note that data appearing in earlier editions of this publication may not always be comparable to data shown in the 2007 edition due to changes in definitions and coverage that were made as a result of the OECD expenditure comparability study (for details on changes, see Annex 3 at *www.oecd.org/edu/eag2007*).

Further references

The following additional material relevant to this indicator is available on line at:

StatLink ⫘⫘ http://dx.doi.org/10.1787/068247218642

- *Table B4.3a. Initial sources of public educational funds and final purchasers of educational resources by level of government for primary, secondary and post-secondary non-tertiary education (2004)*

- *Table B4.3b. Initial sources of public educational funds and final purchasers of educational resources by level of government for tertiary education (2004)*

B4

Table B4.1.
Total public expenditure on education (1995, 2004)
Direct public expenditure on educational institutions plus public subsidies to households (which include subsidies for living costs)
and other private entities, as a percentage of GDP and as a percentage of total public expenditure, by level of education and year

	Public expenditure[1] on education as a percentage of total public expenditure				Public expenditure[1] on education as a percentage of GDP			
	2004			1995	2004			1995
	Primary, secondary and post-secondary non-tertiary education	Tertiary education	All levels of education combined	All levels of education combined	Primary, secondary and post-secondary non-tertiary education	Tertiary education	All levels of education combined	All levels of education combined
Australia	m	m	m	13.7	3.6	1.1	4.8	5.0
Austria	7.2	2.8	10.8	10.8	3.6	1.4	5.4	6.0
Belgium	m	m	m	m	4.0	1.3	6.0	m
Canada	m	m	m	13.1	m	m	m	6.5
Czech Republic	6.7	2.1	10.0	8.9	3.0	1.0	4.4	4.8
Denmark[2]	8.9	4.6	15.3	12.2	4.9	2.5	8.4	7.3
Finland	8.0	4.1	12.8	11.0	4.0	2.1	6.4	6.8
France	7.4	2.3	10.9	m	3.9	1.2	5.8	m
Germany	6.3	2.5	9.8	8.2	3.0	1.2	4.6	4.6
Greece[2]	5.3	2.9	8.5	m	2.1	1.2	3.3	2.2
Hungary	m	m	m	12.9	3.5	1.0	5.4	5.2
Iceland[2]	11.8	3.1	17.0	m	5.3	1.4	7.6	m
Ireland	10.7	3.3	14.0	12.2	3.6	1.1	4.7	5.0
Italy	7.0	1.6	9.6	9.0	3.4	0.8	4.6	4.8
Japan[2]	7.2	1.8	9.8	m	2.7	0.7	3.6	3.6
Korea	12.7	2.1	16.5	m	3.6	0.6	4.6	m
Luxembourg[2]	9.1	m	m	m	3.9	m	m	m
Mexico	16.1	4.0	23.1	22.4	3.8	0.9	5.4	4.6
Netherlands	7.5	2.9	11.1	9.0	3.5	1.4	5.2	5.0
New Zealand	15.1	4.9	21.0	16.5	4.7	1.5	6.5	5.6
Norway	10.0	5.3	16.6	15.5	4.6	2.4	7.6	8.0
Poland	m	m	m	11.9	3.7	1.2	5.4	5.2
Portugal	8.3	1.8	11.4	m	3.9	0.8	5.3	5.1
Slovak Republic[2]	11.6	4.3	18.2	14.1	2.7	1.0	4.2	5.0
Spain	7.2	2.5	11.0	10.6	2.8	1.0	4.3	4.6
Sweden	8.3	3.7	12.9	10.7	4.7	2.1	7.4	7.2
Switzerland	8.7	3.6	13.0	12.8	4.0	1.7	6.0	5.4
Turkey	m	m	m	m	2.9	1.1	4.0	2.4
United Kingdom	8.7	2.3	11.7	11.4	3.9	1.0	5.3	5.3
United States	10.1	3.5	14.4	m	3.7	1.3	5.3	m
OECD average	*9.2*	*3.1*	*13.4*	*12.3*	*3.7*	*1.3*	*5.4*	*5.2*
EU19 average	*8.0*	*2.9*	*11.9*	*10.9*	*3.6*	*1.3*	*5.3*	*5.3*
Brazil[2]	8.9	2.3	12.3	11.2	2.9	0.8	4.0	3.6
Chile[3]	m	m	m	14.5	2.7	0.5	3.5	3.0
Estonia	11.2	2.6	14.9	m	3.8	0.9	5.1	m
Israel	8.9	2.2	13.4	13.5	4.4	1.1	6.6	7.0
Russian Federation	m	m	m	m	2.0	0.7	3.6	m
Slovenia	8.7	2.8	12.6	m	4.1	1.4	6.0	m

1. Public expenditure presented in this table includes public subsidies to households for living costs, which are not spent on educational institutions. Thus the figures presented here exceed those on public spending on institutions found in Table B2.1b.
2. Some levels of education are included with others. Refer to "x" code in Table B1.1a for details.
3. Year of reference 2005.
Source: OECD. See Annex 3 for notes (*www.oecd.org/edu/eag2007*).
Please refer to the Reader's Guide for information concerning the symbols replacing missing data.
StatLink ᱮᱨᱶᱞ http://dx.doi.org/10.1787/068247218642

B4

Table B4.2.
Distribution of total public expenditure on education (2004)
Public expenditure on education transferred to educational institutions and public transfers to the private sector
as a percentage of total public expenditure on education, by level of education

	Primary, secondary and post-secondary non-tertiary education			Tertiary education			All levels of education combined		
	Direct public expenditure on public institutions	Direct public expenditure on private institutions	Indirect public transfers and payments to the private sector	Direct public expenditure on public institutions	Direct public expenditure on private institutions	Indirect public transfers and payments to the private sector	Direct public expenditure on public institutions	Direct public expenditure on private institutions	Indirect public transfers and payments to the private sector
OECD countries									
Australia	75.9	20.3	3.8	67.3	n	32.7	x	x	10.6
Austria	98.0	0.5	1.5	75.2	5.0	19.8	90.9	1.7	7.4
Belgium	44.5	52.9	2.5	35.5	48.8	15.7	43.8	51.1	5.1
Canada	m	m	m	m	m	m	m	m	m
Czech Republic	91.6	3.7	4.7	93.3	1.0	5.8	92.8	2.8	4.4
Denmark[1]	80.9	6.0	13.1	69.7	a	30.3	77.7	3.7	18.6
Finland	90.5	6.4	3.2	75.5	7.3	17.2	85.8	6.7	7.5
France	84.0	12.6	3.4	86.7	5.4	7.9	85.5	10.6	3.9
Germany	84.0	11.1	4.9	80.9	1.2	17.9	80.7	11.6	7.7
Greece[1]	99.7	a	0.3	94.8	a	5.2	98.0	a	2.0
Hungary	84.1	9.8	6.1	78.8	5.4	15.8	85.3	7.7	7.0
Iceland[1]	97.2	1.8	1.0	73.0	4.8	22.2	92.7	2.4	4.8
Ireland	90.8	n	9.2	85.2	n	14.8	89.5	n	10.5
Italy	97.0	1.3	1.6	81.1	2.2	16.7	93.8	1.8	4.4
Japan[1]	96.3	3.5	0.2	69.7	12.1	18.2	90.4	6.1	3.4
Korea	82.3	16.1	1.5	69.9	12.4	17.7	80.3	14.2	5.5
Luxembourg[1]	97.8	m	2.2	m	m	m	m	m	m
Mexico	94.6	n	5.3	93.9	n	6.1	94.9	n	5.1
Netherlands	m	m	m	m	m	m	m	m	m
New Zealand	89.5	3.7	6.8	56.4	1.3	42.3	79.4	5.6	15.0
Norway	86.1	6.2	7.7	56.0	3.2	40.8	75.0	6.5	18.5
Poland	m	m	m	m	m	m	m	m	m
Portugal	91.9	6.7	1.4	94.6	m	5.4	91.5	6.6	1.9
Slovak Republic[1]	89.8	5.9	4.3	89.3	a	10.7	90.8	3.8	5.3
Spain	84.1	14.5	1.5	90.2	1.9	7.8	85.9	11.3	2.9
Sweden	87.1	6.9	5.9	67.0	4.8	28.2	81.4	6.8	11.9
Switzerland	90.5	7.3	2.2	79.9	6.0	14.0	87.6	6.8	5.6
Turkey	99.4	m	0.6	80.7	m	19.3	94.2	n	5.8
United Kingdom	78.9	19.1	2.0	a	76.1	23.9	65.0	28.8	6.1
United States	99.8	0.2	a	71.1	8.2	20.7	92.3	2.6	5.0
OECD average	*88.4*	*8.7*	*3.6*	*73.7*	*8.0*	*18.4*	*85.0*	*8.0*	*7.1*
EU19 average	*86.7*	*9.8*	*4.0*	*74.9*	*10.6*	*15.1*	*83.7*	*9.7*	*6.6*
Partner economies									
Brazil[1]	98.4	n	1.6	87.9	n	12.1	96.5	n	3.5
Chile[2]	59.7	40.1	0.2	35.1	30.0	34.8	56.8	38.2	5.0
Estonia	95.0	0.4	4.6	30.4	69.6	n	83.9	12.6	3.4
Israel	73.6	25.0	1.5	5.1	83.2	11.7	64.4	32.5	3.1
Russian Federation	m	a	m	m	a	m	m	a	m
Slovenia	93.9	0.6	5.5	76.0	0.2	23.7	90.3	0.5	9.2

1. Some levels of education are included with others. Refer to "x" code in Table B1.1a for details.
2. Year of reference 2005.
Source: OECD. See Annex 3 for notes (*www.oecd.org/edu/eag2007*).
Please refer to the Reader's Guide for information concerning the symbols replacing missing data.
StatLink ᴍᴤᴸ http://dx.doi.org/10.1787/068247218642

HOW MUCH DO TERTIARY STUDENTS PAY AND WHAT PUBLIC SUBSIDIES DO THEY RECEIVE?

This indicator examines the relationships between annual tuition fees charged by institutions, direct and indirect public spending on educational institutions, and public subsidies to households for student living costs. It considers whether financial subsidies for households are provided in the form of grants or loans and poses related questions central to this discussion: Are scholarships/grants and loans more appropriate in countries with higher tuitions fees charged by institutions? Are loans an effective means to help increase the efficiency of financial resources invested in education and shift some of the cost of education to the beneficiaries of educational investment? Or are student loans less appropriate than grants in encouraging low-income students to pursue their education? While these questions cannot be fully answered here, this indicator presents information about the policies for tuition fees and subsidies in different OECD countries.

Key results

Chart B5.1. Average annual tuition fees charged by tertiary-type A public institutions (academic year 2004-2005)

This chart shows the annual tuition fees charged by tertiary-type A public institutions for full-time national students in equivalent USD converted using PPPs. Countries in bold indicate that tuition fees refer to public institutions but more than two-thirds of students are enrolled in private institutions. The net entry rate in tertiary-type A (in %) is added next to country names. For example, in the Netherlands, average tuition fees reach USD 1 646 in public tertiary-type A institutions and 59% of students enter this level of education.

There are large differences between OECD countries and partner economies in the average tuition fees charged by tertiary-type A public institutions. There are no tuition fees charged by public institutions in one-third of OECD countries, whereas another third of countries have annual tuitions fees charged by public institutions that exceed USD 1 500. Among the EU19 countries, only the Netherlands and the United Kingdom have annual tuitions fees that represent more than USD 1 500 per full-time student; these relate to government-dependent institutions.

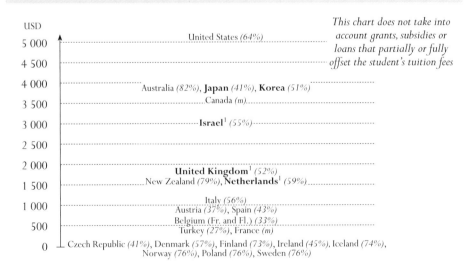

1. Public institutions do not exist at this level of education and most of the students are enrolled in government dependent institutions.
Source: OECD. Table B5.1a and C2.4. See Annex 3 for notes (*www.oecd.org/edu/eag2007*).
StatLink ⬛⬛ http://dx.doi.org/10.1787/068348603526

Other highlights of this indicator

■ An average of 18% of public spending on tertiary education is devoted to supporting students, households and other private entities. In Australia, Denmark, the Netherlands, New Zealand, Norway and Sweden, and the partner economy Chile, public subsidies to households account for about 27% or more of public tertiary education budgets.

■ Low annual tuition fees charged by tertiary-type A institutions are not systematically associated with a low proportion of students that benefit from public subsidies. The tuition fees charged by public educational institutions for national students are negligible (Nordic countries and the Czech Republic) or low (Turkey) in tertiary-type A education but at the same time more than 55% of the students enrolled in tertiary-type A education in these countries can benefit from scholarships/grants and/or public loans. Moreover, Finland, Norway and Sweden are among the seven countries with the highest entry rate to tertiary-type A education.

■ OECD countries where students are required to pay tuition fees and can benefit from particularly large public subsidies do not show lower levels of access to tertiary-type A education compared to the OECD average. For example, Australia (82%) and New Zealand (79%) have one of the highest entry rates to tertiary-type A education and the Netherlands (59%) and the United State (64%) are above the OECD average. The United Kingdom (51%) is just below the OECD average (54%), although entry to tertiary-type A education increased by 4 percentage points between 2000 and 2005.

■ The cost for a government to provide public loans to a significant proportion of students is greater in countries where the average level tuition fees charged by institutions is higher or where the average amount of the public loans available to students is higher than the OECD average. The average amount of public loans is greater than the average tuition fees charged in public institutions in all of the OECD countries with available data, which is an indication that the public loans also serve to support the living expenses of students during their studies.

B5

Policy context

Decisions taken by policy makers on the amount of tuition fees charged by educational institutions have an influence both on the cost of tertiary studies to students and on the resources available to institutions at the tertiary level. Subsidies to students and their families also act as policy levers through which governments can encourage participation in education – particularly among students from low-income families – by covering part of the cost of education and related expenses. Governments can thereby seek to address issues of access and equality of opportunity. The success of such subsidies must therefore be judged, at least in part, through examination of indicators of participation, retention and completion. Furthermore, public subsidies play an important role in indirectly financing educational institutions.

Channelling funding for institutions through students may also help to increase competition between institutions. Since aid for student living costs can serve as a substitute for work, public subsidies may enhance educational attainment by enabling students to study full-time and to work fewer hours or not at all.

Public subsidies come in many forms: as means-based subsidies, as family allowances for all students, as tax allowances for students or their parents, or as other household transfers. Unconditional subsidies (such as tax reductions or family allowances) may provide less of an incentive for low-income students to participate in education than means-tested subsidies. However, they may still help reduce financial disparities between households with and without children in education.

Evidence and explanations

What this indicator does and does not cover

This indicator shows average tuition fees charged in public and private institutions at tertiary-type A level. The indicator does not distinguish tuition fees by type of programmes but shows an overview of tuition fees at tertiary-type A level by type of institution and presents the proportions of students that do or do not receive scholarships/grants fully or partially covering tuition fees. Amounts of tuition fees and associated proportions of students should be interpreted with caution as they result from the weighted average of the main tertiary-type A programmes and do not cover all the educational institutions.

This indicator also shows the proportion of public spending on tertiary education transferred to students, families and other private entities. Some of these funds are spent indirectly on educational institutions – for example, when subsidies are used to cover tuition fees. Other subsidies for education do not relate to educational institutions, such as subsidies for student living costs.

The indicator distinguishes between scholarships and grants, which are non-repayable subsidies, and loans, which must be repaid. It does not, however, distinguish among different types of grants or loans, such as scholarships, family allowances and subsidies in kind.

Governments can also support students and their families by providing housing allowances, tax reductions and/or tax credits for education. These subsidies are not covered here and thus financial aid to students may be substantially underestimated in some countries.

The indicator reports the full volume of student loans in order to provide information on the level of support which current students receive. The gross amount of loans, including scholarships and grants, provides an appropriate measure of financial aid to current participants in education. Interest payments and repayments of the principal by borrowers would be taken into account in order to assess the net cost of student loans to public and private lenders. However, such payments are not usually made by current students but rather by former students. In most countries, moreover, loan repayments do not flow to the education authorities, and thus the money is not available to them to cover other educational expenditures. Nevertheless, some information on repayment systems for these loans is also taken into account, as these can reduce the real costs of loans substantially. The OECD indicators take the full amount of scholarships and loans (gross) into account when discussing financial aid to current students.

It is also common for governments to guarantee the repayment of loans to students made by private lenders. In some OECD countries, this indirect form of subsidy is as significant as, or more significant, than direct financial aid to students. However, for reasons of comparability, the indicator only takes into account the amounts relating to public transfers for private loans that are made to private entities (not the total value of loans generated). Some qualitative information is nevertheless presented in some of the table that can give some insight on this type of subsidy.

Some OECD countries also have difficulties quantifying the amount of loans attributable to students. Therefore, data on student loans should be treated with some caution.

Annual tuition fees charged by tertiary-type A educational institutions for national and foreign students

Large differences are observed among OECD countries and partner economies in the average tuition fees charged by tertiary-type A educational institutions. There are no tuition fees charged by public institutions in the five Nordic countries (Denmark, Finland, Iceland, Norway and Sweden) and in the Czech Republic, Ireland and Poland. By contrast, one-quarter of OECD countries and partner economies have annual tuitions fees for national students charged by public institutions that exceed USD 1 500. In the United States, tuition fees for national students reach more than USD 5 000 in public institutions. Among the EU19 countries, only the Netherlands and the United Kingdom have annual tuitions fees that represent more than USD 1 100 per full-time national student, but these fees related to government dependent private institutions (Table B5.1a and Chart B5.1).

National policies regarding tuition fees and financial aid to students cover generally all students studying in educational institutions of the country. Even if the focus of this indicator is mainly on national students, countries' policies also have to take into account international students: whether in the form of a country's national students going abroad for their studies or other students that enter the country for study reasons. Making differences between national and non-national students in the amount of fees students have to pay or in the financial help students may receive can have, along with other factors, an impact on the flows of international students, attracting students to some countries or, on the contrary, preventing students from studying in other countries.

B5

The amount of tuition fees charged by public educational institutions may differ among students enrolled in the same programme. Several countries make a distinction in the amount of tuition fees charged according to the citizenship of students. In Austria, for example, the average tuition fees charged by public institutions for students who are not citizens of EU or EEA countries are twice the fees charged for citizens of these countries. This kind of differentiation also appears in Australia, Canada, France, Iceland, New Zealand, Turkey, the United Kingdom and the United States, as well as the partner economy Estonia (see Indicator C3), and will appear in Denmark from the 2006-2007 academic year. In these countries, the variation of tuition fees according to citizenship is always significant. This type of policy differentiation may check the flows of international students (see Indicator C3) unless these students receive some financial support from their country of citizenship.

Annual tuition fees charged by private institutions

Annual tuition fees charged by private institutions vary considerably across OECD countries and partner economies as well as within countries themselves. Most OECD countries and partner economies charge higher tuition fees in private institutions than in public institutions. Finland and Sweden are the only countries where there are no tuition fees in either public or private institutions. Variation within countries tends to be highest in countries with the largest proportions of student enrolled in tertiary-type A independent private institutions. By contrast, tuition fees charged by public and government dependent institutions are not so different in most countries and even similar in Austria. The greater autonomy of independent private institutions compared with public and government-dependent institutions partially explains this fact. For example, around three-quarters of students in Korea and Japan are enrolled in independent private institutions and at the same time these two countries show the highest variation between their independent private institutions (Indicator C2 and Table B5.1a).

Public subsidies to households and other private entities

OECD countries spend an average of 0.4% of their GDP on public subsidies to households and other private entities for all levels of education combined. The proportion of educational budgets spent on subsidies to households and private entities is much higher at the tertiary level than at primary, secondary and post-secondary non-tertiary levels and represents 0.3% of GDP. The subsidies are the largest in relation to GDP at tertiary level in Norway (1.0% of GDP), followed by Denmark (0.8%), New Zealand (0.6%), Sweden (0.6%), Australia (0.4%), Finland (0.4%) and the Netherlands (0.4%) (Table B5.2; Table B5.3 available on line at *http://dx.doi.org/10.1787/068348603526*).

OECD countries spend, on average, 18% of their public budgets for tertiary education on subsidies to households and other private entities (Chart B5.2). In Australia, Denmark, the Netherlands, New Zealand, Norway and Sweden, and the partner economy Chile, public subsidies account for 27% or more of public spending on tertiary education. Only Poland spends less than 5% of their total public spending on tertiary education on subsidies (Table B5.2).

Relationships between average tuition fees charged and public subsidies received

When looking at the combination of tuition fees charged by institutions and public subsidies received by national students in tertiary-type A education different patterns emerge in OECD countries. There is no unique model observed in OECD countries and partner economies for the financing of tertiary-type A institutions, as some countries can have similar tuitions fees charged by tertiary-type A educational institutions and differences in the proportion of students benefiting from public subsidies and/or in the average amount of these subsidies (Tables B5.1a and B5.1b and Chart B5.2). Nevertheless, comparing the tuition fees charged by institutions and public subsidies received by students, as well as other factors such as access to tertiary education, level of public expenditure in tertiary education or the level of taxation on income, helps to distinguish four groups of countries. Tax revenue on income (OECD, 2006c) is highly correlated with the level of public expenditure available for education and can provide some information on the possibility to finance public subsidies to students.

Chart B5.2. Public subsidies for education in tertiary education (2004)

Public subsidies for education to households and other private entities as a percentage of total public expenditure on education, by type of subsidy

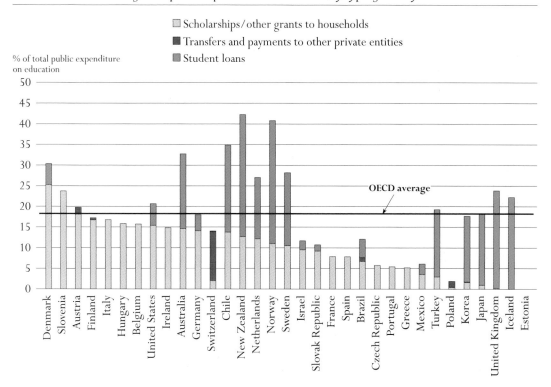

Countries are ranked in descending order of the share of scholarships/other grants to households and transfers and payments to other private entities in total public expenditure on education.
Source: OECD. Table B5.2. See Annex 3 for notes (*www.oecd.org/edu/eag2007*).
StatLink ⬛ᴤ⬛ http://dx.doi.org/10.1787/068348603526

Low tuition fees charged by tertiary-type A institutions (less than USD 300) combined with a high proportion of students (more than 55%) that benefit from public loans or scholarships/grants

The first group includes Nordic countries (Denmark, Finland, Iceland, Norway, Sweden), the Czech Republic and Turkey where there is no (or low) financial barriers for tertiary studies posed by tuition fees and even a high level of aid for students. At 58%, the average entry rate to tertiary-type A education for this group is above the OECD average (see Indicator C2). The tuition fees charged by public educational institutions for national student are negligible (Nordic countries and the Czech Republic) or low (Turkey) in tertiary-type A education and at the same time more than 55% of the students enrolled in tertiary-type A education in this group can benefit from scholarships/grants and/or public loans to finance their studies or for their living expenses (Tables B5.1a and B5.1b and Chart B5.3).

In the Nordic countries, net entry rates in tertiary-type A education are significantly higher than the OECD average and are, on average, 71%. Among the other characteristics of these countries, the proportion of public expenditure allocated to tertiary educational institutions is high compared to the OECD average, whereas both the levels of public expenditure on tertiary education and of taxation on income are also above the OECD average. The Czech Republic and Turkey have a different pattern: low access to tertiary-type A education compared to the OECD average – despite an increase of 16 and 6 percentage points, respectively, in 2000-2005 – combined with low levels (compared to the OECD average) of public spending and of tax revenue on income as a percentage of GDP compared to the OECD average (see Indicators B4 and C2 and Annex 2).

High tuition fees charged by tertiary-type A institutions (more than USD 1 500) combined with a high proportion of students (more than 55%) that benefit from public loans or scholarships/grants

A second group of OECD countries includes four Anglophone countries (Australia, New Zealand, the United Kingdom and the United States) and the Netherlands, where there are potentially quite high financial barriers to enter tertiary-type A education, but also large public subsidies provided to students at this level (Canada could be added to this group of countries, but data on public subsidies are missing). It is noteworthy, however, that the average entry rate to tertiary-type A education for this group of countries is, at 67%, slightly higher than for the group of countries with low tuition fees and high public subsidies.

Tuition fees charged by tertiary-type A educational institutions exceed USD 1 500 in all these countries whereas more than 80% of tertiary-type A students received public subsidies (in the three countries – Australia, the Netherlands and the United States – with available data, see Table B5.1b). The proportion of public subsidies in total public expenditure on tertiary education is higher than the OECD average (18%) in all these five countries: Australia (33%), the Netherlands (27%), New Zealand (42%), the United Kingdom (24%) and the United States (21%) – thus explaining why they are included in this group (Table B5.2). Countries of this group do not have lower access to tertiary-type A education than countries from the previous group. For example, Australia (82%) and New Zealand (79%) have one of the highest entry rates to tertiary-type A education and the Netherlands (59%) and the United States (64%) are above the OECD average (54%), whereas the United Kingdom (51%) is just below the OECD average, though entry to tertiary-type A education increased by 4 percentage points between 2000 and 2005 (see Indicator C2). Finally, the tax revenue on income as a percentage of GDP is relatively high compared to the OECD average in all these countries except in the Netherlands (see Annex 2).

High tuition fees charged by tertiary-type A institutions (more than USD 1 500) combined with a low proportion of students (less than 40%) that benefit from public loans or scholarships/grants

Japan and Korea present a different pattern: high tuition fees charged by tertiary-type A institutions (more than USD 3 500) combined with a relatively low proportion of students that benefit from public subsidies (only one-quarter of students benefit from public subsidies in Japan, see Indicator B5 of *Education at a Glance 2006* for Korea). Tertiary-type A entry rates in those two countries are 41 and 51%, respectively, which is comparatively low. In Japan, some students who excel academically but have difficulty in financing their studies may benefit from reduced tuition and/or admission fees or be exempt from paying these fees entirely. Access for students to tertiary-type A education is below the OECD average in these countries, but is counterbalanced by a higher entry rate than the OECD average to tertiary-type B programmes (see Indicator C2). These two countries are among those with the lowest levels of public expenditure in percentage of GDP allocated to tertiary education (see Table B4.1). This fact partially explains the low proportion of students that can benefit from public loans whereas tax revenue of income as a percentage of GDP is also among the lowest in OECD countries. However, the public subsidies attributable to students represent around 18% of the total public expenditure on tertiary education in these two countries – that is, a proportion equal to the OECD average (Table B5.2).

Low tuition fees charged by tertiary-type A institutions (USD 1 100 or less) combined with a low proportion of students (less than 40%) that benefit from public loans or scholarships/grants

The fourth and last group includes all other European countries for which data are available (Austria, Belgium, France, Ireland, Italy, Poland and Spain) where there are relatively low financial barriers to enter tertiary education combined with relatively low subsidies for students, mainly targeted to specific groups. It is noteworthy that the average tertiary-type A entry rate in this group of countries is, at 48%, relatively low. Similarly, expenditure per student in tertiary-type A education is also comparatively low in this group of countries (see Indicator B1 and Chart B5.1). While high tuition fees can pose potential barriers to student participation, this suggests that the absence of tuition fees, that are assumed to ease the access to education, is not a sufficient condition to entirely relieve challenges for access and quality of tertiary-type A education.

The tuition fees charged by public institutions never exceed USD 1 100 in this group and the proportion of student that benefit from public subsidies is below 40% in countries with available data (Tables B5.1a and B5.1b). In these countries students and their families can benefit from other kinds of subsidies provided by other sources than the ministry of education (*e.g.* housing allowances, tax reductions and/or tax credits for education); these are not covered in this analysis. For example, in France housing allowances may represent a total amount of 90% of the scholarships/grants and about one-third of students benefit from these allowances.

Loan systems (public loans or loan guaranteed by the state) are not available or only available to a small proportion of student in these countries (Table B5.1c). Alongside this, the level of public spending and the tax revenue of income as a percentage of GDP vary significantly more between countries included in this group than in the other groups, but policies on tuition fees and public subsidies are not necessarily the main drivers in the choice of students to enter or not in tertiary-type A education.

Chart B5.3. Relationships between average tuition fees charged by public institutions and proportion of student that benefit from public loans or/and scholarships/grants in tertiary-type A education (school year 2004/2005)

For national full-time national students, in USD converted using PPPs

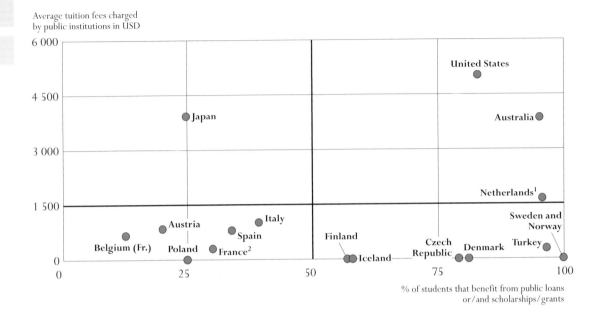

Average tuition fees charged by public institutions in USD

% of students that benefit from public loans or/and scholarships/grants

1. Public institutions do not exist at this level of education and all the students are enrolled in government-dependent institutions.
2. Average tuition fees from 160 to 490 USD.
Source: OECD. Tables B5.1a and B5.1c. See Annex 3 for notes (*www.oecd.org/edu/eag2007*).
StatLink ⫯⫯⫯ http://dx.doi.org/10.1787/068348603526

OECD countries use different mixtures of grants and loans to subsidise students' educational costs

A key question in many OECD countries is whether financial subsidies for households should primarily be provided in the form of grants or loans. Governments subsidise students' living costs or educational costs through different mixtures of grants and loans. Advocates of student loans argue that money spent on loans goes further: if the amount spent on grants were used to guarantee or subsidise loans instead, more aid would be available to students in total and overall access would be increased. Loans also shift some of the cost of education to those who benefit most from educational investment. Opponents of loans argue that student loans are less effective than grants in encouraging low-income students to pursue their education. They also argue that loans may be less efficient than anticipated because of the various subsidies provided to borrowers or lenders, and due to costs of administration and servicing. Cultural differences across and within countries may also affect students' willingness to take out student loans.

Chart B5.2 presents the proportion of public educational expenditure dedicated to loans, grants and scholarships, and other subsidies to households at the tertiary level. Grants and scholarships include family allowances and other specific subsidies, but exclude tax reductions that are part of the subsidy system in Australia, Belgium (Fl.), Canada, the Czech Republic,

Finland, France, Hungary, Italy, the Netherlands, Norway, the Slovak Republic, Switzerland and the United States (see Chart B5.3 in *Education at a Glance 2006*). Around one-half of the 31 reporting OECD countries and partner economies rely exclusively on grants/scholarships and transfers/payments to other private entities. The remaining OECD countries provide both grants or scholarships and loans to students (except Iceland, which relies only on student loans). In general, the highest subsidies to students are provided by those OECD countries offering student loans; in most cases these countries spend an above-average proportion of their budgets on grants and scholarships alone (Chart B5.2 and Table B5.2). Some other countries – Belgium (Fl.), Finland and the partner economy Estonia – do not have public loan systems, but private loans that are guaranteed by the state. This type of subsidy is not taken into account even if it provides some further aid to students, generally through lowest interest rates compared to private loans (see Table B5.1c).

Implementation of public loan systems and amount of public loan

Public loans systems have been relatively recently introduced in most of the countries that report data; the development of these systems occurred in the 1960s and 1980s, corresponding to massive growth of enrolment at tertiary level of education. Since then, public loan systems have developed particularly well in Australia, Sweden and Turkey, where about 80% or more students benefit from a public loan during their tertiary-type A studies. In Norway, public loans are a part of all students' tertiary-type A studies as 100% of students take out loans. Public loan systems are also quite well developed in Iceland (58% of students with a loan), one of the countries – along with Norway and Sweden – where educational institutions at this level do not charge tuition fees to students. In contrast, the United States have the highest level of tuition fees in public tertiary-type A institutions, but less than 40% of students benefit from a public loan during their studies.

The financial support that students receive from public loans during their studies cannot be solely analysed through the proportion of students that have loans. The support for students also depends on the amount they can receive in public loans. In countries with comparable data, the average annual gross amount of public loan available to each students is superior to USD 4 000 in about one-half of the countries and ranges from less than 2 000 in Belgium (Fr.), Hungary and Turkey to more than USD 5 400 in Iceland, Japan, the Netherlands, the United Kingdom and the United States.

The comparison of average tuition fees and average amounts of loans should be interpreted with caution as in a given educational programme the amount of a loan can largely vary between students while that the programmes tuition fees are usually similar between students (Table B5.1d, available on line at *http://dx.doi.org/10.1787/068348603526*). Nevertheless, this can gives some insight into the possibility of loans covering tuition fees and also living expenses. The higher the average level of tuition fees charged by institutions, the bigger the need for a financial support for students through public loans, in order to alleviate financial barriers that may prevent the access to tertiary education. Then the financial pressure for government to support students increases with the amount of tuition fees charged by institutions. In the OECD countries with data available on annual gross amount of loans, the average amount of public loan is superior to the average tuition fees charged in public institutions in all of them showing that the public loans serve also to support a part of the living expenses of the students during their studies.

B5

Among the countries with average tuition fees above USD 1 500 in tertiary-type A public institutions, the average amount of loan is more than twice the average tuition fees in the Netherlands, New Zealand and the United Kingdom. However, this difference in amounts should be counterbalanced in the Netherlands by the fact that only about one-quarter of students benefit from a loan (in the two other countries, the information is not available). The largest differences between average tuition fees and the average amount of loans are observed in Nordic countries that combine no tuition fees charged by institutions, a large proportions of students that can benefit from a public loan and an average amount for this loan that ranges from about USD 2 500 in Denmark to nearly USD 7 000 in Iceland and reach up to nearly USD 9 000 per year in Norway.

The amount that students may get is not the only support related to public loans. Public loan systems offer also some financial aid through the interest rate that students may have to pay, the repayment systems or even through remission/forgiveness mechanisms (Table B5.1c).

Financial support through interest rates

The financial help through reduced interest rates compared to private loans is twofold: there may be some difference between interest rates to be supported by students during their studies and after their studies. Comparing the level of interest rates between countries is quite difficult as the structure of interest rates (public and private) is not known and can significantly vary between countries, so that the given level of interest rate may be considered as high in a country and low in another. However, the difference in rates between studies and after studies seems to aim at lowering the charge due to the loan during the studies of the student. For example, in five countries including Australia, Canada, Iceland, New Zealand and Norway, there is no nominal interest rate on the public loan during the period of studies whereas after the studies, students/ graduates have an interest rate corresponding to the cost of government borrowing or to a higher rate. Nevertheless, there is no systematic difference in interest rate during studies and after studies and six countries – including Belgium, the Netherlands, Sweden, the United Kingdom, the United States and the partner economy Estonia do not differentiate between the interest rate borne by student during their studies and after their studies.

Repayment of loans

Repayment of public loans can be a substantial source of income for governments and can decrease the costs of loan programmes significantly. The current reporting of household expenditure on education as part of private expenditure (see Indicator B3) does not take into account the repayment by previous recipients of public loans.

These repayments can be a substantial burden to individuals and have an impact on the decision to participate in tertiary education. The repayment period vary between countries and ranges from less than 10 years in Belgium (Fr.), New Zealand and Turkey, and the partner economy Estonia, to 20 years or more in Iceland, Norway and Sweden.

Among the 16 OECD countries for which data on repayment system are available, four Anglophone countries (Australia, New Zealand, the United Kingdom and the United States) as well as the Netherlands make the repayment of loans dependent on graduates' level of income. These are also countries where average tuition fees charged by their institutions are higher than USD 1 500 and with average amount of loan amongst the highest in the countries with a public loan system.

Definitions and methodologies

Data refer to the financial year 2004 and are based on the UOE data collection on education statistics administered by the OECD in 2006 (for details see Annex 3 at *www.oecd.org/edu/eag2007*). Data on tuition fees charged by educational institutions and financial aid to students (Tables B1.1a, B1.1b and B1.1c) were collected through a special survey undertaken in 2007 and refer to the school year 2004-2005. Amounts of tuition fees and associated proportions of students should be interpreted with caution as they result from the weighted average of the main tertiary-type A programmes and do not cover all the educational institutions.

Public subsidies to households include the following categories: *i)* grants/scholarships; *ii)* public student loans; *iii)* family or child allowances contingent on student status; *iv)* public subsidies in cash or in kind, specifically for housing, transportation, medical expenses, books and supplies, social, recreational and other purposes; and *v)* interest-related subsidies for private loans.

Expenditure on student loans is reported on a gross basis, that is, without subtracting or netting out repayments or interest payments from the borrowers (students or households). This is because the gross amount of loans including scholarships and grants provides an appropriate measure of the financial aid to current participants in education.

Public costs related to private loans guaranteed by governments are included as subsidies to other private entities. Unlike public loans, only the net cost of these loans is included.

The value of tax reductions or credits to households and students is not included.

Note that data appearing in earlier editions of this publication may not always be comparable to data shown in the 2007 edition due to changes in definitions and coverage that were made as a result of the OECD expenditure comparability study (for details on changes, see Annex 3 at *www.oecd.org/edu/eag2007*).

Further references

The following additional material relevant to this indicator is available on line at:

StatLink ⪎⪎ http://dx.doi.org/10.1787/068348603526

• *Table B5.1d: Variation of tuition fees charged by institutions between students (gross amount) for full-time national students in tertiary type-A education (academic year 2004/2005)*

• *Table B5.3. Public subsidies for households and other private entities as a percentage of total public expenditure on education and GDP, for primary, secondary and post-secondary non-tertiary education (2004)*

Table B5.1a.

Estimated annual average tuition fees charged by tertiary-type A educational institutions[1] for national students (academic year 2004-2005)

In equivalent USD converted using PPPs, by type of institutions, based on full-time students

Amounts of tuition fees and associated proportions of students should be interpreted with caution as they result from the weighted average of the main Tertiary-type A programmes and do not cover all the educational institutions. However, the figures reported can be considered as good proxies and show the difference among countries in tuition fees charged by main educational institutions and for the majority of students.

	Percentage of full-time students enrolled in:			Annual average tuition fees in USD charged by institutions (for full-time students)			
	Public institutions	Government dependent private institutions	Independent private	Public institutions	Government dependent private institutions	Independent private	Comment
	(1)	(2)	(3)	(4)	(5)	(6)	(7)
Australia	98	a	2	3 855	a	7 452	95% of national students in public institutions are in subsidised places and pay an average USD 3 595 tuition fee, including HECS/HELP subsidies.
Austria	88	12	n	837	837	n	
Belgium (Fl.)	x(2)	100	m	x(5)	574	m	
Belgium (Fr.)[2]	32	68	m	661	746	m	
Canada	m	m	m	3 464	m	m	
Czech Republic	93	a	7	No tuition fees	a	3 145	The average fee in public institutions is rather negligible because fees are paid only by student studying too long (more than standard length of the programme plus 1 year): about 4% of students.
Denmark[3]	100	n	a	No tuition fees	m	a	
Finland	89	11	a	No tuition fees	No tuition fees	a	Excluding membership fees to student unions.
France	87	1	12	From 160 to 490	x(6)	From 500 to 8 000	University programmes under the control of the Ministry of Education only.
Germany	m	m	m	m	m	m	
Greece	m	m	m	m	m	m	
Hungary	m	m	m	m	m	m	
Iceland	87	13	a	No tuition fees	From 1 750 to 4 360	a	Excluding registration fees for all students.
Ireland	100	a	n	No tuition fees	a	No tuition fees	The tuition fees charged by institutions are on average of USD 4 470 [1 870 to 20 620] in public institutions and of USD 4 630 [3 590 to 6 270] in private institutions but the government gives the money directly to institutions and the students have not to pay these tuition fees.
Italy	94	a	6	1 017	a	3 520	The annual average tuition fees do not take into account the scholarships/grants that totally cover the tuition fees but partial reductions of fees cannot be excluded.
Japan	25	a	75	3 920	a	6 117	Excludes admission fee charged by the school for the first year (USD 2 267 on average for public, USD 2 089 on average for private institutions) and subscription fee for using facilities (USD 1 510 on average) for private institutions.
Korea	22	a	78	3 883	a	7 406	Tuition fees in first degree programme only. Excludes admission fees to university, but includes supporting fees. A student receiving a scholarship twice a year, is counted as two students.
Luxembourg	m	m	m	m	m	m	
Mexico	66	a	34	m	a	11 359	
Netherlands	a	100	a	a	1 646	a	
New Zealand[3]	98	2	m	1 764	x(4)	x(4)	

1. Without taking into account scholarships/grants that the student may receive.
2. Tuition fees charged for programmes are the same in public than in private institutions but the distribution of students differ between public and private institutions explaining that the weighted average is not the same.
3. Weigthed average for the whole of tertiary education.
Source: OECD. See Annex 3 for notes (*www.oecd.org/edu/eag2007*).
Please refer to the Reader's Guide for information concerning the symbols replacing missing data.
StatLink http://dx.doi.org/10.1787/068348603526

B5

Table B5.1a. *(continued)*
Estimated annual average tuition fees charged by tertiary-type A educational institutions[1]
for national students (academic year 2004–2005)
In equivalent USD converted using PPPs, by type of institutions, based on full-time students

Amounts of tuition fees and associated proportions of students should be interpreted with caution as they result from the weighted average of the main Tertiary-type A programmes and do not cover all the educational institutions. However, the figures reported can be considered as good proxies and show the difference among countries in tuition fees charged by main educational institutions and for the majority of students.

	Percentage of full-time students enrolled in:			Annual average tuition fees in USD charged by institutions (for full-time students)			Comment
	Public institutions	Government dependent private institutions	Independent private	Public institutions	Government dependent private institutions	Independent private	
	(1)	(2)	(3)	(4)	(5)	(6)	(7)
Norway	87	13	a	No tuition fees	From 4 800 to 5 800	a	
Poland	87	a	13	No tuition fees	a	2 710	
Portugal	m	m	m	m	m	m	
Slovak Republic	m	m	m	m	m	m	
Spain	91	a	9	795	a	m	
Sweden	93	7	n	No tuition fees	No tuition fees	m	Excluding mandatory membership fees to student unions.
Switzerland	m	m	m	m	m	m	
Turkey	92	a	8	276	a	14 430 [9 020 to 20 445]	For public institutions, only undergraduate and masters levels.
United Kingdom	a	100	n	a	1 859	1 737	
United States	68	a	32	5 027	a	18 604	Including non-national students.
Brazil	m	m	m	m	m	m	
Chile	m	m	m	m	m	m	
Estonia	a	86	14	a	From 2 190 to 4 660	From 1 190 to 9 765	
Israel	a	87	13	a	From 2 658 to 3 452	From 6 502 to 8 359	Tuition fees charged by institutions are higher for 2nd degree than for 1st degree programmes.
Russian Fed.	m	m	m	m	m	m	
Slovenia	m	m	m	m	m	m	

OECD countries / Partner economies

1. Without taking into account scholarships/grants that the student may receive.
2. Tuition fees charged for programmes are the same in public than in private institutions but the distribution of students differ between public and private institutions explaining that the weighted average is not the same.
3. Weighted average on the whole tertiary education.
Source: OECD. See Annex 3 for notes (*www.oecd.org/edu/eag2007*).
Please refer to the Reader's Guide for information concerning the symbols replacing missing data.
StatLink ᴍᴤ http://dx.doi.org/10.1787/068348603526

Table B5.1b.
Distribution of financial aid to students in tertiary type-A education (academic year 2004-2005)

	Distribution of financial aid to students: Percentage of students that				Eligibility criteria to benefit from scholarships/grants			
	benefit from public loans only	benefit from scholarships/ grants only	benefit from public loans and scholarships/ grants	Do not benefit from public loans nor scholarships/ grants	Progress in study[1,2]	Income of the student[1]	Income of the parents or partner[1]	Other criteria[1]
	(1)	(2)	(3)	(4)	(5)	(6)	(7)	(8)
Australia[3]	71	17	7	5	Never	Always	Always	a
Austria	n	20	n	80	Always	Always	Often for parents, never for partners	Age of student
Belgium (Fl.)	m	m	m	m	Often	Some-times	Often - sometimes	
Belgium (Fr.)	n	12	n	88	Often	Always	Always	Number of dependent persons
Canada	m	m	m	m	Never	Often	Usually-sometimes	According to academic merits
Czech Republic	a	79	a	21	Often	Never	Never	Never
Denmark[4]	1	39	41	19	Always	Always	Never	a
Finland	a	57	a	43	Always	Always	Never-sometimes	Age of the student, student residential status (independently/with parent)
France[4]	n	30	n	70	Always	Always	Always	Age of student
Germany	m	m	m	m	m	m	m	m
Greece	m	m	m	m	m	m	m	m
Hungary	m	m	m	m	m	m	m	m
Iceland	58	n		42	Never	Never	Never	never
Ireland	a	m	m	m	m	m	m	m
Italy	n	39	n	61	Always	Always		Age of student
Japan	24	1	a	75	Some-times	Some-times	Sometimes	Attainment by students of a certain level of education
Korea	m	m	m	m	m	m	m	m
Luxembourg	m	m	m	m	m	m	m	m
Mexico[4]	1	10	m	90	Always	Never	Often-never	
Netherlands	13	68	15	4	Often	Always	Never	
New Zealand[4]	m	m	m	m	Often	Some-times	Never	
Norway	m	m	100	n	Always	Always	Never	
Poland	a	25	n	75	Often	Often	Often	Attainment level for scholarships for learning achivements
Portugal	m	m	m	m	m	m	m	m
Slovak Republic	m	m	m	m	m	m	m	m
Spain	a	34	n	66	Always	Always	Always	
Sweden[4]	n	20	80	n	Always	Always	Never	Always (progress in study and for how long the student had previously received student aid; there is a maximum period of 12 semesters)

OECD countries

1. Possible answers: Never (<5%), sometimes (5 to <40%), usually (40 to <60%), often (60 to <95%), always (95% or more).
2. Progress in studies refer to conditions that lead to limit the duration of studies until graduation or ensure that the students achieved a minimum level.
3. Exclude foreign students.
4. Distribution of students in total tertiary education.
Source: OECD. See Annex 3 for notes (www.oecd.org/edu/eag2007).
Please refer to the Reader's Guide for information concerning the symbols replacing missing data.
StatLink 🔗 http://dx.doi.org/10.1787/068348603526

Table B5.1b. *(continued)*
Distribution of financial aid to students in tertiary type-A education (academic year 2004-2005)

		Distribution of financial aid to students: Percentage of students that				Eligibility criteria to benefit from scholarships/grants			
		benefit from public loans only	benefit from scholarships/ grants only	benefit from public loans and scholarships/ grants	Do not benefit from public loans nor scholarships/ grants	Progress in study[1,2]	Income of the student[1]	Income of the parents or partner[1]	*Other criteria*[1]
		(1)	(2)	(3)	(4)	(5)	(6)	(7)	(8)
OECD countries	Switzerland	m	m	m	m	m	m	m	m
	Turkey	88	6	3	3	Always	Always	Always	Always (dependent from students achievement (25%) and social status (25%)) \ \ If students are not successful (the concept of unsuccessful differs among tertiary institutions), they lose the right to benefit from scholarships.
	United Kingdom	m	m	m	m	m	Always	Always	m
	United States[4]	38	44	m	17	Some-times	Always	Always	a
Partner economies	Brazil	m	m	m	m	m	m	m	m
	Chile	m	m	m	m	m	m	m	m
	Estonia	m	m	m	m	Always	Never	Never	a
	Israel	m	m	m	m	m	m	m	m
	Russian Fed.	m	m	m	m	m	m	m	m
	Slovenia	m	m	m	m	m	m	m	m

1. Possible answers: Never (<5%), sometimes (5 to <40%), usually (40 to <60%), often (60 to <95%), always (95% or more).

2. Progress in studies refer to conditions that lead to limit the duration of studies until graduation or ensure that the students achieved a minimum level.

3. Exclude foreign students.

4. Distribution of students in total tertiary education.

Source: OECD. See Annex 3 for notes (*www.oecd.org/edu/eag2007*).

Please refer to the Reader's Guide for information concerning the symbols replacing missing data.

StatLink ⬛⬛ http://dx.doi.org/10.1787/068348603526

B5

Table B5.1c.
Financial support to students through public loans in tertiary-type A education (academic year 2004-2005)
National students, in USD converted using PPPs

	Year of the creation of a public loan system in the country	Proportion of students that have a loan (%)	Annual gross amount of loan available to each students (USD)	Subsidy through reduced interest rate	
				Interest rate during studies	Interest rate after studies
	(1)	(2)	(3)	(4)	(5)
Australia[1]	1989	79	3 450	No nominal interest rate	No real interest rate (2.4%)
Belgium (Fl.)[2]	m	m	m	1/3 of the interest rate supported by the students (2%)	1/3 of the interest rate supported by the students (2%)
Belgium (Fr.)[3]	1983	1	1 380	4.0%	4.0%
Canada[4]	1964	m	3 970	No nominal interest rate	Interest rates paid by the student (6.7%)
Denmark[5]	1970	42	2 500	4.0%	Flexible rate set by the Central Bank plus 1pt of %
Finland[2]	1969	26	Up to 2 710 per year	1.0%	Full interest rate agreed with the private bank; interest assistance for low-income persons
Hungary[2]	2001	m	1 717	11.95%	11.95%
Iceland	m	58	6 950	No nominal interest rate	1.0%
Japan[6]	1943	24	5 950	Maximum of 3%, rest paid by government	Cost of government borrowing (max. 3%)
Mexico[7]	1970	1	Maximum 10 480	m	m
Netherlands	1986	28	5 730	Cost of government borrowing (3.05%), but repayment delayed until the end of studies	Cost of government borrowing (3.05%)
New Zealand	1992	m	4 320	No nominal interest rate	Cost of government borrowing (max. 7%)
Norway	m	100	Maximum 8 960	No nominal interest rate	Cost of government borrowing
Poland[2]	1998	26	Maximum 3 250	No nominal interest rate	Cost of government borrowing (2.85 to 4.2%)
Sweden	1965	80	4 940	2.80%	2.80%
Turkey	1961	91	1 800	m	m
United Kingdom[8]	1990	m	5 480	No real interest rate (2.6%)	No real interest rate (2.6%)
United States	1970s	38	6 430	5% (interest subsidised for low-income students)	5% (interest subsidised for low-income students)
Estonia[2]	1995	m	2 260	5%, rest paid by government	5%, rest paid by government

1. Including Commonwealth countries.
2. Loan guaranteed by the state rather than public loan.
3. Loan taken by the parents of the student, where only parents have to pay back.
4. Loan outside Quebec. In Quebec, there is only private loans guaranted by the government.
5. The proportion of students refers to all tertiary education. Average amount of loan includes foreign students.
6. Average amount of loan for students in ISCED 5A first qualification programme.
7. Average amount of loan for students in tertiary education.
8. Annual gross amount of loan refers to students in England.
Source: OECD. See Annex 3 for notes (*www.oecd.org/edu/eag2007*).
Please refer to the Reader's Guide for information concerning the symbols replacing missing data.
StatLink 🔗 http://dx.doi.org/10.1787/068348603526

B5

Table B5.1c. *(continued)*
Financial support to students through public loans in tertiary-type A education (academic year 2004-2005)
National students, in USD converted using PPPs

	Repayment system	Annual minimum income threshold (USD)	Duration of typical amortisation period (years)	Average annual amount of repayment (USD)	Percentage of graduates with debt (%)	Average debt at graduation (USD)
			Repayment		**Debt at graduation**	
	(6)	(7)	(8)	(9)	(10)	(11)
Australia[1]	Income contingent	25 750	m	m	67 (domestic graduates)	m
Belgium (Fl.)[2]	m	m	m	m	m	m
Belgium (Fr.)[3]	Mortgage Style	-	5	250	a	a
Canada[4]	Mortgage Style	-	10	950	m	m
Denmark[5]	Mortgage style	-	10-15	830	49	10 430
Finland[2]	Mortgage style		m	1 330	39	6 160
Hungary[2]	Mortgage Style	-	m	640	m	m
Iceland	Fixed part and income contingent part	-	22	3.75% of income	m	m
Japan[6]	Mortgage style	-	15	1 270	m	m
Mexico[7]	m	m	m	m	m	m
Netherlands	Income contingent	17 490	15	m	m	12 270
New Zealand	Income contingent	10 990	6.7	10% of income amount above income threshold	57 (domestic graduates)	15 320
Norway	m	-	20	m	m	20 290
Poland[2]	Mortgage Style	-	m (twice as long as benefiting period)	1950 (+interests)	11	3 250-19 510
Sweden	Income contingent	4 290	25	860	83	20 590
Turkey	Mortgage style	-	1-2	1 780	20	3 560
United Kingdom[8]	Income contingent	24 240	m	9% of income amount above income threshold	79% of eligible students	14 220
United States	Mortgage style	-	10	m	65	19 400
Estonia[2]	Mortgage style	a	7-8	m	m	m

OECD countries (left label for Australia–United States rows)
Partner economy (left label for Estonia row)

1. Including Commonwealth countries.
2. Loan guaranteed by the state rather than public loan.
3. Loan taken by the parents of the student, where only parents have to pay back.
4. Loan outside Quebec. In Quebec, there is only private loans guaranted by the government.
5. The proportion of students refers to all tertiary education. Average amount of loan includes foreign students.
6. Average amount of loan for students in an ISCED 5A first qualification programme.
7. Average amount of loan for students in tertiary education.
8. Annual gross amount of loan refers to students in England.
Source: OECD. See Annex 3 for notes (*www.oecd.org/edu/eag2007*).
Please refer to the Reader's Guide for information concerning the symbols replacing missing data.
StatLink ⧉ http://dx.doi.org/10.1787/068348603526

Table B5.2.
Public subsidies for households and other private entities as a percentage of total public expenditure on education and GDP, for tertiary education (2004)
Direct public expenditure on educational institutions and subsidies for households and other private entities

		Public subsidies for education to private entities						Subsidies for education to private entities as a percentage of GDP
		Financial aid to students						
	Direct public expenditure for institutions	Scholarships/ other grants to households	Student loans	Total	Scholarships/ other grants to households attributable for educational institutions	Transfers and payments to other private entities	Total	
	(1)	(2)	(3)	(4)	(5)	(6)	(7)	(8)
Australia	67.3	14.6	18.1	32.7	1.2	n	32.7	0.37
Austria	80.2	18.1	a	18.1	m	1.7	19.8	0.28
Belgium	84.3	15.7	n	15.7	4.3	n	15.7	0.20
Canada	m	m	m	m	m	m	m	m
Czech Republic	94.2	5.8	a	5.8	m	n	5.8	0.05
Denmark	69.7	25.2	5.1	30.3	a	n	30.3	0.76
Finland	82.8	16.7	n	16.7	n	0.5	17.2	0.36
France	92.1	7.9	a	7.9	2.4	a	7.9	0.10
Germany	82.1	14.1	3.8	17.9	x(4)	n	17.9	0.21
Greece	94.8	5.2	m	5.2	m	a	5.2	0.06
Hungary	84.2	15.8	m	15.8	n	n	15.8	0.16
Iceland[1]	77.8	m	22.2	22.2	m	n	22.2	0.31
Ireland	85.2	14.8	n	14.8	4.5	n	14.8	0.16
Italy	83.3	16.7	n	16.7	5.5	n	16.7	0.13
Japan[1]	81.8	1.0	17.2	18.2	m	n	18.2	0.12
Korea	82.3	1.6	15.9	17.5	1.0	0.1	17.7	0.11
Luxembourg	m	m	m	m	m	m	m	m
Mexico	93.9	3.5	2.6	6.1	1.1	n	6.1	0.06
Netherlands	73.0	12.2	14.9	27.0	1.3	n	27.0	0.37
New Zealand	57.7	12.7	29.6	42.3	m	a	42.3	0.64
Norway	59.2	11.0	29.8	40.8	m	n	40.8	0.99
Poland[2]	98.1	0.4	a	0.4	m	1.5	1.9	0.02
Portugal	94.6	5.4	a	5.4	m	m	5.4	0.05
Slovak Republic[1]	89.3	9.2	1.5	10.7	a	m	10.7	0.11
Spain	92.2	7.8	n	7.8	2.3	n	7.8	0.08
Sweden	71.8	10.5	17.6	28.2	a	a	28.2	0.59
Switzerland[2]	86.0	2.0	0.2	2.2	m	11.9	14.0	0.23
Turkey	80.7	2.9	16.3	19.3	a	m	19.3	0.22
United Kingdom	76.1	0.2	23.7	23.9	x(4)	n	23.9	0.24
United States	79.3	15.4	5.3	20.7	m	m	20.7	0.27
OECD average	*81.9*	*9.9*	*8.6*	*17.5*	*1.6*	*0.7*	*18.1*	*0.26*
Brazil[1,2]	87.9	6.7	4.5	11.2	m	0.9	12.1	0.09
Chile[3]	65.2	13.8	21.0	34.8	10.6	n	34.8	0.17
Estonia[2]	100.0	n	n	n	n	n	n	n
Israel	88.3	9.6	2.2	11.7	9.6	n	11.7	0.13
Russian Federation[2]	m	m	a	m	a	m	m	m
Slovenia	76.3	23.7	n	23.7	m	n	23.7	0.32

1. Some levels of education are included with others. Refer to "x" code in Table B1.1a for details.
2. Public institutions only.
3. Year of reference 2005.
Source: OECD. See Annex 3 for notes (*www.oecd.org/edu/eag2007*).
Please refer to the Reader's Guide for information concerning the symbols replacing missing data.
StatLink ⟦⟧ http://dx.doi.org/10.1787/068348603526

ON WHAT RESOURCES AND SERVICES IS EDUCATION FUNDING SPENT?

INDICATOR B6

This indicator compares OECD countries with respect to the division of spending between current and capital expenditure, and the distribution of current expenditure by resource category. It is largely influenced by teacher salaries (see Indicator D3), pension systems, teacher age distribution, size of the non-teaching staff employed in education (see Indicator D2 in *Education at a Glance 2005*) and the degree to which expansion in enrolments requires the construction of new buildings. It also compares how OECD countries' spending is distributed by different functions of educational institutions.

Key results

Chart B6.1. Distribution of current expenditure on educational institutions for primary, secondary and post-secondary non-tertiary education (2004)

The chart shows the distribution of current spending on educational institutions by resource category. Spending on education can be broken down into capital and current expenditure. Within current expenditure, one can distinguish resource categories compared to other items and service categories such as spending on instruction compared to ancillary and R&D services. The biggest item in current spending – teacher compensation – is examined further in Indicator D3.

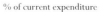 Compensation of all staff ■ Other current expenditure

In primary, secondary and post-secondary non-tertiary education combined, current expenditure accounts for an average of 91% of total spending across OECD countries. In all but four OECD countries and partner economies, 70% or more of primary, secondary and post-secondary non-tertiary current expenditure is spent on staff salaries.

% of current expenditure

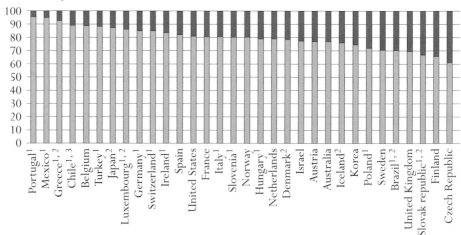

1. Public institutions only.
2. Some levels of education are included with others. Refer to "x" code in Table B1.1a for details.
3. Year of reference 2005.
Countries are ranked in descending order of the share of compensation of all staff on primary, secondary and post-secondary non-tertiary education.
Source: OECD. Table B6.2. See Annex 3 for notes (*www.oecd.org/edu/eag2007*).
StatLink ▓⫘ http://dx.doi.org/10.1787/068352246561

Other highlights of this indicator

- OECD countries spend an average of 34% of current expenditure at the tertiary level on purposes other than the compensation of educational personnel. This is explained by the higher cost of facilities and equipment in higher education.

- On average, OECD countries spend 0.2% of their GDP on subsidies for ancillary services provided by primary, secondary and post-secondary non-tertiary institutions. This represents 6% of total spending. At the high end, Finland, France, the Slovak Republic and Sweden allocate about 10% or more of total spending on educational institutions in percentage of GDP on ancillary services.

- A distinctive feature of tertiary institutions is high spending on R&D, which on average comprises over one-quarter of spending at this level. The fact that some countries spend much more on this item than others helps explain the wide differences in overall tertiary spending. Significant differences among OECD countries in the emphasis on R&D in tertiary institutions also contribute to the observed variation.

- The payment of instructional staff is not as great a share of spending in tertiary institutions as at other levels, because of the higher cost of facilities and equipment as well as the degree to which expansion in enrolments requires the construction of new buildings.

B6

Policy context

How spending is apportioned between different categories of expenditure can affect the quality of services (*e.g.* teachers' salaries), the condition of educational facilities (*e.g.* school maintenance) and the ability of the education system to adjust to changing demographic and enrolment trends (*e.g.* the construction of new schools).

Comparisons of how different OECD countries apportion educational expenditure among the various resource categories can also provide some insight into variation in the organisation and operation of educational institutions. Decisions on the allocation of resources made at the system level – both budgetary and structural – eventually feed through to the classroom and affect the nature of instruction and the conditions under which it is provided.

This indicator also compares how spending is distributed by different functions of educational institutions. Educational institutions offer a range of services in addition to instruction. At the primary, secondary and post-secondary non-tertiary levels, institutions may offer meals and free transport to and from school or boarding facilities. At the tertiary level, institutions may offer housing and often perform a wide range of research activities.

Evidence and explanations

What this indicator does and does not cover

This indicator breaks down educational expenditure by current and capital expenditure and the three main functions typically fulfilled by educational institutions. This includes costs directly attributable to instruction, such as teachers' salaries or school materials, and costs indirectly related to the provision of instruction, such as expenditure on administration, instructional support services, development of teachers, student counselling, or the construction and/or provision of school facilities. It also includes spending on ancillary services such as student welfare services provided by educational institutions. Finally, it includes spending attributable to research and development (R&D) performed at tertiary institutions, either in the form of separately funded R&D activities or in the form of those proportions of salaries and current expenditure in general education budgets that are attributable to the research activities of staff.

The indicator does not include public and private R&D spending outside educational institutions, such as R&D spending in industry. A comparative review of R&D spending in sectors other than education is provided in the *Main OECD Science and Technology Indicators* (OECD 2006). Expenditure on student welfare services at educational institutions only includes public subsidies for those services. Expenditure by students and their families on services that are provided by institutions on a self-funding basis is not included.

Expenditure on instruction, R&D and ancillary services

Below the tertiary level, educational expenditure is dominated by spending on educational core services. At the tertiary level, other services – particularly those related to R&D activities – can account for a significant proportion of educational spending. Variation among OECD countries in expenditure on R&D activities can therefore explain a significant part of the differences in overall educational expenditure per tertiary student (Chart B6.2). For example, high levels of R&D spending (between 0.4 and 0.9% of GDP) in tertiary educational institutions in

Chart B6.2. Expenditure on educational core services, R&D and ancillary services in tertiary educational institutions as a percentage of GDP (2004)

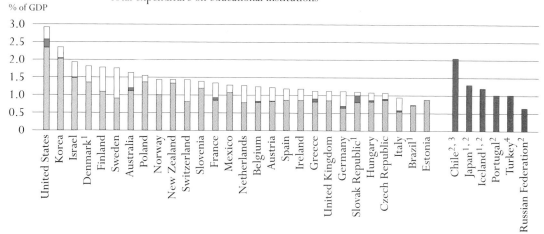

☐ Research and development (R&D)
■ Ancillary services (transport, meals, housing provided by institutions)
☐ Educational core services
■ Total expenditure on educational institutions

1. Some levels of education are included with others. Refer to "x" code in Table B1.1a for details.
2. Total expenditure at tertiary level including R&D expenditure.
3. Year of reference 2005.
4. Total expenditure at tertiary level excluding R&D expenditure.
Countries are ranked in descending order of total expenditure on educational institutions in tertiary institutions.
Source: OECD. Table B6.1. See Annex 3 for notes (*www.oecd.org / edu / eag2007*).
StatLink ⫘⫘⫘ http://dx.doi.org/10.1787/068352246561

Australia, Belgium, Denmark, Finland, France, Germany, the Netherlands, Norway, Sweden and Switzerland, and the partner economy Israel, imply that spending on education per student in these countries would be considerably lower if the R&D component were excluded (see Table B1.1b).

Student welfare services

Student welfare services (as well as services for the general public in some cases) are integral functions of schools and universities in many OECD countries. Countries finance these ancillary services with different combinations of public expenditure, public subsidies and fees paid by students and their families.

On average, OECD countries spend 0.2% of their GDP on subsidies for ancillary services provided by primary, secondary and post-secondary non-tertiary institutions. This represents 6% of total spending on these institutions. At the high end, Finland, France, the Slovak Republic and Sweden spend about 10% or more of total spending on educational institutions in percentage of GDP on ancillary services (Table B6.1).

At the tertiary level, ancillary services are more often provided on a self-financed basis. On average, expenditure on subsidies for ancillary services at the tertiary level amounts to less than 0.1% of GDP and represents up to 0.2% in the United States (Table B6.1).

Current and capital expenditures, and the distribution of current expenditure by resource category

B6

Educational expenditure can first be divided into current and capital expenditure. Capital expenditure comprises spending on assets that last longer than one year and includes spending on the construction, renovation and major repair of buildings. Current expenditure comprises spending on school resources used each year for the operation of schools.

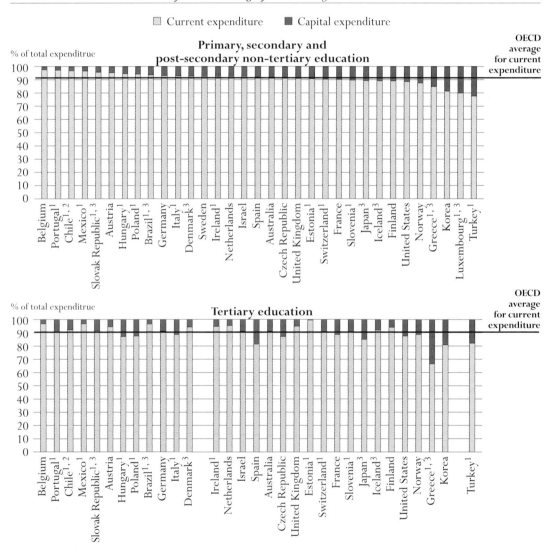

Chart B6.3. **Distribution of current and capital expenditure on educational institutions (2004)**

By resource category and level of education

1. Public institutions only.
2. Year of reference 2005.
3. Some levels of education are included with others. Refer to "x" code in Table B1.1a for details.
Countries are ranked in descending order of the share of current expenditure on primary, secondary and post-secondary non-tertiary education.
Source: OECD. Table B6.2. See Annex 3 for notes (*www.oecd.org/edu/eag2007*).
StatLink ⟨⟨ http://dx.doi.org/10.1787/068352246561

B6

Education takes place mostly in school and university settings. The labour-intensive technology of education explains the large proportion of current spending within total educational expenditure. In primary, secondary, and post-secondary non-tertiary education combined, current expenditure accounts for nearly 91% of total spending on average across all OECD countries.

There is some noticeable variation among OECD countries with respect to the relative proportions of current and capital expenditure: at the primary, secondary and post-secondary non-tertiary levels combined, the proportion of current expenditure ranges from less than 82% in Korea, Luxembourg and Turkey to 97% or more in Belgium, Mexico and Portugal and the partner economy Chile (Chart B6.3).

Proportions of current expenditure allocated to the compensation of teachers and other staff

Current expenditure can be further subdivided into three broad functional categories: compensation of teachers, compensation of other staff, and other current expenditures (*e.g.* teaching materials and supplies, maintenance of school buildings, preparation of student meals and renting of school facilities). The amount allocated to each of these functional categories will depend in part on current and projected changes in enrolment, on the salaries of educational personnel and on costs of maintenance and construction of educational facilities.

The salaries of teachers and other staff employed in education account for the largest proportion of current expenditure in all OECD countries. On average across the OECD countries, expenditure on the compensation of educational personnel accounts for 80% of current expenditure at the primary, secondary and post-secondary non-tertiary levels of education combined. In all except the Czech Republic, Finland, the Slovak Republic and the United Kingdom, 70% or more of current expenditure at the primary, secondary and post-secondary non-tertiary levels is spent on staff salaries. The proportion devoted to the compensation of educational personnel is 90% or more in Greece, Mexico and Portugal (Chart B6.1).

OECD countries with relatively small education budgets (*e.g.* Mexico, Portugal and Turkey) tend to devote a larger proportion of current educational expenditure to the compensation of personnel and a smaller proportion to services that are sub-contracted, such as support services (*e.g.* maintenance of school buildings), ancillary services (*e.g.* preparation of meals for students) and renting of school buildings and other facilities.

In Denmark, France, the United Kingdom and the United States, and the partner economy Slovenia, more than 20% of current expenditure in primary, secondary and post-secondary non-tertiary education combined goes towards compensation of non-teaching staff, while in Austria, Ireland, Korea and the partner economy Chile, this figure is 10% or less. These differences are likely to reflect the degree to which educational personnel such as principals, guidance counsellors, bus drivers, school nurses, janitors and maintenance workers specialise in non-teaching activities (Table B6.2).

OECD countries, on average, spend 34% of current expenditure at the tertiary level on purposes other than the compensation of educational personnel. This is explained by the higher cost of facilities and equipment in higher education (Table B6.2).

B6

Proportions of capital expenditure

At the tertiary level, the proportion of total expenditure spent on capital outlays is larger than at the primary, secondary and post-secondary non-tertiary levels (10.7 versus 9.0%), generally because of more differentiated and advanced teaching facilities. In 13 out of the 31 OECD countries and partner economies for which data are available, the proportion spent on capital expenditure at the tertiary level is 10% or more and in Greece, Korea, Spain and Turkey it is above 17% (Chart B6.3).

Differences are likely to reflect how tertiary education is organised in each OECD country, as well as the degree to which expansion in enrolments requires the construction of new buildings.

Definitions and methodologies

Data refer to the financial year 2004 and are based on the UOE data collection on education statistics administered by the OECD in 2006 (for details see Annex 3 at *www.oecd.org/edu/eag2007*).

The distinction between current and capital expenditure is taken from the standard definition used in national income accounting. Current expenditure refers to goods and services consumed within the current year, and requiring recurrent production in order to sustain the provision of educational services. Capital expenditure refers to assets which last longer than one year, including spending on construction, renovation or major repair of buildings and new or replacement equipment. The capital expenditure reported here represents the value of educational capital acquired or created during the year in question – that is, the amount of capital formation – regardless of whether the capital expenditure was financed from current revenue or by borrowing. Neither current nor capital expenditure includes debt servicing.

Calculations cover expenditure by public institutions or, where available, that of public and private institutions combined.

Current expenditure other than on the compensation of personnel includes expenditure on services which are sub-contracted, such as support services (*e.g.* maintenance of school buildings), ancillary services (*e.g.* preparation of meals for students) and renting of school buildings and other facilities. These services are obtained from outside providers, unlike the services provided by the education authorities or by the educational institutions themselves using their own personnel.

Expenditure on R&D includes all expenditure on research performed at universities and other tertiary education institutions, regardless of whether the research is financed from general institutional funds or through separate grants or contracts from public or private sponsors. The classification of expenditure is based on data collected from the institutions carrying out R&D rather than on the sources of funds.

Ancillary services are services provided by educational institutions that are peripheral to the main educational mission. The two main components of ancillary services are student welfare services and services for the general public. At primary, secondary, and post-secondary non-tertiary levels, student welfare services include meals, school health services, and transportation to and from school. At the tertiary level, it includes residence halls (dormitories), dining halls, and health care. Services for the general public include museums, radio and television broadcasting, sports and recreational and cultural programmes. Expenditure on ancillary services, including fees from students or households, is excluded.

Educational core services are estimated as the residual of all expenditure, *i.e.* total expenditure on educational institutions net of expenditure on R&D and ancillary services.

Note that data appearing in earlier editions of this publication may not always be comparable to data shown in the 2007 edition due to changes in definitions and coverage that were made as a result of the OECD expenditure comparability study (see Annex 3 at *www.oecd.org/edu/eag2007* for details on changes).

B6

B6

Table B6.1.
Expenditure on institutions by service category as a percentage of GDP (2004)
*Expenditure on instruction, R&D and ancillary services in educational institutions and private expenditure
on educational goods purchased outside educational institutions*

| | Primary, secondary and post-secondary non-tertiary education | | | | Tertiary education | | | | |
| | Expenditure on educational institutions | | | Private payments on instructional services/ goods outside educational institutions | Expenditure on educational institutions | | | | Private payments on instructional services/ goods outside educational institutions |
	Core educational services	Ancillary services (transport, meals, housing provided by institutions)	Total		Core educational services	Ancillary services (transport, meals, housing provided by institutions)	R&D at tertiary institutions	Total	
	(1)	(2)	(3)	(4)	(5)	(6)	(7)	(8)	(9)
Australia	3.99	0.17	**4.16**	0.13	1.12	0.08	0.43	**1.63**	0.15
Austria	3.57	0.18	**3.75**	m	0.83	0.01	0.38	**1.22**	m
Belgium	3.97	0.16	**4.13**	0.13	0.80	0.03	0.41	**1.24**	0.17
Canada	m	m	**m**	m	m	m	m	**m**	m
Czech Republic	3.02	0.16	**3.19**	0.12	0.87	0.04	0.16	**1.07**	0.11
Denmark[1]	x(3)	x(3)	**4.33**	0.64	1.35	a	0.46	**1.81**	0.76
Finland	3.51	0.41	**3.92**	m	1.10	n	0.68	**1.78**	m
France	3.58	0.51	**4.09**	0.20	0.86	0.07	0.42	**1.35**	0.08
Germany	3.38	0.08	**3.45**	0.19	0.65	0.05	0.41	**1.11**	0.04
Greece[1]	2.19	0.03	**2.22**	0.85	0.82	0.09	0.21	**1.12**	0.05
Hungary[2]	3.13	0.32	**3.45**	m	0.82	0.04	0.22	**1.08**	m
Iceland[1]	x(3)	x(3)	**5.41**	m	x(8)	x(8)	x(8)	**1.21**	m
Ireland	3.34	0.07	**3.42**	m	0.86	x(8)	0.32	**1.18**	m
Italy[2]	3.30	0.13	**3.44**	0.41	0.55	0.04	0.36	**0.94**	0.14
Japan[1]	x(3)	x(3)	**2.93**	0.79	x(8)	x(8)	x(8)	**1.30**	0.04
Korea	4.04	0.37	**4.41**	m	2.03	0.02	0.30	**2.35**	m
Luxembourg[1,2]	x(3)	x(3)	**3.85**	m	m	m	m	**m**	m
Mexico	4.27	m	**4.27**	0.23	1.07	m	0.21	**1.28**	0.06
Netherlands	3.39	0.04	**3.42**	0.19	0.79	n	0.48	**1.27**	0.07
New Zealand	x(3)	x(3)	**5.01**	0.00	1.34	x(8)	0.10	**1.44**	n
Norway	x(3)	x(3)	**4.22**	m	1.00	n	0.44	**1.44**	m
Poland[2]	3.68	0.11	**3.79**	0.20	1.37	n	0.18	**1.55**	0.06
Portugal[2]	3.80	0.03	**3.82**	0.06	x(8)	x(8)	x(8)	**1.01**	m
Slovak Republic[1]	2.50	0.52	**3.02**	0.73	0.80	0.20	0.10	**1.10**	0.27
Spain	2.88	0.10	**2.98**	m	0.86	m	0.32	**1.18**	m
Sweden	4.03	0.43	**4.46**	m	0.90	n	0.85	**1.76**	m
Switzerland[2]	x(3)	x(3)	**4.51**	m	0.93	x(8)	0.70	**1.63**	m
Turkey[2]	2.89	0.19	**3.09**	0.01	x(8)	x(8)	x(8)	**1.01**	n
United Kingdom	4.21	0.22	**4.44**	m	0.85	m	0.26	**1.12**	0.17
United States	3.77	0.31	**4.08**	a	2.34	0.23	0.34	**2.91**	a
OECD average	*3.48*	*0.22*	*3.84*	*0.29*	*1.04*	*0.05*	*0.36*	*1.40*	*0.13*
Brazil[1,2]	x(3)	x(3)	**2.85**	m	0.66	x(5)	0.01	**0.67**	m
Chile[3]	3.69	0.16	**3.85**	0.03	x(8)	x(8)	x(8)	**2.05**	0.01
Estonia[2]	x(3)	x(3)	**3.66**	m	x(8)	x(8)	n	**0.88**	m
Israel	4.68	0.02	**4.70**	0.29	1.48	0.02	0.43	**1.93**	n
Russian Federation[2]	x(3)	x(3)	**2.01**	m	x(8)	x(8)	x(8)	**0.65**	m
Slovenia[2]	4.12	0.18	**4.30**	m	1.19	n	0.20	**1.39**	m

1. Some levels of education are included with others. Refer to "x" code in Table B1.1b for details.
2. Public institutions only.
3. Year of reference 2005.
Source: OECD. See Annex 3 for notes (*www.oecd.org/edu/eag2007*).
Please refer to the Reader's Guide for information concerning the symbols replacing missing data.
StatLink ⬛📊 http://dx.doi.org/10.1787/068352246561

B6

Table B6.2.
Expenditure on educational institutions by resource category and level of education (2004)
Distribution of total and current expenditure on educational institutions from public and private sources

	Primary, secondary and post-secondary non-tertiary education						Tertiary education					
	Percentage of total expenditure		Percentage of current expenditure				Percentage of total expenditure		Percentage of current expenditure			
	Current	Capital	Compensation of teachers	Compensation of other staff	Compensation of all staff	Other current	Current	Capital	Compensation of teachers	Compensation of other staff	Compensation of all staff	Other current
	(1)	(2)	(3)	(4)	(5)	(6)	(7)	(8)	(9)	(10)	(11)	(12)
OECD countries												
Australia	92.1	7.9	60.2	16.8	77.0	23.0	90.9	9.1	31.8	27.8	59.7	40.3
Austria	95.6	4.4	67.0	10.2	77.2	22.8	94.5	5.5	43.3	13.9	57.2	42.8
Belgium	97.8	2.2	70.3	18.5	88.9	11.1	96.9	3.1	54.0	24.1	78.1	21.9
Canada	m	m	m	m	m	m	m	m	m	m	m	m
Czech Republic	91.9	8.1	47.0	14.3	61.3	38.7	87.3	12.7	30.1	20.9	51.0	49.1
Denmark[1]	92.9	7.1	52.3	26.3	78.6	21.4	94.4	5.6	52.1	25.2	77.3	22.7
Finland	89.4	10.6	54.4	11.6	66.0	34.0	94.2	5.8	35.0	28.1	63.1	36.9
France	90.4	9.6	57.6	23.1	80.7	19.3	88.7	11.3	52.7	26.5	79.2	20.8
Germany[2]	93.2	6.8	x(5)	x(5)	85.1	14.9	91.2	8.8	x(11)	x(11)	71.0	29.0
Greece[1,2]	85.0	15.0	x(5)	x(5)	92.7	7.3	66.7	33.3	x(11)	x(11)	40.6	59.4
Hungary[2]	94.9	5.1	x(5)	x(5)	79.1	20.9	87.3	12.7	x(11)	x(11)	69.7	30.3
Iceland	89.4	10.6	x(5)	x(5)	76.2	23.8	92.0	8.0	x(11)	x(11)	79.4	20.6
Ireland[2]	92.7	7.3	75.4	8.1	83.6	16.4	94.7	5.3	49.3	25.1	74.4	25.6
Italy[2]	93.0	7.0	62.5	18.2	80.7	19.3	88.8	11.2	45.4	21.4	66.8	33.2
Japan[1]	89.5	10.5	x(5)	x(5)	87.4	12.6	85.0	15.0	x(11)	x(11)	61.0	39.0
Korea	81.5	18.5	66.8	7.9	74.7	25.3	80.9	19.1	38.2	14.1	52.3	47.7
Luxembourg[1,2]	80.1	19.9	74.9	11.2	86.2	13.8	m	m	m	m	m	m
Mexico[2]	96.9	3.1	84.4	10.7	95.0	5.0	96.9	3.1	60.2	14.8	75.0	25.0
Netherlands	92.7	7.3	x(5)	x(5)	79.1	20.9	95.3	4.7	x(11)	x(11)	74.5	25.5
New Zealand	m	m	m	m	m	m	m	m	m	m	m	m
Norway	87.8	12.2	x(5)	x(5)	80.3	19.7	88.8	11.2	x(11)	x(11)	63.7	36.3
Poland[2]	94.4	5.6	x(5)	x(5)	72.2	27.8	87.6	12.4	x(11)	x(11)	62.1	37.9
Portugal[2]	97.6	2.4	84.2	11.3	95.5	4.5	90.2	9.8	x(11)	x(11)	73.2	26.8
Slovak Republic[1,2]	96.0	4.0	50.8	16.3	67.1	32.9	91.4	8.6	29.0	15.9	44.9	55.1
Spain	92.2	7.8	70.7	11.4	82.2	17.8	81.6	18.4	59.1	19.9	79.0	21.0
Sweden	92.8	7.2	52.1	18.5	70.6	29.4	m	m	x(11)	x(11)	60.1	39.9
Switzerland[2]	90.6	9.4	72.1	13.0	85.1	14.9	90.7	9.3	40.8	36.6	77.5	22.5
Turkey[2]	77.8	22.2	x(5)	x(5)	88.3	11.7	82.3	17.7	x(11)	x(11)	71.5	28.5
United Kingdom	91.1	8.9	49.0	20.7	69.7	30.3	95.0	5.0	32.3	25.7	58.0	42.0
United States	88.9	11.1	55.3	25.7	81.0	19.0	87.6	12.4	29.7	36.9	66.6	33.4
OECD average	*91.0*	*9.0*	*63.5*	*15.5*	*80.1*	*19.9*	*89.3*	*10.7*	*42.7*	*23.6*	*66.2*	*33.8*
Partner economies												
Brazil[1,2]	93.9	6.1	x(5)	x(5)	70.5	29.5	96.7	3.3	x(11)	x(11)	74.6	25.4
Chile[2,3]	97.1	2.9	84.2	4.9	89.1	10.9	92.1	7.9	x(11)	x(11)	64.1	35.9
Estonia[2]	91.0	9.0	m	m	m	m	99.5	0.5	m	m	m	m
Israel	92.7	7.3	x(5)	x(5)	77.5	22.5	91.0	9.0	x(11)	x(11)	75.3	24.7
Russian Federation	m	m	m	m	m	m	m	m	m	m	m	m
Slovenia[2]	90.0	10.0	49.6	30.9	80.4	19.6	90.8	9.2	36.6	34.0	70.5	29.5

1. Some levels of education are included with others. Refer to "x" code in Table B1.1b for details.
2. Public institutions only.
3. Year of reference 2005.
Source: OECD. See Annex 3 for notes (*www.oecd.org/edu/eag2007*).
Please refer to the Reader's Guide for information concerning the symbols replacing missing data.
StatLink ⏤☐☐ http://dx.doi.org/10.1787/068352246561

HOW EFFICIENTLY ARE RESOURCES USED IN EDUCATION?

This indicator examines the relationship between resources invested and outcomes achieved in primary and lower secondary education across OECD countries and thus raises questions about the efficiency of their education systems.

Key results

Chart B7.1. **Efficiency levels in primary and lower secondary education**

This chart shows the potential for increasing learning outcomes at current levels of resources in primary and lower secondary education across OECD countries as a whole.

☐ Input efficiency ■ Output efficiency

The chart indicates that across OECD countries, there is potential for increasing learning outcomes by 22% while maintaining current levels of resources (output efficiency). The scope for reducing the resources devoted to education while maintaining the current levels of outcomes is slightly larger, at 30% (input efficiency).

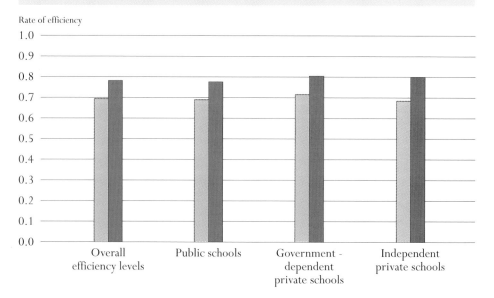

Source: OECD. Table B7.1. See Annex 3 for notes (*www.oecd.org/edu/eag2007*).
StatLink ⟨⟨⟨ http://dx.doi.org/10.1787/068356028750

Other highlights of this indicator

▪ Differences in estimates of efficiency for different types of school (*e.g.* public and private) tend to be modest, when looking at the OECD as whole, though efficiency savings are greater for smaller schools than for larger schools.

B7

Policy context

The relationship between the resources devoted to education and the outcomes achieved has been the focus of much education policy interest in recent years. Seeking to achieve more and better education for the whole population is a goal of governments. However, with increasing pressure on public budgets there is intense interest in ensuring that funding – public funding in particular – is well directed, in order to achieve the desired outcomes in the most effective way possible. Internationally, much attention is of course paid to which education systems achieve most in terms of the quality and equity of learning outcomes, but there is also considerable interest in knowing which systems achieve most given the inputs provided. Could the same outputs be achieved with fewer inputs? Could more outputs be achieved with the same inputs?

Evidence and explanations

This indicator begins with a brief discussion of the issues relevant to measuring efficiency in education. It then examines the correlation between spending and performance and considers what this can say about the efficiency of education systems. Finally, it presents results from analyses conducted by the OECD Economics Department in the context of its "Public Spending Efficiency" project, which applies a modelling approach to measuring educational efficiency. When interpreting the country averages presented in this indicator, it is important to keep in mind that there are substantial differences across countries in the proxy measures of efficiency and that such differences may explain at least part of the observed differences between countries in education outlays.

Student performance and spending per student

Box B7.1 below discusses some of the issues in developing measures of efficiency in education. Given the challenge in properly addressing these issues, it is worth first of all reflecting on what a straightforward comparison of the relationship between education spending and student outcomes indicates about the efficiency of education systems.

Chart B7.2 presents such a comparison by comparing countries' actual spending per student, on average, from the beginning of primary education between the ages of 6 and 15 years, with their average student performance in mathematics from PISA 2003. Spending per student is approximated by multiplying public and private expenditure on educational institutions per student in 2002 at each level of education by the theoretical duration of education at the respective level, between the ages of 6 and 15 years. The results are expressed in USD using purchasing power parities.

Chart B7.2 shows a positive relationship between spending per student and mean mathematics performance. As expenditure per student on educational institutions increases, so also does a country's mean performance. However, the relationship is not a strong one – expenditure per student in fact explains merely 15% of the variation in mean performance between countries.

Deviations from the trend line suggest that moderate spending per student cannot automatically be equated with poor performance by education systems. Spending per student up to the age of 15 years in the Czech Republic is roughly one-third of, and in Korea roughly one-half of, spending levels in the United States, but while both the Czech Republic and Korea are among the top ten performers in PISA, the United States performs below the OECD average. Similarly, Spain and the United States perform almost equally well, but while the United States spends roughly USD 80 000 per student up to the age of 15 years, in Spain this figure is merely USD 47 000.

B7

Box B7.1. **Measuring efficiency in education**

As in any field, measuring efficiency in education is concerned with a comparison of inputs with outputs in order to assess the degree to which goals are achieved while minimising resource usage. Defining appropriate measures of input and output is key in being able to do this and presents a particular challenge in service sectors like education especially with regard to outputs, which are often difficult to measure. Indeed, in measuring education's contribution to Gross Domestic Product in the system of National Accounts only now is there a shift away from the traditional "output equals input" approach to one that attempts to measure the output in volume terms more directly.

Defining inputs and outputs

Two main types of inputs determine educational outcomes. The first type covers discretionary factors under the control of the education system, such as teacher numbers, teacher-student ratios, class sizes, instruction time, teacher quality and other resources in schools. The second type covers non-discretionary or environmental inputs, such as the innate ability of students and students' socio-economic background.

At its most basic level, output can be measured by quantity indicators such as course enrolment and completion rates, study duration or the level of education reached. However, an approach that takes the quality of teaching (and learning) into account focuses more on outcomes, *i.e.* the effective transfer of knowledge and skills – this is, in effect, a quality adjusted output.

The relationship between input volumes (*e.g.* teachers) and outputs provide a measure of technical efficiency, while the relationship between outputs and expenditure inputs provide a measure of cost efficiency.

Approaches to measuring efficiency

The fact that outputs in the public sector are amorphous and intangible in many respects makes it difficult to define a supply function in the conventional sense, while the fact that public sector organisations produce goods that are free at the point of use means that prices of outputs are not determined by market forces. As economic efficiency cannot be directly measured, a technique is needed to proxy an efficiency frontier which would allow relatively accurate benchmarking. One possible approach for doing this is through a non-parametric technique called Data Envelopment Analysis (DEA).

In DEA, efficiency is measured relative to the observed most efficient units (schools or countries). A frontier is constructed such that all observations lie either on or within the frontier so that the frontier represents best practice. Potential efficiency gains for specific countries or schools can then be measured by their position relative to the frontier. Assumptions need to be made about the shape of the efficiency frontier depending on the assumed returns to scale. In Table B7.1, non-increasing returns to scale are assumed. Here, constant returns to scale are assumed between the origin and the observation with the highest input/output ratio and variable returns to scale are assumed thereafter.

Once an efficiency frontier is determined, efficiency shortfalls can be assessed from two perspectives: first, an input oriented measure, which estimates by how much inputs could be scaled back without reducing the level of outputs; second, an output orientation, which estimates how much outputs could be increased given the current levels of inputs.

DEA permits quite robust inferences to be made about relative inefficiencies but they are subject to shortcomings with respect to possible measurement errors. However, techniques for detecting outliers or sample biases can be used to estimate confidence intervals for individual units. In general, the estimates of potential efficiency gains are more certain when the estimated potential gain is greater.

Countries that perform significantly higher than would be expected from their spending per student alone include Australia, Belgium, Canada, the Czech Republic, Finland, Japan, Korea and the Netherlands. Countries that perform significantly below the level of performance predicted from spending per student include Greece, Italy, Mexico, Norway, Portugal, Spain and the United States.

In summary, the results suggest that, while spending on educational institutions is a necessary prerequisite for the provision of high-quality education, spending alone is not sufficient to achieve high levels of outcomes and the effective use of these resources is important in achieving good outcomes.

Chart B7.2. Student performance and spending per student

Relationship between performance in mathematics and cumulative expenditure on educational institutions per student between the ages of 6 and 15 years, in USD, converted using purchasing power parities (PPPs)

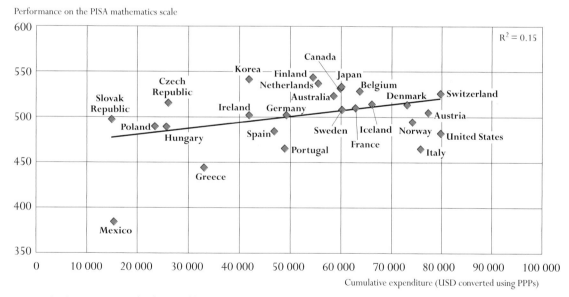

Performance on the PISA mathematics scale

Cumulative expenditure (USD converted using PPPs)

Source: OECD PISA 2003 database. Table 2.6.
StatLink http://dx.doi.org/10.1787/068356028750

Why is it that some countries perform better than others with similar levels of investments?

Many factors influence the relationship between spending per student and student performance. These factors will include the organisation and management of schooling within the system (*e.g.* layers of management and distribution of decision making, geographic dispersion of the population), the organisation of the immediate learning environment of the students (*e.g.* class size, hours of instruction), the quality and remuneration of the teacher workforce as well as characteristics of the students themselves, most notably their socio-economic background. Given this, it is clear that a simple correlational approach between one input and one output variable is insufficient to provide measures of efficiency.

On the input side, there is a need to distinguish between input variables that are within the control of the education providers (teacher numbers, teacher-student ratios, class sizes, instruction time, teacher quality) and those that are not (*i.e.* non-discretionary). In particular, among non-discretionary inputs, the socio-economic background of the students needs to be taken into account as the strength of the influence of this on student outcomes is so great. Student immigrant status and language spoken at home are also important in this regard. In general, it is important to ensure that there is close correspondence between the chosen inputs and the outputs that they are designed to produce.

On the output side, the chosen variables should reflect the goals of the education system, given the chosen input variables. Ideally, then these should cover achievement goals across the curriculum including for example social and civic engagement skills. Importantly, the chosen variables should measures both the quality and equity of achievements within the system.

Inevitably this calls for a more sophisticated assessment of efficiency than can be achieved with simple correlations.

Measures of efficiency in primary and lower secondary public education

The OECD Economics Department has explored the use of Data Envelopment Analysis (DEA) as a means of producing internationally comparative measures of efficiency (OECD, 2007). In DEA, efficiency is measured relative to the observed most efficient units (schools or countries), considering the specified input and output variables (see Box B7.1). As much of this work is exploratory at this stage, only OECD-wide estimates of efficiency are shown in this indicator.

Table B7.1 summarises the estimates of efficiency derived from school level data considering the median school, averaged across all OECD countries. The output variable used in the analysis is the average PISA scores of students and the input variables used are the teacher-student ratio, computer availability, socio-economic backgrounds and language spoken at home of students. By considering volumes rather than values of inputs, these are measures of technical rather than cost efficiency. The model assumes non-increasing returns to scale (see Box B7.1).

The results suggest that the scope for reducing inputs while holding outputs constant (input efficiency) is on average around 30% for the median school. Potential gains from maximising outputs from the current level of inputs are slightly smaller: the average PISA scores of students in the median school is around 22% below the level suggested possible by the efficiency frontier.

Differences in estimates in efficiency for different types of school tend to be modest. The median public school in the overall sample is slightly less efficient than both the median government dependent private school and median independent private school. Schools that rely on public sources for the majority of their funding also tend to be slightly less efficient than other schools. Perhaps as one might expect, smaller schools tend to be less efficient than larger schools, particularly in terms of the extent that inputs could be reduced for the same level of output (Chart B7.1).

In addition to the technical limitations of DEA analysis noted in Box B7.1, the specification of the variables to be used as inputs and outputs is also important to the robustness of the results. As discussed earlier, how well the chosen input and output variables measure, respectively, the resources devoted to education and the intended outputs, is key. Inevitably, the chosen variables in the analysis presented here are limited by the available international datasets. For instance, arguably, the PISA outcome measures provide only a partial measure of the intended goals of education systems and in the case of inputs, to get a fuller picture of these resources devoted to out-of-school learning should perhaps be taken into account also.

Definitions and methodologies

The educational expenditure figures are taken from the UOE data collection on education statistics administered by the OECD (for details see Annex 3 at *www.oecd.org/edu/eag2007*). The student achievement scores are based on assessments administered in 2003 as part of the Programme for International Student Assessment (PISA) undertaken by the OECD.

The cumulative expenditure figures for a given country is approximated as follows: let n(0), n(1) and n(2) be the typical number of years spent by a student from the age of six up to the age of 15 years in primary, lower secondary and upper secondary education. Let E(0), E(1) and E(2) be the annual expenditure per student in USD converted using purchasing power parities in primary, lower secondary and upper secondary education, respectively in 2002. The cumulative expenditure is then calculated by multiplying current annual expenditure E by the typical duration of study n for each level of education i using the following formula:

$$CE = \sum_{i=0}^{2} n(i) * E(i)$$

Estimates for n(i) are based on the International Standard Classification of Education (ISCED).

The estimates of efficiency shown in Table B7.1 and Chart B7.1 have been taken from the papers produced by the OECD Economics Department as part of the project to assess public spending efficiency in primary and secondary education.

The estimates of possible efficiency savings shown in Table B7.1 relate to the median school in each OECD country in terms of PISA 2003 performance and are generated from a Data Envelopment Analysis (DEA) model assuming non-increasing returns to scale. The model uses the PISA score as the output variable and teacher-student ratio, computer availability, socio-economic and language backgrounds as the input variables. In DEA, a frontier is constructed such that all observations (in this case school performance in PISA 2003) lie either on or within the frontier so that the frontier represents best practice. Potential efficiency gains can then be measured by a country's or school's position relative to the frontier.

Further references

For more information see "Performance Indicators for Public Spending Efficiency in Primary and Secondary Education", OECD Economics Department Working Paper No. 546, available on line at *www.oecd.org/eco/Working_Papers*.

B7

Table B7.1.
Estimates of technical efficiency[1] for primary and lower secondary public sector education

	Input efficiency[2]	Output efficiency[3]	Number of schools
Overall level of efficiency	0.693	0.782	6 204
Of which:			
Public schools	0.689	0.777	4 834
Government-dependent private schools	0.715	0.805	672
Independent private schools	0.684	0.799	194
Public funds >50%	0.693	0.780	5 469
Public funds <50%	0.693	0.803	397
Small schools	0.669	0.770	3 102
Large schools	0.712	0.794	3 102

1. Efficiency estimates are for the median school in each OECD country in terms of PISA 2003 performance and are derived from a Data Envelopment Analysis assuming non-increasing returns to scale. The model uses the PISA score as output and the teacher to student ratio, computer availability, socio-economic and language backgrounds as inputs.
2. Indicates scope for scaling back inputs without reducing the level of outputs.
3. Indicates scope for boosting outputs given the current levels of inputs.
Source: OECD Economics Working Paper No. 546, available at *www.oecd.org/eco/working_papers.*
StatLink http://dx.doi.org/10.1787/068356028750

Chapter

C

ACCESS TO EDUCATION, PARTICIPATION AND PROGRESSION

HOW PREVALENT ARE VOCATIONAL PROGRAMMES?

This indicator shows the participation of students in vocational education and training (VET) at the upper secondary level of education and compares the levels of education expenditure per student for general programmes and VET. This indicator also compares the educational outcomes of 15-year-old students enrolled in general education and in vocational education.

Key results

Chart C1.1. **Difference in mathematics performance associated with students' programme orientation (2003)**

■ ☐ Differences in mathematics performances between general programme students and pre-vocational and vocational programme students
Statistically significant differences are marked in darker tone

■ ☐ Differences in mathematics performances between general programme students and pre-vocational and vocational programme students, with accounting for the economic, social and cultural status of students (ESCS)
Statistically significant differences are marked in darker tone

PISA 2003 shows that 15-year-olds in pre-vocational and vocational programmes have statistically significant lower performance in mathematics compared to students enrolled in general programmes in 9 out of the 10 OECD countries for which data are available. On average, across OECD countries, 15-year-olds enrolled in general programmes perform 45 score points higher and after adjusting for socio-economic factors the difference still remains, at 27 score points.

Performance on the PISA mathematics scale

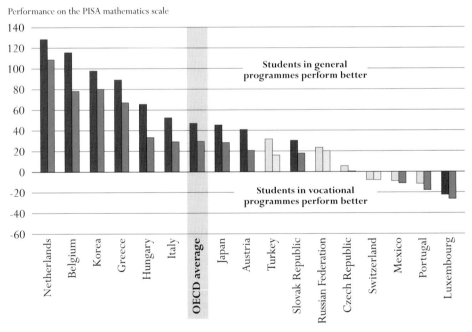

Note: This figure shows data for countries with more than 3 % of students in the aggregated category of pre-vocational and vocational programmes.
Countries are ranked in descending order of performance advantage for students enrolled in general programmes versus students enrolled in vocational programmes.
Source: OECD PISA 2003 database, Table C1.3. See Annex 3 for notes (*www.oecd.org/edu/eag2007*).
StatLink ᘉ⃞ http://dx.doi.org/10.1787/068363750663

Other highlights of this indicator

- In 15 out of the 28 OECD countries and the partner economy Slovenia, the majority of upper secondary students attend pre-vocational and vocational programmes. A significant proportion of vocational education in upper secondary is school-based in most OECD countries.

- The 14 OECD countries for which data are available spend, on average, USD 854 more per student in upper secondary vocational programmes than in general programmes.

Policy context

A range of factors – including better employment outcomes for the more educated – has strengthened the incentive for young people to enroll in school beyond the end of compulsory education and to graduate from upper secondary education. The continued growth in participation in upper secondary education means that countries have to cater to more diverse student populations at that level.

Countries have chosen various approaches to meet these demands. Some have comprehensive lower secondary systems with non-selective general/academic programmes that seek to provide all students with similar opportunities for learning, while others provide more distinct education programmes (*i.e.* academic, pre-vocational and/or vocational programmes) within both lower and upper secondary education. Vocational programmes differ from academic ones not only with regard to their curricula, but also in that they generally prepare students for specific types of occupations and, in some cases, for direct entry into the labour market.

Countries must continuously review their educational systems to ensure that the graduates produced meet the changing demands of their labour market/economy. VET-related issues with which countries are wrestling include increasing the supply of apprentices, specific skill shortages in their workforces, enhancing the status of VET and upgrading its quality.

Today VET encompasses both formal education – secondary programmes (pre-vocational and vocational), post-secondary programmes and even university programmes – and non-formal job-related continuing education and training (see Indicator C5). This indicator will focus on formal education (pre-vocational and vocational programmes) at the upper secondary level.

Evidence and explanations

Participation in upper secondary vocational education

In most OECD countries, students do not follow a uniform curriculum at the upper secondary level. Programmes at the upper secondary level can be subdivided into three categories based on the degree to which they are oriented towards a specific class of occupations or trades and lead to a labour-market relevant qualification:

- General education programmes that are not designed explicitly to prepare participants for specific occupations or trades, or for entry into further vocational or technical education programmes. (Less than 25% of the programme content is vocational or technical.)
- Pre-vocational or pre-technical education programmes that are mainly designed to introduce participants to the world of work and to prepare them for entry into further vocational or technical education programmes. Successful completion of such programmes does not lead to a labour-market relevant vocational or technical qualification. (At least 25% of the programme content is vocational or technical.)
- Vocational or technical education programmes that prepare participants for direct entry into specific occupations without further training. Successful completion of such programmes leads to a labour-market relevant vocational or technical qualification.

Vocational and pre-vocational programmes are further divided into two categories (school-based and combined school- and work-based programmes) on the basis of the amount of training that is provided in-school as opposed to training in the work place:

C1

- In school-based programmes instruction takes place (either partially or exclusively) in educational institutions. These include special training centres run by public or private authorities or enterprise-based special training centres if these qualify as educational institutions. These programmes can have an on-the-job training component, *i.e.* a component of some practical experience at the workplace. Programmes are classified as school-based if at least 75% of the curriculum is presented in the school environment (covering the whole educational programme); this may include distance education.

- In combined school- and work-based programmes, less than 75% of the curriculum is presented in the school environment or through distance education. These programmes include apprenticeship programmes, organised in conjunction with educational authorities or educational institutions that involve concurrent school-based and work-based training, and programmes organised in conjunction with educational authorities or educational institutions that involve alternating intervals of attendance at educational institutions and participation in work-based training (programmes of training in alternation, sometimes referred to as "sandwich" programmes).

The degree to which a programme has a vocational or general orientation does not necessarily determine whether participants have access to tertiary education. In several OECD countries, vocationally oriented programmes are designed to prepare students for further studies at the tertiary level, and in some countries general programmes do not always provide direct access to further education.

In 15 OECD countries and the partner economy Slovenia, the majority of upper secondary students pursue pre-vocational and vocational programmes. In most OECD countries with dual-system apprenticeship programmes (Austria, Germany, Luxembourg, the Netherlands and Switzerland) and in Australia, Belgium, the Czech Republic, Finland, Italy, Norway, the Slovak Republic and the United Kingdom, and the partner economy Slovenia, 60% or more of upper secondary students are enrolled in pre-vocational or vocational programmes. The exceptions are Greece, Hungary, Iceland, Ireland, Japan, Korea, Mexico and Portugal and the partner economies Brazil, Chile, Estonia and Israel, where 60% or more of upper secondary students are enrolled in general programmes even though pre-vocational and/or vocational programmes are offered (Table C1.1).

In many OECD countries, upper secondary vocational education is school based. In Austria, the Czech Republic, Iceland and the Slovak Republic, however, about half of the vocational programmes have combined school-based and work-based elements. In Denmark, Germany, Hungary, Ireland and Switzerland, around 75% or more of students enrolled in vocational programmes have both school-based and work-based elements.

While upper secondary students in many education systems can enrol in vocational programmes, some OECD countries delay vocational training until after graduation from upper secondary education. While vocational programmes are offered as advanced upper secondary programmes in some OECD countries (*e.g.* Austria, Hungary and Spain), they are offered as post-secondary education in others (*e.g.* Canada and the United States).

Apprenticeship (work-based learning) programmes

Table C1.1 includes enrolments in apprenticeship programmes that are a recognised part of the education system in countries. This section provides information on the typical characteristics of these programmes and other work-based learning programmes.

In most OECD countries (Australia, Austria, Belgium, Canada, the Czech Republic, Denmark, Finland, France, Germany, Hungary, Ireland, Luxembourg, Mexico, the Netherlands, New Zealand, Norway, Poland, the Slovak Republic, Switzerland, Turkey and the United Kingdom) and partner economies (Israel, the Russian Federation and Slovenia), some form of apprenticeship system exists. In some countries (*e.g.* Austria, Germany and Hungary), apprenticeship (student) contracts are established between the student (not the vocational training school) and the enterprise. In the United States, there are apprenticeship programmes, but they are not part of the formal education system. For the most part, the majority of countries have combined school and work-based apprenticeship programmes. In contrast, apprenticeship systems do not exist in Japan, Korea, Spain and Sweden.

The minimum entry requirements for entry into apprenticeship programmes vary between countries, however, the typical minimum requirement is usually the completion of lower secondary (in Canada, the Czech Republic, Denmark, Finland, France, Germany, Ireland, Luxembourg, Mexico, the Netherlands, Norway, Poland and the Slovak Republic, and in the partner economies Israel and Slovenia) or upper secondary education (in the partner economy Brazil). In Australia, Austria, Belgium, the Netherlands, the United Kingdom and the United States, entry is governed (in full or in part) by age criteria, while in New Zealand, participants must be in employment. In contrast, the Russian Federation has no legal framework governing entry into apprenticeship programmes.

The duration of apprenticeship programmes is standardised in some countries, ranging from one to four years in Canada, the Czech Republic, Denmark, France, Germany, Ireland, New Zealand, Norway, Poland and the United Kingdom and the partner economies Israel and Slovenia. In other countries (*e.g.* Austria and Belgium), it varies according to subject, the specific qualification being sought, previous knowledge and/or experience.

In most countries, the successful completion of an apprenticeship programme usually results in the awarding of an upper secondary or post-secondary qualification. In some countries, higher level qualifications are also possible (*e.g.* an advanced diploma in Australia).

Differences in educational expenditure per student between general and vocational programmes

In most OECD countries, expenditure per student varies according to whether programmes are general or vocational. In the 14 OECD countries for which data are available, expenditure per student in upper secondary vocational programmes in 2004 was, on average, USD 854 higher than in general programmes (Table C1.2).

The countries with large dual-system apprenticeship programmes (*e.g.* Austria, Germany, Luxembourg, the Netherlands and Switzerland) at upper secondary level tend to be those with a higher difference between expenditure per student enrolled in general and vocational programmes. For example, Germany and Switzerland spend, respectively, USD 6 748 and 5 338 more per student in vocational programmes than in general programmes with employers contributing a large part of these expenditures. Exceptions to this pattern are Luxembourg and the Netherlands, where expenditure per student enrolled in general programmes is higher than that for apprenticeship programmes. The data for Luxembourg and the Netherlands however, is underestimated due to the exclusion of expenditures from private enterprises on dual vocational programmes. Among the four other countries – Australia, the Czech Republic, Finland and the Slovak Republic – with 60% or more of upper secondary students enrolled in vocational programmes, both the Czech Republic and Finland spend more per student enrolled in vocational programmes than in general programmes (Table C1.1 and Table C1.2).

Learning outcomes from vocational education

Is there a difference in the performance of students enrolled in vocational versus general programmes? The analysis below is limited to student performance in mathematics at age 15. Similar patterns were found for PISA 2003 performance in reading and science, but those findings are not reported here in order to simplify the presentation and avoid repetition.

The results in PISA 2003 show that, on average across OECD countries, students in pre-vocational and vocational programmes score 45 points lower than students in general programmes before socio-economic factors have been taken into account. The largest differences are observed in Belgium, Greece, Hungary, Korea and Netherlands. In the Netherlands, the performance of students in general programmes (617 score points) is significantly higher than the overall OECD average (500 score points), while the performance of students in vocational programmes (488 score points) is lower than the overall OECD average. A similar pattern is also found in Belgium, Hungary and Korea. In Greece, however, students enrolled in both general and pre-vocational/vocational programmes performed below the OECD average (with 463 and 374 score points, respectively). Luxembourg is the only country in which students enrolled in pre-vocational and vocational programmes have a statistically significant performance advantage (23 score points).

Given that vocational and general tracking can often reflect social segregation in the education systems, it is also important to examine differences in performance after adjusting for socio-economic factors. After adjusting for socio-economic factors, the performance difference of pre-vocational and vocational programmes is lowered by 18 score points, to remain at 27 score points on average across OECD countries. For 12 OECD countries, there is a statistically significant difference in the performance levels of students enrolled in general programmes compared to students enrolled in pre-vocational and vocational programmes, even after adjusting for socio-economic factors. Students enrolled in pre-vocational and vocational programmes in Luxembourg, Mexico and Portugal still have a statistically significant performance advantage (26, 11 and 18 score points respectively). For the remaining nine countries, students enrolled in pre-vocational and vocational programmes have a performance disadvantage ranging from 18 score points in the Slovak Republic to 109 score points in the Netherlands (Table C1.3 and Chart C1.1).

Nevertheless, it is important to note that the performance disadvantage of those enrolled in pre-vocational and vocational programmes may well have no impact on these students' future careers.

Definitions and methodologies

The student performance data are based on assessments administered as part of the Programme for International Student Assessment (PISA) undertaken by the OECD in 2003.

Data on enrolment is for the school year 2004-2005 and data on finance refer to the financial year 2004 and both are based on the UOE data collection on education statistics administered annually by the OECD.

Data on apprenticeship (work-based learning) programmes are based on a special survey carried out by the OECD in the autumn of 2006.

Table C1.1 shows the distribution of enrolled students in upper secondary education by programme orientation. Pre-vocational and vocational programmes include both school-based programmes and combined school- and work-based programmes that are recognised as part of the education system. Entirely work-based education and training that is not overseen by a formal education authority is not included.

Further references

The following additional material relevant to this indicator is available on line at:

StatLink ⟪⟫ http://dx.doi.org/10.1787/068363750663

- *Table C1.4. Differences in mathematics performances between the different programme orientations (2003)*
- *Table C1.5. Performance of 15-year-old students on the mathematics, reading and science scales by programme orientation (2003)*

Table C1.1.
Upper secondary enrolment patterns (2005)
Enrolment in public and private institutions by programme destination and type of programme

	Distribution of enrolment by programme destination			Distribution of enrolment by type of programme			
	ISCED 3A	ISCED 3B	ISCED 3C	General	Pre-vocational	Vocational	of which: combined school and work-based
	(1)	(2)	(3)	(4)	(5)	(6)	(7)
OECD countries							
Australia	38.5	a	61.5	38.5	a	61.5	m
Austria	43.6	47.1	9.3	21.5	6.2	72.3	32.7
Belgium [1]	49.5	a	50.5	30.4	a	69.6	3.3
Canada	m	m	m	m	m	m	m
Czech Republic	70.3	0.4	29.3	20.5	0.1	79.4	35.5
Denmark	52.1	a	47.9	52.1	a	47.9	47.7
Finland	100.0	a	a	36.1	a	63.9	10.5
France	57.5	10.4	32.1	43.6	a	56.4	11.3
Germany	39.7	59.7	0.6	39.7	a	60.3	45.0
Greece	64.0	a	36.0	64.0	a	36.0	a
Hungary	76.8	a	23.2	75.9	10.9	13.2	13.2
Iceland	50.6	0.6	48.8	63.2	1.6	35.2	16.4
Ireland	71.4	a	28.6	65.7	30.5	3.8	3.8
Italy	80.8	2.9	16.3	38.5	36.6	24.9	a
Japan	75.3	0.9	23.9	75.3	0.9	23.9	a
Korea	71.5	a	28.5	71.5	a	28.5	a
Luxembourg	59.6	15.5	24.8	36.6	a	63.4	13.6
Mexico	89.8	a	10.2	89.8	a	10.2	m
Netherlands	61.8	a	38.2	31.8	a	68.2	20.0
New Zealand	m	m	m	m	m	m	m
Norway	39.2	a	60.8	39.2	a	60.8	13.3
Poland	88.3	a	11.7	55.0	a	45.0	6.5
Portugal	100.0	a	a	69.0	20.5	10.5	m
Slovak Republic	80.7	a	19.3	25.8	a	74.2	31.7
Spain	57.4	n	42.6	57.4	n	42.6	2.8
Sweden	94.8	a	5.2	46.4	0.8	52.7	a
Switzerland	30.5	62.1	7.4	35.3	a	64.7	58.3
Turkey	90.7	a	9.3	57.8	a	42.2	7.4
United Kingdom [2]	43.6	x(1)	56.4	27.8	x(6)	72.2	m
United States	100.0	x(1)	x(1)	100.0	x(4)	x(4)	x(4)
OECD average	*67.1*	*7.7*	*26.7*	*50.3*	*4.2*	*47.5*	*16.2*
EU 19 average	*68.0*	*7.6*	*24.8*	*44.1*	*5.9*	*50.3*	*16.3*
Partner economies							
Brazil	100.0	a	a	93.5	a	6.5	a
Chile	100.0	a	a	63.9	a	36.1	a
Estonia	100.0	a	a	69.0	a	31.0	a
Israel	95.9	a	4.1	65.0	a	35.0	4.1
Russian Federation	57.0	13.3	29.7	57.0	13.3	29.7	m
Slovenia	32.6	44.4	23.0	32.6	n	67.4	3.7

1. Excludes the German-speaking Community of Belgium.
2. Includes post-secondary, non-tertiary education.
Source: OECD. See Annex 3 for notes (*www.oecd.org/edu/eag2007*).
Please refer to the Reader's Guide for information concerning the symbols replacing missing data.
StatLink ᘉᗖ http://dx.doi.org/10.1787/068363750663

Table C1.2.

Annual expenditure on educational institutions per student for all services, by type of programme (2004)

In equivalent USD converted using PPPs for GDP, by level of education, based on full-time equivalents

	Secondary education									Post-secondary non-tertiary education		
	Lower secondary education			Upper secondary education			All secondary education					
	All programmes	General programmes	Vocational/ pre-vocational programmes	All programmes	General programmes	Vocational/ pre-vocational programmes	All programmes	General programmes	Vocational/ pre-vocational programmes	All programmes	General programmes	Vocational/ pre-vocational programmes
	(1)	(2)	(3)	(4)	(5)	(6)	(7)	(8)	(9)	(10)	(11)	(12)
OECD countries												
Australia	7 747	7 753	7 674	8 853	9 227	7 973	8 160	8 212	7 884	7 969	a	7 969
Austria	8 969	8 969	a	9 962	11 082	9 642	9 446	9 329	9 642	m	m	m
Belgium	x(7)	x(7)	x(7)	x(7)	x(7)	x(7)	7 751	x(7)	x(7)	x(7)	x(7)	x(7)
Canada	m	m	m	m	m	m	m	m	m	m	m	m
Czech Republic	4 769	4 752	8 872	4 790	4 200	4 942	4 779	4 659	4 963	2 191	1917	2 223
Denmark	8 224	8 224	a	9 466	x(4)	x(4)	8 849	x(7)	x(7)	m	m	m
Finland	8 918	8 918	a	6 555	5 230	7 314	7 441	7 525	7 314	x(7)	a	x(9)
France	7 837	7 837	a	9 883	x(4)	x(4)	8 737	x(7)	x(7)	4 081	x(10)	x(10)
Germany	6 082	6 082	x(6)	10 459	6 274	13 022	7 576	6 114	13 022	10 573	6712	11 283
Greece	x(7)	x(7)	x(7)	x(7)	x(7)	x(7)	5 213	x(7)	x(7)	5 688	m	m
Hungary[1]	3 433	x(1)	x(1)	3 968	3 575	5 085	3 692	3 475	5 158	6 351	a	6 351
Iceland	8 284	m	a	7 330	m	m	7 721	m	x(7)	x(7)	x(7)	x(7)
Ireland	6 943	x(1)	x(1)	7 309	x(4)	x(4)	7 110	x(7)	x(7)	5 169	x(10)	x(10)
Italy [1]	7 657	7 590	m	7 971	x(4)	x(4)	7 843	x(7)	x(7)	m	m	m
Japan	7 325	7 325	a	7 883	x(4)	x(4)	7 615	x(7)	x(7)	x(7)	m	m
Korea	6 057	6 057	a	7 485	x(4)	x(4)	6 761	x(7)	x(7)	m	m	m
Luxembourg[1]	18 036	18 036	a	17 731	18 285	17 468	17 876	18 102	17 468	m	m	m
Mexico	1 602	1 859	308	2 564	2 528	2 877	1 922	2 093	918	a	a	a
Netherlands	7 948	7 468	8 729	7 037	8 012	6 595	7 541	7 625	7 463	6 624	a	6 624
New Zealand	5 334	x(1)	x(1)	7 424	x(4)	x(4)	6 299	x(7)	x(7)	5 412	m	m
Norway	9 476	9 476	a	12 498	x(4)	x(4)	11 109	x(7)	x(7)	x(4)	x(4)	x(4)
Poland [1]	2 822	2 822	a	2 949	x(4)	x(4)	2 889	x(7)	x(7)	3 147	m	m
Portugal[1]	6 359	x(1)	x(1)	5 962	x(4)	x(4)	6 168	x(7)	x(7)	m	m	m
Slovak Republic	2 389	2 389	a	3 155	3 461	3 052	2 744	2 581	3 052	x(7)	x(8)	x(9)
Spain	x(7)	x(7)	x(7)	x(7)	x(7)	x(7)	6 701	x(7)	x(7)	a	a	a
Sweden	7 836	7 836	a	8 218	7 315	9 092	8 039	7 650	9 092	3 437	11 469	950
Switzerland[1]	9 197	9 197	a	15 368	11 869	17 207	12 176	9 847	17 207	8 401	5 212	10 361
Turkey[1]	a	a	a	1 808	1 434	2 430	1 808	1 434	2 430	a	a	a
United Kingdom	x(7)	x(7)	x(7)	x(7)	x(7)	x(7)	7 090	x(7)	x(7)	x(7)	x(7)	x(7)
United States	9 490	9 490	a	10 468	10 468	a	9 938	9 938	a	m	m	m
OECD average	*6 909*	*7 159*	*6 396*	*7 884*	*7 354*	*8 208*	*7 276*	*7 042*	*8 124*	*4 315*	*6 327*	*6 537*
Partner economies												
Brazil[1]	1 172	x(1)	x(1)	801	x(4)	x(4)	1 033	x(7)	x(7)	a	a	a
Chile [2]	2 106	2 106	a	2 062	2 278	1 680	2 077	2 199	1 680	a	a	a
Estonia [1]	3 579	x(1)	x(1)	3 670	4 118	2 721	3 623	3 798	2 683	3 717	a	3 717
Israel	x(7)	x(7)	x(7)	x(7)	x(7)	x(7)	6 066	m	m	4 272	4 272	a
Russian Federation [1]	x(8)	x(8)	a	x(7)	x(8)	1 766	1 615	1 595	1 766	x(7)	a	x(9)
Slovenia[1]	7 428	x(1)	x(1)	5 062	x(4)	x(4)	6 525	x(7)	x(7)	x(7)	x(7)	x(7

1. Public institutions only.

2. Year of reference 2005.

Source: OECD. See Annex 3 for notes (*www.oecd.org/edu/eag2007*).

Please refer to the Reader's Guide for information concerning the symbols replacing missing data.

StatLink ᴍˢᴾ http://dx.doi.org/10.1787/068363750663

Table C1.3.
Performance of 15-year-old students on the PISA mathematics scales, by programme orientation (2003)
Distinction between programme orientation is based on students' self-reports

C1

	General programmes		Pre-vocational and vocational programmes		Differences in mathematics performances between general programme students and pre-vocational and vocational programme students		Differences in mathematics performances between general programme students and pre-vocational and vocational programme students, accounting for the economic, social and cultural status of students (ESCS)	
	Mean score	S.E.	Mean score	S.E.	Mean score	S.E.	Mean score	S.E.
Australia	c	c	c	c	c	c	c	c
Austria	536	9.3	495	2.5	41	9.5	21	7.7
Belgium	585	2.5	469	3.2	116	4.3	78	3.7
Canada	535	1.7	a	a	a	a	a	a
Czech Republic	519	5.2	513	3.9	6	6.2	1	4.5
Denmark	514	2.7	a	a	a	a	a	a
Finland	544	1.9	a	a	a	a	a	a
France	w	w	w	w	w	w	w	w
Germany	c	c	c	c	c	c	c	c
Greece	463	4.0	374	5.0	89	6.1	67	5.1
Hungary	528	4.4	463	3.9	66	6.0	33	5.2
Iceland	515	1.4	a	a	a	a	a	a
Ireland	c	c	c	c	c	c	c	c
Italy	497	6.1	444	3.7	52	7.3	29	7.4
Japan	545	4.5	500	5.9	45	7.0	28	6.6
Korea	568	3.8	471	5.1	98	6.3	80	6.1
Luxembourg	491	1.0	513	3.2	-23	3.4	-26	3.7
Mexico	382	5.2	391	4.2	-9	6.6	-11	5.1
Netherlands	617	3.2	488	4.5	129	5.5	109	4.7
New Zealand	523	2.3	a	a	a	a	a	a
Norway	495	2.4	a	a	a	a	a	a
Poland	490	2.5	a	a	a	a	a	a
Portugal	465	3.7	477	4.9	-12	6.2	-18	5.4
Slovak Republic	512	4.1	482	5.5	30	7.0	18	5.2
Spain	485	2.4	a	a	a	a	a	a
Sweden	c	c	c	c	c	c	c	c
Switzerland	526	3.3	534	13.2	-8	12.6	-8	13.3
Turkey	431	8.9	400	12.6	32	16.8	16	11.8
United Kingdom	c	c	c	c	c	c	c	c
United States	483	2.9	a	a	a	a	a	a
OECD average	*510*		*466*		*45*		*27*	
Brazil	356	4.8	a	a	a	a	a	a
Russian Federation	473	3.6	450	13.4	23	13.5	20	11.9

Note: The classification of students into programme type is based on self-reports of 15-year-old students, whereas the classification of students into programme type in Table C1.1 is based on national statistics of upper secondary students, and may therefore differ.
Please refer to the Reader's Guide for information concerning the symbols replacing missing data.
Source: OECD PISA 2003 database. See Annex 3 for notes (*www.oecd.org/edu/eag2007*).
StatLink ⊪ http://dx.doi.org/10.1787/068363750663

WHO PARTICIPATES IN EDUCATION?

This indicator examines access to education and its evolution by using information on enrolment rates and trends in enrolments from 1995 to 2005. It also shows patterns of participation at the secondary level of education and the percentage of the youth cohort that will enter different types of tertiary education during their lives. Entry and participation rates reflect both the accessibility of tertiary education and the perceived value of attending tertiary programmes. For information on vocational education and training in secondary education, see Indicator C1.

INDICATOR C2

Key points

Chart C2.1. Entry rates into tertiary-type A education (1995, 2000 and 2005)
Sum of net entry rates for each year of age

The chart shows the proportion of people who enter into tertiary-type A education for the first time, and the change between 1995, 2000 and 2005. Entry rates measure the inflow to education at a particular time rather than the stock of students who are already enrolled.

In Australia, Finland, Hungary, Iceland, New Zealand, Norway, Poland and Sweden, and the partner economy the Russian Federation, more than 60% of young people entered tertiary-type A programmes in 2005. Entry rates in tertiary-type A substantially increased between 1995 and 2005, by 18 percentage points on average in OECD countries. Between 2000 and 2005, the growth exceeds 10 percentage point in more than one-quarter of the 24 OECD countries with available data.

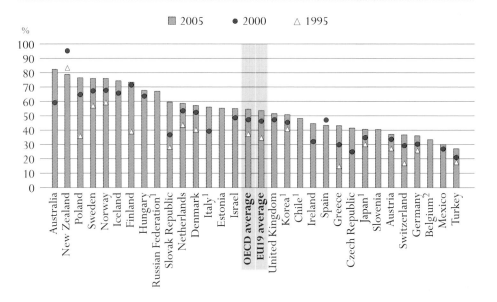

1. Entry rate for tertiary-type A programmes calculated as gross entry rate.
2. Excludes the German-speaking Community of Belgium.
Countries are ranked in descending order of the entry rates for tertiary-type A education in 2005.
Source: OECD. Table C2.5. See Annex 3 for notes (*www.oecd.org/edu/eag2007*).
StatLink http://dx.doi.org/10.1787/068400866631

Other highlights of this indicator

■ In most OECD countries, virtually all young people have access to at least 12 years of formal education. At least 90% of students are enrolled in an age range spanning 14 or more years in Belgium, the Czech Republic, France, Hungary, Iceland, Japan, Spain and Sweden. In contrast, Mexico and Turkey have enrolment rates exceeding 90% for a period of only nine and seven years, and eight and nine years only for partner economies Chile and the Russian Federation.

■ In more than one-half of the OECD countries, 70% of children aged 3 to 4 are enrolled in either pre-primary or primary programmes. A child can expect to be enrolled at age 4 and under more often in the 19 European countries that are members of the OECD (EU19) than in the other OECD countries. On average, the enrolment rate for children aged 3 to 4 is 75.9% for the EU19 whereas the OECD average is 68.5%.

■ Enrolment rates for the age 15 to 19 increased on average from 74 to 82% over the period 1995 to 2005 and in Belgium, the Czech Republic, Greece and Poland, and the partner economy Slovenia, reached 90% or more in 2005 (although Belgium had already reached 90% or more in 1995). A similar pattern is observed with enrolment rates for 20-to-29 year olds, an age group in which most students will be enrolled in tertiary education: between 1995 and 2005, the enrolment rates for 20-to-29-year-olds increased in all OECD countries.

■ The proportion of students who enter tertiary-type B programmes is generally smaller than for tertiary-type A programmes. In OECD countries with available data, 15% of young people, on average, will enter tertiary-type B programmes compared to 54% in tertiary-type A and 2% in advanced research programmes.

■ In Belgium, and to a lesser extent in the partner economy Slovenia, wide access to tertiary-type B programmes counterbalances comparatively low rates of entry into tertiary-type A programmes. In contrast, Iceland, Norway, Poland, and Sweden have entry rates well above the OECD average for tertiary-type A programmes and comparatively very low rates of entry into tertiary-type B programmes. New Zealand stands out as a country with entry rates at both levels that are the highest among OECD countries.

Policy context

A well-educated population is critical for a country's economic and social development. Societies therefore have an intrinsic interest in ensuring broad access to a wide variety of educational opportunities for children and adults. Early childhood programmes prepare children for primary education, and can help combat linguistic and social disadvantages as well as provide opportunities to enhance and complement home educational experiences. Primary and secondary education lay down the foundations for a wide range of competencies, and prepare young people to become lifelong learners and productive members of society. Tertiary education, either directly after initial schooling or later in life, provides a range of options for acquiring advanced knowledge and skills.

A range of factors, including an increased risk of unemployment and other forms of exclusion for young people with insufficient education, has strengthened the incentive for young people to stay enrolled beyond the end of compulsory education and to graduate from upper secondary education. Graduation from upper secondary education is also becoming the norm in most OECD countries. Most of these upper secondary programmes are primarily designed to prepare students for tertiary studies (see Indicator A2).

High tertiary entry and participation rates help to ensure the development and maintenance of a highly educated population and labour force. Moreover, tertiary education programmes are generally associated with better access to employment (see Indicator A8) and higher earnings (see Indicator A9). Rates of entry into tertiary education are a partial indication of the degree to which a population is acquiring high-level skills and knowledge valued by the labour market in today's knowledge society.

As students have become more aware of the economic and social benefits of tertiary education, graduation rates for tertiary-type A and tertiary-type B programmes have risen (see Indicator A3). Tertiary-type A programmes dominate the stock of tertiary enrolments and therefore the volume of resources required as they tend to be longer than other tertiary programmes (see Indicator B1, Table B1.3).

The continued growth in participation and a widening diversity of the backgrounds and interests of those aspiring to tertiary studies means that tertiary institutions will need to expand admissions and adapt their programmes and teaching to the diverse needs of new generations of students.

Evidence and explanations

Virtually all young people in OECD countries have access to at least 12 years of formal education. At least 90% of students are enrolled in an age range spanning 14 or more years in Belgium, the Czech Republic, France, Hungary, Iceland, Japan, Spain and Sweden. By contrast, Mexico and Turkey, and the partner economies Chile and the Russian Federation have enrolment rates exceeding 90% for a period of only 9, 7, 8 and 9 years, respectively (Table C2.1). However, patterns of participation in and progression through education over the life cycle vary widely among countries.

Participation in early childhood education

A child can expect to be enrolled at age 4 and under more often in the EU19 countries than in other OECD countries. On average, the enrolment rate for children aged 3 to 4 is 75.9% for the EU19 countries, whereas the OECD average is 68.5%.

In the majority of OECD countries and partner economies, full enrolment (defined here as enrolment rates exceeding 90%) begins between the ages of 5 and 6. However, in Belgium, the Czech Republic, Denmark, France, Germany, Hungary, Iceland, Italy, Japan, Luxembourg, New Zealand, Norway, Portugal, the Slovak Republic, Spain, Sweden and the United Kingdom, and in partner economies Estonia, Israel and Slovenia, at least 70% of children aged 3 to 4 are already enrolled in either pre-primary or primary programmes. Enrolment rates for early childhood education range from less than 25% in Korea and Turkey to over 90% in Belgium, Denmark, France, Iceland, Italy, New Zealand, Spain and the United Kingdom and the partner economy Estonia (Table C2.1).

Given the impact that early childhood education and care has on building a strong foundation for lifelong learning and on ensuring equitable access to learning opportunities later, pre-primary education is very important, and many countries have recognised this by making pre-primary education almost universal by the age 3. However, institutionally based pre-primary programmes covered by this indicator are not the only form of quality early childhood education and care available. Inferences about access to and quality of pre-primary education and care should therefore be made with caution.

Participation towards the end of compulsory education and beyond

Several factors influence the decision to stay enrolled beyond the end of compulsory education, notably the limited prospects of young people with insufficient education; indeed, in many countries they are at a higher risk of unemployment and other forms of exclusion than their well-educated peers. In many OECD countries, the transition from education to employment has become a longer and more complex process that provides the opportunity or the obligation for students to combine learning and work to develop marketable skills (see Indicator C4).

The age at which compulsory education in OECD countries and partner economies ends, ranges from 14 in Korea, Portugal and Turkey, and the partner economies Brazil and Chile, to 18 in Belgium, Germany and the Netherlands. All other countries lie between the two extremes with compulsory education ending at the ages 15, 16 or 17 (Table C2.1). However, the statutory age at which compulsory education ends does not always correspond to the age at which enrolment is universal.

While participation rates in most OECD countries and partner economies tend to be high until the end of compulsory education, in Belgium, Germany, Mexico, the Netherlands, New Zealand, Turkey and the United States, rates drop to below 90% before the end of compulsory education. In Belgium, Germany, the Netherlands and the United States, this may be due, in part, to the fact that compulsory education ends relatively late at age 18 (age 17, on average, in the United States).

In most OECD countries and partner economies, enrolment rates gradually decline during the last years of upper secondary education. More than 20% of the population aged between 15 and 19 is not enrolled in education in Luxembourg, Mexico, New Zealand, Portugal, Turkey, the United Kingdom and the United States, and in the partner economies Chile, Israel and the Russian Federation (Table C2.1).

There has been a substantial increase of eight percentage points in the proportion of 15-to-19-year-olds enrolled in education on average across OECD countries between 1995 and 2005.

C2

Enrolment rates for the age 15 to 19 increased on average from 74 to 82% over the period 1995 to 2005 and reached 90% or more in 2005 in Belgium, the Czech Republic, Greece, Poland and the partner economy Slovenia, although, Belgium had already reached 90% or more in 1995 (Table C2.2). The growth however differs among countries: while enrolment rate for 15-to-19-year-olds has improved by more than 20 percentage points during the past ten years in the Czech Republic, Greece and Hungary, they remained virtually the same in Australia, Belgium, France, Germany, Luxembourg, the Netherlands, Norway and Switzerland. Of these latter, all (except Luxembourg) have a high proportion of their population of 15-to-19-year-olds enrolled in education (Table C2.2).

Chart C2.2. Enrolment rates of 15-to-19-year-olds (1995, 2000 and 2005)

Full-time and part-time students in public and private institutions

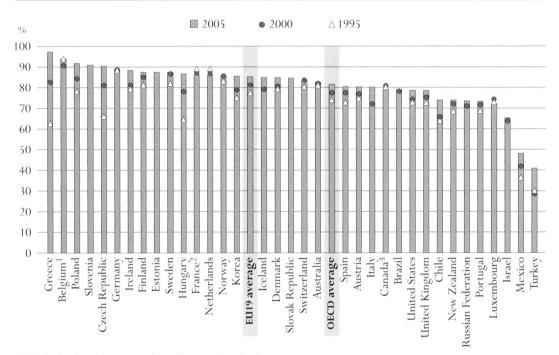

1. Excludes the German-speaking Community of Belgium.
2. Excludes overseas departments for 1995 and 2000.
3. Year of reference 2004.
Countries are ranked in descending order of the enrolment rates of 15-to-19-year-olds in 2005.
Source: OECD. Table C2.2. See Annex 3 for notes (*www.oecd.org/edu/eag2007*).
StatLink ⛓📊 http://dx.doi.org/10.1787/068400866631

Graduates from upper secondary programmes who decide not to enter the labour market directly, as well as people who are already working and want to upgrade their skills, can choose from a wide range of post-secondary programmes.

The transition to post-secondary education

Upper secondary students in many education systems can enrol in relatively short programmes (less than two years) to prepare for a certain trade or specific vocational fields. Some OECD countries delay vocational training until after graduation from upper secondary education. While these programmes are offered as advanced upper secondary programmes in some OECD countries (*e.g.* Austria, Hungary and Spain), they are offered as post-secondary education in others (*e.g.* Canada and the United States), although these post-secondary programmes often resemble upper secondary level programmes.

From an internationally comparable point of view, these programmes straddle upper secondary and tertiary education and are therefore classified as a distinct level of education (post-secondary non-tertiary education).

End of compulsory education and decline in enrolment rates

An analysis of the rate of participation by level of education and single year of age shows that there is no close relationship between the end of compulsory education and the decline in enrolment rates. The sharpest decline in enrolment rates occurs in most of the OECD and partner economies, not at the end of compulsory education but at the end of upper secondary education. After the age of 16, however, enrolment rates begin to decline in all OECD and partner economies. On average in the OECD countries, the enrolment rate in secondary education falls from 91% at the age of 16 to 83% at the age of 17, 53% at the age of 18 and 28% at the age of 19. In Belgium, the Czech Republic, Finland, Germany, Hungary, Japan, Korea, Norway, Poland, the Slovak Republic and Sweden, and in partner economies Estonia, Israel and Slovenia, 90% or more of all 17-year-olds are still enrolled at this level, even though the age at which compulsory education ends is under 17 in most of the countries (Table C2.3).

Overall access to tertiary education

Graduates from upper secondary programmes and those in the workforce who want to upgrade their skills can also choose from a wide range of tertiary programmes.

This indicator distinguishes among different categories of tertiary qualifications: *i)* programmes at tertiary-type B level (ISCED 5B); *ii)* programmes at tertiary-type A level (ISCED 5A); and *iii)* advanced research programmes at the doctorate level (ISCED 6). Tertiary-type A programmes are largely theoretically based and designed to provide qualifications for entry into advanced research programmes and highly skilled professions. Tertiary-type B programmes are classified at the same level of competence as tertiary-type A programmes, but are more occupationally oriented and lead to direct labour market access. The programmes tend not to last as long as type A programmes (typically two to three years), and generally are not deemed to lead to university-level degrees. The institutional location of programmes is used to give a relatively clear idea of their nature (*e.g.* university versus non-university institutions of higher education), but these distinctions have become blurred and are therefore not applied in the OECD indicators.

Today, 54% of young people in OECD countries will enter tertiary-type A programmes during their lifetime, assuming that current entry rates continue. In Australia, Finland, Hungary, Iceland, New Zealand, Norway, Poland and Sweden, as well as in the partner economy the Russian Federation, more than 60% of young people enter tertiary-type A programmes. The United States has an entry rate of 64%, but both type A and type B programmes are included in the type A columns as noted in Table C2.4.

Although Turkey has had a large increase in the number of students entering tertiary-type A programmes for the first time, its entry rate is only 27% and it still remains with Mexico at the bottom of the scale.

The proportion of people who enter tertiary-type B programmes is generally smaller than the proportion entering tertiary-type A programmes. In OECD countries with available data, 15% of young people, on average, will enter tertiary-type B programmes. The OECD country average differs by 4 percentage points from the EU19 country average (11%). The figures range from 4% or less in Mexico, the Netherlands, Norway, Poland and the Slovak Republic to 30% or more in Belgium and Japan, and in the partner economies Chile, Estonia and the Russian Federation, to more than 45% in Korea and New Zealand and the partner economy Slovenia. The share of tertiary-type B programmes in the Netherlands is very small. However it will increase in future years because of a new programme called "associate degrees". Finland and Italy no longer have tertiary-type B programmes in their education system (Table C2.4. and Chart C2.3).

In Belgium and to a lesser extent in the partner economy Slovenia, wide access into tertiary-type B programmes counterbalances comparatively low entry rates into tertiary-type A programmes. Other OECD countries, most notably Iceland, Norway, Poland and Sweden, have entry rates well above the OECD average for tertiary-type A programmes, and comparatively very low rates of entry into tertiary-type B programmes. New Zealand stands out as a country with entry rates at both levels that are the highest among OECD countries.

On average, in all OECD countries with comparable data, six percentage points more of today's young people enter into tertiary-type A programmes compared to 2000, and more than 18 percentage points compared to 1995. Entry rates in tertiary-type A education increased by more than 10 percentage points between 2000 and 2005 in Australia, the Czech Republic, Greece, Ireland, Italy, Poland and the Slovak Republic. New Zealand and Spain are the only OECD countries that shows a decrease of entry rates to tertiary-type A programmes, although in Spain's case, this decrease is counterbalanced by a significant increase of entry rates in tertiary-type B programmes between 2000 and 2005 (Table C2.5. and Chart C2.1).

Changes of net entry rates into tertiary-type B programmes between 1995 and 2005 vary among OECD countries, with an average decrease of one percentage point over this period. This entry rate has decreased slightly in most countries, except in Greece, Korea, New Zealand, the Slovak Republic and Turkey, where it has increased, and in Poland where it has been stable (Chart C2.3). The reclassification of tertiary-type B to tertiary-type A programmes in Denmark after 2000 partly explained the changes observed between 1995 and 2005 (Charts C2.1 and C2.3).

More than 2% of today's young people in the 18 OECD countries with comparable data will enter advanced and research programmes during their lifetime. The figures range from less than 1% in Mexico and Turkey, and in the partner economies Chile and Slovenia, to 3% or more in the Czech Republic, Greece, the Slovak Republic, Spain and Switzerland (Table C2.4).

Rates of entry into tertiary education should also be considered in light of participation in post-secondary non-tertiary programmes, which are an important alternative to tertiary education in some OECD countries.

Chart C2.3. **Entry rates into tertiary-type B education (1995, 2005)**

Sum of net entry rates for each year of age

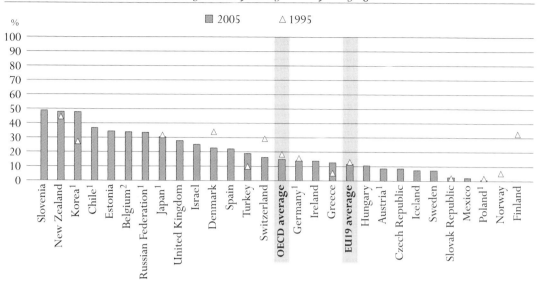

1. Entry rate for tertiary-type B programmes calculated as gross entry rate.
2. Excludes the German-speaking Community of Belgium.
Countries are ranked in descending order of the entry rates for tertiary-type B education in 2005.
Source: OECD. Table C2.5. See Annex 3 for notes (*www.oecd.org/edu/eag2007*).
StatLink ⌖ http://dx.doi.org/10.1787/068400866631

Age of new entrants into tertiary education

The age structure of entrants into tertiary education varies among OECD countries. The typical graduation age for upper secondary education may be different across countries, and/or upper secondary graduates may have gone directly to the labour market before enrolling in a tertiary education programme. People entering tertiary-type B programmes may also enter tertiary-type A programmes later in their lives. Tertiary-type A and B entry rates cannot therefore be added together to obtain overall tertiary-level entry rates because entrants might be counted twice.

Traditionally, students enter tertiary-type A programmes immediately after having completed upper secondary education, and this remains true in many OECD countries. For example, in Greece, Ireland, Italy, Mexico, the Netherlands, Poland and Spain and the partner economy Slovenia, more than 80% of all first-time entrants into tertiary-type A programmes are under 23 years of age (Table C2.4).

In other OECD countries and partner economies, the transition to the tertiary level is often delayed, in some cases by some time spent in the labour force. In these countries, first-time entrants into tertiary-type A programmes are typically older and show a much wider range of age at entry. In Denmark, Iceland and Sweden and the partner economy Israel, more than half the students enter this level for the first time at the age of 22 or older (Table C2.4). The proportion of older first-time entrants to tertiary-type A programmes may reflect, among other factors, the flexibility of these programmes and their suitability to students outside the typical or modal age cohort. It may also reflect a specific view of the value of work experience for higher education studies, which is characteristic of the Nordic countries and common in Australia, the Czech Republic, Hungary, New Zealand and Switzerland, where a sizeable proportion of new entrants is much older than the typical age of entry. It may also reflect that some countries have mandatory military service, which would postpone their entry into tertiary education. For example, Israel has mandatory military service from ages 18 to 21 for men and 18 to 20 for women. In Australia, Denmark, Hungary, Iceland, New Zealand, Norway, Sweden and Switzerland and the partner economy Israel, more than 20% of first-time entrants are aged 27 or older.

Participation in tertiary education

Enrolment rates provide another perspective on participation in tertiary education in that they reflect the total number of individuals entering tertiary education. On average in the OECD countries, 24.9% of the population aged between 20 and 29 are enrolled in education. Enrolment rates for 20-to-29-year-olds exceed 30% in Australia, Denmark, Finland, Iceland, New Zealand, Poland and Sweden, and in the partner economy Slovenia (Table C2.1).

Policies to expand education have put pressure on gaining greater access to tertiary education in many OECD countries and partner economies. Thus far, this pressure has more than compensated the declines in cohort sizes which had led, until recently, to predictions of stable or declining demand from school leavers in several OECD countries. Whereas some OECD countries (Portugal and Spain) are now showing signs of a levelling demand for tertiary education, the overall trend remains on an upward course. On average, in all OECD countries with comparable data, participation rates in tertiary education grew by 7 percentage points from 1995 to 2005. All the OECD countries and partner economies have seen an increase of the participation in 20-to-29-year-olds. This growth is particularly significant in the Czech Republic, Greece and Hungary, which used to be at the bottom of the enrolment rate scale of the OECD countries but have now moved to the middle (Table C2.2 and Chart C2.4).

The relative size of the public and the private sector

In OECD countries and partner economies, education at primary and secondary level is still predominantly publicly provided. On average, 91% of primary education students are enrolled in public institutions in the OECD countries, while the figures decline a bit in secondary education, with 85% of lower secondary students and 82% of upper secondary students being taught in public institutions. An exception, however, can be found at the upper secondary levels in Japan and Mexico, where independent private providers (those who receive less than 50% of their funds from government sources) take on a sizeable role, with 31% and 21 %, respectively, of upper secondary students (Table C2.9, available on line at *http://dx.doi.org/10.1787/068400866631*).

At the tertiary level, the pattern is quite different as private providers generally play a more significant role than at the primary and secondary levels. In tertiary-type B programmes, private sector enrolments account for 35% of the students, and in tertiary-type A and advanced research programmes they account for 21% of students. In the United Kingdom, all tertiary education is provided through government-dependent private institutions and such providers also receive more than half of tertiary students in Belgium and the partner economy Israel. Government-dependent private providers also have a significant share of the provision amongst tertiary-type A and advanced research programmes in the partner economy Estonia (85.4%). Independent private providers are more prominent at the tertiary level than at the pre-tertiary levels

Chart C2.4. Enrolment rates of 20-to-29-year-olds (1995, 2000 and 2005)

Full-time and part-time students in public and private institutions

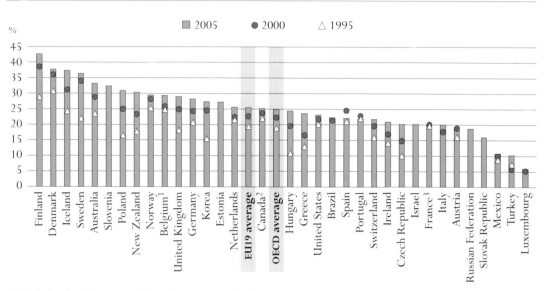

1. Excludes the German-speaking Community of Belgium.
2. Year of reference 2004.
3. Excludes overseas departments for 1995 and 2000.
Countries are ranked in descending order of the enrolment rates of 20-to-29-year-olds in 2005.
Source: OECD. Table C2.2. See Annex 3 for notes (*www.oecd.org/edu/eag2007*).
StatLink ᴍⁱˢ▙ http://dx.doi.org/10.1787/068400866631

(an average of 14% of tertiary students attend such institutions). This is particularly the case in Japan, Korea and partner economy Brazil, where around three-quarters or more of students are enrolled in such institutions (Tables C2.6).

Definitions and methodologies

Data for the school year 2004-2005 are based on the UOE data collection on education statistics administered annually by the OECD.

Except where otherwise noted, figures are based on head counts; that is, they do not distinguish between full-time and part-time study. A standardised distinction between full-time and part-time participants is very difficult because the concept of part-time study is not recognised by some countries. For other OECD countries, part-time education is covered only partially by the reported data.

Net enrolment rates expressed as percentages in Table C2.1 and Table C2.2 are calculated by dividing the number of students of a particular age group enrolled in all levels of education by the size of the population of that age group.

Table C2.4 and Table C2.5 show the sum of net entry rates for all ages. The net entry rate for a specific age is obtained by dividing the number of first-time entrants of that age to each type of tertiary education by the total population in the corresponding age group. The sum of net entry rates is calculated by adding the rates for each year of age. The result represents the proportion of people in a synthetic age cohort who enter tertiary education, irrespective of changes in population sizes and of differences between OECD countries in the typical entry age. Table C2.4 also shows the 20th, 50th and 80th percentiles of the age distribution of first-time entrants, *i.e.* the age below which 20, 50 and 80% of first-time entrants are to be found.

New (first-time) entrants are students who enrol at the relevant level of education for the first time. Foreign students enrolling for the first time in a post-graduate programme are considered first-time entrants.

Not all OECD countries can distinguish between students entering a tertiary programme for the first time and those transferring between different levels of tertiary education or repeating or re-entering a level after an absence. Thus first-time entry rates for each level of tertiary education cannot be added up to a total tertiary-level entrance rate because it would result in counting entrants twice.

In Tables C2.2 and C2.5, data on trends in enrolment and entry rates for the years 1995, 2000, 2001, 2002, 2003 and 2004 are based on a special survey carried out in the OECD countries and four out of six partner economies in January 2007.

Further references

The following additional material relevant to this indicator is available on line at:

StatLink ⬛🔢 http://dx.doi.org/10.1787/068400866631

- *Table C2.7. Education expectancy (2005)*
- *Table C2.8. Expected years in tertiary education (2005)*
- *Table C2.9. Students in primary and secondary education by type of institution or mode of study (2005)*

Table C2.1.
Enrolment rates, by age (2005)
Full-time and part-time students in public and private institutions

	Ending age of compulsory education	Number of years at which over 90% of the population are enrolled	Age range at which over 90% of the population are enrolled	Students aged:					
				4 and under as a percentage of the population aged 3 to 4	5 to 14 as a percentage of the population aged 5 to 14	15 to 19 as a percentage of the population aged 15 to 19	20 to 29 as a percentage of the population aged 20 to 29	30 to 39 as a percentage of the population aged 30 to 39	40 and over as a percentage of the population aged 40 and over
	(1)	(2)	(3)	(4)	(5)	(6)	(7)	(8)	(9)
Australia	15	12	5-16	41.6	99.1	82.5	33.2	14.0	6.2
Austria	15	13	5-17	67.5	98.4	80.3	19.4	3.3	0.3
Belgium[1,2]	18	15	3-17	125.2	99.6	94.0	29.4	8.4	3.5
Canada	16	m	m	m	m	m	m	m	m
Czech Republic	15	14	4-17	83.7	99.8	90.4	20.2	3.8	0.3
Denmark	16	13	3-16	92.3	97.1	84.9	37.7	7.8	1.6
Finland	16	13	6-18	42.3	95.1	87.5	42.6	13.1	3.0
France[1]	16	15	3-17	112.9	101.3	86.2	20.1	2.6	n
Germany	18	12	6-17	78.8	98.3	88.8	28.2	2.5	0.1
Greece	14.5	13	6-19	28.9	97.5	97.4	23.7	6.1	n
Hungary	16	14	4-17	81.7	100.3	86.8	24.4	5.8	0.6
Iceland	16	14	3-16	94.7	98.9	85.0	37.3	11.9	3.2
Ireland	15	12	5-16	23.9	101.1	88.5	20.9	4.0	0.1
Italy[1]	15	13	3-15	105.0	101.2	80.2	20.0	3.2	0.1
Japan	15	14	4-17	82.0	100.7	m	m	m	m
Korea	14	12	6-17	22.5	94.1	85.6	27.3	2.0	0.5
Luxembourg	15	12	4-15	80.7	96.7	72.1	5.9	0.5	0.1
Mexico	15	9	5-13	46.6	99.9	48.2	10.8	3.2	0.5
Netherlands	18	12	5-16	37.1	99.0	86.0	25.6	2.7	0.7
New Zealand	16	12	4-15	90.5	100.9	73.9	30.4	12.3	5.1
Norway	16	13	5-17	85.9	98.4	85.8	29.5	6.9	1.6
Poland	16	13	6-18	34.6	94.6	91.8	30.9	4.6	x(8)
Portugal	14	10	6-15	72.5	103.9	73.4	21.9	3.8	0.7
Slovak Republic	16	12	6-17	77.5	97.1	84.7	16.0	2.8	0.4
Spain[1]	16	14	3-16	120.5	101.4	80.5	22.1	3.6	1.1
Sweden	16	14	5-18	86.5	99.5	87.3	36.4	13.3	3.0
Switzerland	15	12	5-16	26.1	99.6	83.4	21.7	3.6	0.4
Turkey	14	7	7-13	3.7	81.8	40.9	10.3	1.5	0.2
United Kingdom	16	13	4-16	90.6	101.0	78.5	29.0	15.8	7.8
United States	17	11	6-16	50.0	97.7	78.6	23.1	5.2	1.4
OECD average	*16*	*13*		*68.5*	*98.4*	*81.5*	*24.9*	*6.0*	*1.6*
EU19 average	*16*	*13*		*75.9*	*99.1*	*85.2*	*25.0*	*5.7*	*1.3*
Brazil	14	10	7-16	29.4	93.2	79.5	22.5	8.8	2.4
Chile	14	8	9-16	32.7	88.3	74.0	m	m	m
Estonia[1]	15	12	6-17	117.1	104.6	87.5	27.3	9.8	n
Israel[3]	15	13	5-17	79.1	96.0	65.3	20.2	5.2	0.9
Russian Fed.	15	9	7-15	m	81.5	73.5	18.7	0.7	n
Slovenia	15	12	6-17	71.4	96.5	91.0	32.4	6.2	0.7

Note: Ending age of compulsory education is the age at which compulsory schooling ends. For example, an ending age of 18 indicates that all students under 18 are legally obliged to participate in education. Mismatches between the coverage of the population data and the student/graduate data mean that the participation/graduation rates for those countries that are net exporters of students may be underestimated (for instance, Luxembourg) and those that are net importers may be overestimated.
1. The rates "4 and under as a percentage of the population aged of 3-to-4-year-olds" is overestimated. A significant number of students are younger than 3 years old. The net rates between 3 and 5 are around 100%.
2. Excludes the German-speaking Community of Belgium.
3. Excludes programmes for children younger than 3, resulting in substantially lower figures in comparison to previous years.
Source: OECD. See Annex 3 for notes (*www.oecd.org/edu/eag2007*).
Please refer to the Reader's Guide for information concerning the symbols replacing missing data.
StatLink ⫶ http://dx.doi.org/10.1787/068400866631

Table C2.2.
Trends in enrolment rates (1995-2005)
Full-time and part-time students in public and private institutions in 1995, 2000, 2001, 2002, 2003, 2004, 2005

	15-to-19-year-olds as a percentage of the population aged 15 to 19 years							20-to-29-year-olds as a percentage of the population aged 20 to 29 years						
	1995	2000	2001	2002	2003	2004	2005	1995	2000	2001	2002	2003	2004	2005
	(1)	(2)	(3)	(4)	(5)	(6)	(7)	(8)	(9)	(10)	(11)	(12)	(13)	(14)
Australia	81	82	81	83	82	82	82	23	28	28	33	33	33	33
Austria	75	77	77	77	77	79	80	16	18	19	17	18	19	19
Belgium[1]	94	91	91	92	94	95	94	24	25	26	27	29	30	29
Canada	80	81	81	80	80	79	m	22	23	24	25	25	25	m
Czech Republic	66	81	87	90	90	91	90	10	14	15	16	17	19	20
Denmark	79	80	83	82	85	85	85	30	35	36	36	36	36	38
Finland	81	85	85	85	86	87	87	28	38	39	40	40	41	43
France[2]	89	87	86	86	87	87	86	19	19	20	20	20	20	20
Germany	88	88	90	89	89	89	89	20	24	24	26	27	28	28
Greece	62	82	74	83	83	86	97	13	16	22	25	26	28	24
Hungary	64	78	79	81	83	85	87	10	19	20	21	22	24	24
Iceland	m	79	79	81	83	84	85	24	31	30	32	36	37	37
Ireland	79	81	82	83	84	87	89	14	16	18	19	19	23	21
Italy	m	72	73	76	78	79	80	m	17	17	18	20	20	20
Japan	m	m	m	m	m	m	m	m	m	m	m	m	m	m
Korea	75	79	79	80	81	84	86	15	24	25	27	27	28	27
Luxembourg	73	74	75	75	75	75	72	m	5	6	6	6	7	6
Mexico	36	42	42	44	45	47	48	8	9	9	10	10	11	11
Netherlands	89	87	86	87	85	86	86	21	22	23	23	25	26	26
New Zealand	68	72	72	74	74	74	74	17	23	25	28	30	31	30
Norway	83	86	85	85	85	86	86	25	28	26	26	29	29	29
Poland	78	84	86	87	88	90	92	16	24	26	28	29	30	31
Portugal	68	71	73	71	72	73	73	22	22	22	22	23	23	22
Slovak Republic	m	m	74	76	80	83	85	m	m	12	13	13	15	16
Spain	73	77	78	78	78	80	81	21	24	23	23	22	22	22
Sweden	82	86	86	86	87	87	87	22	33	33	34	34	36	36
Switzerland	80	83	83	83	83	83	83	15	19	20	20	21	21	22
Turkey	30	28	30	34	35	40	41	7	5	5	6	6	10	10
United Kingdom	72	75	75	77	75	79	79	18	24	24	27	26	28	29
United States	73	74	76	75	75	76	79	20	21	22	23	22	23	23
OECD average	*74*	*77*	*78*	*79*	*79*	*81*	*82*	*18*	*22*	*22*	*23*	*24*	*25*	*25*
OECD average for countries with 1995 and 2005 data	*74*						*81*	*18*						*26*
EU19 average	*77*	*81*	*82*	*83*	*83*	*84*	*85*	*19*	*22*	*23*	*24*	*24*	*25*	*25*
Brazil	m	78	75	71	74	80	79	m	21	21	23	22	22	23
Chile	64	66	m	66	68	70	74	m	m	m	m	m	m	m
Estonia	m	m	m	m	m	m	87	m	m	m	m	m	m	27
Israel	m	64	63	65	66	65	65	m	m	m	21	21	20	20
Russian Federation	m	71	71	74	m	m	74	m	m	m	13	m	m	19
Slovenia	m	m	m	m	m	m	91	m	m	m	m	m	m	32

1. Excludes the German-speaking Community of Belgium for 2004 and 2005 data.
2. Excludes overseas departments from 1995 to 2004 (DOM).
Source: OECD. See Annex 3 for notes (*www.oecd.org/edu/eag2007*).
Please refer to the Reader's Guide for information concerning the symbols replacing missing data.
StatLink ⫶ http://dx.doi.org/10.1787/068400866631

Table C2.3.
Transition characteristics from age 15 to 20, by level of education (2005)
Net enrolment rates (based on head counts)

C2

	Graduation age at the upper secondary level of education	Age 15	Age 16			Age 17			Age 18			Age 19			Age 20		
		Secondary education	Secondary education	Post-secondary non-tertiary	Tertiary education	Secondary education	Post-secondary non-tertiary	Tertiary education	Secondary education	Post-secondary non-tertiary	Tertiary education	Secondary education	Post-secondary non-tertiary	Tertiary education	Secondary education	Post-secondary non-tertiary	Tertiary education
		(1)	(2)	(3)	(4)	(5)	(6)	(7)	(8)	(9)	(10)	(11)	(12)	(13)	(14)	(15)	(16)
OECD countries																	
Australia	17-18	99	93	n	n	80	1	4	39	3	27	26	3	35	20	2	37
Austria	17-19	95	92	n	n	77	14	n	47	24	5	19	15	14	6	6	21
Belgium[1]	18-19	102	101	n	n	99	n	1	47	6	35	23	7	47	6	2	48
Canada	18	m	m	m	m	m	m	m	m	m	m	m	m	m	m	m	m
Czech Republic	18-19	100	100	n	n	97	n	n	82	4	1	36	12	21	7	8	34
Denmark	19-20	98	93	n	n	85	n	n	81	n	n	61	n	4	37	n	13
Finland	19	99	96	n	n	95	n	n	93	n	n	34	n	20	18	n	32
France	18-20	97	97	n	n	89	n	2	51	n	27	25	1	39	10	1	41
Germany	19	98	96	n	n	92	n	1	83	n	2	41	19	10	20	15	18
Greece	18	96	101	a	a	75	n	16	18	2	61	m	4	71	n	5	73
Hungary	18-20	100	96	n	n	92	n	n	57	9	13	21	16	32	11	12	37
Iceland	18-20	100	94	n	n	83	n	n	75	n	n	68	n	1	38	n	17
Ireland	17-18	99	96	2	n	76	6	6	30	25	35	3	17	42	1	14	42
Italy	17-19	94	88	a	a	83	n	a	72	n	8	9	1	35	6	1	37
Japan	18	103	97	a	a	95	a	m	3	m	m	1	m	m	m	m	m
Korea	17-18	95	95	a	n	93	a	1	8	a	63	1	a	72	n	a	65
Luxembourg	18-19	89	82	n	m	78	n	m	67	n	m	42	n	m	24	1	m
Mexico	18	66	54	a	a	41	a	3	19	a	13	25	a	17	4	a	19
Netherlands	18-19	96	95	n	n	83	n	6	58	n	20	39	n	29	25	n	34
New Zealand	17-18	95	87	1	1	70	2	3	27	4	25	13	4	34	9	3	38
Norway	18-19	99	94	n	n	92	n	n	85	n	n	40	1	14	19	1	29
Poland	18-20	97	97	a	a	95	n	n	92	n	1	38	7	32	16	9	43
Portugal	18	88	80	n	a	76	n	a	47	n	19	27	n	26	15	n	30
Slovak Republic	18-19	99	95	n	n	90	n	n	79	n	3	35	1	24	7	1	32
Spain	17-18	99	94	a	n	82	a	n	42	a	27	23	a	36	13	a	38
Sweden	19	96	97	n	n	98	n	n	94	n	2	30	1	14	21	1	23
Switzerland	18-20	97	90	n	n	86	1	n	76	2	2	46	3	8	19	4	16
Turkey	16-17	59	55	a	n	28	a	5	17	a	14	x(8)	a	21	m	a	23
United Kingdom	16-18	101	94	x(2)	1	80	x(5)	2	37	x(8)	23	24	x(11)	31	19	x(14)	33
United States	18	95	96	m	1	83	n	4	22	n	39	4	m	49	n	m	47
OECD average		*95*	*91*	*n*	*n*	*83*	*1*	*2*	*53*	*3*	*17*	*28*	*4*	*29*	*14*	*3*	*34*
EU19 average		*97*	*94*	*n*	*n*	*86*	*1*	*2*	*62*	*4*	*16*	*29*	*6*	*29*	*14*	*4*	*35*
Partner economies																	
Brazil	17-18	90	87	a	n	83	a	1	60	a	5	39	a	9	27	a	12
Chile	18	98	95	a	n	89	a	n	61	a	m	20	a	m	6	a	m
Estonia	19	98	97	n	n	92	n	n	70	2	10	21	9	37	9	9	40
Israel	17	96	95	n	n	90	n	2	18	n	9	2	n	12	1	1	13
Russian Fed.	17	84	73	x(2)	13	34	x(5)	47	12	x(8)	49	4	x(11)	44	1	x(14)	38
Slovenia	18	98	98	n	n	94	n	n	84	n	5	29	3	44	m	m	50

Note: Mismatches between the coverage of the population data and the student/graduate data mean that the participation/graduation rates for those countries that are net exporters of students may be underestimated (for instance, Luxembourg) and those that are net importers may be overestimated.

1. Excludes the German-speaking Community of Belgium.

Source: OECD. See Annex 3 for notes (*www.oecd.org/edu/eag2007*).

Please refer to the Reader's Guide for information concerning the symbols replacing missing data.

StatLink ᐧᒥᔑ᛭ http://dx.doi.org/10.1787/068400866631

C2

Table C2.4.
Entry rates into tertiary education and age distribution of new entrants (2005)
Sum of net entry rate for each year of age, by gender and mode of participation

| | Tertiary-type B | | | Tertiary-type A | | | | | | Advanced Research Program | | |
| | Net entry rates | | | Net entry rates | | | Age at: | | | Net entry rates | | |
	M+W	Men	Women	M+W	Men	Women	20th percentile[1]	50th percentile[1]	80th percentile[1]	M+W	Men	Women
	(1)	(2)	(3)	(4)	(5)	(6)	(7)	(8)	(9)	(10)	(11)	(12)
Australia	m	m	m	82	74	91	18.7	20.9	27.3	2.8	2.8	2.9
Austria[2]	9	7	10	37	34	41	19.3	20.7	23.7	m	m	m
Belgium[3]	34	29	38	33	29	38	18.5	19.5	23.5	m	m	m
Canada	m	m	m	m	m	m	m	m	m	m	m	m
Czech Republic	8	5	12	41	39	44	19.5	20.4	23.4	3.2	3.7	2.6
Denmark	23	23	23	57	45	69	20.9	22.7	28.3	1.8	2.0	1.6
Finland	a	a	a	73	63	84	19.8	21.4	26.6	m	m	m
France	m	m	m	m	m	m	m	m	m	m	m	m
Germany[2]	14	11	17	36	36	36	20.0	21.4	24.1	m	m	m
Greece	13	13	13	43	39	48	18.1	18.6	20.1	4.6	5.0	4.1
Hungary	11	8	13	68	57	78	19.2	20.9	27.5	1.7	1.8	1.5
Iceland	7	7	7	74	53	96	20.9	23.1	<40	1.7	1.4	2.0
Ireland[4]	14	15	13	45	39	51	18.3	19.0	19.9	m	m	m
Italy[5]	a	a	a	56	49	64	19.2	19.8	22.8	2.0	1.9	2.1
Japan[2,5]	30	23	38	41	47	34	m	m	m	1.2	1.6	0.7
Korea[2,5]	48	46	50	51	54	47	m	m	m	2.1	2.7	1.5
Luxembourg	m	m	m	m	m	m	m	m	m	m	m	m
Mexico	2	2	2	30	30	30	18.4	19.5	22.8	0.2	0.3	0.2
Netherlands	n	n	n	59	54	63	18.4	19.8	22.8	m	m	m
New Zealand	48	41	54	79	64	93	18.7	21.4	<40	1.8	1.7	1.9
Norway	n	1	n	76	63	89	20.0	21.4	<40	2.9	3.0	2.8
Poland[2]	1	n	1	76	70	83	19.5	20.4	22.7	m	m	m
Portugal	m	m	m	m	m	m	m	m	m	m	m	m
Slovak Republic	2	2	3	59	52	67	19.5	20.5	26.3	3.3	3.9	2.8
Spain	22	21	23	43	37	51	18.4	19.0	22.9	4.4	4.2	4.6
Sweden	7	7	8	76	64	89	20.2	22.5	<40	2.6	2.6	2.7
Switzerland	16	19	13	37	36	38	20.0	21.8	27.6	4.4	5.2	3.6
Turkey	19	22	16	27	30	24	18.5	19.8	23.3	0.5	0.6	0.4
United Kingdom	28	19	36	51	45	58	18.5	19.6	25.2	2.2	2.4	2.0
United States	x(4)	x(5)	x(6)	64	56	71	18.4	19.6	26.5	m	m	m
OECD average	*15*	*13*	*16*	*54*	*48*	*61*				*2.4*	*2.6*	*2.2*
EU19 average	*11*	*10*	*13*	*53*	*47*	*60*				*2.9*	*3.0*	*2.7*
Brazil	m	m	m	m	m	m	m	m	m	m	m	m
Chile[2,5]	37	42	31	48	46	50	m	m	m	0.2	0.3	0.2
Estonia[2,5]	34	25	44	55	43	68	m	m	m	2.1	2.0	2.2
Israel	25	24	26	55	51	59	21.3	23.7	27.5	m	m	m
Russian Federation[2,5]	33	x(1)	x(1)	67	x(4)	x(4)	m	m	m	2.0	x(10)	x(10)
Slovenia	49	46	52	40	33	49	19.2	19.7	20.8	0.7	0.7	0.6

OECD countries (left margin, rows Australia–United States)
Partner economies (left margin, rows Brazil–Slovenia)

Note: Mismatches between the coverage of the population data and the student/graduate data mean that the participation/graduation rates for those countries that are net exporters of students may be underestimated (for instance, Luxembourg) and those that are net importers may be overestimated.
1. Respectively 20%, 50% and 80% of new entrants are below this age.
2. Entry rate for tertiary-type B programmes calculated as gross entry rate.
3. Excludes the German-speaking Community of Belgium.
4. Full-time entrants only.
5. Entry rate for tertiary-type A programmes calculated as gross entry rate.
Source: OECD. See Annex 3 for notes (*www.oecd.org/edu/eag2007*).
Please refer to the Reader's Guide for information concerning the symbols replacing missing data.
StatLink http://dx.doi.org/10.1787/068400866631

Table C2.5.
Trends in entry rates at the tertiary level (1995-2005)
Sum of net entry rate for each year of age (1995, 2000, 2001, 2002, 2003, 2004, 2005)

		Tertiary 5A[1]							Tertiary 5B					
		1995	2000	2001	2002	2003	2004	2005	1995	2000	2001	2002	2003	2004	2005
		(1)	(2)	(3)	(4)	(5)	(6)	(7)	(8)	(9)	(10)	(11)	(12)	(13)	(14)
OECD countries	Australia	m	59	65	77	68	70	82	m	m	m	m	m	m	m
	Austria[2]	27	34	34	31	34	37	37	m	m	m	m	8	9	9
	Belgium[3]	m	m	32	33	33	34	33	m	m	36	34	33	35	34
	Canada	m	m	m	m	m	m	m	m	m	m	m	m	m	m
	Czech Republic	m	25	30	30	33	38	41	m	9	7	8	9	10	8
	Denmark	40	52	54	53	57	55	57	33	28	30	25	22	21	23
	Finland	39	71	72	71	73	73	73	32	a	a	a	a	a	a
	France	m	m	m	m	m	m	m	m	m	m	m	m	m	m
	Germany[2]	26	30	32	35	36	37	36	15	15	15	16	16	15	14
	Greece	15	30	30	33	35	35	43	5	21	20	21	22	24	13
	Hungary	m	64	56	62	69	68	68	m	1	3	4	7	9	11
	Iceland	m	66	61	72	83	79	74	m	10	10	11	9	8	7
	Ireland	m	32	39	39	41	44	45	m	26	19	18	17	17	14
	Italy[2,4]	m	39	44	50	54	55	56	m	1	1	1	1	1	a
	Japan[2,4]	30	35	37	39	40	40	41	31	29	29	29	29	30	30
	Korea[2,4]	41	45	46	46	47	49	51	27	51	52	51	47	47	48
	Luxembourg	m	m	m	m	m	m	m	m	m	m	m	m	m	m
	Mexico	m	27	27	35	29	30	30	m	1	2	2	2	2	2
	Netherlands	44	53	54	54	52	56	59	n	n	n	n	n	n	n
	New Zealand	83	95	95	101	107	86	79	44	52	50	56	58	50	48
	Norway	59	67	69	75	75	72	76	5	5	4	3	1	1	n
	Poland[2]	36	65	68	71	70	71	76	1	1	1	1	1	1	1
	Portugal	m	m	m	m	m	m	m	m	m	m	m	m	m	m
	Slovak Republic	28	37	40	43	40	47	59	1	3	3	3	3	2	2
	Spain	m	47	47	49	46	44	43	m	15	19	19	21	22	22
	Sweden	57	67	69	75	80	79	76	m	7	6	6	7	8	7
	Switzerland	17	29	33	35	38	38	37	29	14	13	14	17	17	16
	Turkey	18	21	20	23	23	26	27	9	9	10	12	24	16	19
	United Kingdom	m	47	46	48	48	52	51	m	29	30	27	30	28	28
	United States	m	43	42	64	63	63	64	m	14	13	x(4)	x(5)	x(6)	x(7)
	OECD average	*37*	*47*	*48*	*52*	*53*	*53*	*54*	*18*	*15*	*16*	*16*	*16*	*15*	*15*
	OECD average (for countries with 1995, 2000 and 2005 data)	*37*	*49*					*55*	*19*	*19*					*18*
	EU19 average	*35*	*46*	*47*	*49*	*50*	*52*	*53*	*12*	*11*	*13*	*12*	*12*	*12*	*11*
Partner economies	Brazil	m	m	m	m	m	m	m	m	m	m	m	m	m	m
	Chile[2,4]	m	m	42	48	54	46	48	m	m	15	17	18	25	37
	Estonia	m	m	m	m	m	m	55	m	m	m	m	m	m	34
	Israel	m	48	50	57	58	58	55	m	31	32	m	25	m	25
	Russian Federation[2,4]	m	m	m	65	63	68	67	m	m	m	39	38	34	33
	Slovenia	m	m	m	m	m	m	40	m	m	m	m	m	m	49

1. Entry rate for tertiary-type A programmes included advanced research programmes for 1995, 2000, 2001, 2002, 2003.
2. Entry rate for tertiary-type B programmes calculated as gross entry rate.
3. Excludes the German-speaking Community of Belgium.
4. Entry rate for tertiary-type A programmes calculated as gross entry rate.
Source: OECD. See Annex 3 for notes (*www.oecd.org/edu/eag2007*).
Please refer to the Reader's Guide for information concerning the symbols replacing missing data.
StatLink ᎥᎢᎦᏝ http://dx.doi.org/10.1787/068400866631

C2

Table C2.6.
Students in tertiary education by type of institution or mode of study (2005)
Distribution of students, by mode of enrolment, type of institution and programme destination

	Type of institution						Mode of study			
	Tertiary-type B education			Tertiary-type A and advanced research programmes			Tertiary-type B education		Tertiary-type A and advanced research programmes	
	Public	Government-dependent private	Independent private	Public	Government-dependent private	Independent private	Full-time	Part-time	Full-time	Part-time
	(1)	(2)	(3)	(4)	(5)	(6)	(7)	(8)	(9)	(10)
OECD countries										
Australia	97.7	1.3	1.1	98.6	n	1.4	38.3	61.7	68.1	31.9
Austria	68.7	31.3	n	89.3	10.7	n	m	m	m	m
Belgium[1]	47.0	53.0	m	42.8	57.2	m	69.5	30.5	92.2	7.8
Canada[2]	m	m	m	m	m	m	m	m	74.8	25.2
Czech Republic	67.2	31.5	1.3	93.6	n	6.4	95.5	4.5	96.1	3.9
Denmark	99.1	0.9	a	98.9	1.1	a	54.7	45.3	92.9	7.1
Finland	92.6	7.4	a	89.6	10.4	a	100.0	a	56.2	43.8
France	71.9	8.4	19.7	87.3	0.7	12.0	100.0	a	100.0	a
Germany[3]	64.2	35.8	x(2)	96.3	3.7	x(5)	83.3	16.7	96.2	3.8
Greece	100.0	a	a	100.0	a	a	100.0	a	100.0	a
Hungary	61.2	38.8	a	86.3	13.7	a	76.8	23.2	52.9	47.1
Iceland	66.8	33.2	n	86.6	13.4	n	46.1	53.9	76.5	23.5
Ireland	92.5	a	7.5	92.5	a	7.5	59.5	40.5	84.4	15.6
Italy	84.8	a	15.2	93.7	a	6.3	100.0	n	100.0	n
Japan	7.3	a	92.7	24.4	a	75.6	97.0	3.0	90.0	10.0
Korea	15.8	a	84.2	22.4	a	77.6	m	m	m	m
Luxembourg	m	m	m	m	m	m	m	m	m	m
Mexico	95.9	a	4.1	66.3	a	33.7	100.0	a	100.0	a
Netherlands	n	n	a	m	m	a	n	n	82.2	17.8
New Zealand	69.8	28.5	1.7	98.0	1.9	0.1	41.5	58.5	59.8	40.2
Norway	53.8	46.2	x(2)	86.6	13.4	x(5)	80.7	19.3	72.2	27.8
Poland	77.8	n	22.2	70.5	a	29.5	100.0	a	60.6	39.4
Portugal	56.0	a	44.0	74.3	a	25.7	m	m	m	m
Slovak Republic	89.8	10.2	n	98.0	n	2.0	49.3	50.7	63.7	36.3
Spain	78.4	15.7	5.9	88.0	n	12.0	98.6	1.4	89.0	11.0
Sweden	62.4	37.6	a	93.9	6.1	a	84.5	15.5	50.5	49.5
Switzerland	30.4	38.9	30.8	91.3	7.1	1.6	23.1	76.9	90.2	9.8
Turkey	97.5	a	2.5	94.8	a	5.2	100.0	a	100.0	a
United Kingdom	a	100.0	n	a	100.0	n	24.4	75.6	71.5	28.5
United States	84.8	a	15.2	72.6	a	27.4	48.7	51.3	64.8	35.2
OECD average	*65.5*	*18.5*	*13.9*	*79.1*	*8.9*	*13.0*	*70.9*	*25.1*	*80.2*	*19.8*
EU19 average	*67.4*	*20.6*	*7.2*	*82.1*	*12.0*	*6.3*	*74.8*	*19.0*	*80.5*	*19.5*
Partner economies										
Brazil	29.7	a	70.3	29.7	a	70.3	m	m	m	m
Chile	7.3	3.0	89.7	39.3	16.5	44.1	100.0	a	100.0	a
Estonia	49.8	17.1	33.1	a	85.4	14.6	78.7	21.3	81.5	18.5
Israel	34.3	65.7	a	11.6	78.0	10.5	100.0	a	82.3	17.7
Russian Federation[2]	96.1	a	3.9	85.1	a	14.9	70.6	29.4	55.1	44.9
Slovenia	85.9	6.6	7.5	97.8	0.4	1.7	46.5	53.5	80.1	19.9

1. Excludes the German-speaking Community of Belgium.
2. Year of reference 2004.
3. Excludes advanced research programmes.
Source: OECD. See Annex 3 for notes (*www.oecd.org/edu/eag2007*).
Please refer to the Reader's Guide for information concerning the symbols replacing missing data.
StatLink ᴍˢᴸ http://dx.doi.org/10.1787/068400866631

WHO STUDIES ABROAD AND WHERE?

This indicator is providing a picture of student mobility and the extent of the internationalisation of tertiary education in OECD countries and partner economies. It shows global trends and highlights the major destinations of international students and trends in market shares of the international student pool. Some of the factors underlying students' choice of a country of study are also examined. In addition, the indicator looks at the extent of student mobility in different destinations and presents the profile of the international student intake in terms of their distribution by countries and regions of origin, types of programmes, and fields of education. The distribution of students enrolled outside of their country of citizenship by destination is also examined. Finally, the contribution of international students to the graduate output is examined alongside immigration implications for their host countries. The proportion of international students in tertiary enrolments provides a good indication of the magnitude of student mobility in different countries.

INDICATOR C3

Key results

Chart C3.1. **Student mobility in tertiary education (2005)**

This chart shows the percentage of international students enrolled in tertiary education. According to country-specific immigration legislation and data availability constraints, student mobility is either defined on the basis of students' country of residence or the country where students received their prior education.

Student mobility – *i.e.* international students who travelled to a country different from their own for the purpose of tertiary study – ranges from below 1 to almost 18% of tertiary enrolments. International students are most numerous in tertiary enrolments in Australia, Austria, France, New Zealand, Switzerland and the United Kingdom.

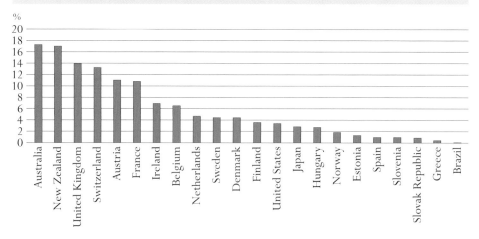

Note: the data on the mobility of international students presented below are not comparable with data on foreign students in tertiary education (defined on the basis of citizenship) presented in pre-2006 editions of *Education at a Glance* or elsewhere in this chapter.
Countries are ranked in descending order of the percentage of international students in tertiary education.
Source: OECD. Table C3.1. See Annex 3 for notes (*www.oecd.org/edu/eag2007*).
StatLink ⋮⋮⋮ http://dx.doi.org/10.1787/068417017111

Other highlights of this indicator

- In 2005, over 2.7 million tertiary students were enrolled outside their country of citizenship. This represented a 5% increase in total foreign student intake reported to the OECD and the UNESCO Institute for Statistics from the previous year.

- France, Germany, the United Kingdom and the United States receive more than 50% of all foreign students worldwide. In absolute numbers, international students from France, Germany, Japan and Korea represent the largest numbers from OECD countries. Students from China and India comprise the largest numbers of international students from partner economies.

- In Spain, Switzerland and the United States, and the partner economy Brazil, more than 15% of international students are enrolled in advanced research programmes.

- 30% or more of international students are enrolled in sciences, agriculture or engineering in Finland, Germany, Hungary, Sweden, Switzerland, the United Kingdom and the United States.

- International graduates contribute to 20% or more of the graduate output for tertiary-type A programmes in Australia and the United Kingdom. The same holds for foreigners graduating in Belgium. The contribution of international and foreign graduates to the tertiary graduate output is especially high for advanced research programmes in Belgium, Switzerland, the United Kingdom and the United States.

Policy context

The general trend towards freely circulating capital, goods and services – coupled with changes in the openness of labour markets – have increased the demand for new kinds of educational provision in OECD countries.

Governments as well as individuals are looking to higher education to play a role in broadening the horizons of students and allowing them to develop a deeper understanding of the multiplicity of languages, cultures and business methods in the world. One way for students to expand their knowledge of other societies and languages and hence to leverage their labour market prospects is to study in tertiary educational institutions in countries other than their own. Indeed, several OECD governments – especially so in the European Union (EU) countries – have set up schemes and policies to promote such mobility to foster intercultural contacts and help to build social networks for the future.

From the macroeconomic perspective, international negotiations on trade liberalisation of services highlight the trade implications of the internationalisation of education service provision. Some OECD countries already show signs of specialisation in education exports. The long term trend towards greater internationalisation of education (Box C3.1) is likely to have a growing impact on countries' balances of payments as a result of tuition fee revenues and domestic consumption of international students. In this perspective, it is worth noting that in addition to student mobility, the cross-border electronic delivery of flexible educational programmes and campuses abroad are also relevant to the trade dimension of international tertiary education, although no comparable data exist yet.

The internationalisation of tertiary education, however, has many more economic outcomes in addition to the short term monetary costs and benefits reflected in the current account balance. It can also provide an opportunity for smaller and/or less developed educational systems to improve the cost efficiency of their education provision. Indeed, training opportunities abroad may constitute a cost-efficient alternative to national provision, and allow countries to focus limited resources on educational programmes where economies of scale can be generated, or expand tertiary education participation despite bottlenecks in education provision.

From the perspective of educational institutions, international enrolments constrain the instructional settings and processes insofar as the curriculum and teaching methods may have to be adapted to a culturally and linguistically diverse student body. These constraints are, however, outweighed by the numerous benefits to host institutions. Indeed, the presence of a potential international client base compels institutions to offer programmes that stand out among competitors, a factor that may contribute to the development of a highly reactive, client-driven quality tertiary education. International enrolments can also help institutions to reach the critical mass needed to diversify the range of educational programmes offered as well as increase tertiary institutions' financial resources when foreign students bear the full cost of their education (Box C3.3). Given these advantages, institutions might favour the enrolment of international students, thereby restricting access to domestic students. Yet there is limited evidence of such a phenomenon, with the exception of some prestigious, highly demanded programmes of elite institutions (OECD, 2004d).

For individuals, the returns to studying abroad depend to a large extent on both the policies of sending countries regarding financial aid to students going abroad and the tuition fee policies of countries of destination (Box C3.3) and their financial support for international

C3

students. The cost of living in countries of study and exchange rates also impact on the cost of international education. In addition, the long-term returns of an international educational experience depend to a large extent on how international degrees are signalled and valued by local labour markets.

The numbers and trends in students enrolled in other countries can provide some idea of the extent of internationalisation of tertiary education. In the future, it will also be important to develop ways to quantify and measure other components of cross-border education.

Evidence and explanations

Concepts and terminology conventions used in this indicator

It is important to specify the concepts and terminology conventions used in this indicator since they have changed, compared with editions of *Education at a Glance* produced before 2006.

Prior to *Education at a Glance 2006*, Indicator C3 focused on foreign students in tertiary education, defined as non-citizens of the country in which they study. This concept of foreign students was inappropriate to measure student mobility to the extent that not all foreign students come to their country of study expressly with the intention to study. In particular, foreign students who are permanent residents in their country of study as a result of immigration – by themselves or by their parents – are included in the total. This results in an overestimation of foreign students' numbers in countries with comparatively low naturalisation rates of their immigrant populations. Moreover, citizens of the country in which they study can be mobile students (*i.e.* nationals who have lived abroad and return to their country of citizenship for the purpose of study).

In an effort to improve the measurement of student mobility and the comparability of internationalisation data, the OECD – together with Eurostat and the UNESCO Institute for Statistics – revised the instruments in 2005 to gather data on student mobility. According to this new concept, the term "international students" refers to students who have crossed borders expressly with the intention to study. Yet, the measurement of student mobility depends to a large extent on country-specific immigration legislations and data availability constraints. For instance, the free mobility of individuals within the EU and broader European Economic Area (EEA) makes it impossible to derive numbers of international students from visa statistics. In acknowledgment of these country specificities, the OECD permits countries to define as international students those who are not permanent residents of their country of study or alternatively students who received their prior education in another country (regardless of citizenship), depending on which operational definition is most appropriate in their national context. Overall, the country of prior education is considered a better operational criterion for EU countries in order not to omit intra-EU student mobility (Kelo, Teichler and Wächter, 2005), while the residence criterion is usually a good proxy in countries that require a student visa to enter the country for educational purposes.

The convention adopted here is to use the terminology "international student" when referring to student mobility while the terminology "foreign student" relates to non-citizens enrolled in a country (*i.e.* comprises some permanent residents and therefore provides an overestimated proxy of actual student mobility). However since not all countries are yet able to report data on student mobility on the basis of students' country of residence or their country of prior education, some tables and charts present indicators on both international and foreign students – albeit separately to emphasize the need for caution in international comparisons.

It should be noted that in this indicator data on total foreign enrolments worldwide are based on the number of foreign students enrolled in countries reporting data to the OECD and to the UNESCO Institute for Statistics and thus may be underestimated. In addition, note that all trend analyses in this indicator are based on numbers of foreign students at different points in time, since no time series on student mobility are available yet. Current work aims at filling this gap and developing retrospective time series on student mobility for future editions of *Education at a Glance*.

Trends in foreign student numbers

Foreign student numbers

In 2005, 2.73 million tertiary students were enrolled outside their country of citizenship, of which 2.30 million (or 84%) studied in the OECD area. This represented a 4.9% increase in total foreign enrolments worldwide since the previous year – or 127 336 additional individuals in absolute numbers. In the OECD area, the increase was slightly smaller with a 4.6% increase in foreign student numbers over just one academic year.

Since 2000, the number of foreign tertiary students enrolled in the OECD area and worldwide increased by 49 and 50%, respectively. This amounts to an 8.2 and 8.4% annual increase on average (Table C3.6).

Compared to 2000, the number of foreign students enrolled in tertiary education increased noticeably in Australia, the Czech Republic, Finland, France, Greece, Ireland, Italy, Japan, Korea, the Netherlands, New Zealand, Norway, Poland, Portugal and Sweden, and in the partner economies the Russian Federation and Slovenia, with indexes of change of 150 or above. In contrast, the number of foreign students enrolled in Austria, Belgium, Iceland, the Slovak Republic, Spain and Turkey, and in the partner economy Estonia, grew by about 20% or less and even shrank in the partner economies Brazil and Chile (Table C3.1).

Interestingly, changes in foreign student numbers between 2000 and 2005 indicate that the growth in foreign enrolments has been larger in the OECD on average than in the 19 EU countries of the OECD with 93 and 61% growth respectively. This pattern suggests that although foreign enrolments increased throughout the OECD, the recent growth in foreign enrolments was even higher outside of the EU area than inside (Table C3.1).

The combination of OECD data with those of the UNESCO Institute for Statistics allows the examination of longer term trends and illustrates the dramatic growth in foreign enrolments over the past 30 years (Box C3.1).

Over the past three decades, the number of students enrolled outside their country of citizenship has grown dramatically from 0.61 million worldwide in 1975 to 2.73 million in 2005 – a more than four-fold increase. This growth in the internationalisation of tertiary education has accelerated during the past ten years, mirroring the growing globalisation of economies and societies.

The growth in the number of students enrolled abroad since 1975 stems from various driving factors. During the early years, public policies aimed at promoting and nurturing academic, cultural, social and political ties between countries played a key role, especially in the context of the European construction in which building mutual understanding between young Europeans

---

Box C3.1. Long term growth in the number of students enrolled outside their country of citizenship

Growth in internationalisation of tertiary education (1975-2005)

1975 0.6M	1980 0.8M	1985 0.9M	1990 1.2M	1995 1.3M	2000 1.8M	2005 2.7M

Source: OECD and UNESCO Institute for Statistics.

Data on foreign enrolment worldwide comes from both the OECD and the UNESCO Institute for Statistics (UIS). UIS provided the data on all countries for 1975-1995 and most of the partner economies for 2000 and 2005. The OECD provided the data on OECD countries and the other partner economies in 2000 and 2005. Both sources use similar definitions, thus making their combination possible. Missing data were imputed with the closest data reports to ensure that breaks in data coverage do not result in breaks in time series.

---

was a major policy objective. Similar rationales motivated North American policies of academic co-operation. Over time, however, driving factors of a more economic nature played an increasing role. Indeed, decreasing transportation costs, the spread of new technologies, and faster, cheaper communication resulted in a growing interdependence of economies and societies in the 1980s and even more so in the 1990s. This tendency was particularly strong in the high technology sector and labour market. The growing internationalisation of labour markets for the highly-skilled fostered individuals' incentives to gain an international experience as part of their studies while the spread of Information and Communication Technology (ICT) lowered information and transaction costs of study abroad and boosted the demand for international education.

In the meantime, the rapid expansion of tertiary education in OECD countries – as well as in most emerging countries more recently (OECD, 2005d) – added financial pressure on education systems. In some countries, foreign students were actively recruited as tertiary institutions increasingly relied upon financial revenues from foreign tuition fees to operate their activities. In a number of other countries, however, education abroad was encouraged as a solution to address unmet demand resulting from bottlenecks in education provision in the context of the rapid expansion of tertiary education.

In the past few years, the rise of the knowledge economy and global competition for skills provided a new driver for the internationalisation of education systems in many OECD countries, whereby the recruitment of foreign students is part of a broader strategy to recruit highly skilled immigrants.

At the institutional level, drivers of international education derive from the additional revenues that foreign students may generate – either through differentiated tuition fees or public subsidies. But tertiary education institutions also have academic incentives to engage in international activities to build or maintain their reputation in the context of academic competition on an increasingly global scale.

Major destinations of foreign students

In 2005, more than five out of ten foreign students went to a relatively small number of destinations. Indeed, only four countries host the majority of foreign students enrolled outside of their country of citizenship: the United States receives the most foreign students (in absolute terms) with 22% of the total of all foreign students worldwide, followed by the United Kingdom (12%), Germany (10%) and France (9%). Altogether, these four major destinations account for 52% of all tertiary students pursuing their studies abroad (Chart C3.2).

Besides these four major destinations, in 2005 significant numbers of foreign students were enrolled in Australia (6%), Japan (5%), Canada (3%), New Zealand (3%) and the partner economy the Russian Federation (3%).

Chart C3.2. Distribution of foreign students by country of destination (2000, 2005)

*Percentage of foreign tertiary students reported to the OECD
who are enrolled in each country of destination*

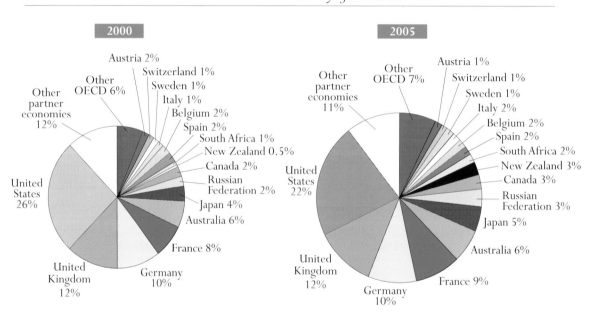

Source: OECD and UNESCO Institute for Statistics for most data on partner economies. Table C3.8 (available on line at the link below). See Annex 3 for notes (*www.oecd.org/edu/eag2007*).
StatLink ᐧ᠊ᜌ᠊ http://dx.doi.org/10.1787/068417017111

Trends in market shares show the emergence of new players on the international education market

The examination of country-specific trends in market shares on the international education market – measured as the percentage of all foreign students worldwide enrolled in a given destination – sheds light on the dynamics of internationalisation of tertiary education.

The United States saw a significant drop as a preferred destination of foreign students, from 26.1 to 21.6% of the global intake. Austria, Belgium, Germany, Spain, Switzerland and the United Kingdom saw a lesser decline, with their market shares dropping by about one-half of a percentage point over the five year period scrutinised. In contrast, the market shares of France,

C3

New Zealand and the partner economies South Africa and the Russian Federation expanded by 1 percentage point or more. The growth in market position was most impressive for New Zealand (2.1%), thereby positioning the country among the big players in the international education market (Chart C3.3).

These trends underline the different dynamics of international education in OECD and partner economies, and reflect different emphases of internationalisation policies, ranging from pro-active marketing policies in the Asia-Pacific region to a more passive approach in the traditionally dominant United States. The United States foreign student intake was also affected by the tightening of the conditions of entry for international students in the aftermath of the events of 11 September 2001 (see Indicator C3, *Education at a Glance 2005* [OECD, 2005d]).

Chart C3.3. **Trends in international education market shares (2000, 2005)**

Percentage of all foreign tertiary students enrolled, by destination

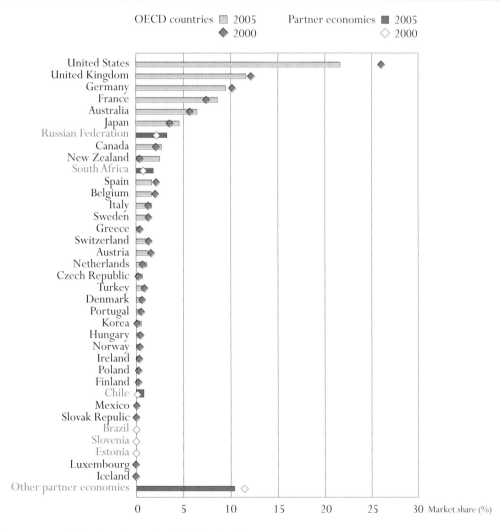

Countries are ranked in descending order of 2005 market shares.

Source: OECD and UNESCO Institute for Statistics for most data on partner economies. Table C3.8 (available on line at the link below). See Annex 3 for notes (*www.oecd.org/edu/eag2007*).

StatLink ᠊ᠠᡨ᠊ http://dx.doi.org/10.1787/068417017111

Underlying factors in students' choice of a country of study

Language of instruction: a critical factor in the choice of a country of study

The language spoken and used in instruction is critical for selecting a foreign country in which to study. Therefore, countries whose language of instruction is widely spoken and read (*e.g.* English, French, German and Russian) dominate in the destinations of foreign students, be it in absolute or relative terms. A notable exception is Japan, which despite a less widespread language of instruction enrols large numbers of foreign students - where 94.2% of its foreign students are from Asia (Table C3.2 and Chart C3.3).

The dominance of English-speaking destinations such as Australia, Canada, the United Kingdom and the United States (in absolute numbers) may be largely attributable to the fact that students intending to study abroad are most likely to have learnt English in their home country, and/or wish to improve their English language skills through immersion and study abroad. The rapid increase in foreign enrolments in Australia (index change of 167), Ireland (174) and, most importantly, New Zealand (845) between 2000 and 2005 can to some extent be attributed to similar linguistic considerations (Table C3.1).

Given this pattern, an increasing number of institutions in non-English-speaking countries now offer courses in English to overcome their linguistic disadvantage in attracting foreign students. This trend is especially noticeable in Nordic countries (Box C3.2).

Impact of tuition fees and cost of living on foreign student destinations

Tuition fees and cost of living are equally important factors for prospective international students when deciding in which country to study.

In Denmark, Finland, Iceland, Norway and Sweden, tuition fees do not exist for domestic and international students alike (Box C3.3). This cost pattern associated with the existence of programmes in English probably explains part of the robust growth in the number of foreign students enrolled in some of these countries between 2000 and 2005 (Table C3.1). However, high unit costs in tertiary education at no fee incur a high monetary burden of international students for their countries of destination (see Table B1.1). As a result, Denmark has recently adopted tuition fees for non-EU and non-EEA international students, as of 2006-2007. Similar debates are currently underway in Finland, Norway and Sweden where foreign enrolments grew by more than 50% between 2000 and 2005.

Indeed, the trade benefits of international education are all the more important as countries charge the full cost of education to their international students. Several countries in the Asia-Pacific region have actually made international education an explicit part of their socio-economic development strategies and have initiated policies to attract international students on a revenue-generating or at least self-financing basis. Australia and New Zealand have successfully adopted differentiated tuition fees for international students. In Japan and Korea, although tuition fees are the same for domestic and international students, foreign enrolments also grew at a robust pace between 2000 and 2005 despite high levels of tuition fees (see Indicator B5). This pattern highlights that tuition costs do not necessarily discourage prospective international students as long as the quality of education provided and its likely returns for individuals make the investment worthwhile. However, in choosing between similar educational opportunities, cost considerations may play a role, especially for students originating from developing countries. In this respect, the comparatively low progress of foreign enrolments in the United Kingdom and the United States between 2000 and 2005 and

C3

> **Box C3.2. OECD countries and partner economies offering tertiary programmes in English (2005)**
>
> | Use of English language in instruction | OECD countries and partner economies |
> |---|---|
> | All or nearly all education programmes in the country are offered in English | Australia, Canada[1], Ireland, New Zealand, United Kingdom, United States |
> | Many education programmes in the country are offered in English | Denmark, Finland, Netherlands, Sweden |
> | Some education programmes in the country are offered in English | Belgium (Fl.), Czech Republic, France, Germany, Hungary, Iceland, Japan, Korea, Norway, Poland, Slovak Republic, Switzerland, Turkey |
> | None or nearly no education programmes in the country are offered in English | Austria, Belgium (Fr.), Greece, Italy, Luxembourg, Mexico, Portugal, Spain
Brazil, Chile, Israel, Russian Federation |
>
> 1. In Canada, tertiary institutions are either French (mostly Quebec) or English-speaking.
>
> *Note:* Assessing the extent to which a country offers a few or many programmes in English is subjective. In doing so, the size of the countries of destination has been taken into account, hence the classification of France and Germany among countries with comparatively few English programmes, despite having more English programmes than Sweden in absolute terms.
>
> *Source:* OECD, compiled from brochures for prospective international students by OAD (Austria), CHES and NARIC (Czech Republic), Cirius (Denmark), CIMO (Finland), EduFrance (France), DAAD (Germany), Campus Hungary (Hungary), University of Iceland (Iceland), JPSS (Japan), NIIED (Korea), NUFFIC (Netherlands), SIU (Norway), CRASP (Poland), Swedish Institute (Sweden) and Middle-East Technical University (Turkey).

the deterioration of its market share on the international education market over the same period may be attributed to the comparatively high level of tuition fees charged to international students in the context of fierce competition from other primarily English-speaking destinations offering similar educational opportunities at a lower cost (Box C3.3).

Other important factors guiding the destinations of foreign students relate to the academic reputation of particular institutions or programmes, the flexibility of programmes with respect to counting time spent abroad towards degree requirements, the limitations of tertiary education provision in the home country, restrictive university admission policies at home, geographical, trade or historical links between countries, future job opportunities, cultural aspirations, and government policies to facilitate credit transfer between home and host institutions. The transparency and flexibility of courses and degree requirements also count. In the recent years, several OECD countries have softened their immigration policies to encourage the temporary or permanent immigration of their international students. As a result, immigration considerations may also guide the directions of some international students choosing between alternative educational opportunities abroad (Tremblay, 2005).

Extent of student mobility in tertiary education

The foregoing analysis has focused on trends in the absolute numbers of foreign students and their distribution by countries of destination since no time series or global aggregates exist on student mobility.

C3

It is also possible to measure the extent of student mobility in each country of destination if not at the global level, then by examining the proportion of international students in total tertiary enrolments. The advantage of this indicator is that it takes the size of the different tertiary education systems into account and highlights the highly internationalised education systems regardless of their size and the importance of their absolute market share.

Box C3.3. Level of tuition fees charged for international students in public universities (academic year 2004-2005)

Tuition fee structure	Countries
Higher tuition fees for international students than for domestic students	Australia, Austria[1], Belgium[1], Canada, Czech Republic, Estonia[1], Netherlands[1], New Zealand, Turkey, United Kingdom[1], United States[3]
Same tuition fees for international and domestic students	France, Italy, Japan, Korea, Mexico[2], Spain
No tuition fees for either international or domestic students	Denmark, Finland, Iceland, Norway, Sweden

Annual average tuition fees charged to international students by public tertiary-type A institutions (2004)

USD PPPs

14 000
13 000 — ◈ United States
12 000
11 000 — ◈ Australia
10 000
9 000 — ◈ Canada / ◈ New Zealand
8 000
7 000
6 000
5 000
4 000 — ◈ Japan, Korea
3 000
2 000 — ◈ Austria[1]
1 000 — ◈ Italy / ◈ Belgium, Czech Republic, France, Spain, Turkey
0 — ◈ Denmark, Finland, Iceland, Norway, Sweden

1. For non-European Union or non-European Economic Area students.
2. Some institutions charge higher tuition fees for international students.
3. International students pay the same fees as domestic out-of-state students. However since most domestic students are enrolled in-state, international students pay higher tuition fees than most domestic students in practice.
Source: OECD. Indicator B5. See Annex 3 for notes (*www.oecd.org/edu/eag2007*).

C3

Wide variations in the proportion of international students enrolled in OECD and partner economies

Australia, Austria, France, New Zealand, Switzerland and the United Kingdom display the highest levels of incoming student mobility, measured as the proportion of international students in their total tertiary enrolment. In Australia, 17.3% of tertiary students enrolled in the country have come to the country expressly to pursue their studies. Similarly, international students represent 11% of total tertiary enrolments in Austria, 10.8% in France, 17% in New Zealand, 13.2% in Switzerland and 13.9% in the United Kingdom. In contrast, incoming student mobility remains 1% or less of total tertiary enrolments in Greece, the Slovak Republic, Spain and the partner economies Brazil and Slovenia. (Chart C3.1).

Among countries where data on student mobility are not available, foreign enrolments constitute a large group of tertiary students in Germany (11.5%), suggesting significant levels of incoming student mobility. However foreign enrolments – and student mobility – represent 1% or less of total tertiary enrolments in Korea, Poland, Turkey and the partner economy Chile (Table C3.1).

Student mobility at different levels of tertiary education

Looking at the proportions of international students at different levels of tertiary education in each country of destination sheds light on patterns of student mobility. A first observation is that with the exception of Japan, New Zealand and Norway, tertiary-type B programmes are far less internationalised than tertiary-type A programmes, suggesting that international students are mostly attracted to traditional academic programmes where degree transferability is often easier. With the exception of Italy, Portugal and Spain, this observation also holds true among countries where data on student mobility are not available (Table C3.1).

In Australia, New Zealand and the Slovak Republic, the proportions of international students are roughly the same in tertiary-type A and advanced research programmes, suggesting that these countries of destination are successful at attracting students from abroad from the start of their tertiary education, and/or keeping them beyond their first degrees. In contrast, other countries display significantly higher incoming student mobility relative to total enrolments in advanced research programmes than in the tertiary-type A programmes that precede advanced research studies. This pattern is most obvious in Belgium, France, Hungary, Japan, Norway, Spain, Switzerland, the United Kingdom and the United States, as well as in Iceland, Poland, Portugal and Turkey, and in the partner economy Chile, among countries where data on student mobility are not available. It may reflect a strong attractiveness of advanced research programmes in these countries, or a preferred recruitment of international students at higher levels of education to capitalise on their contribution to domestic research and development or in anticipation of their subsequent recruitment as highly qualified immigrants.

Profile of international student intake in different destinations

Importance of Asia among regions of origin

Asian students form the largest group of international students enrolled in countries reporting data to the OECD or the UNESCO Institute for Statistics, with 48.9% of the total in all reporting destinations (47.4% of the total in OECD countries, and 57.3% of the total in partner economies). In the OECD, the Asian group is followed by Europeans (24.9%), in particular citizens of the European Union (16.9%). Students from Africa account for 11.0% of all international students, while those from North America account for only 3.7%. Finally, students from South America represent 5.7% of the total. Altogether, 32.0% of international students enrolled in the OECD area originate from another OECD country (Table C3.2).

This predominance of students from Asia is most notable in Australia, Greece, Japan, Korea and New Zealand, where more than 76% of their international or foreign students originate from Asia.

Main countries of origin of international students

The predominance of students from Asia and Europe among international intakes is also notable when looking at individual countries of origin. Students from Japan and Korea comprise the largest groups of international students enrolled in the OECD, at 2.9 and 4.5% of the total respectively, followed by students from France and Germany at 2.1% and 2.9% respectively (Table C3.2).

With respect to international students originating from partner economies, students from China represent by far the largest group, with 16.7% of all international students enrolled in the OECD area (not including an additional 1.4% from Hong Kong, China) The destination of choice for the Chinese is the United States, followed closely by Japan, with 22.8% and 20.6% of all international Chinese students enrolled in each of those two countries respectively. Students from China are followed by those from India (6.2%), Morocco (1.9%), Malaysia (1.9%) and the Russian Federation (1.4%). A significant number of Asians also come from Indonesia, Thailand, Vietnam and Singapore (Table C3.2 and Table C3.8, available on line at *http://dx.doi.org/10.1787/068417017111*).

International students' intake by level and type of tertiary education highlights specialisations

In some countries a comparatively large proportion of international students are enrolled in tertiary-type B programmes. This is the case in Belgium (29.4%), Greece (21.3%), Japan (24.2%), New Zealand (26.1%) and the partner economy Slovenia (26%). Among countries where data on student mobility are not available, foreign enrolments in tertiary-type B programmes also constitute a large group of foreign students in the partner economy Chile (27.2%) (Table C3.4).

In contrast, other countries see a large proportion of their international students enrolling in advanced research programmes. This is most notably the case in Spain (33%), Switzerland (27.1%) and the partner economy Brazil (42.8%). Such patterns suggest that these countries offer attractive advanced programmes to prospective international graduate students. This concentration can also be observed – although to a more limited extent – among international students in Finland (14.3%), France (12%), the United Kingdom (11.5%) and the United States (15.7%). All of these countries are likely to benefit from contributions of these high-level international students to domestic research and development. In addition, this specialisation can also generate higher tuition revenue per international student in the countries charging full tuition costs to foreign students (Box C3.3).

International student intake by field of education underlines magnet centres

As shown in Table C3.5, sciences attract about one in six international students in Australia (17.7%), Germany (17.4%), Switzerland (17.1%) and the United States (18.7%), but less than one in fifty in Japan (1.2%). However, this picture changes slightly when considering scientific disciplines in a broader sense – *i.e.* adding agriculture, engineering, manufacturing and construction programmes. Finland receives the largest proportion of its international students in these fields, at 42.4%. The proportion of international students enrolled in agriculture, sciences or engineering is also high in Australia (29.6%), Germany (38.1%), Hungary (32.6%), Sweden (36.8%), Switzerland (34.7%), the United Kingdom (30.6%) and the United States (34.6%). Similarly, among countries where data on student mobility are not available, agriculture, sciences and engineering attract about one in three foreign students in the Czech Republic (29.0%) and the Slovak Republic (29.1%). In contrast, few foreign students are enrolled in agriculture, sciences and engineering in Poland (Chart C3.4).

Chart C3.4. Distribution of international students by field of education (2005)
Percentage of all international tertiary students enrolled in different fields of education

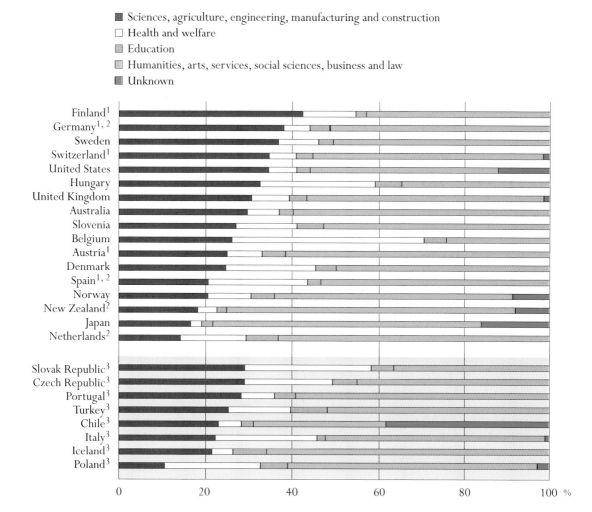

1. Excludes tertiary-type B programmes.
2. Excludes advanced research programmes.
3. Distribution of foreign students by field of education. These data are not comparable with data on international students and are therefore presented separately.
Countries are ranked in descending order of the proportion of international students enrolled in sciences, agriculture, engineering, manufacturing and construction.
Source: OECD. Table C3.5. See Annex 3 for notes (*www.oecd.org/edu/eag2007*).
StatLink http://dx.doi.org/10.1787/068417017111

C3

It is noteworthy that most countries enrolling large proportions of their international students in agriculture, sciences and engineering deliver programmes in the English language. In the case of Germany, the large proportion of foreign students in scientific disciplines may also reflect the strong tradition of the country in these fields.

Non-Anglophone countries, however, tend to enrol a higher proportion of their international students in the humanities and arts fields. Indeed, humanities and arts are favoured by over 20% of the international students in Austria (24.7%), Germany (23%), Japan (25.2%) and the partner economy Slovenia (21%). Among countries where data on student mobility are not available, this is also the case in Iceland (49.2%) and Poland (21.1%).

Social sciences, business and law programmes also attract international students in large numbers. In Australia and New Zealand these fields of education enrol more than half of all international students (at 50.7% and 60.4% respectively). The proportion of international students enrolled in social sciences, business and law is also high in the United Kingdom (40.1%) and the Netherlands (47.1%). Among countries where data on student mobility are not available, Portugal (45.5%) has the highest proportion of its foreign students enrolled in social sciences business and law.

The situation of health and welfare educational programmes is fairly specific since it depends to a large extent on national policies of medical degree recognition. Health and welfare programmes attract large proportions of international students in EU countries, most notably in Belgium (44.4%), Denmark (20.7%), Hungary (26.4%) and Spain (22.9%). Among countries where data on student mobility are not available, health and welfare programmes are also chosen by one-fifth to one-quarter of foreign students in the Czech Republic (20.3%), Italy (23.4%), Poland (22.1%) and the Slovak Republic (29.1%). This pattern is related to the existence of quotas in many European countries restricting access to educational programmes in the medical field. This increases the demand for training abroad in other EU countries to bypass these quotas, and to take advantage of EU countries' automatic recognition of medical degrees under the European Medical Directive.

Overall, the concentration of international students in specific disciplines in each country of destination highlights magnet programmes that attract students from abroad in large numbers. This attraction results from many factors on both the supply and demand side.

On the supply side, some destinations offer centres of excellence or traditional expertise able to attract students from other countries in large numbers (*e.g.* Finland and Germany in sciences and engineering). In the humanities and arts, some destinations also have a natural monopoly on some programmes. This is especially obvious for linguistic or cultural studies (*e.g.* Austria, Germany and Japan).

On the demand side, the characteristics of international students can help to explain their concentration in some fields of education. For instance, students in scientific disciplines are usually less likely to be fluent in many different languages, which may explain their stronger propensity to study in countries offering education programmes in English, and their lesser propensity to enrol in countries where these are less common (*e.g.* Japan). Similarly, the demand of many Asian students for business training may explain the strong concentration of international students in social sciences, business and law in neighbouring Australia and New Zealand – and to a lesser extent in Japan. Last, EU provisions for the recognition of medical degrees clearly drive the concentration of international students in health and welfare programmes in EU countries.

C3

Destinations of citizens enrolled abroad

When studying in tertiary education outside of their country of citizenship, OECD students enrol predominantly in another country of the OECD area. On average, only 3.2% of foreign students from OECD are enrolled in a partner economy to acquire their tertiary education. The proportion of foreign students from partner economies enrolled in another partner economy is significantly higher, with more than 18% of foreign students from Chile, Estonia, Israel and the Russian Federation enrolled in another partner economy. In contrast, students from the Czech Republic (0.7%), France (0.9%), Iceland (0.1%), Ireland (0.2%), and most notably, Luxembourg (0%) display an extremely low propensity to study outside of the OECD area (Table C3.3).

Language considerations, geographic proximity and similarity of education systems are important determinants of the choice of destination. Geographic considerations and differences in entry requirements are likely explanations of the concentration of students from Austria in Germany, from Belgium in France and the Netherlands, from France in Belgium, from Canada in the United States, from New Zealand in Australia, from China in Japan etc. Language issues as well as academic traditions also shed light on the propensity for Anglophone students to concentrate in other countries of the Commonwealth or in the United States, even those geographically distant. Migration networks also play a role, as illustrated by the concentration of students of Portuguese citizenship in France, students from Turkey in Germany or from Mexico in the United States.

Finally, international students' destinations also highlight the attractiveness of specific education systems, be it due to considerations of academic reputation, or as a result of subsequent immigration opportunities. In this respect, it is noteworthy that students from China are mostly concentrated in Australia, Germany, Japan, New Zealand, the United Kingdom and the United States – most of which have set up schemes to facilitate the immigration of international students. Similarly, students from India favour Australia, the United Kingdom and the United States; these three destinations attract 87.1% of Indian citizens enrolled abroad.

International students' contribution to tertiary graduate output and immigration implications

International students' contribution to the graduate output

International students make a significant contribution to the tertiary graduate output of the most internationalised education systems. In some highly internationalised levels of education, this contribution artificially inflates tertiary graduation rates. It is therefore important to examine the contribution of international students to the graduate output of different types of tertiary programmes to assess the extent of this over-estimation (see Indicator A3).

In Australia, Germany, Switzerland and the United Kingdom, more than 30% of tertiary-type A second degrees or advanced research degrees are awarded to international students. This pattern implies that the true domestic graduate output is significantly over-estimated in overall graduation rates. This over-estimation is most important for tertiary-type A second degree programmes in Australia and the United Kingdom and advanced research programmes in Switzerland and the United Kingdom, where international graduates represent more than 35% of the graduate output. The contribution of international students to the graduate output is also significant – although to a lesser extent – in Austria, Japan, New Zealand and the United States, and among countries where student mobility data are not available, in Belgium (Chart C3.5).

However, the contribution of international students to the tertiary graduate output of Denmark, Finland, Norway and Sweden and the partner economy Slovenia is more limited. The same holds for foreign students of the Czech Republic, Hungary, Portugal, the Slovak Republic and Turkey (Table C3.7). This makes it more difficult for these countries to capitalise on this external contribution to domestic human capital production.

Chart C3.5.   Proportion of international and foreign graduates in tertiary graduate output (2005)

Percentage of all tertiary qualifications awarded to international students

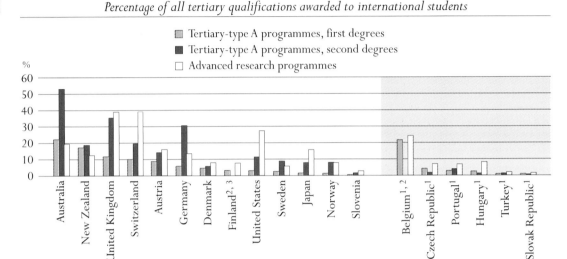

1. Proportion of foreign graduates in tertiary graduate output. These data are not comparable with data on international graduates and are therefore presented separately.
2. First degrees programmes include second degrees.
3. Year of reference 2004.
Countries are ranked in descending order of the proportion of international graduates in tertiary type-A first degree programmes.
Source: OECD. Table C3.7. See Annex 3 for notes (*www.oecd.org/edu/eag2007*).
StatLink ᴍˢᴾ http://dx.doi.org/10.1787/068417017111

Definitions and methodologies

Data sources, definitions and reference period

Data on international and foreign students are based on the UOE data collection on education statistics administered annually by the OECD. Additional data from the UNESCO Institute for Statistics are also included.

Students are classified as international students if they left their country of origin and moved to another country for the purpose of study. Depending on country-specific immigration legislations, mobility arrangements (*e.g.* free mobility of individuals within the EU and EEA areas) and data availability, international students may be defined as students who are not permanent or usual residents of their country of study or alternatively as students who obtained their prior education in a different country (*e.g.* EU countries).

Permanent or usual residence in the reporting country is defined according to national legislations. In practice, this means holding a student visa or permit, or electing a foreign country of domicile in the year prior to entering the education system of the country reporting data. The country of prior education is defined as the country in which students obtained the qualification required to enrol in their current level of education, *i.e.* the country where they obtained their upper secondary or post-secondary non-tertiary education for international students enrolled in tertiary-type A and tertiary-type B programmes and the country where they obtained their tertiary-type A education for international students enrolled in advanced research programmes. Country-specific operational definitions of international students are indicated in the tables as well as in Annex 3 (*www.oecd.org/edu/eag2007*).

Students are classified as foreign students if they are not citizens of the country in which the data are collected. While pragmatic and operational, this classification is inappropriate to capture student mobility as a result of differing national policies regarding the naturalisation of immigrants. For instance, while Australia and Switzerland report similar intakes of foreign students relative to their tertiary enrolments – 20.6 and 18.4% respectively – these proportions reflect significant differences in the actual levels of student mobility – 17.3% of tertiary enrolments in Australia and 13.2% in Switzerland (Table C3.1). This is because Australia is an immigration country and has a higher propensity to grant permanent residence to its immigrant populations than Switzerland. Therefore, interpretations of data based on the concept of foreign students in terms of student mobility and bilateral comparisons need to be made with caution.

Unless mentioned otherwise, data refer to the academic year 2004-2005.

Methodologies

Data on international and foreign students are obtained from enrolments in their countries of destination. The method of obtaining data on international and foreign students is therefore the same as that used for collecting data on total enrolments, *i.e.* records of regularly enrolled students in an educational programme. Domestic and international students are usually counted on a specific day or period of the year. This procedure allows to measure the proportion of international enrolments in an education system, but the actual number of individuals involved in foreign exchange may be much higher since many students study abroad for less than a full academic year, or participate in exchange programmes that do not require enrolment (*e.g.* inter-university exchange or advanced research short-term mobility). On the other hand, the international student body comprises some distance-learning students who are not, strictly speaking, mobile students. This pattern of distance enrolments is fairly common in tertiary institutions of Australia and the United Kingdom (OECD, 2004d).

Since data on international and foreign students are obtained from tertiary enrolments in their country of destination, the data therefore relate to students that are coming in rather than to students going abroad. Countries of destination covered by this indicator include all of the OECD countries (with the exception of Luxembourg and Mexico) and the partner economies Brazil, Chile, Estonia, the Russian Federation and Slovenia, as well as partner economies reporting similar data to the UNESCO Institute for Statistics to derive global figures and to examine the destinations of students and trends in market shares.

Data on students enrolled abroad as well as trend analyses are not based on the numbers of international students, but instead on the numbers of foreign citizens where data consistent across countries and over time are readily available. Yet the data do not include students enrolled in OECD and partner economies that did not report foreign students to the OECD nor to the UNESCO Institute for Statistics. All statements on students enrolled abroad may therefore underestimate the real number of citizens studying abroad (Table C3.3), especially so for countries where numerous citizens study in countries that do not report their foreign students to the OECD or UNESCO Institute for Statistics (*e.g.* China, India).

Table C3.1. displays international as well as foreign enrolments as a proportion of the total enrolment at each level of tertiary education. Total enrolment, used as a denominator, comprises all persons studying in the country (including domestic and international students) but excludes students from that country who study abroad. The table also exhibits changes between 2000 and 2005 in foreign enrolments for all tertiary education.

Tables C3.2, C3.4 and C3.5 show the distribution of international students enrolled in an education system – or foreign students for countries that do not have information on student mobility – according to their country of origin in Table C3.2, according to their level and type of tertiary education in Table C3.4, and according to the field of education they are enrolled in for Table C3.5.

Table C3.3 presents the distribution of citizens of a given country enrolled abroad according to their country of destination (or country of study). As mentioned above, the total number of students enrolled abroad used as a denominator covers only students enrolled in other countries reporting data to the OECD or the UNESCO Institute for Statistics. Therefore, the resulting proportions can be biased and overestimated for countries where large numbers of students study in non-reporting countries.

Table C3.6 shows trends in the absolute number of foreign students reported by OECD countries and worldwide between 2000 and 2005, and the indexes of change between 2005 and the years from 2000 to 2004. It should be noted that the figures are based on the number of foreign students enrolled in countries reporting data to the OECD and to the UNESCO Institute for Statistics. Since data for partner economies that did not report to the OECD were not included in the past, the figures are not strictly comparable with those published in editions of *Education at a Glance* prior to 2006.

Table C3.7 presents the percentage of tertiary qualifications awarded to international students – or foreign students for countries that do not have information on student mobility. It provides an indication of the contribution of international or foreign students to the graduate output of different levels and types of tertiary education.

Table C3.8 (available on line at *http://dx.doi.org/10.1787/068417017111*) provides the matrix of foreign students' numbers by country of origin and country of destination.

Further references

The relative importance of international students in the education system affects tertiary graduation rates and may artificially increase them in some fields or levels of education (see Indicator A3).

In countries where differentiated tuition fees are applied to international students, student mobility may boost the financial resources of tertiary educational institutions and contribute to the financing of the education system. On the other hand, international students may represent a high financial burden for countries where tertiary tuition fees are low or inexistent given the high level of unit costs in tertiary education (see Indicator B5).

International students enrolled in a country different from their own are only one aspect of the internationalisation of tertiary education. New forms of cross-border education have emerged in the last decade, including the mobility of educational programmes and institutions across borders. Yet, cross-border post-secondary education has developed quite differently and in response to different rationales in different world regions. For a detailed analysis of these issues, as well as trade and policy implications of the internationalisation of tertiary education see *Internationalisation and Trade in Higher Education: Opportunities and Challenges* (OECD, 2004d).

Table C3.1.
Student mobility and foreign students in tertiary education (2000, 2005)

International mobile students enrolled as a percentage of all students (international plus domestic), foreign enrolments as a percentage of all students (foreign and national) and index of change in the number of foreign students

Reading the first column: 17.3% of all students in tertiary education in Australia are international students and 13.2% of all students in tertiary education in Switzerland are international students. According to country-specific immigration legislations and data availability constraints, student mobility is either defined on the basis of students' country of residence (*i.e.* Australia) or the country where students received their prior education (*i.e.* Switzerland). The data presented in this table on student mobility represent the best available proxy of student mobility for each country.

Reading the fifth column: 20.6% of all students in tertiary education in Australia are non-Australian citizens, and 18.4% of all students in tertiary education in Switzerland are non-Swiss citizens.

C3

	Student mobility				Foreign enrolments				Index of change in the number of foreign students, total tertiary (2000=100)
	International students as a percentage of all tertiary enrolment				Foreign students as a percentage of all tertiary enrolment				
	Total tertiary	Tertiary-type B programmes	Tertiary-type A programmes	Advanced research programmes	Total tertiary	Tertiary-type B programmes	Tertiary-type A programmes	Advanced research programmes	
	(1)	(2)	(3)	(4)	(5)	(6)	(7)	(8)	(9)
OECD countries									
Australia[1]	17.3	6.8	19.3	17.8	20.6	6.9	23.0	28.3	167
Austria[1,3]	11.0	m	12.1	15.4	14.1	m	15.4	20.2	114
Belgium[1]	6.5	4.4	7.7	19.9	11.7	8.9	13.1	30.8	117
Canada	m	m	m	m	m	m	m	m	m
Czech Republic	m	m	m	m	5.5	1.2	5.9	7.2	339
Denmark[1]	4.4	3.0	4.6	6.9	7.5	9.4	7.0	18.5	135
Finland[2,3]	3.6	m	3.3	7.3	2.8	n	2.4	7.3	152
France[1]	10.8	4.5	11.7	34.4	m	m	m	m	173
Germany[2]	m	m	10.6	m	11.5	4.0	12.8	m	139
Greece[1,3]	0.4	0.3	0.6	m	2.4	2.2	2.7	m	182
Hungary[1]	2.7	0.3	2.8	7.9	3.1	0.4	3.2	8.6	137
Iceland	m	m	m	m	3.2	1.3	3.2	12.7	120
Ireland[2]	6.9	m	m	m	m	m	m	m	174
Italy	m	m	m	m	2.2	6.0	2.1	4.3	180
Japan[1]	2.8	2.8	2.5	16.3	3.1	2.9	2.8	17.1	189
Korea	m	m	m	m	0.5	x(5)	x(5)	x(5)	459
Luxembourg	m	m	m	m	m	m	m	m	m
Mexico	m	m	m	m	m	m	m	m	m
Netherlands[3]	4.7	a	4.7	m	5.6	a	5.7	m	225
New Zealand[1]	17.0	17.5	16.8	16.6	28.9	27.9	29.0	38.3	845
Norway[1]	1.9	4.7	1.7	5.2	4.8	3.1	4.5	18.6	154
Poland	m	m	m	m	0.5	n	0.4	3.2	166
Portugal	m	m	m	m	4.5	5.6	4.3	7.3	152
Slovak Republic[1]	0.9	0.2	0.9	0.7	0.9	0.3	1.0	0.8	107
Spain[1,3]	1.0	m	0.8	7.6	2.5	3.1	1.6	18.9	112
Sweden[1]	4.4	1.2	4.8	n	9.2	5.4	8.7	20.3	154
Switzerland[2,3]	13.2	m	13.1	43.3	18.4	13.1	17.0	43.2	142
Turkey	m	m	m	m	0.9	0.2	1.1	2.9	103
United Kingdom[1]	13.9	5.6	15.1	40.0	17.3	11.2	17.8	41.4	143
United States[1]	3.4	2.1	3.2	24.1	m	m	m	m	124
OECD average	*6.7*	*3.8*	*7.2*	*16.5*	*7.6*	*5.1*	*8.0*	*17.5*	*193*
EU 19 average	*5.5*	*2.2*	*6.1*	*14.0*	*6.3*	*3.8*	*6.5*	*14.5*	*161*
Partner economies									
Brazil[1,3]	0.1	m	m	1.0	m	m	m	m	89
Chile	m	m	m	m	0.3	0.2	0.3	0.8	57
Estonia[1]	1.3	0.1	1.9	2.5	m	m	m	m	103
Israel	m	m	m	m	m	m	m	m	m
Russian Federation[3,4]	m	m	m	m	1.2	0.3	1.4	m	219
Slovenia[1]	1.0	0.5	1.4	4.4	1.1	0.7	1.4	4.9	158

1. For the purpose of measuring student mobility, international students are defined on the basis of their country of residence.
2. For the purpose of measuring student mobility, international students are defined on the basis of their country of prior education.
3. Percentage in total tertiary underestimated because of the exclusion of certain programmes.
4. Excludes private institutions.
Source: OECD. See Annex 3 for notes (*www.oecd.org/edu/eag2007*).
Please refer to the Reader's Guide for information concerning the symbols replacing missing data.
StatLink ᵐˢ⁵ http://dx.doi.org/10.1787/068417017111

Table C3.2.

Distribution of international and foreign students in tertiary education, by country of origin (2005)

Number of international and foreign students enrolled in tertiary education from a given country of origin as a percentage of all international or foreign students in the country of destination, based on head counts

The table shows for each country the proportion of international students in tertiary education who are residents of or had their prior education in a given country of origin. When data on student mobility is not available, the table shows the proportion of foreign students in tertiary education that have citizenship of a given country origin.

Reading the third column: 8.5% of international tertiary students in Denmark are German residents, 0.5% of international tertiary students in Denmark are Greek residents, etc.

Reading the fifth column: 5.1% of international tertiary students in Ireland had their prior education in Germany, 0.4% of international tertiary students in Ireland had their prior education in Greece, etc.

Reading the 14th column: 20.5% of foreign tertiary students in Austria are German citizens, 0.7% of foreign tertiary students in Austria are Greek citizens, etc.

	Countries of destination — OECD countries																	
	International students													Foreign students				
Countries of origin	Australia[1]	Belgium[1,2]	Denmark[1]	Germany[3,4,5]	Ireland[3]	Netherlands[4]	New Zealand[1]	Slovak Republic[1]	Spain[1,5]	Sweden[1]	Switzerland[3,5]	United Kingdom[1]	United States[1]	Austria[5,6]	Czech Republic[6,7]	Finland[6]	France[6]	Greece[6,7]
	(1)	(2)	(3)	(4)	(5)	(6)	(7)	(8)	(9)	(10)	(11)	(12)	(13)	(14)	(15)	(16)	(17)	(18)
OECD countries																		
Australia	a	0.1	2.2	0.2	0.4	0.1	6.7	n	0.1	1.2	0.1	0.5	0.5	0.1	n	0.4	0.1	n
Austria	0.1	n	0.6	2.2	0.4	0.3	0.1	0.4	0.5	1.8	0.9	0.4	0.2	a	0.1	0.4	0.2	n
Belgium	n	a	1.5	0.6	0.5	4.1	n	n	1.8	0.9	0.3	0.8	0.1	0.2	n	0.3	1.1	0.1
Canada	1.9	0.2	1.0	0.3	2.8	0.1	1.1	0.5	0.2	1.2	0.4	1.3	5.0	0.1	0.2	0.8	0.5	0.1
Czech Republic	0.1	0.1	0.1	1.0	0.2	0.2	0.1	26.5	0.2	0.9	0.2	0.2	0.2	1.3	a	0.6	0.3	n
Denmark	0.1	n	a	0.2	0.2	0.2	0.2	n	0.2	0.9	0.1	0.5	0.2	0.2	n	0.6	0.1	n
Finland	n	n	0.6	0.4	0.6	0.4	n	0.2	0.2	2.8	0.1	0.6	0.1	0.5	n	a	0.1	n
France	0.3	36.0	4.4	3.1	5.4	1.0	0.7	0.1	4.6	5.9	6.6	3.7	1.2	1.3	0.1	1.7	a	n
Germany	0.9	0.8	8.5	a	5.1	25.6	2.6	0.7	4.3	9.3	9.4	3.9	1.5	20.5	1.0	3.8	2.5	0.8
Greece	n	0.4	0.5	1.4	0.4	0.4	n	5.3	0.4	0.4	0.3	6.2	0.4	0.7	0.6	0.5	0.9	a
Hungary	n	0.1	0.1	1.2	0.1	0.4	n	1.3	0.1	0.3	0.3	0.2	0.2	3.3	0.2	1.2	0.3	n
Iceland	n	n	7.8	0.1	n	0.2	n	n	0.1	0.2	n	0.1	0.1	0.1	n	0.2	n	n
Ireland	0.1	0.1	1.1	0.2	a	0.1	0.1	0.1	0.3	0.3	n	5.1	0.2	0.1	0.1	0.4	0.2	n
Italy	0.1	0.4	1.3	1.9	1.5	0.6	n	n	3.9	2.0	2.6	1.7	0.6	18.1	0.1	1.4	1.7	0.1
Japan	1.9	0.2	0.3	1.0	0.4	0.3	2.2	0.2	0.3	0.5	0.4	1.9	7.5	0.7	0.1	1.2	0.9	n
Korea	2.4	0.1	0.1	1.8	0.1	0.3	0.1	0.2	0.1	0.4	0.2	1.2	9.4	0.9	0.1	0.5	0.9	n
Luxembourg	n	4.7	0.7	1.1	0.1	0.1	n	n	0.3	n	0.5	0.3	n	1.1	n	n	0.7	n
Mexico	0.2	0.1	0.4	0.6	0.1	0.2	0.2	0.2	9.0	0.5	0.2	0.6	2.3	0.1	n	0.5	0.6	n
Netherlands	0.1	7.5	1.1	0.5	0.6	a	0.1	n	0.7	2.4	0.2	0.8	0.3	0.3	0.1	0.9	0.2	n
New Zealand	1.0	n	0.5	0.1	0.1	n	a	n	0.1	n	0.2	0.2	n	n	n	0.1	n	n
Norway	1.4	n	14.9	0.4	1.4	0.4	0.6	3.3	0.2	0.7	0.1	1.0	0.3	0.2	0.8	0.7	0.1	n
Poland	0.1	0.4	1.2	6.4	0.9	1.2	n	1.6	0.9	1.7	0.7	0.7	0.5	3.7	1.0	1.6	1.4	0.2
Portugal	n	0.1	0.2	0.3	0.1	0.3	n	0.1	9.3	0.5	0.2	0.9	0.2	0.2	0.6	0.3	1.1	n
Slovak Republic	0.1	0.1	n	0.6	0.1	0.2	n	a	0.2	0.1	0.3	0.1	0.1	3.5	54.6	0.3	0.2	n
Spain	0.1	0.4	2.8	2.2	2.7	0.8	n	0.1	a	4.0	0.7	1.9	0.6	1.0	0.1	1.4	1.5	n
Sweden	0.6	n	6.2	0.3	0.7	0.3	0.5	0.2	0.5	a	0.3	1.1	0.5	0.6	0.3	6.4	0.2	n
Switzerland	0.2	0.1	1.4	0.9	0.2	0.2	0.1	0.1	1.2	0.8	a	0.5	0.2	0.8	n	0.5	0.6	n
Turkey	0.1	0.3	0.4	3.3	n	0.8	n	0.2	0.1	0.2	0.6	0.6	2.2	5.4	0.2	0.7	1.0	0.3
United Kingdom	0.9	0.1	13.6	0.9	9.1	0.7	1.0	0.4	2.6	1.5	0.4	a	1.5	0.5	1.8	2.3	1.0	0.1
United States	1.8	0.5	5.5	1.7	16.8	0.5	5.1	0.8	1.8	2.6	0.7	4.5	a	1.0	0.6	2.2	1.0	0.1
Total from OECD countries	14.7	53.3	79.0	34.9	51.4	39.7	21.5	42.4	44.0	44.2	26.8	41.3	35.9	66.6	62.9	31.9	19.3	2.2
Partner economies																		
Brazil	0.2	0.1	0.3	0.8	0.1	0.1	0.1	0.1	3.9	0.1	0.5	0.4	1.3	0.1	n	0.4	0.8	n
Chile	0.1	0.1	0.2	0.4	n	0.1	0.1	0.1	2.8	0.1	0.1	0.1	0.6	n	n	0.2	0.2	n
China	21.1	3.5	7.7	11.9	12.2	8.3	57.0	n	0.6	0.8	1.0	16.5	15.7	3.1	0.2	16.4	6.1	0.1
Estonia	n	0.1	0.2	0.3	0.1	n	n	n	0.9	0.2	n	0.1	0.1	0.1	n	7.1	n	n
India	11.6	0.6	1.0	1.9	2.6	0.2	3.8	0.1	0.1	0.2	0.4	5.2	14.2	0.3	0.4	2.0	0.2	n
Israel	0.2	0.1	0.4	0.6	n	0.4	n	n	9.2	0.2	n	0.1	0.4	0.1	0.8	0.3	0.1	0.2
Russian Federation	0.3	0.4	0.7	5.7	0.9	1.1	0.5	1.5	0.4	0.3	0.8	0.6	0.9	1.1	3.3	13.3	1.1	1.0
Slovenia	n	n	n	0.1	n	0.1	n	0.2	n	0.2	n	n	0.1	1.6	0.1	0.1	n	n
Main geographic regions																		
Total from Africa	3.2	3.4	2.4	8.6	5.4	3.6	0.5	6.6	11.5	0.6	3.8	9.2	6.4	1.6	2.4	11.5	46.4	1.7
Total from Asia	78.5	7.3	13.4	30.8	35.2	15.3	76.6	21.7	3.0	2.9	3.9	46.3	63.2	14.1	8.9	29.3	16.9	83.4
Total from Europe	5.7	53.4	71.9	46.9	33.4	41.3	6.7	69.3	41.6	39.4	28.6	32.8	12.5	81.8	72.0	53.0	20.5	14.5
of which, from EU19 countries	3.7	51.6	44.4	24.7	29.0	36.7	5.5	36.9	31.0	35.9	24.0	28.9	8.3	57.2	60.7	24.2	13.5	1.7
Total from North America	3.8	0.7	6.5	2.0	19.6	0.7	6.1	1.3	2.0	3.8	1.1	5.9	5.1	1.1	0.8	3.0	1.5	0.1
Total from Oceania	2.1	0.1	2.6	0.2	0.5	0.1	9.3	n	0.1	1.3	0.1	0.7	0.8	0.1	n	0.5	0.1	n
Total from South America	1.1	1.1	1.9	3.7	0.7	2.2	0.6	1.1	41.9	1.0	2.5	2.7	12.0	1.1	0.9	2.3	4.1	0.3
Not specified	5.5	34.1	1.3	7.8	5.1	36.8	n	n	n	51.0	59.9	2.4	n	0.2	15.0	0.5	10.5	n
Total from all countries	100.0	100.0	100.0	100.0	100.0	100.0	100.0	100.0	100.0	100.0	100.0	100.0	100.0	100.0	100.0	100.0	100.0	100.0

1. International students are defined on the basis of their country of residence.
2. Excludes data for social advancement education.
3. International students are defined on the basis of their country of prior education.
4. Excludes advanced research programmes.
5. Excludes tertiary-type B programmes.
6. Foreign students are defined on the basis of their country of citizenship, these data are not comparable with data on international students and are therefore presented separately in the table.
7. Excludes tertiary programmes (advance research programmes only).
8. Excludes private institutions.

Source: OECD. See Annex 3 for notes (*www.oecd.org/edu/eag2007*).

Please refer to the Reader's Guide for information concerning the symbols replacing missing data.

StatLink ⧉ http://dx.doi.org/10.1787/068417017111

Table C3.2. *(continued)*

Distribution of international and foreign students in tertiary education, by country of origin (2005)

Number of international and foreign students enrolled in tertiary education from a given country of origin as a percentage of all international or foreign students in the country of destination, based on head counts

The table shows for each country the proportion of international students in tertiary education who are residents of or had their prior education in a given country of origin. When data on student mobility is not available, the table shows the proportion of foreign students in tertiary education that have citizenship of a given country of origin.
Reading the third column: 8.5% of international tertiary students in Denmark are German residents, 0.5% of international tertiary students in Denmark are Greek residents, etc.
Reading the fifth column: 5.1% of international tertiary students in Ireland had their prior education in Germany, 0.4% of international tertiary students in Ireland had their prior education in Greece, etc.
Reading the 14th column: 20.5% of foreign tertiary students in Austria are German citizens, 0.7% of foreign tertiary students in Austria are Greek citizens, etc.

	Countries of destination																
	OECD countries										Partner economies						
	Foreign students									Total OECD destinations	International		Foreign			Total partner economies destinations	Total all reporting destinations
Countries of origin	Hungary[6]	Iceland[6]	Italy[3,6]	Japan[6]	Korea[6]	Norway[6]	Poland[6]	Portugal[6]	Turkey[6]		Estonia[1]	Slovenia[1]	Brazil[6,7]	Chile[6]	Russian Fed.[4,6,8]		
	(19)	(20)	(21)	(22)	(23)	(24)	(25)	(26)	(27)	(28)	(29)	(30)	(31)	(32)	(33)	(34)	(35)
Australia	n	0.4	0.1	0.3	n	0.2	0.1	0.2	0.2	0.4	0.1	0.2	0.1	0.7	n	0.1	0.4
Austria	0.3	1.4	0.5	n	n	0.3	0.3	0.1	0.1	0.4	0.6	1.1	n	0.5	n	0.1	0.4
Belgium	n	0.6	0.4	n	n	0.2	0.1	0.4	n	0.5	0.5	0.1	0.3	0.3	n	n	0.4
Canada	0.6	1.9	0.3	0.2	0.8	0.5	2.0	0.8	n	2.0	0.1	n	0.8	0.6	n	0.1	1.7
Czech Republic	0.1	0.6	0.4	n	n	0.3	2.0	0.1	n	0.3	n	n	0.1	0.1	n	n	0.3
Denmark	n	10.7	0.1	n	n	6.7	0.1	n	n	0.2	0.2	n	0.1	0.2	n	n	0.2
Finland	0.3	5.2	0.2	n	n	2.1	0.1	0.1	n	0.3	31.6	n	n	0.6	n	0.1	0.2
France	0.4	2.9	1.9	0.3	0.1	1.1	0.6	6.0	n	2.1	1.0	0.2	1.2	3.7	n	0.1	1.8
Germany	8.5	12.0	3.1	0.2	0.2	3.6	2.8	2.2	0.8	2.9	2.0	n	2.3	4.3	n	0.2	2.4
Greece	1.0	0.2	14.2	n	n	0.1	0.3	0.1	5.8	1.7	n	0.1	0.1	n	n	1.0	1.6
Hungary	a	0.2	0.4	0.1	n	0.3	0.8	0.1	n	0.3	0.5	0.8	n	n	n	n	0.3
Iceland	0.2	a	n	n	n	2.0	n	n	n	0.1	n	n	n	0.1	n	n	0.1
Ireland	0.2	0.2	n	n	n	0.1	0.1	0.1	n	0.9	n	n	n	n	n	n	0.8
Italy	0.3	2.9	a	0.1	n	0.5	0.3	1.1	0.1	1.3	1.7	8.0	1.5	0.6	n	0.1	1.1
Japan	0.1	1.4	0.4	a	7.1	0.4	0.3	n	0.1	2.9	0.6	n	0.7	0.3	n	0.2	2.5
Korea	0.1	0.4	0.2	17.9	a	0.2	0.3	n	0.2	4.5	0.5	n	0.3	0.4	n	0.3	3.8
Luxembourg	n	n	0.1	n	n	n	n	0.3	n	0.3	n	0.1	n	n	n	n	0.3
Mexico	n	0.6	0.4	0.1	0.1	0.3	0.1	0.1	n	1.0	0.1	n	0.9	2.7	n	0.3	0.9
Netherlands	0.1	1.2	0.2	0.1	n	1.2	0.1	0.4	n	0.4	0.3	0.1	0.3	0.3	n	n	0.4
New Zealand	n	0.2	n	0.1	0.2	0.1	n	n	n	0.2	n	n	n	0.2	n	n	0.1
Norway	5.1	4.8	0.2	n	n	a	5.8	0.1	n	0.6	0.3	n	n	0.3	n	n	0.5
Poland	0.4	3.1	2.6	0.1	0.1	1.1	a	0.6	n	1.3	0.2	0.3	0.2	n	n	0.3	1.1
Portugal	0.1	0.6	0.2	n	n	0.2	0.1	a	n	0.4	0.1	0.1	3.1	n	n	0.2	0.4
Slovak Republic	17.2	1.0	0.4	n	n	0.4	1.2	n	n	0.8	n	0.7	n	n	n	0.2	0.7
Spain	0.2	1.9	1.0	0.1	0.1	0.8	0.2	3.3	n	1.0	1.0	0.4	2.1	2.3	n	0.1	0.9
Sweden	1.2	4.3	0.3	0.1	n	8.4	1.8	0.1	n	0.6	1.5	n	0.1	0.9	n	0.1	0.5
Switzerland	0.1	1.9	2.4	n	n	0.4	0.1	0.6	n	0.4	0.2	n	0.2	0.5	n	0.1	0.4
Turkey	0.3	0.6	0.4	0.1	0.2	0.4	0.2	n	a	1.3	n	n	n	n	n	1.0	1.3
United Kingdom	0.2	2.7	0.6	0.3	0.1	2.5	0.4	0.6	0.6	1.0	0.2	0.2	0.4	0.3	n	0.1	0.9
United States	1.6	5.8	0.7	1.2	2.4	2.4	6.3	1.1	0.1	1.6	1.6	0.3	1.2	25.3	n	0.9	1.5
Total from OECD countries	*38.6*	*69.8*	*31.6*	*21.5*	*11.9*	*36.7*	*26.2*	*18.4*	*8.2*	*32.0*	*44.9*	*12.6*	*15.8*	*44.8*	*n*	*5.8*	*27.9*
Brazil	n	0.4	1.6	0.3	0.1	0.4	0.2	10.6	n	0.8	0.1	0.2	a	3.3	n	0.3	0.7
Chile	n	0.4	0.4	n	0.1	0.6	n	n	n	0.3	n	n	4.9	a	n	0.4	0.3
China	0.8	2.3	0.9	66.1	65.1	3.9	1.7	0.4	0.6	16.7	7.8	0.2	0.9	1.0	n	11.5	15.9
Estonia	0.1	1.4	0.1	n	n	0.6	0.2	n	n	0.1	a	0.1	n	n	1.2	0.4	0.2
India	0.3	n	0.7	0.3	1.6	1.1	1.9	0.1	n	6.2	0.5	0.7	0.2	0.1	n	1.9	5.5
Israel	5.4	0.2	2.2	n	n	0.2	0.3	n	0.1	0.4	0.1	0.2	0.2	0.2	n	0.8	0.5
Russian Federation	1.6	3.5	1.3	0.3	1.2	5.6	4.4	0.3	3.4	1.4	8.9	0.9	0.4	0.4	a	2.7	1.6
Slovenia	0.2	0.2	0.7	n	n	n	0.1	0.1	n	0.1	n	a	0.2	n	n	0.1	0.1
Main geographic regions																	
Total from Africa	*2.0*	*1.9*	*9.2*	*0.7*	*0.9*	*9.3*	*4.1*	*63.7*	*2.0*	*11.0*	*0.7*	*0.3*	*10.7*	*0.2*	*n*	*17.6*	*12.0*
Total from Asia	*14.4*	*8.9*	*10.2*	*94.2*	*92.1*	*15.3*	*17.1*	*2.1*	*53.7*	*47.4*	*9.8*	*1.7*	*3.8*	*2.2*	*34.6*	*57.3*	*48.9*
Total from Europe	*81.1*	*76.9*	*66.4*	*2.2*	*2.4*	*46.4*	*69.5*	*17.8*	*28.8*	*24.9*	*87.3*	*95.8*	*13.5*	*15.5*	*19.4*	*16.8*	*23.7*
of which, from EU19 countries	*30.5*	*51.9*	*26.5*	*1.5*	*0.8*	*30.0*	*11.3*	*15.6*	*7.6*	*16.9*	*41.4*	*12.1*	*11.6*	*13.9*	*n*	*m*	*m*
Total from North America	*2.2*	*7.6*	*1.0*	*1.4*	*3.2*	*2.8*	*8.2*	*1.9*	*0.1*	*3.7*	*1.7*	*0.3*	*2.0*	*25.9*	*n*	*1.0*	*3.3*
Total from Oceania	*0.1*	*0.6*	*0.1*	*0.4*	*0.5*	*0.2*	*0.1*	*0.2*	*0.3*	*0.8*	*0.1*	*0.2*	*0.1*	*0.8*	*n*	*0.1*	*0.7*
Total from South America	*0.3*	*3.9*	*7.9*	*0.9*	*0.9*	*2.4*	*0.8*	*14.3*	*n*	*5.7*	*0.3*	*0.6*	*69.9*	*55.3*	*n*	*7.2*	*5.9*
Not specified	*n*	*0.2*	*5.1*	*n*	*n*	*23.5*	*0.1*	*n*	*15.1*	*6.6*	*n*	*1.1*	*n*	*0.1*	*46.0*	*n*	*5.5*
Total from all countries	*100.0*	*100.0*	*100.0*	*100.0*	*100.0*	*100.0*	*100.0*	*100.0*	*100.0*	*100.0*	*100.0*	*100.0*	*100.0*	*100.0*	*100.0*	*100.0*	*100.0*

1. International students are defined on the basis of their country of residence.
2. Excludes data for social advancement education.
3. International students are defined on the basis of their country of prior education.
4. Excludes advanced research programmes.
5. Excludes tertiary-type B programmes.
6. Foreign students are defined on the basis of their country of citizenship, these data are not comparable with data on international students and are therefore presented separately in the table.
7. Excludes tertiary programmes (advance research programmes only).
8. Excludes private institutions.
Source: OECD. See Annex 3 for notes (www.oecd.org/edu/eag2007).
Please refer to the Reader's Guide for information concerning the symbols replacing missing data.
StatLink ᐧ◖⬛ http://dx.doi.org/10.1787/068417017111

C3

Table C3.3.
Citizens studying abroad in tertiary education, by country of destination (2005)
Number of students enrolled in tertiary education in a given country of destination as a percentage of all students enrolled abroad, based on head counts

The table shows for each country the proportion of students studying abroad in tertiary education in a given country of destination. Reading the second column: 6.3% of Czech citizens enrolled in tertiary education abroad study in Austria, 10.6% of German citizens enrolled in tertiary education abroad study in Austria, etc.

Reading the first row: 2.5% of Australian citizens enrolled in tertiary education abroad study in France, 3.4% of Australian citizens enrolled in tertiary education abroad study in Germany, etc.

| | Countries of destination — OECD countries | | | | | | | | | | | | | | | | | | | |
Countries of origin	Australia[1]	Austria[2]	Belgium[3]	Canada	Czech Republic[5]	Denmark	Finland	France	Germany[4]	Greece[5]	Hungary	Iceland	Ireland[6,7]	Italy[2]	Japan	Korea	Luxembourg	Mexico	Netherlands[4]	New Zealand
	(1)	(2)	(3)	(4)	(5)	(6)	(7)	(8)	(9)	(10)	(11)	(12)	(13)	(14)	(15)	(16)	(17)	(18)	(19)	(20)
Australia	a	0.3	0.4	m	0.1	0.5	0.3	2.5	3.4	0.1	0.1	n	0.6	0.6	3.7	0.5	m	m	0.7	30.0
Austria	1.3	a	0.4	m	0.2	0.4	0.3	3.3	52.5	n	0.3	0.1	0.4	1.8	0.5	n	m	m	1.7	0.3
Belgium	0.6	0.7	a	m	n	0.2	0.2	24.6	9.3	0.2	n	n	0.6	1.8	0.4	0.1	m	m	20.8	n
Canada	8.1	0.1	0.3	a	0.1	0.2	0.2	2.9	1.3	n	0.2	n	0.8	0.3	0.6	0.3	m	m	0.3	1.0
Czech Republic	1.7	6.3	0.8	m	a	0.5	0.7	9.3	34.7	0.1	0.2	n	0.4	2.3	0.5	0.1	m	m	1.4	0.3
Denmark	2.1	0.9	0.7	m	0.1	a	0.7	4.3	9.3	n	0.1	0.8	0.4	0.6	0.3	n	m	m	2.3	1.2
Finland	0.9	1.9	0.4	m	n	1.7	a	3.3	9.7	n	0.4	0.3	0.8	0.8	0.4	n	m	m	1.8	0.1
France	1.1	0.8	28.4	m	n	0.4	0.3	a	12.1	n	0.1	n	1.3	1.6	0.6	n	m	m	1.3	0.5
Germany	2.5	10.6	0.8	m	0.3	1.4	0.5	8.8	a	0.2	1.7	0.1	1.0	2.1	0.5	0.1	m	m	13.8	1.6
Greece	0.1	0.5	1.0	m	0.3	0.1	0.1	4.6	14.7	a	0.3	n	0.1	14.4	n	n	m	m	0.8	n
Hungary	0.7	14.2	1.0	m	0.4	0.6	1.3	7.6	36.4	0.1	a	n	0.2	2.2	1.2	0.1	m	m	3.9	0.1
Iceland	0.6	0.7	1.2	m	n	42.6	0.6	1.3	3.8	n	0.8	a	0.1	0.4	0.2	n	m	m	2.3	0.1
Ireland	0.9	0.2	1.2	m	0.1	0.3	0.2	2.4	2.2	n	0.2	n	a	0.1	0.1	n	m	m	0.5	0.1
Italy	0.5	16.1	6.2	m	0.1	0.3	0.3	10.4	19.9	0.1	0.1	n	0.5	a	0.2	n	m	m	1.3	n
Japan	5.4	0.4	0.3	m	n	0.1	0.2	3.4	3.9	n	n	n	0.1	0.3	a	1.8	m	m	0.3	1.5
Korea	4.4	0.3	0.1	m	n	n	n	2.2	5.5	n	n	n	n	0.1	23.4	a	m	m	0.2	n
Luxembourg	0.2	5.3	21.5	m	n	n	n	23.6	31.0	0.1	n	n	0.1	0.4	n	n	a	m	0.6	n
Mexico	1.7	0.2	0.3	m	n	0.3	0.2	6.0	4.9	n	n	n	0.1	0.7	0.5	0.1	m	a	0.5	0.3
Netherlands	2.3	1.3	1.6	m	0.1	1.6	0.9	6.4	19.2	0.1	0.1	0.1	0.9	1.1	0.8	n	m	m	a	0.4
New Zealand	47.2	0.1	n	m	0.1	0.4	0.2	1.2	1.8	n	n	n	0.4	0.1	1.8	0.6	m	m	0.7	a
Norway	16.6	0.5	1.5	m	1.0	13.2	0.4	1.9	5.2	n	4.7	0.2	1.2	0.5	0.2	n	m	m	1.6	1.7
Poland	0.6	4.0	1.0	m	0.6	1.5	0.4	9.9	49.0	0.1	0.2	n	0.4	3.6	0.3	n	m	m	2.0	n
Portugal	0.3	0.4	6.4	m	0.7	0.2	0.2	18.5	12.7	n	0.1	n	0.1	0.7	0.2	n	m	m	2.0	0.1
Slovak Republic	0.6	6.5	1.2	m	53.9	0.1	0.1	2.2	9.1	n	12.5	n	0.1	0.9	0.2	n	m	m	0.4	n
Spain	0.4	1.4	3.9	m	0.1	0.6	0.5	13.3	21.8	n	0.1	n	1.3	1.7	0.3	n	m	m	3.0	n
Sweden	7.2	1.4	0.4	m	0.4	8.1	3.9	4.1	5.5	0.1	1.2	0.2	0.6	0.9	0.8	n	m	m	1.2	1.5
Switzerland	3.4	2.8	1.8	m	0.1	0.6	0.4	15.3	22.6	0.1	0.1	0.1	0.3	11.0	0.3	n	m	m	1.3	0.3
Turkey	0.5	3.6	0.6	m	0.1	0.4	0.1	4.4	48.9	0.1	0.1	n	n	0.4	0.3	0.1	m	m	1.3	n
United Kingdom	7.6	0.8	0.7	m	1.5	2.1	0.9	10.5	9.0	0.1	0.2	0.1	5.4	1.1	1.8	0.1	m	m	3.3	1.9
United States	8.3	0.9	0.5	m	0.3	0.8	0.5	6.3	8.7	n	0.6	0.1	5.6	0.8	4.0	1.0	m	m	1.1	5.4
Total from OECD countries	*3.4*	*3.0*	*3.2*	*m*	*1.5*	*1.1*	*0.3*	*5.9*	*14.0*	*n*	*0.7*	*n*	*0.9*	*1.8*	*3.5*	*0.2*	*m*	*m*	*2.4*	*1.1*
Brazil	2.0	0.2	0.8	m	n	0.4	0.2	9.3	9.0	n	n	n	n	3.7	2.2	0.1	m	m	0.5	0.2
Chile	1.2	0.1	1.2	m	0.1	0.3	0.2	5.9	6.8	n	n	n	n	1.9	0.5	0.1	m	m	0.5	0.5
China	9.2	0.3	0.4	m	n	0.4	0.3	3.5	6.7	n	n	n	0.4	0.1	20.6	2.5	m	m	1.0	5.7
Estonia	0.2	0.7	0.6	m	0.1	2.7	13.8	2.4	17.8	n	0.2	0.2	0.2	0.8	0.5	n	m	m	0.7	n
India	14.7	n	0.1	m	n	0.2	0.1	0.4	3.1	n	n	n	0.2	0.2	0.2	0.2	m	m	0.1	1.1
Israel	2.1	0.3	0.4	m	1.2	0.4	0.2	2.4	9.6	0.3	5.8	n	n	7.9	0.3	n	m	m	1.9	0.1
Russian Fed.	1.0	0.9	0.5	m	1.4	0.9	2.6	6.2	28.3	0.4	0.5	n	0.3	1.4	0.9	0.4	m	m	1.2	0.5
Slovenia	0.4	20.0	0.9	m	1.0	0.2	0.3	3.1	23.0	n	0.9	n	n	11.2	0.6	n	m	m	1.5	n

Note: The proportion of students abroad is based only on the total of students enrolled in countries reporting data to the OECD and UNESCO Institute for Statistics.

1. Data by country of origin relate to international students defined on the basis of their country of residence.
2. Excludes tertiary-type B programmes.
3. Excludes data for social advancement education.
4. Excludes advanced research programmes.
5. Excludes tertiary programmes (advance research programmes only).
6. Data by country of origin relate to international students defined on the basis of their country of prior education.
7. Excludes part-time students.
8. Excludes private institutions.

Source: OECD. See Annex 3 for notes (*www.oecd.org/edu/eag2007*).

Please refer to the Reader's Guide for information concerning the symbols replacing missing data.

StatLink ⌘ http://dx.doi.org/10.1787/068417017111

Table C3.3. *(continued)*

Citizens studying abroad in tertiary education, by country of destination (2005)

Number of students enrolled in tertiary education in a given country of destination as a percentage of all students enrolled abroad, based on head counts

The table shows for each country the proportion of students studying abroad in tertiary education in a given country of destination. Reading the second column: 6.3% of Czech citizens enrolled in tertiary education abroad study in Austria, 10.6% of German citizens enrolled in tertiary education abroad study in Austria, etc.

Reading the first row: 2.5% of Australian citizens enrolled in tertiary education abroad study in France, 3.4% of Australian citizens enrolled in tertiary education abroad study in Germany, etc.

C3

	Countries of destination																		
	OECD countries											**Partner economies**							
Countries of origin	Norway	Poland	Portugal	Slovak Republic	Spain	Sweden	Switzerland	Turkey	United Kingdom[1]	United States[1]	Total OECD destinations	Brazil[5]	Chile	Estonia[1]	Israel	Russian Federation[4,8]	Slovenia	Total partner economies destinations	Total all reporting destinations
	(21)	(22)	(23)	(24)	(25)	(26)	(27)	(28)	(29)	(30)	(31)	(32)	(33)	(34)	(35)	(36)	(37)	(38)	(39)
OECD countries																			
Australia	0.3	0.1	0.3	n	0.4	3.7	0.6	0.3	17.6	30.3	97.2	n	0.1	n	m	n	n	2.8	100.0
Austria	0.3	0.3	0.1	0.1	1.4	4.4	7.4	0.1	11.1	7.8	96.4	n	0.1	n	m	n	0.1	3.6	100.0
Belgium	0.3	0.1	0.7	n	3.2	2.4	3.0	n	22.5	7.3	98.9	n	n	n	m	n	n	1.1	100.0
Canada	0.2	0.5	0.3	n	0.2	0.9	0.6	n	9.9	69.4	98.7	n	n	n	m	n	n	1.3	100.0
Czech Republic	0.6	2.8	0.3	6.2	1.8	3.4	2.6	n	8.6	13.4	99.3	n	n	n	m	n	n	0.7	100.0
Denmark	14.1	0.1	0.1	n	1.6	16.0	1.7	0.1	26.1	14.6	98.2	n	0.1	n	m	n	n	1.8	100.0
Finland	3.0	0.1	0.1	n	0.8	40.9	1.2	n	18.3	6.2	93.3	n	0.1	2.9	m	n	n	6.7	100.0
France	0.3	0.1	1.9	n	3.2	2.8	7.8	n	21.7	12.7	99.1	n	0.1	n	m	n	n	0.9	100.0
Germany	0.7	0.4	0.6	n	2.2	4.4	11.8	0.2	18.8	13.5	98.5	n	0.1	n	m	n	n	1.5	100.0
Greece	n	0.1	n	0.2	0.3	0.6	0.7	2.4	44.2	4.8	90.3	n	n	n	m	n	n	9.7	100.0
Hungary	0.4	1.0	0.1	0.3	0.8	2.5	2.7	n	7.4	12.3	97.7	n	n	0.1	m	n	0.2	2.3	100.0
Iceland	7.5	n	n	n	0.5	13.9	0.3	n	9.8	12.9	99.9	n	n	n	m	n	n	0.1	100.0
Ireland	0.1	0.1	0.1	n	0.4	0.8	0.2	n	84.4	5.3	99.8	n	n	n	m	n	n	0.2	100.0
Italy	0.2	0.1	0.5	n	6.2	1.8	11.6	n	13.7	8.8	98.9	n	n	n	m	n	0.2	1.1	100.0
Japan	0.1	n	n	n	0.2	0.4	0.4	n	9.8	70.2	98.8	n	n	n	m	n	n	1.2	100.0
Korea	n	n	n	n	0.1	0.1	0.2	n	4.0	57.8	98.7	n	n	n	m	n	n	1.3	100.0
Luxembourg	n	n	0.8	n	0.1	0.1	4.0	n	11.6	0.6	100.0	n	n	n	m	n	n	n	100.0
Mexico	0.1	n	0.1	n	13.3	0.7	0.6	n	7.7	56.7	95.0	n	0.2	n	m	n	n	5.0	100.0
Netherlands	1.8	0.1	0.8	n	2.6	7.8	3.7	0.1	27.4	17.3	98.7	n	0.1	n	m	n	n	1.3	100.0
New Zealand	0.2	n	n	n	0.3	1.2	0.5	n	15.0	25.2	97.1	n	0.1	n	m	n	n	2.9	100.0
Norway	a	4.0	0.1	0.4	1.5	9.8	0.7	n	22.9	10.1	99.0	n	n	n	m	n	n	1.0	100.0
Poland	0.5	a	0.3	0.1	1.5	2.7	1.6	n	6.7	9.2	96.4	n	n	n	m	n	n	3.6	100.0
Portugal	0.2	0.1	a	n	16.6	1.3	6.1	n	20.2	6.4	93.7	0.3	n	n	m	n	n	6.3	100.0
Slovak Republic	0.3	0.7	2.2	a	0.4	0.3	1.1	n	1.9	3.4	95.8	n	n	n	m	n	0.1	4.2	100.0
Spain	0.4	0.1	2.2	n	a	4.1	6.3	n	23.1	14.1	98.6	0.1	0.2	n	m	n	n	1.4	100.0
Sweden	8.1	1.3	0.2	n	1.5	a	1.8	n	24.6	23.3	98.2	n	0.1	0.1	m	n	n	1.8	100.0
Switzerland	0.6	0.1	1.0	n	2.3	2.8	a	n	15.7	14.8	97.7	n	0.1	n	m	n	n	2.3	100.0
Turkey	0.1	n	n	n	n	0.4	1.4	a	3.7	25.0	91.4	n	n	n	m	n	n	8.6	100.0
United Kingdom	1.5	0.2	0.5	n	2.5	3.8	1.7	0.5	a	39.4	97.2	n	n	n	m	n	n	2.8	100.0
United States	0.8	1.6	0.5	n	1.5	2.7	1.1	n	37.2	a	90.3	n	1.3	n	m	n	n	9.7	100.0
Total from OECD countries	*0.6*	*0.3*	*0.4*	*0.1*	*1.9*	*2.6*	*3.3*	*0.2*	*17.0*	*27.3*	*96.8*	*n*	*0.1*	*0.1*	*n*	*n*	*n*	*3.2*	*100.0*
Partner economies																			
Brazil	0.3	0.1	9.1	n	9.3	0.7	1.6	n	5.7	38.3	93.7	a	0.3	n	m	n	n	6.3	100.0
Chile	0.9	n	n	n	15.6	2.9	1.1	n	3.5	38.0	81.6	0.6	a	n	m	n	n	18.4	100.0
China	0.1	n	n	n	0.1	0.3	0.2	n	13.0	22.8	87.8	n	n	n	m	n	n	12.2	100.0
Estonia	1.9	0.4	n	n	2.4	6.7	0.5	n	4.3	6.8	64.0	n	n	a	m	24.3	n	36.0	100.0
India	0.1	0.1	n	n	n	0.4	0.2	n	12.0	60.4	94.2	n	n	n	m	n	n	5.8	100.0
Israel	0.2	0.3	n	1.2	1.0	0.2	0.6	0.2	8.8	27.3	72.7	n	n	n	a	n	n	27.3	100.0
Russian Fed.	1.7	1.1	0.1	n	1.0	1.8	1.4	1.5	4.7	12.3	73.1	n	0.2	m	n	a	n	26.9	100.0
Slovenia	n	0.2	0.5	0.1	1.0	1.8	1.7	n	11.7	11.8	92.0	n	n	n	m	n	a	8.0	100.0

Note: The proportion of students abroad is based only on the total of students enrolled in countries reporting data to the OECD and UNESCO Institute for Statistics.

1. Data by country of origin relate to international students defined on the basis of their country of residence.
2. Excludes tertiary-type B programmes.
3. Excludes data for social advancement education.
4. Excludes advanced research programmes.
5. Excludes tertiary programmes (advance research programmes only).
6. Data by country of origin relate to international students defined on the basis of their country of prior education.
7. Excludes part-time students.
8. Excludes private institutions.

Source: OECD. See Annex 3 for notes (*www.oecd.org/edu/eag2007*).

Please refer to the Reader's Guide for information concerning the symbols replacing missing data.

StatLink ᴍⓢ▮ http://dx.doi.org/10.1787/068417017111

Table C3.4.
Distribution of international and foreign students in tertiary education,
by level and type of tertiary education (2005)

	Tertiary-type B programmes	Tertiary-type A programmes	Advanced research programmes	Total tertiary programmes
	(1)	(2)	(3)	(4)
International students				
Australia[1]	6.2	89.9	3.9	100
Austria[1,2,3]	m	91.0	9.0	100
Belgium[1]	29.4	63.7	7.0	100
Canada	m	m	m	m
Denmark[1]	9.5	87.6	2.9	100
Finland[3,4]	m	85.7	14.3	100
France[1]	10.0	78.0	12.0	100
Greece[1,5]	21.3	78.7	n	100
Hungary[1]	0.5	94.2	5.2	100
Ireland	m	m	m	m
Japan[1]	24.2	65.4	10.5	100
Luxembourg	m	m	m	m
Mexico	m	m	m	m
Netherlands[5]	a	100.0	m	100
New Zealand[1]	26.1	72.0	1.9	100
Norway[1]	3.2	91.2	5.7	100
Slovak Republic[1]	0.7	94.5	4.8	100
Spain[1,3]	m	67.0	33.0	100
Sweden[1]	1.1	98.9	n	100
Switzerland[3,4]	m	72.9	27.1	100
United Kingdom[1]	9.1	79.4	11.5	100
United States	12.7	71.6	15.7	100
Brazil[1,3]	m	57.2	42.8	100
Estonia[1]	4.0	91.0	5.1	100
Israel	m	m	m	m
Slovenia[1]	26.0	70.1	3.9	100
Foreign students				
Czech Republic[6]	2.0	88.3	9.7	100
Germany[5,6]	5.2	94.8	m	100
Iceland[6]	1.7	94.8	3.5	100
Italy[6]	2.9	93.6	3.6	100
Korea[6]	m	m	m	m
Poland[6]	0.1	89.5	10.4	100
Portugal[6]	1.6	90.5	7.9	100
Turkey[6]	6.7	88.9	4.3	100
Chile[6]	27.2	71.7	1.1	100
Russian Federation[5,6,7]	7.2	92.8	m	100

OECD countries / *Partner economies* (row group labels)

1. International students are defined on the basis of their country of residence.
2. Based on the number of registrations, not head-counts.
3. Excludes tertiary-type B programmes.
4. International students are defined on the basis of their country of prior education.
5. Excludes advanced research programmes.
6. Foreign students are defined on the basis of their country of citizenship, these data are not comparable with data on international students and are therefore presented separately in the table.
7. Excludes private institutions.
Source: OECD. See Annex 3 for notes (*www.oecd.org/edu/eag2007*).
Please refer to the Reader's Guide for information concerning the symbols replacing missing data.
StatLink ᴍ𝔰𝕃 http://dx.doi.org/10.1787/068417017111

Table C3.5.
Distribution of international and foreign students in tertiary education, by field of education (2005)

	Agriculture	Education	Engineering, manufacturing and construction	Health and welfare	Humanities and arts	Sciences	Services	Social sciences, business and law	Not known or un-specified	Total all fields of education
International students										
Australia[1]	0.7	3.3	11.3	7.4	7.5	17.7	1.5	50.7	n	100
Austria[1,2]	2.1	5.4	12.0	8.1	24.7	10.9	1.3	35.5	n	100
Belgium[1]	10.8	5.3	7.9	44.4	7.8	7.4	0.9	15.6	n	100
Canada	m	m	m	m	m	m	m	m	m	m
Denmark[1]	2.0	4.8	15.5	20.7	17.6	7.1	0.7	31.5	n	100
Finland[2,3]	2.3	2.4	30.6	12.1	16.4	9.5	3.3	23.4	n	100
France	m	m	m	m	m	m	m	m	m	m
Germany[2,4]	1.5	4.5	19.3	5.9	23.0	17.4	1.3	27.0	0.2	100
Greece	m	m	m	m	m	m	m	m	m	m
Hungary[1]	11.4	6.3	14.1	26.4	13.2	7.1	1.9	19.6	n	100
Ireland	m	m	m	m	m	m	m	m	m	m
Japan[1]	2.5	2.6	12.9	2.5	25.2	1.2	2.4	34.7	16.1	100
Korea	m	m	m	m	m	m	m	m	m	m
Luxembourg	m	m	m	m	m	m	m	m	m	m
Mexico	m	m	m	m	m	m	m	m	m	m
Netherlands[4]	2.4	7.5	5.5	15.1	12.9	6.4	3.2	47.1	n	100
New Zealand[1,4]	0.7	2.3	5.3	4.4	4.9	12.1	1.9	60.4	7.9	100
Norway[1]	1.4	5.5	8.5	9.9	16.9	10.6	3.5	35.1	8.6	100
Spain[1,2,4]	1.8	3.0	10.5	22.9	14.7	8.2	3.2	35.5	n	100
Sweden[1]	1.0	3.4	22.9	9.1	16.8	13.0	1.8	32.0	n	100
Switzerland[2,3]	1.3	3.7	16.3	6.2	18.4	17.1	2.4	33.0	1.5	100
United Kingdom[1]	0.8	4.0	15.1	8.7	14.1	14.6	1.0	40.1	1.4	100
United States[1]	0.3	3.0	15.6	6.5	11.0	18.7	1.8	31.0	12.0	100
Brazil	m	m	m	m	m	m	m	m	m	m
Estonia	m	m	m	m	m	m	m	m	m	m
Israel	m	m	m	m	m	m	m	m	m	m
Slovenia[1]	2.1	6.1	16.1	14.1	21.0	8.8	3.9	28.0	n	100
Foreign students										
Czech Republic[5]	2.4	5.6	15.5	20.3	10.0	11.2	1.6	33.4	n	100
Iceland[5]	1.0	7.9	4.3	4.8	49.2	16.1	1.7	15.1	n	100
Italy[5]	1.9	1.9	13.9	23.4	19.1	6.5	1.4	30.9	1.0	100
Poland[5]	0.8	6.3	4.3	22.1	21.1	5.5	3.2	33.9	2.8	100
Portugal[5]	1.5	4.9	18.8	7.7	8.4	7.9	5.2	45.5	n	100
Slovak Republic[5]	10.8	5.3	11.8	29.1	14.1	6.5	5.6	16.8	n	100
Turkey[5]	2.2	8.3	14.4	14.4	9.2	8.7	3.9	38.8	n	100
Chile[5]	2.7	2.8	9.6	5.3	4.4	10.6	5.6	20.5	38.4	100
Russian Federation	m	m	m	m	m	m	m	m	m	m

1. International students are defined on the basis of their country of residence.
2. Excludes tertiary-type B programmes.
3. International students are defined on the basis of their country of prior education.
4. Excludes advanced research programmes.
5. Foreign students are defined on the basis of their country of citizenship, these data are not comparable with data on international students and are therefore presented separately in the table and chart.
Source: OECD. See Annex 3 for notes (*www.oecd.org/edu/eag2007*).
Please refer to the Reader's Guide for information concerning the symbols replacing missing data.
StatLink 🔗 http://dx.doi.org/10.1787/068417017111

Table C3.6.
Trends in the number of foreign students enrolled outside their country of origin (2000 to 2005)
Number of foreign students enrolled in tertiary education outside their country of origin, head counts

	Number of foreign students						Index of change (2005)				
	2005	2004	2003	2002	2001	2000	2004=100	2003=100	2002=100	2001=100	2000=100
Foreign students enrolled worldwide	2 725 996	2 598 660	2 425 915	2 188 544	1 896 265	1 818 759	105	112	125	144	150
Foreign students enrolled in OECD countries	2 296 016	2 195 550	2 040 574	1 856 600	1 604 565	1 545 534	105	113	124	143	149

Note: Figures are based on the number of foreign students enrolled in OECD and partner economies reporting data to the OECD and UNESCO Institute for Statistics, in order to provide a global picture of foreign students worldwide. The coverage of these reporting countries has evolved over time, therefore missing data have been imputed wherever necessary to ensure the comparability of time series over time. Given the inclusion of UNESCO data for partner economies and the imputation of missing data, the estimates of the number of foreign students may differ from those published in previous editions of *Education at a Glance*.
Source: OECD and UNESCO Institute for Statistics for most data on partner economies. See Annex 3 for notes (*www.oecd.org/edu/eag2007*).
StatLink ᵐˢᵖ http://dx.doi.org/10.1787/068417017111

Table C3.7.
Percentage of tertiary qualifications awarded to international and foreign students, by type of tertiary education (2005)
Calculations based on the number of graduates

	Proportion of international graduates in total graduate output				
	Tertiary type A programmes		Tertiary type B programmes		Advanced research programmes
	First degrees	Second degrees	First degrees	Second degrees	
	(1)	(2)	(3)	(4)	(5)
International graduates					
Australia[1]	22.3	53.2	m	m	19.4
Austria[1]	8.9	14.2	m	m	15.9
Canada	m	m	m	m	m
Denmark[1]	4.7	5.8	3.4	a	7.9
Finland[2,3]	3.3	x(1)	m	a	7.6
France	m	m	m	m	m
Germany[2]	5.8	30.6	m	a	13.4
Greece	m	m	m	m	m
Iceland	m	m	m	m	m
Ireland	m	m	m	m	m
Italy[4]	m	m	m	a	m
Japan[1]	1.5	8.0	2.6	a	15.7
Korea	m	m	m	m	m
Luxembourg	m	m	m	m	m
Mexico	m	m	m	m	m
Netherlands	m	m	m	m	m
New Zealand[1]	17.3	18.8	23.2	n	12.4
Norway[1]	1.4	8.0	1.5	a	7.8
Poland	m	m	m	m	m
Spain	m	m	m	m	m
Sweden[1]	2.6	8.9	0.6	a	5.7
Switzerland[2]	10.1	19.6	m	m	39.1
United Kingdom[1]	11.8	35.4	5.9	x(3)	38.9
United States[1]	3.2	11.4	1.6	a	27.3
Brazil	m	m	m	m	m
Chile	m	m	m	m	m
Estonia	m	m	m	m	m
Israel	m	m	m	m	m
Russian Federation	m	m	m	m	m
Slovenia[1]	0.5	1.5	0.6	1.3	2.7
Foreign graduates					
Belgium[4,5]	21.6	x(1)	5.3	8.1	24.1
Czech Republic[4]	4.2	1.8	2.5	n	7.0
Hungary[4]	2.5	1.3	0.1	a	8.1
Portugal[4]	2.9	4.0	2.2	n	6.8
Slovak Republic[4]	0.9	0.6	m	a	1.4
Turkey[4]	1.0	1.3	0.1	a	2.0

OECD countries / Partner economies / OECD countries

1. International graduates are defined on the basis of their country of residence.
2. International graduates are defined on the basis of their country or prior education.
3. Year of reference 2004.
4. Foreign graduates are defined on the basis of their country of citizenship, these data are not comparable with data on international graduates and are therefore presented separately in the table and chart.
5. Excludes the German-speaking Community of Belgium.
Source: OECD. See Annex 3 for notes (*www.oecd.org/edu/eag2007*).
Please refer to the Reader's Guide for information concerning the symbols replacing missing data.
StatLink ⬛ᴨˢ🔄 http://dx.doi.org/10.1787/068417017111

HOW SUCCESSFUL ARE STUDENTS IN MOVING FROM EDUCATION TO WORK?

This indicator shows the number of years that young people are expected to spend in education, employment and non-employment and examines the education and employment status of young people by gender. During the past decade, young people have spent more time in initial education, delaying their entry into the world of work. Part of this additional time is spent combining work and education, a practice that is widespread in some countries. Once young people have completed their initial education, access to the labour market is often impeded by periods of unemployment or non-employment, although this situation affects males and females differently. Based on the current situation of persons between the ages of 15 and 29, this indicator gives a picture of major trends in the transition from school to work.

Key results

Chart C4.1. Share of 25-to-29-year-olds who are unemployed and not in education, by level of educational attainment (2005)

In this chart the height of the bars indicates the percentage of 25-to-29-year-olds not in education and unemployed, for each level of educational attainment.

☐ Below upper secondary education
▨ Upper secondary and post-secondary non-tertiary education
■ Tertiary education

At the end of the transition period, when most young people have finished studying, access to employment is linked to the education level attained. Not attaining an upper secondary qualification is clearly a serious handicap. Conversely, tertiary education offers a premium for most job seekers (except in Greece, Italy and New Zealand).

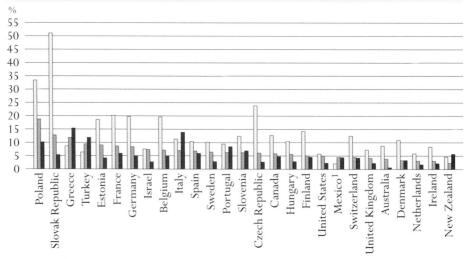

1. Year of reference 2004.
Countries are ranked in descending order of the ratio of the population not in education and unemployed to the 25-to-29-year-old population having attained upper secondary and post-secondary non-tertiary education.
Source: OECD. Table C4.3. See Annex 3 for notes (*www.oecd.org/edu/eag2007*).
StatLink ⸬ http://dx.doi.org/10.1787/068418024204

Other highlights of this indicator

■ On average across OECD countries, a young person aged 15 in 2005 can expect to continue in formal education for about 6.7 years. In 20 of the 29 OECD countries and 3 partner economies for which data are available, this period ranges from five to seven and a half years. However, the range of this figure is wide, from 3.1 years (Turkey) to a high of 8.6 years (Iceland).

■ Among the younger cohort (15-to-19-year-olds) the proportion of individuals in school has increased by 4 percentage points, from 80.5 to 84.5%, between 2000 and 2005 in the OECD countries. This growth has been greatest in the Czech Republic and the Slovak Republic where increases exceed 8 percentage points during the period.

■ In addition to the expected number of years spent in education, a young person aged 15 can expect to hold a job for 6.1 of the 15 years to come, to be unemployed for a total of 0.8 years and to be out of the labour market (not employed, not in education and not looking for a job) for 1.3 years on average in OECD countries.

■ On average, completing upper secondary education reduces unemployment among 20-to-24-year-olds by 7.3 percentage points and that of 25-to-29-year-olds by 7.0 percentage points. Not attaining an upper secondary qualification is clearly a serious impediment to entering employment, while obtaining a tertiary qualification increases the likelihood job seekers will find employment.

Policy context

All OECD countries are experiencing rapid social and economic changes that make the transition to working life more uncertain for younger individuals. In some OECD countries, education and work largely occur consecutively, while in other OECD countries they may be concurrent. The ways in which education and work are combined can significantly affect the transition process. Of particular interest, for example, is the extent to which working (beyond the usual summer jobs for students) while studying may facilitate entry into the labour force.

The transition from education to work is a complex enterprise that not only depends on the length and quality of the schooling received but also on general labour market and economic conditions in a country. High general unemployment rates make the transition substantially more difficult and unemployment rates among those entering the labour market typically reflect this by exhibiting rates that are above those of the more experienced workforce.

General labour market conditions also influence the schooling decisions of younger individuals: in poor labour markets younger individuals tend to stay on longer in education whereas the opposite applies in good labour markets. That employment prospects influence the length and timing of schooling is rational in the sense that high unemployment rates drives down the opportunity costs of education (foregone earnings), which tend to be the most prominent component of the cost of education in most countries.

Taken together, the interaction between the education system and the labour market system makes it difficult to understand the processes of school-to-work transition, but it is nevertheless an important area where policy can make a substantial contribution towards facilitating this transition.

Evidence and explanations

On average, a person aged 15 in 2005 can expect to continue in education for 6.7 years (Table C4.1a). This average figure refers to all 15-year-olds, and some will evidently continue in education for a longer period while others will do so for a shorter time. In 20 of the 29 countries studied, including the partner economy Israel, a 15-year-old can expect to spend from 5.0 to 7.5 additional years in education, on average. However, a large gap separates the groups at each extreme: with Denmark, Finland, Iceland and Poland and the partner economies Estonia and Slovenia (more than eight years in education on average) on the one hand, and Mexico as well as Turkey (with less than five years on average) on the other.

In addition to the average 6.7 years spent in education, a person aged 15 can expect to hold a job for 6.1 of the 15 years to come, to be unemployed for a total of 0.8 years and to be out of the labour market for 1.3 years, neither in education nor seeking work (Table C4.1a).

The average cumulative duration of unemployment varies significantly among countries. This reflects differences in general unemployment rates in countries as well as differences in the duration of education. The cumulative average duration of unemployment is six months or less in Denmark, Iceland, Ireland, Japan, Mexico, the Netherlands, Norway and the United States but around 1.8 years in Poland and the Slovak Republic, which for these two countries is still a large improvement over unemployment figures in recent years.

Chart C4.2. **Expected years in education and not in education for 15-to-29-year-olds (2005)**

Number of years, by work status

☐ Not in education, not in the labour force
■ Not in education, unemployed
■ Not in education, employed
☐ In education, employed (including work-study programmes)
■ In education, not employed

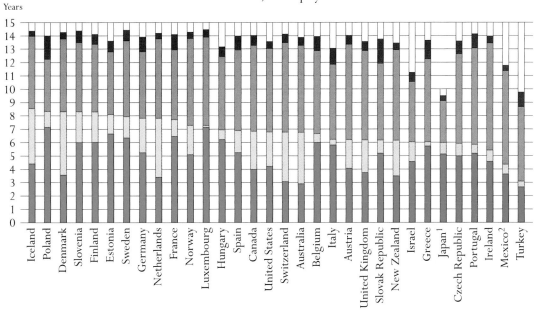

1. Data refer to 15-to-24-year-olds.
2. Year of reference 2004.
Countries are ranked in descending order of the expected years in education of the youth population.
Source: OECD. Table C4.1a. See Annex 3 for notes (*www.oecd.org/edu/eag2007*).
StatLink ⫴⫴ http://dx.doi.org/10.1787/068418024204

The average overall number of expected years in education is higher for females (6.9 years compared with 6.6 for males). In all countries except Austria, Germany, Mexico, the Netherlands, Switzerland and Turkey, and the partner economy Estonia, females spend more years in education than males. In Turkey, female students can expect to receive nearly one year less of education than their male counterparts whereas in Norway, Spain and Sweden the opposite applies (Chart C4.3). However, up to age 29, males are expected to be employed to a much greater extent than females. This difference is close to one and a half years in the OECD countries and also largely reflects the fact that females are more likely to be outside both the education and labour market systems than are males (not in education, not employed and not looking for a job).

However, males and females differ very little in terms of the expected number of years in unemployment, even though expected periods of unemployment tend to be marginally longer for males. While the situation is similar for both genders in many countries, females appear to be at a particular advantage in Canada, Germany, Poland, the Slovak Republic and Turkey. Periods of unemployment for females exceed those for males in only three countries: Greece, Portugal and Spain (Table C4.1a).

Chart C4.3. Gender difference in expected years in education and not in education for 15-to-29-year-olds (2005)

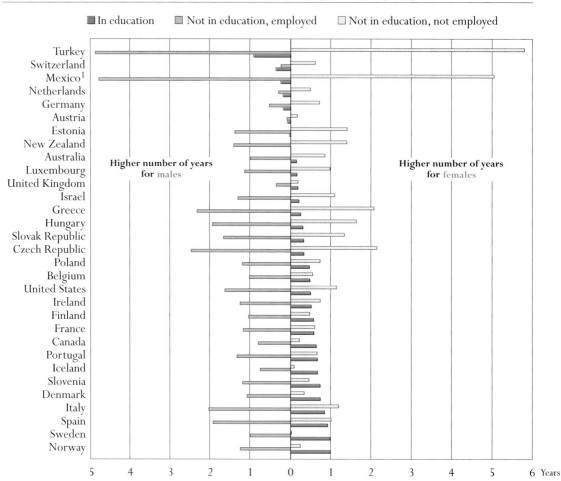

■ In education   ▦ Not in education, employed   ☐ Not in education, not employed

1. Year of reference 2004.
Countries are ranked in descending order of the difference between females and males in expected years in education of 15-to-29-year-olds.
Source: OECD. Table C4.1a. See Annex 3 for notes (*www.oecd.org/edu/eag2007*).
StatLink ⌗ http://dx.doi.org/10.1787/068418024204

Whereas young males can expect to spend 1.6 years neither in education nor in employment between the ages of 15 and 29, the average figure for females is 2.7 years. In the Czech Republic, Hungary, Mexico, New Zealand, the Slovak Republic and Turkey, there is a much stronger tendency for young females to leave the labour market and to spend time out of the educational system and not working. In some countries – Austria, Belgium, Canada, Denmark, Finland, Iceland, Japan, the Netherlands, Norway and Sweden – young males and young females do not differ by more than half a year in this measure.

Conversely, relative to males, females between the ages of 15 and 29 in all OECD countries can expect a lower duration of employment after education; this is partially a consequence of the time spent in education, but is also attributable to other factors such as time spent in childrearing (Table C4.1a).

Unemployment among young non-students

Young people represent the principal source of new skills. In most OECD countries, education policy seeks to encourage young people to complete at least upper secondary education. Since many jobs in the current labour market require ever higher general skill levels, persons with low attainment are often penalised. Differences in unemployment rates among young non-students by level of educational attainment are an indicator of the degree to which further education improves the economic opportunities of young adults.

The unemployment rate by age group is the most common measure used for describing the labour market status of young people. However, unemployment rates do not take educational circumstances into account. For instance, an unemployed young person counted in the numerator may, in some OECD countries, be enrolled in education. And the denominator may include young people in vocational training, provided they are apprenticed. Hence, if almost all young people in a particular age group are still in education, the unemployment rate will reflect only the few present in the labour market. It may therefore appear very high, particularly among the youngest cohort who have usually left the education system with particularly low qualifications.

The ratio of unemployed non-students to the total age cohort is therefore a more appropriate way to reflect the likelihood of youth unemployment (Table C4.3). This is because young people who are looking for a job while still in education are usually seeking part-time or temporary work while studying, unlike those entering the labour market after leaving school.

On average, completing upper secondary education reduces this unemployment ratio (*i.e.* unemployment among non-students as a percentage of the age cohort) among 20-to-24-year-olds by 7.3 percentage points and that of 25-to-29-year-olds by 7.1 percentage points (Table C4.3). In 18 out of 26 OECD countries with available data, the unemployment ratio among 20-to-24-year-olds not in education is equal to or less than 8% for those with upper secondary or post-secondary non-tertiary education. In the same age group, this proportion remains below 8% for those without upper secondary education in only Denmark, Mexico and Turkey. Since it has become the norm in most OECD countries to complete upper secondary education, many young persons who do not complete this level of education are much more likely to have employment difficulties during entry to the labour market. Belgium, France, Ireland, the Slovak Republic and Sweden experience the greatest differences in unemployment rates for 20-to-24-year-olds with an upper secondary level of education and those without.

At the end of the transition period, between the ages of 25 and 29, when most young people have finished studying, differences in access to employment are linked to the education level attained. Not attaining an upper secondary qualification is clearly a serious handicap. Conversely, tertiary education offers a premium for most job seekers.

In 16 OECD countries, for upper secondary graduates aged 25 to 29, the ratio of persons not in education and unemployed to the cohort population is at or above 5%. In a few OECD countries, even young people who have completed tertiary-level education are subject to considerable unemployment risk when they enter the labour market. At the tertiary level of attainment, among 20-to-24-year-olds, the ratio of unemployed non-students to the cohort population is 10% or more – and in some cases significantly more – in Greece, Portugal, the Slovak Republic and Turkey (Table C4.3). Countries that have high unemployment rates among young tertiary educated individuals are also those countries that display high unemployment rates for tertiary educated individuals in the total population (25-to-64-year-olds).

Note that unemployment rates among young individuals largely mirrors those of the labour market in general, but some countries do better than others in terms of providing employment (avoiding unemployment) for the younger cohorts. In having a better understanding of the transition period in general and unemployment rates among the youth population in particular, Indicator A8 provides a good foundation for these types of comparisons.

Entry into the labour market after initial education

The transition from education to work occurs at different points in time in different OECD countries, depending on a range of educational and labour market characteristics. As they grow older, young people spend less time in education and more in the labour force. On average, 83.4% of 15-to-19-year-olds are in education. This average drops to 40.1% for 20-to-24-year-olds and below 14.2% for 25-to-29-year-olds (Table C4.2a). However, in many OECD countries young people begin their transition to work later, and in some cases over a longer period. This reflects not only the demand for education, but also the general state of the labour market, the length and orientation of educational programmes in relation to the labour market and the prevalence of part-time education.

Overall, older non-students are much more likely to be employed than non-students aged 15 to 19, while a higher percentage of male than female non-students are working. A significantly higher share of females than males are out of the labour force. This is particularly so for the 25-to-29-year-old age group, which is likely to reflect, in part, time spent in child-bearing and child-rearing (Tables C4.2b and C4.2c available on line at *http://dx.doi.org/10.1787/068418024204*).

Employment-to-population ratios among young adults not in education provide information on the effectiveness of transition frameworks and thus help policy makers to evaluate transition policies. In 9 out of 26 OECD countries, and in the partner economies Estonia and Slovenia in the year 2005, 90% or more of 15-to-19-year-olds are in education, which suggest that few young people have left school early. While the average of employment-to-population ratios for 20-to-24-year-olds not in education exceeds 42%, the ratios in some OECD countries such as Finland and Poland are considerably lower (Table C4.4a).

Between 2000 and 2005 in the OECD countries, the proportion of individuals in school has increased by 4 percentage points among the younger cohort (15-to-19-year-olds), and focusing on the key transition period (*i.e.* ages 20 to 24) the proportion of individuals in education has increased by 5.4%. Important changes are evident in several countries (Table C4.4) during this period. The proportion of 20-to-24-year-olds in education has risen by more than 10 percentage points in the Czech Republic, Germany, Greece, Hungary, the Netherlands, Poland and the Slovak Republic; at the same time, the proportion of 20-to-24-year-olds not employed has fallen in all of these countries, with the exception of Germany and the Netherlands. The number of individuals in employment has decreased by 5 percentage points in the OECD countries over the period, largely reflecting that more individuals choose to continue their education.

The proportion of 25-to-29-year-olds in education increased between 2000 and 2005, by 2.1 percentage points among the OECD countries, reinforcing the earlier trend of younger

C4

individuals tending to stay on longer in education. On average, however, only 14.6% of 25-to-29-year-olds is in education, 68% are employed and an additional 18% find themselves outside the labour market and not employed. The non-employed ratio has dropped marginally in the OECD countries (from 19 to 17.9%) during this period. In Greece, Hungary, and Spain this decrease in non-employment is around 5 percentage points while 25-to-29-year-olds in Denmark and Turkey have experienced an increase of 4 percentage points. The trends also show that employment prospects play a role in decisions about when to leave the education system in that changes in non-employment are related to changes in proportion of 25-to-29-year-olds in education.

Definition and methodologies

The statistics presented here are calculated from labour force survey data on age-specific proportions of young people in each of the specified categories. These proportions are then totalled over the 15-to-29-year-old age group to yield the expected number of years spent in various states. For countries providing data from the age of 16 only, it is assumed that all 15-year-olds are in education and out of the labour force. This assumption tends to increase the average number of expected years in education compared to *Education at a Glance 2004* (OECD, 2004c).

Persons in education include those attending part-time as well as full-time, where the coverage of education should be as close as possible to that of formal education in administrative sources on enrolment. Therefore, non-formal education or educational activities of very short duration (for example, at the work place) should be excluded.

Data for this indicator are collected as part of the annual OECD Labour Force Survey (for certain European countries the data come from the annual European Labour Force Survey, see Annex 3) and usually refer to the first quarter, or the average of the first three months of the calendar year, thereby excluding summer employment. The labour force status categories shown in this section are defined according to International Labour Organisation (ILO) guidelines, with one exception. For the purposes of these indicators, persons in work-study programmes (see below) have been classified separately as being in education and employed, without reference to their ILO labour force status during the survey reference week, since they may not necessarily be in the work component of their programmes during that week and may therefore not be employed then. The category *other employed* includes individuals employed according to the ILO definition, but excludes those attending work-study programmes who are already counted as employed. Finally, the category *not in the labour force* includes individuals who are not working and who are not unemployed, *i.e.* individuals who are not looking for a job.

Work-study programmes combine work and education as parts of an integrated, formal education or training activity, such as the dual system in Germany; *apprentissage* or *formation en alternance* in France and Belgium; internship or co-operative education in Canada; and apprenticeship in Ireland. Vocational education and training take place both in school settings and working environments. Students or trainees can be paid or not, usually depending on the type of job and the course or training.

The participation rates in education and training are here estimated on the basis of self-reports collected during labour force surveys that often correspond only imprecisely with enrolments obtained from administrative sources shown elsewhere in this publication, for several reasons.

C4

First, age may not be measured in the same way. For example, in administrative data, both enrolment and age are measured on 1 January in OECD countries in the northern hemisphere, whereas in some labour force surveys, both participation in education and age are measured in the reference week, which does not make a significant difference by comparison with the administrative measure. However, in other surveys, the age recorded is the age that will be attained at the end of the calendar year, even if the survey is conducted in the early part of the year; in this case, the rates of participation in education reflect a population that is one year younger than the specified age range. At ages when movements out of education may be significant, this affects the recorded rates of participation in education and training, which are overestimated. From last year onwards, the French data take into account the age measured in the reference week. Second, young people may be enrolled in several programmes and can sometimes be counted twice in administrative statistics but only once in a labour force survey. Moreover, not all enrolments may be captured in administrative statistics, particularly in profit-making institutions. Third, the programme classification used in self-reports in labour force surveys do not always correspond to the qualification standards used for administrative data collections.

The principle behind the estimation of expected years in education is that knowledge of the share of young adults in or out of education is used as a basis for assumptions about how long a typical individual will spend in different labour and educational states.

The unemployment-to-population and the employment-to-population ratios are calculated by dividing the total number of persons unemployed or employed by the number of persons in the population.

With respect to Table C4.4b, a break in the time series is noted for Finland. In 2004, military conscripts in Finland were not included in the data, whereas in previous years conscripts were included in the category "Not in education, not employed".

Further references

The following additional material relevant to this indicator is available on line at:

StatLink ⊞⬚ http://dx.doi.org/10.1787/068418024204

- *Expected years in education and not in education for 15-to 29-year-olds (1998-2005)*
  Table C4.1b: Trends by gender
- *Percentage of the youth population in education and not in education (2005)*
  Table C4.2b: Young males
  Table C4.2c: Young females
- *Trends in the percentage of young population in education and not in education (1995-2005)*
  Table C4.4b: Trends for young males
  Table C4.4c: Trends for young females

Table C4.1a
Expected years in education and not in education for 15-to-29-year-olds (2005)
By gender and work status

		Expected years in education			Expected years not in education			
		Not employed	Employed (including work study programmes)	Sub-total	Employed	Unemployed	Not in the labour force	Sub-total
Australia	Males	3.0	3.7	**6.7**	7.1	0.7	0.5	**8.3**
	Females	2.8	4.0	**6.8**	6.0	0.5	1.8	**8.2**
	M+F	2.9	3.8	**6.8**	6.5	0.6	1.1	**8.2**
Austria	Males	3.8	2.4	**6.2**	7.2	0.8	0.8	**8.8**
	Females	4.3	1.8	**6.2**	7.1	0.6	1.2	**8.8**
	M+F	4.1	2.1	**6.2**	7.2	0.7	1.0	**8.8**
Belgium	Males	5.8	0.6	**6.4**	6.7	1.2	0.7	**8.6**
	Females	6.2	0.7	**6.9**	5.7	1.0	1.4	**8.1**
	M+F	6.0	0.7	**6.7**	6.2	1.1	1.1	**8.3**
Canada	Males	4.1	2.4	**6.6**	6.8	1.0	0.7	**8.4**
	Females	3.9	3.3	**7.2**	6.0	0.5	1.3	**7.8**
	M+F	4.0	2.8	**6.9**	6.4	0.7	1.0	**8.1**
Czech Republic	Males	4.5	1.2	**5.8**	7.9	1.0	0.3	**9.2**
	Females	5.5	0.6	**6.1**	5.4	0.9	2.5	**8.9**
	M+F	5.0	0.9	**5.9**	6.7	1.0	1.4	**9.1**
Denmark	Males	3.3	4.7	**8.0**	6.0	0.6	0.5	**7.0**
	Females	3.9	4.8	**8.7**	4.9	0.4	1.0	**6.3**
	M+F	3.6	4.7	**8.3**	5.4	0.5	0.7	**6.7**
Finland	Males	6.0	2.0	**8.0**	5.6	0.8	0.6	**7.0**
	Females	6.0	2.6	**8.6**	4.5	0.7	1.2	**6.4**
	M+F	6.0	2.3	**8.3**	5.1	0.7	0.9	**6.7**
France	Males	6.1	1.3	**7.4**	5.8	1.3	0.5	**7.6**
	Females	6.8	1.2	**8.0**	4.6	1.0	1.3	**7.0**
	M+F	6.5	1.3	**7.7**	5.2	1.2	0.9	**7.3**
Germany	Males	5.2	2.7	**7.9**	5.2	1.3	0.5	**7.1**
	Females	5.3	2.4	**7.7**	4.7	0.9	1.7	**7.3**
	M+F	5.2	2.6	**7.8**	5.0	1.1	1.1	**7.2**
Greece	Males	5.6	0.3	**5.9**	7.4	1.0	0.7	**9.1**
	Females	5.9	0.3	**6.2**	5.0	1.8	2.0	**8.8**
	M+F	5.7	0.3	**6.0**	6.2	1.4	1.3	**9.0**
Hungary	Males	6.1	0.7	**6.8**	6.4	0.8	0.9	**8.2**
	Females	6.3	0.8	**7.1**	4.5	0.7	2.7	**7.9**
	M+F	6.2	0.7	**6.9**	5.5	0.8	1.8	**8.1**
Iceland	Males	4.9	3.3	**8.2**	5.8	0.5	0.5	**6.8**
	Females	3.9	5.0	**8.9**	5.0	0.2	0.8	**6.1**
	M+F	4.4	4.1	**8.6**	5.4	0.4	0.6	**6.4**
Ireland	Males	4.4	0.7	**5.2**	8.6	0.7	0.5	**9.8**
	Females	4.7	1.0	**5.7**	7.4	0.4	1.5	**9.3**
	M+F	4.6	0.8	**5.4**	8.0	0.5	1.0	**9.6**
Italy	Males	5.5	0.4	**5.8**	6.6	1.2	1.4	**9.2**
	Females	6.2	0.5	**6.6**	4.6	1.2	2.6	**8.4**
	M+F	5.8	0.4	**6.2**	5.6	1.2	1.9	**8.8**
Japan[1]	Males	5.4	0.9	**6.2**	3.0	0.4	0.3	**3.8**
	Females	4.9	0.8	**5.7**	3.3	0.3	0.7	**4.3**
	M+F	5.1	0.8	**6.0**	3.2	0.4	0.5	**4.0**
Luxembourg	Males	7.0	0.2	**7.2**	7.1	0.5	0.1	**7.8**
	Females	7.3	0.1	**7.3**	6.1	0.6	1.0	**7.7**
	M+F	7.1	0.1	**7.3**	6.6	0.6	0.5	**7.7**
Mexico[2]	Males	3.5	1.0	**4.5**	9.5	0.5	0.6	**10.5**
	Females	3.7	0.5	**4.2**	4.7	0.3	5.7	**10.8**
	M+F	3.6	0.7	**4.4**	7.0	0.4	3.2	**10.6**
Netherlands	Males	3.4	4.5	**7.9**	6.1	0.4	0.5	**7.1**
	Females	3.4	4.3	**7.7**	5.8	0.4	1.1	**7.3**
	M+F	3.4	4.4	**7.8**	6.0	0.4	0.8	**7.2**

OECD countries

1. Data refer to 15-to-24-year-olds.
2. Year of reference 2004.
Source: OECD. See Annex 3 for notes (*www.oecd.org/edu/eag2007*).
Please refer to the Reader's Guide for information concerning the symbols replacing missing data.
StatLink ⬛⬛ http://dx.doi.org/10.1787/068418024204

Table C4.1a *(continued)*
Expected years in education and not in education for 15-to-29-year-olds (2005)
By gender and work status

			Expected years in education			Expected years not in education			
			Not employed	Employed (including work study programmes)	Sub-total	Employed	Unemployed	Not in the labour force	Sub-total
OECD countries	New Zealand	Males	3.5	2.7	6.1	7.5	0.6	0.8	8.9
		Females	3.5	2.6	6.1	6.1	0.4	2.3	8.9
		M+F	3.5	2.6	6.1	6.8	0.5	1.6	8.9
	Norway	Males	5.0	1.7	6.8	7.1	0.5	0.6	8.2
		Females	5.1	2.7	7.8	5.9	0.4	0.9	7.2
		M+F	5.1	2.2	7.3	6.5	0.5	0.7	7.7
	Poland	Males	6.8	1.3	8.1	4.5	1.9	0.5	6.9
		Females	7.5	1.1	8.6	3.3	1.6	1.6	6.4
		M+F	7.1	1.2	8.4	3.9	1.8	1.0	6.6
	Portugal	Males	4.8	0.7	5.5	7.9	0.9	0.7	9.5
		Females	5.5	0.6	6.2	6.6	1.2	1.0	8.8
		M+F	5.2	0.7	5.8	7.2	1.1	0.9	9.2
	Slovak Republic	Males	4.9	1.1	6.0	6.6	2.1	0.4	9.0
		Females	5.5	0.9	6.3	4.9	1.6	2.2	8.7
		M+F	5.2	1.0	6.2	5.7	1.8	1.3	8.8
	Spain	Males	4.8	1.6	6.4	7.0	1.0	0.6	8.6
		Females	5.7	1.7	7.3	5.1	1.1	1.5	7.7
		M+F	5.2	1.6	6.9	6.0	1.1	1.0	8.1
	Sweden	Males	6.2	1.3	7.5	6.2	0.9	0.5	7.5
		Females	6.5	1.9	8.4	5.2	0.7	0.7	6.6
		M+F	6.3	1.6	7.9	5.7	0.8	0.6	7.1
	Switzerland	Males	3.1	3.9	6.9	6.8	0.6	0.6	8.1
		Females	3.1	3.5	6.6	6.6	0.7	1.2	8.4
		M+F	3.1	3.7	6.8	6.7	0.6	0.9	8.2
	Turkey	Males	3.0	0.6	3.5	8.0	1.5	1.9	11.5
		Females	2.4	0.3	2.6	3.1	0.7	8.6	12.4
		M+F	2.7	0.4	3.1	5.6	1.1	5.2	11.9
	United Kingdom	Males	3.8	2.3	6.1	7.3	0.9	0.8	8.9
		Females	3.7	2.6	6.3	6.1	0.5	2.1	8.7
		M+F	3.7	2.4	6.2	6.7	0.7	1.4	8.8
	United States	Males	4.2	2.3	6.5	7.1	0.6	0.8	8.5
		Females	4.2	2.8	7.0	5.4	0.5	2.1	8.0
		M+F	4.2	2.6	6.8	6.3	0.5	1.4	8.2
	OECD28 average	*Males*	*4.7*	*1.8*	*6.6*	*6.8*	*0.9*	*0.7*	*8.4*
		Females	*4.9*	*1.9*	*6.9*	*5.4*	*0.8*	*2.0*	*8.1*
		M+F	*4.8*	*1.9*	*6.7*	*6.1*	*0.8*	*1.3*	*8.3*
	EU19 average	*Males*	*5.2*	*1.6*	*6.7*	*6.6*	*1.0*	*0.6*	*8.3*
		Females	*5.6*	*1.6*	*7.2*	*5.3*	*0.9*	*1.6*	*7.8*
		M+F	*5.4*	*1.6*	*6.9*	*6.0*	*1.0*	*1.1*	*8.1*
Partner economies	Estonia	Males	6.6	1.6	8.1	5.4	0.9	0.6	6.9
		Females	6.7	1.3	8.1	4.0	0.7	2.2	6.9
		M+F	6.6	1.5	8.1	4.7	0.8	1.4	6.9
	Israel	Males	4.7	1.2	5.9	4.7	0.7	3.7	9.1
		Females	4.4	1.7	6.1	4.3	0.7	3.8	8.9
		M+F	4.6	1.5	6.0	4.5	0.7	3.8	9.0
	Slovenia	Males	5.6	2.4	8.0	5.7	0.7	0.6	7.0
		Females	6.4	2.3	8.7	4.6	1.0	0.7	6.3
		M+F	6.0	2.3	8.3	5.2	0.9	0.6	6.7

Source: OECD. See Annex 3 for notes (*www.oecd.org/edu/eag2007*).
Please refer to the Reader's Guide for information concerning the symbols replacing missing data.
StatLink ᵐᵻˢᴸ http://dx.doi.org/10.1787/068418024204

Table C4.2a.

Percentage of the youth population in education and not in education (2005)

	Age group	In education					Not in education				Total in education and not in education
		Students in work-study programmes[1]	Other employed	Unemployed	Not in the labour force	Sub-total	Employed	Unemployed	Not in the labour force	Sub-total	
Australia	15-19	8.0	29.8	5.1	35.4	**78.3**	14.3	3.8	3.6	**21.7**	100
	20-24	5.1	22.0	1.8	10.5	**39.4**	49.0	4.4	7.3	**60.6**	100
	25-29	1.3	10.2	1.0	4.1	**16.6**	68.0	3.6	11.8	**83.4**	100
Austria	15-19	23.8	2.0	c	57.8	**84.4**	8.7	4.2	2.7	**15.6**	100
	20-24	1.7	9.7	c	18.0	**30.4**	57.2	4.6	7.8	**69.6**	100
	25-29	c	5.9	c	5.2	**12.0**	74.6	4.5	8.8	**88.0**	100
Belgium	15-19	1.4	2.5	0.4	85.8	**90.1**	3.7	1.8	4.4	**9.9**	100
	20-24	1.1	4.2	0.9	31.9	**38.1**	43.6	11.0	7.3	**61.9**	100
	25-29	0.8	3.4	0.9	2.4	**7.4**	74.9	8.4	9.3	**92.6**	100
Canada	15-19	a	28.8	5.6	47.2	**81.7**	12.1	2.8	3.3	**18.3**	100
	20-24	a	20.7	1.8	19.2	**41.6**	45.2	6.1	7.1	**58.4**	100
	25-29	a	7.5	0.6	6.0	**14.1**	71.0	6.0	9.0	**85.9**	100
Czech Republic	15-19	18.7	c	c	71.2	**90.3**	4.4	3.8	1.5	**9.7**	100
	20-24	0.7	0.7	c	34.4	**35.9**	47.5	8.9	7.7	**64.1**	100
	25-29	a	0.5	c	3.8	**4.4**	72.4	6.7	16.5	**95.6**	100
Denmark	15-19	a	45.2	3.4	39.8	**88.4**	7.3	1.8	2.5	**11.6**	100
	20-24	a	35.1	2.6	16.7	**54.4**	37.2	3.8	4.5	**45.6**	100
	25-29	a	16.8	1.0	9.3	**27.0**	61.3	4.2	7.4	**73.0**	100
Finland	15-19	a	10.9	5.2	74.1	**90.2**	4.5	2.0	3.3	**9.8**	100
	20-24	a	18.6	5.5	28.7	**52.8**	34.1	7.0	6.1	**47.2**	100
	25-29	a	16.1	1.8	7.8	**25.7**	60.3	5.8	8.2	**74.3**	100
France	15-19	5.6	1.9	0.5	82.8	**90.8**	3.0	3.2	3.0	**9.2**	100
	20-24	4.9	5.3	1.2	36.0	**47.4**	36.1	10.6	5.9	**52.6**	100
	25-29	4.4	3.0	1.0	5.4	**13.7**	67.2	9.6	9.5	**86.3**	100
Germany	15-19	16.5	4.8	1.6	70.0	**92.9**	2.7	2.4	2.0	**7.1**	100
	20-24	13.3	7.8	0.9	22.2	**44.2**	37.1	10.3	8.4	**55.8**	100
	25-29	1.6	7.5	0.7	8.7	**18.5**	60.3	9.7	11.5	**81.5**	100
Greece	15-19	a	1.5	c	82.5	**84.5**	5.7	2.8	7.0	**15.5**	100
	20-24	a	3.2	c	38.3	**42.6**	37.3	11.8	8.3	**57.4**	100
	25-29	a	1.6	c	4.8	**6.8**	70.2	12.0	11.0	**93.2**	100
Hungary	15-19	a	c	c	90.0	**90.6**	3.0	1.9	4.5	**9.4**	100
	20-24	a	5.4	0.9	40.3	**46.6**	34.5	7.1	11.8	**53.4**	100
	25-29	a	7.8	c	4.9	**13.1**	63.0	5.7	18.2	**86.9**	100
Iceland	15-19	a	31.8	5.0	49.6	**86.4**	10.7	c	c	**13.6**	100
	20-24	a	32.0	c	19.9	**53.0**	37.1	c	5.4	**47.0**	100
	25-29	a	18.9	c	11.7	**30.9**	61.5	c	5.4	**69.1**	100
Ireland	15-19	a	9.6	c	72.4	**82.5**	13.1	2.2	2.2	**17.5**	100
	20-24	a	6.8	c	20.6	**27.8**	60.0	4.9	7.2	**72.2**	100
	25-29	a	1.2	c	3.8	**5.1**	81.3	3.3	10.3	**94.9**	100
Italy	15-19	c	1.1	0.8	79.9	**81.8**	7.0	3.9	7.2	**18.2**	100
	20-24	0.2	3.4	1.4	33.7	**38.6**	37.3	10.5	13.6	**61.4**	100
	25-29	c	3.4	1.1	9.9	**14.4**	59.8	9.2	16.7	**85.6**	100
Japan	15-24	a	8.5	0.1	51.1	**59.7**	31.5	3.7	5.0	**40.3**	100
Luxembourg	15-19	a	c	c	91.2	**93.4**	4.4	c	c	**6.6**	100
	20-24	a	c	c	46.4	**47.4**	43.3	6.1	3.2	**52.6**	100
	25-29	a	c	m	8.4	**8.6**	81.2	4.0	6.2	**91.4**	100
Mexico[2]	15-19	a	7.1	0.5	47.3	**54.9**	28.0	2.2	14.9	**45.1**	100
	20-24	a	4.7	0.4	15.2	**20.3**	52.3	3.2	24.2	**79.7**	100
	25-29	a	1.9	0.1	2.4	**4.4**	65.4	2.7	27.6	**95.6**	100
Netherlands	15-19	a	43.0	5.6	40.5	**89.2**	7.0	1.3	2.6	**10.8**	100
	20-24	a	32.1	2.3	14.7	**49.1**	41.8	3.9	5.2	**50.9**	100
	25-29	a	13.2	0.7	4.3	**18.2**	70.2	3.5	8.1	**81.8**	100

1. Students in work-study programmes are considered to be both in education and employed, irrespective of their labour market status according to the ILO definition.

2. Year of reference 2004.

Source: OECD. See Annex 3 for notes (*www.oecd.org/edu/eag2007*).

Please refer to the Reader's Guide for information concerning the symbols replacing missing data.

StatLink ⟲ http://dx.doi.org/10.1787/068418024204

Table C4.2a. *(continued)*

Percentage of the youth population in education and not in education (2005)

	Age group	In education					Not in education				Total in education and not in education
		Students in work-study programmes[1]	Other employed	Unemployed	Not in the labour force	Sub-total	Employed	Unemployed	Not in the labour force	Sub-total	
New Zealand	15-19	a	25.7	5.0	39.3	**70.0**	21.5	2.8	5.7	**30.0**	100
	20-24	a	16.2	2.0	14.6	**32.9**	50.5	3.9	12.8	**67.1**	100
	25-29	a	9.7	0.4	5.3	**15.4**	67.9	3.6	13.1	**84.6**	100
Norway	15-19	m	20.4	5.2	61.9	**87.4**	10.1	c	c	**12.6**	100
	20-24	m	16.9	2.2	22.4	**41.5**	48.9	4.4	5.2	**58.5**	100
	25-29	m	6.6	c	8.4	**15.7**	72.0	4.1	8.1	**84.3**	100
Poland	15-19	a	3.3	0.2	94.4	**97.9**	0.4	0.7	1.0	**2.1**	100
	20-24	a	11.8	7.2	43.7	**62.7**	17.2	14.3	5.8	**37.3**	100
	25-29	a	8.1	2.0	6.3	**16.4**	54.3	17.4	11.9	**83.6**	100
Portugal	15-19	a	1.4	c	77.5	**79.3**	12.2	3.1	5.3	**20.7**	100
	20-24	a	5.5	0.7	31.2	**37.4**	48.4	8.8	5.3	**62.6**	100
	25-29	a	5.5	1.0	5.1	**11.5**	73.6	8.4	6.5	**88.5**	100
Slovak Republic	15-19	14.9	c	c	75.4	**90.4**	3.3	4.8	1.5	**9.6**	100
	20-24	0.5	2.6	0.9	27.0	**31.0**	43.8	17.0	8.2	**69.0**	100
	25-29	c	2.3	c	3.4	**6.1**	64.9	14.3	14.8	**93.9**	100
Spain	15-19	a	4.2	2.2	75.4	**81.8**	9.7	4.1	4.4	**18.2**	100
	20-24	a	12.9	3.9	27.6	**44.3**	40.2	8.9	6.6	**55.7**	100
	25-29	a	13.8	2.6	6.3	**22.8**	61.0	7.7	8.6	**77.2**	100
Sweden	15-19	a	11.3	3.8	74.5	**89.6**	5.8	2.1	2.6	**10.4**	100
	20-24	a	11.1	3.1	28.2	**42.5**	44.1	8.7	4.7	**57.5**	100
	25-29	a	9.2	1.7	12.7	**23.6**	66.5	5.6	4.4	**76.4**	100
Switzerland	15-19	33.1	8.9	1.5	41.4	**84.9**	7.9	2.5	4.7	**15.1**	100
	20-24	10.6	11.5	c	14.1	**37.3**	51.7	5.2	5.8	**62.7**	100
	25-29	1.2	9.7	c	4.2	**15.6**	72.3	5.1	7.0	**84.4**	100
Turkey	15-19	a	2.2	0.4	39.9	**42.5**	19.9	4.4	33.3	**57.5**	100
	20-24	a	3.9	1.2	10.2	**15.2**	37.7	9.6	37.6	**84.8**	100
	25-29	a	2.5	0.4	1.4	**4.3**	53.5	8.0	34.2	**95.7**	100
United Kingdom	15-19	4.5	18.7	2.9	49.9	**76.0**	14.6	4.4	5.0	**24.0**	100
	20-24	2.6	13.1	1.1	15.3	**32.1**	51.0	5.8	11.1	**67.9**	100
	25-29	0.9	8.3	0.4	3.7	**13.3**	70.1	3.8	12.8	**86.7**	100
United States	15-19	a	22.0	3.5	60.1	**85.6**	8.3	1.9	4.2	**14.4**	100
	20-24	a	21.0	1.2	13.9	**36.1**	48.4	4.9	10.6	**63.9**	100
	25-29	a	8.0	0.5	3.4	**11.9**	70.0	4.1	14.0	**88.1**	100
OECD28 average	*15-19*		*14.1*	*2.9*	*64.5*	*83.4*	*9.0*	*2.8*	*5.3*	*16.6*	*100*
	20-24		*12.5*	*2.1*	*24.8*	*40.1*	*43.3*	*7.6*	*9.1*	*59.9*	*100*
	25-29		*7.5*	*1.0*	*5.8*	*14.2*	*67.5*	*6.7*	*11.8*	*85.8*	*100*
EU19 average	*15-19*		*10.8*	*2.4*	*72.9*	*87.6*	*6.3*	*2.8*	*3.5*	*12.4*	*100*
	20-24		*10.5*	*2.3*	*29.2*	*42.4*	*41.7*	*8.6*	*7.3*	*57.6*	*100*
	25-29		*7.1*	*1.2*	*6.1*	*14.1*	*67.7*	*7.6*	*10.6*	*85.9*	*100*
Estonia	15-19	a	1.4	c	90.3	**92.0**	2.9	2.5	2.7	**8.0**	100
	20-24	a	18.6	c	31.1	**50.9**	32.7	5.7	10.6	**49.1**	100
	25-29	a	9.7	c	4.3	**14.2**	61.8	8.8	15.2	**85.8**	100
Israel	15-19	a	4.0	0.7	64.3	**68.9**	6.3	1.8	22.9	**31.1**	100
	20-24	a	11.4	1.1	15.8	**28.3**	31.4	7.1	33.2	**71.7**	100
	25-29	a	14.4	0.7	6.3	**21.4**	54.3	5.1	19.2	**78.6**	100
Slovenia	15-19	a	8.6	0.7	83.1	**92.4**	2.7	1.8	3.1	**7.6**	100
	20-24	a	21.2	2.6	31.9	**55.7**	31.3	8.4	4.7	**44.3**	100
	25-29	a	16.0	2.2	6.4	**24.6**	63.9	6.9	4.7	**75.4**	100

1. Students in work-study programmes are considered to be both in education and employed, irrespective of their labour market status according to the ILO definition.

Source: OECD. See Annex 3 for notes (*www.oecd.org/edu/eag2007*).

Please refer to the Reader's Guide for information concerning the symbols replacing missing data.

StatLink ⌨ᴜɪ⁵ᴸ http://dx.doi.org/10.1787/068418024204

Table C4.3.
Percentage of the cohort population not in education and unemployed (2005)
By level of educational attainment, age group and gender

C4

		Below upper secondary education			Upper secondary and post-secondary non-tertiary education			Tertiary education		All levels of education			
		15-19	20-24	25-29	15-19[1]	20-24	25-29	20-24[1]	25-29	15-19	20-24	25-29	15-29
Australia	Males	4.3	12.7	9.9	4.3	3.8	3.8	1.3	1.0	4.3	5.3	4.1	4.6
	Females	3.2	6.2	7.4	3.3	3.5	4.0	1.0	0.3	3.3	3.3	3.0	3.2
	M+F	3.7	9.8	8.8	3.8	3.7	3.9	1.1	0.6	3.8	4.3	3.6	3.9
Austria	Males	4.2	c	c	c	4.7	c	c	c	5.1	6.0	4.3	5.2
	Females	c	c	c	c	3.2	4.6	c	c	3.3	3.3	4.7	3.7
	M+F	3.5	9.2	c	7.3	3.9	3.7	c	c	4.2	4.6	4.5	4.4
Belgium	Males	1.2	19.0	21.3	5.3	10.8	6.6	8.3	5.5	2.1	12.2	8.9	7.8
	Females	1.5	23.7	17.6	c	8.3	7.8	6.6	4.6	1.5	10.1	7.7	6.5
	M+F	1.3	20.9	19.7	3.3	9.6	7.1	7.2	5.0	1.8	11.2	8.3	7.1
Canada	Males	2.7	18.2	14.3	4.8	8.0	6.7	4.8	5.5	3.4	8.6	7.0	6.4
	Females	1.5	7.4	10.7	3.7	3.4	4.7	2.8	4.1	2.2	3.5	4.8	3.5
	M+F	2.1	14.1	12.8	4.3	5.9	5.9	3.6	4.7	2.8	6.1	5.9	5.0
Czech Republic	Males	1.9	22.3	27.0	21.0	9.2	4.9	c	c	4.4	10.3	5.9	6.9
	Females	c	13.3	21.1	16.1	6.7	7.2	c	c	3.1	7.5	7.5	6.2
	M+F	1.5	17.9	23.8	18.7	8.0	6.0	c	2.7	3.8	8.9	6.7	6.5
Denmark	Males	1.4	10.6	14.4	c	4.0	3.2	m	c	1.6	5.5	5.0	4.0
	Females	1.5	c	c	c	c	3.4	m	3.2	2.0	2.2	3.6	2.6
	M+F	1.4	7.7	10.9	c	2.9	3.3	m	3.3	1.8	3.8	4.3	3.3
Finland	Males	c	10.1	13.7	c	7.9	5.2	c	c	2.1	8.4	5.9	5.5
	Females	c	c	c	c	4.9	4.9	c	5.1	1.7	5.7	5.8	4.4
	M+F	c	10.3	14.3	11.9	6.3	5.1	c	4.5	1.9	7.0	5.8	5.0
France	Males	3.4	23.0	22.2	6.0	9.3	8.4	7.2	6.3	4.0	11.5	10.3	8.5
	Females	2.0	22.1	17.7	3.5	8.9	9.1	5.7	5.5	2.4	9.7	8.7	6.9
	M+F	2.7	22.6	20.2	4.6	9.1	8.7	6.4	5.9	3.2	10.6	9.5	7.7
Germany	Males	2.2	16.3	24.6	6.4	11.6	10.0	9.6	5.3	2.4	12.9	11.4	8.8
	Females	2.0	11.1	15.5	6.6	6.4	6.7	9.2	4.7	2.3	7.8	7.8	6.0
	M+F	2.1	13.8	19.8	6.5	9.0	8.4	9.3	5.0	2.3	10.4	9.6	7.4
Greece	Males	c	c	c	c	7.9	7.5	c	11.7	c	8.7	8.5	6.9
	Females	c	c	c	c	12.6	16.2	31.3	18.4	3.2	15.0	15.8	12.0
	M+F	c	13.6	8.7	7.2	10.3	11.8	23.6	15.4	2.8	11.8	12.0	9.4
Hungary	Males	2.0	14.3	11.9	c	7.1	5.3	c	c	2.7	8.4	5.7	5.7
	Females	c	c	8.9	c	5.5	6.1	c	c	c	5.9	5.9	4.5
	M+F	1.4	11.1	10.6	5.0	6.3	5.7	c	2.9	1.9	7.2	5.8	5.1
Iceland	Males	c	c	c	c	c	m	m	c	c	c	c	3.6
	Females	m	c	c	m	c	m	c	c	m	c	c	c
	M+F	c	c	c	c	c	m	c	c	c	c	c	2.7
Ireland	Males	2.8	15.6	11.5	c	4.2	c	c	c	2.7	6.1	4.3	4.4
	Females	c	c	c	c	c	c	c	c	c	3.8	2.4	2.7
	M+F	2.1	13.7	8.4	c	3.5	3.1	3.8	2.2	2.2	5.0	3.4	3.6
Italy	Males	3.7	18.1	10.4	7.9	8.6	6.6	6.3	13.3	4.2	11.4	8.7	8.3
	Females	2.4	14.4	12.6	9.7	8.6	7.3	10.1	14.3	3.6	10.0	9.9	8.1
	M+F	3.1	16.6	11.3	8.9	8.6	6.9	8.6	13.9	3.9	10.7	9.3	8.2
Luxembourg	Males	c	c	c	c	c	c	c	c	c	5.8	3.7	3.7
	Females	c	c	c	c	c	c	c	c	c	6.4	4.4	3.9
	M+F	c	12.6	c	c	4.5	4.6	c	c	c	6.1	4.1	3.8
Mexico[2]	Males	2.6	3.6	2.8	7.3	2.9	5.1	3.1	4.5	2.7	3.5	3.2	3.1
	Females	1.5	2.4	1.4	5.5	6.4	4.3	3.8	4.3	1.6	2.9	2.2	2.2
	M+F	2.1	3.0	2.1	6.1	5.4	4.5	3.4	4.4	2.2	3.2	2.7	2.7
Netherlands	Males	1.2	8.8	5.4	m	2.4	2.6	m	1.2	1.0	4.0	2.7	2.5
	Females	0.8	4.3	3.8	m	2.1	3.7	3.3	2.1	0.6	2.8	3.1	2.2
	M+F	1.1	8.2	5.8	1.1	2.1	3.1	2.7	1.7	1.1	3.7	3.1	2.6

1. Differences between countries in these columns in part reflect the fact that the average age of graduation varies across countries. For instance, in some countries a smaller share of 15-to-19-year-olds attain upper secondary education simply because graduation typically occurs at 19. This means that the denominator in the ratio for the reported columns will be smaller than those where graduation occurs at an earlier age.
2. Year of reference 2004.
Source: OECD. See Annex 3 for notes (*www.oecd.org/edu/eag2007*).
Please refer to the Reader's Guide for information concerning the symbols replacing missing data.
StatLink ⣿⣿⣿ http://dx.doi.org/10.1787/068418024204

C4

Table C4.3. (continued)
Percentage of the cohort population not in education and unemployed (2005)
By level of educational attainment, age group and gender

		Below upper secondary education			Upper secondary and post-secondary non-tertiary education			Tertiary education		All levels of education			
		15-19	20-24	25-29	15-19[1]	20-24	25-29	20-24[1]	25-29	15-19	20-24	25-29	15-29
New Zealand	Males	3.3	9.2	5.8	2.0	2.7	2.6	9.1	8.0	3.0	4.5	4.5	3.9
	Females	2.7	7.6	c	1.9	1.8	2.0	6.4	4.1	2.4	3.4	2.8	2.9
	M+F	3.0	8.4	4.6	2.0	2.3	2.3	7.5	5.7	2.7	4.0	3.7	3.4
Norway	Males	c	c	c	c	c	c	c	c	c	5.1	4.6	3.6
	Females	c	c	c	m	c	c	c	c	c	c	c	2.7
	M+F	c	10.5	10.3	c	c	c	c	c	c	4.4	4.1	3.2
Poland	Males	0.5	23.7	33.6	5.1	15.6	19.1	c	10.0	0.9	16.4	18.5	12.6
	Females	c	18.3	33.2	c	12.2	18.2	4.6	10.3	c	12.2	16.4	10.3
	M+F	0.3	21.6	33.4	3.8	13.9	18.7	5.9	10.2	0.6	14.3	17.5	11.5
Portugal	Males	3.2	9.5	7.8	c	4.6	c	c	7.6	3.0	7.9	6.7	6.1
	Females	3.3	14.2	11.8	c	4.7	8.4	16.1	8.9	3.4	10.0	10.1	8.2
	M+F	3.2	11.4	9.5	c	4.7	6.2	16.6	8.4	3.2	8.9	8.4	7.1
Slovak Republic	Males	3.0	58.1	70.3	19.4	16.8	13.1	c	5.4	5.4	20.4	15.7	14.5
	Females	3.8	29.7	33.5	19.7	11.9	12.4	17.7	5.3	6.2	13.6	12.7	11.2
	M+F	3.4	45.1	51.1	19.5	14.4	12.8	18.8	5.4	5.8	17.1	14.2	12.9
Spain	Males	4.7	12.0	8.9	3.9	5.0	4.9	6.1	5.8	4.6	8.2	6.8	6.6
	Females	4.0	16.7	12.6	2.7	6.5	8.8	6.7	6.1	3.7	9.7	8.6	7.6
	M+F	4.3	13.9	10.4	3.2	5.7	6.8	6.4	5.9	4.1	9.0	7.7	7.1
Sweden	Males	c	20.9	c	c	7.8	7.0	c	c	2.7	9.3	6.6	6.2
	Females	c	c	c	c	7.6	5.8	c	c	c	7.7	4.3	4.6
	M+F	c	18.5	10.2	21.7	7.7	6.4	c	2.8	2.3	8.5	5.5	5.5
Switzerland	Males	c	c	c	c	4.4	3.9	c	c	2.8	4.9	4.6	4.1
	Females	c	c	c	c	4.0	4.9	c	c	c	5.4	5.7	4.4
	M+F	2.2	10.2	12.5	c	4.2	4.4	c	4.2	2.5	5.1	5.1	4.3
Turkey	Males	5.6	14.7	11.4	7.0	10.9	10.6	19.1	11.5	6.0	13.5	11.1	10.0
	Females	1.6	2.5	2.2	6.5	8.7	7.7	20.8	12.3	2.8	6.1	4.5	4.5
	M+F	3.7	7.6	6.4	6.8	9.9	9.5	20.0	11.8	4.5	9.6	8.0	7.3
United Kingdom	Males	5.0	20.5	11.2	5.9	5.9	4.5	6.0	2.6	5.5	7.0	4.3	5.6
	Females	2.1	c	c	3.3	4.7	3.8	c	2.0	2.9	4.2	3.1	3.4
	M+F	3.6	12.0	7.2	4.6	5.3	4.1	4.0	2.3	4.2	5.6	3.7	4.5
United States	Males	c	11.1	c	6.5	5.0	5.0	c	2.6	2.0	5.8	4.1	3.9
	Females	c	8.8	7.2	5.5	3.7	5.0	c	2.1	1.8	4.0	4.1	3.3
	M+F	0.8	10.1	5.8	6.0	4.4	5.0	3.0	2.3	1.9	4.9	4.1	3.6
OECD28 average	*Males*	*2.9*	*16.9*	*16.9*	*7.5*	*7.2*	*6.7*	*7.4*	*6.3*	*3.3*	*8.6*	*6.9*	*6.2*
	Females	*2.2*	*12.7*	*13.6*	*6.8*	*6.4*	*7.0*	*9.7*	*6.2*	*2.7*	*6.8*	*6.5*	*5.3*
	M+F	*2.4*	*13.9*	*13.5*	*7.4*	*6.6*	*6.5*	*8.4*	*5.5*	*2.9*	*7.6*	*6.7*	*5.7*
EU19 average	*Males*	*2.7*	*18.9*	*19.6*	*9.0*	*8.0*	*7.3*	*7.2*	*6.8*	*3.2*	*9.5*	*7.6*	*6.8*
	Females	*2.3*	*16.8*	*17.1*	*8.8*	*7.2*	*7.9*	*11.1*	*7.0*	*2.8*	*7.8*	*7.5*	*6.1*
	M+F	*2.3*	*15.8*	*16.2*	*8.5*	*7.2*	*7.0*	*9.4*	*5.7*	*2.8*	*8.6*	*7.6*	*6.5*
Israel	Males	7.4	9.0	8.8	1.1	6.1	7.8	c	2.3	2.0	5.6	5.4	4.3
	Females	c	c	c	1.2	13.7	7.1	2.5	3.2	1.6	8.4	4.7	4.9
	M+F	6.6	8.3	7.6	1.2	9.4	7.5	2.2	2.8	1.8	7.0	5.1	4.6
Estonia	Males	c	21.9	18.8	29.3	c	8.2	m	c	3.7	5.4	9.4	6.0
	Females	c	m	c	c	8.1	10.1	c	c	c	6.0	8.1	5.0
	M+F	c	14.2	18.6	13.7	4.5	9.1	c	4.1	2.5	5.7	8.7	5.5
Slovenia	Males	1.6	14.3	9.3	4.3	6.1	4.8	m	4.6	2.1	6.9	5.2	4.9
	Females	c	13.9	18.9	4.8	9.9	7.9	c	8.1	1.4	10.2	8.4	6.9
	M+F	1.1	14.2	12.5	4.6	8.0	6.2	c	6.9	1.8	8.5	6.8	5.9

1. Differences between countries in these columns in part reflect the fact that the average age of graduation varies across countries. For instance, in some countries a smaller share of 15-to-19-year-olds attain upper secondary education simply because graduation typically occurs at 19. This means that the denominator in the ratio for the reported columns will be smaller than those where graduation occurs at an earlier age.
Source: OECD. See Annex 3 for notes (*www.oecd.org/edu/eag2007*).
Please refer to the Reader's Guide for information concerning the symbols replacing missing data.
StatLink ⫘⫘ http://dx.doi.org/10.1787/068418024204

Table C4.4a.

Trends in the percentage of the youth population in education and not in education (1995-2005)
By age group and work status

C4

	Age group	1995 In education Total	1995 Not in education Employed	1995 Not in education Not employed	1998 In education Total	1998 Not in education Employed	1998 Not in education Not employed	1999 In education Total	1999 Not in education Employed	1999 Not in education Not employed	2000 In education Total	2000 Not in education Employed	2000 Not in education Not employed	2001 In education Total	2001 Not in education Employed	2001 Not in education Not employed
Australia	15-19	73.4	16.7	9.9	77.3	13.8	8.8	78.2	14.4	7.4	79.5	13.7	6.8	79.5	13.0	7.6
	20-24	27.0	56.1	16.9	32.7	51.3	16.0	34.9	50.6	14.5	35.9	50.9	13.3	36.5	49.6	13.9
	25-29	11.4	67.1	21.5	13.7	67.1	19.2	15.0	66.5	18.5	15.5	65.5	19.0	15.8	67.0	17.2
Austria	15-19	m	m	m	m	m	m	m	m	m	m	m	m	m	m	m
	20-24	m	m	m	m	m	m	m	m	m	m	m	m	m	m	m
	25-29	m	m	m	m	m	m	m	m	m	m	m	m	m	m	m
Belgium	15-19	86.1	3.3	10.5	85.3	3.9	10.8	89.4	3.7	6.8	89.9	3.6	6.5	89.7	4.1	6.2
	20-24	37.5	43.6	19.0	40.6	42.5	16.9	43.7	38.6	17.7	43.8	40.2	16.0	44.2	42.8	13.0
	25-29	6.8	74.2	19.0	9.3	72.4	18.2	14.4	67.7	17.9	11.8	72.5	15.7	15.0	69.5	15.5
Canada	15-19	82.9	9.5	7.6	83.0	9.6	7.5	82.3	10.4	7.3	82.1	10.7	7.2	83.0	10.7	6.3
	20-24	36.2	46.4	17.4	39.0	44.5	16.5	39.0	46.4	14.6	37.9	47.8	14.3	38.7	46.9	14.3
	25-29	12.1	67.0	20.9	12.6	69.2	18.2	12.3	70.5	17.2	12.4	71.5	16.2	13.2	71.3	15.6
Czech Republic	15-19	69.8	23.7	6.5	77.1	15.8	7.2	75.6	14.8	9.7	82.1	10.0	7.9	87.0	6.2	6.8
	20-24	13.1	67.1	19.8	17.1	64.3	18.5	19.6	59.8	20.6	19.7	60.0	20.3	23.1	58.9	18.1
	25-29	1.1	76.1	22.9	1.8	75.1	23.1	2.4	71.7	25.9	2.4	72.1	25.6	3.0	72.1	25.0
Denmark	15-19	88.4	8.7	3.0	90.3	7.9	1.8	85.8	10.8	3.4	89.9	7.4	2.7	86.8	9.4	3.8
	20-24	50.0	39.3	10.7	55.0	38.0	7.0	55.8	36.6	7.6	54.8	38.6	6.6	55.3	38.1	6.6
	25-29	29.6	59.0	11.4	34.5	57.8	7.7	35.5	56.7	7.8	36.1	56.4	7.5	32.4	60.0	7.6
Finland	15-19	m	m	m	m	m	m	m	m	m	m	m	m	m	m	m
	20-24	m	m	m	m	m	m	m	m	m	m	m	m	m	m	m
	25-29	m	m	m	m	m	m	m	m	m	m	m	m	m	m	m
France	15-19	96.2	1.3	2.5	95.6	1.3	3.1	95.7	1.0	3.3	95.3	1.5	3.3	94.9	1.7	3.4
	20-24	51.2	31.3	17.5	53.5	30.0	16.5	53.1	29.4	17.5	54.2	31.7	14.1	53.6	33.1	13.4
	25-29	11.4	67.5	21.0	11.4	66.5	22.1	11.9	66.6	21.4	12.2	69.2	18.6	11.4	70.3	18.3
Germany	15-19	m	m	m	m	m	m	89.5	6.0	4.5	87.4	6.8	5.7	88.5	6.4	5.1
	20-24	m	m	m	m	m	m	34.3	49.0	16.7	34.1	49.0	16.9	35.0	48.7	16.4
	25-29	m	m	m	m	m	m	13.6	68.2	18.1	12.7	69.8	17.5	13.5	68.5	18.0
Greece	15-19	80.0	9.6	10.5	80.1	10.2	9.7	81.8	8.0	10.3	82.7	8.3	9.0	85.4	7.1	7.6
	20-24	29.2	43.0	27.8	28.2	44.7	27.1	30.3	43.7	26.0	31.5	43.7	24.9	35.1	40.9	24.0
	25-29	4.7	65.2	30.2	4.2	66.8	28.9	5.6	66.9	27.5	5.3	66.9	27.8	6.4	67.4	26.3
Hungary	15-19	82.5	6.7	10.8	78.2	10.0	11.8	79.3	9.2	11.6	83.7	7.7	8.6	85.0	6.7	8.3
	20-24	22.5	44.4	33.1	26.5	45.9	27.6	28.6	47.7	23.6	32.3	45.7	22.0	35.0	45.1	20.0
	25-29	7.3	56.8	35.9	7.4	58.9	33.7	8.7	60.1	31.3	9.4	61.4	29.2	9.4	63.4	27.1
Iceland	15-19	59.5	25.7	14.8	82.2	15.1	c	81.6	17.0	c	83.1	14.8	c	79.5	19.0	c
	20-24	33.3	52.6	14.0	47.8	45.9	6.3	44.8	48.4	6.8	48.0	47.7	c	50.3	45.6	c
	25-29	24.1	64.7	11.1	32.8	57.4	9.8	34.7	58.8	6.5	34.9	59.2	5.9	33.8	61.5	c
Ireland	15-19	m	m	m	m	m	m	79.4	15.4	5.2	80.0	15.6	4.4	80.3	15.5	4.1
	20-24	m	m	m	m	m	m	24.6	64.6	10.8	26.7	63.6	9.7	28.3	62.4	9.3
	25-29	m	m	m	m	m	m	3.1	82.4	14.5	3.3	83.4	13.3	3.3	83.1	13.5
Italy	15-19	m	m	m	75.4	9.5	15.2	76.9	8.3	14.8	77.1	9.8	13.1	77.6	9.8	12.6
	20-24	m	m	m	35.8	34.1	30.1	35.6	34.5	29.9	36.0	36.5	27.5	37.0	36.9	26.1
	25-29	m	m	m	16.5	54.1	29.4	17.7	53.4	28.9	17.0	56.1	26.9	16.4	58.0	25.6
Japan	15-19	58.0	34.9	7.1	60.0	32.4	7.6	60.0	31.0	9.0	62.1	29.2	8.8	62.6	28.9	8.4
Luxembourg	15-19	82.7	9.3	8.0	88.6	5.3	6.1	89.2	5.8	5.0	92.2	6.1	c	91.2	7.0	c
	20-24	36.5	52.7	10.8	40.4	50.1	9.5	47.2	43.2	9.6	42.8	48.9	8.2	46.7	44.2	9.0
	25-29	8.3	71.6	20.1	11.9	74.0	14.1	11.3	74.1	14.6	11.6	75.5	12.9	11.6	75.9	12.5
Mexico	15-19	45.0	31.8	23.2	46.9	33.8	19.3	49.6	32.7	17.7	47.9	33.8	18.3	50.3	31.9	17.8
	20-24	15.9	53.4	30.7	17.1	55.4	27.4	19.1	54.8	26.1	17.7	55.2	27.1	19.1	53.8	27.1
	25-29	4.6	62.0	33.4	4.2	65.2	30.6	4.9	65.0	30.1	4.0	65.8	30.2	4.1	64.9	31.0
Netherlands	15-19	m	m	m	89.7	7.6	2.7	88.2	8.9	3.0	80.6	15.7	3.7	86.5	9.9	3.6
	20-24	m	m	m	50.5	42.0	7.5	50.7	42.5	6.7	36.5	55.2	8.2	44.2	47.8	8.0
	25-29	m	m	m	24.4	64.9	10.7	25.0	65.2	9.8	5.0	83.0	12.1	15.3	73.7	11.0

Source: OECD. See Annex 3 for notes (*www.oecd.org/edu/eag2007*).
Please refer to the Reader's Guide for information concerning the symbols replacing missing data.
StatLink ⫶ⅢⓢⅬ http://dx.doi.org/10.1787/068418024204

C4

Table C4.4a. *(continued-1)*

Trends in the percentage of the youth population in education and not in education (1995-2005)
By age group and work status

	Age group	1995 In educa-tion Total	1995 Not in education Employed	1995 Not in education Not employed	1998 In educa-tion Total	1998 Not in education Employed	1998 Not in education Not employed	1999 In educa-tion Total	1999 Not in education Employed	1999 Not in education Not employed	2000 In educa-tion Total	2000 Not in education Employed	2000 Not in education Not employed	2001 In educa-tion Total	2001 Not in education Employed	2001 Not in education Not employed
New Zealand	15-19	m	m	m	m	m	m	m	m	m	m	m	m	m	m	m
	20-24	m	m	m	m	m	m	m	m	m	m	m	m	m	m	m
	25-29	m	m	m	m	m	m	m	m	m	m	m	m	m	m	m
Norway	15-19	m	m	m	92.1	6.0	1.9	91.9	6.4	c	92.4	5.9	c	85.8	11.1	3.0
	20-24	m	m	m	40.2	51.4	8.4	38.4	53.8	7.8	41.7	50.3	8.0	39.6	51.7	8.7
	25-29	m	m	m	14.4	76.1	9.6	17.2	74.4	8.3	17.5	72.1	10.4	13.9	75.9	10.2
Poland	15-19	89.6	4.2	6.2	91.0	4.2	4.8	93.2	2.3	4.6	92.8	2.6	4.5	91.8	2.4	5.8
	20-24	23.7	42.5	33.8	30.8	45.3	23.9	33.1	39.7	27.2	34.9	34.3	30.8	45.2	27.7	27.1
	25-29	3.1	67.5	29.4	5.7	70.5	23.8	5.4	68.0	26.6	8.0	62.9	29.1	11.4	59.9	28.7
Portugal	15-19	72.4	18.5	9.1	71.6	20.1	8.3	72.3	19.6	8.1	72.6	19.7	7.7	72.8	19.8	7.4
	20-24	37.8	46.6	15.6	32.4	55.7	12.0	34.9	53.2	11.9	36.5	52.6	11.0	36.3	53.3	10.4
	25-29	11.6	70.9	17.4	9.5	74.8	15.8	11.5	75.1	13.4	11.0	76.6	12.5	11.2	77.3	11.6
Slovak Republic	15-19	70.1	14.0	15.9	69.4	12.3	18.3	69.6	10.1	20.4	67.3	6.4	26.3	67.3	6.3	26.4
	20-24	14.8	54.9	30.3	17.4	56.3	26.3	17.4	51.2	31.4	18.1	48.8	33.1	19.4	45.7	34.9
	25-29	1.6	65.5	32.9	1.1	71.6	27.2	1.6	70.2	28.2	1.3	66.9	31.8	2.3	65.0	32.7
Spain	15-19	77.3	11.2	11.5	80.2	9.9	9.8	79.3	11.3	9.4	80.6	11.4	8.0	81.4	11.6	6.9
	20-24	40.0	34.2	25.8	44.3	35.7	20.1	43.6	38.8	17.6	44.6	40.3	15.0	45.0	40.7	14.2
	25-29	14.6	51.5	33.9	15.3	57.3	27.5	15.2	59.6	25.1	16.2	62.4	21.4	17.0	63.1	19.8
Sweden	15-19	87.4	6.9	5.6	90.9	4.3	4.7	91.5	4.9	3.7	90.6	5.8	3.6	88.4	7.3	4.3
	20-24	38.8	43.7	17.5	42.6	44.3	13.1	43.8	45.2	11.0	42.1	47.2	10.7	41.2	48.2	10.6
	25-29	19.9	67.0	13.2	24.9	65.0	10.0	22.5	68.1	9.5	21.9	68.9	9.2	22.7	70.0	7.2
Switzerland	15-19	65.6	10.2	24.2	85.5	9.6	4.8	84.4	8.0	7.6	84.6	7.5	7.9	85.7	7.5	6.8
	20-24	29.5	59.2	11.3	34.8	54.2	11.0	35.8	55.8	8.4	37.4	56.7	5.9	39.3	52.3	8.4
	25-29	10.6	76.2	13.2	10.1	77.9	12.1	10.4	79.3	10.3	15.0	73.9	11.1	13.5	75.1	11.4
Turkey	15-19	38.7	34.2	27.2	40.2	32.1	27.7	42.9	30.2	26.9	39.2	29.6	31.2	41.0	26.7	32.3
	20-24	10.3	46.5	43.2	13.4	44.7	42.0	13.1	45.6	41.4	12.7	43.1	44.2	12.7	43.1	44.2
	25-29	2.7	59.6	37.8	2.9	60.4	36.7	3.4	57.7	38.8	2.9	58.8	38.3	2.6	57.1	40.2
United Kingdom	15-19	m	m	m	m	m	m	m	m	m	77.0	15.0	8.0	76.1	15.7	8.2
	20-24	m	m	m	m	m	m	m	m	m	32.4	52.2	15.4	33.5	51.7	14.8
	25-29	m	m	m	m	m	m	m	m	m	13.3	70.3	16.3	13.3	70.6	16.0
United States	15-19	81.5	10.7	7.8	82.2	10.5	7.3	81.3	11.3	7.4	81.3	11.7	7.0	81.2	11.4	7.5
	20-24	31.5	50.7	17.8	33.0	52.6	14.4	32.8	52.1	15.1	32.5	53.1	14.4	33.9	50.5	15.6
	25-29	11.6	71.4	17.0	11.9	72.7	15.4	11.1	73.2	15.7	11.4	72.8	15.8	11.8	70.5	17.7
OECD28 average	*15-19*				*79.7*	*11.5*	*9.1*	*80.4*	*11.3*	*9.0*	*80.5*	*11.2*	*9.2*	*80.7*	*11.1*	*8.8*
	20-24				*35.1*	*46.8*	*18.1*	*35.6*	*46.9*	*17.5*	*35.4*	*47.7*	*17.4*	*37.1*	*46.4*	*17.0*
	25-29				*12.8*	*67.1*	*20.2*	*13.1*	*67.5*	*19.4*	*12.5*	*68.5*	*19.0*	*13.0*	*68.4*	*19.2*
EU19 average	*15-19*				*83.1*	*8.7*	*8.2*	*83.5*	*8.7*	*7.7*	*83.6*	*9.0*	*7.7*	*84.2*	*8.6*	*7.5*
	20-24				*36.8*	*44.9*	*18.3*	*37.3*	*44.9*	*17.9*	*36.5*	*46.4*	*17.1*	*38.7*	*45.1*	*16.2*
	25-29				*12.7*	*66.4*	*20.9*	*12.8*	*67.1*	*20.0*	*11.7*	*69.1*	*19.3*	*12.7*	*68.7*	*18.6*
Estonia	15-19	m	m	m	m	m	m	m	m	m	m	m	m	m	m	m
	20-24	m	m	m	m	m	m	m	m	m	m	m	m	m	m	m
	25-29	m	m	m	m	m	m	m	m	m	m	m	m	m	m	m
Israel	15-19	m	m	m	m	m	m	m	m	m	m	m	m	m	m	m
	20-24	m	m	m	m	m	m	m	m	m	m	m	m	m	m	m
	25-29	m	m	m	m	m	m	m	m	m	m	m	m	m	m	m
Slovenia	15-19	m	m	m	m	m	m	m	m	m	m	m	m	m	m	m
	20-24	m	m	m	m	m	m	m	m	m	m	m	m	m	m	m
	25-29	m	m	m	m	m	m	m	m	m	m	m	m	m	m	m

OECD countries (side label) / *Partner economies* (side label)

Notes: Due to incomplete data, some averages have not been calculated.
Source: OECD. See Annex 3 for notes (*www.oecd.org/edu/eag2007*).
Please refer to the Reader's Guide for information concerning the symbols replacing missing data.
StatLink ⧉ http://dx.doi.org/10.1787/068418024204

Table C4.4a. *(continued-2)*

Trends in the percentage of the youth population in education and not in education (1995-2005)

By age group and work status

C4

	Age group	2002 In education Total	2002 Not in education Employed	2002 Not in education Not employed	2003 In education Total	2003 Not in education Employed	2003 Not in education Not employed	2004 In education Total	2004 Not in education Employed	2004 Not in education Not employed	2005 In education Total	2005 Not in education Employed	2005 Not in education Not employed
Australia	15-19	79.7	13.3	7.0	79.6	13.6	6.8	78.4	14.1	7.5	78.3	14.3	7.4
	20-24	38.7	48.1	13.2	39.7	47.0	13.3	39.0	48.7	12.3	39.4	49.0	11.6
	25-29	16.5	65.7	17.8	17.7	64.7	17.6	17.7	65.0	17.3	16.6	68.0	15.4
Austria	15-19	81.5	12.1	6.3	83.6	10.7	5.6	83.3	9.3	7.3	84.4	8.7	6.9
	20-24	29.4	58.9	11.7	30.3	59.3	10.4	30.3	56.8	12.9	30.4	57.2	12.4
	25-29	10.3	77.3	12.4	12.5	75.2	12.3	13.0	72.6	14.4	12.0	74.6	13.4
Belgium	15-19	89.6	3.6	6.8	89.1	3.8	7.1	92.1	3.1	4.9	90.1	3.7	6.2
	20-24	38.2	44.4	17.4	39.9	43.0	17.1	38.8	44.4	16.9	38.1	43.6	18.3
	25-29	5.8	77.0	17.2	8.9	72.8	18.3	6.0	74.3	19.7	7.4	74.9	17.7
Canada	15-19	82.2	11.2	6.6	81.9	11.3	6.9	81.0	11.5	7.5	81.7	12.1	6.1
	20-24	38.8	47.2	14.0	39.0	48.0	12.9	40.2	46.7	13.0	41.6	45.2	13.2
	25-29	14.5	69.0	16.5	14.4	70.4	15.3	13.5	71.0	15.5	14.1	71.0	14.9
Czech Republic	15-19	88.3	5.7	6.0	89.0	5.2	5.8	89.9	4.4	5.7	90.3	4.4	5.3
	20-24	25.7	56.2	18.1	28.7	53.3	18.0	32.3	49.2	18.5	35.9	47.5	16.6
	25-29	2.9	73.3	23.8	3.0	73.0	24.1	3.8	71.6	24.5	4.4	72.4	23.2
Denmark	15-19	88.7	8.9	2.4	89.8	7.7	2.5	89.5	8.4	2.1	88.4	7.3	4.3
	20-24	55.3	37.4	7.3	52.1	36.1	11.8	54.0	34.8	11.3	54.4	37.2	8.3
	25-29	35.0	58.3	6.7	23.9	64.6	11.5	28.3	59.8	11.9	27.0	61.3	11.6
Finland	15-19	m	m	m	88.1	5.7	6.2	88.9	5.2	5.9	90.2	4.5	5.2
	20-24	m	m	m	52.5	33.1	14.4	53.1	31.5	15.4	52.8	34.1	13.0
	25-29	m	m	m	27.2	58.7	14.1	25.7	58.8	15.5	25.7	60.3	14.0
France	15-19	94.6	1.9	3.4	m	m	m	91.5	3.2	5.4	90.8	3.0	6.2
	20-24	53.2	32.5	14.4	m	m	m	45.2	37.2	17.6	47.4	36.1	16.5
	25-29	11.7	70.1	18.2	m	m	m	13.2	66.7	20.0	13.7	67.2	19.1
Germany	15-19	90.1	5.2	4.7	91.2	4.1	4.7	93.4	3.0	3.6	92.9	2.7	4.4
	20-24	38.1	46.0	15.9	41.2	43.1	15.6	44.0	38.5	17.5	44.2	37.1	18.7
	25-29	16.3	66.3	17.4	17.9	63.7	18.4	17.6	62.8	19.6	18.5	60.3	21.2
Greece	15-19	86.6	7.1	6.3	84.2	6.3	9.5	83.5	6.5	10.0	84.5	5.7	9.8
	20-24	35.6	41.8	22.6	38.4	39.9	21.7	36.3	41.9	21.8	42.6	37.3	20.1
	25-29	5.7	68.7	25.5	7.0	68.8	24.3	5.8	68.9	25.3	6.8	70.2	23.0
Hungary	15-19	87.5	4.5	8.0	89.7	3.5	6.8	90.4	3.4	6.2	90.6	3.0	6.4
	20-24	36.9	42.6	20.5	40.5	39.6	19.9	43.8	37.6	18.6	46.6	34.5	18.9
	25-29	8.6	63.1	28.3	12.6	59.9	27.5	12.9	63.2	23.9	13.1	63.0	24.0
Iceland	15-19	80.9	14.8	c	88.5	7.6	c	85.4	11.8	c	86.4	10.7	c
	20-24	53.8	40.1	6.2	57.1	35.1	7.8	56.1	37.5	6.4	53.0	37.1	10.0
	25-29	36.5	58.8	c	26.8	61.7	11.5	30.2	64.0	5.8	30.9	61.5	7.6
Ireland	15-19	81.6	13.6	4.8	81.4	13.4	5.2	79.3	10.8	9.9	82.5	13.1	4.4
	20-24	29.0	60.2	10.8	30.3	58.3	11.3	34.6	53.2	12.2	27.8	60.0	12.2
	25-29	3.5	81.8	14.7	4.8	80.2	14.9	12.3	73.2	14.5	5.1	81.3	13.6
Italy	15-19	80.8	8.7	10.5	83.8	6.9	9.3	81.2	7.8	11.0	81.8	7.0	11.2
	20-24	38.2	37.5	24.3	44.1	34.2	21.7	37.7	38.7	23.6	38.6	37.3	24.1
	25-29	15.6	59.5	24.8	22.8	54.7	22.5	15.4	59.8	24.8	14.4	59.8	25.8
Japan	15-24	58.6	32.0	9.5	58.4	31.7	9.8	59.1	31.7	9.2	59.7	31.5	8.8
Luxembourg	15-19	91.3	5.7	3.0	92.2	5.7	2.1	91.4	5.5	3.2	93.4	4.4	2.2
	20-24	47.8	45.2	7.0	46.0	45.9	8.1	49.1	40.8	10.1	47.4	43.3	9.3
	25-29	13.9	74.5	11.6	7.6	82.2	10.2	6.1	81.5	12.4	8.6	81.2	10.3
Mexico	15-19	53.4	29.0	17.5	54.0	28.2	17.8	54.9	28.0	17.0	m	m	m
	20-24	20.8	52.6	26.6	19.8	52.6	27.6	20.3	52.3	27.4	m	m	m
	25-29	4.6	64.8	30.6	4.2	64.8	31.0	4.4	65.4	30.3	m	m	m
Netherlands	15-19	86.7	9.5	3.8	87.0	8.7	4.3	89.2	7.5	3.3	89.2	7.0	3.9
	20-24	45.1	47.7	7.3	44.2	46.5	9.4	46.6	44.2	9.3	49.1	41.8	9.1
	25-29	16.2	71.6	12.2	16.5	71.4	12.1	16.9	71.2	11.9	18.2	70.2	11.6

Notes: The break in Austrian time series is due to a change in survey methodology from 2003 to 2004; the break in French time series is due to a change in methodology: age is measured in the reference week from 2004, as the participation in education.

Source: OECD. See Annex 3 for notes (*www.oecd.org/edu/eag2007*).

Please refer to the Reader's Guide for information concerning the symbols replacing missing data.

StatLink ⟐⟐⟐⟐ http://dx.doi.org/10.1787/068418024204

C4

Table C4.4a. *(continued-3)*
Trends in the percentage of the youth population in education and not in education (1995-2005)
By age group and work status

	Age group	2002			2003			2004			2005		
		In education Total	Not in education Employed	Not in education Not employed	In education Total	Not in education Employed	Not in education Not employed	In education Total	Not in education Employed	Not in education Not employed	In education Total	Not in education Employed	Not in education Not employed
New Zealand	15-19	m	m	m	m	m	m	m	m	m	70.0	21.5	8.5
	20-24	m	m	m	m	m	m	m	m	m	32.9	50.5	16.7
	25-29	m	m	m	m	m	m	m	m	m	15.4	67.9	16.7
Norway	15-19	85.3	11.5	3.2	86.9	10.4	2.7	87.2	9.9	2.8	87.4	10.1	2.5
	20-24	38.5	51.8	9.7	38.7	50.8	10.6	40.6	49.6	9.8	41.5	48.9	9.6
	25-29	14.2	75.0	10.7	15.4	71.9	12.7	15.4	71.5	13.1	15.7	72.0	12.3
Poland	15-19	95.9	1.0	3.1	95.6	1.1	3.3	96.5	0.9	2.6	97.9	0.4	1.7
	20-24	53.8	20.8	25.4	55.7	18.8	25.5	57.5	18.4	24.1	62.7	17.2	20.1
	25-29	14.9	53.3	31.8	17.3	52.4	30.2	15.5	53.7	30.8	16.4	54.3	29.3
Portugal	15-19	72.4	20.3	7.3	74.8	16.4	8.8	75.1	15.1	9.8	79.3	12.2	8.4
	20-24	34.7	53.3	12.0	35.2	52.5	12.3	38.7	47.8	13.5	37.4	48.4	14.1
	25-29	10.7	77.1	12.2	11.7	73.7	14.6	11.0	75.0	14.0	11.5	73.6	14.9
Slovak Republic	15-19	78.6	5.8	15.6	82.2	5.2	12.6	87.8	4.3	7.9	90.4	3.3	6.3
	20-24	22.1	44.0	33.9	24.0	46.4	29.6	27.5	44.7	27.8	31.0	43.8	25.2
	25-29	2.9	66.6	30.5	2.6	68.3	29.1	4.5	66.6	28.9	6.1	64.9	29.0
Spain	15-19	81.9	11.0	7.2	82.6	10.1	7.3	82.2	10.1	7.6	81.8	9.7	8.5
	20-24	43.4	41.5	15.1	43.5	41.8	14.8	41.3	43.2	15.6	44.3	40.2	15.5
	25-29	16.1	64.2	19.8	15.4	65.0	19.5	15.3	66.2	18.5	22.8	61.0	16.2
Sweden	15-19	88.4	7.0	4.6	88.7	7.0	4.2	89.4	5.8	4.8	89.6	5.8	4.7
	20-24	41.7	47.0	11.2	42.3	46.0	11.8	42.8	43.6	13.6	42.5	44.1	13.4
	25-29	22.4	69.5	8.1	22.8	67.9	9.4	21.5	68.0	10.5	23.6	66.5	10.0
Switzerland	15-19	86.2	8.0	5.8	83.6	8.4	8.0	84.9	7.9	7.2	84.9	7.9	7.2
	20-24	38.0	52.3	9.7	35.8	51.5	12.7	37.3	51.7	11.0	37.3	51.7	11.0
	25-29	12.7	74.7	12.6	12.2	73.6	14.2	15.6	72.3	12.1	15.6	72.3	12.1
Turkey	15-19	42.2	24.8	32.9	45.9	21.3	32.8	43.5	21.2	35.3	42.5	19.9	37.7
	20-24	14.1	40.6	45.3	15.8	36.5	47.8	13.0	39.1	47.8	15.2	37.7	47.1
	25-29	3.0	56.2	40.7	3.7	53.2	43.1	3.1	54.0	42.8	4.3	53.5	42.2
United Kingdom	15-19	75.3	16.2	8.6	76.3	14.3	9.4	74.3	16.7	9.0	76.0	14.6	9.3
	20-24	31.0	53.7	15.3	32.6	52.1	15.3	31.1	54.1	14.8	32.1	51.0	16.8
	25-29	13.3	70.7	16.0	15.0	68.7	16.3	14.2	69.0	16.8	13.3	70.1	16.6
United States	15-19	82.9	10.2	7.0	m	m	m	83.9	9.2	6.9	85.6	8.3	6.1
	20-24	35.0	48.5	16.5	m	m	m	35.2	47.9	16.9	36.1	48.4	15.5
	25-29	12.3	70.3	17.4	m	m	m	13.0	68.7	18.4	11.9	70.0	18.1
OECD28 average	*15-19*	*82.0*	*10.4*	*7.7*	*82.8*	*9.5*	*7.9*	*83.3*	*9.1*	*7.9*	*84.5*	*8.3*	*7.3*
	20-24	*37.6*	*45.8*	*16.6*	*38.7*	*44.5*	*16.8*	*39.5*	*43.5*	*17.0*	*40.8*	*43.0*	*16.2*
	25-29	*13.1*	*68.4*	*19.1*	*13.8*	*67.3*	*19.0*	*13.8*	*67.2*	*19.0*	*14.6*	*67.5*	*17.9*
EU19 average	*15-19*	*85.5*	*8.2*	*6.3*	*86.1*	*7.5*	*6.4*	*86.8*	*6.9*	*6.3*	*87.6*	*6.3*	*6.1*
	20-24	*38.8*	*45.0*	*16.1*	*40.1*	*43.9*	*16.0*	*41.3*	*42.1*	*16.6*	*42.4*	*41.7*	*15.9*
	25-29	*12.5*	*69.1*	*18.4*	*13.9*	*67.8*	*18.3*	*13.6*	*67.5*	*18.8*	*14.1*	*67.7*	*18.1*
Estonia	15-19	m	m	m	94.4	2.3	3.3	91.0	1.4	7.6	92.0	2.9	5.2
	20-24	m	m	m	39.7	42.3	18.0	48.6	31.9	19.5	50.9	32.7	16.3
	25-29	m	m	m	14.7	59.8	25.5	14.9	65.3	19.8	14.2	61.8	24.0
Israel	15-19	69.4	6.0	24.6	69.0	5.7	25.2	68.9	5.6	25.6	68.9	6.3	24.7
	20-24	26.8	31.7	41.6	28.1	27.7	44.2	28.6	30.5	40.9	28.3	31.4	40.3
	25-29	19.1	52.2	28.7	19.6	52.7	27.7	20.9	53.9	25.3	21.4	54.3	24.2
Slovenia	15-19	m	m	m	92.8	2.4	4.8	92.2	3.5	4.3	92.4	2.7	4.9
	20-24	m	m	m	56.8	30.2	13.0	60.9	27.9	11.2	55.7	31.3	13.0
	25-29	m	m	m	25.3	63.1	11.5	26.6	61.8	11.5	24.6	63.9	11.5

Source: OECD. See Annex 3 for notes (*www.oecd.org/edu/eag2007*).
Please refer to the Reader's Guide for information concerning the symbols replacing missing data.
StatLink ⫶⫶⫶⫶ http://dx.doi.org/10.1787/068418024204

DO ADULTS PARTICIPATE IN TRAINING AND EDUCATION AT WORK?

This indicator examines the participation of the adult population in non-formal job-related education and training by showing the expected number of hours in such education and training. A particular focus of this indicator is the time that a hypothetical individual (facing current conditions in terms of adult learning opportunities at different stages in life) is expected to spend in such education and training over a typical working life (a 40-year period).

Key results

Chart C5.1. Expected hours in non-formal job-related training (2003)

This chart shows the hours that people in different countries can expect to spend in non-formal job-related education and training over the course of a typical working life.

Across countries, there are major differences in the time that individuals can expect to spend in non-formal job-related education and training over a typical working life.

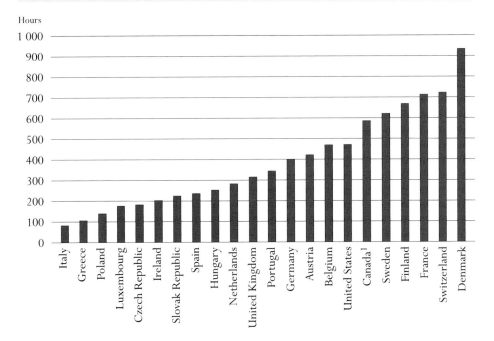

1. Year of reference 2002.
Countries are ranked in ascending order of the expected hours in non-formal job-related education and training.
Source: OECD. Table C5.1a. See Annex 3 for notes (*www.oecd.org/edu/eag2007*).
StatLink ᐧᐧᔕᐧ http://dx.doi.org/10.1787/068423487063

Other highlights of this indicator

▪ Adults with higher levels of educational attainment are more likely to participate in non-formal job-related continuing education and training than adults with lower educational attainment.

▪ Across countries, there are major differences in the number of hours that individuals can expect to spend in non-formal job-related education and training over a typical working life. At the tertiary level, this ranges from below 350 hours in Greece, Italy and the Netherlands to more than 1 000 hours in Denmark, Finland, France and Switzerland.

▪ In all but six countries – Finland, France, Greece, Hungary the Netherlands and Portugal – men can expect to spend more hours in non-formal job-related continuing and education and training than women.

Policy context

The ageing of the population and the skill demands in OECD economies – associated with new technologies, globalisation and organisational change – are among the key reasons why lifelong learning occupies a prominent position in today's policy foreground. Many observers also hold that changes in workplace organisation are leading to shifts in the demand for different types of skills, underpinning the importance of continuing education and training.

Evidence and explanations

Variation across countries in participation rates

There is substantial cross-country variation in participation rates in non-formal job-related continuing education and training. In the OECD, four countries – Denmark, Finland, Sweden and the United States – take the lead, with more than 35% of the population between 25 and 64 years of age having participated in some type of non-formal job-related continuing education and training over the previous 12 months. The participation rate is lower than 10% in Greece, Hungary, Italy, the Netherlands, Poland, Portugal and Spain. Between these two extremes, the incidence of participation in education and training varies greatly; for example, the figure is about 11% in the Czech Republic and Ireland, but over twice this rate in Canada and the United Kingdom (Table C5.1a).

Training leads to further training

In addition to these large variations in participation rates, a striking pattern is that adult education and training increases with one's level of initial education (Table C5.1a). In all countries, the participation rate varies significantly according to prior levels of educational attainment. In other words, all countries share inequalities in the incidence of adult learning. On average for the OECD countries surveyed, participation in adult non-formal job-related education and training is 14 percentage points higher for individuals who have attained a tertiary level of education than for persons who have only attained an upper secondary or post-secondary non-tertiary education. Similarly, participation is 10 percentage points higher for individuals who have attained an upper secondary and post-secondary non-tertiary education than for persons who have only attained education below the upper secondary level. A greater understanding of the underlying causes of this participation differential by initial education could assist with strategies for promoting lifelong learning among the less qualified.

Expected hours in non-formal job-related education and training

Chart C5.2 shows major differences across countries in the number of hours that individuals of different levels of educational attainment can expect to spend in non-formal job-related education and training over a typical working life. At the tertiary level of attainment, this ranges from below 350 hours in Greece, Italy and the Netherlands to more than 1 000 hours in Denmark, Finland, France and Switzerland. In a few countries – Denmark, France and Finland – individuals with attainment below the upper secondary level can expect to spend considerably more hours in non-formal job-related continuing education and training than persons in other countries who have attained a tertiary level of education.

It is illustrative to consider these data in relation to the average annual hours of work. For instance, in Switzerland, individuals at the tertiary level of attainment can expect to register over 1 300 hours in non-formal job-related education and training over a typical working life,

Chart C5.2. **Expected hours in non-formal job-related education and training by level of educational attainment (2003)**

Expected number of hours in non-formal job-related education and training for 25-to-64-year-olds, by level of educational attainment

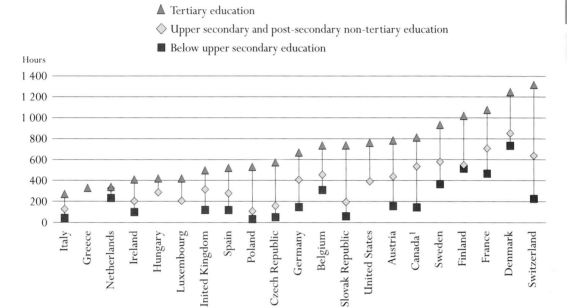

▲ Tertiary education

◇ Upper secondary and post-secondary non-tertiary education

■ Below upper secondary education

1. Year of reference 2002.
Countries are ranked in ascending order of the expected hours in non-formal job-related training at the tertiary level of education.
Source: OECD. Table C5.1a. See Annex 3 for notes (*www.oecd.org/edu/eag2007*).
StatLink 🔍 http://dx.doi.org/10.1787/068423487063

the highest figure among all OECD countries (Table C5.1a). This implies that during the working life, such individuals can expect to spend the equivalent of over 83% of an average year of work in continuing education and training. Considering all levels of education, lifetime hours in non-formal job-related education and training as a percentage of average annual hours in work range from below 10% in the Czech Republic, Greece, Italy and Poland to 40% and above in Denmark, France, Sweden and Switzerland.

Expected hours in non-formal job-related education and training by age and gender

In most countries, participation in non-formal job-related learning declines with age, although the extent of the decline varies across countries (Chart C5.3). In only four countries is there an increase in expected non-formal job-related learning between the ages of 25 to 34 and 35 to 44: the Czech Republic, Denmark, Finland and Sweden. Only one country, the United States, registers an increase in the expected hours in non-formal job-related education and training between the ages of 35 to 44 and 45 to 54. In Austria, Belgium, France, Hungary and Spain, individuals in the oldest age group (55-to-64-year-olds) have substantially fewer expected hours in non-formal education and training than their younger peers. In these countries, the number of expected hours is only around one-quarter or less of those of the next youngest age group. This may be due to older adults placing less value on investment in training and also to employers

Chart C5.3. Expected hours in non-formal job-related education and training for the population, by selected age group (2003)

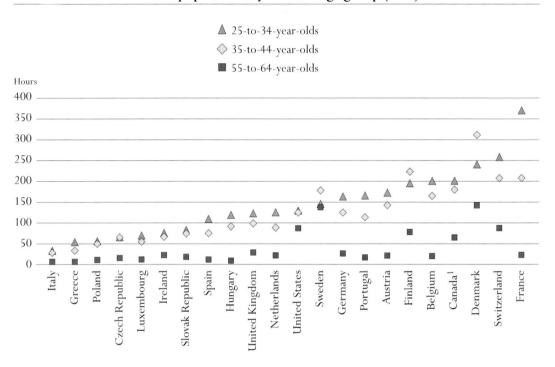

1. Year of reference 2002.
Countries are ranked in ascending order of the expected hours in non-formal job-related education and training of the 25-to-34 age group.
Source: OECD. Table C5.1b. See Annex 3 for notes (*www.oecd.org/edu/eag2007*).
StatLink http://dx.doi.org/10.1787/068423487063

proposing training less frequently to older workers (possibly in light of the shorter time available for capturing returns on this investment). By presenting data on how hours in training are distributed across age cohorts, Tables C5.1b and C5.1c shed light on whether the concept of lifelong learning is being put into practice in a country (both the absolute number of hours in training and their distribution should be examined in this connection). To have a complete picture of lifelong learning, additional information on labour market participation rates among older workers is informative in many respects.

Canada, Denmark, Finland, Sweden, Switzerland and the United States are notable in the extent to which they achieve relatively high expected hours in non-formal learning across age groups. Denmark and Sweden are exceptional as regards the high number of expected hours in non-formal learning in the oldest age group, with about 140 hours.

In all but three countries – France, Hungary and Finland – employed men can expect to spend more hours in non-formal job-related education and training than employed women (Chart C5.4). By far the largest gender difference is seen in Switzerland, with employed males registering almost 360 more expected hours than employed females. In all countries except Austria, Belgium and Switzerland the difference between the genders is less than one hundred hours (in favour of males).

Chart C5.4. Gender difference in expected hours in non-formal job-related education and training for 25-to-64-year-olds in the labour force (2003)

C5

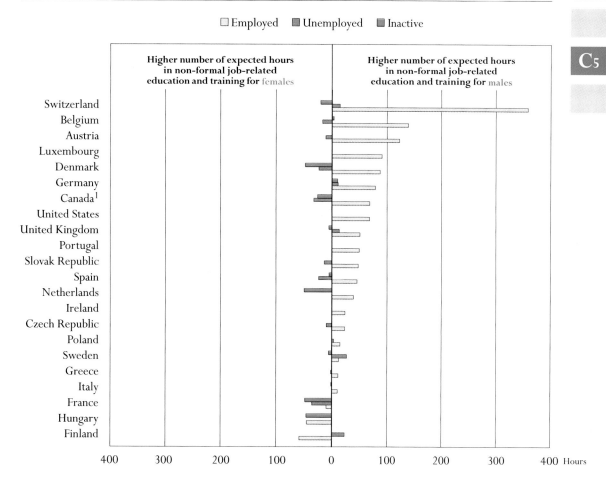

1. Year of reference 2002.

Countries are ranked in descending order of the difference between employed females and males in expected hours of non-formal job-related education and training.

Source: OECD. Table C5.1b. See Annex 3 for notes (*www.oecd.org/edu/eag2007*).

StatLink ⬛ᴍˢ⬛ http://dx.doi.org/10.1787/068423487063

Job-related education and training may also be an effective mechanism for combating unemployment, as it can permit individuals to develop skills that make them more attractive to employers. In the face of changing technologies, work practices and markets, policy-makers in many countries are promoting more general work-related training and informal learning by adults. However, employed workers accumulate many more hours of non-formal job-related education and training than unemployed workers. In all countries, employed workers register significantly higher expected hours in job-related education and training than do the unemployed (Table C5.1b). This is mainly because the time spent in unemployment is generally much shorter than the time spent in employment. Nevertheless, the time spent in non-formal job-related learning activities during the most recent year was significantly higher for the unemployed participants than for the employed participants in all countries (Table C6.3 in *Education at a Glance 2005* [OECD, 2005d). However, significantly fewer of the unemployed than the employed participated in these activities.

C5

Definition and methodologies

Data for non-European countries were calculated from country-specific household surveys (see Annex 3 at *www.oecd.org/edu/eag2007*). Data for countries in the European statistical system come from the January 2006 version of the European Labour Force Survey *ad hoc* module "Lifelong Learning 2003". For most European countries, data on hours in job-related activities are available for up to three most recent non-formal learning activities. Data for Canada cover up to five job-related training activities per training participant. Data for the United States cover up to four job-related training activities per training participant.

The analysis in this indicator is focused on non-formal job-related continuing education and training. *Non-formal education* is defined as any organised and sustained educational activities that cannot be considered as formal education according to ISCED and do not lead to a corresponding qualification. Non-formal education may therefore take place both within and outside educational institutions, and may cater to persons of all ages. Depending on country contexts, it may cover educational programmes to impart adult literacy, basic education for out-of-school children, life skills, work skills and general culture. Non-formal education programmes do not necessarily follow the educational ladder system. The term "job-related" refers to education and training activities intended mainly for work reasons as opposed to personal or social reasons. That is, the respondent takes part in the activity in order to obtain knowledge and/or learn new skills for a current or a future job, increase earnings, improve career opportunities and generally improve his or her opportunities for advancement and promotion.

The calculation of time spent in non-formal job-related learning activities by labour force status (Table C5.1C) is weighted by the time that a hypothetical person is expected to spend as "employed", "unemployed" and "inactive" respectively. For most countries the data refer to the labour force status during a reference week, while the time spent in learning activities refers to all activities during a one-year reference period (prior to the interview), regardless of the labour force status when participating in the learning activity.

Table C5.1a.

Participation rate and expected number of hours in non-formal job-related education and training by level of educational attainment (2003)

Participation rate and expected number of hours in non-formal job-related education and training for a forty-year period for 25-to-64-year-olds in the population, by gender and educational attainment

		Participation rate during one year				Expected hours in non-formal job-related education and training between the ages of 25 and 64				Average hours of work	Ratio (%) of hours in training to annual hours of work
		Lower secondary education	Upper secondary and post-secondary non-tertiary education	Tertiary education	All levels of education	Lower secondary education	Upper secondary and post-secondary non-tertiary education	Tertiary education	All levels of education		
Austria	M+F	5	19	37	19	140	420	767	422	1550	27
	Males	7	20	34	21	157	468	722	470	m	m
	Females	4	17	40	17	131	366	834	374	m	m
Belgium	M+F	6	15	30	16	293	437	719	469	1542	30
	Males	8	17	33	18	353	543	768	540	m	m
	Females	4	14	28	14	230	327	668	397	m	m
Canada [1]	M+F	6	20	35	25	128	517	796	586	1740	34
	Males	8	22	35	25	126	486	863	590	m	m
	Females	5	19	36	25	c	549	738	582	m	m
Czech Republic	M+F	3	10	21	11	34	142	556	182	1986	9
	Males	6	12	20	13	28	134	562	186	m	m
	Females	2	9	22	9	39	150	553	179	m	m
Denmark	M+F	22	36	54	39	719	836	1 230	934	1475	63
	Males	25	36	54	39	726	884	1 197	946	m	m
	Females	20	36	54	39	722	780	1 260	922	m	m
Finland	M+F	20	32	54	36	497	530	1 003	669	1718	39
	Males	18	31	52	33	503	514	975	637	m	m
	Females	21	33	56	39	486	545	1 035	701	m	m
France	M+F	9	19	33	19	450	692	1 061	713	1441	49
	Males	11	20	34	20	458	567	1 093	664	m	m
	Females	8	17	33	17	440	833	1 039	760	m	m
Germany	M+F	3	10	24	12	130	390	650	398	1441	28
	Males	3	10	23	12	149	431	672	447	m	m
	Females	3	9	25	11	114	348	626	348	m	m
Greece	M+F	n	3	11	4	c	c	312	106	1936	5
	Males	1	3	11	4	c	c	316	106	m	m
	Females	n	3	11	3	c	c	c	106	m	m
Hungary	M+F	1	4	9	4	c	270	402	253	m	m
	Males	2	3	8	4	c	177	384	192	m	m
	Females	1	5	10	5	c	370	422	312	m	m
Ireland	M+F	5	10	20	11	82	185	392	203	1646	12
	Males	6	12	20	11	98	c	401	209	m	m
	Females	3	9	20	10	c	190	385	197	m	m
Italy	M+F	1	6	12	4	26	111	254	82	1591	5
	Males	2	6	13	4	31	113	264	87	m	m
	Females	1	6	12	4	21	110	244	77	m	m
Luxembourg	M+F	3	12	27	12	c	189	402	176	1592	11
	Males	4	13	29	13	c	212	436	207	m	m
	Females	2	11	26	10	c	c	c	c	m	m
Netherlands	M+F	5	11	13	9	216	308	322	283	1354	21
	Males	6	11	12	10	227	292	298	277	m	m
	Females	4	10	14	9	211	328	357	289	m	m
Poland	M+F	1	7	29	9	16	90	513	139	1984	7
	Males	2	8	27	9	c	104	531	147	m	m
	Females	1	6	31	9	c	76	495	131	m	m

1. Year of reference 2002.

Source: OECD. See Annex 3 for notes (*www.oecd.org/edu/eag2007*).

Please refer to the Reader's guide for information concerning the symbols replacing missing data.

StatLink ᠁ᠰ᠘ http://dx.doi.org/10.1787/068423487063

C5

Table C5.1a. *(continued)*
Participation rate and expected number of hours in non-formal job-related education and training by level of educational attainment (2003)
Participation rate and expected number of hours in non-formal job-related education and training for a forty-year period for 25-to-64-year-olds in the population, by gender and educational attainment

		Participation rate during one year				Expected hours in non-formal job-related education and training between the ages of 25 and 64				Average hours of work	Ratio (%) of hours in training to annual hours of work
		Lower secondary education	Upper secondary and post-secondary non-tertiary education	Tertiary education	All levels of education	Lower secondary education	Upper secondary and post-secondary non-tertiary education	Tertiary education	All levels of education		
Portugal	M+F	4	15	27	7	232	c	c	343	1678	20
	Males	4	17	27	8	159	c	c	316	m	m
	Females	3	14	27	7	302	c	c	367	m	m
Slovak Republic	M+F	6	19	37	19	43	178	721	225	1931	12
	Males	10	21	37	22	c	190	741	240	m	m
	Females	4	16	38	16	c	165	699	212	m	m
Spain	M+F	3	7	14	6	102	261	503	237	1800	13
	Males	4	9	14	7	116	265	503	247	m	m
	Females	2	6	14	6	87	257	506	226	m	m
Sweden	M+F	24	37	57	40	350	562	917	622	1563	40
	Males	24	36	56	39	368	617	932	641	m	m
	Females	23	38	58	42	324	502	911	603	m	m
Switzerland	M+F	8	27	44	29	212	621	1 301	723	1556	46
	Males	9	29	45	33	256	760	1 422	912	m	m
	Females	7	26	43	26	184	514	1 085	551	m	m
United Kingdom	M+F	7	26	46	27	103	297	480	315	1672	19
	Males	8	26	45	28	131	323	494	344	m	m
	Females	7	27	48	26	81	272	471	287	m	m
United States	M+F	12	32	56	37	c	374	746	471	1822	26
	Males	c	32	58	37	c	c	790	499	m	m
	Females	c	34	58	39	c	351	704	446	m	m
OECD average	*M+F*	*7*	*17*	*31*	*18*	*210*	*371*	*669*	*389*	*1668*	*25*
	Males	*8*	*18*	*31*	*19*	*243*	*393*	*684*	*405*	*m*	*m*
	Females	*6*	*17*	*32*	*17*	*241*	*370*	*686*	*384*	*m*	*m*

Source: OECD. See Annex 3 for notes (*www.oecd.org/edu/eag2007*).

Please refer to the Reader's guide for information concerning the symbols replacing missing data.

StatLink ⛶ http://dx.doi.org/10.1787/068423487063

Table C5.1b.
Expected number of hours in non-formal job-related education and training by age group and labour force status (2003)
Expected number of hours in non-formal job-related education and training by gender, age group and labour force status for all levels of educational attainment

C5

		Expected hours in non-formal job-related education and training between the ages of 25 and 64							
		Age group				Labour force status			
		25-34	35-44	45-54	55-64	Employed	Unemployed	Inactive	Total
Austria	M+F	169	141	92	20	373	20	29	422
	Males	187	154	101	28	434	13	n	470
	Females	150	127	83	14	312	25	26	374
Belgium	M+F	197	163	89	20	378	53	37	469
	Males	208	202	100	29	447	30	34	540
	Females	185	123	79	11	308	47	30	397
Canada [1]	M+F	197	178	148	64	497	51	38	586
	Males	210	161	146	73	531	34	25	590
	Females	184	195	149	55	463	67	51	582
Czech Republic	M+F	62	63	42	15	170	8	4	182
	Males	65	61	39	21	182	2	n	186
	Females	59	65	45	11	158	12	7	179
Denmark	M+F	236	309	248	141	745	94	95	934
	Males	248	314	233	152	787	82	66	946
	Females	224	305	262	130	701	106	115	922
Finland	M+F	191	221	180	77	528	85	55	669
	Males	199	200	167	72	499	93	n	637
	Females	182	243	193	83	557	70	68	701
France	M+F	366	206	118	23	493	102	117	713
	Males	355	181	105	23	488	83	93	664
	Females	377	230	131	22	499	119	141	760
Germany	M+F	159	123	91	26	263	92	44	398
	Males	188	134	93	32	301	97	50	447
	Females	129	111	89	19	223	86	39	348
Greece	M+F	50	32	18	6	92	6	4	106
	Males	49	28	20	9	96	5	n	106
	Females	51	35	16	4	85	7	4	106
Hungary	M+F	115	89	40	9	171	10	63	253
	Males	93	59	32	9	148	n	30	192
	Females	138	119	47	9	194	17	76	312
Ireland	M+F	72	64	44	22	181	n	11	203
	Males	71	68	45	25	194	n	n	209
	Females	73	61	44	19	170	n	9	197
Italy	M+F	29	26	20	6	73	3	4	82
	Males	30	28	21	8	78	3	3	87
	Females	28	25	19	5	68	3	5	77
Luxembourg	M+F	66	53	46	12	162	n	n	176
	Males	79	64	45	19	205	n	n	207
	Females	53	41	47	c	115	n	n	141
Netherlands	M+F	122	87	53	21	231	10	41	283
	Males	125	78	59	15	250	n	10	277
	Females	118	95	47	28	211	5	61	289
Poland	M+F	52	48	29	10	127	9	2	139
	Males	57	47	29	15	135	10	n	147
	Females	47	48	29	7	120	7	n	131

1. Year of reference 2002.

Source: OECD. See Annex 3 for notes (*www.oecd.org/edu/eag2007*).

Please refer to the Reader's guide for information concerning the symbols replacing missing data.

StatLink ⓢⓟ http://dx.doi.org/10.1787/068423487063

Table C5.1b. *(continued)*
Expected number of hours in non-formal job-related education and training by age group and labour force status (2003)
Expected number of hours in non-formal job-related education and training by gender, age group and labour force status for all levels of educational attainment

			Expected hours in non-formal job-related education and training between the ages of 25 and 64							
			Age group				Labour force status			
			25-34	35-44	45-54	55-64	Employed	Unemployed	Inactive	Total
OECD countries	**Portugal**	M+F	162	111	54	16	260	n	23	**343**
		Males	168	91	41	16	286	n	n	**316**
		Females	156	130	65	16	237	n	n	**367**
	Slovak Republic	M+F	79	72	56	18	207	13	n	**225**
		Males	81	75	57	28	232	2	n	**240**
		Females	77	70	55	10	184	16	n	**212**
	Spain	M+F	105	73	47	11	177	37	20	**237**
		Males	107	76	48	16	200	25	17	**247**
		Females	103	70	46	7	154	49	22	**226**
	Sweden	M+F	142	176	167	137	580	29	12	**622**
		Males	151	196	155	139	586	39	4	**641**
		Females	133	156	179	135	574	12	11	**603**
	Switzerland	M+F	254	205	177	87	637	47	39	**723**
		Males	328	262	203	119	825	50	24	**912**
		Females	187	152	153	58	467	36	44	**551**
	United Kingdom	M+F	119	97	71	28	269	14	33	**315**
		Males	131	104	74	35	294	20	29	**344**
		Females	107	90	68	22	244	7	35	**287**
	United States	M+F	126	123	136	86	428	n	n	**471**
		Males	135	126	137	102	463	n	n	**499**
		Females	118	121	135	72	396	n	n	**446**
	OECD average	***M+F***	***139***	***121***	***89***	***39***	***320***	***38***	***35***	***389***
		Males	***148***	***123***	***89***	***45***	***348***	***37***	***32***	***405***
		Females	***131***	***119***	***90***	***35***	***293***	***38***	***44***	***373***

Source: OECD. See Annex 3 for notes (*www.oecd.org/edu/eag2007*).
Please refer to the Reader's guide for information concerning the symbols replacing missing data.
StatLink http://dx.doi.org/10.1787/068423487063

Table C5.1c.
Expected number of hours in non-formal job-related education and training, by level of educational attainment (2003)
Expected number of hours in non-formal job-related education and training, by age group and labour force status

C5

| | | Expected hours in non-formal job-related education and training between ages of 25 and 64 | | | | | | | |
| | | Age group | | | | Labour force status | | | |
	Level of education	25-34	35-44	45-54	55-64	Employed	Unemployed	Inactive	Total
Austria	Below upper secondary (0/1/2)	58	48	29	5	110	c	c	**140**
	Upper secondary (3/4)	175	136	89	21	368	22	29	**420**
	Tertiary (5/6)	241	250	212	64	714	c	c	**767**
Belgium	Below upper secondary (0/1/2)	127	115	49	3	186	59	48	**293**
	Upper secondary (3/4)	151	171	95	21	340	57	41	**437**
	Tertiary (5/6)	286	205	159	69	640	43	37	**719**
Canada [1]	Below upper secondary (0/1/2)	m	m	m	m	m	m	m	**m**
	Upper secondary (3/4)	m	m	m	m	m	m	m	**m**
	Tertiary (5/6)	m	m	m	m	m	m	m	**m**
Czech Republic	Below upper secondary (0/1/2)	14	7	12	1	23	c	c	**34**
	Upper secondary (3/4)	47	45	38	12	129	9	4	**142**
	Tertiary (5/6)	186	186	114	70	546	c	c	**556**
Denmark	Below upper secondary (0/1/2)	239	243	171	65	455	c	184	**719**
	Upper secondary (3/4)	205	284	199	147	685	86	65	**836**
	Tertiary (5/6)	282	379	362	207	1 011	116	103	**1 230**
Finland	Below upper secondary (0/1/2)	194	149	118	36	273	c	c	**497**
	Upper secondary (3/4)	147	175	146	62	389	102	39	**530**
	Tertiary (5/6)	247	309	277	170	889	c	51	**1 003**
France	Below upper secondary (0/1/2)	245	118	75	12	247	107	96	**450**
	Upper secondary (3/4)	324	227	123	18	470	106	116	**692**
	Tertiary (5/6)	488	291	206	76	809	105	146	**1 061**
Germany	Below upper secondary (0/1/2)	54	39	32	5	46	59	24	**130**
	Upper secondary (3/4)	162	120	87	22	230	109	52	**390**
	Tertiary (5/6)	243	187	153	66	522	86	42	**650**
Greece	Below upper secondary (0/1/2)	11	c	c	c	12	c	c	**15**
	Upper secondary (3/4)	48	26	15	c	76	10	8	**94**
	Tertiary (5/6)	98	91	79	45	285	15	c	**312**
Hungary	Below upper secondary (0/1/2)	45	31	11	c	56	c	c	**90**
	Upper secondary (3/4)	118	99	42	11	170	21	79	**270**
	Tertiary (5/6)	176	120	81	25	337	c	49	**402**
Ireland	Below upper secondary (0/1/2)	29	28	18	8	66	c	c	**82**
	Upper secondary (3/4)	60	56	43	27	161	c	c	**185**
	Tertiary (5/6)	109	113	102	69	371	c	c	**392**
Italy	Below upper secondary (0/1/2)	10	9	5	1	25	c	c	**26**
	Upper secondary (3/4)	27	34	32	17	102	5	3	**111**
	Tertiary (5/6)	90	72	65	28	222	12	21	**254**
Luxembourg	Below upper secondary (0/1/2)	17	6	10	c	33	c	c	**34**
	Upper secondary (3/4)	64	56	57	12	165	c	c	**189**
	Tertiary (5/6)	128	126	98	50	396	c	c	**402**
Netherlands	Below upper secondary (0/1/2)	92	73	41	11	134	c	78	**216**
	Upper secondary (3/4)	131	87	55	34	254	17	37	**308**
	Tertiary (5/6)	130	103	67	22	294	c		**322**
Poland	Below upper secondary (0/1/2)	6	6	3	1	12	c	c	**16**
	Upper secondary (3/4)	32	32	20	6	78	10	c	**90**
	Tertiary (5/6)	145	169	132	68	497	10	c	**513**

1. Year of reference 2002.
Source: OECD. See Annex 3 for notes (*www.oecd.org/edu/eag2007*).
Please refer to the Reader's guide for information concerning the symbols replacing missing data.
StatLink ⌐⌐⌐⌐ http://dx.doi.org/10.1787/068423487063

C5

Table C5.1c. *(continued)*
Expected number of hours in non-formal job-related education and training, by level of educational attainment (2003)
Expected number of hours in non-formal job-related education and training, by age group and labour force status

| | Level of education | Expected hours in non-formal job-related education and training between ages of 25 and 64 | | | | | | | |
| | | Age group | | | | Labour force status | | | |
		25-34	35-44	45-54	55-64	Employed	Unemployed	Inactive	Total
Portugal	Below upper secondary (0/1/2)	88	92	41	10	149	c	c	**232**
	Upper secondary (3/4)	261	145	79	c	463	c	c	**529**
	Tertiary (5/6)	336	226	169	c	764	c	c	**835**
Slovak Republic	Below upper secondary (0/1/2)	11	21	10	1	27	c	c	**43**
	Upper secondary (3/4)	61	58	44	15	159	15	c	**178**
	Tertiary (5/6)	217	218	185	101	703	c	c	**721**
Spain	Below upper secondary (0/1/2)	48	29	19	6	73	22	7	**102**
	Upper secondary (3/4)	86	83	73	18	188	40	33	**261**
	Tertiary (5/6)	180	151	129	43	409	62	32	**503**
Sweden	Below upper secondary (0/1/2)	106	73	107	64	325	c	c	**350**
	Upper secondary (3/4)	123	164	149	125	504	46	12	**562**
	Tertiary (5/6)	183	249	244	241	889	18	10	**917**
Switzerland	Below upper secondary (0/1/2)	108	62	25	17	126	56	c	**212**
	Upper secondary (3/4)	214	175	164	68	552	35	34	**621**
	Tertiary (5/6)	407	352	317	225	1 171	76	54	**1 301**
United Kingdom	Below upper secondary (0/1/2)	30	35	27	12	56	c	c	**103**
	Upper secondary (3/4)	101	93	67	35	254	16	27	**297**
	Tertiary (5/6)	161	140	117	62	442	10	27	**480**
United States	Below upper secondary (0/1/2)	c	c	c	c	c	c	c	**c**
	Upper secondary (3/4)	98	107	97	72	337	c	c	**374**
	Tertiary (5/6)	190	186	223	148	695	c	c	**746**

Source: OECD. See Annex 3 for notes (*www.oecd.org/edu/eag2007*).
Please refer to the Reader's guide for information concerning the symbols replacing missing data.
StatLink ᴍᴍ🔊 http://dx.doi.org/10.1787/068423487063

Chapter

D

THE LEARNING ENVIRONMENT
AND ORGANISATION
OF SCHOOLS

HOW MUCH TIME DO STUDENTS SPEND IN THE CLASSROOM?

This indicator examines the amount of instruction time that students are expected to receive between the ages of 7 and 15. It also discusses the relationship between instruction time and student learning outcomes.

INDICATOR **D1**

Key results

Chart D1.1. **Total number of intended instruction hours in public institutions between the ages of 7 and 14 (2005)**

☐ Ages 7-8   ▨ Ages 9-11   ■ Ages 12-14

Students in OECD countries are expected to receive, on average, 6 898 hours of instruction between the ages of 7 and 14, of which 1 586 hours are between ages 7 and 8, 2 518 hours between ages 9 and 11, and 2 794 hours between ages 12 and 14. The large majority of intended hours of instruction are compulsory.

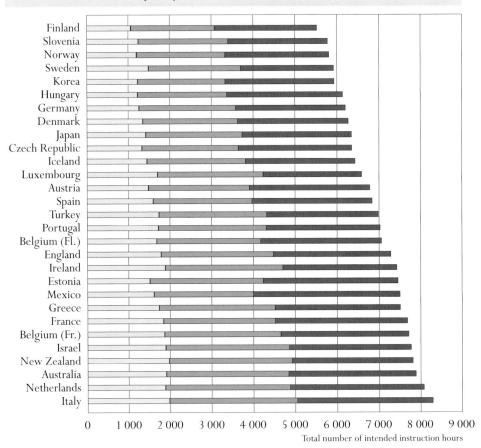

Countries are ranked in ascending order of total number of intended instruction hours.
Source: OECD. Table D1.1. See Annex 3 for notes (www.oecd.org/edu/eag2007).
StatLink ⟨⟩ http://dx.doi.org/10.1787/068453733667

Other highlights of this indicator

- In OECD countries, students between the ages of 7 and 8 receive an average of 769 hours per year of compulsory instruction time and 793 hours per year of intended instruction time in the classroom. Students between the ages of 9 and 11 receive about 45 hours more per year (than those aged between 7 and 8 years) and those aged between 12 and 14 receive just over 90 hours more per year than those aged between 9 and 11.

- On average among OECD countries, the teaching of reading, writing and literature, mathematics and science comprises nearly 50% of the compulsory instruction time of students aged 9 to 11 and 40% for students aged 12 to 14. For 9-to-11-year-olds, there is great variation among countries in the proportion of compulsory curriculum devoted to reading and writing: from 13% or less in Australia and the partner economies Chile and Israel to 30% or more in France, Mexico and the Netherlands.

Policy context

The amount and quality of time that people spend learning between early childhood and the start of their working lives shape much of their lives both socially and economically. Countries make a variety of choices about instruction, concerning the length of time devoted to instruction overall and the subjects that are compulsorily taught at schools. These choices reflect national priorities and preferences for the education received by students at different ages, as well as general priorities placed on different subject areas. Countries usually determine statutory or regulatory requirements of instruction hours. These are most often stipulated as the minimum number of hours of instruction that a school must perform. A central notion in the setting of minimum levels is that the provision of sufficient teaching time is a prerequisite for achieving good learning outcomes.

Instruction time in formal classroom settings comprises a large part of the public investment in student learning. Matching resources with students' needs and using time in an optimal manner, from the perspective of the learner and of public investment, are major challenges for education policy. The costs of education primarily include teachers' labour, institutional maintenance and other educational resources. The length of time during which these resources are made available to students (as partly shown in this indicator) is thus an important factor in the allocation of funding.

Evidence and explanations

What this indicator shows

Intended instruction time is an important indicator of students' opportunity to learn as well as the public resources invested in education. This indicator captures intended instruction time as a measure of exposure to learning in formal classroom settings as per public regulations. It does not show the actual number of hours of instruction received by students and does not compare learning outside of the formal classroom setting. Discrepancies could exist across countries between the regulatory minimum hours of instruction and the actual hours of instruction received by students. There is some research showing that factors such as school timetable decisions, lesson cancellations (Box D1.1) and teacher absenteeism may mean that the minimum instruction hours are not reached.

The indicator also illustrates how minimum instruction times are allocated to different curricular areas. However, the instruction time in classroom settings is only one aspect of student learning time and this indicator does not cover out-of-school learning activities. The indicator is calculated as the intended net hours of instruction for the grades in which the majority of students are 7 to 15 years of age. Although such data are difficult to compare among countries because of different curriculum policies, they nevertheless provide an indication of how much formal instruction time is considered necessary in order for students to achieve the desired educational goals.

Total intended instruction time: an average of 6 898 hours between ages of 7 and 14

Total intended instruction time is an estimate of the number of hours during which students are taught both compulsory and non-compulsory parts of the curriculum.

D1

The total number of instruction hours that students are intended to receive between ages 7 and 14 averages 6 898 hours among OECD countries. However, formal requirements range from 5 523 hours in Finland to over 8 000 hours in Italy and the Netherlands. These hours comprise compulsory and non-compulsory hours during which the school is obliged to offer instruction to students. Whereas the total intended instruction time within this age range is a good indicator of students' theoretical workload, it cannot be interpreted as actual instruction students receive over the years they spend in initial education. In some countries with greater student workload, the age band of compulsory education is less and students drop out of the school system earlier, whereas in other countries a more even distribution of study time over more years amounts in the end to a larger number of total instruction hours for all. Table D1.1 shows the age range at which over 90% of the population is in education and Chart D1.1 shows the total amount of intended instruction time students receive between ages 7 and 14.

In some countries, intended instruction time varies considerably among regions or different types of schools. In many countries, local education authorities or schools can determine the number and allocation of hours of instruction. Additional teacher time is often planned for individual remedial teaching or enhancement of the curriculum. On the other hand, time may be lost due to a lack of qualified substitutes to replace absent teachers, or due to student absences (Box D1.1).

Annual instruction time should also be examined together with the length of compulsory education, which measures the time during which young people receive full-time educational support from public resources, and during which more than 90% of the population participates in education (see Indicator C1). Intended instruction time does not capture the quality of learning opportunities being provided nor the level or quality of human and material resources involved (for some insight on human resources, see Indicator D2, number of teachers relative to the student population).

Box D1.1. **Intended and actual instruction time in the Netherlands**

A study conducted by Regioplan Beleidsonderzoek in the Netherlands analysed the prevalence of lesson cancellations and their effect upon instruction time. The study analysed data from the 2005-2006 school year from 96 secondary schools and/or secondary school auxiliary branches.[1] A distinction was made between two types of instruction time: timetabled instruction time and the instruction time achieved.

Timetabled instruction time measured the amount of time in clock hours that schools timetable for lessons or face-to-face instruction. Instruction time achieved is calculated by subtracting the cancelled lessons from the timetabled instruction time. Lessons are considered to be cancelled when the school deviates from its instruction time timetable. This usually

....

1. The participants all use the Cover Planning module of the GP Untis timetabling programme or the Gepro *Roosterexpert* programme. Using these programmes, schedulers can plan and keep up to date with what lessons have to be cancelled or replaced and for what reason. Interviews and secondary analyses were also carried out using other sources of information regarding sick leave, unfilled vacancies, staff policy, staff turnover and educational yields.

refers to daily timetable changes. The cancellation of lessons can take place in two ways: true cancellation of lessons whereby the children are given time off, and substitution and replacement whereby the lessons are not given as planned but either a substitute teacher is provided for the lesson or a replacement activity is scheduled. For this analysis, substitution and replacement are taken into account as instruction time and is distinguished from the cancellation of lessons without substitution and replacement.

Using these two measures permits a calculation of the "instruction time achieved". It is important to note that a low cancellation rate for lessons does not necessarily mean that sufficient hours of face-to-face instruction will be achieved. On the other hand, a high rate of lesson cancellation does not necessarily mean that too little instruction time is achieved.

Timetabled instruction time

The study showed that very few schools timetable sufficient instruction time. On average, only 17% of the schools sampled had timetabled sufficient instruction time. In this regard, there is a clear distinction between education levels in the school system (defined in this study of Dutch schools as the lower years, the upper years and the final years of secondary school). The largest discrepancies were evident in the lower years of school education in which only 6% of schools had timetabled sufficient instruction time. In the upper years, 35% of schools had timetabled sufficient instruction time and 65% of schools had for the final exam classes. On average, 87% of the required instruction time is timetabled in the lower years versus 94% in the upper years. For final exam classes, the required time is actually exceeded at 107%.

Cancellation of lessons

On average 6.7% of the lessons at the secondary schools sampled were cancelled. Replacement and substitution accounted for 1.2% of the cancelled lessons. This varies across schools. There are schools at which less than 5% of the lessons are cancelled as well as schools at which more than 9% of the lessons are cancelled. The major reasons for cancellation are operational (organisational, leave and refresher/training courses) (found for 47% of cancellations) and the illness of teachers (43% of cancellations).

Instruction time achieved

In the lower years, on average 81% of the minimum instruction time is achieved, compared to 87% in the upper years and 99% in final exam years. It is, however, not the case that schools with many lessons on the timetable are also subsequently the ones with the most cancelled lessons. At many schools, teachers are timetabled in for additional hours for which they can be deployed as substitutes to reduce the cancellations of lessons and the reduction of instruction time received by students.

Compulsory instruction time: an average of 6 672 hours between ages 7 and 14

Total compulsory instruction time is an estimate of the number of hours during which students are taught both the compulsory core and compulsory flexible parts of the curriculum.

For 7-to-8-year-olds and 9-to-11-year-olds, total intended instruction time equals total compulsory instruction time in most countries, while for older age groups this is less frequently the case. However, intended instruction time is fully compulsory for all age groups between 7 and 14 years

D1

in the Czech Republic, Denmark, Germany, Greece, Iceland, Japan, Korea, Luxembourg, Mexico, the Netherlands, Norway, Spain and Sweden as well as partner economies Estonia and Slovenia (also in the Russian Federation in the two age groups for which data are available). Except Greece, Mexico and the Netherlands and partner economy Estonia, these countries have a total number of intended instruction time between the age of 7 and 14 below the OECD average. In these countries, except for Greece and Mexico as well as Japan and the Netherlands where data are missing, education is also fully compulsory at age 15.

Within the formal education system, OECD countries show an average annual amount of total compulsory instruction time in classroom settings of 769 hours for 7-to-8-year-olds, 814 hours for 9-to-11-year-olds and 898 hours for 12-to-14-year-olds. The average number of compulsory instruction hours per year is 911 for the typical programme in which most 15-year-olds are enrolled (Table D1.1).

Teaching of reading and writing, mathematics and science: at least 40% of compulsory instruction time, on average for 12-to-14-year-olds

In OECD countries students aged 9 to 11, for which study areas are not necessarily organised as separate subject classes, spend an average of nearly 50% of the compulsory curriculum to three basic subject areas: reading, writing and literature (23%), mathematics (16%) and science (8%). On average, 7% of the compulsory curriculum is devoted to modern foreign languages. Together with social studies, the arts and physical education, these seven study areas form part of the curriculum in all OECD countries for these age cohorts (Table D1.2a and Chart D1.2a).

Chart D1.2a. **Instruction time per subject as a percentage of total compulsory instruction time for 9-to-11-year-olds (2005)**

Percentage of intended instruction time devoted to various subject areas within the total compulsory curriculum

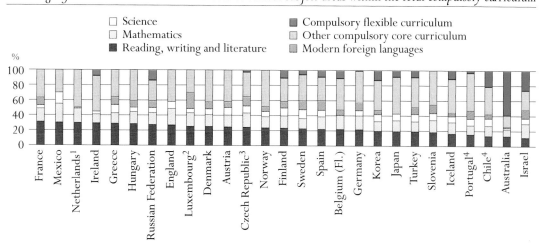

1. Includes 9 and 11-year-olds only.
2. German as a language of instruction is included in "Reading, writing and literature" in addition to the mother tongue Luxemburgish.
3. For 9-to-10-year-olds, social studies is included in science.
4. Includes 10-to-11-year-olds only.
Countries are ranked in descending order of number of compulsory instruction hours devoted to reading, writing and literature.
Source: OECD. Table D1.2a. See Annex 3 for notes (*www.oecd.org/edu/eag2007*).
StatLink ⌐ʃ▄ http://dx.doi.org/10.1787/068453733667

D1

Chart D1.2b. Instruction time per subject as a percentage of total compulsory instruction time for 12-to-14-year-olds (2005)

Percentage of intended instruction time devoted to various subject areas within the total compulsory curriculum

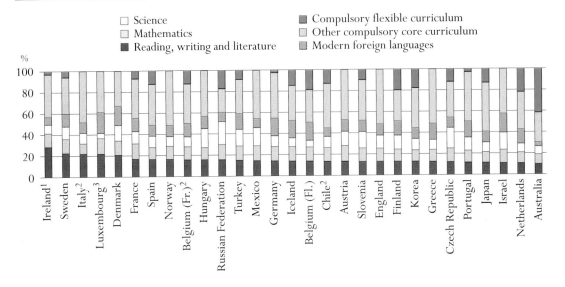

1. For 13-to-14-year-olds, arts is included in non-compulsory curriculum.
2. Includes 12-to-13-year-olds only.
3. German as a language of instruction is included in "Reading, writing and literature" in addition to the mother tongue Luxemburgish.
Countries are ranked in descending order of number of compulsory instruction hours devoted to reading, writing and literature.
Source: OECD. Table D1.2b. See Annex 3 for notes (*www.oecd.org/edu/eag2007*).
StatLink ᕵᓵᔨ http://dx.doi.org/10.1787/068453733667

On average, reading and writing account for the greatest share of the curriculum for 9-to-11-year-old students, but the variation in this share among countries is greater than for other subjects; reading and writing accounts for 13% or less of instruction time in Australia and partner economies Chile and Israel, compared with 30% or more in France, Mexico and the Netherlands. Sizeable variation is also evident in modern foreign languages, which account for 1% or less of instruction time in Australia, England, Japan and Mexico but represent 21% of total compulsory instruction time in Luxembourg and over 10% in the Czech Republic, Portugal, Spain and Sweden as well as in partner economies Israel and Slovenia.

For 12-to-14-year-old students in OECD countries, an average of 40% of the compulsory curriculum is devoted to three basic subject areas: reading, writing and literature (15%), mathematics (13%) and science (11%). In these age cohorts, a relatively larger part of the curriculum is devoted to modern foreign languages (12%) and social studies (12%), whereas somewhat less time is devoted to the arts (8%). Together with physical education, these seven study areas form part of the compulsory curriculum for lower secondary students in all OECD countries (Table D1.2b and Chart D1.2b).

The variation between countries in the percentage share of subjects within the curriculum for 12-to-14-year-olds is less than it is for 9-to-11-year-olds. Again, the greatest variation is evident in reading and writing with a range from 10% or less in Australia and the Netherlands to 28% in Ireland (where reading and writing includes work in both English and Irish).

D1

There is also substantial variation in the percentage of compulsory instruction time devoted to particular subjects for 9-to-11-year-olds compared to 12-to-14-year-olds. On average across OECD countries, the time of compulsory instruction for 12-to-14-year-olds devoted to reading, writing and literature is one-third lower than for 9-to-11-year-olds. However, the difference is reversed in the time devoted to social studies and modern foreign languages.

For some countries, these differences are larger than in other countries. The percentage of compulsory instruction time devoted to reading, writing and literature for 12-to-14-year-olds is equal to or less than one-half of that for 9-to-11-year-olds in the Czech Republic, England, Greece, Mexico and the Netherlands. Yet, for Ireland, Sweden and the partner economies Chile and Israel, the difference between the shares is less than 5%. Clearly, countries place a different emphasis upon particular subjects and when those subjects should be taught to students.

On average among OECD countries, the non-compulsory part of the curriculum comprises 2 to 4% of the total intended instruction time for 9-to-11-year-old students as well as for 12-to-14-year-old students. Nevertheless, a considerable amount of additional non-compulsory instruction time can sometimes be provided. For 9-to-11-year-old students, all intended instruction time is compulsory for students in most countries, but the additional non-compulsory time is as high as 15% in Hungary, 20% in Turkey, and 32% in the partner economy Israel. For 12-to-14-year-old students, non-compulsory instruction time is a feature in Australia, Belgium (French community), England, Finland, France, Hungary, Ireland, Italy, Portugal and Turkey, and ranges from 2% in Finland to 29% in Hungary (Tables D1.2a and D1.2b).

On average, 4% of compulsory instruction time belongs to the flexible part of the curriculum in the grades where most students are 9-to-11 years of age while the corresponding proportion is 9% for students aged 12 to 14.

In most OECD countries, the number of hours of compulsory instruction is defined. Within the compulsory part of the curriculum, students have varying degrees of freedom to choose the subjects they want to learn. However, for 9-to-11-year-olds, up to 59% of the compulsory curriculum is operated on a flexible basis in Australia. For 12-to-14-year-olds, Australia again has the highest degree of flexibility in the compulsory curriculum (41%), although several other countries allow more than 10% flexibility in the compulsory curriculum (Belgium, the Czech Republic, Finland, Iceland, Japan, Korea, the Netherlands and Spain, and the partner economies Chile, the Russian Federation and Slovenia) (Tables D1.2a and D1.2b).

Definitions and methodologies

Data on instruction time are from the 2006 OECD-INES Survey on Teachers and the Curriculum and refer to the school year 2004-2005.

Instruction time for 7-to-15-year-olds refers to the formal number of 60-minute hours per school year organised by the school for class instructional activities for students in the reference school year 2004-2005. For countries with no formal policy on instruction time, the number of hours was estimated from survey data. Hours lost when schools are closed for festivities and celebrations, such as national holidays, are excluded. Intended instruction time does not include non-compulsory time outside the school day, homework, individual tutoring, or private study done before or after school.

- Compulsory curriculum refers to the amount and allocation of instruction time that almost every public school must provide and almost all public sector students must attend. The measurement of the time devoted to specific study areas (subjects) focuses on the minimum common core rather than on the average time spent on study areas, since the data sources (policy documents) do not allow more precise measurement. Total compulsory curriculum comprises the compulsory core curriculum as well as the compulsory flexible curriculum.

D1

- The non-compulsory part of the curriculum refers to the average time of instruction to which students are entitled above the compulsory hours of instruction. These subjects often vary from school to school or from region to region, and may take the form of "non-compulsory elective" subjects.

- Intended instruction time refers to the number of hours per year during which students receive instruction in the compulsory and non-compulsory parts of the curriculum.

For 15-year-olds in Table D1.1, typical instruction time refers to the programme in which most 15-year-olds are enrolled. This can be a programme in lower or upper secondary education, and in most countries it refers to a general programme. If the system channels students into different programme types at this age, an estimation of the average instruction time may have been necessary for the most important mainstream programmes weighted by the proportion of students in the grade level where most 15-year-olds are enrolled. Where vocational programmes are also taken into account in typical instruction time, only the school-based part of the programme should be included in the calculations.

The instruction time for the least demanding programme refers to programmes stipulated for students who are least likely to continue studying beyond mandatory school age or beyond lower secondary education. Such programmes may or may not exist in a country depending on streaming and selection policies. In many countries students are offered the same amount of instruction time in all or most programmes, but there is flexibility in the choice of study areas or subjects. Often such choices have to be made quite early if programmes are long and differ substantially.

Further references

Specific notes on definitions and methodologies regarding this indicator for each country are given in Annex 3 at *www.oecd.org/edu/eag2007*. In addition, a more comprehensive analysis of decision making was published in Indicator D6 of *Education at a Glance 2004* (OECD, 2004c). Information on the underlying decision-making survey is available in *Education at a Glance 2004*, Annex 3 (*www.oecd.org/edu/eag2004*) under the heading "Indicator D6 Locus of decision making at lower secondary levels". The complete decision-making data are available under the heading "Underlying data on decision making for Indicator D6".

Table D1.1.
Compulsory and intended instruction time in public institutions (2005)
*Average number of hours per year of total compulsory and non-compulsory instruction time in the curriculum
for 7-to-8, 9-to-11, 12-to-14 and 15-year-olds*

D1

	Age range at which over 90% of the population are enrolled	Average number of hours per year of total compulsory instruction time					Average number of hours per year of total intended instruction time				
		Aged 7 to 8	Aged 9 to 11	Aged 12 to 14	Aged 15 (typical programme)	Aged 15 (least demanding programme)	Aged 7 to 8	Aged 9 to 11	Aged 12 to 14	Aged 15 (typical programme)	Aged 15 (least demanding programme)
	(1)	(2)	(3)	(4)	(5)	(6)	(7)	(8)	(9)	(10)	(11)
OECD countries											
Australia	5-16	952	979	970	966	952	952	979	1 014	1 022	1 008
Austria	5-17	690	767	913	1 005	960	735	812	958	1 050	1 005
Belgium (Fl.)	3-17	a	a	a	a	a	835	835	960	960	450
Belgium (Fr.)[1]	3-17	840	840	960	m	m	930	930	1 020	1 020	m
Czech Republic	4-17	661	774	902	970	396	661	774	902	970	396
Denmark	3-16	671	763	880	840	a	671	763	880	840	a
England	4-16	880	900	900	760	a	890	900	933	950	a
Finland	6-18	530	654	796	858	a	530	673	815	858	a
France	3-17	918	894	959	1 042	a	918	894	1 053	1 147	a
Germany	6-17	627	777	872	897	m	627	777	872	897	m
Greece	6-19	864	928	998	1 089	926	864	928	998	1 307	1 144
Hungary	4-17	555	624	717	763	763	611	718	921	1 106	1 106
Iceland	3-16	720	792	872	888	a	720	792	872	888	a
Ireland	5-16	941	941	848	802	713	941	941	907	891	891
Italy	3-15	990	957	1 016	1 069	m	990	1 023	1 082	1 069	m
Japan	4-17	707	774	869	m	a	707	774	869	m	a
Korea	6-17	612	703	867	1 020	a	612	703	867	1 020	a
Luxembourg	4-15	847	847	782	750	a	847	847	782	750	a
Mexico	5-13	800	800	1 167	1 058	a	800	800	1 167	1 124	a
Netherlands	5-16	940	1 000	1 067	m	a	940	1 000	1 067	m	a
New Zealand	4-15	a	a	a	a	a	985	985	962	950	950
Norway	5-17	599	713	827	855	a	599	713	827	855	a
Poland	6-18	m	m	m	m	m	m	m	m	m	m
Portugal	6-15	855	849	880	821	m	855	866	905	872	m
Scotland	4-16	a	a	a	a	a	a	a	a	a	a
Slovak Republic	6-17	m	m	m	m	m	m	m	m	m	m
Spain	3-16	793	794	956	979	978	793	794	956	979	978
Sweden	5-18	741	741	741	741	a	741	741	741	741	a
Switzerland	5-16	m	m	m	m	m	m	m	m	m	m
Turkey	7-13	720	720	791	959	a	864	864	887	959	a
United States	6-16	m	m	m	m	m	m	m	m	m	m
OECD average		*769*	*814*	*898*	*911*	*812*	*793*	*839*	*931*	*968*	*881*
EU19 average		*785*	*826*	*893*	*892*	*789*	*799*	*845*	*931*	*965*	*853*
Partner economies											
Brazil	7-16	m	m	m	m	m	m	m	m	m	m
Chile	9-16	m	m	m	m	m	m	m	m	m	m
Estonia	6-17	752	910	1 073	1 190	980	752	910	1 073	1 190	980
Israel	5-17	666	749	971	919	a	944	990	971	919	a
Russian Federation	7-15	m	748	884	m	m	m	748	884	m	m
Slovenia	6-17	621	721	791	908	888	621	721	791	908	888

1. Aged "12 to 14" covers aged 12 to 13 only.

Source: OECD. See Annex 3 for notes *(www.oecd.org / edu / eag2007).*

Please refer to the Reader's Guide for information concerning the symbols replacing missing data.

StatLink ⫶⫶⫸ http://dx.doi.org/10.1787/068453733667

D1

Table D1.2a.
Instruction time per subject as a percentage of total compulsory instruction time for 9-to-11-year-olds (2005)
Percentage of intended instruction time devoted to various subject areas within the total compulsory curriculum

	Compulsory core curriculum											TOTAL compulsory core curriculum	Compulsory flexible curriculum	TOTAL compulsory curriculum	Non-compulsory curriculum
	Reading, writing and literature	Mathematics	Science	Social studies	Modern foreign languages	Technology	Arts	Physical education	Religion	Practical and vocational skills	Other				
	(1)	(2)	(3)	(4)	(5)	(6)	(7)	(8)	(9)	(10)	(11)	(12)	(13)	(14)	(15)
OECD countries															
Australia[1]	13	9	2	3	1	2	4	4	1	n	1	41	59	100	n
Austria	24	16	10	3	8	n	18	10	8	x(12)	3	100	x(12)	100	m
Belgium (Fl.)[1]	22	19	x(11)	x(11)	7	n	10	7	7	n	18	89	11	100	n
Belgium (Fr.)[1]	a	a	a	a	5	a	a	7	7	a	81	100	n	100	11
Czech Republic[2]	24	19	9	11	13	n	14	8	n	n	n	97	3	100	n
Denmark	25	16	8	4	9	n	21	10	4	n	3	100	n	100	n
England	27	22	10	8	n	9	8	7	5	n	5	100	n	100	n
Finland	23	16	11	2	9	n	14	9	6	n	n	90	10	100	3
France	31	18	5	10	10	3	11	13	n	n	n	100	n	100	n
Germany	21	18	7	5	10	1	15	11	7	n	3	99	1	100	n
Greece	29	14	11	11	10	n	8	7	7	n	2	100	n	100	n
Hungary	28	16	6	7	9	n	15	11	n	4	4	100	n	100	15
Iceland	16	15	8	8	4	6	12	9	3	5	2	89	11	100	n
Ireland	29	12	4	8	x(13)	n	12	4	10	n	14	92	8	100	n
Italy[3]	a	a	a	a	a	a	a	a	a	a	a	a	a	100	7
Japan	19	15	9	9	n	n	10	9	n	n	21	92	8	100	m
Korea	19	13	10	10	5	2	13	10	n	2	3	87	13	100	n
Luxembourg[4]	25	18	6	2	21	n	11	10	7	n	n	100	n	100	n
Mexico	30	25	15	20	n	n	5	5	n	n	n	100	n	100	n
Netherlands[5]	30	19	x(4)	15	2	2	10	7	4	n	12	100	n	100	n
New Zealand	a	a	a	a	a	a	a	a	a	a	a	a	a	a	a
Norway	23	15	7	8	6	n	16	7	9	n	9	100	n	100	n
Poland	m	m	m	m	m	m	m	m	m	m	m	m	m	m	m
Portugal[6]	15	12	9	6	11	x(7)	18	9	n	n	17	97	3	100	3
Scotland	a	a	a	a	a	a	a	a	a	a	a	a	a	a	a
Slovak Republic	m	m	m	m	m	m	m	m	m	m	m	m	m	m	m
Spain	22	17	9	9	13	n	11	11	x(13)	n	n	91	9	100	n
Sweden	22	14	12	13	12	x(3)	7	8	x(4)	7	n	94	6	100	n
Switzerland	m	m	m	m	m	m	m	m	m	m	m	m	m	m	m
Turkey	19	13	10	10	9	n	7	7	7	9	1	91	9	100	20
United States	m	m	m	m	m	m	m	m	m	m	m	m	m	m	m
OECD average[1]	*23*	*16*	*8*	*8*	*7*	*1*	*12*	*8*	*4*	*1*	*4*	*92*	*4*	*100*	*2*
EU19 average	*25*	*16*	*8*	*8*	*9*	*1*	*13*	*9*	*4*	*1*	*4*	*97*	*3*	*100*	*2*
Partner economies															
Brazil	m	m	m	m	m	m	m	m	m	m	m	m	m	m	m
Chile[6]	13	13	10	10	5	5	8	5	5	a	2	79	21	100	m
Estonia	m	m	m	m	m	m	m	m	m	m	m	m	m	m	m
Israel	11	19	7	11	11	x(13)	n	7	7	n	n	74	26	100	32
Russian Federation	27	16	7	7	9	7	7	7	n	n	n	86	14	100	n
Slovenia	18	16	10	8	11	2	11	11	n	3	10	100	n	100	n

1. Australia, Belgium (Fr.) and Belgium(Fl.) are not included in the averages.
2. For 9-to-10-year-olds, social studies is included in science.
3. For 9 and 10-year-olds the curriculum is largely flexible, for 11-year-olds it is about the same as for 12 and 13-year-olds.
4. German as a language of instruction is included in "Reading, writing and literature" in addition to the mother tongue Luxemburgish.
5. Includes 9 and 11-year-olds only.
6. Includes 10-to-11-year-olds only.
Source: OECD. See Annex 3 for notes *(www.oecd.org/edu/eag2007)*.
Please refer to the Reader's Guide for information concerning the symbols replacing missing data.
StatLink ⫘⫸ http://dx.doi.org/10.1787/068453733667

Table D1.2b.
Instruction time per subject as a percentage of total compulsory instruction time for 12-to-14-year-olds (2005)
Percentage of intended instruction time devoted to various subject areas within the total compulsory curriculum

		Compulsory core curriculum														
		Reading, writing and literature	Mathematics	Science	Social studies	Modern foreign languages	Technology	Arts	Physical education	Religion	Practical and vocational skills	Other	TOTAL compulsory core curriculum	Compulsory flexible curriculum	TOTAL compulsory curriculum	Non-compulsory curriculum
		(1)	(2)	(3)	(4)	(5)	(6)	(7)	(8)	(9)	(10)	(11)	(12)	(13)	(14)	(15)
OECD countries	Australia	9	9	8	7	4	6	6	6	1	n	3	**59**	41	**100**	5
	Austria	13	15	13	12	11	n	16	10	7	2	n	**100**	x(12)	**100**	m
	Belgium (Fl.)	14	14	6	9	17	4	4	6	6	1	n	**81**	19	**100**	n
	Belgium (Fr.)[1]	16	13	9	13	13	3	3	9	6	n	3	**88**	13	**100**	6
	Czech Republic	12	13	20	16	10	3	8	7	n	n	n	**88**	12	**100**	n
	Denmark	20	14	15	9	18	n	9	8	3	n	3	**100**	n	**100**	n
	England	13	12	12	13	11	12	11	8	4	n	4	**100**	n	**100**	4
	Finland	13	12	13	5	14	n	9	7	4	4	n	**80**	20	**100**	2
	France	17	15	12	13	12	6	7	11	n	n	n	**93**	7	**100**	10
	Germany	14	14	10	12	17	3	10	9	5	2	2	**98**	2	**100**	n
	Greece	12	11	10	10	15	5	6	8	6	1	16	**100**	n	**100**	n
	Hungary	15	12	18	12	12	3	10	8	n	4	6	**100**	n	**100**	29
	Iceland	14	14	8	6	17	4	7	8	2	4	3	**85**	15	**100**	n
	Ireland[2]	28	13	8	17	7	x(15)	4	5	9	x(15)	5	**97**	3	**100**	7
	Italy[1]	22	10	10	15	10	10	13	7	3	n	n	**100**	n	**100**	10
	Japan	11	10	9	9	10	3	7	9	n	n	18	**87**	13	**100**	m
	Korea	13	11	11	10	10	4	8	8	n	4	5	**82**	18	**100**	n
	Luxembourg[3]	22	15	5	10	20	n	10	8	6	n	5	**100**	n	**100**	n
	Mexico	14	14	17	26	9	n	6	6	n	9	n	**100**	n	**100**	n
	Netherlands	10	10	8	11	14	5	7	9	n	3	n	**78**	22	**100**	n
	New Zealand	a	a	a	a	a	a	a	a	a	a	a	**a**	a	**a**	a
	Norway	16	13	9	11	10	n	8	10	7	n	16	**100**	n	**100**	n
	Poland	m	m	m	m	m	m	m	m	m	m	m	**m**	m	**m**	m
	Portugal[4]	11	11	12	13	15	4	7	9	n	n	14	**97**	3	**100**	3
	Scotland	a	a	a	a	a	a	a	a	a	a	a	**a**	a	**a**	a
	Slovak Republic	m	m	m	m	m	m	m	m	m	m	m	**m**	m	**m**	m
	Spain	16	11	11	10	10	8	11	7	x(13)	x(13)	3	**87**	13	**100**	n
	Sweden	22	14	12	13	12	x(3)	7	8	x(4)	7	n	**94**	6	**100**	n
	Switzerland	m	m	m	m	m	m	m	m	m	m	m	**m**	m	**m**	m
	Turkey	15	14	16	10	15	n	4	6	5	4	3	**91**	9	**100**	12
	United States	m	m	m	m	m	m	m	m	m	m	m	**m**	m	**m**	m
	OECD average	*15*	*13*	*11*	*12*	*12*	*3*	*8*	*8*	*3*	*2*	*4*	*91*	*9*	*100*	*4*
	EU19 average	*16*	*13*	*11*	*12*	*13*	*4*	*8*	*8*	*4*	*1*	*3*	*93*	*7*	*100*	*4*
Partner economies	Brazil	m	m	m	m	m	m	m	m	m	m	m	**m**	m	**m**	m
	Chile[1]	13	13	11	11	8	5	11	5	5	a	5	**87**	13	**100**	m
	Estonia	m	m	m	m	m	m	m	m	m	m	m	**m**	m	**m**	m
	Israel	11	13	16	21	18	x(3)	4	5	13	n	n	**100**	n	**100**	m
	Russian Federation	15	14	22	9	9	4	4	6	n	n	n	**83**	17	**100**	m
	Slovenia	13	13	15	15	11	2	6	6	n	n	9	**90**	10	**100**	m

1. Includes 12-to-13-year-olds only.
2. For 13-to-14-year-olds, arts is included in non-compulsory curriculum.
3. German as a language of instruction is included in "Reading, writing and literature" in addition to the mother tongue Luxemburgish.
4. Technology is included in Arts for 14-year-olds.
Source: OECD. See Annex 3 for notes *(www.oecd.org/edu/eag2007).*
Please refer to the Reader's Guide for information concerning the symbols replacing missing data.
StatLink http://dx.doi.org/10.1787/068453733667

INDICATOR D2

WHAT IS THE STUDENT-TEACHER RATIO AND HOW BIG ARE CLASSES?

This indicator examines the number of students per class at the primary and lower secondary levels, and the ratio of students to teaching staff at all levels; it distinguishes between public and private institutions. Class size and student-teacher ratios are much discussed aspects of the education students receive and – along with the total instruction time of students (see Indicator D1), teachers' average working time (see Indicator D4) and the division of teachers' time between teaching and other duties – are among the determinants of the size of the teaching force within countries.

Key results

Chart D2.1. **Average class size in primary education (2000, 2005)**

☐ 2005   ◆ 2000

The average class size in primary education is 22 students per class, but varies between countries from 33 in Korea to less than half that number in Luxembourg and the partner economy the Russian Federation. From 2000 to 2005, the average class size did not vary significantly, but the differences in class size between OECD countries seem to have diminished. Class size tends to have decreased in countries that had relatively large class sizes (for example, Japan, Korea and Turkey) whereas class size tends to have increased in countries with relatively small class sizes (for example, Iceland).

Number of students per class

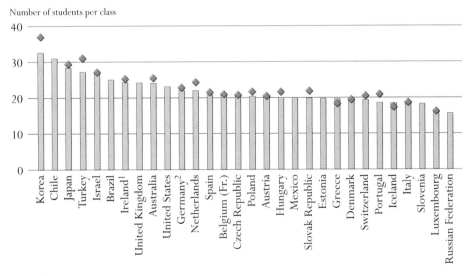

1. Public institutions only.
2. Years of reference 2001 and 2005.
Countries are ranked in descending order of average class size in primary education.
Source: OECD. 2005 data: Table D2.1, present edition. 2000 data: Table D2.1, *Education at a Glance 2002*. See Annex 3 for notes (*www.oecd.org/edu/eag2007*).
StatLink ⇄ http://dx.doi.org/10.1787/068464517374

Other highlights of this indicator

- The average class size in lower secondary education is 24 students per class, but varies from 30 or more in Japan, Korea and Mexico and the partner economies Brazil, Chile and Israel to 20 or less in Denmark, Iceland, Ireland (public institutions), Luxembourg and Switzerland, and the partner economy the Russian Federation.

- The number of students per class increases by an average of nearly three students between primary and lower secondary education, but ratios of students to teaching staff tend to decrease with increasing levels of education due to more annual instruction time, though this pattern is not uniform among countries.

- On average across OECD countries, the availability of teaching resources relative to student numbers in secondary education is more favourable in private institutions than in public institutions. This is most striking in Mexico where, at the secondary level, there are around 14 more students per teacher in public institutions than there are in private institutions. Consistently, at the lower secondary level, there is one student more per class on average across OECD countries in public institutions than in private institutions.

Policy context

Class size, education quality and education systems

Class size is a hotly debated topic and an important aspect of education policy in many OECD countries. Smaller classes are often perceived to allow teachers to focus more on the individual needs of students and reduce the amount of class time teachers spend dealing with disruptions. Smaller class sizes may also influence parents when they choose schools for their children. In this respect, class size would be an indicator of the quality of the school system.

Yet evidence on the effects of variations in class size upon student performance is very mixed. In what has evolved as a contentious area of research that has produced little in the way of consistent results, there is some evidence that smaller classes may have an impact upon specific groups of students (*e.g.* disadvantaged students).

A further reason why there is mixed evidence on the impact of class size may be because there is not sufficient variation in class size to estimate the true effects of this variable on student performance. In addition, policies to group lower performing students into smaller classes in order to devote more attention to them may reduce the observed performance gains that may otherwise be expected from smaller classes. Finally, the fact that the relationship between class size and student performance is often non-linear makes the effects difficult to estimate.

Numerous factors influence the interaction between teachers and students with class size being just one of them. Other influences include the number of classes or students for which a teacher is responsible, the subject taught, the division of the teacher's time between teaching and other duties, the grouping of students within classes and the practice of team-teaching.

The ratio of students to teaching staff is also an important indicator of the resources devoted to education. A smaller ratio of students to teaching staff may have to be weighted against higher salaries for teachers, increased professional development and teacher training, greater investment in teaching technology, or more widespread use of assistant teachers and other paraprofessionals whose salaries are often considerably lower than those of qualified teachers. Moreover, as larger numbers of children with special educational needs are integrated into normal classes, more use of specialised personnel and support services may limit the resources available for reducing the ratio of students to teaching staff.

The ratio of students to teaching staff is obtained by dividing the number of full-time equivalent students at a given level of education by the number of full-time equivalent teachers at that level and in similar types of institutions. However, this ratio does not take into account instruction time compared to the length of a teacher's working day nor how much time teachers spend teaching and therefore it cannot be interpreted in terms of class size (Box D2.1).

Evidence and explanations

Average class size in primary and lower secondary education

At the primary level, the average class size across OECD countries is 22 students per class, but varies widely among countries. It ranges from 33 students per primary class in Korea to fewer than 20 in Denmark, Greece, Iceland, Italy, Luxembourg, Mexico, Portugal, the Slovak Republic and Switzerland and partner economies Estonia, the Russian Federation and Slovenia. At the lower

D2

secondary level, the average class size across OECD countries is 24 students per class and varies from 36 students per class in Korea to fewer than 20 in Denmark, Iceland, Ireland (public institutions), Luxembourg and Switzerland and the partner economy the Russian Federation (Table D2.1).

Box D2.1. **Relationship between class size and ratio of students to teaching staff**

The number of students per class results from a number of different elements: the ratio of students to teaching staff, the number of classes or students for which a teacher is responsible, the instruction time of students compared to the length of teachers' working days, the proportion of time teachers spend teaching, the grouping of students within classes and team teaching.

For example, in a school of 48 full-time students and 8 full-time teachers, the ratio of students to teaching staff equals 6. If teachers' working week is estimated to be 35 hours including 10 hours teaching, and if instruction time for each student is 40 hours per week, then whatever the grouping of students in this school, average class size can be estimated as follows:

Estimated class size = 6 students per teacher * (40 hours of instruction time per student/ 10 hours of teaching per teacher) = 24 students.

Compared to this estimated figure, class size presented in Table D2.1 is defined as the division of students who are following a common course of study, based on the highest number of common courses (usually compulsory studies), and excludes teaching in sub-groups. Thus, the estimated class size will be close to the average class size of Table D2.1 where teaching in sub-groups is less frequent (as is the case in primary and lower secondary education).

Because of these definitions, similar student-to-teacher ratios between countries can lead to different class sizes. For example, in lower-secondary education, Germany and Greece have very similar average class sizes (24.7 students in Germany and 24.5 students in Greece – see Table D2.1), but the ratio of students to teaching staff differs substantially with 15.5 students per teaching staff member in Germany compared to 7.9 in Greece (see Table D2.2). The explanation for this may lie in the higher number of teaching hours required for teachers in Germany compared to Greece (758 hours in Germany compared to 583 hours in Greece – see Table D4.1).

The number of students per class tends to increase, on average, by nearly three students between primary and lower secondary education. In Austria, Greece, Japan, Mexico, Poland and Portugal, and the partner economies Brazil and Israel, the increase in average class size exceeds four students, while Switzerland and the United Kingdom show a small drop in the number of students per class between these two levels (Chart D2.2). The indicator on class size is limited to primary and lower secondary education because class sizes are difficult to define and compare at higher levels of education, where students often attend several different classes, depending on the subject area.

Between 2000 and 2005, average class size in primary education did not vary significantly (21.5 in 2005 against 22.0 in 2000). However, among countries with comparable data, class size decreased in countries among those with larger class sizes in 2000 (Korea, Japan and Turkey), whereas class size increased (or stayed constant) in countries among those with the lowest class sizes in 2000 (Iceland, Italy and Luxembourg). At secondary level of education, variations in class sizes between 2000 and 2005 follow a similar trend leading to narrowing the range of class sizes (2000 data in *Education at a Glance 2002,* Table D2.1 available on line at: *www.oecd.org/edu/eag2002*).

Chart D2.2. Average class size in educational institutions, by level of education (2005)

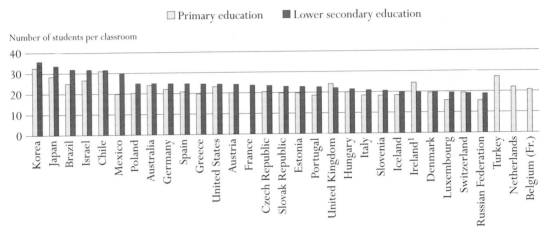

☐ Primary education   ■ Lower secondary education

1. Public institutions only.
Countries are ranked in descending order of average class size in lower secondary education.
Source: OECD. Table D2.1. See Annex 3 for notes (*www.oecd.org/edu/eag2007*).
StatLink ⌐⌐⌐⌐ http://dx.doi.org/10.1787/068464517374

Ratio of students to teaching staff

In primary education, the ratio of students to teaching staff, expressed in full-time equivalents, ranges from equal to or more than 26 students per teacher in Korea, Mexico, Turkey and partner economy Chile to less than 11 in Hungary, Italy and Portugal. The OECD average in primary education is 17 students per teacher (Chart D2.3).

There is similar variation among countries in the ratio of students to teaching staff at the secondary level, ranging from 31 students per full-time equivalent teacher in Mexico to less than 11 in Austria, Belgium, Greece, Italy, Luxembourg, Portugal and Spain. On average among OECD countries, the ratio of students to teaching staff at the secondary level is 13, which is close to the ratios in Australia (12), the Czech Republic (13), Finland (14), France (12), Japan (14), Poland (13), the Slovak Republic (14), Sweden (13) and the United Kingdom (14), and the partner economies Israel (13) and Slovenia (13) (Table D2.2).

As the difference in the mean ratios of students to teaching staff between primary and secondary education indicates, there are fewer full-time equivalent students per full-time equivalent teacher in higher levels of education. The ratio of students to teaching staff decreases between primary and secondary levels of education, despite a tendency for class sizes to increase. This was found to be true in all but seven OECD countries (Hungary, Italy, Mexico, the Netherlands, Poland, Sweden and the United States, and the partner economy Chile).

Chart D2.3. Ratio of students to teaching staff in educational institutions, by level of education (2005)

D2

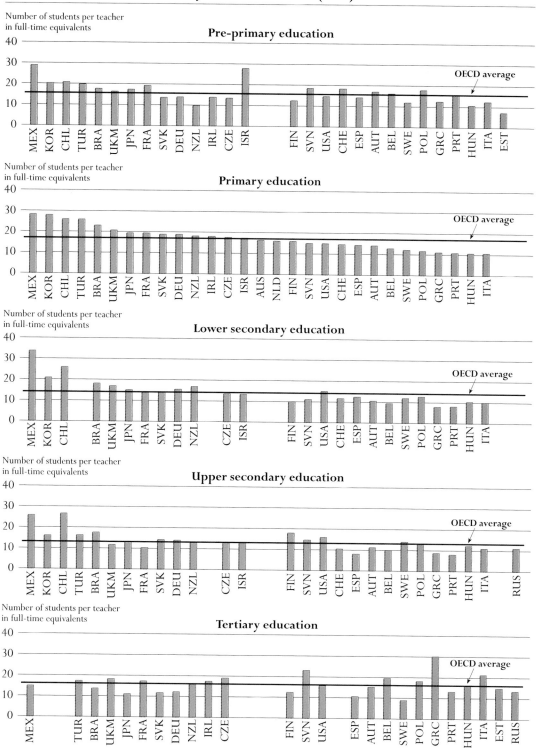

Note: Please refer to the Reader's Guide for list of country codes and country names used in this chart.
Countries are ranked in descending order of number of students per teacher in primary education.
Source: OECD. Table D2.2. See Annex 3 for notes (*www.oecd.org/edu/eag2007*).
StatLink ᴍᴤᴵ http://dx.doi.org/10.1787/068464517374

The decrease in the ratio of students to teaching staff from the primary to the secondary level reflects differences in annual instruction time, which tend to increase with the level of education. It may also result from delays in matching the teaching force to demographic changes, or from differences in teaching hours for teachers at different levels. The general trend is consistent among countries, but it is not obvious from an educational perspective why a smaller ratio of students to teaching staff should be more desirable at higher levels of education (Table D2.2).

The ratios of students to teaching staff in pre-primary education are shown in Table D2.2. For the pre-primary level, information is also presented on the ratio of students to contact staff (teachers and teachers' aides). Some countries make extensive use of teachers' aides at the pre-primary level. Eight OECD countries and two partner economies reported smaller ratios of students to contact staff (column 1 of Table D2.2) than students to teaching staff. For countries such as the Slovak Republic, Sweden and the United Kingdom, this difference is not substantial. But in Austria, France, Germany, Japan and the United States as well as in partner economies Chile and Israel and there are larger numbers of teachers' aides. The use of these staff means that student to contact staff ratios are substantially lower than student to teacher ratios particularly in France and partner economy Israel.

At the tertiary level, the ratio of students to teaching staff ranges from 30 students per teacher in Greece to 11 or below in Iceland, Japan, Spain and Sweden (Table D2.2). Such comparisons in tertiary education, however, should be made with caution since it is still difficult to calculate full-time equivalent students and teachers on a comparable basis at this level.

In 12 out of the 15 OECD countries and partner economies with comparable data, the ratio of students to teaching staff is lower in the more occupationally specific tertiary-type B programmes than in tertiary-type A and advanced research programmes (Table D2.2). Hungary, the Slovak Republic and Turkey are the only countries with a higher ratio in tertiary-type B programmes.

Teaching resources in public and private institutions

Table D2.3 focuses on the secondary level and illustrates the comparative provision of teaching resources between public and private institutions by examining the ratio of students to teaching staff between the two types of providers. On average across the OECD countries (and also in partner economies) for which there are data, there are smaller ratios of students to teaching staff in private institutions at both lower secondary and upper secondary levels, with just over than one more student per teacher in public institutions than in private institutions. The most striking examples of this are Mexico and the United Kingdom where, at the lower secondary level, there are at least 11 more students per teacher in public institutions than in private institutions. The difference in Mexico at the upper secondary level is similarly large. But this is not true in all countries.

Smaller ratios of students to teaching staff in the public sector relative to the private sector are evident in some countries. This is most pronounced in Spain at the lower secondary level where there are some 16 students per teacher in private institutions compared with only 11 students per teacher in public institutions.

In terms of average class size (Chart D2.4 and Table D2.1), on average across the OECD countries for which there are data, average class sizes do not differ between public and private institutions

Chart D2.4. Average class size in public and private institutions by level of education (2005)

■ Public institutions   □ Private institutions

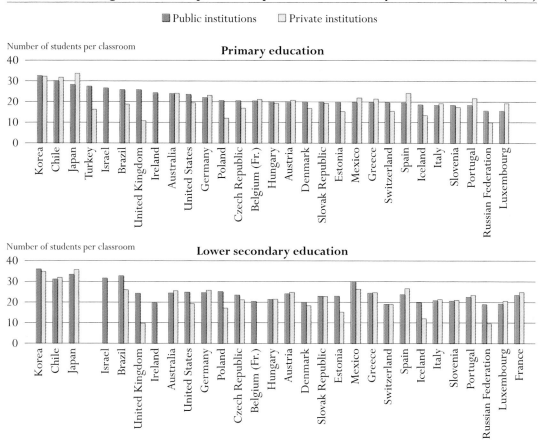

Countries are ranked in descending order of number of students per classroom in public institutions in primary education.
Source: OECD. Table D2.1. See Annex 3 for notes (*www.oecd.org/edu/eag2007*).
StatLink ⟍⟍⟍ http://dx.doi.org/10.1787/068464517374

from more than 1-2 students per class for primary and lower secondary education. However, this trend disguises marked variation between countries. At the primary level, in the Czech Republic, Iceland, Poland, Switzerland, Turkey, the United Kingdom and the United States, and in partner economies Brazil, Estonia and the Russian Federation, for example, average class sizes in public institutions are notably higher – four students or more per class – though in all these countries except partner economy Brazil, the private sector is small (at most 5% of students at the primary level). In contrast, class sizes in private institutions exceed those in public institutions to a similar degree or larger in Japan, Luxembourg and Spain.

The class size comparison between public and private institutions also shows a mixed picture at the lower secondary level, where private education is more prevalent. Lower-secondary average class sizes are larger in private institutions than in public institutions in 11 OECD countries and 2 partner economies, though differences tend to be smaller than is the case in primary education.

There are numerous reasons why countries encourage public and private school sectors. In many countries, a rationale for encouraging growth in both sectors is to facilitate school choice. That is, to broaden the choices available to students and families in their schooling. Considering the importance of class size in discussions of schooling in many countries, differences in class size between public and private schools and institutions may be a driver of differences in enrolment between these sectors. It is interesting to note that in the OECD countries and partner economies with a substantial private sector in primary and lower secondary education (Australia, Belgium [Fr.], Denmark, Korea, and Luxembourg and the partner economy Chile; see Table C2.9), there are, on average, only marginal differences in class size between public and private institutions. Where large differences do exist, they tend to show private institutions having more students per class than public institutions. This indicates that in countries where a substantial proportion of students and families have decided to choose private education institutions, class size would not be a major determinant of those decisions.

Definitions and methodologies

Data refer to the school year 2004-2005, and are based on the UOE data collection on education statistics that is administered annually by the OECD.

Class sizes have been calculated by dividing the number of students enrolled by the number of classes. In order to ensure comparability among countries, special needs programmes have been excluded. Data include only regular programmes at primary and lower secondary levels of education and exclude teaching in sub-groups outside the regular classroom setting.

The ratio of students to teaching staff has been calculated by dividing the number of full-time equivalent students at a given level of education by the number of full-time equivalent teachers at that level and in the specified type of institution.

The breakdown of the ratio of students to teaching staff by type of institution distinguishes between students and teachers in public institutions and in private institutions (government-dependent private institutions and independent private institutions). In some countries the proportion of students in private institutions is small (see Table C2.9).

Instructional personnel:

• Teaching staff refers to professional personnel directly involved in teaching students. The classification includes classroom teachers; special education teachers; and other teachers who work with a whole class of students in a class, in small groups in a resource room, or in one-to-one teaching situations inside or outside a regular class. Teaching staff also includes department chairpersons whose duties include some teaching, but excludes non-professional personnel who support teachers in providing instruction to students, such as teachers' aides and other paraprofessional personnel.

• Teachers' aides and teaching/research assistants include non-professional personnel or students who support teachers in providing instruction to students.

Table D2.1
Average class size, by type of institution and level of education (2005)
Calculations based on number of students and number of classes

D2

	Primary education					Lower secondary education (general programmes)				
		Private institutions					Private institutions			
	Public institutions	Total private institutions	Government-dependent private institutions	Independent private institutions	TOTAL: Public and private institutions	Public institutions	Total private institutions	Government-dependent private institutions	Independent private institutions	TOTAL: Public and private institutions
	(1)	(2)	(3)	(4)	(5)	(6)	(7)	(8)	(9)	(10)
Australia	24.0	24.1	24.1	a	**24.0**	24.5	25.5	25.5	a	**24.9**
Austria	20.0	20.7	x(2)	x(2)	**20.1**	24.1	24.8	x(7)	x(7)	**24.2**
Belgium	m	m	m	m	**m**	m	m	m	m	**m**
Belgium (Fr.)	20.4	21.2	21.2	a	**20.8**	20.4	m	m	a	**m**
Canada	m	m	m	m	**m**	m	m	m	m	**m**
Czech Republic	20.6	16.9	16.9	a	**20.5**	23.5	21.2	21.2	a	**23.4**
Denmark	19.9	16.8	16.8	a	**19.5**	19.9	18.3	18.3	a	**19.7**
Finland	m	m	m	a	**m**	m	m	m	a	**m**
France	m	m	m	m	**m**	23.4	24.8	25.0	13.1	**23.7**
Germany	22.0	23.1	23.1	x(3)	**22.0**	24.7	25.8	25.8	x(8)	**24.7**
Greece	19.6	21.4	a	21.4	**19.7**	24.5	24.7	a	24.7	**24.5**
Hungary	20.1	19.1	19.1	a	**20.0**	21.4	21.5	21.5	a	**21.4**
Iceland	18.5	13.3	13.3	n	**18.4**	19.8	12.0	12.0	n	**19.7**
Ireland	24.3	m	a	m	**m**	19.7	m	a	m	**m**
Italy	18.3	19.1	a	19.1	**18.3**	20.9	21.4	a	21.4	**20.9**
Japan	28.3	33.7	a	33.7	**28.4**	33.4	35.7	a	35.7	**33.5**
Korea	32.6	32.3	a	32.3	**32.6**	36.0	34.8	34.8	a	**35.7**
Luxembourg	15.6	19.2	20.0	19.1	**15.8**	19.2	20.6	20.1	21.3	**19.5**
Mexico	19.8	21.9	a	21.9	**19.9**	30.0	26.4	a	26.4	**29.7**
Netherlands	x(5)	x(5)	x(5)	a	**22.0**	m	m	m	a	**m**
New Zealand	m	m	m	m	**m**	m	m	m	m	**m**
Norway	a	a	a	a	**a**	a	a	a	a	**a**
Poland	20.6	12.0	12.1	12.0	**20.4**	25.1	17.2	27.0	15.2	**24.9**
Portugal	18.2	21.7	24.8	20.7	**18.5**	22.5	23.5	24.2	22.3	**22.6**
Slovak Republic	19.9	19.2	19.2	n	**19.8**	23.0	22.9	22.9	n	**23.0**
Spain	19.4	24.2	24.2	23.8	**20.8**	23.8	26.7	27.0	24.1	**24.7**
Sweden	m	m	m	m	**m**	m	m	m	m	**m**
Switzerland	19.5	15.4	14.5	15.5	**19.4**	19.1	19.1	21.1	18.7	**19.1**
Turkey	27.5	16.2	a	16.2	**27.2**	a	a	a	a	**a**
United Kingdom	25.8	10.7	a	10.7	**24.2**	24.3	9.7	18.4	9.2	**22.1**
United States	23.6	19.4	a	19.4	**23.1**	24.9	19.3	a	19.3	**24.3**
OECD average	*21.7*	*20.1*	*19.2*	*20.4*	***21.5***	*23.8*	*22.7*	*23.0*	*21.0*	***24.1***
EU19 average	*20.3*	*18.9*	*19.7*	*18.1*	***20.2***	*22.5*	*21.6*	*22.9*	*18.9*	***22.8***
Brazil	25.9	18.7	a	18.7	**25.0**	32.7	25.9	a	25.9	**31.9**
Chile	30.2	31.8	33.5	23.5	**31.0**	31.1	31.9	33.5	24.6	**31.5**
Estonia	19.9	15.2	a	15.2	**19.7**	23.0	15.1	a	15.1	**22.8**
Israel	26.6	a	a	a	**26.6**	31.7	a	a	a	**31.7**
Russian Federation	15.6	9.9	a	9.9	**15.6**	18.9	9.6	a	9.6	**18.8**
Slovenia	18.2	17.3	17.3	n	**18.2**	20.6	21.0	21.0	n	**20.6**

Source: OECD. See Annex 3 for notes *(www.oecd.org/edu/eag2007).*
Please refer to the Reader's Guide for information concerning the symbols replacing missing data.
StatLink ⬛ᵢₗ⬛ http://dx.doi.org/10.1787/068464517374

D2

Table D2.2
Ratio of students to teaching staff in educational institutions (2005)
By level of education, calculations based on full-time equivalents

	Pre-primary education			Secondary education				Tertiary education		
	Students to contact staff (teachers and teachers aides)	Students to teaching staff	Primary education	Lower secondary education	Upper secondary education	All secondary education	Post-secondary non-tertiary education	Tertiary-type B	Tertiary-type A and advanced research programmes	All tertiary education
	(1)	(2)	(3)	(4)	(5)	(6)	(7)	(8)	(9)	(10)
Australia[1,2]	m	m	16.2	x(6)	x(6)	12.1	m	m	15.0	m
Austria	14.3	17.0	14.1	10.6	11.3	10.9	10.7	7.5	16.3	15.3
Belgium	16.1	16.1	12.8	9.4	9.9	9.8	x(5)	x(10)	x(10)	19.6
Canada	m	m	m	m	m	m	m	m	m	m
Czech Republic	13.5	13.5	17.5	13.5	12.8	13.2	16.9	16.9	19.2	19.0
Denmark	m	6.6	x(4)	11.9	m	m	m	m	m	m
Finland	m	12.5	15.9	10.0	18.0	13.9	x(5)	x(5)	12.5	12.5
France	13.7	19.3	19.4	14.2	10.3	12.2	m	x(10)	x(10)	17.3
Germany	10.5	13.9	18.8	15.5	14.0	15.1	16.3	11.6	12.3	12.2
Greece	12.5	12.5	11.1	7.9	8.8	8.3	7.4	23.2	35.8	30.2
Hungary	m	10.7	10.6	10.4	12.2	11.2	12.8	24.8	15.5	15.9
Iceland	m	m	x(4)	11.3	10.8	11.2	x(5, 10)	x(10)	x(10)	11.0
Ireland	m	13.9	17.9	x(6)	x(6)	15.5	x(6)	x(10)	x(10)	17.4
Italy	12.4	12.4	10.6	10.1	11.0	10.7	m	8.5	21.7	21.4
Japan	16.7	17.4	19.4	15.1	13.0	13.9	x(5, 10)	8.5	12.3	11.0
Korea	20.2	20.2	28.0	20.8	16.0	18.2	a	m	m	m
Luxembourg[2]	m	m	m	x(6)	x(6)	9.0	m	m	m	m
Mexico	28.9	28.9	28.3	33.7	25.8	30.6	a	13.7	15.0	14.9
Netherlands	m	x(3)	15.9	x(6)	x(6)	16.2	x(6)	m	14.3	m
New Zealand	9.8	9.8	18.1	16.8	12.9	14.8	15.8	13.9	17.2	16.3
Norway	m	m	m	m	m	m	m	m	m	m
Poland	m	17.9	11.7	12.7	12.9	12.8	11.0	12.5	18.3	18.2
Portugal	m	15.4	10.8	8.2	8.0	8.1	m	x(10)	x(10)	13.2
Slovak Republic	13.5	13.6	18.9	14.1	14.3	14.2	10.9	12.5	11.7	11.7
Spain	m	14.1	14.3	12.5	8.1	10.6	a	7.0	11.9	10.6
Sweden	11.7	11.9	12.2	12.0	14.0	13.0	18.5	x(10)	x(10)	8.9
Switzerland[1,2]	m	18.3	14.6	11.7	10.5	11.4	m	m	m	m
Turkey	m	19.7	25.8	a	16.2	16.2	a	52.7	13.6	17.3
United Kingdom[1,3]	16.1	16.3	20.7	17.0	11.8	14.1	x(5)	x(10)	x(10)	18.2
United States	11.9	14.5	14.9	15.1	16.0	15.5	21.5	x(10)	x(10)	15.7
OECD average	14.8	15.3	16.7	13.7	13.0	13.4	14.2	16.4	16.4	15.8
EU19 average	13.4	14.0	14.9	11.9	11.8	12.2	13.1	13.8	17.2	16.4
Brazil	m	17.6	22.9	18.1	17.6	17.9	a	x(10)	x(10)	13.6
Chile	19.3	20.8	25.9	25.9	26.6	26.3	a	m	m	m
Estonia	7.3	7.3	m	m	m	m	m	13.3	15.9	14.9
Israel	12.7	27.8	17.3	13.4	13.4	13.4	m	m	m	m
Russian Federation[4]	m	m	m	m	11.2	m	x(5)	11.2	14.4	13.4
Slovenia	9.6	9.6	15.0	11.1	14.6	12.9	x(5)	x(10)	x(10)	23.0

1. Includes only general programmes in upper secondary education.
2. Public institutions only (for Australia, at ISCED level 5A/6 only).
3. The ratio of students to contact staff refers to public institutions only.
4. Excludes general programmes in upper secondary education.
Source: OECD. See Annex 3 for notes (www.oecd.org/edu/eag2007).
Please refer to the Reader's Guide for information concerning the symbols replacing missing data.
StatLink ⫘⊐ http://dx.doi.org/10.1787/068464517374

Table D2.3
Ratio of students to teaching staff, by type of institution (2005)
By level of education, calculations based on full-time equivalents

D2

	Lower secondary education				Upper secondary education				All secondary education			
		Private				Private				Private		
	Public	Total private institutions	Government-dependent private institutions	Independent private institutions	Public	Total private institutions	Government-dependent private institutions	Independent private institutions	Public	Total private institutions	Government-dependent private institutions	Independent private institutions
	(1)	(2)	(3)	(4)	(5)	(6)	(7)	(8)	(9)	(10)	(11)	(12)
OECD countries												
Australia[1]	x(9)	x(10)	x(11)	a	x(9)	x(10)	x(11)	a	12.3	11.9	11.9	a
Austria	10.5	11.8	x(2)	x(2)	11.0	13.2	x(6)	x(6)	10.7	12.5	x(10)	x(10)
Belgium[2]	9.1	m	9.7	m	10.3	m	9.7	m	9.9	m	9.7	m
Canada	m	m	m	m	m	m	m	m	m	m	m	m
Czech Republic	13.5	11.4	11.4	a	12.6	14.5	14.5	a	13.1	14.0	14.0	a
Denmark[3]	11.8	12.6	12.6	a	m	m	m	a	m	m	m	a
Finland[4,5]	9.9	12.5	12.5	a	17.6	20.6	20.6	a	13.5	18.8	18.8	a
France	13.9	15.5	x(2)	x(2)	9.6	12.5	x(6)	x(6)	11.7	13.8	x(10)	x(10)
Germany	15.8	13.0	13.0	x(3)	14.2	12.8	12.8	x(7)	15.3	12.9	12.9	x(11)
Greece	7.9	7.8	a	7.8	8.9	6.9	a	6.9	8.4	7.3	a	7.3
Hungary	10.4	10.3	10.3	a	12.3	11.5	11.5	a	11.3	11.1	11.1	a
Iceland[3]	11.3	10.9	10.9	n	10.7	11.4	11.4	n	11.2	11.3	11.3	n
Ireland[2]	x(9)	x(10)	a	x(12)	x(9)	x(10)	a	x(12)	15.5	16.3	a	16.3
Italy	10.3	7.3	a	7.3	11.9	4.4	a	4.4	11.2	5.2	a	5.2
Japan[4]	15.2	13.2	a	13.2	12.3	14.9	a	14.9	13.7	14.6	a	14.6
Korea	20.8	20.8	20.8	a	15.3	16.7	16.7	a	18.5	17.8	17.8	a
Luxembourg	x(9)	m	m	m	x(9)	m	m	m	9.0	m	m	m
Mexico	35.8	23.8	a	23.8	30.2	16.6	a	16.6	33.8	19.8	a	19.8
Netherlands	m	m	m	a	m	m	m	a	m	m	m	a
New Zealand	17.0	15.9	17.1	13.6	13.2	12.0	14.2	7.7	15.2	13.5	15.3	10.0
Norway	m	m	m	m	m	m	m	m	m	m	m	m
Poland	12.8	9.8	12.5	9.2	13.1	10.2	16.0	9.7	12.9	10.1	14.3	9.5
Portugal	8.0	10.2	11.4	8.9	8.5	6.3	9.5	5.6	8.2	7.5	10.5	6.3
Slovak Republic	14.1	13.2	13.2	n	14.5	13.2	13.2	n	14.3	13.2	13.2	n
Spain	11.2	16.2	16.4	15.0	7.4	11.5	11.5	11.5	9.5	14.7	15.3	12.5
Sweden	12.1	11.4	11.4	a	14.0	14.5	14.5	a	13.0	13.0	13.0	a
Switzerland[6]	11.7	m	m	m	10.5	m	m	m	11.4	m	m	m
Turkey	a	a	a	a	16.7	7.9	a	7.9	16.7	7.9	a	7.9
United Kingdom[1]	18.6	7.2	a	7.4	12.5	7.8	9.8	7.7	15.2	7.6	5.9	7.6
United States	15.7	10.7	a	10.7	16.5	12.2	a	12.2	16.1	11.4	a	11.4
OECD average	*13.8*	*12.7*	*13.1*	*9.8*	*13.2*	*12.0*	*13.3*	*8.1*	*13.5*	*12.4*	*13.0*	*9.2*
EU19 average	*11.9*	*11.4*	*12.2*	*9.3*	*11.9*	*11.4*	*13.1*	*7.6*	*11.9*	*11.9*	*12.6*	*9.2*
Partner economies												
Brazil	19.3	11.2	a	11.2	20.1	10.4	a	10.4	19.6	10.8	a	10.8
Chile	26.6	25.2	27.4	16.7	27.5	25.8	29.8	13.8	27.1	25.6	29.0	14.6
Estonia	m	m	a	m	m	m	a	m	m	m	a	m
Israel	13.4	a	a	a	13.4	a	a	a	13.4	a	a	a
Russian Federation	m	m	a	m	m	m	a	m	m	m	a	m
Slovenia[2]	11.1	8.2	8.2	n	13.2	14.9	14.6	27.0	12.2	14.6	14.3	27.0

1. Includes only general programmes in lower and upper secondary education.
2. Upper secondary includes post-secondary non-tertiary education.
3. Lower secondary includes primary education.
4. Upper secondary education includes programmes from post-secondary education.
5. Upper secondary education includes tertiary-type B education.
6. Includes only general programmes in upper secondary education.
Source: OECD. See Annex 3 for notes (www.oecd.org/edu/eag2007).
Please refer to the Reader's Guide for information concerning the symbols replacing missing data.
StatLink ⫙⫘ http://dx.doi.org/10.1787/068464517374

HOW MUCH ARE TEACHERS PAID?

This indicator shows the starting, mid-career and maximum statutory salaries of teachers in public primary and secondary education, and various additional payments and incentive schemes used in teacher reward systems. It also presents information on aspects of teachers' contractual arrangements. Together with average class size (see Indicator D2) and teachers' working time (see Indicator D4), this indicator presents some key measures of the working lives of teachers. Differences in teachers' salaries, along with other factors such as student to staff ratios (see Indicator D2) provide some explanation for differences in expenditure per student (see Indicator B1).

Key results

Chart D3.1. **Teachers' salaries in lower secondary education (2005)**

Annual statutory teachers' salaries in public institutions in lower secondary education, in equivalent USD converted using PPPs, and the ratio of salary after 15 years of experience to GDP per capita

Salaries of teachers with at least 15 years experience at the lower secondary level range from less than USD 16 000 in Hungary to USD 51 000 or more in Germany, Korea and Switzerland, and exceed USD 88 000 in Luxembourg.

Salaries of teachers with at least 15 years experience in lower secondary education are over twice the level of GDP per capita in Korea and Mexico, whereas in Iceland and Norway, and the partner economy Israel, salaries are 75% or less than GDP per capita.

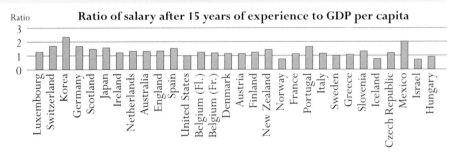

Countries are ranked in descending order of teachers' salaries in lower secondary education after 15 years of experience and minimum training.
Source: OECD. Table D3.1. See Annex 3 for notes (*www.oecd.org/edu/eag2007*).
StatLink ᵐˢᴾ http://dx.doi.org/10.1787/068520240747

Other highlights of this indicator

- Teachers' salaries have risen in real terms between 1996 and 2005 in virtually all countries, with the largest increases evident in Finland, Hungary and Mexico and in starting salaries in Australia. Salaries at the primary and upper secondary levels in Spain fell in real terms over the same period, even though they remain above the OECD average level.

- On average in OECD countries, upper secondary teachers' salary per teaching hour exceeds that of primary teachers by 42%, though the difference is minimal in New Zealand and Scotland and is equal to or greater than 75% in Hungary and the Netherlands.

- Salaries at the top of the scale are on average around 70% higher than starting salaries for both primary and secondary education, though this differential usually varies between countries largely in line with the number of years it takes for a teacher to progress through the scale. Nevertheless, top-of-the-scale salaries in Korea are almost three times that of starting salaries, but it takes 37 years to reach the top of the scale. In Portugal, however, the ratio of salaries at the top of the scale to starting salaries is close to that in Korea, but teachers reach the top of the salary scale after 26 years of service. But it is important to consider that not all teachers will reach the top of the salary scale. For example, in the Netherlands in 2005, 13% of the teachers in secondary education were at the maximum salary level.

- On average in OECD countries, about one in six teachers in primary and lower secondary education that are working in public institutions are employed part-time. Part-time employment represents about one-third or more teachers in Germany, Norway and Sweden and about one-half of the teachers in the Netherlands.

- Fifteen OECD countries have mandatory probation periods for teachers. The average length of probation periods is 12 months. In seven OECD countries, teachers are granted tenure after successfully completing their probationary period. On average across OECD countries, teachers must be employed for 20 months until their tenure is reached.

D3

Policy context

Teachers' salaries are the largest single cost in providing school education, making compensation a critical consideration for policy makers seeking to maintain both the quality of teaching and a balanced education budget. The size of education budgets naturally reflects trade-offs among many interrelated factors, including teachers' salaries, the ratio of students to teaching staff, the instruction time planned for students and the designated number of teaching hours.

Ensuring a sufficient number of skilled teachers is a key concern in all OECD countries. In competitive labour markets, the equilibrium rate of salaries paid to different types of teachers would reflect the supply and demand for those teachers. This is often not the case in OECD countries where salaries and other conditions are often set centrally to cover all teachers. Teachers' salaries and conditions are therefore a policy malleable factor that can affect both the demand for and supply of teachers. In addition, salaries and working conditions can be important influences in attracting, developing and retaining skilled and effective teachers.

Comparing salary levels at different career points allows some analysis of the structure of the career progression and promotion possibilities available within the teaching profession. Theoretically, a career structure with an age-earnings profile (which depicts salary increases across workers' age) that is steep offers stronger salary incentives to teachers throughout their careers. A salary structure can provide salary incentives that attract high quality teachers and increase job satisfaction and performance with stronger rewards for teachers. Additional important aspects of teachers' career structure are the role of probationary periods at the beginning of their careers and the issue of tenure.

Evidence and explanations

Comparing teachers' salaries

The first part of this indicator compares the starting, mid-career and maximum statutory salaries of teachers with the minimum level of qualifications required for certification in public primary and secondary education. First, teachers' salaries are examined in absolute terms at three career points: starting, mid-career, and top-of-the-scale. The changes in these salaries between 1996 and 2005 are then presented. Contractual arrangements and additional payments made to teachers provide further insight into the career structures of teachers.

International comparisons of salaries provide simplified illustrations of the compensation received by teachers for their work. This provides only a snapshot of the complete system of compensations and the resultant welfare inferences that can be made. Large differences between the taxation and social benefit systems in OECD countries as well as the use of financial incentives (including regional allowances for teaching in remote regions, family allowances, reduced rates on public transportation, tax allowances on purchasing cultural goods, and other quasi-pecuniary entitlements that contribute to a teacher's basic income) make it important to exercise caution when comparing teachers' salaries.

Statutory salaries as reported in this indicator must be distinguished from the actual wage expenditures incurred by governments and from teachers' average salaries, which are also influenced by other factors such as the age structure of the teaching force or the prevalence of part-time work. Indicator B6 shows the total amounts paid in compensation to teachers. Furthermore, since

Chart D3.2. Teachers' salaries (minimum, after 15 years experience and maximum) in lower secondary education (2005)

Annual statutory teachers' salaries in public institutions in lower secondary education, in equivalent USD converted using PPPs, and the ratio of salary after 15 years of experience to GDP per capita

○ Starting salary/minimum training
▨ Salary after 15 years of experience/minimum training
● Salary at the top of scale/minimum training

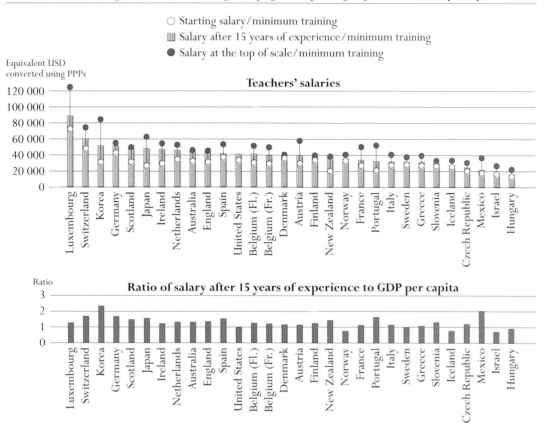

Countries are ranked in descending order of teachers' salaries in lower secondary education after 15 years of experience and minimum training.
Source: OECD. Table D3.1. See Annex 3 for notes (*www.oecd.org/edu/eag2007*).
StatLink ⟲⟲⟲ http://dx.doi.org/10.1787/068520240747

teaching time, teachers' workload and the proportion of teachers in part-time employment can vary considerably among countries, these factors should be considered when using comparisons of statutory salaries to make judgements about the benefits received by teachers in different countries (see Indicator D4). When considering the salary structures of teachers it is also important to consider that not all teachers will reach the top of the salary scale. For example, in the Netherlands in 2005, 13% of the teachers in secondary education were at the maximum salary level.

The annual statutory salaries of lower secondary teachers with 15 years of experience range from less than USD 16 000 in Hungary to over USD 51 000 in Germany, Korea and Switzerland and exceed USD 88 000 in Luxembourg (Table D3.1).

In most OECD countries, teachers' salaries increase with the level of education being taught. For example, in Belgium (Fl.), Belgium (Fr.), Finland, Hungary, Luxembourg, the Netherlands and Switzerland, the salary of an upper secondary teacher with at least 15 years experience is at least 25% higher than that of a primary school teacher with the same experience. In contrast, in Australia, the Czech Republic, England, Greece, Ireland, Japan, Korea, New Zealand, Portugal, Scotland, Turkey and the United States, and the partner economies Israel and Slovenia, upper secondary and primary teachers' salaries are more comparable (less than 5% difference, see Table D3.1). The extent of the variation would be influenced by the structure of teachers' salaries up to the mid-career point. In some countries, such as the United States, teachers' salaries are influenced by the educational attainment of teachers. As this attainment is not constant among teachers at all levels across their career, care should be taken in interpreting the extent of differences in salaries of teachers at different levels of school education.

Comparatively large differences in the salaries of teachers at different levels may influence how schools and school systems attract and retain teachers of different levels. It may also influence the extent to which teachers move across different education levels and, with that, the degree of segmentation in the teacher labour market.

Statutory salaries relative to GDP per capita

Among other considerations, countries invest in teaching resources relative to their ability to fund educational expenditure. Comparing statutory salaries to GDP per capita is thus another way of assessing the relative value of teachers' salaries among countries. Comparative data on salaries for comparable professions would provide a better benchmark for teacher salaries; since such data are not yet available, comparisons with GDP per capita provide some basis for standardised comparisons.

Salaries for teachers with at least 15 years experience (in primary and lower secondary education) relative to GDP per capita are relatively low in Hungary (0.89), Iceland (0.75) and Norway (0.74), and the partner economy Israel (0.70) and highest in Korea (2.34 in primary and 2.33 in lower secondary), Mexico (2.01 in lower secondary) and Turkey (2.54 in primary). In upper secondary general education, the lowest ratios are found in Iceland (0.88) and Norway (0.80) and partner economy Israel (0.70), and mid-career salaries relative to the GDP are highest in Korea (2.33) and Turkey (2.57) (Table D3.1).

Some countries, such as the Czech Republic, Hungary and Turkey, as well as the partner economy Israel, have both relatively low GDP per capita and low teachers' salaries. Others (*e.g.* Korea, New Zealand, Portugal and Spain) have a relatively low GDP per capita but teachers' salaries that are comparable to those in countries with much higher GDP per capita. Germany, Luxembourg and Switzerland have a high GDP per capita and high teachers' salaries (Chart D3.2 and Table D3.1), whereas Norway has a high GDP per capita, but average mid-career salaries.

Statutory salaries per hour of net teaching time

An alternative measure of salaries and the cost of teaching time is the statutory salary for a full-time classroom teacher relative to the number of hours per year that a teacher is required to spend teaching students (see Indicator D4). Although this measure does not adjust salaries for the amount of time that teachers spend in various teaching-related activities, it can nonetheless provide a rough estimate of the cost of the actual time teachers spend in the classroom.

The average statutory salary per teaching hour after 15 years of experience is USD 47 in primary, USD 59 in lower secondary, and USD 68 in upper secondary general education. In primary education, the Czech Republic, Hungary and Mexico and partner economy Israel have the lowest salary costs per teaching hour (USD 30 or less). By contrast, salaries are relatively high in Denmark, Germany, Japan, Korea and Luxembourg (USD 60 or more). There is even more variation in salaries per teaching hour in general upper secondary schools, ranging from about USD 35 or less in Hungary and Turkey, and the partner economy Israel, to USD 80 or more in Denmark, Japan, Korea, Luxembourg and the Netherlands (Table D3.1).

Even in countries where statutory salaries are the same in primary and secondary education, salaries per teaching hour are usually higher in upper secondary education than in primary education, since in most countries, secondary teachers are required to teach fewer hours than primary teachers (see Indicator D4). On average among OECD countries, upper secondary teachers' salary per teaching hour exceeds that of primary teachers by around 42%. In New Zealand and Scotland, this difference is only 5% or less, whereas it is around 60% or more in Finland, France, Greece, Hungary and Portugal and over 80% in the Netherlands (Table D3.1). However, the large difference between primary and upper secondary teachers' salary per teaching hour does not necessarily exist when comparing salary per hour of working time. For example, in Portugal where there is a large difference in salary per teaching hour between primary and upper secondary teachers, the difference between teaching time at primary and upper secondary level is among the greatest in OECD countries, even though their statutory salaries and their the working time required at school is the same (Table D4.1).

Teaching experience and qualifications influence teachers' salary scales

Salary structures illustrate the salary incentives available to teachers at different points in their careers. There is some evidence that a sizeable proportion of teachers and school administrators do not want to progress to higher levels in their careers (OECD, 2005). Presumably, this is because the negative aspects of such a promotion outweigh the positive aspects such as increased salaries, prestige and other rewards. To address this problem, salary structures could be adjusted to ensure that appropriate incentives are offered throughout teachers' careers.

As can be seen from Table D3.1, OECD data on teachers' salaries is limited to information on statutory salaries at three points of the salary scale: starting salaries, salaries after 15 years of service and salaries at the top of the scale. These salaries correspond to teachers with the minimum required training. Therefore, interpretation must be undertaken with caution as further wage increases can occur in some OECD countries with further qualifications.

Theoretically, a system that offers greater rewards to experience and performance provides salary incentives that may influence job motivation and satisfaction and school effectiveness. Deferred compensation is a key incentive for many workers across numerous industries. Organisations can design complex deferred compensation schemes to attract high-quality workers and then provide them with the most appropriate incentives throughout their careers within the organisation. Deferred compensation rewards the most effective employees for staying within particular organisations or professions and for meeting the established performance criteria.

Pensions are an important form of deferred compensation. In most OECD countries, teachers receive some form of pension that accrues with their experience in the teaching profession. This pension provides an incentive to stay in the profession. A monetary incentive is also provided in those systems where the amount of a pension that a teacher receives depends upon the level they reach in the career structure. This is a form of deferred compensation that provides a key incentive for workers as the greatest benefits they receive in the future depend upon their current ability to meet established performance criteria (if they are established). However, the pension schemes are not considered in this analysis.

Deferred compensation exists in the salary structure of teachers in OECD countries. On average among OECD countries, statutory salaries for primary, lower and upper secondary general teachers with 15 years of experience are 36, 37 and 41% higher, respectively, than starting salaries. The increases from starting salary to the top of the salary scale are, on average, 69, 70 and 71%. For lower secondary teachers, the average starting salary was USD 29 772. After 15 years experience, with minimum training, this figure increases to USD 40 322, and then it reaches USD 48 983 at the top of the salary scale. A similar increase is therefore evident between first, the starting salary and that at 15 years of experience and second, the salary at 15 years of experience and at the top of the salary scale (reached, on average, after 24 years of experience).

It is clear that there are large differences in salary structures across countries. A number of countries have relatively flat structures that offer a lower amount of salary increases for teachers. For example, most of the teachers at the top of the salary scale in Denmark (except at the upper secondary level), Finland, Germany, Norway and Turkey, and the partner economy Slovenia, only earn up to 30% more than teachers at the bottom of the salary scale.

Increases in salaries between points on a salary structure should be seen in the context of the number of years that it takes for a teacher to proceed through the salary scale, a factor which varies substantially across countries. In lower secondary education, teachers in Australia, Denmark, England, New Zealand and Scotland reach the highest step on the salary scale relatively quickly (within 5 to 9 years). In these countries, the monetary incentives that come with promotion and commensurate wage increases disappear relatively quickly compared to other countries. If job satisfaction and performance are determined, at least in part, by prospects for salary increases, then difficulties could arise as teachers approach the peak in their age-earnings profiles. Alternately, this may be part of a system whereby policymakers consider that this system better reflects the job of a teacher and the stages of teachers' careers that are considered most productive.

In Austria, the Czech Republic, France, Greece, Hungary, Italy, Japan, Korea, Luxembourg and Spain, and the partner economy Israel, teachers in lower secondary education reach the top of the salary scale after 30 or more years of service (Table D3.1). It is difficult to categorise countries simply by whether they have steep or flat salary structures. Most countries have steep and flat portions that vary across teachers' tenure. For example, teachers in Germany and Luxembourg have the opportunity for similar salary increases in the first 15 years of the tenure but then face very different growth rates after 15 years. In Luxembourg the rate of growth of salaries increases while teachers in Germany face relatively small increases. Policy makers in these countries face different issues for these more experienced teachers.

While the salary opportunities available to teachers are emphasised in this discussion, it should be acknowledged that there can also be benefits to compression in pay-scales. It is often considered that greater levels of trust and information flows exist in organisations where employees have smaller difference in their salaries as this can facilitate greater levels of collegiality. These benefits need to be weighed against the benefits of increased salary incentives.

Teachers' salaries between 1996 and 2005

In comparing the index of change between 1996 and 2005 in teachers' salaries, it is evident that salaries have grown in real terms at both primary and secondary levels in virtually all countries.

The biggest increases across all levels have taken place in Hungary, though these salaries remain below the OECD average. In some countries, however, salaries have fallen in real terms between 1996 and 2005, most notably at the primary and upper secondary levels in Spain (Table D3.2 and Chart D3.3), even though they remain above the OECD average level.

Chart D3.3. **Changes in teachers' salaries in lower secondary education, by point in the salary scale (1996, 2005)**

Index of change between 1996 and 2005 (1996=100, 2005 price levels using GDP deflators)

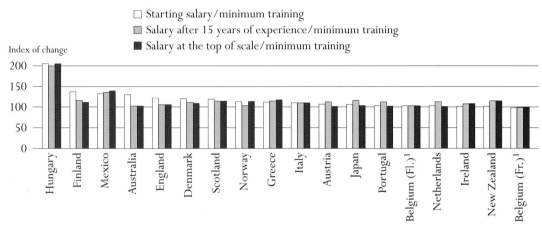

1. The data for Belgium in 1996 are based on Belgium as a whole.
Countries are ranked in descending order of index of change between 1996 and 2005 in teachers' starting salaries.
Source: OECD. Table D3.2. See Annex 3 for notes (*www.oecd.org/edu/eag2007*).
StatLink ⫘⫘ http://dx.doi.org/10.1787/068520240747

Salary trends have also varied between different points on the salary scale. For instance, starting salaries have risen faster than mid-career or top-of-the-scale salaries for all education levels in Australia, Denmark, England, Finland and Scotland. By contrast, salaries of teachers with at least 15 years experience have risen relatively more quickly (than both starting and top-of-the-scale salaries) in Austria, Japan, the Netherlands and Portugal. In the case of New Zealand, top-of-the-scale salary has risen faster than starting salary and in the same proportion as salary of teachers with at least 15 years of experience. However, with a relatively short salary scale (eight years to reach the top of the scale), teacher recruitment is in fact a key focus in New Zealand.

The rationale for these differences would vary across countries. For some countries that have increased starting salaries, these increases have had the objective of attracting greater numbers of graduates to teaching. A danger exists with this policy if salaries are not also increased at other points of the salary structure. If this does not occur, then it has a negative impact upon salary incentives at these points which can have a negative impact upon teacher retention. The efficiency considerations of utilising resources to attract more early-career teachers to the profession need to be considered against the potential implications for teacher retention. It is important to note that comparing changes in salaries at three points of the salary structure may not account for changes in other aspects of the structure of teachers' salaries. For example, in Finland an additional component of salaries may now be paid based upon the personal performance of teachers. This is not captured in the comparison discussed above but is an important change in the structure of teachers' salaries.

D3

Additional payments: Incentives and allowances

In addition to basic pay scales, many school systems have developed schemes that offer additional payments for teachers, which may take the form of financial remuneration and/or a reduction in the number of teaching hours. Together with the starting salary, such additional payments may affect a person's decision to enter into or stay in the teaching profession. Early career additional payments for graduate teachers may include family allowances and bonuses for working in certain locations, and higher initial salaries for higher-than-minimum teaching certification or qualifications such as holding educational qualifications in multiple subjects or with certification to teach students with special educational needs.

In some countries, the reduction of required teaching hours is used to reward experience or long service (*e.g.* in Greece and Iceland). In other countries such as Portugal, teachers can be compensated by a reduction of teaching hours for carrying out special tasks or activities (leading a drama club, or acting as teacher supervisor of student teachers, etc.). Adjustments to base salary may be awarded to teachers in public schools either by the head teacher or school principal, or by government at the local, regional or national level.

Types of additional payments

Data on additional payments can be grouped into three broad areas:

1. Additional payments based on responsibilities assumed by teachers and particular conditions of teaching (*e.g.* additional management responsibilities or teaching in high-need regions, disadvantaged schools)

2. Additional payments based upon the demographic characteristics of teachers (*e.g.* age and/or family status)

3. Additional payments based upon teachers' qualifications, training and performance (*e.g.* holding higher than the minimum qualifications and/or completing professional development activities)

Data have not been collected on payment amounts but on whether they are available to teachers and at what level the decision to award such payments are taken (see Table D3.3a; see also Tables D3.3b, D3.3c and D3.3d [available on line at: *http://dx.doi.org/10.1787/068520240747*] and Annex 3 at *www.oecd.org/edu/eag2007*).

Additional payments are most often given for particular responsibilities or working conditions. A clear example is teaching in more disadvantaged schools, particularly in schools that are located in very poor neighbourhoods or have a large proportion of students that speak languages other than the language of instruction, means teachers face particular demands on their job that teachers in other schools may not encounter. It has been shown that these schools often have trouble attracting teachers and that the least experienced teachers in an education system often work in these schools (OECD, 2005). Additional payments for teaching in disadvantaged schools are provided in about two-thirds of OECD and partner economies, and ten countries also offer additional payments for teachers who teach in certain fields. These payments may be offered in response to a shortage of teachers in these areas.

More than one-half of OECD countries offer additional payments based on demographic characteristics of teachers. Additional payments to teachers based upon their qualifications, training and performance are even more common across OECD countries and partner economies.

D3

Of these, five types of additional payments are offered based upon teachers' initial education and qualifications. The most common types of these payments are available for holding either an initial education qualification higher than the minimum requirement and/or a higher than minimum level of teacher certification and training. These are available in nearly one-half of OECD countries and partner economies with one-third of countries offering both types of additional payments. Thirteen OECD countries and partner economies offer additional payments for the successful completion of professional development activities.

Additional payments that are made to teachers for outstanding performance in teaching are available in 13 OECD countries and 1 partner economy – the only additional payment that could be classified as a performance incentive. In 9 of the 14 countries (the Czech Republic, Denmark, England, Finland, Hungary, the Netherlands, New Zealand and Sweden and the partner economy Slovenia) that offer this incentive, the decision to award the additional payment can be made at the school-level.

The form of incentive and the method for identifying outstanding performance varies across the 14 countries that offer this incentive. In Mexico, outstanding performance is calculated based upon the learning achievements of students as well as criteria relating to teachers experience, performance and qualification. Performance rewards can also be based on the assessment of the head teacher (Portugal), or on assessments performed by education administrations (the provincial directorate of education and the ministry of education in Turkey).

Aspects of teachers' contractual arrangements

When analysing the income received by teachers it is not sufficient to compare statutory teacher salaries. An important consideration is to compare teachers' contractual arrangements, and in particular the proportion of part-time employment among teachers. This will give some further insight on the real amount of salary received by teachers rather than simply the statutory salaries. From an organisational perspective, a desire for increased flexibility in the labour market has led to increased part-time employment across many sectors of the economy. In addition, opportunities for part-time employment are important for many people who do not wish to pursue full-time employment due to other commitments or preferences.

On average in OECD countries about one in six teachers work on a part-time basis in public institutions at primary and lower secondary levels of education. This average hides large differences among the 20 OECD countries and partner economies with available information. In Greece and Mexico (primary education only), it is not possible for teachers to teach on a part-time basis. In nine OECD countries and one partner economy, part-time employment is possible but is marginal with less than 10% of the teachers with this employment status. In the ten remaining countries, part-time represents a larger proportion of teachers: less than one out of five teachers in Austria and Luxembourg, between one out of five and one out of three teachers in Australia, Belgium (Fl.), Iceland, and New Zealand, slightly more than one-third of teachers in Norway and Sweden and nearly half the teachers in Germany (primary education) and the Netherlands (Table D3.4).

In the majority of countries with available information, part-time employment opportunities depend upon a decision at school level or from local authorities/government and in five of the countries with the largest proportions of part-time employment, the decision is taken at school level. This may indicate that part-time employment is used to increase the flexibility of the teaching force. Schools recognise that their teaching and school organisation requirements change and they need flexibility in their teacher workforce that reflects the changing requirements of the school. School-based decisions on part-time employment of teachers may allow for this flexibility to be created and facilitate meeting the changing demands placed upon schools.

Probationary periods offer both teachers and schools the opportunities to assess if they are satisfied with their employment arrangements. It permits a degree of learning about the teacher and the school that may facilitate a better "fit" between the teacher and their role in the school. Job tenure guarantees employment security for teachers. Guaranteed employment is being phased-out of many sectors in some OECD countries as it can hinder flexibility in the labour market and reduce accountability. Job tenure should also be viewed in the context of the incentives offered to teachers. The granting of job tenure can be a strong incentive to teachers and even outweigh the incentive effects discussed in relation to salary progression. Moreover, once teachers have job tenure, this would have an impact upon the incentive effects of increased salary.

Among the 26 OECD countries and partner economies for which comparable information is available, teachers have a mandatory probation period in 16 countries. This period usually lasts for one year, but can reach two years (Greece, Luxembourg) and even be extended to three years (Germany). In seven OECD countries, teachers receive job tenure after completing their probationary period. But in some countries such as Austria, six years are necessary to achieve job tenure whereas there is only a one month probation period. In some countries a period of time is necessary to hold the tenure even if there is no probation period. For example, a teacher needs six months to get tenure without any probation period in Mexico, two years to achieve tenure in Iceland and three years in Belgium (Fl.).

Definitions and methodologies

Data are from the 2006 OECD-INES Survey on Teachers and the Curriculum and refer to the school year 2004-2005.

Data on statutory teachers' salaries and bonuses (Tables D3.1 and D3.3a) are derived from the 2006 OECD-INES Survey on Teachers and the Curriculum. Data refer to the school year 2004-2005, and are reported in accordance with formal policies for public institutions.

Statutory salaries (Table D3.1) refer to scheduled salaries according to official pay scales. The salaries reported are gross (total sum of money paid by the employer) less the employer's contribution to social security and pension (according to existing salary scales). Salaries are "before tax" (*i.e.* before deductions for income taxes). In Table D3.1 salary per hour of net contact divides the annual statutory salary of a teacher (Table D3.1) by the annual net teaching time in hours (Table D4.1).

Gross teachers' salaries were converted using GDP and purchasing power parities (PPPs) exchange rate data from the OECD National Accounts database. The reference date for GDP per capita is the calendar year 2005, while the period of reference for teachers' salaries is 30 June 2004 to 30 June 2005. The reference date for PPPs is 2004-2005. Data are adjusted for inflation with reference to January 2005. For countries with different financial years (*i.e.* Australia and New Zealand) and countries with slightly different salary periods (*e.g.* Hungary, Iceland, Norway and Spain) from the general OECD norm, a correction to the deflator is made only if this results in an adjustment of over 1%. Small adjustments have been discounted because even for salaries

D3

referring to 2004-2005, the exact period for which they apply will only be slightly different. Reference statistics and reference years for teachers' salaries are provided in Annex 2.

For the calculation of changes in teacher salaries (Table D3.2), the GDP deflator is used to convert 1996 salaries to 2005 prices.

Starting salaries refer to the average scheduled gross salary per year for a full-time teacher with the minimum training necessary to be fully qualified at the beginning of the teaching career.

Salaries after 15 years of experience refer to the scheduled annual salary of a full-time classroom teacher with the minimum training necessary to be fully qualified plus 15 years of experience. The maximum salaries reported refer to the scheduled maximum annual salary (top of the salary scale) of a full-time classroom teacher with the minimum training to be fully qualified for the job.

An adjustment to base salary is defined as any difference in salary between what a particular teacher actually receives for work performed at a school and the amount that he or she would be expected to receive on the basis of level of experience (*i.e.*, number of years in the teaching profession). Adjustments may be temporary or permanent, and they can effectively move a teacher off the scale and onto a different salary scale or onto a higher step on the same salary scale.

The data on decision making are taken from the 2004 OECD-INES survey on decision making in public, lower secondary education and refer to the school year 2004-2005. On teacher salary scales, the survey asked which level in the education system decides on the salary scales (excluding bonuses) of teaching staff and how autonomously these decisions are taken.

Further references

The following additional material relevant to this indicator is available on line at:

StatLink ⫘⫘ http://dx.doi.org/10.1787/068520240747

- *Table D3.3b Adjustments to base salary for teachers in public schools made by head teacher / school principal (2005)*
- *Table D3.3c Adjustments to base salary for teachers in public schools made by local or regional authority (2005)*
- *Table D3.3d Adjustments to base salary for teachers in public schools made by national authority (2005)*

See also: OECD (2005), *Teachers Matter: Attracting, Developing and Retaining Effective Teachers*, OECD, Paris.

Specific notes on definitions and methodologies regarding this indicator for each country are given in Annex 3 at *www.oecd.org / edu / eag2007*.

In addition, a more comprehensive analysis of decision making was published in *Education at a Glance 2004* (OECD, 2004c), Indicator D6. Information on the underlying decision-making survey is available in *Education at a Glance 2004*, Annex 3 (*www.oecd.org / edu / eag2004*) under the heading Indicator D6 "Locus of decision making at lower secondary levels". The complete decision-making data are available under the heading "Underlying data on decision making" for Indicator D6 (*www.oecd.org / edu / eag2004*). As a complement to Table D3.1, which presents teachers salaries in equivalent USD using PPPs, a table with teachers salaries in equivalent euros converted using PPPs is included in Annex 2.

D3

Table D3.1.
Teachers' salaries (2005)
Annual statutory teachers' salaries in public institutions at starting salary, after 15 years of experience and at the top of the scale by level of education, in equivalent USD converted using PPPs

	Primary education				Lower secondary education				Upper secondary education			
	Starting salary / minimum training	Salary after 15 years of experience / minimum training	Salary at top of scale / minimum training	Ratio of salary after 15 years of experience to GDP per capita	Starting salary / minimum training	Salary after 15 years of experience / minimum training	Salary at top of scale / minimum training	Ratio of salary after 15 years of experience to GDP per capita	Starting salary / minimum training	Salary after 15 years of experience / minimum training	Salary at top of scale / minimum training	Ratio of salary after 15 years of experience to GDP per capita
	(1)	(2)	(3)	(4)	(5)	(6)	(7)	(8)	(9)	(10)	(11)	(12)
OECD countries												
Australia	30 858	44 423	44 423	1.30	31 092	44 526	44 526	1.30	31 092	44 526	44 526	1.30
Austria	27 094	35 823	53 938	1.04	28 379	38 805	56 139	1.13	28 589	39 531	59 151	1.15
Belgium (Fl.)	29 270	41 007	50 001	1.24	29 270	41 007	50 001	1.24	36 327	52 451	63 054	1.59
Belgium (Fr.)	27 754	38 901	47 452	1.18	27 865	39 335	48 190	1.19	34 729	50 601	61 039	1.53
Czech Republic	18 654	24 423	29 078	1.19	18 654	24 423	29 078	1.19	18 955	24 868	29 663	1.21
Denmark	34 517	38 911	38 911	1.14	34 517	38 911	38 911	1.14	33 902	47 374	47 374	1.39
England	29 992	43 835	43 835	1.33	29 992	43 835	43 835	1.33	29 992	43 835	43 835	1.33
Finland	27 806	32 406	32 406	1.05	32 273	38 159	38 159	1.23	34 681	43 346	43 346	1.40
France	23 212	31 224	46 071	1.03	25 711	33 723	48 692	1.11	25 960	33 974	48 967	1.12
Germany	40 125	49 930	52 062	1.62	41 630	51 240	53 493	1.66	45 022	55 195	57 671	1.79
Greece	25 823	31 439	37 772	1.06	25 823	31 439	37 772	1.06	25 823	31 439	37 772	1.06
Hungary	11 818	15 622	20 682	0.89	11 818	15 622	20 682	0.89	13 706	19 541	25 508	1.12
Iceland	24 134	27 295	31 925	0.75	24 134	27 295	31 925	0.75	25 952	31 966	33 917	0.88
Ireland	28 198	46 709	52 930	1.20	28 198	46 709	52 930	1.20	28 198	46 709	52 930	1.20
Italy	24 224	29 301	35 641	1.04	26 108	31 917	39 135	1.14	26 108	32 813	40 917	1.17
Japan	25 593	47 855	61 054	1.56	25 593	47 855	61 054	1.56	25 593	47 863	62 865	1.56
Korea	30 183	51 641	82 915	2.34	30 058	51 516	82 790	2.33	30 058	51 516	82 790	2.33
Luxembourg	49 219	67 779	100 314	0.96	70 908	88 634	123 187	1.26	70 908	88 634	123 187	1.26
Mexico	12 753	16 784	27 824	1.58	16 351	21 347	35 286	2.01	m	m	m	m
Netherlands	32 195	41 835	46 734	1.19	33 298	45 960	51 207	1.31	33 630	61 511	67 848	1.75
New Zealand	19 071	36 894	36 894	1.42	19 071	36 894	36 894	1.42	19 071	36 894	36 894	1.42
Norway	31 382	35 058	39 044	0.74	31 382	35 058	39 044	0.74	33 589	37 778	40 950	0.80
Poland	m	m	m	m	m	m	m	m	m	m	m	m
Portugal	19 704	32 275	50 634	1.62	19 704	32 275	50 634	1.62	19 704	32 275	50 634	1.62
Scotland	30 213	48 205	48 205	1.47	30 213	48 205	48 205	1.47	30 213	48 205	48 205	1.47
Slovak Republic	m	m	m	m	m	m	m	m	m	m	m	m
Spain	31 847	37 056	46 623	1.35	35 840	41 588	51 904	1.52	36 611	42 552	53 120	1.55
Sweden	26 234	30 802	35 750	0.96	26 756	31 585	36 153	0.98	28 387	34 108	38 785	1.06
Switzerland	40 657	52 743	63 899	1.48	46 751	60 061	72 706	1.68	54 973	70 300	83 900	1.97
Turkey	17 909	19 577	21 623	2.54	a	a	a	a	18 179	19 847	21 893	2.57
United States	33 521	40 734	m	0.97	32 225	41 090	m	0.98	32 367	41 044	m	0.98
OECD average	*27 723*	*37 603*	*45 666*	*1.28*	*29 772*	*40 322*	*48 983*	*1.30*	*31 154*	*43 239*	*51 879*	*1.41*
EU19 average	*28 311*	*37 762*	*45 739*	*1.19*	*30 366*	*40 177*	*48 332*	*1.25*	*31 655*	*43 629*	*52 263*	*1.36*
Partner economies												
Brazil	m	m	m	m	m	m	m	m	m	m	m	m
Chile	m	m	m	m	m	m	m	m	m	m	m	m
Estonia	m	m	m	m	m	m	m	m	m	m	m	m
Israel	14 716	18 055	25 131	0.70	14 716	18 055	25 131	0.70	14 716	18 055	25 131	0.70
Russian Federation	m	m	m	m	m	m	m	m	m	m	m	m
Slovenia	25 148	29 766	31 664	1.30	25 148	29 766	31 664	1.30	25 148	29 766	31 664	1.30

Source: OECD. See Annex 3 for notes (*www.oecd.org/edu/eag2007*).
Please refer to the Reader's Guide for information concerning the symbols replacing missing data.
StatLink ᵐˢ⁵ http://dx.doi.org/10.1787/068520240747

Table D3.1. *(continued)*
Teachers' salaries (2005)
Annual statutory teachers' salaries in public institutions at starting salary, after 15 years of experience and at the top of the scale
by level of education, in equivalent USD converted using PPPs

		Ratio of salary at top of scale to starting salary				Salary per hour of net contact (teaching) time after 15 years of experience			
		Primary education	Lower secondary education	Upper secondary education	Years from starting to top salary (lower secondary education)	Primary education	Lower secondary education	Upper secondary education	Ratio of salary per teaching hour of upper secondary to primary teachers (after 15 years of experience)
		(1)	(2)	(3)	(4)	(5)	(6)	(7)	(8)
OECD countries	Australia	1.44	1.43	1.43	9	50	55	55	1.10
	Austria	1.99	1.98	2.07	34	46	64	67	1.45
	Belgium (Fl.)	1.71	1.71	1.74	27	51	57	78	1.53
	Belgium (Fr.)	1.71	1.73	1.76	27	54	54	76	1.41
	Czech Republic	1.56	1.56	1.56	32	30	38	40	1.34
	Denmark	1.13	1.13	1.40	8	61	61	85	1.39
	England	1.46	1.46	1.46	5	m	m	m	m
	Finland	1.17	1.18	1.25	16	48	64	79	1.65
	France	1.98	1.89	1.89	34	34	53	54	1.60
	Germany	1.30	1.28	1.28	28	62	68	77	1.25
	Greece	1.46	1.46	1.46	33	40	63	66	1.63
	Hungary	1.75	1.75	1.86	40	20	28	35	1.75
	Iceland	1.32	1.32	1.31	18	41	41	57	1.40
	Ireland	1.88	1.88	1.88	22	51	64	64	1.25
	Italy	1.47	1.50	1.57	35	40	53	55	1.37
	Japan	2.39	2.39	2.46	31	83	95	112	1.35
	Korea	2.75	2.75	2.75	37	64	90	93	1.46
	Luxembourg	2.04	1.74	1.74	30	88	138	138	1.58
	Mexico	2.18	2.16	m	14	21	20	m	m
	Netherlands	1.45	1.54	2.02	18	45	61	82	1.82
	New Zealand	1.93	1.93	1.93	8	37	38	39	1.04
	Norway	1.24	1.24	1.22	16	47	53	72	1.53
	Poland	m	m	m	m	m	m	m	m
	Portugal	2.57	2.57	2.57	26	38	57	63	1.67
	Scotland	1.60	1.60	1.60	6	54	54	54	1.00
	Slovak Republic	m	m	m	m	m	m	m	m
	Spain	1.46	1.45	1.45	38	42	58	61	1.46
	Sweden	m	m	m	a	m	m	m	m
	Switzerland	1.57	1.56	1.53	26	m	m	m	m
	Turkey	1.21	a	1.20	a	31	a	35	1.14
	United States	m	m	m	m	w	w	w	w
	OECD average	*1.69*	*1.70*	*1.71*	*24*	*47*	*59*	*68*	*1.42*
	EU19 average	*1.65*	*1.63*	*1.70*	*26*	*47*	*61*	*69*	*1.48*
Partner economies	Brazil	m	m	m	m	m	m	m	m
	Chile	m	m	m	m	m	m	m	m
	Estonia	m	m	m	m	m	m	m	m
	Israel	1.71	1.71	1.71	36	18	23	27	1.54
	Russian Federation	m	m	m	m	m	m	m	m
	Slovenia	1.26	1.26	1.26	13	43	43	47	1.09

Note: Ratio of salary at the top of the scale to starting salary has not been calculated for Sweden because the underlying salaries are estimates derived from actual rather than statutory salaries.
Source: OECD. See Annex 3 for notes *(www.oecd.org/edu/eag2007).*
Please refer to the Reader's Guide for information concerning the symbols replacing missing data.
StatLink ⟨⟩ http://dx.doi.org/10.1787/068520240747

Table D3.2.
Change in teachers' salaries (1996 and 2005)
Index of change[1] between 1996 and 2005 in teachers' salaries at starting salary, after 15 years of experience and at the top of the salary scale, by level of education, converted to 2005 price levels using GDP deflators (1996=100)

	Primary education			Lower secondary education			Upper secondary education, general programmes		
	Starting salary/minimum training	Salary after 15 years of experience/minimum training	Salary at top of scale/minimum training	Starting salary/minimum training	Salary after 15 years of experience/minimum training	Salary at top of scale/minimum training	Starting salary/minimum training	Salary after 15 years of experience/minimum training	Salary at top of scale/minimum training
	(1)	(2)	(3)	(4)	(5)	(6)	(7)	(8)	(9)
OECD countries									
Australia	130	103	103	131	103	103	131	103	103
Austria	106	109	105	107	113	102	102	105	96
Belgium (Fl.)[2]	106	110	113	103	103	103	103	103	103
Belgium (Fr.)[2]	100	105	107	98	99	100	99	100	100
Czech Republic	w	w	w	w	w	w	w	w	w
Denmark	121	112	109	121	112	109	109	107	102
England	123	106	106	123	106	106	123	106	106
Finland	134	118	114	138	117	112	143	127	120
France	w	w	w	w	w	w	w	w	w
Germany	w	w	w	w	w	w	w	w	w
Greece	116	118	121	112	115	118	112	115	118
Hungary	206	201	206	206	201	206	187	202	211
Iceland	m	m	m	m	m	m	m	m	m
Ireland	107	114	110	102	108	108	102	108	108
Italy	111	111	112	110	110	111	110	110	110
Japan	107	117	104	107	117	104	107	117	104
Korea	m	m	m	m	m	m	m	m	m
Luxembourg	m	m	m	m	m	m	m	m	m
Mexico	133	132	133	133	137	140	m	m	m
Netherlands	105	112	102	103	113	102	103	109	101
New Zealand	102	115	115	102	115	115	102	115	115
Norway	114	104	114	114	104	114	112	109	110
Poland	m	m	m	m	m	m	m	m	m
Portugal	104	113	103	104	113	103	104	113	103
Scotland	120	115	115	120	115	115	120	115	115
Slovak Republic	m	m	m	m	m	m	m	m	m
Spain	95	94	93	m	m	m	94	93	93
Sweden	w	w	w	w	w	w	w	w	w
Switzerland	101	98	104	m	m	m	m	m	m
Turkey	w	w	w	a	a	a	w	w	w
United States	m	m	m	m	m	m	m	m	m
Partner economies									
Brazil	m	m	m	m	m	m	m	m	m
Chile	m	m	m	m	m	m	m	m	m
Estonia	m	m	m	m	m	m	m	m	m
Israel	m	m	m	m	m	m	m	m	m
Russian Federation	m	m	m	m	m	m	m	m	m
Slovenia	m	m	m	m	m	m	m	m	m

1. The index is calculated as teacher salary 2005 in national currency * 100 / Teacher salary 1996 in national currency * GDP deflator 2005 (1996=100). See Annex 2 for statistics on GDP deflators and salaries in national currencies in 1996 and 2005.
2. Data for 1996 based on Belgium as a whole.
Source: OECD. See Annex 3 for notes *(www.oecd.org/edu/eag2007).*
Please refer to the Reader's Guide for information concerning the symbols replacing missing data.
StatLink ⫯⫯⫯ http://dx.doi.org/10.1787/068520240747

Table D3.3a.
Adjustments to base salary for teachers in public institutions (2005)
Types of criteria to adjust base salary awarded to teachers in public institutions

D3

	Criteria based on teaching conditions/ responsibilities						
	Management responsibilities in addition to teaching duties	Teaching more classes or hours than required by full-time contract	Special tasks (career guidance or counselling)	Teaching in a disadvantaged, remote or high cost area (location allowance)	Special activities (e.g. sports and drama clubs, homework clubs, summer school etc.)	Teaching students with special educational needs (in regular schools)	Teaching courses in a particular field
OECD countries							
Australia	■	■	■	■		■	
Austria	■	■	■		■		
Belgium (Fl.)		■					
Belgium (Fr.)				■			
Czech Republic	■	■				■	
Denmark	■	■	■		■		■
England	■			■		■	■
Finland	■	■	■	■	■	■	■
France	■	■	■	■	■		
Germany	■	■					
Greece		■	■	■			
Hungary	■	■	■		■	■	■
Iceland	■	■	■	■		■	
Ireland	■						
Italy	■	■	■				
Japan	■	■		■	■	■	
Korea	■	■				■	
Luxembourg		■	■		■	■	
Mexico	■			■			■
Netherlands	■	■		■	■	■	■
New Zealand	■	■		■	■	■	■
Norway	■						■
Poland	m	m	m	m	m	m	m
Portugal	■		■				
Scotland				■			
Slovak Republic	m	m	m	m	m	m	m
Spain	■		■	■			
Sweden	■						
Switzerland	■	■			■	■	
Turkey		■	■		■		
United States	■			■	■		■
Partner economies							
Brazil	m	m	m	m	m	m	m
Chile	m	m	m	m	m	m	m
Estonia	m	m	m	m	m	m	m
Israel	■	■	■	■		■	
Russian Federation	m	m	m	m	m	m	m
Slovenia	■	■		■	■	■	■

■: Exists in the country.
Source: OECD. See Annex 3 for notes *(www.oecd.org/edu/eag2007)*.
Please refer to the Reader's Guide for information concerning the symbols replacing missing data.
StatLink ⏸ http://dx.doi.org/10.1787/068520240747

D3

Table D3.3a. *(continued)*

Adjustments to base salary for teachers in public institutions (2005)

Types of criteria to adjust base salary awarded to teachers in public institutions

	Criteria related to teachers' qualifications, training and performance						Criteria based on demography		
	Holding an initial educational qualification higher than the minimum qualification required to enter the teaching profession	Holding a higher than minimum level of teacher certification or training obtained during professional life	Outstanding performance in teaching	Successful completion of professional development activities	Reaching high scores in the qualification examination	Holding an educational qualification in multiple subjects	Family status (married, number of children)	Age (independent of years of teaching experience)	Other
OECD countries									
Australia	■	■					■		■
Austria							■	■	■
Belgium (Fl.)		■							■
Belgium (Fr.)									■
Czech Republic			■					■	
Denmark	■	■	■	■		■			
England	■		■						
Finland	■		■	■		■			■
France							■		
Germany							■	■	
Greece	■	■					■		
Hungary	■	■	■	■		■		■	■
Iceland	■	■		■				■	■
Ireland	■	■			■				
Italy							■		
Japan							■		■
Korea							■		
Luxembourg		■		■			■	■	
Mexico	■	■	■	■	■				■
Netherlands	■	■	■	■	■	■			■
New Zealand		■	■	■					■
Norway	■	■							
Poland	m	m	m	m	m	m	m	m	m
Portugal	■	■	■	■			■		
Scotland		■							
Slovak Republic	m	m	m	m	m	m	m	m	m
Spain				■			■		
Sweden			■						
Switzerland							■		■
Turkey	■		■	■			■		■
United States	■	■							
Partner economies									
Brazil	m	m	m	m	m	m	m	m	m
Chile	m	m	m	m	m	m	m	m	m
Estonia	m	m	m	m	m	m	m	m	m
Israel	■	■		■			■	■	
Russian Federation	m	m	m	m	m	m	m	m	m
Slovenia	■	■	■	■					■

■: Exists in the country.

Source: OECD. See Annex 3 for notes *(www.oecd.org/edu/eag2007)*.

Please refer to the Reader's Guide for information concerning the symbols replacing missing data.

StatLink 🔗 http://dx.doi.org/10.1787/068520240747

Table D3.4.
Contractual arrangements of teachers (2005)

		Contractual arrangements			Part-time employment		
		Mandatory probation period (Yes "Y" or No "N")	Number of months of probation	Number of months until tenure is reached	Proportion of part-time employment in primary education(%)	Proportion of part-time employment in lower secondary education (%)	Level of decision-making for part-time employment
		(1)	(2)	(3)	(4)	(5)	(6)
OECD countries	Australia	Y	12	a	20	20	School, school board or committee
	Austria[1]	Y	1	72	19	16	State government
	Belgium (Fl.)	N	a	36	29	29	School, school board or committee
	Belgium (Fr.)	m	m	m	m	m	m
	Czech Republic	Y	3	3	m	m	School, school board or committee
	Denmark	N	a	m	m	m	School, school board or committee
	England	N	a	6	5	5	School, school board or committee
	Finland	N	a	a	2	7	Local authorities or governments
	France	Y	12	12	7	11	Provincial/regional authorities or governments
	Germany[2]	Y	18-36	18-36	47	36	m
	Greece	Y	24	24	a	a	Central government
	Hungary	N	3	n	7	7	School, school board or committee
	Iceland	N	a	24	24	x(4)	Local authorities or governments
	Ireland	m	m	m	m	m	m
	Italy	Y	12	12	2	1	Central government
	Japan	Y	12	a	5	7	Provincial/regional authorities or governments or Local authorities or governments
	Korea	m	m	m	m	m	m
	Luxembourg[3]	Y	24	24	17	7	m
	Mexico	N	a	6	a	m	Local authorities or governments
	Netherlands	N	a	12	55	46	School, school board or committee
	New Zealand	N	a	a	26	25	School, school board or committee
	Norway	N	a	n	35	35	School, school board or committee
	Poland	m	m	m	m	m	m
	Portugal	Y	12	a	3	8	Provincial/regional authorities or governments
	Scotland	Y	12	m	7	5	Local authorities or governments
	Slovak Republic	m	m	m	m	m	m
	Spain	Y	12	m	5	5	Provincial/regional authorities or governments
	Sweden[1]	Y	12	m	34	x(4)	Local authorities or governments
	Switzerland	m	m	m	m	m	m
	Turkey[4]	Y	12	12	m	a	Provincial/regional authorities or governments
	United States	Y	m	36	a	a	Local authorities or governments
	OECD average	~	12	20	18	16	
	EU19 average	~	12	22	17	14	
Partner economies	Brazil	m	m	m	m	m	m
	Chile	m	m	m	m	m	m
	Estonia	m	m	m	m	m	m
	Israel	m	m	m	m	m	m
	Russian Federation	m	m	m	m	m	m
	Slovenia	Y	10	m	1	6	School, school board or committe

1. Where a difference in requirements exists between teachers employed as civil servants and teachers employed as salaried employees, the figure reported represents the category of teachers that comprise the greater proportion of the teacher workforce.
2. For the number of months of probation and until tenure is reached, the figure represents primary and lower secondary teachers only.
3. For the number of months until tenure is reached, the figure represents lower secondary teachers only.
4. For the number of months until tenure is reached, the figure represents primary teachers only.
Source: OECD. See Annex 3 for notes *(www.oecd.org/edu/eag2007).*
Please refer to the Reader's Guide for information concerning the symbols replacing missing data.
StatLink ᴀᴍˢᴸ http://dx.doi.org/10.1787/068520240747

INDICATOR D4

HOW MUCH TIME DO TEACHERS SPEND TEACHING?

This indicator focuses on the statutory working time of teachers at different levels of education as well as their statutory teaching time. Although working time and teaching time only partly determine the actual workload of teachers, they do give some valuable insights into differences among countries in what is demanded of teachers. Together with teachers' salaries (see Indicator D3) and average class size (see Indicator D2), this indicator presents some key measures of the work lives of teachers.

Key results

Chart D4.1. **Number of teaching hours per year in lower secondary education (2005)**

Net contact time in hours per year in public institutions

The number of teaching hours per year in public lower secondary schools averages 707 hours but ranges from 505 hours per year in Japan to over 1 000 hours in Mexico (1 047 hours) and the United States (1 080 hours).

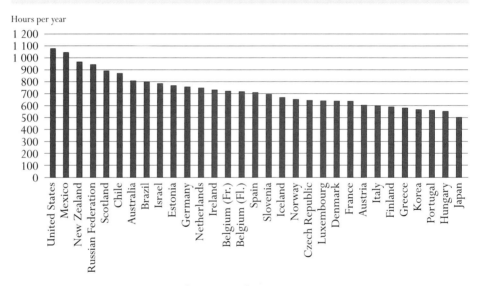

Hours per year

Countries are ranked in descending order of the number of teaching hours per year in lower secondary education.
Source: OECD. Table D4.1. See Annex 3 for notes (*www.oecd.org/edu/eag2007*).
StatLink http://dx.doi.org/10.1787/068521306487

Other highlights of this indicator

- The number of teaching hours per year in public primary schools averages 803 hours (2 less than in 2004), but ranges from less than 650 hours in Denmark, Japan and Turkey to 1 080 hours in the United States.

- The average number of teaching hours in upper secondary general education is 664 hours, but ranges from less than 450 in Japan (429 hours) to more than 1 000 hours in the United States (1 080 hours).

- The composition, in terms of days, weeks and hours per day, of teachers' annual teaching time varies considerably. For instance, while teachers in Denmark teach for 42 weeks in the year (in primary and secondary education) compared with 35-36 weeks per year in Iceland, the total teaching time (in hours) for teachers in Iceland is greater than for teachers in Denmark (or equal for upper secondary education).

- Regulations concerning teachers' working time also vary. In most countries, teachers are formally required to work a specific number of hours; in others, teaching time is only specified as the number of lessons per week and there may be assumptions made on the amount of non-teaching time required per lesson (at school or elsewhere). For example, in Belgium (Fr.), the additional non-teaching hours within the school are set at the school level and the government defines only the minimum and maximum number of teaching periods per week at each level of education.

INDICATOR D4

D4

Policy context

In addition to class size and the ratio of students to teaching staff (see Indicator D2), students' hours of instruction (see Indicator D1) and teachers' salaries (see Indicator D3), the amount of time teachers spend teaching affects the financial resources which countries need to invest in education. Teaching hours and the extent of non-teaching duties are also important elements of teachers' work and may be related to the attractiveness of the teaching profession.

The proportion of working time spent teaching provides information on the amount of time available for other activities such as lesson preparation, correction, in-service training and staff meetings. A high proportion of working time spent teaching may indicate that less time can be devoted to work such as student assessment and lesson preparation. Alternately, these duties may be performed at the same level as teachers with a lower proportion of teaching time but conducted outside of regulatory working time hours.

Evidence and explanations

Teaching time in primary education

In both primary and secondary education, countries vary in the number of teaching hours per year required of the average public school teacher. Teaching hours in primary education are usually higher than in secondary education.

Chart D4.2. Number of teaching hours per year, by level of education (2005)
Net contact time in hours per year in public institutions

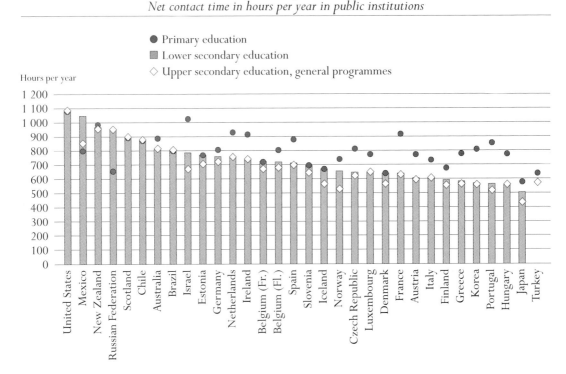

Countries are ranked in descending order of the number of teaching hours per year in lower secondary education.
Source: OECD. Table D4.1. See Annex 3 for notes (*www.oecd.org/edu/eag2007*).
StatLink ⟳⟲ http://dx.doi.org/10.1787/068521306487

In OECD countries, a primary school teacher teaches an average of 803 hours per year (2 less than the previous year), but this varies from less than 650 hours in Denmark, Japan and Turkey to 900 hours or more in France, Ireland, the Netherlands and New Zealand and over 1 000 hours in the United States and in the partner economy Israel (Chart D4.2 and Table D4.1) (see Annex 3 for details at *www.oecd.org/edu/eag2007*).

Teaching time can be distributed quite differently throughout the year. Korea is the only country in which primary teachers may teach for six days per week and yet total annual teaching time is less than the average because the hours taught per day is less than average. Denmark and Iceland provide an interesting contrast in this respect as both countries have similar annual net teaching time in hours (Chart D4.3). However, teachers in Denmark must complete in principle 200 days of instruction in 42 weeks, compared to 180 days in 36 weeks in Iceland. The number of hours taught per day of instruction provides the explanation for this difference.

Primary teachers in Iceland must complete 20 less days of instruction than teachers in Denmark, but these days would each include, on average, 3.7 hours of teaching compared to 3.2 in Denmark. These teachers in Iceland must provide just over half-an-hour more teaching time per day of instruction than teachers in Denmark. A relatively small difference in teaching time per day can lead to a substantial difference in the number of days of instruction per year teachers must complete.

Teaching time in secondary education

In lower secondary education in OECD countries teachers teach an average of 707 hours per year. The teaching load ranges from less than 600 hours in Finland (592 hours), Greece (583 hours), Hungary (555 hours), Japan (505 hours), Korea (570 hours) and Portugal (564) to more than 1 000 hours in Mexico (1 047 hours) and the United States (1 080 hours) (Chart D4.2 and Table D4.1).

The upper secondary general education teaching load is usually lighter than in lower secondary education. A teacher of general subjects has an average statutory teaching load of 664 hours per year among OECD countries. Teaching loads range from less than 450 hours in Japan to more than 800 hours in Australia (810), Mexico (848) and Scotland (893), and the partner economy Chile (873), over 900 hours in New Zealand (950) and partner economy the Russian Federation (946) and over 1 000 hours in the United States (1080) (Chart D4.2 and Table D4.1).

As is the case for primary teachers, the number of hours of teaching time and the number of days of instruction vary across countries. As a consequence, the average hours per day that teachers teach vary widely, ranging at the lower secondary level from three or less hours per day in Hungary and Korea to five hours or more per day in Mexico and New Zealand and partner economy the Russian Federation and six hours per day in the United States. Similarly, at the upper secondary general level, teachers in Denmark, Finland, Greece, Hungary, Korea, Norway and Portugal teach for on average three hours or less per day, compared to five hours per day in New Zealand and the partner economy the Russian Federation and six hours per day in the United States. Korea provides an interesting example of the differences in the organisation of teachers' work. In Korea, teachers must complete the highest number of days of instruction (220 days) but have the fourth lowest required number of hours of teaching time for lower secondary teachers and fifth lowest for upper secondary teachers (Chart D4.3). The inclusion of breaks between classes as teaching time by some countries but not others may explain some of these differences.

D4

Chart D4.3. **Net teaching time in hours by the number of days of instruction (2005)**

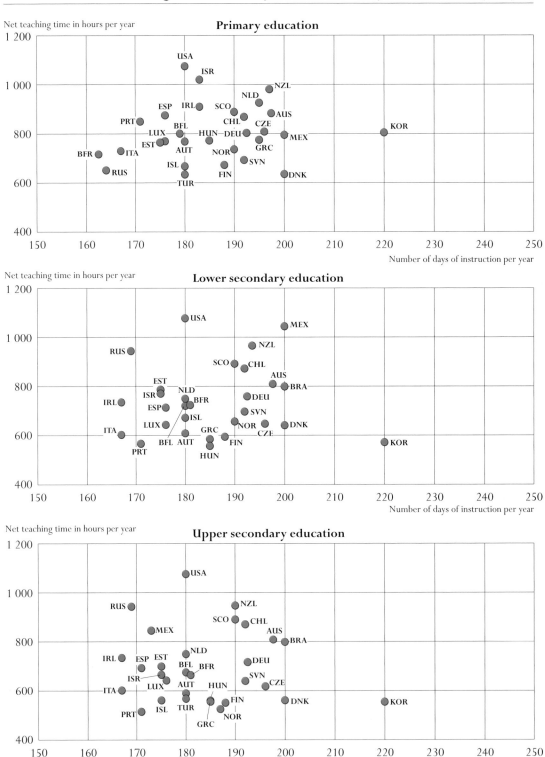

Note: Please refer to the Reader's Guide for the list of country codes used in this chart.

Source: OECD. Table D4.1. See Annex 3 for notes (*www.oecd.org / edu / eag2007*).

StatLink ⫶⫶ http://dx.doi.org/10.1787/068521306487

Teaching time contrasts between levels

In France, Hungary, Korea, Portugal and partner economy Israel, a primary teacher is required to teach over 220 hours more than a lower secondary teacher and, except in Hungary, 250 hours more than an upper secondary teacher (general programmes). By contrast, there is little or no difference in Belgium (Fr.), Denmark, Iceland, New Zealand, Scotland and the United States, and the partner economies Brazil, Chile, Estonia and Slovenia between the number of required instruction hours for primary and secondary teachers, particularly between primary and lower-secondary teachers. Mexico is the only OECD country and the Russian Federation the only partner economy that have secondary teachers who complete a substantially larger number of hours of instruction than primary teachers. In Mexico, required teaching hours for lower secondary teachers is just over 30% greater than for primary teachers. Upper secondary teachers in Mexico have a lower number of hours teaching than lower secondary teachers but their required teaching hours are still 6% higher than for primary teachers (Chart D4.1). This is largely because of larger daily contact time.

In interpreting the differences in teaching hours between countries, it should be noted that net contact time, as used for the purpose of this indicator, does not necessarily correspond to teaching load. Whereas contact time in itself is a substantial component, the preparation for classes and necessary follow-up (including correcting students' work) also need to be included in comparisons of teaching loads. Other elements of teaching load (such as the number of subjects taught, the number of students taught, and the number of years a teacher teaches the same students) should also be taken into account. These factors can often only be assessed at the school level.

Teachers' working time

The regulation of teachers' working time varies widely among countries. While some countries formally regulate contact time only, others establish working hours as well. In some countries, time is allocated for teaching and non-teaching activities within the formally established working time.

In most countries, teachers are formally required to work a specified number of hours per week to earn their full-time salary; this includes teaching and non-teaching time. Within this framework, however, countries differ in the allocation of time to teaching and non-teaching activities (Chart D4.4). Typically, the number of hours for teaching is specified (except in England and Sweden and in Switzerland where it is specified at district level only), but some countries also regulate at the national level the time that a teacher has to be present in the school.

Australia, Belgium (Fl. for primary education), Denmark (primary and lower secondary education), England, Greece, Iceland, Ireland, Luxembourg, Mexico, New Zealand, Portugal, Spain, Sweden, Turkey and the United States, and the partner economy Israel, specify the working time during which teachers are required to be available at school, for both teaching time and non-teaching time. In Greece, legislation requires a reduction of teaching hours in line with years of service. Early-career teachers undertake a teaching time of 21 teaching hours per week. After six years, this is reduced to 19 teaching hours per week and after 12 years, teaching time is reduced to 18 teaching hours per week. Finally, after 20 years of service, teaching time is 16 teaching hours per week, nearly three-quarters that of early career teachers. However, the remaining hours of teachers' working time must be spent within school.

Chart D4.4. Percentage of teachers' working time spent teaching, by level of education (2005)

Net teaching time as a percentage of total statutory working time

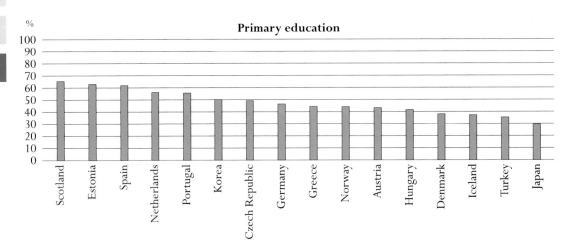

Primary education

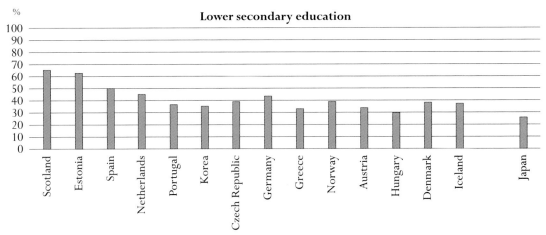

Lower secondary education

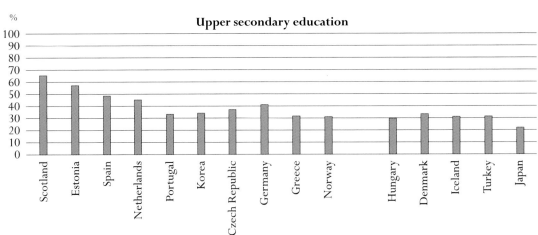

Upper secondary education

Countries are ranked in descending order of the percentage of teachers' working time spent teaching in primary education.
Source: OECD. Table D4.1. See Annex 3 for notes (*www.oecd.org/edu/eag2007*).
StatLink http://dx.doi.org/10.1787/068521306487

D4

In Austria (primary and lower secondary education), the Czech Republic, Germany, Hungary, Japan, Korea, the Netherlands, Norway and Scotland and in the partner economy Estonia the total working time that teachers have to work per year at school or elsewhere is specified (but the split between time spent at school and time spent elsewhere is not specified). In addition, in some countries the number of hours to be spent on non-teaching activities is also (partly) specified. However, it is not specified whether the teachers have to spend the non-teaching hours at school or outside school.

Non-teaching time

In Belgium (Fr.), Finland, France, Italy and New Zealand there are no formal requirements for how much time should be spent on non-teaching duties. However, this does not mean that teachers are totally free in carrying out other tasks. In Austria, provisions concerning teaching time are based on the assumption that the duties of the teacher (including preparing lessons and tests, marking and correcting papers, examinations, and administrative tasks) amount to a total working time of 40 hours per week. In Belgium (Fr.), the additional non-teaching hours within the school are set at the school level. There are no regulations regarding lesson preparation, correction of tests and marking students' papers, etc. The government defines only the minimum and maximum number of teaching periods (of 50 minutes each) per week at each level of education (Table D4.1).

Definitions and methodologies

Data are from the 2006 OECD-INES Survey on Teachers and the Curriculum and refer to the school year 2004-2005.

Teaching time

Teaching time is defined as the number of hours per year that a full-time teacher teaches a group or class of students according to policy. It is normally calculated as the number of teaching days per annum multiplied by the number of hours a teacher teaches per day (excluding periods of time formally allowed for breaks between lessons or groups of lessons). Some countries, however, provide estimates of teaching time based on survey data.

At the primary level, short breaks between lessons are included if the classroom teacher is responsible for the class during these breaks.

Working time

Working time refers to the normal working hours of a full-time teacher. According to formal policy in a given country, working time can refer to:

• The time directly associated with teaching (and other curricular activities for students such as assignments and tests, but excluding annual examinations); or

• The time directly associated with teaching and also hours devoted to other activities related to teaching, such as lesson preparation, counselling students, correcting assignments and tests, professional development, meetings with parents, staff meetings and general school tasks.

Working time does not include paid overtime.

D4

Working time in school

Working time in school refers to the time teachers are supposed to spend at work, including teaching and non-teaching time.

Number of teaching weeks and days

The number of teaching weeks refers to the number of weeks of instruction excluding holiday weeks. The number of teaching days is the number of teaching weeks multiplied by the number of days a teacher teaches per week, less the number of days that the school is closed for holidays.

Further references

The following additional material relevant to this indicator is available on line at:

StatLink ██🖿 http://dx.doi.org/10.1787/068521306487

• *Table D4.2. Number of teaching hours per year (1996, 2005)*

Specific notes on definitions and methodologies regarding this indicator for each country are given in Annex 3 (*www.oecd.org/edu/eag2007*).

D4

Table D4.1.
Organisation of teachers' working time (2005)
Number of teaching weeks, teaching days, net teaching hours, and teacher working time over the school year

	Number of weeks of instruction			Number of days of instruction			Net teaching time in hours			Working time required at school in hours			Total statutory working time in hours		
	Primary education	Lower secondary education	Upper secondary education, general programmes	Primary education	Lower secondary education	Upper secondary education, general programmes	Primary education	Lower secondary education	Upper secondary education, general programmes	Primary education	Lower secondary education	Upper secondary education, general programmes	Primary education	Lower secondary education	Upper secondary education, general programmes
	(1)	(2)	(3)	(4)	(5)	(6)	(7)	(8)	(9)	(10)	(11)	(12)	(13)	(14)	(15)
OECD countries															
Australia	40	40	40	197	198	198	888	810	810	1 209	1 233	1 233	a	a	a
Austria	38	38	38	180	180	180	774	607	589	a	a	a	1 792	1 792	a
Belgium (Fl.)	37	37	37	179	180	180	806	720	675	931	a	a	a	a	a
Belgium (Fr.)	37	37	37	163	181	181	722	724	664	a	a	a	a	a	a
Czech Republic	40	40	40	196	196	196	813	647	617	a	a	a	1 659	1 659	1 659
Denmark	42	42	42	200	200	200	640	640	560	1 306	1 306	m	1 680	1 680	1 680
England	38	38	38	190	190	190	a	a	a	1 265	1 265	1 265	a	a	a
Finland	38	38	38	188	188	188	677	592	550	a	a	a	a	a	a
France	35	35	35	m	m	m	918	639	625	a	a	a	a	a	a
Germany	40	40	40	193	193	193	808	758	717	a	a	a	1 742	1 742	1 742
Greece	40	38	38	195	185	185	780	583	559	1 500	1 425	1 425	1 762	1 762	1 762
Hungary	37	37	37	185	185	185	777	555	555	a	a	a	1 864	1 864	1 864
Iceland	36	36	35	180	180	175	671	671	560	1 650	1 650	1 720	1 800	1 800	1 800
Ireland	37	33	33	183	167	167	915	735	735	1 036	735	735	a	a	a
Italy	40	38	38	167	167	167	735	601	601	m	m	m	a	a	a
Japan	35	35	35	m	m	m	578	505	429	a	a	a	1 960	1 960	1 960
Korea	37	37	37	220	220	220	810	570	553	a	a	a	1 613	1 613	1 613
Luxembourg	36	36	36	176	176	176	774	642	642	1 022	890	890	a	a	a
Mexico	41	41	36	200	200	173	800	1 047	848	800	1 167	971	a	a	a
Netherlands	40	37	37	195	180	180	930	750	750	a	a	a	1 659	1 659	1 659
New Zealand	39	39	38	197	194	190	985	968	950	985	968	950	a	a	a
Norway	38	38	37	190	190	187	741	656	524	m	m	m	1 680	1 680	1 680
Poland	m	m	m	m	m	m	m	m	m	m	m	m	m	m	m
Portugal	36	36	36	171	171	171	855	564	513	855	616	564	1 540	1 540	1 540
Scotland	38	38	38	190	190	190	893	893	893	a	a	a	1 365	1 365	1 365
Slovak Republic	m	m	m	m	m	m	m	m	m	m	m	m	m	m	m
Spain	37	37	36	176	176	171	880	713	693	1 140	1 140	1 140	1 425	1 425	1 425
Sweden	a	a	a	a	a	a	a	a	a	1 360	1 360	1 360	1 767	1 767	1 767
Switzerland	m	m	m	m	m	m	m	m	m	m	m	m	m	m	m
Turkey	37	a	37	180	a	180	639	a	567	870	a	756	1 808	a	1 808
United States	36	36	36	180	180	180	1 080	1 080	1 080	1 332	1 368	1 368	a	a	a
OECD average	*38*	*38*	*37*	*187*	*186*	*184*	*803*	*707*	*664*	*1 151*	*1 163*	*1 106*	*1 695*	*1 687*	*1 688*
EU19 average	*38*	*38*	*37*	*184*	*183*	*182*	*806*	*668*	*643*	*1 157*	*1 092*	*1 054*	*1 660*	*1 660*	*1 646*
Partner economies															
Brazil	40	40	40	200	200	200	800	800	800	m	m	m	m	m	m
Chile	40	40	40	192	192	192	873	873	873	m	m	m	m	m	m
Estonia	35	35	35	175	175	175	770	770	700	a	a	a	1 225	1 225	1 225
Israel	43	42	42	183	175	175	1 025	788	665	1 221	945	945	a	a	a
Russian Fed.	34	35	35	164	169	169	656	946	946	m	m	m	m	m	m
Slovenia	39	39	39	192	192	192	697	697	639	a	a	a	a	a	a

Source: OECD. See Annex 3 for notes *(www.oecd.org/edu/eag2007)*.
Please refer to the Reader's Guide for information concerning the symbols replacing missing data.
StatLink ᎦᎢᏚᎵ http://dx.doi.org/10.1787/068521306487

INDICATOR D5

HOW DO EDUCATION SYSTEMS MONITOR SCHOOL PERFORMANCE?

This indicator focuses on the evaluation and accountability arrangements for lower secondary public schools that exist across countries. The focus is upon the collection, use and availability of student and school performance information. This indicator complements the quantitative information relating to teacher salaries and working and teaching time (Indicators D3 and D4), instruction time of students (Indicator D1), and the relationship between number of students and numbers of teachers (Indicator D2) by providing qualitative information on the type and use of particular school accountability and evaluation arrangements.

Key results

▪ Student assessments in school accountability and evaluation arrangements are increasingly common across OECD countries. Just over half of OECD countries and the partner economy Israel have national examinations that are completed by lower-secondary school students. More common amongst OECD countries are periodic national assessments of students in compulsory education. These occur in two-thirds of OECD countries and the partner economy Israel. In some countries such as Australia, schools implement standardised tests as a requirement to obtain government funding.

▪ Two-thirds of OECD countries and partner economy Israel have regulations that require lower-secondary schools to be inspected regularly. Slightly fewer countries (19 OECD countries) have regulatory requirements for schools to conduct periodic school self-evaluations.

▪ Only three OECD countries utilise school evaluation and accountability information to provide financial rewards (Korea and the United States) and/or sanctions to schools (Belgium [Fl.], Korea and the United States).

D5

Policy context

In the last decade, moves toward greater decentralisation of responsibilities in the education sector and attempts to increase the focus of the public sector on outputs, as opposed to inputs, have led to changes in monitoring systems within the public sector. In some countries this is evident in extent and manner in which the operations and performance of schools are evaluated.

The decentralisation of responsibilities and activities to schools can create a need for greater school evaluation and accountability. Activities that were previously conducted centrally need to be monitored to ensure the effectiveness of operations. The greater freedom given to schools to develop the education they offer can create a need for evaluation of school performances in order to ensure that standards are maintained and that improvements are monitored and perhaps more fully developed. Outputs in education can be difficult to measure. Numerous countries have historically utilised school inspectorates to monitor and evaluate the performance of schools. Increasingly, countries are also using student results in standardised tests to gauge the performance of schools.

The objectives of school evaluation and accountability differ across countries. At times, these arrangements are viewed as policy levers that can drive educational effectiveness and school improvements. Other objectives include holding institutions accountable for the use of public funds. An important aspect of this issue is the role of school choice and whether school evaluation and accountability information is used to promote school choice for parents and families. Again, there can be differing objectives for promoting school choice. A general belief that people should have the right to choose the school education that best suits their needs is common in many countries. Moreover, increasing school choice could increase the effectiveness of the school education system and facilitate school improvement. For this to occur it is assumed that parents and students would move to those schools that best suit their needs, assumed to be those schools that are considered to provide the best education. This would act as a signal both to the school that is receiving more students and to the school that students are leaving. It would also provide signals throughout the school education system concerning the school education that best suits the needs of students and families.

Evidence and explanations

Student assessment and performance information

A variety of information can be used to both create a system of school accountability and to evaluate schools. The information can focus on students, teachers and/or schools. Data was collected from countries to identify if and how information on student performance was collected. Three categories of student information were identified: national examinations that have a civil effect on students; periodic national assessments; and, the existence of follow-up statistics on students' post-lower secondary education and labour-market activities.

Just over half of the OECD countries, as well as the partner economy Israel, have national examinations that are completed by lower secondary school students that have some civil effect or consequence (such as proceeding to a higher level of education). More common are periodic national assessments of students in compulsory education that occur in two-thirds of OECD countries as well as partner economy Israel. In some countries, such as Australia, conducting standardised tests are a requirement of the government funding that schools receive.

The reporting of student assessment results also varies across countries, with some countries emphasising minimum standards and others emphasising the proportion of students in schools who have reached specific achievement levels.

Austria, the Czech Republic, Japan, Spain and Switzerland have neither national examinations nor periodic student assessments. In these countries, at least in regard to lower-secondary public schools, there appears to be relatively little information on student performance (as measured through national examinations and assessments).

D5

School inspection and evaluation

Information about the performance and activities within schools, as opposed to the performance of students, can be used in a school accountability and evaluation framework. School inspections and evaluations provide information on the performance of schools in a variety of criteria. They are distinguished from each other through the organisation of the performance evaluation.

Two-thirds of OECD countries, as well as the partner economy Israel, have regulations that require lower-secondary schools to be inspected regularly. Slightly fewer countries (19 OECD countries) have regulatory requirements for schools to conduct periodic school self-evaluations. One-half of OECD countries have both of these regulatory requirements. In some countries these are used as complementary sources of information. For example, in England, school inspectors utilise school self-evaluation information in designing their inspections of schools and the specific aspects they may focus upon in their inspections. Utilising both sources of data could be viewed as both an efficiency measure and/or as a sign of deeper school evaluation and accountability mechanisms.

In Denmark, Hungary, Japan and Norway there are regulations requiring school self-evaluation but none for a regular school inspection. Conversely, Belgium (Fl.), the Czech Republic, Mexico, Switzerland, Turkey and partner economy Israel have regulations requiring the inspection of lower-secondary schools but no requirements for school self-evaluation (Table D5.1). These systems may choose to focus on specialised inspectors or have a more top-down management approach as opposed to systems that focus on self-evaluations with information being generated and analysed within schools.

The interpretation of these evaluation requirements should be made with caution as the focus is on regulatory requirements that may differ from actual practice. In Austria, for example, there are no requirements for school self-evaluation but it occurs quite frequently and the school inspectorate provides some assistance in such self-evaluations. This assistance is normally in the form of guidance or a 'template' with which schools can perform self-evaluations. In Japan, starting in 2002, the Standard for Lower Secondary School Establishment and other regulations have stipulated that schools must attempt to implement self-evaluation concerning their educational activities and the status of other aspects of school management, and disclose the results. It is also stipulated that schools must actively provide school information to parents and guardians. However, less than 50% of the public schools at the lower secondary level of education disclose or provide the information.

Information was also collected on the organisational framework of evaluation and accountability arrangements. Eighteen OECD countries and partner economy Israel have a specific national or regional school inspectorate. Twenty-four OECD countries and the partner economy Israel have a specific unit in the central administration that deals with systemic school or student evaluations. To evaluate schools, it is assumed that the person or organisation conducting the evaluation has the required capabilities. It is clear that some countries have these capabilities in the central administration and school inspectorates while other countries either believe these capabilities already exist or are trying to develop them within schools.

Use of school evaluation information

The collection of information is perhaps of little use if nothing is done with that information. Information from student assessments and school evaluation can be used for various ends by different categories of people involved in the educational system. For example, educational authorities such as the central administration might use such information to assess the efficient functioning of the school education system, educational institutions may use the information for school and system development, and parents of students may use the information for school choice. This section looks at the use of this information across countries to facilitate school choice, to provide school rewards and sanctions, and to influence school improvement decisions.

Central to facilitating the development of school choice for parents and families is the availability of information regarding student performance and school inspection and evaluation. If this information is made available to parents and families then it can inform their decisions of which school best meets their needs. Eighteen OECD countries make information on school evaluation available to the local school community or general public. Italy and Turkey make this information available to targeted groups such as parents but not to the general public (Table D5.2).

As discussed above, there are numerous reasons why data on school evaluation is collected and why it could be made available to targeted groups and/or the general public. Ten OECD countries reported making this information available to parents for the purpose of informing school choice. Germany, Mexico, Portugal, and Spain make this information available to the general public or to targeted groups, but the intention in these countries is not to inform school choice. There can be numerous objectives for making information available to parents that may not be related to school choice. For example, providing further information to key stakeholders may be part of broader accountability and evaluation arrangements. In addition, in some countries parents have little choice of schools and some countries reported large variations in the degree of school choice. For example, the degree of school choice can differ substantially between parents and families living in consolidated urban areas and those living in more regional or remote areas with lower population densities. It should also be noted that this data does not rule out the possibility of the information being used by parents to choose the school that best suits their needs. For example, in Belgium (Fl.), school evaluations are not intended by law to be used for school choice, but in reality are used in this manner by parents.

The provision of financial rewards and sanctions can be a feature of systems of school evaluation and accountability. But only Belgium (Fl.), Korea and the United States utilise such information to provide financial rewards and/or sanctions to schools. Across these three countries, different information is used to determine the level of financial rewards and sanctions. In Belgium (Fl.) only financial sanctions can be provided and in most situations, when the result of the evaluation is insufficient, a financial sanction is not immediately imposed. Instead, the school is given a period of three years to work on their weaknesses. After that time, the definitive evaluation will be conducted. Only in the case of unsatisfactory improvement, can a financial sanction may be imposed.

Many more OECD countries use this information to motivate decisions on school improvement. Indeed, nineteen OECD countries and the partner economy Israel utilise information on student assessment and school evaluation for school improvement. The use of this information in this manner is important, considering that the focus of discussion of school evaluation and national student testing is often upon school accountability. However, it should be noted that countries that use information to provide financial rewards or sanctions to schools may also have the ultimate objective of school improvement. A key aspect of these rewards and sanctions may be the incentives created for school improvement. In fact, the three countries (Belgium [Fl.], Korea and the United States) that provide financial rewards and sanctions from this information also used the information to motivate decisions on support for school improvement. This may be an indication of more comprehensive school improvement and accountability systems. However, in some countries such as the United States, the focus may remain on school accountability measures that aim to increase standards.

Definitions and methodologies

Data are from the 2006 OECD-INES Survey on Teachers and the Curriculum and refer to the school year 2004-2005.

Public institutions

An institution is classified as public if it is:

• Controlled and managed directly by a public education authority or agency, or

• Controlled and managed either by a government agency directly or by a governing body (a council, committee, etc.), most of whose members are either appointed by a public authority or elected by public franchise.

National examinations, assessments and follow-up statistics

National examinations are to be seen as assessments that have a formal civil effect for students. Countries were instructed to respond "Yes" irrespective of the scope of the examinations in terms of subject matter areas covered; so the answer should be yes, even if the examinations covers just one or two subject matter areas. As for examinations, national assessments are most likely based on student achievement testing; however, where examinations have a formal civil effect for students, this is not the case for national assessments.

Follow-up statistics may be based on census data, involving all students, or on representative surveys.

School inspections and evaluations

Requirements for school inspection are the legal frameworks that may operate from the central administrative level or from lower administrative levels, such as regional offices or municipalities. A school inspection could be done by inspectors, visitation committees or review panels. School self-evaluation is internal evaluation of schools to improve their own practice and/or to inform parents and the local community.

School evaluation and accountability information

School evaluation and accountability information is defined as any kind of systematic descriptive information to which an evaluative interpretation is given; it may depend on test scores, inspection reports, audits, or statistical data.

Further references

Specific notes on definitions and methodologies regarding this indicator for each country are given in Annex 3 (*www.oecd.org/edu/eag2007*).

D5

D5

Table D5.1.
Evaluation of public schools at lower secondary education (lower secondary education, 2005)

	Student information			School information		Organisational framework	
	Existence of national examinations	Existence of a periodical national assessment in compulsory education	Existence of follow-up statistics on student careers[1]	Requirements that schools be regularly inspected[2]	Requirement that schools conduct regular self-evaluation[3]	Existence of national/regional school inspectorate	Central administration undertakes systemic school or student evaluations[4]
OECD countries							
Australia		■	■	■	■	■	■
Austria						■	■
Belgium (Fl.)		■	■	■		■	
Belgium (Fr.)	m	m	m	m	m	m	m
Czech Republic				■		■	■
Denmark	■	■	■		■		■
England		■	■	■	■	■	■
Finland		■					■
France	■	■	■	■	■	■	■
Germany[5]	■	■		■	■	■	■
Greece	■			■	■	■	■
Hungary		■			■		■
Iceland	■	■		■	■		■
Ireland	■		■	■	■	■	■
Italy		■	■				■
Japan					■		
Korea	■	■	■	■	■	■	■
Luxembourg	■	■	■	■	■		■
Mexico	■	■		■			■
Netherlands	■		■	■	■	■	■
New Zealand	■	■	■		■	■	■
Norway	■	■	■		■		■
Poland	m	m	m	m	m	m	m
Portugal	■	■		■	■	■	■
Scotland	■	■		■	■	■	■
Slovak Republic	m	m	m	m	m	m	m
Spain				■	■	■	■
Sweden	■		■	■	■	■	■
Switzerland				■		■	
Turkey	■	■		■		■	■
United States		■					
Partner economies							
Brazil	m	m	m	m	m	m	m
Chile	m	m	m	m	m	m	m
Estonia	m	m	m	m	m	m	m
Israel	■	■		■		■	■
Russian Federation	m	m	m	m	m	m	m
Slovenia	m	m	m	m	m	m	m

■: Exists in the country.
1. Existence of follow-up statistics on student careers in follow-up education or/and labour market.
2. Existence of a legal or formal administrative framework that requires schools to be inspected regularly.
3. Existence of a legal or formal administrative framework that requires schools to carry out school self-evaluation regularly.
4. Existence, in the central administration, of unit(s) that deal with systemic, school or student evaluations.
5. A positive response if 50% or more of the reporting Lander provided a positive response.
Source: OECD. See Annex 3 for notes *(www.oecd.org/edu/eag2007).*
Please refer to the Reader's Guide for information concerning the symbols replacing missing data.
StatLink ⧉ http://dx.doi.org/10.1787/068530238142

Table D5.2.
Use of information from school evaluation and accountability of public schools
(lower secondary education, 2005)

	Availability of school evaluation and accountability information			Use of school-evaluation information by higher administrative levels	
	Information made available to the local school community or the general public	Information made available to targeted groups (*e.g.* parents)	Information made available to parents to inform school choice	To provide financial rewards or sanctions to the school	To motivate decisions on support for school improvement
OECD countries					
Australia	■	■	■		
Austria	a	a	a	a	a
Belgium (Fl.)	■	■	■	■	■
Belgium (Fr.)	m	m	m	m	m
Czech Republic	■	■	a		■
Denmark	■	■	■		■
England	■	■	■		■
Finland	a	a	a	a	a
France	■	■	a	a	
Germany[1]	■	■			■
Greece					■
Hungary					
Iceland	■	■	a		■
Ireland					■
Italy		■	■		
Japan					
Korea			a	■	■
Luxembourg	■	■	a		■
Mexico	■	■			
Netherlands	■	■	■		m
New Zealand	■	■	■		■
Norway	■	■	a		■
Poland	m	m	m	m	m
Portugal	■	■			■
Scotland	■	■	■		■
Slovak Republic	m	m	m	m	m
Spain	■	■			■
Sweden	■	■	■		■
Switzerland					
Turkey		■	a		
United States	■	■	■	■	■
Partner economies					
Brazil	m	m	m	m	m
Chile	m	m	m	m	m
Estonia	m	m	m	m	m
Israel					■
Russian Federation	m	m	m	m	m
Slovenia	m	m	m	m	m

■: Exists in the country.
1. A positive response if 50% or more of the reporting Länder provided a positive response.
Source: OECD. See Annex 3 for notes *(www.oecd.org/edu/eag2007).*
Please refer to the Reader's Guide for information concerning the symbols replacing missing data.
StatLink ⫘⫘ http://dx.doi.org/10.1787/068530238142

Annex

CHARACTERISTICS
OF EDUCATIONAL SYSTEMS

The typical graduation age is the age at the end of the last school/academic year of the corresponding level and programme when the degree is obtained. The age is the age that normally corresponds to the age of graduation. (Note that at some levels of education the term "graduation age" may not translate literally and is used here purely as a convention.)

Table X1.1a.
Typical graduation ages in upper secondary education

	Programme orientation		Educational/labour market destination			
	General programmes	Pre-vocational or vocational programmes	ISCED 3A programmes	ISCED 3B programmes	ISCED 3C short programmes[1]	ISCED 3C long programmes[1]
OECD countries						
Australia	17-18	17-18	17-18	17-18	17-18	17-18
Austria	18	18	18	18	18	a
Belgium	18	18	18	a	18	18
Canada	m	m	m	m	m	m
Czech Republic	18-19	18-19	18-19	18-19	a	18-19
Denmark	19-20	19-20	19-20	a	19-20	19-20
Finland	19	19	19	a	a	a
France	m	m	m	m	m	m
Germany	19	19	19	19	19	a
Greece	17-18	17-18	17-18	a	16-17	17-18
Hungary	18	18	18-20	a	16-17	18
Iceland	20	20	20	19	18	20
Ireland	17-18	18	17-18	a	19	17-18
Italy	19	19	19	19	17	a
Japan	18	18	18	18	18	18
Korea	17-18	17-18	17-18	a	a	17-18
Luxembourg	17-19	17-19	17-19	19	17-19	17-19
Mexico	18	18	18	a	a	18
Netherlands	18-20	18-20	17-18	a	18-19	18-20
New Zealand	17-18	17-18	18	17	17	17
Norway	18-19	18-19	18-19	a	m	18-19
Poland	18	20	19-20	a	a	19-20
Portugal	17-18	17-18	17-18	17-18	17-18	17-18
Slovak Republic	18-20	18-20	19-20	a	17	18-19
Spain	17	17	17	a	17	17
Sweden	19	19	19	a	a	19
Switzerland	18-20	18-20	18-20	18-20	m	17-19
Turkey	16-17	16-17	16-17	a	m	a
United Kingdom	m	m	m	m	m	m
United States	m	m	m	m	m	m
Partner economies						
Brazil	17	18	19	18	a	a
Chile	18	18	18	a	a	a
Estonia	19	19	19	a	a	a
Israel	18	18	18	a	a	18
Russian Federation	17	17	17	17	17	17-18
Slovenia	19	19	19	19	17-18	a

1. Duration categories for ISCED 3C - Short: at least one year shorter than ISCED 3A/3B programmes; Long: of similar duration to ISCED 3A or 3B programmes.
Source: OECD.
Please refer to the Reader's Guide for information concerning the symbols replacing missing data.

Table X1.1b.
Typical graduation ages in post-secondary non-tertiary education

Annex 1

		Educational/labour market destination		
		ISCED 4A programmes	**ISCED 4B programmes**	**ISCED 4C programmes**
OECD countries	Australia	a	a	18-19
	Austria	19	20	20
	Belgium	19	19	19-21
	Canada	m	m	m
	Czech Republic	20	a	20
	Denmark	21-22	a	a
	Finland	a	a	25-29
	France	m	m	m
	Germany	22	22	a
	Greece	a	a	19-20
	Hungary	a	a	19-22
	Iceland	a	a	21
	Ireland	a	a	18-19
	Italy	a	a	20
	Japan	m	m	m
	Korea	a	a	a
	Luxembourg	a	a	20-25
	Mexico	a	a	a
	Netherlands	a	a	18-20
	New Zealand	18	18	18
	Norway	19	a	20
	Poland	a	a	21
	Portugal	m	m	m
	Slovak Republic	20-21	a	a
	Spain	18	a	a
	Sweden	a	a	19-20
	Switzerland	19-21	21-23	a
	Turkey	a	a	a
	United Kingdom	m	m	m
	United States	m	m	m
Partner economies	Brazil	a	a	a
	Chile	a	a	a
	Estonia	a	a	21
	Israel	m	m	a
	Russian Federation	a	a	19
	Slovenia	20	20	a

Source: OECD.
Please refer to the Reader's Guide for information concerning the symbols replacing missing data.

Table X1.1c.
Typical graduation ages in tertiary education

	Tertiary-type B (ISCED 5B)	Tertiary-type A (ISCED 5A)			Advanced research programmes (ISCED 6)
		3 to less than 5 years	5 to 6 years	More than 6 years	
Australia	23-29	20	20	22	24-28
Austria	20-22	22	23	25	25
Belgium	21-23	22-24	23-24	25-27	25-29
Canada	m	22	23	25	29
Czech Republic	23-24	22-23	24-25	a	27-28
Denmark	21-25	22-24	25-26	26-28	30-34
Finland	21-22	22-26	24-28	30-34	29
France	20-21	m	m	m	25-26
Germany	21-22	25	26	a	28
Greece	24	21-22	22-24	22-24	24-28
Hungary	21	m	m	m	30
Iceland	22-24	23	25	a	29
Ireland	20	21-22	23-24	24	27
Italy	22-23	22	23-25	a	27-29
Japan	20	22	24	a	27
Korea	20	m	m	m	26
Luxembourg	m	m	m	m	m
Mexico	m	m	m	m	24-28
Netherlands	19-20	22-23	22-24	25-26	25
New Zealand	20	21-22	22-24	23-24	28
Norway	20	22	24	25	27
Poland	24-25	24	25	a	26
Portugal	21	22	23	25-26	m
Slovak Republic	21-22	21-22	23-24	a	27
Spain	19	20	22	24	25-27
Sweden	22-23	23-25	25-26	a	27-29
Switzerland	23-29	23-26	23-26	28	29
Turkey	19	22-24	24-28	30-34	30-34
United Kingdom	20-21	21	23	24	24
United States	20	22	24	25	27
Brazil	24	m	m	m	27
Chile	m	m	m	m	25
Estonia	m	m	m	m	28
Israel	20-22	22-26	a	a	28-30
Russian Federation	m	m	m	m	25-30
Slovenia	m	m	m	m	28

Note: Where tertiary-type A data are available by duration of programme, the graduation rate for all programmes is the sum of the graduation rates by duration of programme.
Source: OECD.
Please refer to the Reader's Guide for information concerning the symbols replacing missing data.

Table X1.2a.
School year and financial year used for the calculation of indicators, OECD countries

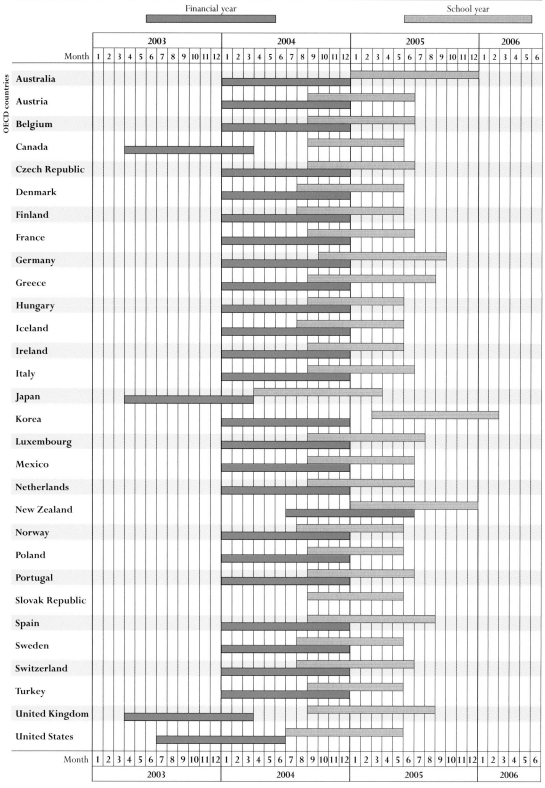

Source: OECD.

Annex 1

Table X1.2b.
School year and financial year used for the calculation of indicators, partner economies

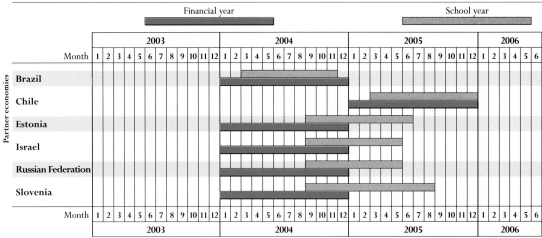

Source: OECD.

Table X1.3.
Summary of completion requirements for upper secondary (ISCED 3) programmes

	ISCED 3A programmes				ISCED 3B programmes				ISCED 3C programmes			
	Final examination	Series of examinations during programme	Specified number of course hours, AND examination	Specified number of course hours only	Final examination	Series of examinations during programme	Specified number of course hours, AND examination	Specified number of course hours only	Final examination	Series of examinations during programme	Specified number of course hours, AND examination	Specified number of course hours only
OECD countries												
Australia[1,2]	Y/N	Y	Y	N	N	Y	N	N	N	Y	N	N
Austria	Y	Y	Y	N	Y	Y	Y	N	N	Y	Y	N
Belgium (Fl.)[3]	Y	Y	N	N	a	a	a	a	Y	Y	N	N
Belgium (Fr.)	Y	Y	N	N	a	a	a	a	Y	Y	N	N
Canada (Québec)[1]	N	Y	Y	N					N	Y	Y	N
Czech Republic[1]	Y	Y	Y	N	N	Y	Y	N	Y	Y	Y	N
Denmark[1]	Y	Y	Y		a	a	a	a	Y	Y	Y	
Finland	Y/N	Y	Y	N								
France	Y	N	Y	N	a	a	a	a	Y/N	Y	N	
Germany	Y	Y	N	N	Y	Y	N	N	a	a	a	a
Greece[1]	N	Y	N	N					N	Y	N	N
Hungary	Y	N	Y	N	Y	N	Y	N	Y	N	Y	N
Iceland[1]	Y/N	Y	N	N	Y	Y	N	N	Y/N	Y	N	N
Ireland[1]	Y	N	N	N	a	a	a	a	Y	Y	Y	N
Italy	Y	N	Y/N	N	Y	Y/N	Y/N	N	Y	N	Y/N	N
Japan	N	N	Y	N	N	N	Y	N	N	N	Y	N
Korea	N	N	N	Y					N	N	N	Y
Luxembourg	Y	Y	Y	N	Y	Y	Y	N	Y	Y	Y	N
Mexico	N	Y	Y	N					Y/N	Y	Y	N
Netherlands[1]	Y	Y	Y	N	a	a	a	a	Y	Y	Y	N
New Zealand	Y	N	N	N								
Norway	N	Y	Y	N	a	a	a	a	N	Y	Y	N
Poland	Y/N	N	N	N	a	a	a	a	Y	N	N	N
Portugal	m	m	m	m	m	m	m	m	m	m	m	m
Slovak Republic[1]	Y	N	Y	N					Y	N	Y	N
Spain	N	Y	Y	N					Y/N	Y/N	Y/N	N
Sweden	Y/N	Y/N	N	Y/N								
Switzerland	Y	Y	Y		Y	Y	Y		Y		Y	
Turkey[1]	N	N	Y	N	N	N	Y	N	N	N	Y	N
United Kingdom[1]	N[4]	Y	N	N	a	a	a	a		Y	N	N
United States[1]	20Y/30N	SS	SS	Y[5]	a	a	a	a	a	a	a	a
Partner economy												
Israel[1]	Y/N	Y	Y	N	a	a	a	a	Y/N	Y	Y	

Note: Y = Yes; N = No; SS = Some states

1. See Annex 3 for additional notes on completion requirements (*www.oecd.org/edu/eag2007*).

2. Completion requirements for ISCED 3A vary by state and territory. The information provided represents a generalisation of diverse requirements.

3. Covers general education only.

4. There is usually no final examination, though some ISCED 3A programmes can be completed this way.

5. Almost all states specify levels of Carnegie credits (*i.e.* acquired through completion of a two-semester course in specific subjects, which vary by state).

Source: OECD.

Please refer to the Reader's Guide for information concerning the symbols replacing missing data.

Annex

REFERENCE STATISTICS

Table X2.1.

Overview of the economic context using basic variables (reference period: calendar year 2004, 2004 current prices)

	Total public expenditure as a percentage of GDP	GDP per capita (in equivalent USD converted using PPPs)	GDP deflator (1995 =100)	Number of full-time equivalents students enrolled in educational institutions as a percentage of total population
OECD countries				
Australia	m	30 875	125.00	22.5
Austria	50.3	33 235	110.38	19.4
Belgium	m	31 975	114.47	25.3
Canada	39.9	32 413	118.03	m
Czech Republic	44.4	19 426	156.29	21.3
Denmark	55.1	32 335	120.47	25.5
Finland	50.3	29 833	114.18	24.5
France	53.2	29 006	113.63	24.1
Germany	47.1	29 916	105.67	20.3
Greece	39.4	27 691	146.56	19.3
Hungary	m	16 519	248.77	20.9
Iceland	44.7	33 271	139.66	30.7
Ireland	33.9	36 536	143.12	24.5
Italy	47.8	27 744	129.18	19.0
Japan	37.2	28 930	91.56	16.5
Korea	28.1	20 723	131.51	24.2
Luxembourg	43.1	64 843	118.67	m
Mexico	23.4	10 145	302.43	30.2
Netherlands	46.4	33 571	126.12	21.9
New Zealand	31.1	24 834	119.95	27.0
Norway	45.8	41 880	141.74	25.1
Poland	m	13 089	187.56	23.9
Portugal	46.7	19 324	134.11	20.7
Slovak Republic	23.1	14 651	163.63	22.6
Spain	38.7	26 018	135.65	19.2
Sweden	56.8	31 072	112.11	24.9
Switzerland	46.0	34 740	105.04	m
Turkey	m	7 212	3 972.22	19.7
United Kingdom	43.3	31 780	126.15	24.8
United States	36.4	39 660	118.84	22.9
Partner economies				
Brazil	32.7	9 054	224.69	27.2
Chile[1]	m	12 635	150.09	27.9
Estonia	34.2	14 441	187.99	24.7
Israel	49.2	24 512	146.38	30.1
Russian Federation	m	9 899	868.01	14.8
Slovenia	47.4	21 536	184.81	20.1

1. Year of reference 2005.
Source: OECD.
Please refer to the Reader's Guide for information concerning the symbols replacing missing data.

Table X2.2.
Basic reference statistics (reference period: calendar year 2004, 2004 current prices)[1]

	Gross Domestic Product (in millions of local currency)[2]	Gross Domestic Product (adjusted to financial year)[3]	Total public expenditure (in millions of local currency)	Total population in thousand (mid-year estimates)	Purchasing Power Parity for GDP (PPP) (USD=1)	Purchasing Power Parity for GDP (PPP) (Euro Zone=1)	Purchasing Power Parity for private consumption (PPP) (USD=1)
OECD countries							
Australia	857 765	848 008	m	20 204	1.359422	1.5698	1.4
Austria	235 819		118 664	8 175	0.867975	1.0023	0.89
Belgium	288 089		m	10 421	0.864572	0.9984	0.91
Canada	1 290 788		515 468	31 989	1.24549	1.4382	1.26
Czech Republic	2 781 060		1 235 094	10 207	14.02564	16.1959	15.06
Denmark	1 467 310		807 820	5 403	8.398717	9.6983	8.94
Finland	151 935		76 484	5 227	0.974275	1.1250	1.07
France	1 659 020		883 116	62 324	0.917704	1.0597	0.95
Germany	2 207 200		1 039 600	82 501	0.89429	1.0327	0.9
Greece	212 734		83 801	11 062	0.694512	0.8020	0.75
Hungary	20 712 284		m	10 107	124.053262	143.2486	133.39
Iceland	915 286		409 233	293	94.023652	108.5723	103.46
Ireland	147 569		50 072	4 059	0.99503	1.1490	1.08
Italy	1 388 870		663 443	58 175	0.860514	0.9937	0.91
Japan[4]	496 050 500	491 920 250	183 222 000	127 751	133.100917	153.6962	152.31
Korea	779 380 500		218 768 500	48 082	782.194214	903.2266	888.8
Luxembourg	26 996		11 647	453	0.918444	1.0606	0.9
Mexico	7 709 096		1 802 610	104 000	7.306949	8.4376	7.9
Netherlands	489 854		227 535	16 276	0.896506	1.0352	0.91
New Zealand	148 484		46 234	4 063	1.471595	1.6993	1.5
Norway	1 716 933		786 170	4 591	8.929665	10.3114	9.72
Poland	922 157		m	38 180	1.845321	2.1309	2.07
Portugal	143 478		66 975	10 502	0.706991	0.8164	0.75
Slovak Republic	1 355 262		312 732	5 382	17.186158	19.8454	18.89
Spain	840 106		325 095	42 692	0.756343	0.8734	0.78
Sweden	2 565 056		1 456 493	8 994	9.178642	10.5989	9.57
Switzerland	447 309		205 981	7 454	1.727346	1.9946	1.86
Turkey	430 511		m	71 789	0.831471	0.9601	0.9
United Kingdom	1 176 527	1 126 854	509 421	59 835	0.618715	0.7145	0.61
United States	11 657 300	11 469 975	4 243 239	293 933	1	1.1547	1
Euro Zone					*0.866*	*1.0000*	*m*
Partner economies							
Brazil	1 941 498		634 416	182 937	1.1722	1.3536	m
Chile[5]	64 549 001		m	16 295	313.522	362.0346	m
Estonia	146 694		50 217	1 351	7.5186	8.6820	m
Israel	548 936		270 251	6 809	3.289	3.7979	m
Russian Federation	17 008 400		m	143 850	11.9443	13.7925	m
Slovenia	6 271 795		2 974 939	1 996	145.8705	168.4417	m

1. Data on GDP, PPPs and total public expenditure in countries in the Euro zone are provided in EUR.
2. GDP calculated for the fiscal year in Australia and GDP and total public expenditure calculated for the fiscal year in New Zealand.
3. For countries where GDP is not reported for the same reference period as data on educational finance, GDP is estimated as: wt-1 (GDPt - 1) + wt (GDPt), where wt and wt-1 are the weights for the respective portions of the two reference periods for GDP which fall within the educational financial year. Adjustments were made in Chapter B for Australia, Canada, Japan, the United Kingdom and the United States.
4. Total public expenditure adjusted to financial year.
5. Year of reference 2005.
Source: OECD.
Please refer to the Reader's Guide for information concerning the symbols replacing missing data.

Annex 2

Table X2.3.
Basic reference statistics (reference period: calendar year 1995, 1995 current prices)[1]

	Gross Domestic Product (in millions of local currency)[2]	Gross Domestic Product (adjusted to financial year)[3]	Gross Domestic Product (2004 constant prices, base year=1995)[2]	Total public expenditure (in millions of local currency)	Total population in thousand (mid-year estimates)	Purchasing Power Parity for GDP (PPP) (USD=1)	Purchasing Power Parity for private consumption (PPP) (USD=1)
Australia	518 144	502 361	686 212	184 270	18 193	1.319122	1.37969
Austria	175 526		213 639	98 374	7 948	0.949892	0.98335
Belgium	207 782		251 680	107 927	10 137	0.921861	0.95232
Canada	810 426	771 914	1 093 593	381 542	29 302	1.214619	1.27027
Czech Republic	1 466 522		1 779 434	783 678	10 331	10.857984	12.26405
Denmark	1 019 545		1 217 947	606 983	5 230	8.589436	8.91466
Finland	95 916		133 067	59 039	5 108	0.979608	1.13104
France	1 194 808		1 460 042	650 674	59 419	0.959259	1.02936
Germany	1 848 450		2 088 821	1 012 330	81 661	1.02654	0.99959
Greece	102 790		145 150	m	10 634	0.578868	0.64704
Hungary	5 767 686		8 325 998	2 327 299	10 329	59.296251	61.86322
Iceland	454 213		655 371	186 845	267	75.172041	87.62692
Ireland	53 147		103 107	21 840	3 601	0.817283	0.89372
Italy	947 339		1 075 108	499 713	56 844	0.775789	0.82553
Japan[4]	493 271 700	488 212 650	541 780 074	m	125 472	174.850793	197.74651
Korea	398 837 700		592 620 667	83 080 800	45 093	690.03741	685.20741
Luxembourg	15 110		22 748	5 996	410	1.002795	0.96317
Mexico	1 837 019		2 549 055	380 924	90 164	2.928674	3.17044
Netherlands	305 261		388 412	170 327	15 460	0.903208	0.91699
New Zealand	93 387		123 793	31 743	3 676	1.462794	1.47642
Norway	937 445		1 211 317	483 072	4 358	9.012985	9.53392
Poland	337 222		491 667	147 561	38 588	1.147401	1.25985
Portugal	85 138		106 983	m	10 030	0.61231	0.63843
Slovak Republic	585 784		828 265	189 100	5 363	13.140138	13.24353
Spain	447 205		619 337	192 633	39 388	0.708614	0.75011
Sweden	1 787 889		2 287 929	1 199 338	8 827	9.421095	10.211
Switzerland	372 250		425 849	157 093	7 081	1.997352	2.10287
Turkey	7 762		10 838	m	61 644	0.022613	0.02584
United Kingdom	719 747	690 268	932 671	322 934	58 025	0.623732	0.64311
United States	7 342 300	7 261 100	9 809 217	2 717 835	266 588	1	1
Brazil	646 192		745 444	224 283	152 945	0.63	m
Chile	25 875 699		43 007 633	5 265 291	14 210	247.49	m
Estonia	43 061		78 031	m	1 448	4.8101	m
Israel	283 038		389 898	147 374	5 545	2.986	m
Russian Federation	1 540 493		1 959 467	m	147 613	1.63	m
Slovenia	m		3 393 643	m	1 990	0.4017	m

(Left margin: OECD countries; Partner economies)

1. Data on GDP, PPPs and total public expenditure in countries in the Euro zone are provided in EUR.
2. Australia and New Zealand : GDP and total public expenditure calculated for the fiscal year.
3. For countries where GDP is not reported for the same reference period as data on educational finance, GDP is estimated as: wt-1 (GDPt - 1) + wt (GDPt), where wt and wt-1 are the weights for the respective portions of the two reference periods for GDP which fall within the educational financial year. Adjustments were made in Chapter B for Canada, Japan, the United Kingdom and the United States.
4. Total public expenditure adjusted to financial year.
Source: OECD.
Please refer to the Reader's Guide for information concerning the symbols replacing missing data.

Table X2.4.
Annual expenditure on educational institutions per student for all services (2004)
In equivalent USD converted using PPPs for private consumption, by level of education, based on full-time equivalents

	Pre-primary education (for children 3 years and older)	Primary education	Secondary education			Post-secondary non-tertiary education	Tertiary education (including R&D activities)			All tertiary education excluding R&D activities	Primary to tertiary education
			Lower secondary education	Upper secondary education	All secondary education		Tertiary-type B education	Tertiary-type A & advanced research programmes	All tertiary education		
	(1)	(2)	(3)	(4)	(5)	(6)	(7)	(8)	(9)	(10)	(11)
Australia	m	5 609	7 522	8 596	7 923	7 738	8 181	14 565	13 629	9 953	7 820
Austria	5 955	7 479	8 747	9 715	9 213	x(4)	9 823	13 927	13 614	9 358	9 561
Belgium	4 670	6 304	x(5)	x(5)	7 364	x(5)	x(9)	x(9)	11 250	7 524	7 619
Canada	m	m	m	m	m	m	m	m	m	m	m
Czech Republic	2 959	2 600	4 441	4 461	4 451	2040	3 048	6 651	6 288	5 319	4 176
Denmark	5 001	7 592	7 726	8 893	8 313	x(4, 9)	x(9)	x(9)	14 303	10 698	9 174
Finland	3 899	5 081	8 120	5 968	6 775	x(5)	7 948	11 388	11 386	7 009	7 101
France	4 770	4 909	7 570	9 547	8 440	3 943	8 803	10 814	10 305	7 121	7 612
Germany	5 454	4 917	6 043	10 393	7 528	10 506	6 372	13 134	12 177	7 675	7 753
Greece	x(2)	4 255	x(5)	x(5)	4 828	5 267	2 360	6 667	5 179	4 186	4 755
Hungary[1]	3 935	3 572	3 193	3 690	3 434	5 906	4 733	6 694	6 599	5 215	4 023
Iceland	5 556	7 665	7 528	6 662	7 017	x(4, 9)	x(9)	x(9)	8 071	m	7 510
Ireland	4 559	4 996	6 397	6 734	6 550	4762	x(9)	x(9)	9 408	6 859	6 185
Italy[1]	5 646	6 988	7 240	7 538	7 417	m	7 922	7 296	7 303	4 550	7 303
Japan	3 447	5 725	6 401	6 889	6 655	x(4, 9)	6 658	12 039	10 655	m	7 120
Korea	2 218	3 952	5 331	6 587	5 950	a	3 752	7 568	6 220	5 416	5 275
Luxembourg[1]	x(2)	13 734	18 406	18 094	18 242	m	m	m	m	m	m
Mexico	1 659	1 567	1 481	2 371	1 777	a	x(9)	x(9)	5 345	4 471	1 968
Netherlands	5 721	6 130	7 830	6 933	7 429	6 526	a	13 641	13 641	8 508	7 881
New Zealand	5 016	5 092	5 233	7 283	6 179	5 310	5 681	9 648	8 698	8 084	6 179
Norway	3 975	7 839	8 705	11 482	10 206	x(5)	x(9)	x(9)	13 777	9 599	9 850
Poland[1]	3 606	2 791	2 516	2 629	2 576	2 806	2 457	3 986	3 933	3 471	2 962
Portugal[1]	4 205	4 413	5 994	5 621	5 815	m	x(9)	x(9)	7 297	m	5 476
Slovak Republic	2 343	1 886	2 173	2 870	2 496	x(4)	x(4)	5 945	5 945	5 404	2 782
Spain	4 477	4 814	x(5)	x(5)	6 498	x(5)	8 109	9 291	9 093	6 645	6 399
Sweden	4 236	7 164	7 516	7 882	7 710	3 296	x(9)	x(9)	15 555	8 013	8 714
Switzerland[1]	3 326	7 959	8 541	14 272	11 307	7 801	5 545	21 726	20 399	11 622	11 035
Turkey[1]	m	1 035	a	1 670	1 670	a	x(9)	x(9)	m	3 909	1 410
United Kingdom	8 037	6 026	x(5)	x(5)	7 191	x(5)	x(9)	x(9)	11 648	8 917	7 374
United States	7 896	8 805	9 490	10 468	9 938	m	x(9)	x(9)	22 476	19 842	12 092
OECD average	*4 503*	*5 548*	*6 566*	*7 490*	*6 927*	*4 393*	*~*	*~*	*10 526*	*7 575*	*6 682*

1. Public institutions only.
Source: OECD. See Annex 3 for notes (*www.oecd.org/edu/eag2007*).
Please refer to the Reader's Guide for information concerning the symbols replacing missing data.

Annex 2

Table X2.5.
Annual expenditure on educational institutions per student for all services (2004)
In equivalent EUR converted using PPPs for GDP, by level of education, based on full-time equivalents

| | Pre-primary education (for children 3 years and older) | Primary education | Secondary education | | | Post-secondary non-tertiary education | Tertiary education (including R&D activities) | | | All tertiary education excluding R&D activities | Primary to tertiary education | Proportion of students enrolled, based on full-time equivalents in | | |
			Lower secondary education	Upper secondary education	All secondary education		Tertiary-type B education	Tertiary-type A & advanced research programmes	All tertiary education			Pre-primary education (for children 3 years and older)	Primary, secondary and post-secondary non-tertiary education	All tertiary education
	(1)	(2)	(3)	(4)	(5)	(6)	(7)	(8)	(9)	(10)	(11)	(12)	(13)	(14)
Australia	m	5 002	6 709	7 667	7 066	6 901	7 296	12 990	12 155	8 876	6 974	2.9	81.5	15.5
Austria	5 288	6 641	7 767	8 627	8 181	x(4)	8 723	12 367	12 089	8 310	8 490	13.2	71.9	15.0
Belgium	4 257	5 746	x(5)	x(5)	6 713	x(5)	x(9)	x(9)	10 255	6 859	6 945	15.3	71.4	13.2
Canada	m	m	m	m	m	m	m	m	m	m	m	m	m	m
Czech Republic	2 752	2 417	4 130	4 148	4 139	1 897	2 834	6 185	5 847	4 946	3 884	13.3	72.2	14.5
Denmark	4 610	6 998	7 122	8 198	7 663	x(4.9)	x(9)	x(9)	13 185	9 861	8 457	20.5	64.5	15.0
Finland	3 708	4 833	7 723	5 676	6 444	x(5)	7 559	10 831	10 829	6 666	6 753	10.8	71.8	17.4
France	4 276	4 401	6 787	8 559	7 566	3 535	7 892	9 694	9 238	6 384	6 824	17.3	67.7	15.0
Germany	4 754	4 285	5 267	9 057	6 561	9 156	5 554	11 447	10 613	6 689	6 757	13.4	73.1	13.4
Greece	x(2)	3 979	x(5)	x(5)	4 515	4 926	2 207	6 235	4 843	3 915	4 447	x(13)	71.2	28.8
Hungary[1]	3 664	3 327	2 973	3 436	3 197	5 500	4 407	6 234	6 144	4 856	3 747	16.4	71.0	12.7
Iceland	5 295	7 304	7 174	6 348	6 687	x(4, 9)	x(9)	x(9)	7 691	m	7 157	12.8	73.7	13.5
Ireland	4 285	4 696	6 012	6 330	6 157	4476	x(9)	x(9)	8 843	6 447	5 814	0.1	82.6	17.3
Italy[1]	5 171	6 400	6 631	6 903	6 792	m	7 255	6 682	6 688	4 167	6 688	11.7	69.6	18.7
Japan	3 416	5 673	6 343	6 827	6 595	x(4, 9)	6 598	11 930	10 559	m	7 056	8.4	71.9	18.6
Korea	2 183	3 889	5 245	6 482	5 855	a	3 692	7 447	6 121	5 330	5 191	4.7	67.4	27.9
Luxembourg[1]	x(2)	11 655	15620	15 355	15 481	m	m	m	m	m	m	m	m	m
Mexico	1 554	1 467	1 387	2 220	1 664	a	x(9)	x(9)	5 004	4 186	1 843	12.3	80.2	7.5
Netherlands	5 029	5 388	6 883	6 094	6 531	5 737	a	11 991	11 991	7 479	6 927	9.9	76.0	14.1
New Zealand	4 427	4 495	4 619	6 429	5 455	4 687	5 015	8 516	7 678	7 136	5 454	6.0	79.1	14.9
Norway	3 747	7 389	8 206	10 823	9 620	x(5)	x(9)	x(9)	12 987	9 049	9 285	11.5	72.2	16.0
Poland[1]	3 503	2 711	2 444	2 554	2 502	2 725	2 386	3 872	3 821	3 372	2 877	9.2	75.4	15.3
Portugal[1]	3 863	4 054	5 507	5 163	5 342	m	x(9)	x(9)	6 703	m	5 030	7.8	76.2	16.1
Slovak Republic	2 230	1 796	2 069	2 732	2 376	x(4)	x(4)	5 659	5 659	5 144	2 648	12.6	76.5	10.9
Spain	3 998	4 299	x(5)	x(5)	5 803	x(5)	7 242	8 298	8 121	5 935	5 715	16.8	66.3	16.9
Sweden	3 825	6 469	6 786	7 117	6 962	2 976	x(9)	x(9)	14 045	7 235	7 868	14.7	71.8	13.5
Switzerland[1]	3 102	7 422	7 964	13 309	10 544	7 275	5 171	20 260	19 023	10 838	10 290	10.6	77.8	11.6
Turkey[1]	m	970	a	1 565	1 565	a	x(9)	x(9)	m	3 664	1 322	1.6	89.6	8.8
United Kingdom	6 862	5 145	x(5)	x(5)	6 140	x(5)	x(9)	x(9)	9 945	7 614	6 296	4.3	83.5	12.2
United States	6 838	7 626	8 218	9 065	8 607	m	x(9)	x(9)	19 464	17 183	10 472	8.7	72.4	19.0
OECD average	*4 105*	*5 051*	*5 983*	*6 827*	*6 301*	*3 986*	~	~	*9 613*	*6 886*	*6 115*	*10.5*	*74.3*	*15.5*
Brazil[1]	1 014	1 004	1 015	694	894	a	x(4)	7 811	7 810	7 710	1 128	9.9	87.5	2.6
Chile[2]	2 131	1 836	1 823	1 786	1 799	a	3 786	7 006	5 952	m	2 480	8.8	76.6	14.6
Estonia[1]	1 027	2 506	3099	3 178	3 137	a	3 632	n	3 942	m	2 946	19.2	76.7	4.1
Israel	3 705	4 496	x(5)	x(5)	5 253	3 700	7 511	10 324	9 776	7 596	5 664	16.0	68.0	15.7
Russian Fed.[1]	m	x(5)	x(5)	x(5)	1 398	x(5)	1 613	2 460	2 218	m	1 537	m	m	m
Slovenia[1]	5 515	x(3)	6 433	4 384	5 651	x(4)	x(9)	x(9)	6937	5 946	5 910	10.4	71.6	18.0

1. Public institutions only.
2. Year of reference 2005.
Source: OECD. See Annex 3 for notes (*www.oecd.org/edu/eag2007*).
Please refer to the Reader's Guide for information concerning the symbols replacing missing data.

Table X2.6a.
Reference statistics used in the calculation of teachers' salaries, by level of education (1996, 2005)

	Teachers' salaries in national currency (1996)[1]								
	Primary education			Lower secondary education			Upper secondary education, general programmes		
	Starting salary / minimum training	Salary after 15 years of experience / minimum training	Salary at top of scale / minimum training	Starting salary / minimum training	Salary after 15 years of experience / minimum training	Salary at top of scale / minimum training	Starting salary / minimum training	Salary after 15 years of experience / minimum training	Salary at top of scale / minimum training
Australia	25 693	46 781	46 781	25 693	46 781	46 781	25 693	46 781	46 781
Austria	19 911	25 522	40 136	20 598	26 791	42 910	21 891	29 334	48 204
Belgium (Fl.)[2]	20 479	27 542	32 721	20 950	29 346	35 781	25 998	37 534	45 119
Belgium (Fr.)[2]	20 479	27 542	32 721	20 950	29 346	35 781	25 998	37 534	45 119
Czech Republic	w	w	w	w	w	w	w	w	w
Denmark	200 000	244 000	250 000	200 000	244 000	250 000	218 000	310 000	325 000
England	12 113	20 423	20 423	12 113	20 423	20 423	12 113	20 423	20 423
Finland	17 660	23 378	24 051	19 846	27 751	28 928	20 519	28 928	30 610
France	w	w	w	w	w	w	w	w	w
Germany	w	w	w	w	w	w	w	w	w
Greece	10 772	12 854	15 148	11 141	13 223	15 518	11 141	13 223	15 518
Hungary	341 289	462 618	597 402	341 289	462 618	597 402	435 279	574 067	717 756
Iceland	m	m	m	m	m	m	m	m	m
Ireland	18 235	28 189	33 362	19 141	29 872	33 679	19 141	29 872	33 679
Italy	14 939	18 030	21 864	16 213	19 796	24 233	16 213	20 412	25 442
Japan	3 462 000	5 917 000	8 475 000	3 462 000	5 917 000	8 475 000	3 462 000	5 917 000	8 733 000
Korea	w	w	w	w	w	w	w	w	w
Luxembourg	m	m	m	m	m	m	m	m	m
Mexico	29 105	38 606	63 264	37 092	47 174	76 196	m	m	m
Netherlands	21 772	26 537	32 627	22 925	28 847	35 840	23 120	40 273	47 756
New Zealand	23 000	39 220	39 220	23 000	39 220	39 220	23 000	39 220	39 220
Norway	165 228	201 446	204 211	165 228	201 446	204 211	178 752	207 309	222 078
Poland	m	m	m	m	m	m	m	m	m
Portugal	9 970	15 001	25 902	9 970	15 001	25 902	9 970	15 001	25 902
Scotland	12 510	20 796	20 796	12 510	20 796	20 796	12 510	20 796	20 796
Slovak Republic	m	m	m	m	m	m	m	m	m
Spain	18 609	21 823	27 940	m	m	m	21 582	25 327	31 780
Sweden	w	w	w	w	w	w	w	w	w
Switzerland	65 504	87 585	100 847	m	m	m	m	m	m
Turkey	w	w	w	a	a	a	w	w	w
United States	m	m	m	m	m	m	m	m	m
Brazil	m	m	m	m	m	m	m	m	m
Chile	m	m	m	m	m	m	m	m	m
Estonia	m	m	m	m	m	m	m	m	m
Israel	m	m	m	m	m	m	m	m	m
Russian Federation	m	m	m	m	m	m	m	m	m
Slovenia	m	m	m	m	m	m	m	m	m

OECD countries / *Partner economies*

1. Data on salaries for countries now in the Euro zone are shown in EUR.
2. Data on teachers' salaries for 1996 refer to Belgium.
Source: OECD.
Please refer to the Reader's Guide for information concerning the symbols replacing missing data.

Table X2.6a. *(continued)*

Reference statistics used in the calculation of teachers' salaries, by level of education (1996, 2005)[1]

| | Teachers' salaries in national currency (2005)[2] | | | | | | | | | |
| | Primary education | | | Lower secondary education | | | Upper secondary education, general programmes | | | |
	Starting salary / minimum training	Salary after 15 years of experience / minimum training	Salary at top of scale / minimum training	Starting salary / minimum training	Salary after 15 years of experience / minimum training	Salary at top of scale / minimum training	Starting salary / minimum training	Salary after 15 years of experience / minimum training	Salary at top of scale / minimum training	GDP deflator 2005 (1996 = 100)
OECD countries										
Australia	43 234	62 240	62 240	43 562	62 384	62 384	43 562	62 384	62 384	130
Austria	23 485	31 050	46 752	24 598	33 635	48 660	24 780	34 265	51 270	111
Belgium (Fl.)	25 280	35 417	43 185	25 280	35 417	43 185	31 375	45 301	54 459	117
Belgium (Fr.)	23 970	33 598	40 984	24 066	33 973	41 621	29 995	43 704	52 719	117
Czech Republic	262 181	343 266	408 694	262 181	343 266	408 694	266 417	349 521	416 924	142
Denmark	294 528	332 015	332 015	294 528	332 015	332 015	289 274	404 229	404 229	121
England	18 558	27 123	27 123	18 558	27 123	27 123	18 558	27 123	27 123	125
Finland	27 020	31 490	31 490	31 360	37 080	37 080	33 700	42 120	42 120	114
France	21 109	28 395	41 896	23 381	30 667	44 280	23 608	30 895	44 530	114
Germany	35 656	44 370	46 264	36 994	45 534	47 536	40 008	49 048	51 249	107
Greece	17 640	21 476	25 802	17 640	21 476	25 802	17 640	21 476	25 802	141
Hungary	1 470 996	1 944 576	2 574 420	1 470 996	1 944 576	2 574 420	1 706 028	2 432 388	3 175 116	209
Iceland	2 275 524	2 573 556	3 010 140	2 275 524	2 573 556	3 010 140	2 447 000	3 014 000	3 198 000	139
Ireland	28 127	46 591	52 796	28 127	46 591	52 796	28 127	46 591	52 796	145
Italy	20 862	25 234	30 694	22 484	27 487	33 703	22 484	28 259	35 238	126
Japan	3 335 000	6 236 000	7 956 000	3 335 000	6 236 000	7 956 000	3 335 000	6 237 000	8 192 000	90
Korea	23 211 000	39 712 000	63 762 000	23 115 000	39 616 000	63 666 000	23 115 000	39 616 000	63 666 000	125
Luxembourg	45 123	62 139	91 966	65 007	81 258	112 936	65 007	81 258	112 936	129
Mexico	94 282	124 082	205 700	120 878	157 816	260 864	m	m	m	244
Netherlands	28 636	37 210	41 568	29 617	40 880	45 547	29 913	54 712	60 348	125
New Zealand	28 419	54 979	54 979	28 419	54 979	54 979	28 419	54 979	54 979	122
Norway	277 032	309 480	344 664	277 032	309 480	344 664	296 508	333 492	361 488	148
Poland	m	m	m	m	m	m	m	m	m	164
Portugal	13 905	22 775	35 731	13 905	22 775	35 731	13 905	22 775	35 731	134
Scotland	18 694	29 827	29 827	18 694	29 827	29 827	18 694	29 827	29 827	125
Slovak Republic	m	m	m	m	m	m	m	m	m	162
Spain	24 169	28 122	35 382	27 199	31 561	39 390	27 784	32 293	40 313	136
Sweden	241 200	283 200	328 700	246 000	290 400	332 400	261 000	313 600	356 600	112
Switzerland	69 749	90 483	109 622	80 203	103 037	124 731	94 308	120 602	143 934	105
Turkey	15 703 400 000	17 166 140 000	18 960 140 000	a	a	a	15 939 800 000	17 402 540 000	19 196 540 000	2 353
United States	33 521	40 734	m	32 225	41 090	m	32 367	41 044	m	120
Partner economies										
Brazil	m	m	m	m	m	m	m	m	m	m
Chile	m	m	m	m	m	m	m	m	m	m
Estonia	m	m	m	m	m	m	m	m	m	m
Israel	46 240	56 731	78 966	46 240	56 731	78 966	46 240	56 731	78 966	134
Russian Fed.	m	m	m	m	m	m	m	m	m	m
Slovenia	15 156	17 939	19 083	15 156	17 939	19 082	15 156	17 939	19 083	m

1. For the computation of teachers' salaries in equivalent USD shown in Indicator D3, teachers' salaries are converted from national currencies to USD using January 2004 PPPs **for GDP** and adjusted for inflation where necessary. Teachers' salaries in equivalent USD based on January 2004 PPPs for **final consumption** are shown in table X2.6b of Annex 2.

2. Data on salaries for countries now in the Euro zone are shown in EUR.

Source: OECD.

Please refer to the Reader's Guide for information concerning the symbols replacing missing data.

Table X2.6b.
Reference statistics used in the calculation of teachers' salaries (1996, 2005)

		Purchasing power parity for GDP (PPP) (2004)[1]	Purchasing power parity for GDP (PPP) (2005)[1]	Purchasing power parity for GDP (PPP) (January 2005)[1]	Gross domestic product (in millions of local currency, calendar year 2005)[1]	Total population in thousands (calendar year 2005)	GDP per capita (in equivalent USD, calendar year 2005)[2]	Reference year for 2005 salary data	Adjustments for inflation (2005)
OECD countries	Australia	1.36	1.38	1.37	965 969	20 474 000	34 240	2005	0.98
	Austria	0.87	0.87	0.87	245 103	8 233 306	34 393	2004/2005	1.00
	Belgium (Fl.)[3]	0.86	0.86	0.86	298 180	10 473 901	32 996	Jan 2005	1.00
	Belgium (Fr.)[3]	0.86	0.86	0.86	298 180	10 473 901	32 996	2004/2005	1.00
	Czech Republic	14.03	14.08	14.06	2 970 261	10 234 092	20 606	2004/2005	1.00
	Denmark	8.40	8.40	8.40	1 551 967	5 419 000	34 091	2005	0.98
	England[4]	0.62	0.62	0.62	1 224 461	60 218 000	32 860	Jan 2005	1.00
	Finland	0.97	0.97	0.97	157 377	5 245 100	30 959	01 oct. 2004	1.00
	France	0.92	0.90	0.91	1 710 024	62 702 400	30 266	2004/2005	1.00
	Germany	0.89	0.88	0.89	2 241 000	82 464 000	30 777	2004/2005	1.00
	Greece	0.69	0.69	0.69	228 156	11 103 924	29 578	2004	1.02
	Hungary	124.05	124.90	124.47	22 026 763	10 087 452	17 483	May 2005	1.00
	Iceland	94.02	94.55	94.29	1 012 201	295 864	36 183	2004/2005	1.00
	Ireland	1.00	1.00	1.00	161 163	4 148 662	38 850	2004/2005	1.00
	Italy	0.86	0.86	0.86	1 417 241	58 530 300	28 094	2005	1.00
	Japan	133.10	127.52	130.31	501 402 600	127 773 000	30 773	2004/2005	1.00
	Korea	782.19	755.82	769.01	806 621 900	48 294 000	22 098	2005	1.00
	Luxembourg	0.92	0.92	0.92	29 396	457 300	70 244	2004/2005	1.00
	Mexico	7.31	7.48	7.39	8 369 246	105 300 000	10 627	2004/2005	1.00
	Netherlands	0.90	0.88	0.89	505 646	16 316 000	35 120	2004/2005	1.00
	New Zealand	1.47	1.46	1.47	155 885	4 101 000	25 950	2005	0.99
	Norway	8.93	8.73	8.83	1 903 841	4 622 000	47 207	2004/2005	1.00
	Poland	1.85	1.85	1.85	979 191	38 161 000	13 894	2003/2004	1.00
	Portugal	0.71	0.70	0.71	147 787	10 549 424	19 889	2004/2005	1.00
	Scotland[4]	0.62	0.62	0.62	1 224 461	60 218 000	32 860	2004/2005	1.00
	Slovak Republic	17.19	17.09	17.14	1 471 131	5 387 099	15 983	2002/2003	1.00
	Spain	0.76	0.76	0.76	905 455	43 398 200	27 400	2004/2005	1.00
	Sweden	9.18	9.21	9.19	2 670 547	9 030 000	32 111	2005	1.00
	Switzerland	1.73	1.70	1.72	455 594	7 501 000	35 650	2005	1.00
	Turkey	831471.00	876766.00	854119	487 202	72 065 000	7 711	2005	0.97
	United States	1.00	1.00	1.00	12 397 900	296 677 000	41 789	2004/2005	1.00
Partner economies	Brazil	m	m	m	m	m	m	m	m
	Chile	m	m	m	m	m	m	m	m
	Estonia	m	m	m	m	m	m	m	m
	Israel	3.16	3.12	3.14	553 970	6 909 000	25 670	2004/2005	1.00
	Russian Federation	m	m	m	m	m	m	m	m
	Slovenia	0.60	0.60	0.60	27 625	2 001 000	22 908	2004/2005	1.00

1. Data on PPPs and GDP for countries now in the Euro zone are shown in EUR.

2. GDP per capita in national currencies (2005) has been calculated from total population (2005) and total GDP (2005), and has been converted to USD using PPPs **for GDP** (2005). These data are available in this table.

3. Data on gross domestic product and total population refer to Belgium.

4. Data on gross domestic product and total population refer to the United Kingdom.

Adjustments for inflation are used if the reference year deviates from 2004/2005 and the inflation between the actual reference year and 2004/2005 would deviate more than 1 per cent.

Source: OECD.

Please refer to the Reader's Guide for information concerning the symbols replacing missing data.

Table X2.6c.
Teachers' salaries (2005)
Annual statutory teachers' salaries in public institutions at starting salary, after 15 years of experience and at the top of the scale by level of education, in equivalent EUR converted using PPPs

	Primary education				Lower secondary education				Upper secondary education			
	Starting salary / minimum training	Salary after 15 years of experience / minimum training	Salary at top of scale / minimum training	Ratio of salary after 15 years of experience to GDP per capita	Starting salary / minimum training	Salary after 15 years of experience / minimum training	Salary at top of scale / minimum training	Ratio of salary after 15 years of experience to GDP per capita	Starting salary / minimum training	Salary after 15 years of experience / minimum training	Salary at top of scale / minimum training	Ratio of salary after 15 years of experience to GDP per capita
	(1)	(2)	(3)	(4)	(5)	(6)	(7)	(8)	(9)	(10)	(11)	(12)
Australia	27 093	39 003	39 003	1.30	27 298	39 093	39 093	1.30	27 298	39 093	39 093	1.30
Austria	23 789	31 452	47 357	1.04	24 917	34 071	49 290	1.13	25 101	34 708	51 934	1.15
Belgium (Fl.)	25 699	36 004	43 901	1.24	25 699	36 004	43 901	1.24	31 895	46 052	55 361	1.59
Belgium (Fr.)	24 368	34 155	41 663	1.18	24 465	34 537	42 310	1.19	30 492	44 428	53 592	1.53
Czech Republic	16 378	21 443	25 530	1.19	16 378	21 443	25 530	1.19	16 642	21 834	26 044	1.21
Denmark	30 306	34 164	34 164	1.14	30 306	34 164	34 164	1.14	29 766	41 594	41 594	1.39
England	26 333	38 487	38 487	1.33	26 333	38 487	38 487	1.33	26 333	38 487	38 487	1.33
Finland	24 414	28 453	28 453	1.05	28 335	33 504	33 504	1.23	30 450	38 057	38 057	1.40
France	20 380	27 415	40 450	1.03	22 574	29 609	42 752	1.11	22 793	29 829	42 993	1.12
Germany	35 229	43 838	45 710	1.62	36 551	44 989	46 967	1.66	39 529	48 461	50 635	1.79
Greece	22 673	27 603	33 164	1.06	22 673	27 603	33 164	1.06	22 673	27 603	33 164	1.06
Hungary	10 376	13 716	18 159	0.89	10 376	13 716	18 159	0.89	12 034	17 157	22 396	1.12
Iceland	21 189	23 965	28 030	0.75	21 189	23 965	28 030	0.75	22 786	28 066	29 779	0.88
Ireland	24 758	41 010	46 472	1.20	24 758	41 010	46 472	1.20	24 758	41 010	46 472	1.20
Italy	21 269	25 726	31 293	1.04	22 923	28 023	34 360	1.14	22 923	28 810	35 925	1.17
Japan	22 470	42 017	53 606	1.56	22 470	42 017	53 606	1.56	22 470	42 023	55 196	1.56
Korea	26 501	45 340	72 799	2.34	26 391	45 231	72 690	2.33	26 391	45 231	72 690	2.33
Luxembourg	43 214	59 510	88 075	0.96	62 257	77 820	108 158	1.26	62 257	77 820	108 158	1.26
Mexico	11 197	14 736	24 430	1.58	14 356	18 743	30 981	2.01	m	m	m	m
Netherlands	28 267	36 731	41 032	1.19	29 235	40 353	44 960	1.31	29 527	54 007	59 570	1.75
New Zealand	16 744	32 393	32 393	1.42	16 744	32 393	32 393	1.42	16 744	32 393	32 393	1.42
Norway	27 554	30 781	34 280	0.74	27 554	30 781	34 280	0.74	29 491	33 169	35 954	0.80
Poland	m	m	m	m	m	m	m	m	m	m	m	m
Portugal	17 300	28 337	44 457	1.62	17 300	28 337	44 457	1.62	17 300	28 337	44 457	1.62
Scotland	26 527	42 324	42 324	1.47	26 527	42 324	42 324	1.47	26 527	42 324	42 324	1.47
Slovak Republic	m	m	m	m	m	m	m	m	m	m	m	m
Spain	27 962	32 535	40 935	1.35	31 468	36 514	45 572	1.52	32 144	37 361	46 640	1.55
Sweden	23 033	27 044	31 389	0.96	23 492	27 731	31 742	0.98	24 924	29 947	34 053	1.06
Switzerland	35 697	46 308	56 104	1.48	41 047	52 733	63 836	1.68	48 266	61 723	73 664	1.97
Turkey	15 724	17 189	18 985	2.54	a	a	a	a	15 961	17 426	19 222	2.57
United States	29 431	35 764	m	0.97	28 294	36 077	m	0.98	28 419	36 037	m	0.98
OECD average	*24 341*	*33 015*	*40 094*	*1.28*	*26 140*	*35 403*	*43 007*	*1.30*	*27 353*	*37 964*	*45 550*	*1.41*
EU19 average	*24 857*	*33 155*	*40 159*	*1.19*	*26 661*	*35 276*	*42 435*	*1.25*	*27 793*	*38 307*	*45 887*	*1.36*
Brazil	m	m	m	m	m	m	m	m	m	m	m	m
Chile	m	m	m	m	m	m	m	m	m	m	m	m
Estonia	m	m	m	m	m	m	m	m	m	m	m	m
Israel	12 921	15 852	22 065	0.70	12 921	15 852	22 065	0.70	12 921	15 852	22 065	0.70
Russian Federation	m	m	m	m	m	m	m	m	m	m	m	m
Slovenia	22 080	26 134	27 801	1.30	22 080	26 134	27 801	1.30	22 080	26 134	27 801	1.30

Source: OECD. See Annex 3 for notes *(www.oecd.org/edu/eag2007)*.
Please refer to the Reader's Guide for information concerning the symbols replacing missing data.

Table X2.7
Tax revenue of main headings as percentage of GDP, 2004

	Income & Profits	Social Security	Payroll	Property	Goods & Services	Other
Australia	18.2	~	1.4	2.7	8.9	~
Austria	12.5	14.4	2.6	0.6	12.0	0.4
Belgium	17.4	14.1	~	1.8	11.3	0.0
Canada	15.6	5.1	0.7	3.4	8.7	0.1
Czech Republic	9.7	16.2	~	0.4	12.0	0.0
Denmark[1]	29.5	1.2	0.2	1.8	16.0	0.0
Finland	17.1	11.9	~	1.1	14.0	0.0
France[1]	10.1	16.1	1.1	3.3	11.1	1.6
Germany	9.5	14.1	~	0.9	10.1	0.0
Greece	8.2	12.1	~	1.5	13.0	~
Hungary	9.0	11.5	0.9	0.9	15.5	0.3
Iceland	17.0	3.2	~	2.5	15.9	0.1
Ireland	11.8	4.5	0.2	2.1	11.4	~
Italy	12.9	12.5	~	2.5	10.8	2.3
Japan	8.5	10.0	~	2.6	5.3	0.1
Korea	6.9	5.1	0.1	2.8	8.9	0.9
Luxembourg	12.6	10.7	~	3.0	11.5	0.1
Mexico	4.7	3.1	0.2	0.3	10.5	0.1
Netherlands	9.2	13.8	~	2.0	12.0	0.2
New Zealand	21.7	~	~	1.8	12.0	~
Norway[1]	20.3	9.5	~	1.1	13.1	~
Poland	6.1	14.0	0.3	1.3	12.4	~
Portugal[1]	8.3	11.0	~	1.6	13.3	0.2
Slovak Republic[1]	5.7	11.9	~	0.6	12.1	~
Spain[1]	9.8	12.1	~	2.8	9.8	0.2
Sweden	19.0	14.3	2.4	1.6	13.0	0.1
Switzerland	12.7	7.1	~	2.5	6.9	~
Turkey	6.9	7.5	~	1.0	14.9	1.0
United Kingdom	13.2	6.8	~	4.3	11.5	~
United States	11.1	6.7	~	3.1	4.7	~
OECD Average	*12.5*	*9.4*	*0.3*	*1.9*	*11.4*	*0.2*

OECD countries

1. The total tax revenues have been reduced by the amount of capital tranfer. The capital transfer has been allocated between tax headings in proportion to the report tax revenue.
Source: OECD REVENUE STATISTICS 1965-2005 – ISBN9264028129 – © OECD 2006 (Table 6).
Please refer to the Reader's Guide for information concerning the symbols replacing missing data.

General notes

Definitions

Gross domestic product (GDP) refers to the producers' value of the gross outputs of resident producers, including distributive trades and transport, less the value of purchasers' intermediate consumption plus import duties. GDP is expressed in local money (in millions). For countries which provide this information for a reference year that is different from the calendar year (such as Australia and New Zealand), adjustments are made by linearly weighting their GDP between two adjacent national reference years to match the calendar year.

The **GDP deflator** is obtained by dividing the GDP expressed at current prices by the GDP expressed at constant prices. This provides an indication of the relative price level in a country. Data are based on the year 1995.

GDP per capita is the gross domestic product (in equivalent USD converted using PPPs) divided by the population.

Annex 2

Purchasing power parity exchange rates (PPP) are the currency exchange rates that equalise the purchasing power of different currencies. This means that a given sum of money when converted into different currencies at the PPP rates will buy the same basket of goods and services in all countries. In other words, PPPs are the rates of currency conversion which eliminate the differences in price levels among countries. Thus, when expenditure on GDP for different countries is converted into a common currency by means of PPPs, it is, in effect, expressed at the same set of international prices so that comparisons between countries reflect only differences in the volume of goods and services purchased.

Total public expenditure as used for the calculation of the education indicators, corresponds to the non-repayable current and capital expenditure of all levels of government. Current expenditure includes final consumption expenditure (*e.g.*, compensation of employees, consumption intermediate goods and services, consumption of fixed capital, and military expenditure), property income paid, subsidies, and other current transfers paid (*e.g.*, social security, social assistance, pensions and other welfare benefits). Capital expenditure is spending to acquire and/or improve fixed capital assets, land, intangible assets, government stocks, and non-military, non-financial assets, and spending to finance net capital transfers.

Sources

The 2007 edition of the *National Accounts of OECD Countries: Main Aggregates*, Volume I.

The theoretical framework underpinning national accounts has been provided for many years by the United Nations' publication *A System of National Accounts*, which was released in 1968. An updated version was released in 1993 (commonly referred to as SNA93).

OECD Analytical Data Base, January 2007.

Annex

3

SOURCES, METHODS AND TECHNICAL NOTES

Annex 3 on sources and methods is available
in electronic form only. It can be found at:
www.oecd.org/edu/eag2007

REFERENCES

Bowles, S. and **H. Gintis** (2000), "Does Schooling Raise Earnings by Making People Smarter?", K. Arrow, S. Bowles and S. Durlauf (eds.), *Meritocracy and Economic Inequality,* Princeton University Press, Princeton.

Eccles, J.S. (1994), "Understanding women's educational and occupational choices: Applying the Eccles *et al.* model of achievement-related choices", *Psychology of Women Quarterly,* Vol. 18, Blackwell Publishing, Oxford.

Kelo, M., U. Teichler and **B. Wächter** (eds.) (2005), "EURODATA: Student Mobility in European Higher Education", Verlags and Mediengesellschaft, Bonn, 2005.

OECD (2002), *Education at a Glance: OECD Indicators – 2002 Edition,* OECD, Paris.

OECD (2004a), *Learning for Tomorrow's World – First Results from PISA 2003,* OECD, Paris.

OECD (2004b), *Problem Solving for Tomorrow's World – First Measures of Cross-Curricular Competencies from PISA 2003,* OECD, Paris.

OECD (2004c), *Internationalisation and Trade in Higher Education: Opportunities and Challenges,* OECD, Paris.

OECD (2004d), *Education at a Glance: OECD Indicators – 2004 Edition,* OECD, Paris.

OECD (2005a), *Trends in International Migration – 2004 Edition,* OECD, Paris.

OECD (2005b), *PISA 2003 Technical Report,* OECD, Paris.

OECD (2005c), *Education at a Glance: OECD Indicators – 2005 Edition,* OECD, Paris.

OECD (2006a), *Education at a Glance: OECD Indicators – 2006 Edition,* OECD, Paris.

OECD (2006b), *Where Immigrant Students Succeed: A Comparative Review of Performance and Engagement in PISA 2003,* OECD, Paris.

OECD (2006c), *OECD Revenue Statistics 1965-2005,* OECD, Paris.

Tremblay, K. (2005) "Academic Mobility and Immigration", *Journal of Studies in International Education,* Vol. 9, No. 3, Association for Studies in International Education, Thousands Oaks, pp. 1-34.

Contributors to this Publication

Many people have contributed to the development of this publication. The following lists the names of the country representatives, researchers and experts who have actively taken part in the preparatory work leading to the publication of *Education at a Glance – OECD Indicators 2007*.
The OECD wishes to thank them all for their valuable efforts.

National Co-ordinators

Mr. Brendan O'REILLY (Australia)
Mr. Mark NEMET (Austria)
M. Dominique BARTHÉLÉMY (Belgium)
Ms. Maddy BOLLEN (Belgium)
Ms. Oroslinda Maria GOULART (Brazil)
Ms. Amanda SPENCER-HODGKINSON (Canada)
Mr. Atilio PIZARRO (Chile)
Mr. Lubomir MARTINEC (Czech Republic)
Mr. Jakob Birklund ANDERSEN (Denmark)
Ms. Sylvia KIMMEL (Estonia)
Mr. Matti KYRÖ (Finland)
M. Claude SAUVAGEOT (France)
Ms. Barbara MEYER-WYK (Germany)
Ms. Evelyn OBELE (Germany)
Mr. Gregory KAFETZOPOULOS (Greece)
Ms. Judit KÁDÁR-FÜLÖP (Hungary)
Ms. Margrét HARÐARDÓTTIR (Iceland)
Mr. Pat MAC SITRIC (Ireland)
Mr. Yosef GIDANIAN (Israel)

Ms. Fiorella FARINELLI (Italy)
Mr. Kenji SAKUMA (Japan)
Mr. Sun-Ho KIM (Korea)
M. Jérôme LEVY (Luxembourg)
Mr. Rafael FREYRE MARTINEZ (Mexico)
Mr. Marcel SMITS VAN WAESBERGHE (Netherlands)
Mr. David LAMBIE (New Zealand)
Mr. Kjetil MÅSEIDE (Norway)
Mr. Jerzy WISNIEWSKI (Poland)
Mr. João Trocado MATA (Portugal)
Mr. Mark AGRANOVITCH (Russian Federation)
Mr. Vladimir POKOJNY (Slovak Republic)
Ms. Helga KOCEVAR (Slovenia)
Mr. Enrique ROCA COBO (Spain)
Mr. Dan ANDERSSON (Sweden)
Ms. Dominique Simone RYCHEN (Switzerland)
Mr. Ibrahim Z. KARABIYIK (Turkey)
Ms. Janice ROSS (United Kingdom)
Ms. Valena White PLISKO (United States)

Technical Group on Education Statistics and Indicators

Mr. Brendan O'REILLY (Australia)
Mr. Lars STAHRE (Australia)
Ms. Sabine MARTINSCHITZ (Austria)
Mr. Wolfgang PAULI (Austria)
Ms. Ann VAN DRIESSCHE (Belgium)
Mr. Philippe DIEU (Belgium)
Ms. Nathalie JAUNIAUX (Belgium)
Mr. Liës FEYEN (Belgium)
Mr. Guy STOFFELEN (Belgium)
Mr. Raymond VAN DE SIJPE (Belgium)
Ms. Carmilva FLORES (Brazil)
Mr. Williams MACIEL (Brazil)
Ms. Vanessa NESPOLI DE OLIVEIRA (Brazil)
Mr. Jean-Claude BOUSQUET (Canada)
Ms. Lynn BARR-TELFORD (Canada)
Mr. Patrice DE BROUCKER (Canada)
Mr. Eduardo CORREA (Chile)
Mr. Cesar MUÑOZ HERNANDEZ (Chile)
Mr. Vladimir HULIK (Czech Republic)

Ms. Michaela KLENHOVÁ (Czech Republic)
Mr. Felix KOSCHIN (Czech Republic)
Mr. Leo JENSEN (Denmark)
Mr. Jakob Birklund ANDERSEN (Denmark)
Ms. Kristi PLOOM (Estonia)
Ms. Tiiu-Liisa RUMMO-LAES (Estonia)
Mr. Jean-Louis MERCY (EUROSTAT)
Ms. Lene MEYER (EUROSTAT)
Mr. Timo ERTOLA (Finland)
Ms Riitta LEHTOMAA (Finland)
Mr. Miikka PAAJAVUORI (Finland)
Mr. Mika TUONONEN (Finland)
Mr. Matti VÄISÄNEN (Finland)
Ms. Michèle JACQUOT (France)
Ms. Christine RAGOUCY (France)
Ms. Fabienne ROSENWALD (France)
Mr. Heinz-Werner HETMEIER (Germany)
Ms. Kirsten OTTO (Germany)
Mr. Alexander RENNER (Germany)

Mr. Martin A. SCHULZE (Germany)
Ms. Vassilia ANDREADAKI (Greece)
Mr. Konstantinos STOUKAS (Greece)
Mr. Angelos KARAGIANNIS (Greece)
Ms. Judit KOZMA-LUKÁCS (Hungary)
Mr. László LIMBACHER (Hungary)
Ms. Ásta URBANCIC (Iceland)
Ms. Mary DUNNE (Ireland)
Ms. Gillian GOLDEN (Ireland)
Mr. Yosef GIDANIAN (Israel)
Ms. Anna HEFETZ (Israel)
Ms. Gemma DE SANCTIS (Italy)
Ms. Giuliana MATTEOCCI (Italy)
Ms. Teresa MORANO (Italy)
Ms. Paola DI GIROLAMO (Italy)
Mr. Paolo TURCHETTI (Italy)
Mr. Kazuhiko TAKEDA (Japan)
Ms. Midori MIYATA (Japan)
Mr. Tokuo OGATA (Japan)
Mr. Junichiro HAYASHI (Japan)
Ms. Jeongwon HWANG (Korea)
Dr. Kwanghyun LEE (Korea)
Mr. Jérôme LEVY (Luxembourg)
Ms. Manon UNSEN (Luxembourg)
Mr. David VALLADO (Luxembourg)
Ms. Erika VALLE BUTZE (Mexico)
Mr. Egon DIETZ (Netherlands)
Mr. Jaco VAN RIJN (Netherlands)
Mr. Dick TAKKENBERG (Netherlands)
Ms. Daphne DE WIT (Netherlands)
Mr. Paul GINI (New Zealand)

Mr. David SCOTT (New Zealand)
Ms. Marie ARNEBERG (Norway)
Ms. Birgitta BØHN (Norway)
Mr. Geir NYGÅRD (Norway)
Mr. Terje RISBERG (Norway)
Ms. Alina BARAN (Poland)
Ms. Anna NOWOZYNSKA (Poland)
Mr. Jose PAREDES (Portugal)
Mr. João PEREIRA DE MATOS (Portugal)
Mr. Mark AGRANOVITCH (Russian Federation)
Ms. Alzbeta FERENCICOVÀ (Slovak Republic)
Mr. Vladimir POKOJNY (Slovak Republic)
Ms. Elena REBROSOVA (Slovak Republic)
Mrs. Helga KOCEVAR (Slovenia)
Ms. Tatjana SKRBEC (Slovenia)
Mr. Eduardo DE LA FUENTE (Spain)
Mr. Jesus IBANEZ MILLA (Spain)
Ms. Karin ARVEMO-NOTSTRAND (Sweden)
Mr. Henrik ENGSTROM (Sweden)
Ms. Christina SANDSTROM (Sweden)
Ms. Katrin HOLENSTEIN (Switzerland)
Ms. Katrin MUEHLEMANN (Switzerlan)
Ms. Nilgün DURAN (Turkey)
Mr. Michael BRUNEFORTH (UNESCO)
Mr. Said OULD A VOFFAL (UNESCO)
Mr. Anthony CLARKE (United Kingdom)
Mr. Steve HEWITT (United Kingdom)
Mr. Steve LEMAN (United Kingdom)
Ms. Mary Ann FOX (United States)
Ms. Lauren GILBERTSON (United States)
Mr. Thomas SNYDER (United States)

Network A on Educational Outcomes

Lead Country: United States
Network Leader: Mr. Jay MOSKOWITZ
Ms. Wendy WHITHAM (Australia)
Mrs. Helene BABEL (Austria)
Mr. Jürgen HORSCHINEGG (Austria)
Mrs. Christiane BLONDIN (Belgium)
Ms. Liselotte VAN DE PERRE (Belgium)
Mr. Luc VAN DE POELE (Belgium)
Ms. Oroslinda Maria GOULART (Brazil)
Mr. Don HOIUM (Canada)
Ms. Tamara KNIGHTON (Canada)
Mr. Jerry MUSSIO (Canada)
Mr. Lubomir MARTINEC (Czech Republic)
Ms. Pavla ZIELENIECOVA (Czech Republic)
Mr. Joern SKOVSGAARD (Denmark)
Mr. Aki TORNBERG (Finland)
Mr. Thierry ROCHER (France)
Mr. Botho PRIEBE (Germany)
Mr. Panyotis KAZANTZIS (Greece)
Ms. Zsuzsa HAMORI-VACZY (Hungary)
Mr. Julius K. BJORNSSON (Iceland)
Mr. Gerry SHIEL (Ireland)

Mrs. Anna Maria CAPUTO (Italy)
Mr. Ryo WATANABE (Japan)
Ms. Mee-Kyeong LEE (Korea)
Ms. Iris BLANKE (Luxembourg)
Mr. Felipe MARTINEZ RIZO (Mexico)
Mr. Renze PORTENGEN (Netherlands)
Ms. Lynne WHITNEY (New Zealand)
Ms. Anne-Berit KAVLI (Norway)
Ms. Glória RAMALHO (Portugal)
Mr. Vladislav ROSA (Slovak Republic)
Ms. Lis CERCADILLO PÉREZ (Spain)
Ms. Anna BARKLUND (Sweden)
Ms. Anita WESTER (Sweden)
Mr. Erich RAMSEIER (Switzerland)
Mr. Sevki KARACA (Turkey)
Ms. Lorna BERTRAND (United Kingdom)
Mr. Eugene OWEN (United States)
Ms. Elois SCOTT (United States)
Ms. Maria STEPHENS (United States)

Network B on Education and Socio-economic Outcomes

Lead country: Sweden
Network Leader: Mr. Dan ANDERSSON
Ms. Oon Ying CHIN (Australia)
Mr. Brendan O'REILLY (Australia)
Mr. Mark NÉMET (Austria)
Ms. Ariane BAYE (Belgium)
Ms. Isabelle ERAUW (Belgium)
Ms. Oroslinda Maria GOULART (Brazil)
Mr. Patrice DE BROUCKER (Canada)
Ms. Shannon DELBRIDGE (Canada)
Ms. Zuzana POLAKOVA (Czech Republic)
Mr. David Tranekær KLEMMENSEN (Denmark)
Ms. Irja BLOMQVIST (Finland)
Ms. Aila REPO (Finland)
Ms. Pascale POULET-COULIBANDO (France)
Ms. Christiane KRÜGER-HEMMER (Germany)
Mr. Nikolaos BILALIS (Greece)
Mr. Evangelos INTZIDIS (Greece)
Mr. Angelos KARAGIANNIS (Greece)
Ms. Éva TÓT (Hungary)
Ms. Asta URBANCIC (Iceland)
Mr. Philip O'CONNELL (Ireland)
Ms. Liana VERZICCO (Italy)
Mrs. Paola UNGARO (Italy)
Ms. Jihee CHOI (Korea)
Mr. Jérôme LEVY (Luxembourg)

Mme. Astrid SCHORN (Luxembourg)
Mr. Roy TJOA (Netherlands)
Mr. Johan VAN DER VALK (Netherlands)
Mr. Marcel SMITS VAN WAESBERGHE (Netherlands)
Ms. Cheryl REMINGTON (New Zealand)
Mr. Erik DAHL (Norway)
Mr. Lars NERDRUM (Norway)
Mr. Terje RISBERG (Norway)
Ms. Anne Brit UDAHL (Norway)
Ms. Malgorzata CHOJNICKA (Poland)
Mr. José Luis ALBUQUERQUE (Portugal)
Ms. Rute GUERRA (Portugal)
Ms. Isabel FARIA VAZ (Portugal)
Ms. Slavica CERNOSA (Slovenia)
Ms. Raquel ÁLVAREZ-ESTEBAN (Spain)
Mr. Dan ANDERSSON (Sweden)
Ms. Anna JÖNSSON (Sweden)
Mr. Kenny PETERSSON (Sweden)
Mr. Russell SCHMIEDER (Sweden)
Ms. Anna BORKOWSKY (Switzerland)
Mr. Ali PANAL (Turkey)
Mr. David MCPHEE (United Kingdom)
Mr. Stephen LEMAN (United Kingdom)
Mr. Abe GEORGE (United States)
Ms. Lisa HUDSON (United States)
Mr. Dan SHERMAN (United States)

Network C on School Features and Processes

Lead Country: Netherlands
Network Leader: Mr. Jaap SCHEERENS
Mr. Lars STAHRE (Australia)
Mr. Christian KRENTHALLER (Austria)
Mr. Philippe DELOOZ (Belgium)
Ms. Ann VAN DRIESSCHE (Belgium)
Mr. Raymond VAN DE SIJPE (Belgium)
Ms. Maria Aparecida CHAGAS FERREIRA (Brazil)
Mrs. Carmilva SOUZA FLORES (Brazil)
Ms. Oroslinda Maria GOULART (Brazil)
Ms. Nelly MCEWEN (Canada)
Ms. Michaela KLENHOVA (Czech Republic)
Mr. Lubomir MARTINEC (Czech Republic)
Ms. Pavlina STASTNOVA (Czech Republic)
Mr. Jørgen Balling RASMUSSEN (Denmark)
Ms. Maria HRABINSKA (European Commission)
Mr. Hannu-Pekka LAPPALAINEN (Finland)
Mrs. Dominique ALLAIN (France)
Mr. Gerd MÖLLER (Germany)
Mr. Vassilios CHARISMIADIS (Greece)
Ms. Anna IMRE (Hungary)
Mr. Pat MAC SITRIC (Ireland)
Ms. Annamaria FICHERA (Italy)

Dr. Kwanghyun LEE (Korea)
Ms. Jeongwon HWANG (Korea)
Mme Astrid SCHORN (Luxembourg)
Mr. Jean-Claude FANDEL (Luxembourg)
Ms. Erika VALLE BUTZE (Mexico)
Ms. Maria HENDRIKS (Netherlands)
Mr. Hans RUESINK (Netherlands)
Mr. Marcel SMITS VAN WAESBERGHE (Netherlands)
Ms. Robyn SMITS (New Zealand)
Ms. Bodhild BAASLAND (Norway)
Mr. Jerzy CHODNICKI (Poland)
Mr. Helder GUERREIRO (Portugal)
Mr. Mitja SARDOC (Slovenia)
Mr. Ignacio ÁLVAREZ PERALTA (Spain)
Ms. Ulla LINDQVIST (Sweden)
Mrs. Annika HAGLUND (Sweden)
Mr. Eugen STOCKER (Switzerland)
Ms. Nilgün DURAN (Turkey)
Ms. Alison KENNEDY (UNESCO)
Mr. Anthony CLARKE (United Kingdom)
Mrs. Kerry GRUBER (United States)
Ms. Laura SALGANIK (United States)

Others contributors to this publication

Ms. Fung-Kwan TAM (Layout)

RELATED OECD PUBLICATIONS

Where Immigrant Students Succeed: A Comparative Review of Performance and Engagement in PISA 2003
ISBN 92-64-02360-7

Are Students Ready for a Technology-Rich World?: What PISA Studies Tell Us
ISBN 92-64-03608-3

Learning for Tomorrow's World – First Results from PISA 2003 (2004)
ISBN 92-64-00724-5

Problem Solving for Tomorrow's World – First Measures of Cross-Curricular Competencies from PISA 2003 (2004)
ISBN 92-64-00642-7

From Education to Work: A Difficult Transition for Young Adults with Low Levels of Education (2005)
ISBN 92-64-00918-3

Education Policy Analysis 2005-2006 (2006)
ISBN 92-64-02269-4

OECD Handbook for Internationally Comparative Education Statistics: Concepts, Standards, Definitions and Classifications (2004)
ISBN 92-64-10410-0

Completing the Foundation for Lifelong Learning: An OECD Survey of Upper Secondary Schools (2004)
ISBN 92-64-10372-4

OECD Survey of Upper Secondary Schools: Technical Report (2004)
ISBN 92-64-10572-7

Internationalisation and Trade in Higher Education: Opportunities and Challenges (2004)
ISBN 96-64-01504-3

Classifying Educational Programmes: Manual for ISCED-97 Implementation in OECD Countries (1999)
ISBN 92-64-17037-5

OECD publications can be browsed or purchased at the OECD Online Bookshop (*www.oecdbookshop.org*).

This book has...

StatLinks

A service that delivers Excel® files from the printed page!

Look for the *StatLinks* at the bottom right-hand corner of the tables or graphs in this book. To download the matching Excel® spreadsheet, just type the link into your Internet browser, starting with the *http://dx.doi.org* prefix.
If you're reading the PDF e-book edition, and your PC is connected to the Internet, simply click on the link.
You'll find *StatLinks* appearing in more OECD books.

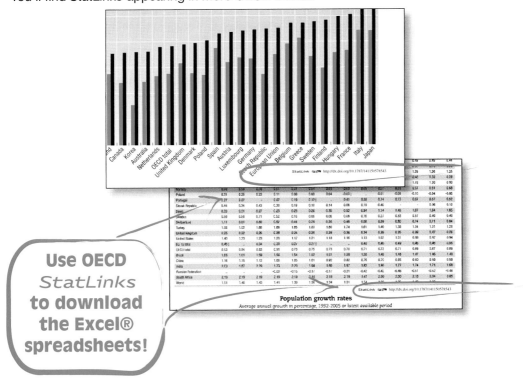

Use OECD *StatLinks* to download the Excel® spreadsheets!

StatLinks : another innovation from OECD Publishing.

Learn more at *www.oecd.org/statistics/statlink*

We'd like to hear what you think about our publications and services like *StatLinks*: e-mail us at oecdpublishing@oecd.org

OECD PUBLICATIONS, 2, rue André-Pascal, 75775 PARIS CEDEX 16
PRINTED IN FRANCE
(96 2007 05 1 P) ISBN 978-92-64-03287-3 – No. 55593 2007